PEASANT STRUGGLES IN INDIA

By the same author

1. *Gandhi's Truth and Non-violence X-rayed*
2. *Indian Feudal States and National Liberation Struggle*
3. *Social Background of Indian Nationalism*
4. *Recents Trends in Indian Nationalism*
5. *Rural India in Transition*
6. *Rural Sociology in India*
7. *Essays on Modernization Underdeveloped Societies (2 vols. Ed.)*
8. *Slums and Urbanization (with S. Devadas Pillai)*
9. *A Profile of an Indian Slum (with S. Devadas Pillai)*
10. *State and Society in India—Essays in Dissent*
11. *A Positive Programme for the Indian Revolution (Ed.)*

Peasant Struggles
in
India

edited by
A.R. DESAI

BOMBAY
OXFORD UNIVERSITY PRESS
DELHI CALCUTTA MADRAS
1979

Oxford University Press
OXFORD LONDON GLASGOW
NEW YORK TORONTO MELBOURNE WELLINGTON
NAIROBI DAR ES SALAAM CAPE TOWN
KUALA LUMPUR SINGAPORE JAKARTA HONG KONG TOKYO
DELHI BOMBAY CALCUTTA MADRAS KARACHI

© Oxford University Press 1979

Printed in India
by Jay Print Pack (P) Ltd., New Delhi 110 015
and published by R. Dayal, Oxford Univerity Press
2/11 Ansari Road, Daryaganj, New Delhi 110 002

To
Kathleen Gough
who pioneered to give the
heroic struggles of the
exploited and oppressed
rural poor of India
their place in history

Contents

Introduction XI

PART I

Tribal and Peasant Struggles: An Overview

Introduction 3

1. Background of Tribal Struggles in India   *V. R. Raghavaiah*   12

2. Tribal Revolts in Chronological Order: 1778 to 1971   *V. R. Raghavaiah*   23

3. Messianic Movements   *Fr. Stephen Fuchs*   28

4. Agrarian Revolts   *N. G. Ranga and Swami Sahajanand Saraswathi*   47

5. Indian Peasants Struggles and Achievements   *N. G. Ranga*   66

6. Indian Peasant Uprisings   *Kathleen Gough*   85

PART II

Agrarian Struggles in the 19th Century

Introduction 129

7. The Santhal Insurrection: 1855–56   *L. Natrajan*   136

8. Indigo Cultivators' Strike: 1860   *L. Natrajan*   148

9. Maratha Uprising: 1875   *L. Natrajan*   159

10	Conclusion	*L. Natrajan*	170
11	Unrest in Andhra Pradesh	*V. R. Raghavaiah*	174
12	Peasant Struggle in Patna, 1873: Its Legalistic Character	*Kalyan Kumar Sengupta*	179
13	Agrarian Disturbances in 19th Century Bengal	*Kalyan Kumar Sengupta*	189

PART III

Agrarian Struggles in the Early 20th Century

	Introduction		211
14	Early Struggles: 1905–18	*Sukhbir Choudhary*	221
15	Post-War Awakening: 1919–21	*Sukhbir Choudhary*	237

PART IV

Agrarian Struggles in the Twenties and Thirties

	Introduction		277
16	Sreerama Raju's Uprising-1922–24	*V. Raghavaiah*	291
17	Village Repression by British Rulers	*Report of India League Delegation in 1932*	303
18	Agrarian Movements in Bengal and Bihar: 1919–39	*Binay Bhushan Chaudhuri*	337
19	Damodar Canal Tax Movement	*Buddhadeva Bhattacharyya with Tarunkumar Bannerjee and Dipak Kumar Das*	375

PART V

Agrarian Struggles on the Eve of British Withdrawal

	Introduction		415
20	The Kisan Sabha	*Sunil Sen*	428
21	Tebhaga Chai	*Sunil Sen*	442
22	The Bargadars Bill	*Sunil Sen*	453
23	The Dilemma	*Sunil Sen*	461
24	Kakdwip Tebhaga Movement	*Krishnakant Sarkar*	469
25	Social Origins of the Peasant Insurrection in Telangana: 1946–51	*D. N. Dhanagare*	486
26	The Postwar Situation and Beginning of Armed Struggle	*C. Rajeshwar Rao*	517
27	Telangana	*P. Sundarayya*	532
28	Hyderabad State—Its Socio-Political Background	*P. Sundarayya*	537
29	The Communist Movement in Andhra: Terror Regime—1948–51	*P. Sundarayya*	545
30	Entry of Indian Army and Immediately After	*P. Sundarayya*	565
31	The Liberation Movement Among Varlis	*S. V. Parulekar*	569
32	The Struggle of 1946	*S. V. Parulekar*	583

PART VI

An Overview

Introduction		597
33	Peasant Revolts in Malabar in the Nineteenth and Twentieth Centuries *K. N. Panikkar*	601
34	Peasants of the Paraganas *Asim Mukhopadhyay*	631
35	Peasants and Revolution *Hamza Alavi*	671
36	Peasant Resistance and Revolt in South India *Kathleen Gough*	719
37	Peasant Movement in India *Uday Mehta*	743
38	The 'Two-Stages' Theory of Revolution in the Third World: Need for its Evaluation *A. R. Desai*	751
39	Unconventional Anthropology of 'Traditional' Peasantry *A. R. Desai*	760
	Index	767

Introduction

(1)

THIS BOOK attempts to provide a panoramic view of tribal and peasant struggles in India during the colonial period. It is not a source book, but the readings give an insight into various sources, some of which are rare documents, not easily available and have acquired the character of archival importance.

Recently, a number of books and articles have been published on peasant movements in India.[1] They deal with various categories of struggles in different parts of the country launched by various sections of the agrarian population through different periods of British rule. Some of the books and articles give excellent detailed accounts of specific struggles. However, there is no work which provides an all-India picture of tribal and peasant struggles which took place during various phases of British rule. Nor do we find an account, which portrays the historical development of these movements during this period, which can reflect the varieties of forms and methods adopted by these movements. Similarly, there is no systematic analytical work which examines these struggles from the point of view of delineating the roles of specific sections and classes of the rural population which took leadership, provided guidance, raised specific issues and elaborated various forms of mobilization and struggle.

The present volume, through its arrangement of selections and sectional introductions, endeavours to sketch such an outline. In the absence of a comprehensive, historical account of tribal and peasant movements, a work attempting such a perspective and delineating the historical development of these movements, will hopefully prove valuable for a proper appraisal of agrarian movements and their contribution to the nationalist movement in India.

The choice in highlighting particular movements (and omitting others) was made with a view to exploring the inner dynamic of the various social movements that emerged, revealing the methods adopted, levels of involvement of various sections, types of alliances and conflicts, ingenous devices adopted for mobilization, organizational innovations and forms, changing nature of issues around which struggles were launched and the nature and types of leadership which emerged in the course of agrarian struggles. The present work is thus an endeavour to provide a perspective of the dialectical development of the agrarian movement in India during the British period.

(2)

The volume is also prepared to subserve a number of other objectives. There is a widely held assumption even among a large section of the academicians and students of rural India, that unlike its counterparts in other countries, the Indian peasant has been passive, fatalistic, docile, unresisting and bogged down in the quagmire of superstitions and other-wordly fantasies. Various explanations have been projected to uphold this belief. It is my view, based on a considerable survey of the agrarian situation in India, that this assumption is wrong and requires to be refuted. The Indian rural scene during the entire British period and thereafter, has been bristling with protests, revolts, and even large scale militant struggles involving hundreds of villages and lasting for years.

The present volume has been prepared to highlight the fact that rural India has been a theatre of varieties of struggles involving various categories of rural population during the entire period of British domination. This provides enough evidence to refute the prevalent assumptions of a 'passive' peasantry.

(3)

Literature on peasant agitations, peasant struggles, peasant revolts and rebellions in other countries of the Third World is available on a fairly extensive scale.[2] We now have useful accounts of such struggles from Latin America, some countries of Africa and South East Asia. Similarly, there are a number of studies portraying the significant and important role played by the agrarian poor in the Russian, Chinese, Yugoslavian, Cuban, Vietnamese and other revolutions which broke through the capitalist-colonial or semi-colonial framework, bypassed the bourgeois phase of social organization and transformed those societies into non-capitalist, social formations. In fact, during and after the Second World War, the peasantry in a large number of colonial and semi-colonial countries participated on a massive scale both in the national liberation struggles to overthrow imperialism, and to counteract the brazen intervention by these powers, either to reconquer the territories or subject them to newly evolved forms of indirect domination.

Thus, while vivid, comprehensive accounts of peasant struggles have come to light from other countries, there is almost a total neglect by scholars in systematically studying the agrarian movements and struggles which took place in India—the most populous, most comprehensively and systematically ruled country by the then most powerful colonizing power—Britain. In fact, scholarship both of the west and of independent India, managed to gloss over this aspect of the agrarian history of India. Operating under the 'modernization' syndrome, and evolving an a-historical structural-functional approach, they conducted rural studies in a manner wherein peasant struggles were treated almost as a non-issue. Rural researches focussed on various kinds of surveys of villages, of the operation of the caste system, on the impact of land reforms, on Community Development, Panchayati Raj, elections, and the impact of technological inputs, basically accepting the postulates of the post-independence rulers who were developing the Indian union on the basis of a capitalist mixed-economy. For scholarship, the historical epoch of British domination and its impact on rural Indian society was outside the scope of its research. In fact, for these scholars, the rural population was treated as 'traditional', to be modernized by the new rulers in consonance with their major assumptions of 'development'. For them tribal and peasant struggles were considered as disfunctional, anomic, and disintegrative phenomena, obstructing the rapid and smooth development of the capitalist path since independence. In short, the established scholarship, with few exceptions, treated tribal and peasant struggles as a law and order problem.

This is evidenced by the fact that while there are hundreds of studies which are described as village studies, there is not even a simple enumerative document listing the tribal and peasant movements, both during British period and Independent India.

The entire scholarly exercise of Indian and western scholarship supported massively by the Indian State and international organizations and academies, successfully diverted attention from conducting methodically, large scale studies of the vital and crucial theme of the deepening and widening struggles launched by various categories of the rural population which played a significant role in weakening the foundations of British colonialism in India. This also prevented scientific studies of the increasing resistance organized by various sections of the rural populace, who are being subjected to subtle, varied and complex forms of exploitation, oppression and repression in the post-independence period.

It should be acknowledged that a small group of historically oriented radical social scientists and Marxists is attempting to counteract this lacuna in scholarship. These researchers are trying to focus their studies on tribal and peasant struggles during the British and post-British period. This endeavour however is diffused, scattered and concentrates on specific episodes and movements. Except for the pathbreaking effort by Kathleen Gough (reproduced in the present work) nobody to my knowledge has ventured to analyse the struggles of various strata of rural population in a total historical context. I have given my reasons for this in the sectional introductions. The present volume, as pointed out earlier, is specially prepared to highlight the urgent necessity of further study on the question of the role of the peasantry. By organizing the material in historical order, and attempting to provide explanations in sectional introductions, I have tried to draw a sketch, however elementary, of this phenomenon in its overall matrix. I consider such an exercise very necessary for a very important practical reason. Without a proper comprehension of the tribal and peasant movements in their overall context, it will not be possible to evolve a correct strategy and tactics for shaping these movements as a part of the larger struggle to end the evolving exploitative and oppressive, socio-economic order and to replace it by a non-capitalist, socialist, socio-economic formation in India.

(4)

India was considered the brightest jewel in the British crown. India a country of continental dimensions was subjected to the most systematic and forceful transformation process by British colonizers to suit their needs. They reduced this complex and historically one of the few continuously enduring precapitalist civilizations into a classic colony of the British empire. Unfortunately a systematic analysis of the British impact on India is still not available. The massive literature delineating this impact portrays segmental pictures of the impact of various measures adopted by the British, on different facets of rural life.

A synthesis of the British impact on reshaping the socio-economic framework, class configuration as well as Indian political administrative and cultural life of rural India is still not available. Jawaharlal Nehru[3], Dr K.S. Shelvankar[4], and Rajni Palme Dutt[5] endeavoured to evolve such an outline. The present author has also tried to capture the overall impact in his *Social Background of Indian Nationalism*.[6]

The credit for the first serious attempt to assess the overall impact of British rule in India, goes to Marx who hinted at the double mission of this rule—one destructive and the other positive. However, after the emergence of the independent Indian union, an intense debate has been launched particularly among various sections of Marxists to reappraise the nature of the transformation that took place in India under British rule. This debate has great relevance in shaping the programmes and policies for action launched by various Communist and Marxist parties.

The issues round which this debate is carried on can be formulated in following manner:

1. Characterization of the socio-economic formation which emerged during the British period.
2. Nature of the dominant mode of production generated by the British impact on India.
3. Nature of changes generated by the British as consequences of adopting measures such as the introduction to private property in land; new modes of revenue collection; transformation of land and asset into commodities; enforcing change in the objective of production; introduction of commercialization in agriculture, ushering in a novel principle of governance, based on a rule of law, a bourgeois legal framework and an administration composed of a hierarchy of offices, constituted of Imperial, provincial, and local units and further composed of Class I, II, III employees and other categories founded on the new principle of recruitment, promotion and retirement.

4. Whether the British expropriated political power from kings, feudal lords, nobles and others or created new feudal classes and shared power with them.

5. Whether the British introduced a bourgeois economic system, without facilitating a capitalist mode of production in agriculture or adequate industrialization of the country or perpetuated and strengthened the feudal and seni-feudal mode of production as the dominant mode.

6. Characterization of the strata and classes such as zamindars, with a chain of intermediaries such as tenants, sub-tenants, share croppers, bonded labour, and agricultural labourers in zamindari areas and the categories like absentee owners, rich peasants, middle peasants, poor peasants, agricultural proletariat, and others in Ryatwari areas, emerged as a direct consequence of the policies and measures adopted by the British rulers.

7. Characterization of working conditions in rural areas which appear to be precapitalist in the sense of non-free labour, but operating and serving the capitalist world market, not unsimilar to slave labour in southern U.S.A. or indentured and bonded labour which emerged in the process of proletarianization and pauperization in a large number of colonial countries.

How does one describe a peasantry which is indebted and bonded and which in the context of pauperization and proletarianization in colonial countries, provides extremely cheap labour, and is subjected to super-exploitation, in forms reminiscent of descriptions provided by Marx in *Capital* (in the chapter on primitive accumulation)? Should this labour be designated as indicative of a feudal and semi-feudal mode of production, or a type of labour, which assists expansion of the sphere of the capitalist mode of production? Should this mode of exploitation be described as initiating and strengthening feudal and semi-feudal relations of productions for keeping colonies backward and thereby creating feudal and semi-feudal allies, or should it be considered as a peculiar way in which a capitalist socio-economic formation was ushered in without the capitalist mode of production being made dominant in the agricultural sector?

8. Characterization of the type of socio-economic formation which has emerged in India, after independence. Is it a neo-colony, a peri-

pheral capitalism, a satellite formation or a backward capitalist social formation?

9. Characterization of the nature of the state which has emerged after independence and which has been reshaping the economy and society of India on the basis of a 'mixed economy'.

10. Nature of the revolution that is sought to be brought about in India. Whether it will be National Democratic, Peoples' Democratic, New Democratic or Socialist Revolution?

11. Method of making Revolution: peaceful, realized through parliamentary path, using extra-parliamentary methods as mere pressure techniques to accelerate the pace of the parliamentary path of struggle, or a forcible smashing of the power of the ruling class basically via extra-parliamentary militant class and mass struggles.

12. The class which will be the leader of the revolution, the classes which will ally with the leading class, will remain neutral or act as an enemy against whom revolutionary movements will have to be directed.

Views held about the issues indicated above are not merely academic discussions. They determine strategies, shape policies, organize actions and frame approaches towards different sections of the rural population. Holders of different views ranging from Gandhian to Marxist, are locked in tense battles to implement their concept of transformation.

The present volume attempts to bring together information about the various agrarian struggles launched by the holders of different views, and described by the architects of the movements, as well as their evaluation of these very struggles when they subsequently split into different parties or became independent. It also includes descriptions and evaluations of some of the struggles by scholars specializing in this aspect of study.

(5)

The debate going on in India around the issues indicated above is not restricted to that country, alone. It is a part of the great debate going on around the world about the 'revolutionary potentiality' of various sections of agrarian populations in different types of struggles going on largely in the underdeveloped world.

The massive participation of various sections of the agrarian population, particularly rich, middle, and poor peasantry as well as the agrarian proletariat in various types of struggles in colonial and semi-colonial countries, have raised a number of crucial issues which are discussed in academic circles in various countries and international forums.

We will restrict our discussion to only three concepts which are germane to our theme. The first concept is 'revolution'. Concepts like 'peasant rebellion', 'peasant revolt', 'peasant protest', 'peasant guerilla warfare', 'peasant movement' etc. also need to be properly defined. The term 'peasant' is also variously used. In fact a prominent section of scholarship is trying to restrict the term 'peasantry' to a specific section of the agrarian population, and have started designating entire societies as 'Peasant Societies'.

The concept 'Revolution' is being used in such stereotyped, ambiguous, jargonized manner that it looses its heuristic value. Douglas Deal in his very thought provoking article reviewing the discussion on 'Are Peasants Revolutionary?' defines the word 'Revolution' as suggested by Perez Zagorin. 'Revolution is any attempt by subordinate groups to bring about, by violent means, a change in (1) government (i.e., personnel) or policies (2) regime (i.e., form of government), or (3) society (i.e., social structure, system of property relations, or dominant values), whether this attempt is justified by reference to past conditions or as an unattained ideal.'[7]

The attempt by Douglas Deal to define 'revolution', itself reveals how many categories are subsumed under this concept even by him, making the definition vague, connoting large varieties of peasant struggles, which are not aimed at a structural transformation of social order, nor a transfer of power from one class to another.

The term 'revolution' is used even to describe political upheaval which changes personnel of the government, (the term would deprive the concept of its essential characteristics). Marxism has provided a very fruitful definition of revolution by pointing out two crucial elements—change in property relations, and transfer of power from one class to another. In this context it has given a clue towards defining revolution, which in recent times has taken two forms, viz., bourgeois-democratic revolutions and socialist revolutions. Marxism has also pointed out that in the context of colonial and semi-colonial countries, bourgeois revolution or colonial revolution meant national liberation struggles from foreign rule, establishment of a bourgeois regime to launch an independent bourgeois socio-economic order, sometimes described as completing the task of the bourgeois democratic revolution. The concept of socialist or proletarian revolution is made clear by defining it as a revolution, wherein bourgeois property relations are overturned and political power is transferred from the bourgeoisie to the proletariat.

During the imperialist phase of capitalism and particularly after the great socialist October Revolution in a backward, predominantly peasant country, an acute controversy has been going on about the nature of revolution which would complete even the bourgeois-democratic tasks. Can the bourgeoisie initiate development which can lift the economy and social order from colonial underdevelopment to even a bourgeois type of development experienced by advanced capitalist countries, or has the revolution to be a socialist one, even in order to complete bourgeois democratic tasks.

Whatever the discussions and differences among Marxists, the major criterion adopted by them to define Revolution still appears to me heuristically the most scientific and fruitful one. It helps us to locate the role of different sections of rural population in a struggle for bringing about a revolutionary transformation of society.

One of the peculiar developments that had taken place in colonial and the semicolonial countries particularly after the October Revolution, with regard to nationalist movements to secure freedom from imperialism, deserves careful attention.

The fear that the masses of the Third World may overthrow even the indigenous bourgeois-landlord classes in the process of overthrowing imperialism, and thereby usher in a Socialist Revolution, has led the national bourgeois and the bourgeois intelligentsia to evolve a compromising 'transfer of power' from colonialism to independence. This path of compromise is generally characterized by bargaining and negotiating with imperialism backed by varieties of reformist pressure struggles, wherein the exploited and oppressed classes and masses are often pressed in the service of 'nationalism' to build up pressure, but not permitted to take to the road of radical and revolutionary class and militant mass struggles which may operate against the local exploiters, and may lead to the overthrow of the very bourgeois-landlord-rich farmer leadership along with the overthrow of imperialism. The pressure movement, may take violent forms, but even in unleashing the violent forms, the bourgeois leaders of these movements ensure that the exploited poor and propertyless sections do not carry this struggle against local exploiting classes. In fact, this leadership carefully regulates the movement, gives a definite direction to it, carefully chooses allies, and even presses into service the poor and propertyless, who are carefully harnessed to specific forms of struggles which are withdrawn as soon as they get out of hand. The Indian subcontinent encompassing India, Pakistan, Bangladesh, Sri Lanka, and Burma, which were part of the administrative unit of the British Empire, provide a classic illustration of the operation of this path of bargain and compromise backed by pressure to secure freedom from British rule.

Under the leadership of Gandhi, the most astute, farsighted and most consistent architect of this path, the Indian National Congress followed this 'non-violent' road to compromise and with all its subtle manoeuvrings, enabled it to secure a transfer of power from the British rule and stave off the possibility of the subcontinent following the other militant path of revolutionary class and mass struggles.

It is my submission that adequate attention has not been paid to the consequences of following one or the other path. The withdrawal of direct rule of imperialism and the nature of development after independence, particularly with regard to various sections of the rural population has its roots in the subjugation of the rural population throughout this period of its politicization—firmly guided and controlled by Gandhi and the Indian National Congress.

Inadequate recognition of this phenomenon, has created great confusion in discussions of the peasantry as a revolutionary class. The concept of revolution needs clarification, because when a panegyric assessment of the revolutionary potential of the peasantry is projected, it is not clear as to the type of revolution to which this potential is related. Similarly when the discussion about the role of peasantry is carried on with regard to anti-colonial, anti-imperialist national movement, it is not clear whether one discusses this role in the context of a nationalist movement taking to the path of bargain, backed with pressure, where various sections of the rural people are pressed in the movement, without being permitted to take to class struggles against local exploiters or it refers to the role of peasantry in the context of a nationalist movement wherein the leadership adopts the path of militant class and mass struggles, based on the exploited and oppressed rural strata developing their own strength and fighting power, and in the process sharpening class struggles against local exploiters and oppressors. This volume attempts to clarify the differences between revolution, rebellion, revolt, protest and other forms of agrarian struggles. This point has been rightly emphasized by a large number of scholars such as E. Wolf[8], Shanin[9], Douglas Deal[10] and others[11]. This differentiation is vital because it will indicate whether the various forms of struggles are oriented to secure reform and partial demands or a structural transformation of society. Similarly it will give us an idea whether the specific form of struggle helps to augment the bargaining strength of the native capitalist landlord classes against the imperialists and thereby reduce the movement to a pawn in the bargaining procedure, or whether the struggle is a genuine force which will prepare the peasantry for a revolutionary social transformation of property relations and state power.

(6)

Similarly, a proper clarification is necessary as to who should be characterized as peasants from the various categories of agrarian population in a society. This is all the more necessary to assess the role and potentiality of various sections of the agrarian population in different phases and types of revolutions.

As rightly pointed out by Douglas Deal, certain types of peasants will revolt under certain conditions and circumstances. 'The task of measuring their revolutionary potential (in a qualitative sense) thus involves the analysis of peasant participation in specific revolutions: one must discover who revolts, why they revolt, and what their actions amount to in the short and long run. And if the behaviour of peasants in response to revolutionary stimuli around the world is to be fully understood, their failure to rise, their messianic lunges, sullen withdrawals, obeisance to paternalistic superiors and their explosions of fury spent in vain must also be thrown into relief.'[12]

A section of outstanding students of agrarian society are attempting to define the peasantry in a very limited sense. Teodor Shanin, representing this school of scholarship, defines this position. 'The peasantry consists of small agricultural producers, who with the help of simple equipment and the labour of their families produce mainly for their own consumption and for the fulfilment of obligations to holders of political and economic power.' He further clarifies the implication of his definition by stating that, 'such a definition implies a specific relation to land, the peasant family farm and the peasant village community as the basic units of social interaction, a specific occupational structure and particular influence of past history and specific patterns of development.[13] A massive body of literature has emerged which has assumed that peasants constitute that section of rural population constituting 'small-scale agriculturists mainly occupied with family subsistence and the rendering of obligations to landlords and states.' In fact, on the basis of the acceptance of this definition, entire theoretical models of societies are being built which are characterized as 'peasant societies.' However, it is my submission that defining peasants in this manner, irrespective of the context of whether they belonged to the 'Asiatic', slave, feudal, colonial capitalist, capitalist or non-capitalist socialist societies, creates considerable confusion about various categories of the rural population, with regard to their position, role and future, particularly in the context of capitalist, colonial and emerging non-capitalist societies during the last two to three hundred years. Such a definition does not clearly reveal the qualitative impact and differentiation that takes place in the agrarian arena, as a result of the impact of the capitalist system through an expansion of the market, changed objectives of production, commercialization, introduction of a capitalist type of private property in land resulting in the vital process of differentiation within the agrarian population—resulting in the emergence of rich, middle and poor peasants, a massive process of pauperization and proletarianization creating a qualitatively new category of agricultural proletariat, which as Wolf rightly points out cannot be described as 'peasant', and which is clearly a consequence of the impact of capitalist penetration in rural areas. Douglas Deal has very succinctly pointed out the difficulties involved in the limited definition with regard to examining the position, role and the nature of participation of various strata of peasants in the development of struggles in rural areas.

'More troublesome and numerically significant are the rural proletariat, who work on haciendas, plantations, capitalist farms, and plots of better-off peasant proprietors; they may be permanent or casual day labourers but they can earn a money wage and are normally landless. Wherever there is population pressure on land in a suitably commercialized economy, this proletariat will exist in one form or another and may include, as part-time members, poor peasants with less than subsistence holdings who are driven to seek a supplementary income in order to survive. This proletariat's existence heralds the development of capitalism in the countryside as some or most of the peasants lose their land to larger and more commercially inclined owners responding to national and international market forces. Indeed, this process of proletarianization has itself been one of the major causes of agrarian revolutions in the modern world. Whatever their differences, the fortunes of landless labourers and peasant cultivator are so intertwined as to render absurd the examination of each group without the other.'[14]

This approach neglects the dialectical process of stratification and variations which develop within the peasantry as a result of capitalist development and the possibility or otherwise of various sections to improve their conditions within the framework of that social order. In the context of the Indian situation, this approach obscures the role and future of various sections of the rural population in the context of the type of society which has developed in India.

I strongly feel that the larger definition of peasants as adopted by Marxists is still fruitful. The division of the agrarian population, as formulated by eminent Marxists like Lenin, Trotsky, Mao-Tse-Tung and others, as landlords, absentee or otherwise, rich, middle and poor peasant and the distinct class of agrarian proletariat, gives a more productive and objectively more authentic approach to understanding the role of the peasantry in colonial and post-colonial societies.

This definition clarifies more sharply the dynamic of transformation in capitalistically reforged agrarian structures in colonial and semi-colonial countries. It helps to understand the capacities, and potentialities of different categories of rural population and to identify issues around which the rural population will mobilize and the manner in which it will organize its struggles. It also provides the tools for conceiving a type of socio-economic formation within which the basic problems of pauperization and proletarianization can be eliminated and the preconditions established for a society within which the bulk of the rural population can meet its requirements of employment, education, health, housing etc.

The present volume, describing a wide variety of struggles, involving different categories of the agrarian population and based on varieties of issues, in a country which is probably the largest, most complex and most systematically colonized will, I hope, contribute to the clarification of the debate around the relation of the 'peasant' to 'revolution'.

It is hoped that this endeavour to present tribal and peasant struggles in India for the first time in one place will serve the purposes highlighted in this introduction. The inadequacies of this collection will be more than compensated if it serves to stimulate more competent and comprehensive studies. The historically crucial role of the Indian revolution not only in ending the prevalent exploitative social system, but also in terms of the impact it would have on the world capitalist system makes further study of the role of peasant struggles, and the role of the proletariat in it, a vital issue.

(9)

I am thankful to those who permitted me to publish their valuable works. I am also conscious of my debt to my young friends Dr Uday Mehta, Dr M.N.V. Nair, Sunil Gavaskar and a number of other friends who helped me in preparing this volume. I cannot forget the enormous pains taken by my young friend Chandra Sen Momaya in the difficult task of preparing the Index.

To my friends at the Oxford University Press, goes the credit of publishing this work in its present elegant form. Their assistance in editing and organizing this volume is warmly appreciated. Finally, I affectionately acknowledge the stimulating, and warm atmosphere provided by my family members.

A. R. Desai

Bombay,
August 1978.

NOTES

1. It is difficult to list these books and papers. Some of the selections in the present volume contain valuable foot-notes indicating such works.
2. Douglas Deal's article 'Peasant Revolts and Resistance in the Modern World — A Comparative View, in *Journal of Contemporary Asia* contains in foot-notes and Bibliography, one of the most useful list of such publications. pp. 435–45.
3. Pandit Jawaharlal Nehru, *Discovery of India*, Asia Publishing House, Bombay.
4. Dr K.S. Shelvankar, *Problem of India*.
5. R. Palme Dutt, *India Today*, Peoples Publishing House, Bombay.
6. A.R. Desai, *Social Background of Indian Nationalism*, Bombay, 1977.
7. Douglas Deal, op. cit., p. 415.
8. E. Wolf, 'On Peasant Rebellions' *International Social Science Journal*, Vol. 21, 1969.
9. Shanin Tedor, 'Peasantry as a Political Factor', *Sociological Review*, Vol. 14 no. 1, pp. 5–27.
10. Douglas Deal, op. cit. pp. 414–45.
11. See Douglas Deal, op. cit. Bibliography.
12. Douglas Deal, op. cit. pp. 414.
13. Shanin Tedor (Ed.), 'Peasants and Peasant Societies', pp. 240, *Penguin Modern Sociology Readings Reprint 1976.*
14. Douglas Deal, op. cit. pp. 417.

PART I
Tribal and Peasant Struggles: An Overview

Introduction

(1)

THE FIRST SELECTION by Raghaviah, a noted social worker attached to Adim Sevak Samaj is a very valuable work which provides a picture of Tribal Revolts on an all-India scale. Excepting Fr Stephen Fuch's book, *Rebellious Prophets*, this is perhaps the only work which gives a useful account of Tribal movements enveloping every state in India.

The first article, 'Background of Tribal Struggles in India' describes British strategies in confronting tribal populations. Raghaviah begins with a brief informative account of the tribal population and describes the impact on them of various measures adopted by the British. He briefly examines how these measures uprooted the very foundations of tribal socio-economic structure and hit at the basis of tribal communal-cultural life, generating among them a deep sense of frustration, resentment and inevitable need to struggle for sheer survival. Raghaviah summarizes the observations made by various scholars and administrators like B.S. Guha, Verrier Elwin, O'Malley and others. He also points out the role of the Missionary Complex which evolved in the tribal belt. V. Raghaviah is, however, silent over the non-revolutionary, class-collaborationist and pro-Hindu role of Ashramas created by Gandhian social workers endeavouring to assimilate the tribals in the Hindu social system. However, his highlighting the functions of Missions to directly or indirectly subserve the interests of the British rulers gives a proper perspective for analyzing the role of Missionary Complexes in India. A brief account of the tribal struggles and also the non-tribal peasant struggles given by him is valuable for seeing how the same forces operated on the tribal and non-tribal rural population compelling them to rise in revolt.

(2)

The second selection, 'Tribal Revolts in Chronological Order,

1778 to 1971'—is reproduced from the Appendix in V. Raghaviah's abovementioned book. Its utility need not be stressed. It is the first effort, to my knowledge, to compile in such a form the listing of important Tribal Revolts. It demonstrates how the scholars, social and political workers might prepare similar chronological and other tabular materials for every state. It also suggests the vital need of similar chronological and tabular material on peasant revolts in the country.

(3)

The third selection, 'Messianic Movements' reproduced from *Rebellious Prophets* by Stephen Fuchs, is included here to highlight specific features of certain categories of Tribal Revolts. Fuchs has ably analyzed 'characteristic common features found in certain tribal movements. It helps us to grasp why certain types of tribal revolts take on specific forms, and also point out their limitations. While Fuchs's work is valuable in this respect, he ignores the following major elements in his delineation: (i) Colonial Capitalist exploitative setting provided by the British rulers; (ii) Role of Missions in helping British rule; (iii) the type of all-India socio-economic structure which would ensure economic and social liberation of tribal populations from their plight; and (iv) the need for an all-India political organization to provide leadership to organize movements.

(4)

The fourth selection 'Agrarian Revolts' is reproduced from *History of the Kisan Movement* by N.G. Ranga and Swami Sahajanand Saraswathi. The book was published by All-India Kisan Sabha which acquired importance during the mid-thirties as one of the series of publications brought out as a part of an educational campaign launched by the organization. As it has gone out of print for quite some time, it has acquired an archival significance.

The value of the selection lies in the fact that it is one of the first systematic reviews of agrarian revolts in India. It also presents the assessment of these struggles by the chief architects of the All-India Kisan Sabha.

The value of this article lies in its analysis of Gandhi as a conscious strategist, utilizing the peasantry for reformist pressure and as a consistent opponent of any class struggle against local exploiters having the support of the British arms, laws and the police. It also hints at how after the withdrawal of the Non-cooperation movement most of the subsequent militant struggles of the peasantry were launched by groups and associations not basically approved by Gandhi and his orthodox wing of leadership.

The article which brings the story of peasant struggles upto the middle of 1930's is useful because it indirectly raises some important theoretical issues such as: (i) the inability of the peasantry in evolving by itself an independent all-India political party; (ii) the peasantry being led by parties representing either Bourgeois, Pettie-Bourgeois or Proletariat interests; (iii) the necessity of understanding properly the role of various classes in rural areas and their links with various classes on a national scale; (iv) an appraisal of the Indian National Congress from its inception as a party of the Indian bourgeoisie, attempting to bring the peasantry into the vortex of a larger national movement and taking up certain issues and stimulating specific types of movements, associations, institutions to channalize peasant struggles into specific, limited, reformist movements to strengthen the bargaining position of the Indian bourgeoisie.

The selection classifies struggles which emerged in India during the British period upto 1936-37, into a number of major phases: (i) Revolts upto and including 1857 i.e. during the regime of East India Company were launched by the tribals and the peasants in a crude and primitive fashion, but secured some concessions from the government.
(ii) Revolts from 1857 upto the beginning of the twentieth century against the British economic and political policies in the background of famines, a new land-revenue system which was very harsh, new administrative machinery and civil and criminal laws.
(iii) Peasant struggles in the first two decades of the 20th century comprizing of two currents; (a) the earlier spontaneous basically economic struggles against immediate foes like moneylenders, traders, zamindars, British administrators and others; (b) conscious agitation led by Indian National Congress taking up specific issues like the Indenture System and subsequent struggles launched by Mahatma Gandhi and his associates in places like Champaran, Khaira, Borsad, Bardoli. During this period Gandhi endeavoured

to provide specific direction to the peasant struggles within a consciously evolved political matrix.

The authors point out how the Indian National Congress under the leadership of Gandhi kept silent and systematically eschewed the struggles of landless labourers, tenants and others against their local exploiters. They also point out how the Indian National Congress, avoided purposely, transforming the spontaneous types of class struggles against local exploiting classes into more organized, deepened and politically linked struggles with other exploited strata on a national scale, which could have made the anti-Imperialist struggle more broad based, militant and revolutionary.

(iv) The crucial impact of the Non-cooperation Movement the first All-India Nationalist mass movement launched and subsequently withdrawn by Indian National Congress under the guidance of Mahatma Gandhi is also discussed.

According to the authors the Non-cooperation Movement was a watershed in the history of peasant movements in India for the following reasons:—

(a) The Non-cooperation Movement revealed the importance of peasant movement in the political struggle against Imperialism.

(b) It also pointed out how participation in larger national movements by the vast bulk of peasantry comprising of landless labourers, tenants, poor and indebted middle peasants, ruined artisans and others, enhanced their struggle not merely against foreign rule but also against local exploiters like Princes, zamindars, landlords, traders, moneylenders supported by the government.

(c) It also revealed how the Indian National Congress, evolved under Mahatma Gandhi a new broader strategy of consciously involving the peasantry in the nationalist movement, but stearing clear of the revolutionary possibilities offered by an organized peasantry. If necessary it was even prepared to withdraw the larger national movement so that such a development would not take place. It also exposed how the Indian National Congress under the leadership of Mahatma Gandhi never permitted the peasant movements to go beyond reformist pressure for economic relief or a pressure movement for political bargaining with the British rulers.

(d) Withdrawal of the Non-cooperation Movement by Gandhi

generated two major currents in the organization of peasant movements:

(i) The non-Swarajist wing of the Indian National Congress under the conscious direction of Gandhi evolved a strategy of elaborating institutional devices to help Congress to systematically reach out to the rural masses, give immediate relief to certain sections and train a cadre of constructive workers who could take leadership in rural areas for launching some political movements on non-class lines. This strategy simultaneously enabled the Indian National Congress to obstruct the exploited strata from taking to the path of revolutionary class struggles both against foreign rulers and local exploiters which could have uprooted both the foreign and local exploitative socio-economic system.

(ii) Some leaders who were organizing the struggles of the peasantry and did not mind broadening and deepening the struggles even against local exploiters got disillusioned. This eventually led to the emergence of various political tendencies within and outside the Indian National Congress. Such leaders endeavoured to elaborate various institutional and organizational devices broadly subsumed under Kisan Sabhas and Kisan Organizations.

(e) Ranga and Swami Sahajanand then describe the next phase in the peasant movements wherein a number of political tendencies develop. They hint at the emergence of communal political parties, regional political parties, parties standing for some reforms with regard to certain sections and specific grievances and the emergence of socialist and communist groups and currents both within the Congress and outside under Marxist ideology. With all their limitations, these political parties and groups posed an alternative programme to the Gandhian constructive programme strategy and directed the struggles of various sections of the poor and the exploited peasantry towards militant movements, both to end foreign rule and also to fight the capitalist-landlord-moneylenders' exploitation and oppression.

(5)

The fifth article is reproduced from N.G. Ranga's book, *Revolutionary Peasants* first published in 1949. This article is significant for a number of reasons: By this time Ranga had disassociated himself with Kisan Sabhas which were now dominated by Communists and Socialists. He became anti-Communist for two major reasons: (a) Stalinist policy of forced collectivization led to tremendous suffering and uprooting of the peasantry in the Soviet Union; (b) Communist Party of India's betrayal of national liberation struggles in India by discouraging and sabotaging the heroic peasant and workers struggles in the name of supporting the British Government in the Second World War after 1941. Ranga battled to evolve an alternate model viz. the Kisan Mazdur Praja Raj, based on faith in cooperatives as the institutional mechanism to save and strengthen the peasantry from both capitalist and what he called communist depredation.

Revolutionary Peasants from which this selection is reproduced was written during a transitional period when Ranga was dreaming of building an international peasant organization to strengthen the peasantry as an independent class to withstand the impact both of Capitalism and Communism which, according to him, were urban and therefore inimical to the interests of the peasantry. He tried to discover the revolutionary potential of the peasantry by locating its manifestation in their various struggles in the past and the present. This article belongs to this phase of his search. We need not analyse here the subsequent change in Ranga after 1949, into a spokesman of the rich farmer class and also his subsequent association with various parties in India which increasingly expoused the cause of the rising Kulak class in India.

What is important about his article is that Ranga as an active participant of peasant movements during various periods of the Indian national movement upto Independence, provides a very useful account of peasant movements which took place in India since the Revolt of 1857. He also highlights the direct and indirect impact of the Nationalist movements in stimulating, broadening and unleashing a number of peasant struggles both against the British rulers and the local exploiters, and which as a consequence brought various strata of the peasantry on the broader national stage generating a broadened all-India and even international political consciousness. The present selection is a rare account which prominently brings out the role of peasant struggles in Non-cooperation Movement, Civil Disobedience Movement, Quit India Movement and the movements launched in various Indian

Feudal States known as State's People's Struggles to either establish constitutional governments or abolish these feudal relics perpetuated by British Rule in India in its own interest. Ranga's article draws attention to the movements which are either ignored or underestimated by even Marxist scholars.

The selection reproduced here, is noteworthy on following counts: (i) It strives to distinguish the struggles which were essentially meant for redressing economic, social and political oppression in local areas exhibiting an immediate, unorganized and spontaneous character from the struggles (particularly from the second decade of the 20th century) which were politically directed and which attempted to unify, transform and elevate them from the status of being limited, purely sectional and economic or other grievances into the status of a larger national struggle. (ii) It draws attention to the Tribal and the Peasants' struggles not only in British territory, but also in various princely states. (iii) It draws attention to a number of organizational experiments and political and national perspectives which emerged to rouse the peasantry; (iv) It warns against ignoring the role of the Nationalist Movement, the Congress and other organizations in stimulating various types of peasant movements. (v) It emphasizes the need to recognize the importance of peaceful struggles, satyagrahas, marches, conferences, meetings, processions, demonstrations, various educational and training programmes and the emergence of various institutions in contributing to the growth of peasant movements and elevating peasant consciousness, (vi) It provides a corrective and a balance to the one-sided picture of peasant movements drawn by some of the Gandhian or communist groups.

(6)

The sixth selection 'Indian Peasant Uprising' is by Katheleen Gough, who is well-known for her valuable studies on *Indian Village Communities* and *Peasant Movements in India*. This article sums up her views on Indian peasant struggles. This article is noteworthy for following reasons:

(i) It clearly defines the scope of her study—examining social movements which involved peasants as the sole or main force, and where class struggles against those who extracted surplus from peasants led to armed struggles in due course. (ii) It challenges those scholars who underestimate the scope and significance of Indian peasant uprisings. The author disagrees with those who consider that the relative non-development of peasant movements in India as compared to say China was due to the existence of the caste system and the strength of bourgeois leadership against the landlords and the British and the pacifying influence of Gandhiji on the peasantry. (iii) It establishes her proposition by asserting that even a cursory study reveals a history of 77 revolts—the smallest of which engaged several thousand peasants in active support and combat; about 30 revolts affecting several tens of thousands; and about 12, several hundreds of thousands. While recognizing that in China peasant uprisings had larger coverage than India, she explains why this was so: (4) *It points out thirteen major features of colonial background created by British Rule*, which came unevenly and by stages, but once operative, created a structure of underdevelopment which became endemic and which though modified could never be eradicated even after independence. (v) It endeavours to classify peasant revolts during the British period into five types of actions in terms of goals, ideology and methods of organization: viz. (a) Restorative rebellions, to drive out the British and restore earlier rulers and social relations; (b) religious movements for the liberation of a region or ethnic group under new forms of government; (c) social banditry (to use Hobsbawn's term); (d) terrorist venegence with ideas of winning collective justice; (e) mass insurrections for the redressal of partiticular grievances. (vi) It attempts to classify uprisings of peasants, except early revolts, to drive out the British and restore traditional principalities, as pre-political or premature, but progressive in the sense that they sought a new form of peasant society which would be free from alien rule and would be based on some traditional virtues and modern technology, and above all there would be a popular government and would not revert to the pre-British social structures. (vii) It attempts to highlight remarkable organizing abilities, potential discipline and solidarity of the peasants and their determined militancy in opposing imperialism and exploitative class relations. It also points to the peasant's inventiveness and potential military prowess and their aspirations for a more democratic and egalitarian society, and even their capacity for cooperating in class struggles cutting across caste, religion and linguistic lines to redress their common grievances. (viii) It points out how peasant revolts since 1920's have been coordinated within policies of oppositional political parties and forming two major types: (a) political movements for independence or for national and regional autonomy among blocks of Tribal people like nationalist wars for independence in Kashmir, Nagaland, Mizoram and Jharkhand Movement in Tribal Bihar, (b) peasant struggles which were primarily class struggles and were guided by one or another of India's communist parties. (ix) It refers to seven major uprisings under Communist guidance, first by the undivided Communist Party of India and later by the Marxist groups, which broke away from CPI (Marxist) in 1967. Katheleen Gough points out how peasant movements led by communists differed in many respects from peasant struggles either fought earlier or under the leadership of other parties and groups, and how they were started or stopped according to national or even international changes in party line. She highlights the strength and weaknesses of these movements.

Katheleen Gough's article is worth studying because it attempts to place the various peasant revolts in a certain framework. In spite of the deliberate eschewing of reference to peasant struggles launched under the auspicies of Indian National Congress or Congress socialist party and numerous other political groups in different part of the country, the article focuses attention on certain aspects of peasant struggles hitherto ignored.

1 Background of Tribal Struggles In India

V. R. Raghavaiah

OF ALL THE TRIBES in India, it is the fight with the Assam tribes that drew the British rulers into the vortex of an India-wide struggle with the tribal people, which necessitated a drastic change in their approach to the tribes and their problems. After getting a foretaste of the intricacies involved in a struggle with the primitive peoples, the British East India Company's Government had to face perhaps the biggest of tribal insurrections in India, with the great Santal people in 1855. By this time, the Britisher who had till then not known what a clash with tribal people meant, had to set himself to seriously think about this problem. That is why we find them more cautious and more careful in dealing with the Santals and about the same time with the Mundas, another great tribe of this country. Soon followed a spate of revolts spearheaded by the Indian war of Independence of 1857 which rocked the British Empire to its foundations. The tribals too initiated struggles to safeguard their honour, to protect their cherished freedom, and to get redress against the moneylender, the Zamindar, and other parasitic landholders, who tried to deprive them of all they had. It cannot be said that they under-rated the strength of the enemy nor were they over-estimating their own strength. They knew that their primitive arms could not silence the Britishers' guns. They also realized that non-tribal India would not make common cause with their struggle. They should have also been aware that ultimately they have to rely upon their own strength and yet they gave a heroic fight for the simple reason that they could not avoid it much less postpone it.

The Santals are one of the six largest tribes of India—in fact the second largest tribe, with a population of 28,11,578 in 1951 which

Reproduced from *Tribal Revolts* by V. Raghavaiah, Andhra Rashtra Adimajati Sevak Sangh, Nellore (A.P.), 1971, pp. 13-26.

rose to 31,54,107 in 1961. The largest tribe in this country are the Gonds with a population of 32,01,004 in 1941, and 39,91,767 in 1961. The other large tribes of this country are Bhils with a population of 38,38,371, the Oraons numbering 14,44,554, the Mundas claiming a population of 10,19,098 and the Khonds having a population of 8,45,981. The total population of the Scheduled tribes of India has been estimated in 1961 to be 29,88,347, though taking into account many unscheduled but nevertheless possessing all the characteristics of primitive people, the total tribal population in this country, scheduled and unscheduled, can be roughly estimated to be four crores. Madhya Pradesh is the State claiming the largest tribal population of 66,78,410, that is, 20.63% of the total State Population, Orissa closely following with a tribal population of 42,04,770. The States having the largest percentage of tribal population to the total population are Nagaland with 93.09 per cent, Orissa with 24.07, Madhya Pradesh with 20.63, Assam with 17.42, Gujerat with 13.35 and Rajasthan with 11.46.

The late Dr B.S. Guha, for a long time, the Director of the Department of Anthropology, Government of India, who contributed a great deal to the anthropological lore in this country, reviewing the disturbances that occurred in the Tribal areas, observed that 'the underlying causes of these uprisings were the deep dissatisfaction created among the tribal people, against exploitation by their more advanced neighbours. Following the measures taken principally in the U.S.A., after the initial stage of exploitation was over, to segregate the tribes into special areas of reservation, to protect their lives and interests, the Government of India passed an Act in 1874 to specify the tribal areas into 'Scheduled Tracts'. These areas were reconstituted under Section 52(A) of the Government of India Act of 1919 and finally in 1935 more stringent provisions for special treatment of Tribal areas were incorporated by converting them into total and partially excluded areas'. Enumerating a few of these uprisings the learned Anthropologist stated 'several uprisings of the tribal people took place beginning from Mal Paharia rising in 1772, the mutiny of the Hos of Singbhum in 1831, the Khond uprising in 1846, to the Santal rebellion of 1855. In like manner a punitive expedition was sent to the Jaintia Hills in 1744 by the Company's Government and in 1833 the confederacy of the Khasi Chiefs was defeated by the

British army. Other expeditions were sent, such as those to Chin-Lushai Hills between 1850 and 1890, the Naga Hills expedition of 1878, the Abhor expedition of 1912, and finally the column sent to the unadministered areas of the Naga Hills as late as 1939'.

Just as there has been a clash of economic interests in the various tribal uprisings, there has been a clash of cultures also between the tribals and their non-tribal vested interests, bulwarked by the ruling authorities, who in their initial stages of administration and unsettled authority had to lean upon the educated and the landed classes, who were potential trouble makers—a policy continuously followed by the British throughout their rule in this country, which even the present administration is not yet quite able to replace by a thoroughly democratic people's rule. The two types of interests were closely entwined and were sometimes supplying the necessary momentum to each other. The tribal reacted fiercely when his religious beliefs were scoffed at, when his independence was attacked, when his traditional, customs and manners, civic rights, judicial systems, standards of etiquette and prestige and code of honour were brushed aside and deep rooted conventions ignored and insulted and violated.... According to the Santal's and other tribals' conception, particularly that of the Assamese tribal people, the cultivable land of any village was not alienable by any one individual and was the common property of all. Distribution and redistribution of all village land was effected by the village council of elders and all clearings of the jungle, as well as the sowing and harvesting were carried out under the supervision and initiation of the village priests and elders. The residents of any village could use and improve separate plots of land allotted to them and if any family had more members and required more land they could under instructions from the elders annex more land. When these well-established conventions were ignored by the European rulers who had been given to an individualistic and not to a collective pattern of living, the clash became inevitable.

Tribal justice was summary. It was meted out by the village elders, who could be expected to know the merits of each case personally in some cases and by reliable hearsay in others, and do full justice to the disputing parties.* The trials did not cost the

---

*See Verrier Elwin, *Maria Murder and Suicide*, Oxford University Press (1943), 1977. [ed.]

tribal anything and he had no need to walk scores of miles to the British Law Courts, for numerous adjournments, pay lawyers and argue out his case not by himself as he would do in his own village tribal enquiry, but in a different language, through an intermediary who could not have grasped the implication of tribal customs and culture and before a judge who lived miles away from the scene of offence and could not have had any knowledge of the locality or its surroundings. In civil matters even when he at last got relief, it was only on paper and he had to wait for longer durations executing his decrees and meeting endless hair-splitting technical objections relating to irregularities in the process of attachment, sale etc.

This naturally vexed the tribal and when he ultimately realized that it was not the course of events, so much as it was the skill of the lawyer and the length of the client's purse that brought him success in the law courts, he got quite bewildered and lost faith in the fairness of British justice.

In the tribal's view the jungle is his ancestral home. It was his birth place and cradle. In fact, he took to the jungle like fish to water. Every sound was familiar to him in the woods. He could recognize and name every bird, plant, animal and even insect. He loved the jungle and was in turn loved and adored by it. He never slew an animal for the mere love of hunt. He never cut any tree for satisfying his whim or fancy. He was Nature's child and like a loving mother, Nature fed him, nursed him, lulled him and protected him as a mother. In fact he is the overlord of it, an axiom, so well understood by the primitive since the emergence of Man. He had his collective ceremonial hunts in it. He worshipped the Goddess of the jungle before each hunt as for instance the Garela Misemma of the Chenchus of Andhra Pradesh, and after each hunt, offered selected parts of the kill to the Goddess. He loved the jungle and was least afraid of its carnivorous denizens. He collected a large part of his food from it in the shape of yams he could dig, edible nuts, fruits, flowers and leaves he could pluck to satisfy his hunger. He could also gather from the jungle several items of forest produce, including medicinal herbs, fuel, honey and housing material.

One of the main reasons why tribal people in this sub-continent feel disunited, isolated, and thwarted, is the gradual and steady temptation to which they succumbed in the past one hundred years, by allowing themselves to be easily converted by powerful religious Missions, foreign as well as indigenous, not because they really believed that their pattern of faith was inferior to that of others, but because through conversion they fondly hoped to secure economic betterment, freedom from exploitation and relief from the Sowcar's or Mahajan's (money-lender) harassment. The earlier Christian missionaries who felt that the tribal areas served as fertile fields for their proselytizing operations, worked in close cooperation with the British administrators, that the impression was inevitably created that redress from wrongs could be secured quicker and more effectively from the Government through the intervention and influence of these intermediaries. This happened in the State of Assam, in the Naga Land, in the Ranchi and surrounding areas of Bihar, in Madhya Pradesh, Andhra Pradesh and in every other part of this vast country where the Missions operated. Criminal tribes' settlements which were formed in every State by the State Governments were entrusted for management to these Missionary agencies some of which had no compunctions in offering all manner of baits for procuring converts from these miserable and helpless convicts. Possessing as Settlement Managers, very wide powers in making or marring the future of thousands of convicts entrusted to their care, the missionaries conferred favours on those who accepted their faith and even unlawfully exercised criminal and civil judicial powers against the prisoners. This occurred on a large scale in the Lushai, Khasi and Jaintia hills as well as in Madhya Pradesh, Bihar and Travancore-Cochin, thus not only undermining the numerical strength of the tribal population as such, but also in effectively destroying the sense of tribal culture solidarity, discipline and self-confidence among the tribal people. Consequent on conversions, the tribals' racial and national feeling suffered a set back and duel loyalties came to be established among the converts. With this jolt suffered in the tribal's self-confidence, he could not face his opponents, the indigenous exploiters and their patrons, the alien rulers, and this naturally resulted in eventual surrender to the wielders of superior skill and greater might. It is this painful realisation that elicited the following heartfelt warning from Mahatma Gandhi to the Indian Nation. The Mahatma observed:

'If we can bestow a little serious thought we will realize what a great and pressing problem it is to improve the social and economic or moral and material condition of the Aborigines. We can ill-afford to allow such a huge population as that of the Adivasis to remain any longer illiterate, ignorant and labouring under great hardships like abject poverty, unsympathetic administration, serfdom to Sowcars and landlords and unkind exploitation by more advanced sections of the general population'.

If the elite of the Society represented by the intelligentia, the native chiefs, and the subordinate officials had evinced a fraction of interest in tribal welfare as they did in feathering their own nests in the widespread chaos that prevailed in the country in the wake of the British conquest and their 'divide and rule' policies, or if the destiny holders of this vast country here or in England had at least a humanitarian interest, if not wise and far-reaching statemanship, in dealing with their forlorn tribal populations, the massacre of Santals and the pillage and arson perpetrated in their villages would not have occurred. Dr Verrier Elwin writing in his admirable book '*A Philosophy for NEFA*' has the following observations on tribal land and its cultural and psychological significance to the owners thereof. He remarked:

'In other parts of India (than NEFA) where the tribal communities have declined, in many ways, the first cause of their depression was the loss of their land and forests. This had the effect of so enervating the tribal organism that it had no interior resistance against infection by a score of other evils. To the tribal mind, Government's attitude about land and forests is as important as any scheme of development or education. If we look back over the long series of Tribal rebellions against authority in other parts of tribal India, we see that the majority of them arose over this one point. Thus the Kol insurrection of 1833 was caused by encroachment on tribal land. The Tamar rebellions repeated seven times between 1789 and 1832 were primarily due to the illegal deprivation of their rights in land, which the Hos, Mundas and Oraons had suffered.' (pp. 62-3)

Dr J.H. Hutton too had remarked in his work *Modern India and the West*, that 'the best land (of the tribals) passed into the hand of outsiders....'

It may not be correct to suppose that the tribal revolts were unconnected with the general popular discontent resulting from the ruthless exploitation engineered by the British East India Company's unscrupulous and commercial administration. Though the eruptions of this unrest took firm shape from the mid-nineteenth century onwards, trouble was undoubtedly brewing virtually in every part of the country among almost every section of the people, like the peasants, intelligentia, trading communities, the military, the scions of native royal dynasties, who were deprived of their territories by the application of the Doctrine of Lapse, conquest and various other pretexts found for justifying annexation. The peasants were badly hit by rack-renting by the Zamindars and rich landholders and reduced to poverty owing to the unhelpful attitude of the Company's courts, which were mostly supporting the claims of the vested interests of the creditors. It was clear to every litigant that the then Government was solidly behind the vested interests though they took shelter under some law or other, either imported from their own country or by a tortuous interpretation of the prevailing local laws, which did not take notice of the Indian conditions of tenancy, collective, inalienable ownership of land, and other time-honoured practices, which assured the actual tiller undisturbed and continued right to enjoy the land, which his ancestors tilled.

The revolts of the tribal people were not isolated and on the other hand, shared many features in common with the revolts of non-tribal, agrarian and small trading communities. For various reasons that particular period might have been chosen by the suffering masses to ventilate their grievances in an organized manner. The country was disturbed all over with wars between one ruler and another, mostly formented by the Company's skilful civil servants, militant lieutenant Governors and adventurers, with previous experience of raking up trouble as well as fanning it. There were also other causes like wars between the Company and the native rulers like Tippu, the fading remnants of the Maharashtra Peshwas, Oudh's ruling chiefs, Ranjit Singh's petulant and belligerent forces, the potential foreign rivals and festering discontent among low paid Indian sepoys, the much exploited indigo farmers and labourers of Bengal and Bihar, not to mention the wholesale evictions from their lands carried on by the Jenmi Namboodri Brahmin wealthy land-lords of Kerala whose rights in land were suddenly converted from a pattern of partnership with the Mopla Muslim tenants and landless labourers, into one of absolute ownership with right to evict the tenants at will. In addition, the disbanded soldiery of the dispossessed native chiefs swept across the country under the names of Pindaris, Thugs etc., committing dacoities and rendering the highways unsafe every where. Added to this, the textile and other artisans whose ancient cottage industries were ruthlessly destroyed by the Company's officials, to promote import of British fabrics, iron and steel goods etc., caused unheard of unemployment and acute misery and poverty.

Popular and country-wide uprisings occurred among the indigo-cultivators of Bihar and Bengal in 1860, among the rack-rented peasants in Bogra and Pabna in 1872 in Bengal, among the farmers of Poona and Ahmednagar in Maharashtra in 1875, and among the Moplas of Malabar in 1836, 1849, 1851, 1852, 1854, 1855, 1873, 1880, 1894, 1896 and 1921. L. Natarajan has given a brief account of these uprisings in his pamphlet *Peasant Uprisings in India*. The indigo-cultivators of Bihar struck against the European land-owners and merchants, who, using their influence with the East India Company's administration, began to compel the ryots of Bihar to cultivate indigo, which they exported on a monopoly scale to Britain, for colouring her textiles, as the chemical dyes were not invented by that time, They purchased huge estates from the Zamindars and compelled the tenants not to grow any other crop including food crops. The prices offered were so ridiculously small that the tenants loudly protested and forced the Governor-General of the Company on 13-7-1810 to concede that the European Zamindars were committing acts of violence, causing death to the farmers, were unlawfully detaining and confining them for refusing to cultivate the land with indigo, were engaged in large scale violent attacks hiring unruly elements, and were even causing death and severely injuring the farmers frequently. The Governor-General in Council, therefore, resolved to 'adopt such measures as appeared to him under existing circumstances, best calculated to prevent the repetition of offences equally injurious to the English character and to the peace and happiness of our native subjects'.

This promise remained a dead letter until the harassed cultivators rose in revolt in 1860. It was further conceded by the Judge of Nadia in his letter to the Secretary to the Bengal Government on

20-4-1854, that every two and half bighas of land were considered by planters as only one bigha and not content with this, the planters took away two bundles from their fields. The agitation soon assumed the proportions of a rebellion driving the surprised Europeans into panic, and they sought the Government's intervention, which was not forthcoming readily, in view of the violent Santal revolt of 1855-6 and the Indian War of Independence of 1857, which left unforgetable impressions on the foreigner as well as on the sons of the soil. The Lieutenant Governor of Bengal gave assurance to the ryots to protect them against the hooliganism of the Europeans and after meeting a rebellious assembly of 2,000 angry tenants in one of his tours, and realizing the gravity of the situation, announced that the peasants were free to raise any crops they liked and that all the harassment and restrictions in vogue till then were removed. In 1917-8 the indigo planters' problem again cropped up and under Mahatma Gandhi's leadership the peasants once again repeated their struggle against the European planters and by adopting the weapon of Satyagraha known as the Champaran Satyagraha, came out victorious.

Enhancement of rent and cesses was the root cause of the conflict that broke out between the Zamindars and the peasants in Pabna and Bogra in 1872-3. The landlords began to force the tenants to enter into registered agreements relating to the conditions of tenancy, taking advantage of the ignorance and illiteracy of the latter, by inserting new terms, injurious to the tenants and dragging them into costly litigation in distant courts, where unfamiliar laws foreign to the country's genius held mastery over illiteracy and poverty. Taught by bitter experience the courts fell in line with the spirit of the times and the agitation of the peasants and ultimately passed orders justly and in favour of the tenants.

The Sapa rising of peasants (1875) was due to same or similar causes that erupted the other insurrections. The land settlements of the East India Company were motivated with a commercial basis, namely of squeezing as much revenue from the peasant as one could secure, irrespective of his ability to pay the enhanced assessments fixed at an exaggerated estimate of the yield of the soil. This, the ryots could not pay, not only that, the required payment was directed to be paid in cash which again affected him adversely owing to fluctuating prices. The convenience of the Government was evidently not the same as the facility of the subject. This new method of collecting land revenue was at variance with that of the traditional Moghul rulers and drove the cultivators into the greedy hands of money-lenders, whose rates of usury ranged between fifty and hundred percent. Indebtedness resulted in suits for taking possession of the peasants' lands, through law courts, whose decisions were taken far away from the villages of the ryots and in utter ignorance and disregard of the conditions prevailing, involving costs which the poor peasant could not afford to incur. Between 1851 and 1865 the number of suits in Poona and Ahmednagar, where the discontent prevailed, rose seven to eight and half times. Even the Company's Governor-in-council was obliged to acknowledge that 'our Civil Courts have become hateful to the masses of our Indian subjects from being made the instruments of almost incredible rapacity of usurious capitalists. Nothing can be more calculated to give rise to widespread discontent and disaffection to the British Government than the practical working of the present laws'. This warning did not produce any visible effect, as the peasants had to wait for 12 years more i.e., in 1870 in which another high Government official thought it necessary to sternly warn that:

'The Santal rebellion arose out of the things precisely similar to that now existing in the west of Khandesh'. Even this did not move the Government to a realization of the discontent prevailing. It again slept over the matter quite unmoved by the warnings even of its own officials. In December 1874 the peasants of village Kardeh of the Sirur Taluka fired the first shot. They took the law into their own hands by attacking the moneylenders so that they might destroy the agreements relating to debts and sales of land, effected under pressure and in ignorance. A severe social boycott was organized against the Sahukars who became helpless and quietly surrendered the documents and cash they possessed. In some cases even violence was used by the villagers against Marwari moneylenders. There were other uprisings in several neighbouring villages in Shrigonda, Parner, Nagar and Karjat talukas. The Government now came down upon the peasants heavily and arrested more than a thousand of them. As expected, the revolt was quelled in less than three weeks.

Yet another revolt that rocked South India was that of the combustible Mopla muslims who were descendants of both early

Arab settlers as well as converted Hindus. The struggle here was against the Zamindar Nambudiris by the peasant tenants, the cause being the conversion by the British Indian Government of the status of a Jenmi from that of the traditional partner to that of an absolute owner of the land, with right to evict the Mopla tenants, a right he had not before. This resulted in the enhancement of rents and wholesale evictions for non-payment of rents.

The Moplas revolted under the able leadership of a young lawyer Shri Narayana Menon and struck against the land-holders. Between 1836 and 1854 there were twenty two uprisings resulting in pitched battles in which several Moplas lost their lives at the hands of the security forces. There were riots in 1851 and 1852, 1855, 1873, 1880, 1883 to 1885, 1894 and 1896 and finally in 1921 when thousands of rebels who were guilty of arson, and murder of land-holders and their supporters were arrested and hundreds executed by the British authorities. Shri Narayana Menon who entered the Coimbatore jail at the age of 30 for leading the peasant revolt secured his release only when he served a long term of more than twenty years for a life sentence. It is thus seen that in every one of the revolts, tribal or non-tribal, the parties to the disputes were originally the tenant and the land-grabber and as revolt and violence flared up, the Government invariably stepped in to safeguard the vested interests of moneylenders, zamindars, and the intelligentsia.

Undoubtedly revolt was not only in the air but got into the blood of every one's veins in the mid-nineteenth century period of India's chequered history. There is, therefore, no point in trying to find out who ignited the first spark, the tribal or the non-tribal? Surely the Santal revolt of 1855 should have taught a few lessons to the leaders of the National revolt of 1857, and this must have been of immense help in estimating the seriousness of events that happened subsequent to it. Both tribal and non-tribal revolts could not dislodge their common adversary namely British Government from its entrenched position in India until its dissolution was accomplished in 1946-7...

2 Tribal Revolts in Chronological Order: 1778 to 1971

V. Raghavaiah

1778	:	Revolt of the Pahariya Sirdars of Bihar against the British Government.
1784-5	:	Koli disturbances (Maharashtra) at the instigation of a Rani of Jawahar.
1789, 1794-5	:	Revolt in Tamar of Chota Nagpur.
1795-1800	:	Revolt of the Chuari Movement in Bihar.
1798	:	Panchet estate sale revolt.
1801	:	Tamar revolt in Bihar.
1803	:	Koya uprising in the Rampa area of the East Godavari Agency, Andhra Pradesh.
1807-8	:	Chota Nagpur Tribal revolt.
1809-28	:	Bhil revolt in Gujarat.
1811, 1817, 1820	:	Bihar agrarian Tribal revolts.
1818	:	The Koli revolt (Maharashtra) after a conspiracy.
1816-24	:	Burmese invasions of Assam and their reign of terror.
1824-6	:	First Burmese war against the Burmese occupation of Assam in which the British first espoused Assam's cause and after defeating Burmese, usurped Assam.

Reproduced from *Tribal Revolts* by V. Raghavaiah *op. ct.* pp. 261-66.

1825	: Singphos attacked and set fire to the British magazine at Sadiya.
1827	: Mishmis murdered explorer Wilcox.
1828	: First revolt of Assam tribes against the British under Gomdhar Konwar who was defeated by Lt. Rutherford.
1828	: Singpho's Chief attacked Sadiya with 3000 tribal warriors.
1829	: Revolt of Khasis of Assam.
1829	: Teerut Singh (Assam) massacred the British generals and their Indian Sepoys.
1833	: Teerut Singh's surrender.
March 1834	: Teerut Singh's death.
1831-2	: The Great Kol insurrection.
1820, 1832, 1867	: Munda revolts in Bihar.
1832-3	: The Kherwar rising under the leadership of Bhagirath in Bihar. Hazari Bagh rising of Kherwars-leader Dubia Gossaian-Bihar. Phatel Singh of Palmau was later risings' leader in Bihar.
1834-41	: Lushais (Assam) raid British subjects.
1835	: Daflas of NEFA (Assam) raided British Plains' subjects and British took to reprisals to revenge.
1835	: Raja of Jaintia hills (Assam) was deposed by the British owing to his anti-British activities, and given a pension.
1836	: Mishmis (Assam) killed botanist Griffith suspecting his intentions.
1838	: Naik revolt in Gujarat.
1839-43	: Khampti (Assam) rising.
1839	: Khamptis attacked and killed the British

	Agent, Adam White and 80 other officers and soldiers.
1842	: British annex Sadiya and Muttock country in Assam.
1842	: Captain Blunt's troops attacked by Bastar Gonds. Blunt had to withdraw.
1842	: Lushais (Assam) raided the British territory of Arakan, Sylhet and defeated the British forces.
1843	: Singpho Chief Nirang Phidu attacked the British garrison and killed several soliders.
1844	: Lushais attack Manipuri villagers and massacred taking 20 heads as trophies. Reprisal by the British followed. Lushai leader Lal Sukla arrested and transported for life.
1846	: Bhil revolt under Kuwar Jive Vasavo in Gujarat.
1849	: Kadma Singpho attacked British villages in Assam and was captured.
1850	: Lushais were punished by the British raid under Colonel Lister.
1850	: Revolt of Chakra Bisoyi, the Kondh tribal leader in Orissa.
1854	: Kachari chief in North Kachari hills of Assam submitted and permitted the British to annex his territory.
1855	: The revolt of the Santals in Bihar.
1855	: Eden's punitive expedition against Mishmis to avenge their killing of 2 Missionaries.
1858	: Naikdas' revolt against the British in Gujarat.
1857-8	: Bhil revolt (Gujarat) under the leadership of Bhagoji Naik and Kajar Singh.

7-9-1857	:	Revolt of Maniram Dewan and Saring Raja of Assam, their arrest by the British Government.
1860	:	Lushai Chief raided—British Tripura and killed 186 British subjects.
1860-2	:	Revolt of Syntengs of Jaintia Hills.
1861	:	The Phulaguri uprising of tribal peasants.
1861	:	The Juang revolt in Orissa.
1862	:	Syntengs of Jaintia Hills revolt.
1862	:	Andhra Agency Koya tribal revolt against Muttadars (Petty tribal Zamindars) and their supporters, the British.
1867, March	:	Sentinal islanders (Andaman group) attack Humphrey.
1868	:	Naiks' revolt under Joria's leadership in Gujarat.
1868	:	Revolt of the Raig-Mels of Kamrup and Darrang.
1869	:	Final peace between the British and the Singphos.
1869-70	:	Dhanbad Santal unrest (Bihar) against Raja of Tundi subsequently settled by Colonel Dalton.
1871-2	:	Treaty signed between Lushais and British.
1872-3	:	Daflas quelled by British military: expedition.
1879	:	Naga revolt.
1879	:	Andhra Agency Koya revolt against Muttadars and the British.
1880	:	Koya's revolt under Tammandora's leadership Malkangiri, Orissa.

7-8-1883	:	Sentinal islanders attack Humphrey (Andamans).
1889	:	Sardari (Munda leaders) agitation against the British Government.
1891	:	Manipur revolt led by Tikendrajit Singh against the British.
1892	:	Eastern Lushais rising against the British.
27-8-1895	:	Birsa Munda's arrest.
1911	:	Bastar tribal uprising.
1913, 1914, 1920, 1921	:	Tana Bhagat rebellion in Bihar.
1922	:	Rampa rebellion of Koyas under Alluri Sree Rama Raju against the British.
1932	:	Rani Guidallo's Naga non-Christian revolt (Assam).
1941	:	Gond and Kolam revolt against the British Government, in Adilabad district of Andhra Pradesh, led by Bhimu.
1942	:	Lakshmana Naik's Koraput revolt in Orissa.
1942-5	:	Revolts against Jap occupation army by the Tribes of Andaman group of islands:
1946-8	:	Warli revolt (Maharashtra).
1963-71	:	Naga revolt.
1966-71	:	Mizo revolt.
1967-71	:	Naxalite revolt.

3 Messianic Movements

Fr Stephen Fuchs

IT IS DIFFICULT, if not impossible, to give a precise definition of messianic movements. But it is possible to enumerate and describe certain characteristic features which, either together or at least in part, can be found active in these movements. The characteristic common features which in greater or lesser prominence appear in almost all these movements are: (1) A society intensely dissatisfied with the social and economic conditions which it is forced to accept; (2) the existence in this society of emotional unrest with certain hysterical symptoms; (3) the appearance of a charismatic leader; (4) the demand of this leader for implicit faith and obedience from his followers; (5) the test of this unquestioned faith and obedience consisting either in a radical change of life (cessation of cultivation of land, change of occupation, etc.) or even the wholesale destruction of property (furniture, houses, livestock, etc.); (6) the rejection of established authority and call for rebellion against it; (7) the threat of severe punishment of opponents of, and traitors to, the movement; (8) the remembrance of a 'Golden Age' in the distant past; (9) 'Revivalism', i.e. a renewed interest in the traditional religion, coming as a rule after a period of indifference or decline, and accompanied with expressions of great emotional excitement; (10) 'Nativism', i.e. the attempt of a backward people to restore selected parts of its pristine culture and to reject certain alien elements adopted from foreign cultures; (11) 'Vitalism', i.e. the desire of the members in the movement for alien goods, especially spiritual ones, from 'heaven', through magic or supernatural powers; (12) 'Syncretism', i.e. the indiscriminate adoption of various cultural traits of a superior civilization by a backward people; (13) 'Eschatologism', i.e. the expectation of a world renewal through world-wide catastrophic

Reproduced from *Rebellious Prophets* by Stephen Fuchs, Asia Publishing House, Bombay, 1965, pp 1-20.

revolutions and upheavals; (14) 'Millenarianism' or 'Chiliasm', i.e. the hope or expectation of a paradise on earth for a thousand years or some such long period of time.
(1) A society intensely dissatisfied with the social and economic conditions which it is forced to accept.

This is the result of a clash between two cultures, on vastly superior and the other retarded. The members of the backward culture often live in very simple and primitive economic and social conditions, with no incentive nor prospect for improvement, relief or progress. In the past, before the clash with the superior form of culture, they were quite content with their lot and desired nothing better. They realized their backward condition only after seeing a class of people leading a life entirely above their own, often radically different, incomprehensible and unattainable for them by natural effort.

Such a clash of cultures took place nearly always in colonized countries which were economically underdeveloped, highly isolated, politically acephalous, i.e. without centralized polity and, on the whole, in a state of passive acceptance of alien rule. In India, prior to the advent of the European powers, we do not speak of 'colonizers' and the 'colonized' but the effort of high-caste Hindu and Muslim rule on the low castes and aborigines was practically the same as in other countries colonized by Europeans.

The backward communities when confronted with the superior alien society became aware of their own abject poverty and began to feel the desire to alleviate it.

The emotional reactions of the backward and colonized communities are of jealousy and, often enough, hatred of the aliens who neither share the good things they possess as friends nor initiate them into the mysteries of their production or purchase.

Their intellectual problem is first to explain the aliens' success and secondly to find a way to achieve similar success. But the problem must be solved in terms of the experience of the backward societies.

They attribute the aliens' wealth to their religion, or magic, or their peculiar way of life; they never think it could be due to hard work and an inventive mind. When, consequently, they adopt the foreigners' religion, or ape their customs and way of life, the results are disastrous. They break loose from their own culture and lose their mental bearings, while at the same time they enter only very superficially into the mentality of the foreigners' religion and culture. Moreover, they are not accepted by the foreigners as equals. They thus lose their mental security and equilibrium, and become a prey to insecurity and anxiety, emotions which express themselves in hysterical symptoms. This leads us to the next point.

(2) The existence in this society of emotional unrest with certain hysterical symptoms

This emotional unrest is caused by a confusion in spiritual and social values. This confusion is the consequence of the influx of a new and dominating culture, and of the rules and regulations enforced by this dominating power. These new ideas are not properly understood by the dominated subjects, and often are contrary to their old beliefs and practices. This clash places them in a dilemma and makes it difficult for them to choose between the old and the new values. Should they, for instance, give up growing food for their families and seek employment as servants or labourers of the foreigners? Should they change their old methods of farming as the agricultural officers suggest? Or should they still continue to increase fertility by magic or religious means? Should they get married according to tribal law, or should they follow the laws of the new religion which they have adopted? Should they in case of murder take blood-revenge or call in the police?

Intellectually bewildered and perplexed, their culture in which their ethical values are imbedded partially disrupted by the impact of the alien culture, yet desirous of the aliens' wealth, the members of the subject-culture attempt, within the terms of their knowledge and based on their ancient traditions, to grasp the modern techniques of making wealth.

But the aliens share neither the technique nor the wealth with their colonized subjects. The latter believe that this is deliberate; and with their traditional ideas of a cooperative social system they consider this withholding to be profoundly immoral. The aliens, on the other hand, have different property concepts and regard the demands of the subject people as arrogant and unjust. Moreover, they are often incapable of teaching their subjects the essentials of their culture, because they do not understand their difficulties and their way of reasoning.

The same is true with regard to their ethical values. They are told that their ethical values and rules of behaviour are wrong, immoral, repulsive and ridiculous. Many of their actions in obedience to their ancient traditional ethics are punished, sometimes very severely, in the courts of law set up by the dominating culture. Blood-revenge, head-hunting, human sacrifices, cannibalism, bride-capture, duels, etc. fall under this heading.

Their tribal mythology—myths are primitive forms of explanatory theories for the events of nature—which have hitherto satisfied their naive curiosity about the origin of the world and of man and of human institutions, are ridiculed and judged to be foolish, inadequate and wrong.

This mental confusion and despair, often aggravated by economic oppression and social degradation, leads to mass hysterias which may express themselves in mental disturbances, acts of violence or suicides.

Similar conditions prevailed in India in pre-colonial times: the Hindu high-castes treated the backward classes as half-human brutes or as untouchables, while the Muslims regarded them as despicable 'infidels'. In this respect Hindus and Muslims scarcely differed from the haughty Anglo-Saxon administrative officials and army officers of the British colonial period.

To increase the confusion, Christian missionaries, on the other hand, insisted on equal rights for all, and condemned racial and social discrimination; so did the Muslim missionaries according to whom a convert acquired the right to humane treatment on entering the Muslim brotherhood. But there were also Hindu sects, particularly the Vaishnavas, who insisted on social equality and preached fraternity and abolition of caste.

The privileged position which the aliens claim for themselves as their heritage is thus exposed by the missionaries as unjustified usurpation, as criminal expropriation of a helpless people by the strong and dominating invaders. This awareness among the backward classes leads them to envy, hatred and injured resentment.

If in this perplexity and mental confusion a strong, authoritarian leader arises who pretends to know 'all the answers' and takes the lead, a messianic movement is generated.

(3) The appearance of a charismatic leader

The position of the leader starting and continuing a messianic movement requires careful investigation. Sometimes the ostensible leader is only a figurehead and not the real driving force behind a movement. There is a sort of Machiavelli-like figure behind him who is the real—often purely—political force behind the prophet. Religion is used intentionally and deliberately in the service of politics.

In some cases it is the leader who inaugurates a movement, while in other cases a social group is responsible for the rise of a movement who then search for and find a leader. But it may also be that the movement is the result and outcome of the situation in which both leader and followers find themselves and which forces them to concerted action.

It may happen that when the founder of a movement is not very successful, or loses his life early in his career, a successor takes over and leads the movement to success and gains many adherents.

The leader of the movement is usually a member of the community in which the movement rises, but sometimes he is an outsider who, however, identifies himself completely with the aims of the people he is leading.

The inaugurator of a movement has often had an intimate knowledge of the community against which the movement is directed; he has either received his education from its members, or worked for them, or lived with them for a shorter or longer period.

His messianic vocation is either the result of an inner conversion, and conscious aversion from the alien oppressor, or he has been rejected or slighted by him, and the messianic movement is initiated in revenge. Leader and followers need not always have the same motives and aims.

Most of the self-styled leaders are hardly educated, and often they are seriously mistaken about the extent of their own powers and abilities and about the power of the community which they are going to oppose.

A typical feature in all these movements is the claim of the founders—whether men or women—to be recipients of divine revelations regarding doctrines, ceremonies and policy. They possess the greatest self-confidence in their mission and are unshakable in their convictions and decisions.

Generally theirs was a youth spent in poverty and obscurity; sometimes they are sickly; often they suffer from nervous disturbance or disease. Some are epileptics.

Often they claim for themselves—and are granted by their followers—a sort of divine veneration. In India, Hindu Messiahs often claim to be incarnations of one or other of the powerful Hindu gods, Vishnu, Krishna or even Durga. The Muslim Messiahs claim to be Mahdis, Imams or great saints of the Sufi Orders. A few others claim to be incarnations of God, or of Christ on his second arrival as promised and foretold by Christ himself.

Most Messiahs claim to possess magic power, or the power to work miracles; they can heal the sick, make people invulnerable, turn bullets into water, multiply food, foretell the future, and the like.

Very impressive to perplexed and drifting minds is the authority and self-assurance with which these self-styled leaders carry themselves. Guided by a divine inspiration, they inspire hope and confidence in their followers. They pretend to know the root and cause of the evils which beset the community and to know also the way out of the trouble. If success fails to follow their remedial intervention they have an explanation and excuse ready. Generous assurance is given that all obstacles will presently be removed. Success is always just round the corner. This hope is infused into all new disciples of the movement; it inspires those interested in the cause to exert themselves and in fact stimulates unexpected energies and abilities.

(4) The demand of this leader for implicit faith and obedience

In all messianic movements the leader demands implicit faith and obedience from his followers. This is an indispensable condition for admission into the brotherhood. This absolute obedience and devotion to the cause are demanded because the leader is convinced either of his superhuman dignity or of the divine guidance and inspiration which he receives. Opposition to his utterances and decisions is consequently regarded as blasphemy. When the movement is successful, the leader often assumes royal dignity and rights. He behaves like a king and expects to be treated like one.

The recruitment of his followers is in most cases selective; at least at the beginning of the movement only such disciples join who are easily led and gladly obey. Later on, when the movement gathers impetus and becomes large, these early and most trusted followers advance into important positions for which they are grateful to the leader and which they repay by redoubled devotion and submission.

Naturally, not all the disciples and intimates of the leader are sincere. There may be a large degree of hypocrisy and sycophancy in this; but the retinue of adoring disciples and cringing followers increases the self-assurance and inflates the ego of the leader. No doubt, even the most self-confident leaders have their hours of doubt and depression, especially after disappointment or defeat, but the group of devoted followers is usually able to reassure the leader and to enwrap him in an atmosphere of exaltation from which he rarely escapes to judge his true position realistically.

Although these leaders are anxious to gain many followers to their movements, almost invariably they make high claims and demand heavy sacrifices as an indispensable condition for admission into the brotherhood. The higher the price the candidates have to pay, the greater their subsequent devotion and the more absolute their submission to the cause of the leader.

In many instances the intimate disciples of such a leader are tempted into committing actions which bring them into collision with the established authority in the country, i.e. with the government of the dominating culture against which their movement is directed. They then see their only salvation in a victory for their movement. A failure of their agitation would probably land them in jail; even a worse fate may await them. Hence their extreme devotion to the cause and their utter submission to the leader to whom they transfer all responsibility for their own actions. He will, as they hope, take on himself all responsibility and blame if the movement ultimately should fail.

(5) The test of this unquestioned faith and obedience consists either in a radical change of life or a wholesale destruction of property

The leader advises methods by which his followers can achieve their revolutionary objectives. These methods are often radically different from their former ways of life.

For the inner circle of disciples the movement means a whole-time job. They must abandon their former way of life and devote all their time and energy to the movement. Since most of these individuals up to the time of joining the movement had an occupation by which they earned their livelihood, they are now forced to give this up and to take on the duties which the leader assigns to each of them.

For the great majority of followers this change of occupation may become a necessity only when the movement reaches the climax. At that moment all men have to be engaged in carrying out the task set before them. It is the aim proposed by the leader of the movement, which has caught their imagination and found their approval. In fact that was their motive in joining the movement. Now that the moment has come to attain the desired goal, all are called up for concerted action to realize it. This often means giving up the occupation by which followers had previously earned their livelihood for themselves and for their dependents.

Another motive for giving up their former occupation is the conviction that a new era is being inaugurated in which everything will be changed. To pursue one's old occupation is a sign that the follower does not really believe in the movement and doubts its success. The test, therefore, lies in giving up all independent resources and in relying completely and without reservations on the leader and on the group carrying on the movement.

It may also be that the pursuance of certain occupations is being made responsible for the decline of the whole community (in the case of the Chamars, for instance, the dealing in hides and leather-work). A ritually pure job must be pursued in place of the old polluting occupations.

If a certain messianic movement is connected, as it often is, with the belief in a coming Golden Age, or a Millennium, no labour or physical exertion would in future be required, nor would there be any need to preserve and store food, clothing, etc. Everything would be provided in the coming age of plenty; any individual effort and initiative would only be an expression of doubt in the leader and in his helpers. In the Golden Age soon to come better goods would be offered to the followers; why then keep the present inferior goods? It is a declaration of faith in the leader to renounce one's property before the Golden Age has really arrived and before the prophecy of the leader has been fulfilled.

On the other hand, if the messianic movement contains the element of eschatologism, or in other words, if the followers of the movement believe that the change of things will come through a great catastrophe, there is in that case still no need for further exertion or provision for the future.

Sometimes the radical change of life for the followers, even the wholesale destruction of property, livestock, houses, etc. is the outcome of their complete rootlessness and despair. They hope by turning everything upside down to regain their loss of balance and security, and to get a hold on reality. This is often accompanied by an expression of intolerance, and where non-members refuse to join the movement they carry out the desperate act of destruction. Subconsciously they attribute a magic value to this act of despair; any refusal to join in it means a weakening of the magic effect, and is therefore strongly resented and severely punished.

(6) Rejection of the established authority and call for rebellion against it

From the outset any established and properly functioning authority or government will be against any violent change which brings disorder and confusion in its wake. Consequently it is opposed to messianic movements. But such a movement has been created just for the purpose of bringing about a change and forcing the self-established authority to abrogate its privileges and to hand over control and power. It even aims at a violent overthrow of the imposed domination.

Where the subject societies are weakly organized politically and without powerful chiefs or kings, it is easy for a messianic movement to forge a new hierarchical system of its own which completely cuts across old ties and boundaries between peoples and thus channelizes their loyalty in a new direction. In this way messianic movements easily become political.

Messianic movements, being in their very essence revolutionary, become provocative and dangerous to the established government if the leaders are strong and militant. The established government often reacts violently to such provocation and suppresses the movement with great severity. If this is done when the movement is still in its initial stage, and when the government succeeds in eliminating the ring-leaders, such a movement can be completely suppressed. But once the movement has gained momentum and spread over a wide area and attracted many followers, even the removal of the leader is abortive. New leaders rise in place of the old one, and often they are more violent and extreme, more efficient and more capable of leadership than their predecessor.

Not infrequently the religious leader of a messianic movement assumes the political role forced on him by circumstances or by his followers. He then more or less abandons his religious aims and aspirations. But it may also happen that another individual takes over from the religious leader, and pursues the political aims either in close cooperation with or even in complete supersession of the religious leader. Often there is an almost dynastic succession of messianic leaders, the father being the creator and inaugurator of the movement and aiming at a religious change, while the succeeding sons or adopted disciples later turn the religious movement into a political one.

Where the dominating culture which causes the confusion and despair in the inferior community is at the same time the established authority and government (often indeed a self-imposed authority which the subjects have never really accepted) opposition to the domination of the superior community appears also as rebellion against the established authority and government. A messianic movement, born out of the clash of two vastly different cultures and supported by the inner rejection and smouldering hatred of the subject community against its masters, is essentially a revolutionary movement. A religious revolution will in such a predicament always turn into a political revolution.

(7) Threat of severe punishment of opponents of, and traitors to, the movement

Opponents offend a God, or a representative of God, and reject the inspirations of God. Moreover, opposition implies criticism of the justification of the cause. It is blasphemy and sacrilege.

The conviction is strong that corporate action is required, and all must fall in line. The movement must be an action of the whole community, as it is for the salvation and benefit of the whole society.

If members of the community keep aloof they weaken the cause, endanger its success, bring on the disapproval and anger of the divine agency that decreed the movement. They also impair the magic effect of corporate action.

There is an innate intolerance in primitive society, and in heavily oppressed social groups because they are mainly ruled by public opinion which enforces the sanctions. Moreover, such communities cannot tolerate indiscipline nor afford to take liberties with tribal laws. This would endanger the survival of the whole group. Thus the sanctions are severe and must be strictly enforced. A messianic movement which is accepted and approved by the whole community enjoys therefore all the privileges of tribal action in the vital interest of the society. Non-cooperation, and even more so defection are crimes in the eyes of the community. The greater the movement and the more important the position of its leader, the more heinous the crime.

(8) The remembrance of a 'Golden Age' in the beginning of mankind

Remembrance of a 'Golden Age' or paradise in the earliest times of mankind is found among many peoples all over the world. It is almost universal. The descriptions of this 'Golden Age' differ widely, and they change with the cultural standards of the peoples relating such myths. But all describe it as a place of pure and unmixed happiness, without suffering, without sorrow and death. Almost always the emphasis is on material and physical happiness, combined with sensual pleasures; though spiritual and intellectual enjoyments are also mentioned. Moreover it is always clearly stated that man in this 'Golden Age' is good, innocent, a friend of God, and obedient to his commandments.

Almost all the myths about a 'Golden Age' include the story of its tragic conclusion, either through human guilt, or through the seduction of man by an evil spirit, or by some unfortunate coincidence. Thus such myths explain satisfactorily the existence of pain and sorrow, suffering and death in the world.

The consequences of this loss of the 'Golden Age' are, however, not final. For in many of the myths the promise of a return of the 'Golden Age' in the fullness of time is held out to mankind.

It is exactly this 'Golden Age', or paradise, which the founder of the messianic movement wants to inaugurate. He usually makes a deep impression on his audience because this tradition is still very much alive in the community and his promises therefore do not sound unrealistic or unbelievable. The preacher usually promises an earthly paradise, with material benefits in abundance. His preaching is clothed in popular language, easily understood by his audience. He uses expressions which vividly appeal to the longing of the masses for happiness and for freedom from suffering and want. Poor and rootless people, the sick and needy are promised immediate relief.

Hatred against the superior community is incited by a description of the paradise as it existed in times previous to the arrival of the invaders. Loss of the paradise is often attributed to the invaders. In strong contrast to the Golden Age in the past stands the present age with all its misery, degradation and oppression. The blame for all this is put on the superior community. The messianic movement is meant to restore the Golden Age destroyed or filehed from them by the invasion of the superior community.

(9) Revivalism, i.e. a renewed interest in the traditional religion, coming as a rule, after a period of indifference or decline, accompanied with expressions of great emotional excitement

Revivalism is a result of calling back to mind the lost existence of a 'Golden Age'. It is often believed that the Golden Age will return if the conditions are restored of that life in which man lived in those happy days. Thus the revivalists try to reconstruct, as related in the myths, the times and conditions of life in the Golden Age.

This results in a renewed interest in the traditional religion, as also in the whole culture of the community. It leads to a practice of the religious rites and even to the restoration of obsolete social and cultural institutions.

The old religious cults especially are repeated, and with much wishful thinking the revivalists pretend that they have already the feeling of happiness. It is a dangerous make-belief because it leads to a rather artificial excitement of the emotions and the creation of a happy feeling which does not have any foundation in reality. The situation has not really improved; the revivalists only dream of it.

These rites of revivalism are often accompanied by parapsychological phenomena, such as visions, trances and ecstasies, hysterical weeping, glossalalia, etc.

This revivalism comes after a period of indifference or decline of traditional religion and culture. The messianic leaders now attribute the present unhappy state of the community to this neglect of traditional religion and to the abandonment of its practice. They therefore insist on the faithful performance of these rites with renewed vigour. This leads not seldom to an emotional excitement with hysterical symptoms. Frequently in these ceremonies decorum is offended, and the excitement may lead to sexual licence and debauchery.

(10) Nativism, i.e. the conscious attempt of a backward people to restore selected aspects of its pristine culture and to reject alien elements previously adopted from foreign cultures

A messianic movement, accompanied as it usually is by a rebellious attitude of its members against foreign overlordship, is not solely prompted by the resentment of a certain class in the community such as chiefs and medicine men whose vested interests had been most affected. It arises chiefly out of the deep-reaching changes which the new way of life had been bringing into the rhythm of daily life, with inevitable but unwanted obligations that it laid upon individuals.

This led to the conviction that they were happy, powerful, and of strong vitality, before they had ever heard of the disturbing new-comers and before they had been tempted by them to abandon their old ways of life, their religion and their social habits. The logical conclusion out of this is the belief that a return to pristine habits of thinking, believing and living will restore their lost paradise and wipe out the nightmare of present misery. This thought finally leads to a deliberate rejection of all that is new and to an exaggerated evaluation of the old values.

The messianic movement is consequently often strongly grounded in the indigenous culture. For example, all leaders of the movement claim some sort of contact with the spirit world, or the gods, or ancestors, or culture heroes, etc. of the community. They claim to have received their vocation and mission from these divine or semi-divine patrons and protectors of the community and they pretend to derive their authority from them. Thus the means and rites by which they try to placate the gods and spirits of their old religion and by which they hope to regain their goodwill are often magical. Supernatural techniques are employed, such as prophecy, divine possession and exorcism of evil spirits. On the other hand, adoptions from alien cultures are discredited and discarded as polluting and harmful, and making the old gods angry and jealous.

(11) Vitalism, i.e. the desire of the members in the movement for alien goods, especially spiritual ones, from 'heaven', through magic or supernatural powers

The leaders of messianic movements become quickly aware that their resources for a campaign against their alien and vastly superior masters are pitifully inadequate and insufficient. Thus they try to provide quick and easy solutions of all their problems through magic and supernatural means. When these means fail to achieve their object (as they invariably do) the effect on the adherents of the movement is usually complete demoralization, passive resignation and despair.

(12) Syncretism, i.e. the indiscriminate adoption of various cultural traits of the superior culture by a backward people

In spite of all nativism (i.e. return to the traditional culture and the weeding-out and condemnation of all alien culture traits) there is a large amount of indiscriminate borrowing of various elements from the dominating culture by a backward and subject people.

The leaders of a messianic movement attribute the economic and social superiority of their masters to their religion. They believe that certain elements in their religion are responsible for their superiority, consequently they adopt them and graft them on to their old beliefs and practices.

Social considerations also come into play here. It is believed that borrowings from the dominating culture will raise the status of the subordinate community. Through the adoption of these traits they will be able to put themselves on an equal footing with their masters and reduce the extent of subordination under which they suffer.

Concomitantly with the introduction of such new elements the leaders stress the necessity of abandoning certain old ways, which do not go well with the innovations. Since these leaders, uneducated as they are, usually fail to understand the true nature of the salient features in the alien superior culture, and hit on very unessential, though perhaps superficially striking culture traits, their new cult doctrine is hopelessly illogical, contradictory and greatly over-simplified.

(13) Eschatologism, i.e. the expectation of a world renewal and improvement after a world-wide catastrophic revolution and upheaval

Eschatologism is based on the largely mystical belief that things can only improve after they have become really and extremely bad.

Moreover, the inner unrest and insecurity of the mind is transferred to nature, and a natural cataclysm is expected because it takes place in the mind of the leaders of a movement.

Hidden in this expectation of a general upheaval and wholesale destruction is the hope that in such an event the social and economic positions would change, the superior community would lose its dominating position and the backward society would come out on top, without much personal effort.

(14) Millenarianism, or Chiliasm, i.e. the hope or expectation of a paradise on earth, lasting a thousand years or some indefinitely long period

Millenarianism, or Chiliasm, is based on the belief in a Golden Age which is going to return or which can be restored in the fullness of time.

It is often expressly stated by the founder of a messianic movement that it is he who can hasten the arrival of the Golden Age. He expects to become the ruler in this Golden Age, in which pure, unmixed happiness, perfect harmony and peace, devoid of sorrow and suffering, want and death, will be maintained for a thousand years or at least for a very long time.

This Golden Age is frequently to be inaugurated by a preliminary world catastrophe in which almost the whole of mankind is destroyed and only the faithful followers of the movement survive.

These fourteen traits are found more or less strongly represented in almost all messianic movements all over the world, as in India.

These common features, characteristic of messianic movements, are often strikingly similar down to small details. But this similarity need not be explained always in terms of diffusion or mutual borrowings. It may be attributed rather to similar social and economic situations, to which the human mind reacts the world over in a similar manner. In fact, in a number of cases the mutual influence of such movements can positively be ruled out.

Messianic Movements in India

It goes without saying that in India live large population groups which are fertile soil for the growth of messianic movements. Such population groups in India are mainly of two types: one type can be classified under the term 'primitive tribes', officially 'scheduled tribes', or 'aboriginals' (*adivasi*), while the so-called 'scheduled castes' (untouchables and other low castes) belong to the second category. The 'scheduled tribes' differ from the 'scheduled castes' in their culture and religion. The tribes have retained more of their original tribal culture and religion, while the 'scheduled castes' have been much more 'Hinduized', though for certain ritually unclean habits and practices they are excluded by orthodox Hindus from participation in Hindu worship and social life.

These two categories constitute since immemorial times the under-privileged populations of India. However, a few revolutionary movements of a messianic type can also be found among peoples who for one reason or another have suffered a temporary eclipse and have for some time experienced economic, social or political oppression.

While the Hindu (and Muslim) 'scheduled classes' are distributed in almost equal numerical strength all over India, the 'scheduled tribes' are found mainly in three areas: they are in greater concentration in the north-eastern part of Central India, in Assam (including West Bengal), and in the hilly parts of South India. Western and northern India also have their contingent of primitive groups, but they are scattered in small communities and are, with the exception of the Bhils, almost completely detribalized under the influence of the overpowering Hindu and Muslim populations.

The most important and fairly compact group of primitive tribes is found in Central India. Indeed, in certain areas the primitives form the majority of the population. Here the tribes have preserved their tribal culture and tradition to a remarkable extent. Numbering over twelve million, they have so far successfully resisted any attempts at assimilation and detribalization, though they were subjected for centuries to the domination and arrogant interference of Hindu and Muslim overlords. Needless to say most of the messianic movements in Central India have arisen among these tribes. Only one movement can be reported of a powerful untouchable caste (Chamars) in Central India.

The second largest group of aboriginals is found in Assam (including West Bengal) and the North-East Frontier Agency. Until a few decades ago the tribes in the Frontier Agency enjoyed much freedom and suffered little disturbance in their traditional manner of living. Only since independence has the Indian Government earnestly attempted to introduce its administration into this frontier region of India and tried to integrate the tribes in the national Indian culture. The Nagas—as the tribes are called in this part of India—resist vigorously and fight for complete independence or at least a partial autonomy. No messianic movements are reported from the Frontier Agency, but they may arise in the near future. In Assam and West Bengal several such movements have arisen among the tribal people as well as among the low caste population. Some centuries ago, when Vaishnavism was young and vigorous, some of its apostles assumed a messianic role while spreading their gospel of human equality and the right of all to worship God in devotion and love. They were ready even to take up arms and to fight for their rights. In more recent times the leaders of messianic movements have come mainly from Muslim sects with strong reformative tendencies.

In northern India, where today the tribals form a negligible minority, messianic movements were active among the Mohammedan and Sikh converts from the lower castes of Hinduism. In pre-British times such movements owed their origin often to Mahdavi conceptions, while later they began with reformative attempts of an allegedly adulterated Islamic or Sikh faith, but in their later phases these movements turned invariably against the British colonizers who not only appeared to disturb their religious and cultural traditions, but also restrained their political ambitions, and imposed their rule and law upon them.

In western India, in Maharashtra and Gujarat, we find messianic movements among the primitive Naikdas and Warlis, the low-caste Kolis, and some stray Muslim groups under the influence of Mahdavi conceptions while the insurrection headed by Wasudeo Balwant Phadke is of a unique and extraordinary type. A number of Hindu reform movements can be reported to have taken place in the large and important Bhil tribe, which here and there have developed into revival or even messianic movements. Their leaders were often outsiders, not Bhils.

The primitive tribes of South India are divided into numerically small and insignificant groups; they have been decimated and scattered and so completely subdued by the superior cultivating Hindu castes that they have lost all their fighting spirit. They are everywhere on the retreat. Their disappearance as tribal entities or their assimilation by the lowest strata of a classless Indian proletariat is only a question of time. Naturally few messianic movements can be expected from the primitive tribes of South India.

The situation is different with regard to the untouchable and backward Hindu castes of this region. They are much stronger in numbers and have preserved their caste solidarity in spite of their ages-long oppression by the superior Hindu castes. Several times they have tried to assert their social and political position in South India on the strength of their numbers and their ancient history. Some castes of this category have preserved memories of former greatness and glory. Still, so far only the low castes of Kanara could be stirred up by a great religious leader, the Brahmin Basava, the second founder of the Lingayats. A more recent movement in South Kanara and North Coorg, among the Gaudos failed to develop. In Kerala only the Ezhavas have produced leaders who claimed the charismatic role of saviour for their community.

A similar movement can be reported of the Nairs who, though never low-caste, experienced a temporary setback of their social and political importance.

The lowest castes in South India, like the Pulayas and Parayas in Kerala and the Madigas in Andhra, are apparently still too much demoralized by centuries of severe economic exploitation and social degradation to stand up and fight for a place in the sun. A solitary Parayan leader styled himself Messiah, but he was not able to create a movement strong enough to survive him long. The same is true of the Madiga Messiah, Virabramham.

It goes without saying that the eventuality of the appearance of a Messiah or Saviour depends on a combination of numerous factors. The history of the messianic movements in India shows that in some cases it was the individual who, gifted with the peculiar abilities required for such a role, placed himself willingly at the helm of the movement and often provoked and inspired it. In other cases it was severe economic distress, coupled with social degradation and political oppression, that gave birth to it. The role of the Saviour or Messiah was assigned by the members of the community to an individual adjudged by public consent to possess the necessary qualities for such leadership. Sometimes the leaders thus chosen did not really possess the necessary qualifications and sometimes even lacked the ambition to lead such movements. In this latter category of leadership are consequently found most of the failures of messianic movements.

4 Agrarian Revolts

N.G. Ranga and Swami Sahajanand Saraswathi

THE KISAN MOVEMENT has had a history of at least 120 years since the British regime came to be established in India. To those of us who are used to peasant agitations organized and led by some conscious leaders having a political ideology and struggling for the collective and progressive welfare of peasants, the earlier agitations of peasants may seem to be rather unorganized and spasmodic groupings of the semi-conscious masses in the dark. Yet a brief review of such groupings will be of great interest to us who are anxious to develop a conscious, organized and militant kisan movement bent upon the achievement of Kisan and Muzdoor Raj.

Mass Emigration

The Districts of Cuddapah, Kurnool, Anantapur and Bellary were ceded to the British by the Nizam about the beginning of the 19th Century. The local peasants were made to pay in full the excessive land revenue and other innumerable cesses and imposts previously imposed by the Nizam, where as in the past, the Nizam's Collections were not so regular; the burden of such taxes became too heavy. But all the complaints made by peasants were of no avail and the British administrators were anxious only to increase their collections year after year. In their unholy anxiety to increase their collections, the Collectors insisted upon every ryot taking a particular portion of waste land, whose extent was increasing into cultivation and paying tax on it in proportion to the land cultivated by him whether such land is cultivated or not and desired or not by the peasant. In despair large numbers of peasants of these districts, now known as Rayalasima had begun to emigrate to the neighbouring forests and Mysore, only to escape from

Reproduced from *History of Kisan Movement* by N.G. Ranga and Swami Sahajanand Saraswathi, All India Kisan Publications, Madras G.T.

these increasing burdens of taxes. They had abandoned their lands and homes and beloved surroundings since at that time, the possession of land became more a burden than an asset. This naturally opened the eyes of the Government. Hundreds of deserted villages and lakhs of acres of abandoned land smote the rulers in the face and threatened the solvency of the Provincial Government. In a hurry, Sir Thomas Munro was sent to settle the land revenue payable by peasants and the Government agreed to his proposals and carried out in 1820-30 the drastic reduction of land revenue and he systematized the survey and settlement and land records. This was the first triumph of our peasants during the nineteenth Century.

Famines and Peasants

Between 1770-1897 there were several disastrous famines all over India; those of Rayalasima were the worst, resulting in the death of lakhs of workers and peasants. Special mention has to be made of the famine years 1770, 1896 and 1897 when millions of poor people died for want of food and water. The advent of railways had only slowly enabled the State to import cereals and pulses to the famine stricken areas and so in most places the prices of food grains had gone up and even the higher and lower middle classes were being hopelessly impoverished by their attempts to purchase food and raiment and maintain themselves during times of unemployment. It is a sad commentary on the political capacity of our people that despite such terrible sufferings of the masses and the mass-deaths of workers and peasants and the outbreaks of cholera and other epidemics, in the wake of starvation and consumption of horrible things (ending in cannibalism also) no real and effective mass protest was organized by anyone or any organization against such inhuman state of things.

Yet some dare-devils preferred dacoity to degrading death as a result of starvation and a large number of bandits began to infest the towns and countryside, striking terror into the hearts of not only the townsmen and rich people but also the big landlords and even the local officials. Coupled with the new spirit of philanthrophy and public spirit that was slowly manifesting itself in the towns and through the newspapers, this growing danger to the property and safety of the propertied classes was responsible for forcing

Government to appoint successive Famine Commissions and to devise and enforce the Famine Relief System. That this system was devised not so much with any laudable philanthrophic sentiments as by the anxiety of Government to protect the institution of property and stave off the growing threat to the established order is indicated by the content of this Famine Relief system.

To ascertain whether there is any famine at all in any area, Test Works have to be run for 15 days to employ workers on the hardest and most cruel task of breaking stones for 8 to 10 hours a day in burning sun and blinding winds, on a payment of $\frac{3}{4}$ anna per day i.e. a wage which is not enough to give even half of a full meal a day. If the suffering workers flock to such test works in ever growing numbers for those 15 days, then alone is a famine considered to exist. Even after a state of famine is declared to exist and famine relief works are opened, workers are paid only $1\frac{1}{2}$ annas per head per a day of ten to twelve hours for work that breaks anyone's strengths and spirit. Thus the most meanminded and cruel relief has been provided for our famished masses with a view just to prevent them from defying the society as a whole because of gnawing hunger and also to tie them down to work, which succeeds in weakening them. Thus the very potential revolutionary capacity of peasants and workers was met first by some relief and next by a process which weakens them every moment.

Famines occurred in 1868 in Northern India.

1876-8 in South India.

1888-9 in Madras.

Again there were famines in 1891, 1896, 1899, 1906, 1907.

1877 famine:— area affected 200,000 square miles. Population affected:— 360 lakhs.*

1878. N.W.F.P. and Punjab—220 lakhs of people were affected. Mortality 55 lakhs.

Expenditure Rs 8 crores and loss of revenue Rs 3 crores.

1874. Bengal Famine. Cost Rs 6.75 crores.

1875-8. South Indian famine. Cost Rs 9.25 crores.

Estimate of annual cost of famine in loss of revenue and actual expenditure made in 1878—150 lakhs of pounds (sterling).

Three Famine Commissions were appointed in 1880, 1898, 1901.

*10 lakhs = 1 million; 100 lakhs = 1 crore.

Recommendations of Famine Commissions
1. Extension of irrigation at a total cost of Rs 44 crores.
2. Granting loans and advances to cultivators to enable them is execute private agricultural improvements.
3. Emigration.
4. Promotion of agriculture.

Action taken by Government:
1. Famine Code.
2. Agricultural Loans Act.
   Land Improvement Act.
3. Deputation of Sir Frederick Nicholson and his report on Continental cooperative Movement.
4. Passing of the Indian Co-operative Act 1911.
5. Development of Minor Irrigation and unproductive Irrigation Works.

Bengal Tenants Outburst

The Bengali Zamindars prospered under the aegis of Permanent Settlement at the expense of the industry and of the hard working peasants. The special gift of nature to Bengal, the culture of jute which came to be in great demand in the world has only enriched these zamindars and served only as another lever with which rents can be forced upon them. Legal and illegal imposts were multiplied and Nazaranas or premiums were heaped upon peasants. Owing to the tightened alliance between the British and zamindars during and after the Indian Mutiny, even the Courts had begun to decree that the land itself had also belonged to Zamindars and peasants were only tenants-at-will. There seemed to be no limit to the capacity of zamindars and their persecution of the peasants. Just about 1870-80, the economic depression had also contributed its share towards the growth of poverty of peasants.* Naturally peasants—the various grades of them began first to fall into arrears of rent, then to be threatened with the loss of lands and eviction from their homesteads. It thus so happened that thousands of peasants came to consciously refuse the rents, disobey the dictates of Courts, obstruct their eviction and finally to fight with whatever weapons were available, (the agents of Courts and Zamindars). A regular state of anarchy came to prevail in a large part of Bengal

---

*See also W.W. Hunter's *Annals of Bengal.*

and Santal countryside and a reign of terror was set afoot. The state rushed to the rescue of its allies, the Zamindars, mowed down thousands of peasants and established a counter and more cruel and organized state of official terrorism. Thus in blood and fire was the great uprising of suffering tenants of Bengal and Santhal Parganas suppressed.

But it only served as a warning to the British Government and so an enquiry Committee was appointed and the first statute the Bengal Tenancy Act was passed, conferring permanency of tenure upon some classes of tenants and thus staying off the immediate danger.

The next agitation came from Mahratta in 1875. The Mahratta peasants to their horror, learnt that according to the British Civil Law, they could be imprisoned for their failure to pay off their debts, whenever demanded by their creditors. They were hard hit by the slump in cotton prices after the cessation of Civil War in America and, so the burden of their debts became too unbearable. Just at that time, the moneylenders began to take advantage of the Civil Laws and purchase the lands of peasants, evict their debtors from their ancestral houses and consign those of them who became unable to pay in time to Civil Debtors Jails. This was the limit for the patience of the warlike Mahratta Peasants. So they rose in their thousands against these moneylenders. They raided the houses of moneylenders, tore away almost in a frenzy the promissary notes and other papers, pertaining to their debts to them. In many places, they were obstructed by some moneylenders and so resorted to violence. Several moneylenders and their supporters were killed or beaten badly. Even a large number of police were severely dealt with, whenever they had tried to save moneylenders or whenever they attempted to harass peaceful peasants. For a time, it looked as if the whole Mahratta countryside was up in arms against the British Raj itself. When the British Government took its cue from this fury of the masses and hurriedly passed the Deccan Agriculturists Relief Act, whereby no peasant of Mahratta could be sent to the Civil Debtors jail for failure to repay debts.

Protection of Punjab Peasants

A similar uprising took place in the Punjab in 1890-1900 against the growing alienation of peasants' lands to the moneylenders of towns. The Sikh, Muhammaden and Hindu peasants who had till recent past enjoyed an independent Sikh state could not brook the superiority of the moneylenders, conferred upon them by the British Civil Laws. No wonder the murders or assaults on moneylenders began to increase rather alarmingly. The British Government quickly passed the Punjab Land Alienation Act in 1902-03 prohibiting the transferring of land from Kisan tribes or other classes and prohibiting the usufruct mortagages for more than twenty years.

Similarly because the Punjab peasants began to protest against the oppressive incidence of land revenue, the Government passed the Shaharanpur Rules, according to which the Land Revenue should never exceed 50 per cent of net-income from land, either at the original settlement or at any resettlement.

Thus it can be seen that the four major fights apart from the war of Independence put up by our peasants in their crude and primitive fashion have resulted in considerable concessions from Government. The British Government had also shown itself quite capable of meeting mass movements more than half way, lest the masses should either through their struggles develop their political consciousness or fall into the hands of politicians. There were neither political organisations nor class organisations at that time either to stimulate, engineer and develop peasants' risings, or to exploit the spontaneous uprisings of peasants with a view to strengthen any political movement for freedom.

Hence the extraordinary vigilence displayed by Lord Curzon to examine the complaints made by Ramesh Chandra Dutt, C.I.E. that the land Revenue Assessment was too heavy, that British Government did wrong in undermining the strength and influence of Zamindars and that Government should not have refused to extend Permanent Settlement of land revenue to all parts of India. He obtained fairly detailed reports of land revenue practices from all provincial Governments and in the resolution of the Governor General in Council, he laid down general principles, to guide, the settlement officers and Provincial Governments in making settlements and resettlements. It was through that resolution that Lord Curzon insisted that in no case the resettlements ought to exceed 18 per cent of the original assessment. At the same time, he laid it down as the policy of Government to protect peasants as against the rapacity of Zamindars. The Resolution of Government of India on 'Land Revenue Policy.' This he did, in 1905 in order to prevent the Indian National Congress, of which R.C. Dutt was the economist, to capture the heart of the peasants. He wanted to make the Government pass for the real champion of peasants. But unfortunately the Indian National Congress did not follow up its advantage by adopting a bold and forward policy in regard to the protection of peasants.

There was, however, one great struggle engineered by our nationalists under the leadership of the Congress on behalf of our voiceless peasants. It was aimed at the abolition of the *Indenture System*. According to this system, lakhs of our peasants and workers used to be somehow or other induced to sign some indenture bonds, agreeing to work for a specified number of years for some specified employer on his estate and in his province or country and consenting to all the penalties that the employer might inflict upon them for any breach of the bonds. Under this system our rural folk used to be recruited for work in South Africa, Malaya, Ceylon and other overseas countries and also for plantation work in Assam, Bengal, Madras and U.P. For years, lakhs of these unfortunate people who had agreed to go and work on the estates of employers, most of whom were Europeans, were persecuted in an unspeakable manner. There was not an indignity that could not be hurled at them and not a punishment that could not be procured by their influential employers from the too willing courts for even petty offences. The criminal law of our country and the legal systems of other countries were so criminal in their conception and effect that in actual practice, our indentured labourers were converted into virtual slaves of their employers. Against this inhuman system, our Indian National Congress waged a relentless war and the great Bankim Chandra Chaterjee brandished his powerful pen for espousing the cause of these sufferers. At last the Congress had triumphed and the indenture system was abolished by Government which had agreed to shoulder the responsibility for the safety, economic well-being and cultural uplift of all immigrant and emigrant labour. Today Government of India has its agents in Ceylon, Malaya, Burma and South Africa to look after the interests of our emigrants and Protectors in Assam to watch the interests of our plantation labourers. Thus

Government of India also seeks to secure a minimum wage for our workers in ceylon and Malaya, in addition to fighting for their political status.

1905-19: It is however true to say that the Indian National Congress did not lay as much stress on the need for relief for our peasants, during 1905-19 as it did on the needs of our industrialists. There were many causes for this but the most important of them was the predominent voice our industrialists and disciples of Justice Ranade led by Ferozshah Mehta, and Gokhale, were then having in the counsels of the Congress. Our nationalists continued to press for the establishment of permanent settlement of land revenue, the abolition of salt-tax and excise revenue; but since they were preoccupied with their fight for protection for our industries and state assistance to our industrialists, they could not do anything more than formally reiterating these demands on behalf of our agriculturists. Even in this regard, for some reason, not easily explicable, they kept themselves scrupulously silent about the fate of our crores of zamindari tenants of U.P., C.P., Orissa, Bihar, Bengali Assam and Madras. Lord Curzon's challenge to Ramesh Chandra Dutt, an ex-President of the Congress that it was the Government which had done more to protect tenants from the rapacity of Zamindars, remained unanswered probably because the then leadership of the Congress was so over-whelmingly zamindari and capitalistic in its class content.

Champaran Struggle 1917-8

The next phase in the awakening of our Kisan owed its development and success to the leadership of Mahatma Gandhi and Rajendra Prasad in the famous Champaran struggle against the indigo planters, many of whom were Europeans, who were persecuting the local Bihari peasants to grow Indigo against their will on (Tinkathia) pain of paying higher taxes and collecting several illegal exactions. Mahatma Gandhi initiated the method for that time extremely novel and original, of conducting a systematic and authoritative enquiry into the real nature and degree of the sufferings of the peasants at the hands of the planters. Thousands of suffering peasants flocked round the Mahatma and Rajendra Prasad and detailed their woes. But the Provincial Government took fright and prohibited them from pursuing their enquiries.

On their refusal to obey this prohibitory order, there arose a crisis, in which the arrest of Mahatma Gandhi and subsequent release were followed by the appointment of an enquiry Committee with Mahatmajee as one of its members. Eventually the Bihar Government accepted the recommendations of the Committee whose report bears the imprint of Mahatma's personality. An enactment based on the Report relieved peasants from their most immediate and pressing troubles and freed them from the special impost laid on them by the Indigo planters. But just as the earlier Congress agitation led by Ramesh Chunder Dutt against temporary settlements did not embrace the exploitation of our peasants by zamindars, so also this agitation led by the Mahatma in Champaran did not lead up to any fight against the main causes for the terrible poverty and sufferings of Champaran peasants, namely the excessive rents and exorbitant incidence of debts. It may be because of Mahatmaji's growing habit which later on came to be considered as one of his political virtues of concentrating upon one thing at a time. But it does strike one as rather significant that both he and Rajendra Prasad should have remained scrupulously silent upon the ravages of the zamindari system and the extreme need for liberating peasants from its cluches. Anyhow, this Champaran satyagraha movement of 1917 i.e. during the Great War had the excellent result of awakening not only of the Bihar peasantry but also the general public of India to the tremendous revoluntionary potentialities latent in the bosom of our peasants.

Kaira Satyagraha

Soon the Kaira and Bardoli drought and the consequent failure of crops claimed the attention of Mahatama Gandhi. The half-blind Bombay Government insisted upon its pound of flesh by demanding the payment of land revenue despite the inability of peasants to pay. Gandhiji's Satyagraha came to the rescue of these much harassed kisans and Bombay Government had also to eat the humble pie in the face of this rising peasant revolt led by such an implacable fighter. It suspended the kist collection. It was during this campaign that Com. Indulal Yagnik, now the Joint Secretary of the All India Kisan Committee received his first lessons in field work for our kisans. Even here Mahatmaji did not complicate his campaign by trying to tackle the other troubles of our kisans such as their indebtedness, alienations of lands.

These two campaigns succeeded in establishing Mahatmaji as a magic man of peasant satyagraha and to some extent awakening our peasants to the use of satyagraha for achieving their purposes. It is true that the great majority of our peasantry was still unaware of politics, and was therefore not politically affected by these triumphs. But they did open the eyes of a growing number of the educated kisans, like myself, to the political possibilities of our peasants' mass-action.

Non-Co-operation Movement

But it was left to the great nation-wide Non-co-operation movement, which succeeded in drawing in one effort millions of peasants with its magical slogan of 'Swaraj in one year,' into its orbit. It shook our peasants free from their age old political slumber and dragged them, almost against their traditions into the whirlpool of our national political life. For the first time they were told, to their great satisfaction and wonder, that it was quite legitimate for them to refuse to pay land revenue, the payment of which they had come to look upon almost as a religious duty. To them, in those early days of our national movement of direct action and in that first flush of their political awakening, Swaraj meant freedom from all tax burdens and especially the abolition of land revenue. Naturally they hugged to their hearts both Mahatmaji's name and the slogan of 'Non-payment of Taxes.' When therefore Gandhiji commenced his preparations for his open conspiracy of 'Non-payment of taxes' campaign in Bardoli, the whole Kisan India opened its eyes and began to spontaneously refuse or delay the payment of land revenue or rent. Throughout India millions of peasants, believing that the end of the British Raj was within sight, abstained from paying their rents or revenue and began to watch political developments with bated breath. If only Mahatmajee had given the much wanted command to our Kisans not to pay their taxes, as was feared by the British and anticipated by our kisans, who knows if Lord Lloyd's fear of the destruction of British power in India might not have actually materialised. As it was, instead of that command, Mahatmaji suddenly withdrew the whole non-co-operation movement and thus left millions of our peasants as well as the country in mid-air.

With what consequences? Those lakhs of peasants alone know to their bitter cost. They came to be penalised in thousand and one ways by their zamindars, who not so long ago had been so terror-stricken and who were only too glad to wreak vengeance upon their kisans who had the temerity to hope for a better future; those millions of peasants and workers alone can tell what terrible disappointment they suffered when their very first hope of a bright life was frustrated and their aspiration of winning Swaraj was dashed to the ground. With the imprisonment of thousands of active congress-men whose association with the peasantry was very intimate and with the return to quasi-normal life of the other disappointed and dazed congressmen, our peasants found so few to fend for them and almost none to lead them in their struggles against the enraged British Government and its more cruel allies, the Zamindars.

Pedanandipad Campaign
The real revolutionary significance of this first mass upsurge of our peasantry can be guessed from the phenomenal and dramatic success of the following uprisings in particular. One took place in Pedanandipad area of Guntur District. There for a good few weeks, there was virtually Kisan Raj. In that area even the British mounted police and regular Military forces could not make peasants give them even information regarding the direction to any village pond or well, not to speak of giving any supplies of food or water or payment of taxes.

Oudh Kisan Rising
Laljee made an eloquent mention of this in his autobiography. There lakhs of peasants rose spontaneously against the oppressive zamindars and demanded not only Swaraj but also the removal of their sufferings. It did not subside, even after the Bardoli debacle until the Government hurriedly passed the Oudh Rent Act of 1921 which conferred the permanency of tenure upon the tenants. Luckily for the Government, its ruse, played once before in Maharashtra soon after the Deccan riots of 1897, negotiating with a peasant rising by offering something to appease it, succeeded in Oudh also, with the result that the Agra tenants of the same Province have had to go without the benefit of permanency of

tenure until in 1938 the Congress Government has introduced its bill to that effect.

Two other struggles need a mention in this connection, the No-tax campaign of Karnatak and the Mopplla Rebellion of Malabar. The former bode fair to become as frighful an affair as that of Pedanandipad but the withdrawal of non-cooperation movement sabotaged it at its very early stage.

Mopplla Rebellion

The latter proved to be disastrous to all concerned, except the British. In Malabar, Mopllas who are moslems by religion are mostly either agricultural workers, or tenants or the most depressed section of intermediary landholders with or without personal cultivation. They were then being exploited mercilessly by the Nambudris who were the virtual owners of the land and who had the absolute right of electing any intermediary peasant, known as Kanamdar or any of the actual cultivators. In fact these Nambudris, who were Brahmins were often aided by Kanamdars, most of whom were Nairs and they were freely exercising their right to evict peasants from their homesteads and raising the rents at their will and pleasure. No wonder an agitation sprang up in the wake of the Religious Revivalist movement which later on was prostituted by the Justice Party. Its leaders were the late Sir M. Krishnan Nair and Mr M.P. Narayana Menon. One joined the Justice party and rose to be an executive Councillor of the Madras Government and the other entered the Congress and came to be condemned for transportation for life for the alleged crime of having incited Mopplas to wage war against His Majesty's Government to be released only in 1936.

This rent reduction and permanency of tenure agitation, awakened the peasants, both Hindus and Moslems to the need for political action. It helped Krishnan Nair to be returned to the Madras Legislative Council. It gave a tremendous initial significance to the Non-cooperation Movement of Malabar. But soon a communal turn was given by some very responsible Moslem leaders and all the pent up enemity and disgust of peasants in general and Moppllas in particular burst up like a volcano, and resulted in blood-shed. The frightened Nambudris had in the meanwhile made common cause with the leaders of Kanamdars agreed with the Justice Party, of which the earstwhile leader of tenants M. Krishnan Nair was an important pillar, over a compromise tenancy legislation and rallied all the Hindus to aid them and thus helped to make the whole thing a communal fight. The poor peasants who were thus mislead by their religious leaders and intrigued by their landlords and deceived by their colleagues, the Hindu tenants who were in their turn humbugged by the Justice Party, rushed headlong with their false religious slogans of hostility and war against Hindus in general and their suicidal means of blood and fire. Thus in a few months the heroic peasants of Malabar were either mowed down by British fire or consigned to Andamans in all their thousands. This fight has become notorious for the train-tragedy in which nearly 80 Moppllas died of suffocation in a closed railway wagon and also for the treachery perpetrated upon our innocent peasants by religious leaders, reformist tenant agitators and the withdrawal of all Congress adivce, leadership and support from the sufferers just at the right nick of time.

Sitarama Raju's Fight

In the wake of the failure of the Non-cooperation Movement and the six year sentence upon Mahatma Gandhi, a dreadful gloom had set in all over the Country, except in a tiny quarter, it lies on one of the broad backs of the Eastern Ghats, in the Jeypore Zamindari and on the Borders of the Narsipatam Taluk. There was enacted one of the most romantic dramas of revolutionary life of modern India. Alluri Sitarama Raju a Kshatriya of west Godavari District, went there and befriended with the Koyas and other hill-people of that tract. He became a Sadhu, and an expert healer both by spiritual powers and herbs. He saw the sufferings of those ignorant but militant people helpless at the hands of forest and excise officials. His appeals to officials for mercy were in vain. Those hill-tribes were not allowed to carry on their 'Podu' or 'Jungle' cultivation. They were made to pay too many dues upon so many of their activities such as gathering fuel, grazing their cattle in forests, felling fuel, grass, fruit, or gum, gathered in the forest to any outsiders. Thus their very traditional mode of life was threatened by Government. Raju saw no way out of it except through rebellion. When all his appeals for justice were in vain, he welcomed the spontaneous rising of those proud, martial and brave Koyas against the Government. That rising soon became a violent revolution and it was suppressed at great cost to human life on both sides and to the Indian finances, by a merciless and ruthless use of fire and iron by the British Government.

Thanks to the post-autonomy and Congress Governments, M.P. Narayan Menon and hundreds of other Malabar victims, and the few survivers of the Sitarama Raju's 'Pituri' were released recently.

Kamagatamaru

After the war another epoch of our peasant struggle began. Just after the war the magic word went abroad that the British Prime Minister's plighted promise to India that Swaraj would be granted soon after the war was over was broken and that the word came for all patriots to strike their last blow at British Imperialism to wrest from it India's Swaraj. Mahatma Gandhi's weapon of Satyagraha evoked tremendous hopes in the hearts of our nationalists. It was in that atmosphere that hundreds of Punjab peasants flocked to the banner of revolution. Their brethren who had emigrated to Canada, U.S.A. and South America not only sent large sums of money but also despatched a shipload of men, money and ammunition to aid their revolutionary work. Hopes were raised all over the Punjab countryside of the impending struggle and advent of Swaraj. But alas, the British got scent of it, captured those famous Kamagatamaru heroes, clapped many more peasants of Punjab villages into jails and persecuted in an unspeakable fashion many thousands of the brave Sikh peasants for their share in that adventurous scheme.

The Aka movement of Hardoi in U.P. stirred up the peasantry of Sitapur, Raibarelli, Fyzabad and several other Districts in 1922-3 i.e. just after the Bardoli withdrawal of Satyagraha and at the time of the Mopplla and Sitarama-Raju's 'Pituri'. It was led by Nadari Pari, an actual peasant and the whole countryside responded to him to a man. Government found it so hard to tackle it since actual peasants were at its head and the leaders were not specially wedded to the Gandhian ideas of non-violence in regard to every detail. Eventually it was suppressed as all other peasant struggles by the blood and fire of Government.

But all these great and spontaneous risings of our peasants from one end of the country to the other succeeded as nothing else had during the previous sixty years since the great Indian war of Independence, to bestir our peasants bring them into the whirlpool of our national politics, evoked in their hearts great and even extravagant hopes and encouraged them to dream glorious dreams of peace, plenty and prosperity on the advent of Swaraj. If not for anything else, atleast for having opened the eyes of crores of our peasants who would otherwise have continued to vegetate with their Curzonian contentment and sense of atrophy, and brought them once for all into our political area, the great Non-Cooperation Movement and Mahatmaji's slogan of 'Swaraj within one year' were more than justified. But how one wishes that the Congress had provided some defence forces to protect our peasants on their retreat. How one deplores the failure of our leaders to take a more realistic view of things and prevented such a sudden and almost heartless (one is almost tempted to say, irresponsible) withdrawal of Congress support from our peasants. Three conclusions force themselves upon our minds as a result of this cursory survey of the effect of introduction of national politics into the life of our peasants, since 1917, by Mahatma Gandhi and his followers, working through the Indian National Congress. That our peasants were taken by suprise, they had either to absorb the political thought of the day even if there were one or were not provided with any political machinery in the shape of a self-confident, self-conscious and local autonomous Congress or Kisan organisation to stand up for them through thick and thin and to constantly guide them. Instead as soon as Mahatmaji withdrew his Non co-operation movement and abandoned all aggressive political action, the local congress committees went limp and congressmen became devoid of any initiative or leadership. Indeed Congress had fought shy of having anything more to do with Moppllas or Koyas or U.P. or Punjab Kisans or others and Congressmen instantly dropped all Kisan work. Need one wonder then if all over India, our peasantry quickly relapsed into their traditional political somnombulence, nursing an awful bitterness against our politicians and their own miserable fate.

The second conclusion is that in too many cases were our peasants struggles exploited either by communalists or religious maniacs who had little respect to the creed of non-violence, that our peasants were defenceless against their bad leadership, denied as they had been of any political training, organisational ability or knowledge of the effects and consequences of agitational work, which could be gained only through their active participation in their class or political organisations. Naturally there was too much exhibition of violence at the fag end of our kisan struggles of those hectic days of 1920-3 and it frightened away our Congressmen and thus denied them of any active sympathetic, day to day support and guidance of the Congress, which they then needed much more than at any other time.

The third conclusion is that owing to their abandonment by the Congress once their revolutionary temper went beyond the mild expectations of the Congress leaders and thus upset the calculations of the reformist leaders of the Congress of different provinces of these days by threatening to shake to their roots the very economic foundations of society, our peasants came in for the cruel intentions of Government and zamindars and were persecuted hopelessly for years in many a way.

It was in 1923 July-December, just when the members of Moppla rebellion were dying out and the Sitarama Raju's fight was going on that I had begun to organize Ryots Associations (or Kisan Sabhas as they had later on come to be known all over India) Agricultural and Labour Unions in the Andhra on my return from England. I met with instantaneous success in Guntur District with the ryots since they were all disillusioned about the Government and the Justice Party which persuaded them into the belief that no reprisals would be taken against them for their support to the Pedanandipadu No-tax campaign and later on, inflicted heavy penal-rates of assessment for their having dared to support the Congress to bring 'Swaraj within one year' also helped them to rally to my call to organize themselves into Ryots Associations.

It was just at that time that a very bitter controversy was going on between the pro-changers headed by the late Moti Lal Nehru and C.R. Das and No-changers led by Srijit C. Rajagopalachari as to whether Congress should enter the legislatures or not. Though in several provinces, Swaraj parties were organised the Congressmen went into legislatures under their auspices, in the Andhra and in Guntur District in particular, orthodox Congress leaders succeeded in preventing any great development of the Swaraj Party. Naturally this gave an opportunity to our Ryots Association to formulate its Election Manifesto, set up a selection committee and nominate its candidates and make them sign the peasants pledge and conduct the electioneering on purely peasants' lines. At all the stages, even orthodox Congress leaders cooperated with our Ryots Association. While the Non-Brahmin Party eschewed all Brahmin candidates, our Ryots Association selected a Brahmin candidate, thus demonstrating at its very inception, its non-communal character and politics. Three out of its four candidates were successful. One was sent to the Central Assembly and two to the local council and two of them eventually joined the congress and distinguished themselves in the country's cause. This unexpected success of the Ryots Association and the splendid response given by peasants to its call excited the fear of Government and jealously of some congressmen and most of the Justicites. So from all sides we were attacked about the further need for such associations. We could have gone on developing Ryots Associations all over the province if only we had a sufficient number of workers to carry on propaganda. Unfortunately we had none and we did not then think of organising a Kisan school to train youths for this work and to develop a selfrelient and independent cadre of comrades for this extra congress work. Since neither the local congress workers who were themselves few in number and hard-pressed for time and resources nor peasants themselves were forthcoming to aid us. Our Ryots Associations marked very little progress between 1924-196, beyond spreading themselves to West Godavari and Krishna Districts also and spreading and popularising the idea of independent class organizations for peasants and workers.

Bihar and U.P. Kisan Sabhas of 1926-7

In 1926-7, some comrades began to organise Kisan Sabhas in Bengal, Punjab and U.P. on more or less idealistic lines with a revolutionary programme. As they were too often mistaken for communist organizations by the local Governments which were only too anxious to nip in the bud everything that savoured of revolutionary temper, they were banned before they could take deep roots. Somehow the Bihar and U.P. Kisan Sabhas managed to keep up their existence until 1928, when they presented their memoranda to the All Parties Conference presided over by the late Pt. Moti Lal Nehru. So far as one could ascertain, these Kisan Sabhas seemed to have favoured universal franchise, complete independence and fundamental rights. It is significant that when Dr Annie Beasant declined to provide for universal franchise (when some of us suggested it to her in 1925 soon after the Delhi conference) in her scheme for an Indian Commonwealth, the Nehru Committee favoured it, especially when our Kisan Sabhas also pleaded for it.

Andhra Ryots Association

The Andhra Provincial Ryots Association was organised by some of us in 1928 under the Presidentship of B.V. Ratnam M.L.C. and M.B. Needu M.Sc. One of the Parliamentary Secretaries of Madras Ministry came out with a pamphlet on 'Why Peasants Associations?' and strongly advocated their establishment on the lines of the American Farmers Unions. As he took an active part in that Provincial Ryots conference, he was elected the General Secretary. Even at that time there was a trial of strength between the Justicities and Congressites over the issue of Congress boycott and so the justicites staged a walk-out saying that Ryots conferences ought not to meddle with politics.

Andhra Zamindari Ryots Association

In 1929 the Conference met under my presidentship and supported the stand taken by the Congress in regard to politics and concerned itself mostly with land revenue, agricultural indebtedness, unemployment and internal social reforms but did not try to tackle the zamindari ryot problem. That was taken up by the Andhra Zamindari Ryots conference organized by Mr R.M. Sharma with the co-operation of some of us. But the conference only demanded a radical revision of the Estates Land Act so as to minimize the sufferings of tenants. Our peasant workers were not then prepared to demand the abolition of the zamindari system, so unprepared was the political world to grapple with such problems at that time.

The 1930 Civil Disobedience Movement, the preciptious fall of prices of our agricultural commodities due to the economic depression and the consequent pressure sudden and stunning brought to bear upon them by money-lenders and landlords and the heroic struggles and achievements of Bardoli peasants in 1928-9 and 1930-1 had all prepared the field for the spread of bolder ideas among the peasantry and for the acceptance by our peasants of our revolutionary lead and also for the adoption by them of our tactics.

1928-9 Bardoli Triumph

It is impossible to over estimate the electrical effect the triumph of Bardoli ryots of 1928-9 had upon our Indian peasantry. There the Bardoli peasants rose against the unjust enhancement of land revenue sought to be imposed upon them by the Bombay Government. They were led by Sardar Vallabhai Patel and assisted by Mahatma Gandhi and financed by President Vithalbhai Patel. But the chief factor which ultimately won for them their complete success was their own limitless sacrifices and unexampled discipline and determination. At last the Bombay Government had to yield to the demand of peasants to appoint an impartial Enquiry Committee. The Committee gave its award mostly in favour of peasants. This well advertised triumph of Bardoli peasants put heart into the Indian peasantry and evoked again their hopes of being able to successfully rise against the Government.

*10 lakhs = 1 million, 100 lakhs = 1 crore

*See also W.W. Hunters' *Annals of Bengal*.

5 Indian Peasants' Struggles and Achievements

N.G. Ranga

WAR OF INDEPENDENCE: In all the areas in which the first war of Indian Independence was in progress (1857-60) peasants played quite a heroic part, suffered terribly, displayed great military skill, prowess and achieved victories. But they were made to pay bitterly for their display of patriotism. To this day, the peasants of Meerut Division pay certain abwabs which were then levied as punitive imposts for their participation in that revolution.

During that struggle, large numbers of peasants threw themselves valiantly into the fray with such abandon that they did not mind leaving their holdings in the care of their landlords. So many of them forgot the wrongs done to them by their landlords and made common cause with them in fighting for freedom. But alas, when later the British had triumphed, their lands were treated as the property of the Zamindars since the latter were found in actual control and they were reduced from the status of proprietors to that of tenants-at-will of their own former lands; so heavy were their sacrifices. And the Zamindars had no scruples in grabbing their lands so unjustly.

Unfortunately they could not rise beyond the limitations of their feudal environment and hence were reduced to dust before the British arms. And as yet, they had not developed the political aspect of their cultural and traditional conception of unity of the whole of India nor could they anticipate the later twentieth century idea of achievement of a nation-wide organization, consciousness and unified patriotic endeavour.

We can understand the magnitude of the sacrifice offered by peasants in that struggle when we remember from what a high state of customary rights, individual and collective, Indian peasants

Reproduced from *Revolutionary Peasants* by N.G. Ranga, *op. cit.* pp 33-59.

fell by deciding to join the war against the British. They had been members of village communities which, according to Elphinstone, contained 'in miniature all the materials of a State within themselves and are sufficient to protect their members if all other Governments were withdrawn'.

That the lands were recognized even by the Mughals to be the property of kisans is proved by the fact that Akbar and Aurangazeb had to purchase lands from cultivators.

Todar Mal's revenue settlement conducted under the order of Akbar was made with individual peasants and not with any of the Zamindars or even the headmen of a village. No wonder Holt Mackenzie grew eloquent over the permanence of the rights of these peasants. He observed 'the village Zamindars... were the immemorial occupants of the soil.... They sold, and mortgaged their lands at will. They may have been bound in some cases to a lower class of cultivators, who had by distinct engagements or long usage acquired the right of occupancy so long as they paid the customary rent.... Nothing but violence appears to have disturbed the tenure of the village Zamindars; neither the exile nor the longest absence, dissolved the tie that bound them to the fields of their ancestors, nor destroyed their right to resume possession when they returned.'

The British came to upset all this. Their early administrators recognised the Taluqdars as the prototypes of English landlords to subserve their political ends. But when they found that these Taluqdars were also undependable, Lord Dalhousie decreed that 'the settlement should be made village by village with the parties actually in possession but without any recognition, either formal or indirect, of their proprietary right so as to deal with the actual occupants of the soil'.

Thus the U.P. peasants were being re-instated in their traditional rights and holdings by the British who were losing faith in the so-called landed aristocracy, as a political stabilising force. Lord Canning who was no friend of the peasants had to confess that 'as a question of justice the lands and villages taken from the Talooqdars had, for the most part, been usurped by them through fraud and violence.'

Naturally the British expected gratitude from those U.P. kisans. They hoped that the kisans who were being helped to get back to their lands from which they had been forcibly ejected by the Taluqdars would betray the national cause and side with them, the new beneficent rulers.

Lord Canning observed in 1858 that 'it might have been expected that, when insurrection first arose in Oudh...the village occupants who had been so highly favoured by the British Government and in justice to whom it had initiated a policy distasteful to the most powerful class in the province, would have come forward in support of the Government who had endeavoured to restore them to their hereditary rights and with whose interests their interests were identical. Such, however, was not the case. So far as I am informed, not an individual dared to be loyal to the Government which had befriended him.'

On the other hand, lakhs of peasants made common cause with that war of independence. The British naturally decided that 'the lands of men who have taken an active part against us should be largely confiscated in order, among other reasons, to enable us to reward others.' 'The Governor-General proclaims to the people of Oudh that...the proprietory right in the soil of the province is confiscated to the British Government which will dispose of that right in such manner as to it may seem fitting.'

The consequence was that the great class of kisans fell, the Taluqdars who were the usurpers and adventurers, rose and within the course of a year, the kisans' 'rights had ceased to exist or were reduced to a mere shadow; they were completely in the power of the Taluqdars and were subject to every kind of oppression, tyranny and exaction.'

Such was the bitter price paid by kisans for having made common cause with Taluqdars in that first war of independence and such indeed was the reward reaped by the faithless Taluqdars for their rebellion against the British and their eventual submission to the foreign rulers. Is this not typical of what happened in England after Cromwell's yeomen's revolution, in the U.S.A. after the attainment of independence and in the U.S.S.R. after the 1917 revolution and 1920-1 counter-revolution? Wherever and whenever peasants have gone into any revolution without their own leadership, ideological stand and definite political objectives but under the leadership of other classes, they have uniformly been cheated of the fruits of revolution or been the worst victims of the failure of a revolution.

Santhals' Revolution

Later came the 1855-73 Santhal and Bengal revolts, this time not only against the British Raj as such but also against the Zamindars who were invested with unjustified and undreamt of powers of ownership of land that peasants had customarily considered and cultivated for millenniums as their own and also against money-lenders who were given powers to get peasants imprisoned for failure to repay their debts and against the autocracy of officials. The Santhals never thought that they could be evicted from their ancestral homesteads, holdings and forests for failure to pay taxes and debts but that had come to happen.

The self-respecting, proud, if unorganized, Indian peasant never could reconcile himself to the preposterous right conferred by the British Government on the Zamindar to distrain his properties, including his draught cattle, grain crops and that too came to be the order of the day. So he rose in revolt against that unjust order of the day, imposed upon them by British imperialism through the convenient media of its allies, the Indian Zamindars and money-lenders.

The peasants 'banded themselves (especially in Patna District) to resist short measures; illegal cesses, and forced deliveries of agreement (one-sided) to pay enhanced rents.' And also 'there had been combination of Raiyats (peasants) in East Bengal, refusing to payments except what they considered just.'

The Santhals found their leaders in two brothers who claimed to have received some occult blessings from the gods to put an end to the zhulum of officers and to the deceit of merchants. As many as 35,000 Santhals formed their bodyguard. They armed themselves with their traditional weapons of bows, arrows, axes and swords. They began to march to Calcutta to place their petition before the Governor to free them from their oppressors. But one Government Inspector obstructed their march and provoked them on 7-7-1855 into violence. Thus had commenced their rebellion and their resultant massacre at the hands of the British. The British officers who had been smitten with remorse later confessed that 'it was not war, it was execution; we had orders to go out whenever we saw the smoke of a village rising about the jungle. The Magistrate used to go with us...I surrounded the village with my sepoys and the Magistrate called upon the rebels to surrender.' To such an unjust and peremptory order, the brave Santhals knew only one answer to give. That was defiance. There upon they were brutally fired upon and butchered *en masse*.

The Santhals displayed such exceptional courage and military discipline that they faced successive vollies of British bullets with reckless heroism and abandon.

Government had however to yield to these peasants, despite its gratitude to the Bengal Zamindars for their treacherous betrayal of the War of Independence and pass the Bengal Tenancy Act which had come to re-establish the lost permanency of tenure and fixity of feudal exactions.

Mahratta Peasant Awakening

With equal fury and fervour rose the Mahratta peasants in the same generation, against the oppressions of money-lenders. They could not brook the idea of obedience to the new laws which gave such coercive powers to money-lenders that any money-lender could with impunity move a court to imprison any one of his peasant debtors. So they revolted, burnt down the houses, destroyed other properties of money-lenders, killed a good many such oppressors and even attacked those Government officials who were supporting their oppressors.

Bombay Peasants' Revolts in 1871-75

These revolts were not well planned, nor were they widespread. They took place haphazardly and in many districts like Kaira, Ahmednagar, Poona, all unconnected with each other. The peasants aimed their blows not on Government, but on money-lenders and even when whole villages were in revolt, great care was taken not to harm anyone else but marwari money-lenders. Generally 'object of the rioters was to obtain and destroy the bonds, decrees, etc., in the possession of their creditors; when these were peaceably given up to the assembled mob there was usually nothing further done. When the money-lender refused or shut himself up, violence was used to frighten him into surrender or to get possession of the papers'.

Again the might of British Raj came down on them and suppressed their risings. Yet it had to yield and redress their grievances as least in part. Hence the passing of the Deccan Agriculturists' Relief Act, whereby an exception was made for the Mahratta peasants from the operations of the Civil Procedure Code in that they could not be imprisoned for failure to repay debts—a great concession indeed.

Punjab Discontent

Similarly the Punjab peasants too agitated and threatened to revolt to prevent the rapid alienation of their lands to the urban money-lenders for failure to repay debts. The British Government could not await a similar rebellion as had taken place in Bengal and Maharashtra since the armed and martial Sikhs might make a formidable enemy. So it hastened to pass the Punjab Land Alienation Act to prevent the alienation of peasants' lands to non-agricultural sections.

South India in Ferment

Similarly the Krishna and Godavari Deltaic peasants and the Karnataka and Rayalaseema peasants too revolted several times from the beginning of the 19th century to protest against the exorbitant land revenue exactions, the neglect of irrigation facilities and the extortionate method of tax collections. G. Lakshminarasu Chetti organized a grand constitutional agitation against the Madras Tortures Act and succeeded in getting it repealed and this saved the South Indian peasants from being put to several cruel and inhuman tortures for failure to pay taxes. The South Indian peasants resorted to their ancestral method of *satyagraha* by abandoning their lands and villages (a method of satyagraha adopted by the Lohara peasants in 1936, and by those of the Orissa States in 1939 with much less success) and migrating to the neighbouring Indian States or even British districts. Since peasant solidarity was so great in those days and also since the cultivation of land under the then prevailing tax burdens was such an unwelcome task none would go and occupy their lands and houses and Government had to climb down and agree to a reduction of their tax burdens in order to persuade them to return to their lands and villages.

Contribution of the Indian National Congress

With the beginning of the 20th century, the Indian National Congress began to champion the cause of the oppressed peasants.

It imported a political significance—common cause with the nation-wide freedom movement and anti-imperialist bias—into every one of the struggles that peasants have had to wage in order to free themselves from new imperialist impositions and machinations. Thus country-wide campaigns were organised with nationalism as their dynamo and economic pressure as their propellers against the vicious indenture labour system, contract labour in plantations, exploitation by European planters in India and other parts of the British Empire. Now that political consciousness and organisation were added to economic grievances, success began to dawn on the horizon of Indian peasants. The indenture system was abolished and some relief was got for plantation labour. A large number of risings took place in Malabar both in the last and present centuries. They were misnamed communal riots and their basic causes, the political and economic grievances of peasants against the local landlords were not sought to be removed. Of course there was always the tendency for communal leaders to exploit these basic factors. But thanks to the sacrifices made by the Mopilla (Moslem) peasants, the Madras Government had had to pass the Malabar Tenancy Act which conferred permanency of tenancy upon a very large section of peasantry.

Gandhiji and Peasant Satyagraha

An entirely new dynamic and political revolutionary tendency has come to be imported into peasant struggles by Mahatma Gandhi since his advent on the Indian politico-economic theatre in 1916. He familiarised the peasants of Champaran in Bihar and Kaira in Gujerat with his new weapon of Satyagraha, an open, non-violent, organised, politically alive revolt against injustice—in their struggles against the indigo planters and land revenue collectors respectively. He introduced the technique of first enquiring into the essential facts of the peasants' grievances, then formulating their demands, educating them as to the nature and magnitude of their needs and immediate demands, training them in the art of internal self-sufficiency pointing out the need for economy in case of a prolonged struggle against the authorities and steeling their mind to the rigours to jails, and other harassments of imperialism. He would convince the peasants that the satisfaction of their carefully moderated minimum demands was most urgently called for by Dharma or social justice, and that it would be their sacred duty to force the authorities to perform their Dharma towards them. The injection of this inspiring and ennobling conception of serving Dharma by revolting against injustice and by seeking redress for their own grievances, would steel the determination and fighting morale of the peasants. As the champions of Dharma, peasants would go ahead, to face all their enemies without fear and with perfect confidence in their own cause and in their duty to and capacity for teaching their opponents how to conform to Dharma. As Calvin strengthened the bourgeoisie by his casuistry proving that they were helping society by helping themselves; as Marx put new life into the proletariat by demonstrating that they were the heirs of capitalism, chosen by Dame History, so Mahatma Gandhi invested the peasants as well as the colonial peoples with the saintly staff of satyagraha to achieve the protection to Dharma for themselves and to oblige their opponents to conform to Dharma and thus save humanity from injustice.

Bardoli Satyagraha
With the blessings of Mahatma Gandhi, his greatest kisan disciple, Vallabhbhai Patel organised and led the Bardoli peasants against the resettlement enhancements proposed by Government. Under his inspiring guidance, peasants braved all risks, faced with courage the loss of their beloved cattle and ancestral lands and even risked eviction from their villages. At last, they triumphed over the Government. That was in 1929.

Again in 1930, when Mahatmaji gave this call to the people to rise against Imperialism to achieve national independence, the Bardoli peasants rose to a man, refused to pay taxes, faced the auction sales and eventual loss of almost all their lands and refused to have any truck with Government. Such was the marvellous strength of their political revolt led by their great Sardar. When the Congress was in Ministry in 1937-9 the loyal Sardar saw to it that all their lands were returned. Thus did our peasants gain their initiation in both economic and political Satyagraha.

Vizag Revolution and Raju's Leadership
The Vizag Agency tribes waged a two-year war against British imperialism with the help of an extraordinary revolutionary leader

Sitarama Raju. They made the fullest military use of the strategic advantages of the hills and valleys and impassable gorges and their own special knowledge of the terrain. They were strictly non-violent. They made full use of their traditional weapons. But strangely enough, they pursued the Hindu Dharmic way of liberating their enemies, once they fell into their hands and asked for excuse, with the result that their secret dens came to be known and their ways of organisation understood by their enemy.

What did they fight for? At first they started asking for free use of the forest lands and produce. Rapidly their demands went up and they wanted to establish Swaraj for the whole of the Agency area, if not for the whole of India.

The tragedy of it all was that their struggle came off a year after the great non-co-operation movement (1920-2) was over and when nationalist India was just recovering from the shock of reaction. The British Government was very cruel towards those brave tribal people. It used all the modern weapons and killed thousands of those unfortunate Koya and Savara people.

Great trouble set in upon these people after their noble and resourceful leader Raju was killed. Most of their other leaders were killed, several others were sent to jail and great reprisals were hurled upon the masses. Yet the spirit of resistance of these hill tribes did not die. It only awaited another inspired leader and a suitable opportunity. This became clear in the August 1942 Revolution when again these people gave a fine account of their anti-imperialist spirit.

But owing to the special attention paid by the police to this area and its people, even such Congress constructive work as hand-spinning was not allowed. Government encouraged the local Muthadars or village tribal chiefs to tyrannise over the people and thus destroy their will to revolt. Despite all such repression, Congress-men like P. Kodandaramayya and R.M. Sarma had been doing yeoman service to these people. As a result of their work, the Gothi system by which the hill tribes were kept down as hereditary servants (bordering on slavery) of those Muthadars and others who advanced small sums of money to these ignorant and helpless people either for marriage or for drink has come to be abolished since 1940. Yet so many of these people are even now unable to take advantage of it. Secondly, the last Congress ministry has declared their lands inalienable. But during the war, the Advisers' regime again had allowed alienation of their lands subject to the Collector's permission.

The present Congress Ministry is trying to help these tribal peoples. The All-India Adibasis and Excluded Areas Association was founded in 1936. It has now become a powerful organisation developing the political consciousness of these 20 million Adibasis in our country.

Satyagraha Struggle between 1921-30
Ever since the Non-co-operation movement a number of Satyagraha campaigns have come to be organised against so many unjust laws and imposts; such struggles as those of Bardoli and Pedanandipadu and Duddukuru in 1921 against the land tax; the struggles against Karnataka forest laws in 1921 and 1931-4; the rent exactions in U.P. and Bihar in 1921 and 1931-3; the anti-resettlement campaigns of Godavari and Kistna Deltas and a number of peasant struggles against landlords of Venkatagiri (1931) Tsadumu and Munagala (1939) were organised in the South by some of us. There were also the Land Satyagraha in Bihar (1939), the anti-Zamindari fight in Bengal, and Andhra, and Canal Duties struggle of the Punjab and Bengal (1939), the Jute prices struggle (1937-42), and the Debt Relief Agitation of Bengal. All these campaigns shared the same new features.

Aboriginal Kisans
There are more than 200 lakhs of aboriginal kisans in India. The Santhal rebellion of the last century and the Koya revolt of the thirties of this century and the recent agitation among the Bhils of Dahanu, the tribes of Mymensingh, and Mayurbhanj have shown that these aboriginal tribes too have in them the irrepressible spirit of revolt that can shake up modern capitalist hegemony to its very roots.

The pity is that the Santhal tribal people are not fully aware of their legal rights accruing from the Chota Nagpur Tenancy Act. 'Even were they aware of it, not one in a thousand would have the means and the courage to risk the Rajah's displeasure by having recourse to the law. Hence, Rajahs and landlords ruthlessly exploit this helplessness of the ryots' observed Rev. Kanjiya in 1946. *(Modern Review)*.

These Santhals are losing their lands to the plainsmen, whether they be money-lenders, landlords or touts. Many are the causes for this. The following are mentioned by Mr Ece Mculder in his article in the *New Review* of February 1947.

(*i*) Rent suits and executions, (*ii*) loans, (*iii*) surrender by fraud, (*iv*) wilfully defective settlement, (*v*) Zhulum and brute force of landlords, officials, etc., (*vi*) illegal mutilation of kisans' names on landlords' registers, (*vii*) misunderstanding of the tribal peoples' rights by the courts, (*viii*) starting penshops on aboriginal land and then quietly or suddenly rebuilding these shops into pucca buildings, (*ix*) covering aboriginal areas with grogshops, instead of providing wells, tanks and other forms of irrigation, (*x*) the threat of leasing out forest and grazing lands to companies of financiers, bankers or landlords.

As a result of the growing but forced landlessness of kisans caused by the above methods pursued by money-lenders, landlords and corrupt officials, the area of *bakhast* lands is increasing almost in every tribal village, on which the landlord comes to have the right to settle new kisans.

These complaints are to be met with in every tribal area all over India. I conducted enquiries into the conditions of tribes in Hyderabad in 1927 and in Nilgiris in 1929 and in the Andhra hills in 1931-3 and again in 1936; everywhere the same vicious economic forces were found to be at work to deprive the tribal kisans of their rights.

To relieve their social and economic distress and win for them the same political freedom and status as was being granted to the other peoples of India, there was founded in 1936, the All-India Excluded Area and Tribal Peoples' Association and Sri P. Kodandaramayya has been its soul ever since. A number of provincial conferences also have been held. The Provincial Congress Ministries, notably of Orissa, Bombay, and Assam have been trying to improve educational facilities for these tribal peoples. A few co-operative societies too have been formed. But because we have not yet succeeded in grafting our new organisations on to the traditional love of their own martyrs and heroes who had fought for their freedom and their tribal democratic organisations, as apart from their so-called Rajahs or Chiefs or Muthadars, our modern organisations have as yet remained largely beyond the affections and reach of their masses.

Recently, we have put ourselves in touch with the natural leaders of some of these tribes, such as Samant, Jaipal Singh, Nichols Roy and with the Tribal or Adibasi organisations they have been building up and we trust that very soon these tribal peoples too will be able to march hand in hand with all other sections in our revolutionary attempts to achieve Kisan Mazdoor Praja Raj.

We are encouraged in this hope by our recent discoveries of the revolutionary traditions, legends and ballads that some of these tribal people have built up. For instance, the Manipuri kisan women became so adept in the modern intricacies of markets for their agricultural produce that when the merchants and consumers of Manipur refused to pay them reasonable prices, they organised and went on a strike. For weeks, they maintained their strike and saw to it that there were no blacklegs. In the end, the Manipuri merchants had to accept the demands of those worldly-wise tribal women.

Secondly, when I visited Akola in 1945, and again Udaipur in 1946, I came across the inspiring dance recital of a Bhil kisan cum tribal revolt against their Jaipur and Udaipur Maharanas. According to this recital, which, by the way, is based upon a popular ballad woven by the Bhil poets several centuries ago, the Maharana heaped so many taxes on the Bhils, oppressed them so much and in the end his officers violated their hearths and the modesty of their women, that they rose against his oppression. Their leader, Ram Gopal, organized them for an armed rebellion. For weeks, a guerilla fight went on between the State troops and the Bhils. In the end, their leaders were killed, many of their ranks too fell on the battlefields and out of disgust they left the State in a mass exodus. But after a time, the son of the Maharaja, when he came to the gadi, repented for the sins of his father and begged the Bhils to return to the State.

This legend is woven into such a powerful and eloquent ballad and it is sung, to the tune of a mass dance which inspires the Bhils even today into such crescendoes of emotion, anger and abandon that one can easily get an idea of the passionate mass movement their rebellion must have been in its own day.

The Adibasis who could organize such a movement and who could perform such heroic deeds in an organized manner not only in the Bhil area under their own Bhil leadership, and in the far distant Manipuri under the leadership of their women but also under the inspiration of an outsider like Sitarama Raju on Koraput hills of the Andhra can be expected to take once again their place in the vanguard of our present-day revolutionary struggle for the democratic Kisan Mazdoor Praja Raj.

Indian States Peasants Rebel

Between 1937-46, the peasants of a number of Indian States were in revolt against their horrible conditions of life, which were not in any way different from the intolerable conditions, prevalent in the days of Charlemagne, as described in the chapter on 'The Peasant Bodo,' in medieval Europe by Eileen Power.

The following few quotations from her book on Bodo's life will give us a realistic picture of a part of the misery of the Indian peasants in almost all our Indian States and also in a number of Zamindaris of British India.

'Every year each man was bound to do a fixed amount of ploughing on the domain land and also to give—Carvee—an unfixed amount of ploughing every week when it was needed.'

In addition, there was 'handwork—he had to help repair building or cut down trees or gather fruits or make ale or carry loads. It was by these services that the monks got their own seigniorial farm cultivated.'....(p. 16).

The farmers 'had to carry a load of wood to the big house (of the landlord) in return for being allowed to gather firewood in the woods; they had to pay some hogsheads of wine for the right to pasture their pigs in the same precious woods; every third year, they had to give up one of their sheep for the right to graze upon the fields of the chief. Every farmer had also to pay other rents in produce; every year he owed the big house three chickens and fifteen eggs and a large number of planks to repair its buildings; often he had to give it a couple of pigs; sometimes corn, wine, honey, wax, soap or oil. Even the wives of the farmers were kept busy, if they happened to be serfs; for the servile women were obliged to spin cloth or to make a garment for the big house every year.'....(pp. 16, 17).

The sufferings of the peasants in the Indian States were even more intolerable and they have had to bear the burden of the continually accumulating illegal *abwabs* or imposts. Their feudalism has inherited all the evils of the Mughal empire and had been maintained by British arms and the Indian princes!

Against this terrible order, Indian peasants began to protest. At first the Loharu, Patiala and Nabha peasants revolted. They organized a 'Farm Strike', abandoned their villages and ran into the neighbouring forests. The States sent out their armed police and military on horse-back, to hunt the peasants as it were, and force them to go back to their villages and cultivate their lands. After some fight, the peasants gave up their Satyagraha. There came the prolonged Mansa Peasants' Satyagraha for rent reductions. Partial success came their way after a three month struggle.

The Mysore and Travancore State peoples waged their state-wide struggles for responsible governments. Many were the atrocities committed by the governments. Hundreds of peasants and workers died in those shooting outrages. Only a few political concessions were made and the feudal dues were reduced.

The struggle then spread to the Orissa States. For a while some of the princes fled their states, so furious and all-enveloping were the peasants' revolts, and so helpless were their local police and military forces. The princes hastened to promise to abolish a number of feudal dues, such as forest fees, free supply of fuel, wood, grass, forced labour and supply of animals. Rents too were offered to be reduced. Soon the British forces went to their rescue and the former concessions were mostly withdrawn. Thereupon, the peasants again rebelled, and marched on the princes' capitals and demanded various economic and political concessions. But the British military fired on them, killed large numbers and suppressed their risings. Cruel reprisals were thereafter instituted by the princes. I had an occasion to see large numbers of peasants who fell victims to those barbarities and they were such as to bring shame upon the princes and their protectors, the British. Women were raped, young boys were whipped on their tender parts, peasants were immersed for many moments in rivers, houses and villages were burnt down and grain was looted and cattle confiscated.

Unable to bear these indignities, more than 30,000 peasants

left their villages in a number of States including Nilgiris, Dhenkenal, and marched into the neighbouring forests of Orissa Province; built small huts out of the forest leaves and branches and lived in those improvised camps for many months. At long last, the States had to agree not to resort to any reprisals or indulge in incendiarism or looting and also to abandon their demands for forced labour and some of its more oppressive forms before those peasants could be persuaded to return to their villages.

I visited their camps and interviewed their men, women and leaders. It was an eye-opener to us. Those camps were perfectly orderly. They were built according to the traditional village planning of our peasants. They were ruled by their peasant panchayats. A number of their leaders were women—old and bold. They displayed their inherent qualities of leadership, organisation, discipline and unity. Under the stress of that revolution, their traditional caste distinctions were gone and untouchability was abolished and they learnt to live as one united equalitarian society.

In the wake of these revolutions, rose the peasants of a number of Maharashtra and Karnatak States. They too achieved a number of triumphs and concessions.

Then rose the Jaipur, Gwalior and Udaipur peasants against their local Thakors and other feudal lords. They made use of the internal quarrels and contradictions between the States, princes and the Thakors of Jaipur. They were led by the late Jamnalal Bajaj, a merchant prince and a great follower of Mahatma Gandhi. They achieved victory on their economic front. The Udaipur revolt was put down cruelly. But forced labour had to be abandoned.

During the latter half of 1946, the Hyderabad peasants have risen against their local feudal chiefs, the Deshmukhs. The Communists and Congressmen provided the requisite leadership. But as it is always the case with Communists, they tried to elbow out the Congressmen and achieve a 'closed shop' for their organisation, with the result that the ranks of the peasants were split and a large section of the middle classes and merchants were forced to join hands with the State authorities in order to save themselves from Communist repression.

The State authorities and their local feudal and other allies perpetrated many horrors on the Warrangal, Nalgonda and Bidar peasants. Lootings, rapings, incendiarism and murders of peasants became the order of the day. It was after the States' Peoples' Organisation and the Andhra Congress had begun to champion the cause of these peasant sufferers, that the State has called a halt to its campaign of repression. But this freedom from the feudal lords of the States is being won at great cost by States peasants. All over the Rajasthan States, peasants have had to struggle hard for months after August 1947 to get rid of forced labour, *abwabs* and eventually the Jagirdari or Thakurdari systems.

The sufferings of Hyderabad peasants were of a sterner type. Owing to the intransigence of the Nizam and his ministry, the States people had to offer heroic resistance to the Nazi terrorism of Razakars, a gang of power-mad Moslems. The tribal people, known as Koyas of Palvancha Taluk, the kisans of Nalgonda, Warrangal, Mahaboobnagar districts struggled heroically against the State's campaign of violence and repression. The Koyas offered many pitched battles in their mountain fastnesses on the banks of the Godavari.

Fortunately the statesmanship and strong 'Police Action' organised by Sardar Patel, the hero of Bardoli peasant Satyagraha of 1928, forced the Nizam to surrender. With his fall has come down the Razakar terror and the power of the landlords.

The liberation of practically the whole princely order and the consequent liberation of 70 million States peoples and their attainment of democratic government is the biggest and most romantic achievement of post-partition India and it is significant that it has been achieved by Sardar Patel, the kisan statesman. The Indian States' peasant masses have been in the vanguard of the States' peoples fight for economic and political freedom and thanks to the attainment of freedom by India on 15th of August 1947 and the statesmanship and revolutionary capacity of Sardar Vallabhabhai Patel, the States peoples have also attained control of the government and the feudalism of the zamindari and jagirdari orders is being liquidated.

Veera Gunnamma

An indomitable spirit of revolt and Satyagraha was displayed by Veera Gunnamma of Mandasa. On the 31st March 1940, even as I was being interned and imprisoned by the Madras Government, the local police and Magistrate were arresting seven of the local peasant leaders of Mandasa on very flimsy grounds. The gathering of peasants consisted of more women than men, since the village was stormed by surprise while men were at work in the field. The women protested against the unjust arrests. The police insulted them. Gunnamma roundly abused them for their behaviour. They fired on her. She sprung upon them like a lioness. She was being shot at and she continued to vigorously protest against that police brigandage and injustice until she was felled by the sixth gunshot wound. Today the Vizagapatam peasants cherish the memory of this great heroine, who, unarmed as she was, put to shame, without flinching under the fusillade of shots tearing at her body, the whole beastly might of British Imperialism. When on the 1st of September 1941, Bharatidevi, the peasants' president was offering to Gunnamma's memory at her grave, the highest honours due to a peasant martyr, there was a gathering of one hundred thousand peasants. Peasants have learnt how to die nobly and heroically and also how to honour their martyrs. It is in the fitness of things that a woman, Gunnamma should preside over their growing lists of martyrs.

Even in the realm of practical politics, peasants have achieved quite a lot. Between 1937-40, a number of Provincial Governments had to declare moratoria for rural debts, scale down debt burdens. improve the rights of Zamindari tenants, reduce rents and land revenue burdens for all peasants and grant educational and cultural facilities for landless Harijans and prohibit the alienation of the lands of the aboriginal peasantry and so on.

August Revolution and Peasants

During the 1942 August Revolution, it was the Indian peasant who played the most heroic, dynamic and effective role. Students and urban middle classes too contributed much. But peasants excelled themselves. They rose spontaneously and simultaneously, as if by design and upset the means of transport of the British war machine. Police stations and other local officers of Government were captured. Wherever they succeeded in overcoming the local governmental forces and agencies, they proceeded to establish their panchayats and in several areas in United Provinces, Bihar, Bengal, Maharashtra and Tamilnad, they established their rival Governments. The most famous achievements were witnessed in

Midnapore and Satara Districts where for years, the British were unable or regain their control over whole regions consisting of the masses of peasants.

Thus the 20th century and post-August revolutionary peasants have shown that they are bent upon achieving political power and that they are no longer content with mere looting and occasional displays of their discontent and fury. One remarkable feature of this peasant regime of post-August revolution is that no harm was done to private properties, ordinary individuals or their interests and only Government agents and properties were attacked. Underground activities were highly developed and both criminal and civil agencies of their Panchayat Raj were used to maintain law and order in their emancipated peasant India. Thus the peasant became the central figure of the 1942 revolution.

One other interesting feature of peasant revolution is the rapidity with which peasant revolutionaries were able to construct the whole edifice of separate panchayats for political, administrative and judicial purposes and make them all work efficiently and in harmony. In Satara district from the villages right upto the district level, these tiers of panchayats were built up. And they did remarkable work. They were able to make and enforce laws. They could collect taxes and cesses and administer public funds. All this was possible because the hoary traditions of Panchayat Raj and democracy were still there with the peasants in their folk-lore and day-to-day settlement of village affairs and disputes. And they served as foundations. So, neither the exercise of political power through panchayat democracy nor the management of administration were new. This is another proof, if proof were needed, to demonstrate the capacity of Indian and Chinese and African peasants to run their administration, if and when they capture political and economic power.

No longer are our peasants' satyagraha campaigns isolated struggles unobserved by the peasants of other parts, as Lenin found Russians to be. Wherever there was a struggle, the peasants of the whole of India came to be interested in it, collected funds, observed sympathetic All-India Days and helped the sufferers in every possible manner. Thus the Mandasa State subjects, the Orissa State subjects, Refugee Camps, the Bengali Flood victims, the Rayalaseema famine-stricken peasants, the Malabar peasants and so many others were helped on an all-India basis. True, the All-India Peasants Congress had come to knit all the peasants together under the aegis of a National Peasant unity. But it was Mahatma Gandhi and the National Congress which laid the foundations for the growth of the new consciousness and familiarized the peasants with the potent idea of their national unity.

6 Indian Peasant Uprisings

Kathleen Gough

IN KILVENMANI village in eastern Thanjavur, Tamil Nadu, in 1969, a group of Harijan landless labourers, influenced by the CPI(M), struck for higher wages in view of the increased production and price inflation brought about by the 'green revolution'.[1] Goons hired by their landlords arrived on their street at night, imprisoned 42 men, women and children in a hut and burnt these people to ashes.[2] Again, in Chandwa-Rupaspur village, Bihar, in November 1971, a movement of Santhal tribespeople resisting encroachment of their land was met by landlords' thugs. Four Santhals were roasted alive, 10 were shot dead or hacked to pieces, 33 were severaly wounded and 45 huts burned down.[3] These incidents and many similar ones have illustrated a process of peasant resistance and landlord reprisals that has intensified in India during the past seven years. Since the Naxalbari uprising in West Bengal in 1967 and the emergence of rebel and revolutionary groups among both townsfolk and peasantry, several peasant struggles have erupted, hundreds of landlords, police and moneylenders have been assassinated, and thousands of peasants have died by violence.[4]

Social movements among the peasantry have been widely prevalent in India during and since British rule. We may define a social movement as 'the attempt of a group to effect change in the face of resistance'[5] and peasants as people who engage in agricultural or related production with primitive (palaeotechnic) means and who surrender part of their produce or its equivalent to landlords or to agents of the state. This article is confined to social movements which (a) involved peasants as the sole or main force, (b) were class struggles against those who exacted surplus from peasants and (c) undertook or were provoked to armed struggle in the course of their careers.

Reprinted from *Economic and Political Weekly* Vol. IX 32-4, Special Number, August 1974, pp. 1391-1412.

Generally, the scope and significance of India's peasant uprisings have been understressed. Barrington Moore, Jr, for example, in spite of acknowledging at some length instances of peasant revolts described in recent Indian writings, concludes that China forms 'a most instructive contrast with India, where peasant rebellions in the premodern period were relatively rare and completely ineffective and where modernisation impoverished the peasants at least as much as in China and over as long a period of time'.[6] Moore attributes the alleged weakness of Indian peasant movements to the caste system with its hierarchical divisions among villagers and to the strength of bourgeois leadership against the landlords and the British and the pacifying influence of Gandhi on the peasantry.[7] I would argue that peasant revolts have in fact been common both during and since the British period, every state of present-day India having experienced several over the past two hundred years. Thus in a recent brief survey I discovered 77 revolts, the smallest of which probably engaged several thousand peasants in active support or in combat. About 30 revolts must have affected several tens of thousands, and about 12, several hundreds of thousands. Included in these revolts is the 'Indian Mutiny' of 1857-8, in which vast bodies of peasants fought or otherwise worked to destroy British rule over an area of more than 500,000 square miles.[8] The frequency of these revolts and the fact that at least 34 of those I considered were solely or partly by Hindus, cause me to doubt that the caste system has seriously impeded peasant rebellion in times of trouble.

There does seem no doubt that, apart from the Mutiny, peasant uprisings in China usually had a wider geographical scope than those in India. At least since late Moghul times the reasons for this may have included political fragmentation as well as diversity of language and culture among India's people. During the later decades of Moghul rule the country had already disintegrated into a number of virtually autonomous, mutually warring kingdoms and principalities between whose peasants there was little contact. The British conquered India piecemeal over a hundred year period from the mid-eighteenth to the mid-nineteenth centuries. Early revolts against their rule therefore tended to occur at different dates in different regions, although there was inter-regional coordination among the largest—for example, those led by Raja

Chait Singh in Oudh and other areas in 1778-81, by Vizier Ali in Gorakhpur in 1799, and by the military chiefs (*poligars*) of Madras and Andhra in 1801-5.[9]

Shortly after the British had subdued most of India a huge uprising, widely backed by the peasantry, did sweep over most of Northern and Central India in the shape of the Mutiny, but even in this case resistance tended to be strongest in the areas more recently conquered, while those which had earlier had revolts that had been crushed, played lesser roles.[10]

After the Mutiny, British rule and military preparedness became stronger than ever and the rural upper classes of landlords and princes were either crushed totally or co-opted by the British through concessions. At the same time, political disunity was perpetuated by the division of India into British provinces interspersed with 'native states' having separate judicial systems. Popular action was difficult to organise across these boundaries as well as across ethnic and linguistic lines. Between the Mutiny and Independence, the British government and army were also better co-ordinated than those of China and India was not disturbed by invasions. In these circumstances, politically disunited, under a despotic Central government and opposed by their landed aristocrats, after 1858 peasants engaged only in regional uprisings led by religious figures or by local peasant committees until political parties began to form peasant unions in the 1930s. Even so, some of these revolts were impressive and wrung concessions from the rulers. Since the mid-1930s peasant uprisings as well as non-violent resistance by peasants have usually been at least partly guided by political parties, especially by communists, or else by nationalist and separatist movements of the formerly primitive tribes. In brief, I would argue that the limitations of Indian peasant revolts have sprung more from broader political forces at the level of the province and the colonial and post-colonial state than from the caste system or from peculiarities of village structure. At least two Indian authors have, indeed, argued that the caste system provided a framework for the organisation of peasant rebellions, since in many cases peasants were able to assemble quickly through the medium of their caste assemblies.[11]

When peasant uprisings figure in the British literature, they are often obscured under such headings as 'communal riots' between major religions, fanatical religious cults, or the activities of 'criminal' castes and tribes. While the armed struggles of peasants *have* often had these characteristics, a large proportion of such movements has also, and primarily, been concerned with the struggles of tenants, agricultural labourers, plantation workers, or tribal cultivators, against the exactions of landlords, bureaucrats of the state, merchants, moneylenders, or their agents, the police and the military.

The Colonial Background
Information is limited about peasant uprisings and other forms of violence against the rich and powerful in remote pre-British times. Whatever the earlier record, revolts broke out in many areas during the seventeenth and eighteenth centuries, as the Moghul bureaucracy became more oppressive and exacted harsher taxes, as commercial relations penetrated the country side, and as local rulers made increasing incursions into tribal hill territories.[12] Prominent among the peasant rebellions against the Moghuls were those of the Jats of the Ganges-Jamuna region from the 1660s to 1690s, and of the Satnami religious sect in Narnaul in 1672. In some, but not all, of the revolts against the Moghul power, peasants placed themselves under the leadership of local princes or land managers (zamindars) who rebelled because the imperial land revenue pressed so heavily on the peasants that there was little left for these local dignitaries. In the eighteenth century, the rapid expansions of Sikh and Maratha power and the growth of Thuggee bands in the heartland of the empire owed much to the fervent support of peasants suffering under Moghul revenue exactions.[13] Outside the empire, peasant opposition to encroaching royal authority in the eighteenth century was instanced in the revolts of the Maomoria movement against the kings of the Assam valley,[14] and in south India, in the resistance of the Kallar (literally, 'Robber') tribespeople against the efforts of the rulers of Ramnad and Madura to extract taxes from them in traditionally independent hill regions.[15]

As it spread gradually throughout India, however, British rule brought a degree of disruption and suffering among the peasantry which was, it seems likely, more prolonged and widespread than had occurred in Moghul times.[16] The effects of British rule came, of course, unevenly and in stages, but once operative, they created a structure of underdevelopment in the Indian countryside which became endemic, and which has been modified but never eradicated since Independence. Although I cannot analyse this structure in detail here, the following seem to me to have been the major changes that have affected Indian peasants during the 200-odd years between the beginning of British rule and the present time.

1 The early decades of rule by the East India Company saw outright plunder of the country's wealth coupled with ruinous taxation of the peasantry, in some areas up to twice that imposed by the Moghuls. These no doubt contributed to the Bengal famine of 1770 in which a third of the people died. The collection of heavy revenues was subsequently regularised in the Permanent Settlement of Bengal, Bihar and Orissa in 1793 and in comparably harsh settlements in other regions. Revenues in the early decades were used chiefly for government expenses, wars, private fortunes, remittances to Britain and public works designed to increase imperial trade.[17]

2 In later decades, land revenue declined to a much smaller proportion of the crop than was exacted by the Moghuls, but by that time surplus was being removed from the peasants by other kinds of agents such as moneylenders, noncultivating intermediary tenants, landlords, merchants, the new professional classes such as lawyers, and particularly, although less directly, by British firms engaged in export crop farming, banking, shipping, exports and imports and internal trade.[18]

3 The British land settlements for the first time made land private property of a capitalist kind. The new landlords included zamindars who had previously been revenue collectors under the Moghuls, a variety of princes or subordinate rulers, village headmen, military tenants, religious or secular functionaries of former governments, in some cases peasant cultivators who had hitherto merely leased land under customary regulation, and in other cases merchants or moneylenders who bought land rights, along with the right to collect revenue, in government auctions when previous revenue collectors proved unable to bring in the tax. While such persons gained private landownership, the lower ranks of cultivating tenants, village servants, and serfs lost their hereditary rights to work and to share the produce of village lands, and could be evicted if their landlords found them unnecessary, recalcitrant or unable to pay their rents.

4 During and since British rule, there has been increasing encroachment on tribal hill territories and oppression of tribespeople by European and Indian planters, by government usurpa-

tion of forest areas, by landlords, merchants, and moneylenders from the plains, and by government agents. To the loss of large tribal areas was added exploitation in such forms as rack-renting, unequal terms of trade, usury, corvee and even slave labour, and the obligation to grow cash crops for little or no return.[19]

5 The British effected a reduction in the scale of at least some Indian handloom and handicraft industries, especially those for the production of luxury goods, through discriminatory internal and external tariffs. Such measures virtually destroyed India's export of manufactured goods and also obliged Indians to buy British industrial manufactures, notably cotton textiles.[20] Reports indicate that centres of manufacture such as Dacca and Agra, as large or larger than London in the mid-eighteenth century, shrank as a result of these and other British policies to a fraction of their former size.[21] Craftsmen deprived of their livelihood were driven back upon the land as tenants or landless labourers or joined the modern urban lumpen proletariat. Peasants had to sell their produce for cash, often to moneylenders in return for advance loans, in order to buy imported goods as well as to pay rents and revenues.

6 On balance, India was plundered through the export of capital to Britain by such methods as the repatriation of profits and salaries, debt services for colonial wars and public works, 'home charges' and adverse terms of trade with respect to raw materials exported from India and to imported manufactured goods.

7 In many regions various means were used to encourage or compel cultivators to grow industrial crops, and even food crops, for export. In addition to highland plantations for tea, coffee, cinnamon, and later, rubber, large areas of the plains were at different periods turned over to indigo, opium, cotton, oilseeds, jute, pepper, coconuts, and other export crops.[22] Landlords and local merchants profited from their sales to British export firms, and brought pressure on peasants to grow them in their roles as wage labourers, serfs, tenants or indebted smallholders. Despite the expansion of the total cultivated area, the production of export crops reduced the area available for subsistence farming in at least some regions such as Kerala.

8 Speculation and investment in land by merchants, bureaucrats, landlords, and successful cash crop farmers made land sales increa-

singly common. The growth of absentee landlordism and of cultivation for private profit meant that traditional paternalistic relations of landlords and their tenants were disrupted in many villages, and that tenants and labourers were exposed to new and more alienating forms of exploitation, resulting in greater resentment on their part.

9 Population increase occurred, especially after 1921, as modern medical supplies and services reduced epidemics and infant mortality. Thus, the population of former British India more than doubled between 1891 and 1951. At the same time, industry developed very slowly, so that there came to be too many villagers for a palaeotechnic agriculture to feed adequately and large-scale unemployment or underemployment in the villages. In India as a whole, per capita agricultural output declined between 1911 and 1947.[23] Some of the consequences of 'agricultural overpopulation' were fragmentation of landholdings leading to dwarf-tenancies; competition for land among share-croppers and other tenants, which encouraged rack-renting; moneylending and chronic rural indebtedness; and the growth of debt bondage in some areas and of poorly paid day labour in others. Although the data are imperfect, it seems probable that there has been, both during and since British rule, a decline in the proportions of landlords, rich peasants and middle peasants and an increase in the proportions of poor peasants and landless labourers.[24] Today, India has everywhere overburdened villages and underemployed and ill-nourished villagers.[25]

10 From the 1850s with the building of the railways, the increased movement of goods and people had profound effects. It further undermined the unity and self-sufficiency of villages. The modern transport of foodgrains reduced the danger of severe regional famines; at the same time, by permitting grain stocks to be removed from prosperous areas it appears to have allowed the growth of chronic malnutrition throughout the country. Concomitantly, however, modern transport fostered the movement of ideas between town and country and created links between urban and rural people. Such links strengthened the Indian nationalist movement led by the bourgeoisie; they also permitted a degree of unity between peasants and urban workers in the more recent revolts.

11 The most brutal feature of the British period was the famines.[26] There were serious regional famines before British rule, notably in the Deccan in 1630-32 and in 1702-4. It seems certain, however, that the famines of the British period were more frequent. Thus, 14 major famines are known to have occurred between the early eleventh and the late seventeenth centuries. During the period of government by the East India Company, by contrast, in addition to the catastrophic Bengal famine of 1770, there were twelve serious famines and four periods of acute scarcity before the Mutiny of 1857, while Indian peasants were being tormented by excessive revenue exactions. Still more devastating famines followed the Mutiny. The worst occurred between 1865 and 1899, and the most severe of all in 1896-7, when 97 million were seriously affected and at least 4.5 million died. Another 650,000 died in 1898, and a further 3.25 million in 1899. In the famines of the 1860s the principal victims were landless labourers and unemployed weavers, but by 1900 tenant cultivators formed the largest category employed in government relief works during famines in the Deccan and Gujarat, while landless labourers formed the next largest category, and weavers were still prominent. The data suggest that by the end of the century tenant cultivators had no reserves left and that in famines they suffered almost equally with landless labourers and with artisans thrown out of work by British industrial policies. Using figures collected by Bhatia, and selecting only those which record the deaths of more than 100,000 people in any single famine year and region. I have calculated a total of 20,687,000 famine deaths in India between 1866 and 1943. Because of the omission of smaller figures this is undoubtedly far too low.

Probably thanks to improved transportation, there was no very large famine between 1908 and 1943, when the stoppage of rice imports from Burma by the Japanese invasion, coupled with hoarding and speculation, produced the Bengal famine in which 3.5 million died. Since 1947 no catastrophic major famine has occurred in India proper (as distinct from Bangladesh), but unknown millions annually die untimely deaths as a result of illness compounded with chronic malnutrition. A United Nations report of 1963 charged that five million Indian children still died of malnutrition each year.[27] Severe shortages occurred in 1964-6, and since 1971 the situation has become increasingly critical, with famine deaths, suicides by starving people, food riots and other forms of agitation in many parts of India.

Since Independence, and especially since 1954, foreign food loans have augmented India's food supply, but have also helped plunge the country hopelessly into debt.[28] India's own food production has roughly doubled since Independence. This is no mean achievement, but even when combined with foreign imports the increase is barely adequate to meet the needs of a population which grew from 356 million in 1951 to 556 million in 1971. When combined with hoarding, speculation and widening inequality in incomes, it is not at all adequate.

12 Since Independence, land reforms have removed some of the biggest landlords—the zamindars—and some of the non-cultivating intermediary tenants, but in general laws on land ceilings have been evaded.[29] Before and after each act, landlords have evicted numerous tenants on the grounds that they needed the land for 'personal cultivation' and have created new paper owners' to conform with the acts while leaving the real control undisturbed. At least in some areas, therefore, land reforms have resulted in an increase in the proportions of poor peasants working part-time for wages, of landless labourers, and of both rural and urban casual workers and unemployed.[30]

13 During 1965-71 the 'green revolution' increased productivity in some regions. Reports indicate, however, that it tended still further to polarise agricultural incomes, for it enriched the larger owners while tenants and labourers gained little or none of the increase during a period in which they were also being affected by generalised inflation. As farms are consolidated and operate as industrial capitalist enterprises, the green revolution dispossesses some tenants, disemploys some landless labourers and drives out of business small farmers who cannot afford the new technology and cannot compete.[31] In 1972-4, moreover, the gains of the green revolution have for the most part been wiped out by seasonal drought and flooding or, most recently, by shortages of fertilisers.

The above conditions form the background of agrarian revolt from the late eighteenth century until the present. Directly or indirectly, all of them have been either created or severely exacerbated by British colonial policies or by the policies of the Indian government, under the influence of imperialism, in the post-colonial period.[32]

Types of Peasant Uprisings

Seventy-seven revolts, including the Mutiny, were considered in preparation for this article. Eight of them occurred in East Bengal (present-day Bangladesh); as it happened, none were selected from regions lying in present-day Pakistan. The East Bengal revolts help to illustrate general processes at work in British India. This paper does not cover agrarian unrest in what became East Pakistan and later, Bangladesh; it is evident, however, that there have been peasant uprisings there since the end of British rule, especially during the invasion by Yahya Khan's forces in 1971, and revolutionary movements based on peasants are continuing there.[33]

A rough classification of the revolts during British rule yields five types of action in terms of goals, ideology and methods of organisation: (1) Restorative rebellions to drive out the British and restore earlier rulers and social relations; (2) religious movements for the liberations of a region or an ethnic group under a new form of government; (3) social banditry (to use Hobsbawm's term);[34] (4) terrorist vengeance, with ideas of meting out collective justice; (5) mass insurrections for the redress of particular grievances.

The first and second of these types are transformative, in the sense that they sought from the beginning—and sometimes briefly achieved—a largescale restructuring of society.[35] Restorative revolts were, however, backward looking, whereas India's religious peasant movements have been 'nativistic' in combining traditional cultural elements and values with new themes, sometimes derived from the oppressing groups, in a utopian vision of a Golden Age. The third, fourth and fifth types are initially reformative in the sense that they aim at only partial changes in society. Both the third and the fifth types have, however, sometimes become transformative and have led to the seizure of a liberated zone. The fourth type, terrorist vengeance, can take place sporadically and spontaneously with little or no organisation; it has probably occurred thousands of times in all parts of the country in the form of small outbursts of retaliation against landlords, moneylenders, etc. Occasionally, however, terrorist vengeance seems to develop into an organised movement, sometimes involving a religious cult; it is also usually present to some degree in all of the other four types. Religious movements (type 2) are thus not completely confined to attempts to liberate an ethnic group or a region: some bandit groups, indeed, have special religious cults, as well as some terrorist movements, and both restorative rebellions and insurrections have usually been regarded as sanctioned by 'normal' religion. The religious movements for liberation are, however, a sufficiently distinctive group, bearing messianic and millenarian messages, to be placed in a separate category. Finally, both messianic religious movements and agitations for the redress of special grievances have, of course, occurred very frequently in non-violent forms; but this paper deals only with armed revolts, or (in two or three cases) with armed movements which engaged in forceful action without actually resorting to fighting.

Since the mid-1930s peasant unions have been organised by a variety of socialist and social democratic groups and since the mid-1940s several armed peasant uprisings have occurred under communist influence. Some of these outbreaks took place in regions already shaken by peasant uprisings in the British period—notably, in Bengal, in various tribal hill regions and in Kerala. With modifications, the communist-inspired outbreaks have partaken of the character of types 3, 4 and 5, coupled with a consciously revolutionary and transformative ideology having some elements akin to type 2. There have thus been continuities as well as changes between the earlier revolts and the modern communist ones. The most significant changes have, of course, been the attempt at leadership by a vanguard political party, together with the possession of a view of world history, an analysis of India, a strategy of revolution and a plan for the nation state at large, derived from the theories of Marx and Lenin and, more recently, of Mao Tse-tung.

The goals and methods of those engaged in revolt varied with their circumstances. Although no neat correlations are evident I shall suggest some connections between contexts and types of revolt. All of the revolts seem to have occurred under conditions of relative deprivation,[36] that is of deprivation considered outrageous by comparison with the past or with the condition of others in the present. All of them embodied ideas of freedom from undue economic exploitation or deprivation; of some form of collective independence from a domination conceived of as foreign and unjustified; and of a just social order sanctioned by some religious faith or all-embracing modern ideology, especially that of Marxism. It is true of course that Marxism differs from religious belief in its denial of the supernatural, and that the work of Marx and his successors points a way towards non-dogmatic, scientific analysis of social phenomena. As a political ideology, however, especially when translated into the language and concepts of peasants, Marxism has similarities to religious movements in that it purports to offer a complete explanation of society and especially of social evils, and in that parts of the explanation are accepted on faith. Marxist movements are also dedicated to a future state of ethical virtue, providing new relationships for a 'blessed community'. Finally, as in chiliastic religious movements, its followers are ideally willing to sacrifice their lives to bring this state about. Contrary to Cohn,[37] I do not regard these qualities as undesirable in times of oppression, nor as necessarily linked with lack of realism or with collective paranoia.

Restorative Movements

Between 1765 and 1857 a large proportion of revolts were led by Hindu or Muslim petty rulers, former revenue agents under the Moghuls, tribal chiefs in hill regions and local landed military officers (*poligars*) in south India. They were supported by masses of peasants and sometimes of former soldiers. The revolts were either against the conquest itself and the imposition of heavy revenues on existing nobles, or retaliatory attempts to drive out the British after they had dispossessed a zamindar or a raja for failing to pay the revenues and had replaced him with some other claimant to the estate, with a Company officer, or with a merchant, moneylender or adventurer who had bought the estate at auction. The goals of these revolts were complete annihilation or expulsion of the British and reversion to the previous government and agrarian relations. The peasants were not blind loyalists. Their own grievances were bitter, for in their efforts to squeeze out the revenue the Company's officers often completely pauperised the peasants or had them starved, flogged or jailed.[38]

Twenty-nine revolts involving peasants as the main force were counted for this period, 12 by tribal chiefs and 17 by Hindu or

Muslim rulers or other former officials.³⁹ Six took place in Bengal, five in Bihar, three in Assam and 15 in central and south India. The enemies in these rebellions included all British officials and troops, British plantation owners, revenue agents, pro-British landlords, moneylenders, and police. Rebel armies of peasants and former soldiers holed up in forts, in the forests, or on hill tops with stocks of grain, and from there made forays in bands of a few hundred to several thousand, robbing and killing officials, looting and burning treasuries, plundering merchant boats or the homes of landlords and moneylenders, and ambushing or fighting off police and troops with matchlocks, knives, swords, or bows and arrows. All of the movements involved several thousand armed rebels and supporting populations of tens or hundreds of thousands. The largest rebellions produced alliances of nobles in several districts, peasant insurrections over wide areas, the capture of towns and the temporary expulsion of the British from one or more local government centres.

Among these major uprisings were the revolt of Raja Chait Singh and other Hindu and Muslim zamindars of Oudh in 1778-81; the subsequent revolt of Vizier Ali, the deposed Nawab of Oudh, in Banaras, Gorakhpur and surrounding areas in 1799; the massive uprisings of the *poligars* and their peasants in Tinnevelly, North Arcot, and the ceded districts of Andhra in 1801-5; the uprising of the Chuar tribesmen of Midnapore in 1799;⁴⁰ the revolt of the Pazhassi Raja, which commanded tens of thousands of guerilla fighters and affected most of the population of Malabar in 1796-1805; and almost immediately afterwards, an insurrection further south in Travancore and Cochin by Velu Thampi, the prime minister of Travancore state, with professional army of 30,000 and even larger numbers of cultivators. The last of these major rebellions before the Mutiny was the famous Santhal tribal revolt of 1855-6, involving a peasant army of between 30 and 50 thousand, village assemblies in groups of 10,000, and tens of thousands of government troops. All these revolts were, of course, eventually crushed by the British. Some rebel leaders fled into banditry or, very rarely, were reinstated with less exacting revenue settlements. More commonly they were wiped out with exemplary savagery; Velu Thampi was hanged publicly after his death. The Pazhassi Raja was executed and his lineage dispossessed; his palace was razed and a road built over the site. After a few of the revolts the revenue exactions on the peasants were reduced, but more often 'pacification' was brutally effected. Half the Santhal army was murdered and the victors randomly flogged or imprisoned peasants as examples to others. The Oudh revolt of 1778-81 ended with the zamindars' forts destroyed, their owners expelled into banditry and fierce plunderings and revenue exactions in the countryside which led to the famine of 1784.

The largest restorative rebellion was, of course, the 'Mutiny' of 1857-8. Begun by Hindu and Muslim soldiers in revolt against their conditions and against offences to their religions, it engaged millions of impoverished peasants, ruined artisans, dispossessed nobles, estate managers, tribal chiefs, landlords, religious leaders (Hindu, Muslim, tribal and Sikh), civil servants, boatmen, shopkeepers, mendicants, low caste labourers and workers in European plantations and factories. The leaders included rajas and nawabs with the emperor of Delhi as figurehead, native gentry, tribal chiefs and village headmen some of whom set themselves up as kings. The revolt was not centrally co-ordinated, but leaped from district to district throughout most of northern and central India and inspired scattered uprisings in the south.[41] The racism of the conquerors, their insults to religion, their eviction of rulers and managers, and above all their ruination of agriculture and manufactures, combined to provoke an anti-imperialist cataclysm. For the peasants, years of rack-renting, famines, high prices, tariffs, debts, land seizures and physical brutality were the main grievances; for the artisans, loss of livelihood; for the workers, low wages and sub-human conditions; and for the hill chiefdoms, incursions, taxes and loss of land. The prime enemies were of course the British government, military and planters, the big 'loyal' princes who allied with them, the revenue officers, the wealthier merchants and the money lenders. The revolt raged most fiercely in areas which had been conquered after 1800, for example, Oudh (conquered in 1856), Chota Nagpur (1831-3), Jabalpur (1818), Nagpur (1854), Jhansi (1853) and Berar (1853-60). Bengal, Orissa, the ceded districts of Andhra and Madras, Kerala, Mysore and Bombay, which had been conquered earlier and had already undergone rebellions and repression, played lesser roles.

In the heart of the rebel area mass insurrections of armed peasants, in addition to the mutinying troops and the private armies of rulers, combined to massacre the British and to destroy government buildings, revenue and court records, coffee and indigo plantations and factories, telegraphs, railways and churches—in short, every organ of British rule. The war was a holy war, so announced repeatedly by rulers and religious leaders, but it was also most interestingly a war in which Hindu and Muslim, tribesman and Sikh, explicitly foreswore mutual enmity and combined in defence of their own and each others' customs and honour against infidel conquest and oppression. Contrary to standard British accounts, it seems to have come within an ace of ending the Company's rule.[42] It failed, apparently, because it did not spread to all of India and was not centrally co-ordinated (as was the British government and army), and because, spreading at different dates from region to region, the rebellion lost some strongholds, in particular Delhi, before it could properly take hold in others. Nevertheless, for several months it raged over a 500,000-square-mile region in which the peasantry, including the lowest castes and the landless labourers, formed the backbone of resistance.

Religious Movements

After the failure of the Mutiny and the annexation of India by the Crown, rebel princes and chiefs were for the most part executed, driven into exile, or co-opted by the government. Tribal chiefs played a part in some of the later uprisings and also some religious leaders with claims to royal or noble descent. In general, however, peasant rebels from the Mutiny to the 1930s joined bandit troops, engaged in insurrections under their own committees or local popular leaders, or else took part in movements for local liberation under charismatic religious leaders. A number of such religious movements had already occurred before the Mutiny.

Hobsbawm,[43] Cohn,[44] and Worsley[45] have suggested that millenarian movements were rare or absent in India and the view is widespread that they stem usually from Judaeo-Christian origins or influences. In the strict sense of belief in a thousand year period in which the Evil One will be chained, this is probably true, but most writers give a wider meaning to millenarian. Cohn cites five characteristics: such movements are collective; they look forward to a reign of bliss on this earth; the transformation from the present evil age is to be total; it is imminent, its followers waiting in 'tense expectation of the millennium'; and it will come about by super natural means.[46]

In this sense, a number of millenarian movements have arisen among Hindus, Muslims and tribal peoples in India over the past two centuries and probably earlier, although their prevalence has until recently been overlooked by researchers. Stephen Fuchs' 'Rebellious Prophets: A Study of Messianic Movements in Indian Religions'[47] describes more than 50 movements with messianic and millenarian overtones. All had divine or prophetic leaders who were believed to possess supernatural powers and looked forward to a terrestrial state of righteousness and justice in which their enemies would be removed or defeated. Most were transformative rather than reformative in their expectation of a sudden, total change, and most believed the Golden Age to be imminent and subject to some kind of supernatural intervention.

Fuchs records 19 such movements among peasants which resorted to armed struggle against the British and against those familiar foes, the landlords, merchants, moneylenders, revenue agents and other bureaucrats, troops, and police. The Moplah (or Mappilla) revolts of Malabar which took place between 1836 and 1896—actually 22 in number and varying somewhat in ideology —are here counted as one further instance, for a total of twenty.[48]

Of these 20 revolts involving armed struggle, 10 occurred among tribal peoples and 10 among predominantly Muslim or Hindu populations. Ten arose before the Mutiny and 10 afterwards. Four of the non-tribal movements occurred in Bengal, one in Gujarat, one in Maharashtra, one in Malwa, one in Patiala, one in Kerala and one in Assam. Six of the 10 non-tribal movements were Muslim and only four predominantly Hindu, although most of the tribal peoples were affected by Hinduism as well as Christianity and a few by Islam. It is probable that other millenarian revolts may yet come to light among the Hindu peoples of various regions; certainly, there were some non-violent Hindu millenarian movements.[49] At present it seems, however, that tribal and Muslim minorities, especially in eastern India, were those most liable to violent uprisings on a millenarian kind.

If this is true, I suggest that fervent chiliastic movements may be most likely to arise among cultural minorities who have lost their customary security, occupations or statuses and have suffered unusual deprivation by comparison with their own past and with those around them.[50] This would apply particularly to the Muslim cultivators of Bengal and Kerala who suffered acutely, often under Hindu landlords, both as rack-rented or evicted peasants, and as religious groups who were hated by those in authority because their co-religionists had earlier wielded political power. I would also apply to the tribal peoples, who, more than most groups in India, suffered incursions, loss of land, swindling, bankruptcy, and the undermining of their culture by literate and technologically superior invaders, both British and Indian. It is noteworthy that the Hindus who have joined religious movements with an egalitarian and millenarian flavour, for example, the Vaishnavite Maomorias of Assam in 1769-1839 and the followers of the Bengal Sanyasis in the late eighteenth century, were also predominantly low caste or of tribal origin, suffering unusual deprivation from evictions, famine, and excessive rents or revenues.[51]

It seems likely that the more hopeless the real prospects of the religious movement and the fewer its means of practical rehabilitation or redress, the greater the tendency to seek an imminent millenarian outcome through nonempirical means, and to invest the leader with marvellous, indeed magical, powers. Thus five of the 19 movements studied were classically millenarian in character, waiting in tense expectation of imminent deliverance, chiefly by supernatural means. These movements included the early movement of Moplah tenants in the 1830s to 1850, led by the Mambram Tangal,[52] the Naikda tribal movement in Gujarat under the Hindu religious leader Joria Bhagat in 1867-70,[53] the Munda tribal movement under Birsa in the 1890s,[54] and the Bhil tribal movement under Govindgiri, a tribal convert to Hinduism, in 1900-12, following a severe famine in 1900. The Bhil groups of the Panch Mahals and the Naikdas, both of whom probably number fewer than 10,000, came to believe that their leader was himself an incarnation of the supreme deity (Parameswar or Siva among the Naikdas and Vishnu among the Bhils). Both groups thought that their divine leader would deliver them from British rule and establish an independent, ethical tribal kingdom, which the Naikdas called *dharmraj* (kingdom of virtue), a Hindu term. The Muslim Moplah tenants, suffering from rack-renting, evictions and famine with the spread of cash crop farming and the disruption of their formerly stable tenancies,[56] were taught by the Tangal that if they would give up cultivating, pray diligently, and organise for battle, a ship bearing arms and modern equipment for 40,000 men would miraculously appear on the horizon and the British would be driven out of Malabar—a clear case of a millenarian cargo cult. Birsa received teaching from both Lutheran missionaries and Hindu ascetics but then reverted to his Munda religion, bringing with him beliefs and images from both major faiths. He taught the Mundas first that he was a divinely appointed messenger come to deliver them from foreign rule, and later that he was an incarnation of God (Bhagwan) himself. His mission was to save the faithful from destruction in imminent flood, fire and brimstone by leading them to the top of a mountain. Beneath them, all the British, Hindus and Muslims would perish, after which a Munda kingdom would be ushered in.

Although their religious predictions failed, all of these movements organised such numbers of fervent followers that they took instead to empirical means and made armed attacks on their oppressors. Birsa assembled a force of 6,000 Mundas armed with swords and bows and arrows, some of whom burned Hindu temples and Christian houses and churches, killed a constable and were finally defeated in battle by government troops. Joria's followers were organised for revolt by Rupsing Gobar, a rebel leader who actually founded a Naikda kingdom, collected revenues, and sacked two nearby police stations before his army was subdued by British forces. Govindgiri collected an army in the Mangarh hills in 1911 and plundered the surrounding Hindu and Muslim landowners, but was conquered by state troops and British artillery. Bands of Moplah devotees numbering from three hundred to several hundred, chiefly tenants facing eviction, carried out 22 uprisings over a period of 60 years in several talukas of Malabar, in which they assassinated numerous police, government officials, Hindu landlords and British and Indian troops. Faced with insuperable odds, but driven to frenzied action by continuing economic misery, the Moplah movement became sustained by a redemptive ideology. It was believed that the rebels, having first purified themselves by religious ceremonies, would gain instant salvation by assassinating their British and landlord oppressors until they themselves fell in martyrdom.

All of the religious movements believed in a coming realm of righteousness and invested their leaders with supernatural powers, but the more powerful ones seem from the beginning to have relied chiefly on their own efforts to usher in the new society. These movements were especially prominent during the famines and harsh exploitation of peasants in the early decades of Company rule in Bengal. They included the Muslim Maulvis under Titu Miyan, who spread over Barasat, Nadia, Faridpur, Jessore and Calcutta regions in 1827-31; the Muslim Pagal Panthis, converts from the Garo and Hajong tribes, under Tipu Shah in northern Mymensingh in 1824-33; and the Muslim Faraizis of Bogra and Faridpur in 1838-51. All of these movements attracted tens of thousands of rack-rented and evicted peasants, recruited armed bands of many thousands, and strove to drive out their Hindu landlords and British rulers and establish a reign of Islamic righteousness. Tipu Shah and Titu Miyan conquered large territories, set up administrations and levied tribute from the landlords. Dudu Miyan, the Faraizi leader, ran a parallel administration to that of the British from Bahadarpur in East Bengal, which he divided into circles of villages under deputies. Each deputy settled disputes among the tenants, forced Muslims to convert to the Maulvi sect, and protected cultivators from the zamindars' excesses through a mixture of litigation and armed intimidation. The British defeated Tipu Shah and Titu Miyan in battle and imprisoned Dudu Miyan in Alipore jail—a site of confinement and ill-treatment of revolutionary prisoners down to the present day.[57]

Social Bandits

Five of the revolts studied are best classified by Hobsbawm's term 'social banditry'. They are the Thuggee of north and central India of 1650-1850 or later,[58] the Sanyasis and Fakirs of Bengal in the late eighteenth century,[59] the dispossessed military chief Narasimha Reddi and his followers in Kurnool, Andhra Pradesh, in 1846-7,[60] the tribal Lodhas of Midnapore, who became a 'criminal caste' in the nineteenth century after being evicted from their homelands,[61] and the tribal Kallar of South India, some of whom operated as bandits from their hill country in Madura into lowland Madura, Pudukottai and Thanjavur in the late eighteenth to the twentieth centuries.[62] These groups form only a small proportion of the large numbers of peasants, tribesmen, disinherited landlords and disbanded soldiers who turned to part-time or full-time banditry in the eighteenth and nineteenth centuries when they were deprived of their livelihood, evicted from their homelands, or squeezed in their tribal territories.

The Thuggee were the most colourful and numerous of Indian bandits, the best of them combining a rather distant millenarian prospect with a certain Robin Hood gallantry and a genius for swift assassination. They arose about 1650 in the area between Delhi and Agra and multiplied in late Moghul times as revenue exactions became harsher. During British rule they spread throughout Bihar and into Oudh, Bengal, Orissa, Rajputana, the Punjab, Mysore and the Karnatak. Operating in bands of about a dozen, they left their home villages periodically and waylaid wealthy travellers many miles away, decoyed them by stealth and then strangled them with yellow scarves, robbed them and burried them. Precisely what was done with the booty is unclear, but in some cases at least the Thuggee must have shared it with their fellow villagers, for they had the peasants' loyalty in their own territories. Thuggee were recruited from outlaws of the state, peasants and disbanded soldiers—chiefly from the most oppressed classes of their regions. Each band customarily contained members of several Hindu castes, Muslims, and in the Punjab, Sikhs. Band members observed normal social distinctions in their own communities but ate, smoked and drank together on their outings. They were initiated into a movement devoted to the service of their goddess, seen as Kali by the Hindus and Fatima by the Muslims, by whom they believed their order to have been created so as to root out evil beings and save humanity from destruction. As in the case of the Moplahs and no doubt most of the other armed religious movements, rites of dedication and purification preceded each assassination. Thuggee were forbidden by their religion to kill women, children, youth, Hindu and Muslim holy men, carpenters, poor people, beggars, bards, water-carriers, oil-vendors, dancers, sweepers, laundry workers, musicians and cripples—in short almost every productive or defenceless category in the population. They confined their assaults chiefly to merchants, soldiers, money-carriers and servants of the Company. They are reported to have assassinated more than a million people and plundered many millions of rupees.

The Thuggee, like the Kallar, the Lodhas and many other tribes who raided rich plainsmen when their lands were invaded, must be classed as reformative, since they sought not a liberated kingdom but only short-term relief for themselves and their fellows, and believed only vaguely in a Golden Age hereafter. The Sanyasis and Fakirs became, however, a transformative movement and for a short time a highly successful one. These religiosi were originally peasants, evicted and made homeless during the wars, depredations and revenue exactions of the East India Company and various rival Indian princes in the late eighteenth century. They first formed bands of Hindu and Muslim holy men and survived as mendicants. As their numbers swelled in the great famine of 1770, they gathered together with disbanded soldiers and dispossessed zamindars, formed bandit troops and scoured the countryside, raiding the grain stocks and treasuries of the wealthy and distributing them to the starving peasantry.[63] In trying to consolidate its rule the Company met with a large Sanyasi and Fakir rebellion in 1771 between Rangpur and Dacca which defeated a company of sepoys and killed the commander. Bands of five thousand to seven thousand bandits then spread over most of Bengal and eastern Bihar, set up an independent government in Bogra and Mymensingh and almost wiped out another British detachment in 1773. Further frequent encounters took place between the Sanyasis-Fakirs and British forces all over West Bengal and Bihar until the movement finally disintegrated about 1800; according to Stephen Fuchs, its survivors are believed to have migrated to join the Marathas in their wars against the British.

The militant religious movements discussed in type 2 strove for the liberation of an ethnic region—both from the British and from 'foreign' Indian predators and invaders—and for the establishment of a divinely ordained kingdom of righteousness and justice. They arose among severly exploited minorities most of whom, nevertheless, remained in their home territories and were numerically preponderant within a region. Many bandit movements resembled the ethnic religious movements in possessing special religious cults, charismatic leaders and a belief that their struggles would eventually release the world from pain. Bandits apparently differed from local religious movements for liberation, however, in being recruited from displaced or outcast groups and individuals—disbanded soldiers, unseated nobles, evicted peasants, unemployed artisans, outlaws of the state although not necessarily of the local community, and those who had lost all through war or famine. They were thus men who, although they might maintain a home or shelter in their villages, had no livelihood except plunder and were free to roam far afield. Alternatively, bandits arose part-time among tribal peoples squeezed by plains invaders and by the government, who could combine vengeance with predation by raising plains' landlords from their own base areas.

Being foot-loose, bandits had great adaptability and therefore an ambiguous status in the larger society. As Hobsbawm stresses, only some of them, probably a minority, were 'social bandits', that is engaged essentially in class struggle and concerned with the interests of the poor from whom they sought protection and with whom they shared their loot.[64] Many bandit groups, including some Thuggee, served as mercenaries for established landlords and princes as well as for dispossessed rebel nobles or for adventurers seeking fortune and political power.[65] Others served religious messiahs bent on driving out the British.[66] The Kallar of Madura exemplify the diverse potentialities of bandits. Having fought unsuccessful wars to maintain their tribal lands tax-free from the Nayak rulers of Madura and the British in the mid-eighteenth century, some Kallar became bandits (perhaps 'social') who robbed merchants and officials on the high roads out of Madura. Others hired themselves as mercenaries to the Maratha Raja of Thanjavur. After British rule became established around 1800, bandit troops from Kallar settlements of both Madura and Thanjavur became cattle thieves operating among high caste rich peasants and landlords of these districts. In their attempts to reduce cattle losses, the plains landlords even appointed single families of Kallar as watchmen (*kavalgar*) in their villages. These collected annual bribes from the villagers on behalf of bandit groups to ward off the bandits' predations, or when cattle did disappear, arranged their ransom.[67] The system persisted in western Thanjavur as late as 1953. The Kallar *Kavalgar* of one village where I worked had earlier murdered his cousin in a family dispute and had served sentence in the Andaman Islands. On his return he came to live in his wife's village which belonged to Brahman landlords and obtained the post of 'watchman' there. At that date, small groups of youth of Kallar communities long resident as tenants in Thanjavur villages still engaged in plundering landlords and rich peasants through cattle thefts, highway robberies and thefts from grain carts far from home in the famine season and shared their loot with their kinsfolk. Their untouchable servants of the Palla (landless labourer) caste, specially trained in dacoity, sometimes assisted them. Two miles from my place of work lived a famous (but retired) Palla multi-murderer who told wondrous anecdotes. His neighbours protected him with amused pride as a kind of village marvel.

When whole regions were ravaged by famine or excessive revenue exactions, bandits sometimes led ordinary peasants in driving out the rulers and landlords, as in the Sanyasi and Fakir rebellion. The relationship of peasants to these liberators seems, however, to have been characteristically uneasy. During the Bengal famine of 1769-70 a third of the villages of Birbhum and Bishnupur districts were wiped out, yet the Company still further increased its revenue demands by twelve per cent between 1770 and 1776. Thousands of peasants ruined by famine or rack-renting scoured the countryside as bandits and in 1787 and 1788 sacked the Bishnupur treasury, carrying off more than three thousands sterling pounds' worth of silver.[68] In November 1789 the peasantry made common cause with the bandits and drove out the British from Rajnagar and Bishnupur. Very soon, however, the peasants came to be at odds with the bandits and fell upon them, slaughtering them unmercifully, and in 1790 peasants co-operated with the government to restore 'peace and order'. The reason for this clash is unclear: perhaps bandit rule proved less 'social' than the peasants anticipated, or perhaps the peasants resisted bandit demands for division of their lands.

Terrorist acts with ideas of vengeance and justice
Banditry involves assassination, whether routine or occasional, but which is mainly for survival and predation, while restorative and religious movements for liberation kill or terrorise in pursuit of their aim to drive out the oppressor. The simplest, if least effective, form of revolt, however, is that in which peasants rise up and kill or maim the oppressors without plans for the future—often, indeed, in the certain knowledge of being annihilated. In India every village has its legends of individual or small group acts of violence against landlords, revenue agents, moneylenders,

bailiffs, or other authorities or wealthy persons. More rarely, when there is extreme suffering yet when it is impossible to drive out the enemy, patterns of violence may emerge in which members of a minority or even a whole region, engage in epidemic assassinations of key enemies, or burn buildings, stacks, or other property. The individual terrorist kills and risks his life for his community, in vengeance but also partly with a sense of group pride and natural justice; sometimes, with a religious belief that this is his unavoidable destiny and his road to salvation. Although the custom was ancient among them, some of the Lushai Kukis' headhunting raids into Sylhet and Cachar in the first half of the nineteenth century seem to have been in vengeance, 'not [as some charged] to get heads to bury with [their dead chief] Laroo, but to avenge unfair dealing of Bengalis at the frontier marts'.[69] And although they sprang originally from a millenarian ideology, most of the nineteenth century Moplah killings of British officials, landlords and revenue agents were carried out to avenge specific wrongs, to mete out rural justice and to afford desperate paupers escape to salvation through martyrdom.[70] The British correctly estimated the element of collective justice, for they levied heavy fines on the entire village of those who died fighting after they had assassinated some high ranking person.

Mass insurrections
Fourteen of the revolts studied were mass insurrections in which peasants provided the leadership and were the sole or dominant force.[71] These revolts were sudden and dramatic. They lacked a religious movement ideology and a single charismatic religious leader. They aimed initially at the redress of particular grievances and thus were at first reformative. They started characteristically with peaceful mass boycotts or demands for the righting of wrongs, but fought when reprisals were taken against them. Seven of the revolts occurred in Bengal, two in the Punjab, three in the Deccan, one in Mysore and one in Kerala. Several became revolutionary in aim as they progressed and four actually achieved a temporarily liberated zone. These were the revolts of the peasants and bandits of Bishnupur and Birbhum in 1789,[72] of the Jat peasants of Haryana in 1809,[73] of the peasants of Khandesh in 1852,[74] and of the Moplahs of Kerala in 1921.[75] One revolt, that of the Santhals of

Bengal in 1870, was predominantly tribal, although plains' peasants took part in it.[76] The rest involved Hindus, Muslims, or Sikhs, usually a combination of members of two religions. Six occurred before the Mutiny, and eight afterwards. The biggest revolts, those of Rangpur in 1783, of Bishnupur in 1789, of the Jats in 1809, of the Mysore peasants in 1830-31, of the indigo growers in Bengal in 1860, of the Deccan peasants in 1875, and of the Moplahs in 1921, probably affected populations of more than a million. The revolts characteristically lasted for several weeks, but the Moplah revolt continued for six months.

All the uprisings involved tenants or small owner-cultivators. All were against economic deprivations resulting from British policies and in most cases also from landlords' exactions. The revolt in Rangpur and Dinajpur of 1783 and the Deccan peasant uprising of 1875 provide earlier and later examples of features characteristic of all these uprisings. In Rangpur in the early years of Company rule, revenue exactions under the revenue contractor Debi Singh were outrageous—his agents chained and imprisoned selected peasants, then flogged and starved them until their villages paid the assessment. On January 18, 1783, peasants of many villages assembled in Tepah and elected a leader—the son of a peasant who had served as leader in a previous insurrection. The mob then stormed a prison and released the prisoners and marched with drumbeats to demand revenue concessions from the local agent. When his police fired and killed a peasant a fight ensued in which the agent Gaurmohan was captured and several peasants killed before the crowd could withdraw. Although the peasants made clear that they wanted justice, not bloodshed, and later presented a written petition to the government, they met only attempts to renew the revenue collections. The situation was so bad that, as they claimed, 'we then sold our cattle and the trinkets belonging to our women. We have since sold our children...' Failing to get relief, they killed two revenue agents[77] and raised a huge armed force which marched through the countryside. The revolt spread to Dinajpur, where peasants elected two more leaders and sacked and robbed a revenue office. After five weeks British troops put down the rebellion after killing many peasants, burning their homes and hanging a village headman. No relief seems to have been forthcoming from this uprising.

The Deccan revolt of 1875 was joined by water-carriers, barbers and even the house-servants of moneylenders in addition to cultivators. It covered Poona and Ahmednagar districts and spread into Gujarat. Excessive revenue exactions, low prices of grain and cotton crops and evictions and land mortgages to moneylenders drove the peasants to a three week insurrection. Tens of thousands met in public gatherings in market places and vowed to boycott the claims of moneylenders and to seize their documents. Some moneylenders fled the area. Those who resisted the armed bands who came for documents had their fodder stacks burned down, although the peasants carried on very little personal violence. After three weeks troops moved against the boycotters, hundreds were arrested in each centre, and the government levied collective fines throughout the area. The revolt produced some respite in the Deccan Agriculturalists' Relief Act of 1879.[78]

The famous Bengal indigo strike of 1860 was the first large strike in India and one of the most successful. It illustrates the initiative and discipline of which peasants are capable. It involved hundreds of thousands of tenants on British plantations. The tenants were forced to grow indigo at very low prices for the British textile industry, to the exclusion of most other crops. When they refused, slave drivers—some trained on United States southern plantations—kidnapped or flogged them, exposed them in stocks, or murdered them. Once decided upon, the strike spread rapidly. Tenants assembled with staffs, swords, bows and arrows and matchlocks to defend their settlements. In Pabna an army of 2,000 peasants appeared and wounded a magistrate's horse; otherwise, there was little violence. The strike stopped indigo planting in Bengal and forced the planters to move west to Bihar.

The Moplah rebellion of 1921 lasted longer than any other peasant insurrection I have examined. It bridged the period of 'pre-political-party, peasant uprisings and that of peasant actions sponsored by political parties. In its first large all-India struggle towards Independence, the Indian National Congress joined with Muslims of the Khilafat movement[79] to boycott British instituted councils, law courts, titles, educational institutions and the purchase of foreign goods. The boycott allied Hindu and Muslim middle class leaders, a few landlords, high ranking non-cultivating tenants and a large mass of poverty stricken cultivating tenants and landless labourers, especially Moplahs, who formed a majority of the population in the Earnad and Walluvanad taluks and who followed the Khilafat leaders. Both the Congress and the Khilafat parties had begun to organise a movement for tenancy reforms, which was strongly opposed by Malabar's big landlords with their memories of the nineteenth century Moplah revolts. The manager of a large Hindu princely estate persuaded the police to search the local Khilafat secretary's house for a gun that he alleged had been stolen from the palace. Thousands of armed Moplahs were summoned by drumbeats to prevent their leader's arrest. When police broke into a mosque in search of the fugitive, Moplahs throughout the two taluks rose in insurrection, sacking police stations, looting government treasuries and destroying records of debts and mortgages in courts and registries. For six months British rule became inoperative throughout the region. A leader emerged to govern it who was known as Raja by the Hindus, Amir by the Muslims, and Colonel of the Khilafat army. He administered the territory, supervised the execution of police, both Hindu and Muslim, who had committed atrocities, and of traitors who helped the British forces, put an end to the looting, and announced the suspension of land revenue and rents for one year. He commanded poor peasants to harvest their landlords' crops and used the surplus to feed his army. He issued passports to travellers entering and leaving his kingdom and edicts against the harming of Hindus by Muslims.

The Congress party under Gandhi withdrew its support from the movement as soon as it resorted to violence and tried ineffectively to mediate between the British and the revolutionaries. The resultant wavering among Hindu followers roused suspicion among the Moplahs and when British troops attacked and engaged in espionage among the Hindus the movement acquired a communal flavour. The rebels killed some 500 alleged traitors, chiefly Hindus, sacked about a hundred temples and forcibly converted 2,500 Hindus to Islam. A fierce struggle followed between British and Gurkha troops on one side and the rebel army on the other, in which according to A. Sreedhara Menon about 10,000 were estimated to have died. There was prolonged guerilla warfare and two large battles were fought. On reconquering the region the British took savage reprisals. The rebel leaders were shot, hundreds of their followers were hanged or deported to the Andamans and 61 prisoners suffocated as a result of being enclosed in a railway goods-wagon on their way from Tirur to Coimbatore jail. Considering the violent enmity of the Hindu landlords, the wavering of the (largely Hindu) Indian National Congress and the terror instituted by the British, the rebel leaders' conduct must be considered moderate and the rebels' communal reprisals a minor part of the revolt, which was essentially a peasants' insurrection. The Moplah rebellion illustrates the fact that in India as elsewhere, agrarian classes usually have a partial isomorphism with major ethnic categories, whether these are Hindu and Muslim or culturally distinct blocks of Hindu castes, or even, in some areas, co-resident linguistic groups.[80] What is labelled inter-religious or inter-communal strife is often, perhaps usually, initially a class struggle, but unity in the class struggle is all too often broken by the upper classes' appeal to and manipulation of cultural differences, and under duress those most oppressed may turn on all the co-religionists of their oppressors.

Modern Peasant Uprisings

Except for the early revolts to drive out the British and re-establish traditional principalities, the uprisings so far discussed were 'pre-political' or 'primitive' in the special sense that they were not addressed to the future of the nation state and thus were doomed to failure when they aimed at revolution. These revolts were, however, politically progressive in that they sought a new state of peasant society which would combine freedom from alien rule together with some traditional virtues and modern technology and popular government, rather than merely reverting to pre-British social structures. The revolts also amply illustrated the remarkable organising abilities of the peasantry, their potential discipline and solidarity, their determined militancy in opposing imperialism and exploitative class relations, their inventiveness and potential military prowess and their aspirations for a more democratic and egalitarian society. The more impressive uprisings also show that even in India, where inter-ethnic strife has produced some of the most tragic modern holocausts, peasants are capable of co-operating in class struggles across caste, religious and even linguistic lines to redress their common grievances.

Peasant revolts since the 1920s have been co-ordinated within the policies of oppositional political parties. They have formed two major types. On the one hand, there have been political movements for independence or for national or regional autonomy among blocks of tribal peoples. The most notable of these have been the struggle for an independent state in Kashmir, the nationalist war of the Naga and Mizo tribal peoples, and the Jarkhand movement for the political autonomy of the Santhals, Oraons and other tribes. On the other hand, there have been peasant uprisings which were primarily class struggles and were guided by one or another of India's communist parties.

Seven major peasant uprisings or episodes of revolutionary struggle in the Indian countryside have occurred to my knowledge under communist guidance. The first four were conducted by the Communist Party of India before it split into two wings in 1964. These were Tebhaga uprising in the north of Bengal in 1946, the Telengana peasant war in former Hyderabad state (now part of Andhra Pradesh) in 1946-8,[81] a strike of tenants and landless labourers in eastern Thanjavur for several weeks in 1948,[82] and a series of short strikes followed by attacks on granaries and grain trucks in Kerala in 1946-8.[83] The other three uprisings were led by Maoist groups which began to break away from the Communist Party of India (Marxist) in 1967. They included prolonged peasant struggles involving land claims and harvest shares in 1966-71 led by the Andhra Pradesh Revolutionary Communist Committee; the uprising in Naxalbari in West Bengal in 1967; and the 'annihilation campaign' of the Communist Party of India (Marxist-Leninist) against landlords, moneylenders, police and a variety of political enemies of the party, especially in Srikakulam, Mushahari and Debra-Gopivallabpur in 1969-70.[84]

Communist sponsored uprisings differ in many respects from those of earlier periods. First, of course, they are led at least ostensibly by a vanguard party which recruits members from urban petty bourgeois, urban working class, or even landlord origins as well as from the peasants and which draws on the theories of Marx and Lenin as well as, more recently, Mao Tse-tung. In each uprising the party involved has had as its ultimate goal the revolutionary attainment of a People's Democracy as a prelude to the transition to socialism throughout India.[85] Peasant revolts have been coordinated, and sometimes started, in accordance with current party policy, and have sometimes been stopped by the party because of national or even international changes of party line.[86]

Nevertheless, just as modern tribal nationalist movements, in their goal of ethnic liberation, share common features with and may even draw experience and organisational strength from earlier tribal religious movements,[87] so various communist struggles among the peasants have had features in common with early peasant movements involving social banditry, terrorist vengeance with ideas of popular justice, or mass insurrections for the redress of grievances.

The most successful communist led peasant actions were those of Tebhaga in 1946, Telengana in 1946-8, Naxalbari in 1967, and Andhra Pradesh in 1969-71. All of them involved a large component of tribal people. All of these revolts began as strikes or other forms of popular action initiated by the peasants or with their willing consent for the redress of specific grievances. The Tebhaga revolt began with a demand for reduction of the occupying tenants' (jotedars')[88] rights in the crop from half to one-third and a corresponding increase in the rights of poor peasant sharecroppers (adhiars or bargadars). It had been preceded in the late 1930s by a campaign on behalf of middle peasants (the better-off tenants) to abolish 'feudal' levies over and above the legal rents. In Telengana, too, the initial demands were for abolition of illegal exactions by the deshmukhs and nawabs—the feudal lords—and later on for cancellation of peasants' debts.[89] In Thanjavur the demands were for halving the rents paid by cultivating tenants and doubling the wages of landless labourers. In Naxalbari the peasant unions began by taking over land which the communist-led West Bengal government had already decreed should be removed from the jotedars, the former occupancy tenants who by this time had become outright owners of the land with the abolition of zamindari rights. The land act provided for this land to be distributed to the landless, but the proprietors refused to surrender it. Having driven out the landlords, the peasant unions then went on to distribute all the land among the peasants.[99] Similarly, in Warangal, Khammam and Karimnagar districts of Andhra Pradesh in 1969, the communist peasant unions began their armed struggle by occupying land which had been taken from them by neighbouring landlords and redistributing it among the tribal peasants.[91]

In all these struggles, much as in more successful of the traditional peasant insurrections referred to earlier, the peasant unions were able to secure temporary liberated zones which they governed for several weeks or months through peasant committees supervised by the Communist Party. In Thanjavur landlords, police and bureaucrats remained in the area but obeyed the village committees; in the other regions the peasants killed or drove out these figures during the period of revolutionary government. The largest and longest revolt was that of Telengana, which is reported to have engulfed 2,000 villages in an area of 15,000 square miles, with a population of four million and a peasant army of 5,000. In the more recent Andhra Pradesh uprising of the late 1960s under the Andhra Pradesh Revolutionary Communist Committee, which took place partly in the same area, the revolutionaries claimed in mid-1970 a liberated area of 7,000 to 8,000 square miles with a population of 500,000 to 600,000.[92] Repression has since greatly increased and the movement appears to be temporarily crushed.

In contrast with these efforts, communist armed action has been less successful when it employed tactics suggestive of banditry or of terrorist vengeance, unaccompanied by mass insurrection or by demands for redress of specific grievances and popular control by peasant committees. These tactics predominated in the party's struggles among the peasants in 1948-9 in Kerala and in those of the CPI(ML) in eastern India and elsewhere in 1969-72.[93] In the former instance the communists had earlier, in 1946, conducted successful mass strikes for higher wages among landless labourers and mass cultivation of the forest lands of big landlords. (As in Bengal, they had also successfully organised strikes of middle peasants against illegal levies during the late 1930s.) When, however, police reprisals became heavy and several communists and peasants were killed, the party went partly underground and squads of party members and peasant leaders began to rob grain trucks and ransack the granaries of landlords and distribute food to the people. Although poor peasants admired these exploits—much as they admire those of dacoits who pillage the rich and powerful—the peasants did not become organised through these actions and had no control over them. In the course of these actions the police and the armed goons of (Congress-supporting) landlords killed several leading peasants and party members and arrested most of the others, and the Communist Party became temporarily isolated from the villagers.

In the second instance, the CPI(ML) moving away from its earlier policy of mass struggles in Naxalbari and to some extent in Srikakulam, developed the policy of 'annihilation' of landlords, police, moneylenders, oppressive bureaucrats and enemies of other political parties by secret squads recruited from young party members and their associates in the cities, and, where possible, from the most oppressed groups of poor peasants and landless labourers in the countryside. Several dozens and probably hundreds of landlords in eastern India were assassinated in a three-year period. In their size, secrecy, primitive weaponry, utter devotion and in the fact that they tended to operate some distance from home, these revolutionary squads resembled those of the Moplah peasant insurgents who carried out acts of terrorist vengeance in Malabar in the nineteenth century—and no doubt also other Indian terrorist groups in urban uprisings of the early twentieth century. While commanding admiration in many villages, the squad tactic, unaccompanied by mass organisation around specific economic grievances, isolated the cadres and exposed a defenceless populace to police and later to military reprisals. The annihilation policy, along with other shortcomings, was criticised in a letter from the Chinese government in November 1970, and helped provoke a split in the party in 1971. Since the death of Charu Mazumdar, the party chairman and the main exponent of the annihilation tactic, in July 1972, it has been repudiated by most of the party's remaining leaders.[94] At present, most of the CPI(ML)'s cadres appear to have been arrested, or to have left the party, or to have been killed in action or in jails.[95]

Conclusions

Indian peasants have a long tradition of armed uprisings, reaching back at least to the initial British conquest and the last decades of Moghul government. For more than 200 years peasants in all the major regions have repeatedly risen against landlords, revenue agents and other bureaucrats, moneylenders, police and military forces. The uprisings were responses to relative deprivation of unusually severe character, always economic, and often also involving physical brutality or ethnic persecution. The political Independence of India has not brought surcease from these distresses, for imperial extraction of wealth from India and oppression by local property owners continue to produce poverty, famine, agricultural sluggishness and agrarian unrest. Major uprisings under communist leadership since British rule not unnaturally show a continuity of tactics with earlier peasant revolts. Of these, the more successful have involved mass insurrections, initially against specific grievances, and the less successful, social banditry and terrorist vengeance. Both in the case of communist revolts and in that of earlier peasant uprisings, social banditry and terrorist vengeance, when they occurred, appear to have happened in the wake of repression of other forms of revolt.

Although revolts have been widespread, certain areas have an especially strong tradition of rebellion. Bengal has been a hotbed of revolt, both rural and urban, from the earliest days of British rule. Some districts in particular such as Mymensingh, Dinajpur, Rangpur and Pabna in Bangladesh, and the Santhal regions of Bihar and West Bengal, figured repeatedly in peasant struggles and continue to do so. The tribal areas of Andhra Pradesh, and the state of Kerala, also have long traditions of revolt. Hill regions where tribal or other minorities retain a certain independence, ethnic unity, and tactical manoeuverability, and where the terrain is suited to guerilla warfare, are of course especially favourable for peasant struggles, but these have also occurred in densely populated plains regions such as Thanjavur, where rack-renting, land hunger, landless labour and unemployment cause great suffering.

The more successful revolts of the recent period occurred under irregular conditions which are unlikely to be repeated. The Tebhaga revolt took place three years after a famine had killed three and a half million Bengalis, leaving a labour shortage. The British government was nervous of offending the peasantry because of the Japanese invasion; it failed to move against the rebels until the Japanese had been defeated and the proportions of the rebellion had become alarming.[96] In Telengana in 1946-7 the change of government created an emergency, as the Nizam of Hyderabad refused to accede to the Indian Union, and it was some time before the Indian government decided to invade the state and mop up both the Nizam's forces and the communists. In Thanjavur in 1948 the government was occupied in invading Hyderabad and did not immediately institute repression.

Today the Indian government is more heavily militarised than it has ever been. It has the experience of crushing recent peasant struggles, of years of police repression in West Bengal and of the invasion of Bangladesh. It also has the example of US methods of repression in Indochina.[97] The increasing poverty, famine and unemployment make it seem certain that India's agrarian ills can be solved only by a **peasant-backed revolution leading to socialism**, but the struggle will be very long and hard.

References

1 An earlier version of this paper was presented at a Conference on Peasants of Asia and Latin America at the University of British Columbia in February, 1973.
2 The hut and charred bodies were photographed and are reproduced in Lasse and Lisa Berg, 'Face to Face: Fascism and Revolution in India', **Ramparts Press**, California, 1971, p. 55. For more details and an account of recent class struggles in Thanjavur, see Mythily Shivaraman, 'Rumblings of Class Struggle in Thanjavur', in Kathleen Gough and Hari P Sharma, eds, 'Imperialism and Revolution in South Asia', Monthly Review Press, New York, 1973.
3 Rupert M Moser, 'The Situation of the Adivasis of Chota Nagpur and Santal Parganas, Bihar, India', International Work Group for Indigenous Affairs Document No 4, Frekderiksholms Kanal 4 A, DK 1220 Copenhagen K, Denmark, 1972.
4 A supporter of the Communist Party of India (Marxist-Leninist), one of the main Maoist groups, reported that an estimated 10,000 peasants and others had been killed on the communist side in the three years from 1967 to 1970 (personal communication).
5 David F Aberle, 'The Peyote Religion Among the Navaho', Wenner-Gren Foundation for Anthropological Research, 1966, p. 315.
6 Barrington Moore, Jr, 'The Social Origins of Dictatorship and Democracy', Beacon Press, 1966, p. 202.
7 *Op cit*, p. 383. Moore is actually equivocal about the effects of caste on peasant unrest, for on page 382 he writes, 'Any notion to the effect that caste or other distinctive traits of Indian peasant society constitutes an effective barrier to insurrection is obviously false', but on page 383, 'Caste was also a way of organising a highly fragmented society... Though this fragmentation could at times be overcome in small ways and in specific localities, it must have been a barrier to widespread rebellion. Furthermore, the system of caste did enforce hierarchical submission. Make a man feel humble by a thousand daily acts and he will behave in a humble way. The traditional etiquette of caste was no mere excrescence; it had definite political consequences. Finally, as a safety valve, caste does provide a form of collective upward mobility through Sanskritization'. My view is that an enforced etiquette of submission does not necessarily engender submissive feelings; if the subordinate comes to feel unjustly deprived, having to observe the etiquette may engender rebellious feelings which

sometimes burst forth. In Thanjavur in 1952 I lived on a street of low ranking and poverty stricken cowherds and sharecroppers, servants of Brahman landlords. The caste etiquette was the most subservient I have seen outside of Kerala. In private the sharecroppers often raged against their landlords as 'evil'. In spite of severe reprisals involving flogging and being forced to drink pints of cowdung and water, lower caste men in this village had frequently resorted to violence. One once smote his landlord across the face; another cut off his landlord's leg; two more bound their landlord to a cart-wheel, thrashed him and drove him out of the village for seducing a kinswoman. Sanskritisation permits upward mobility but only for a small minority. The conflicts of interest among castes which are respectively composed predominantly of smallholders, sharecroppers, and landless labourers, are a serious matter for revolutionary organisers, but such class conflicts among peasants are worldwide.

8 S.B. Chaudhuri, 'Civil Rebellion in the Indian Mutinies, 1857-9', World Press, Calcutta, 1957, p. 32.
9 See S.B. Chaudhuri, 'Civil Disturbances During the British Rule in India (1765-1857)', World Press, Calcutta, 1955, pp. 56-8, 74-6 and 125-32 for accounts of these revolts.
10 The Punjab appears to have been an exception. Although recently conquered, the Sikhs in particular provided soldiers loyal to the British.
11 See E.M.S. Namboodiripad, 'The National Question in Kerala', Bombay, 1952, pp. 102-3; Irfan Habib, 'The Agrarian System of Moghul India', Asia Publishing House, London, 1963, p. 332.
12 The formerly primitive tribes of India number about 45 million and form about one-twelfth of the population.
13 For peasant revolts in the Moghul period see Irfan Habib, *op cit*, pp. 330-3, 337-51. See also Ramkrishna Mukherjee, 'The Rise and Fall of the East India Company', Veb Deutscher Verlag der Wissenschaften, Berlin, 1957, p. 217. Information on the Thuggee is taken mainly from an unpublished paper by the late Saghir Ahmad, 'Thuggees: Rebels or Criminals?', which is being edited for publication. Major sources include W.H. Sleeman, 'History and Practices of the Thug', Philadelphia, 1839; W.H. Sleeman, 'Reports on the Depredation Committed by the Thug Gangs of Upper and Central India', Calcutta, 1840, Francis Tuker 'The Yellow Scarf', London, 1961; and John Masters, 'The Deceivers', London, 1960.
14 Stephen Fuchs, 'Rebellious Prophets: A Study of Messianic Movements in Indian Religions', Asia Publishing House, 1965, pp. 143-4.
15 W. Francis, *Madras District Gazetteers*, Madura, Madras Government Press, 1906, pp. 88-91.
16 See, eg, Michael Barratt Brown, 'After Imperialism', Heinemann, 1963, pp. 58-60; Amiya Kumar Bagchi, 'Foreign Capital and Economic Development in India: A Schematic View', in Kathleen Gough and Hari P. Sharma, eds, *op cit*, for analysis.
17 S.B. Chaudhuri, *op cit*, 1955, p. 15.
18 See, eg, Barratt Brown, *op cit*, pp. 174-7; and A.K. Bagchi, *loc cit*.
19 See, for example, Martin Orans, 'The Santal', Wayne State University Press, 1965, pp. 30-6; Rupert M. Moser, *loc cit*; S.B. Chaudhuri, *op cit*, 1955, pp. 51-3.
20 The century old dispute regarding the extent, or even the occurrence, of 'deindustrialisation' in nineteenth century India has not abated. Most writers acknowledge that there was certainly a decline in the proportion of Indian craftsmen relative to the total population in the first half of the nineteenth

century, and some, that the decline continued throughout the century. The agrument regarding the earlier period, in particular, seems unquestionable in view of the staggering decline in exports of Indian craft goods and the staggering increases in Indian exports of raw materials and in British imports to India of manufactured goods. For evidence and figures see Barratt Brown, *op cit*; A.K. Bagchi, *loc cit;* B.B. Misra, 'The Indian Middle Classes', Oxford University Press, 1961; and Daniel Thorner, 'Deindustrialisation in India,' in 'Land and Labour in India', Asia Publishing House, 1962, chapter VI. Romesh Chandra Dutt's classic study, 'The Economic History of India under Early British Rule, 1757-1837', Routledge and Kegan Paul, 1963, first published in 1901, is still of great value, especially pp. 176-200. Dharma Kumar, who is mainly concerned about stressing the existence of landless labour in India from pre-British times, nevertheless points out that the agriculturally dependent population increased from about 60 per cent to 69 per cent between 1800 and 1901. It had reached about 75 per cent by 1951 ('Land and Labour in South India', Cambridge University Press, 1965, p. 181). In Kerala and Thanjavur in the 1950s I found many families in castes traditionally designated as Weavers, Goldsmiths, Traders, Tile-Makers, high class Potters, Oil-mongers, Basket and Mat-Makers, or other craftsmen, who became unable to ply their crafts at some time during British rule and who became tenant farmers, landless labourers, or casual workers in towns. Saghir Ahmad found the same in West Punjab (see 'Peasant Classes in Pakistan', in Gough and Sharma, eds, *op cit.* 1973, pp. 203-21). Morris D. Morris has argued more strongly than other recent writers against 'deindustrialisation', but I believe his arguments to have been ably answered by several Indian authors. See Morris D. Morris, ed, 'The Indian Economy in the Nineteenth Century: A Symposium', Indian Economic and Social History Association, Delhi School of Economics, Delhi 7, 1969.)

21 The population of Dacca is reported to have fallen from 150,000 in 1757 to between 30,000 and 40,000 in 1840. In 1787 the exports of Dacca muslins to England amounted to three million rupees, but in 1817 they had ceased altogether. Murshidabad, Surat, Agra and also southern cities such as Thanjavur suffered correspondingly (R. Mukherjee, *op cit*, pp. 337-9).

22 Opium, for example, was the chief agricultural crop in Malwa and lower Rajputana in 1817-8 (S.B. Chaudhuri, *op cit*, 1955, p. 217), and this was still true in 1860-80. Indigo in Bengal and Bihar, cotton in the north-west provinces, central India and the Karnatak, jute and sugarcane in Bengal, and tea, tobacco and coffee in north-east and south-east India, were among the export crops that were greatly expanded in the first half of the nineteenth century. In Bombay province in 1834-45 cotton occupied 43 per cent of cultivated land in Broach and 22 per cent in Surat but the cultivators were reported to receive little or no profit (R.C. Dutt, 'The Economic History of India in the Victorian Age, 1837-1900', Routledge and Kegan Paul, 1960, p. 98). Today about 40 per cent of the land in Kerala state is devoted to export crops and Assam is similarly dominated by a plantation economy; export crops occupy at least one-fifth of the cultivable land of India as a whole (A.K. Gopalan, 'Kerala Past and Present', Lawrence and Wishart, 1959, pp. 79-96). In addition to the expansion of industrial crops for export, India also exported increasing amounts of foodgrains during the nineteenth century, in spite of the growing population and the virtual stagnation of subsistence agriculture. Thus, India exported 1.25 million tons of foodgrains in 1879-80, whereas it had exported only 0.65 million pounds sterling worth in 1842, 3.58 million in 1860 and 27.26 million in 1880 (B.M. Bhatia, 'Famines in India, 1860-1965', Asia Publishing House, 1967, p. 38).

23 For a detailed treatment of trends in both commercial and subsistence agriculture during British rule, see George Blyn, 'Agricultural Trends in India, 1891-1947', Philadelphia, 1966.
24 There is uncertainty about the exact proportions of the different classes of peasants and agricultural workers in various decades because of imperfect records and differences in modes of classification. Dharma Kumar rightly points out that there was a substantial class of agricultural labourers at the beginning of British rule, usually enslaved and mainly untouchable. She estimates its size at about 10 to 15 per cent of the total population. Although she emphasises continuities in the agrarian structure of India in the nineteenth century, Kumar notes that, agricultural labourers had increased to an estimated 15 to 20 per cent of the total population in the period between 1871 and 1901. Landless labourers were estimated at 28 per cent of the total workforce in 1951 and 26 per cent in 1971. It is also relevant to estimate the proportions of agricultural labourers in relation to the total population *dependent on agriculture* in the various periods, and the latter in relation to the total population of India. Rough estimates are as follows. Dharma Kumar estimates the agriculturally dependent population at 60 per cent of the total population in 1800 or even less. Agricultural labourers were probably about 17 to 25 per cent of the agricultural population. In 1901 the agricultural population was about 69 per cent of the total with agricultural labourers about 27 to 29 per cent of the agricultural population. In 1951 the agricultural population was about 75 per cent of the total population and agricultural labourers about 38 per cent of the agricultural population. In 1971 the agricultural population had declined again to 69 per cent of the total; agricultural labourers still formed about 38 per cent of the agriculturally dependent population, but a larger proportion of them were probably totally landless than were in 1951. (See Dharma Kumar, 'Land and Caste in South India', Cambridge University Press, 1965, especially pp. 168-93; Charles Bettelheim, 'India Independent', Monthly Review Press, 1969, p. 25; and Government of India *Censuses* for the various decades.) In some states where the agricultural population's density is very high, the numbers of agricultural labourers have risen quite rapidly in recent decades. In Thanjavur district, for example, they increased by 60 per cent between 1951 and 1961. (See, eg, Mythily Shivaraman, 'Rumblings of Class Struggle in Thanjavur', in Gough and Sharma, eds, *op cit*, p. 252.) When middle and poor peasants lose their lands, moreover, not all of them show up in the category of landless labourers. Some, like some former landless labourers, are forced to migrate to cities, where they often join the lumpen proletariat of beggars, casual labourers and underemployed craftsmen or service workers. The urban population increased from about 25 per cent to 31 per cent of the total between 1951 and 1971.
25 See, eg, V.M. Dandekar and Nilakantha Rath, 'Poverty in India: Dimensions and Trends', *Economic and Political Weekly*, Bombay January 2, 1971, pp. 106-46. (P. Bardhan, 'Green Revolution and Agricultural Labourers: A Correction', *Economic and Political Weekly*, January 2, 1971, pp. 25-48).
26 See B.M. Bhatia, *op cit*, for the following information, especially pp. 10-13, 239-42 and 308-39.
27 *Newsweek*, June 17, 1963, reporting on the World Food Congress held in Washington, DC, under the auspices of the United Nations.
28 P.L. Eldridge, 'The Politics of Foreign Aid in India,' Vikas Publications, Delhi, 1969, especially pp. 112-16. India imported only 2.6 per cent of its foodgrains in the First Five Year Plan (1951-5), but this was increased, chiefly under US

Public Law 480 loans, to 4.9 per cent in the Second Plan and 7.5 per cent in the Third.

29 For the impact of land reforms, see, eg, Bhowani Sen, 'Evolution of Agrarian Relations in India', People's Publishing House, Delhi, 1962; Grigory Kotovsky, 'Agrarian Reforms in India', People's Publishing House, 1964; and Charles Bettelheim, *op cit*, pp. 146-233.

30 See Hari P. Sharma, 'Green Revolution in India: Prelude to a Red One?' in Gough and Sharma, eds, *op cit*, pp. 88 and 94. Observations in Kerala in 1964 convinced me that these processes were widely at work there, partly as a result of landlords' reactions to successive land reform acts. In one north Kerala village, for example, I found that whereas in 1948 poor peasants, landless labourers and casually employed non-agricultural day labourers, having no land or only one small garden, were 72.1 per cent of the population, by 1964 they were 88.2 per cent.

31 See, eg, Francine Frankel, 'India's Green Revolution: Economic Gains and Political Costs', Princeton University Press, 1971, for the increasing gap in incomes brought about by the green revolution and the fact that it chiefly benefits the larger farmers. Mohan Ram, ('Maoism in India', Vikas, Delhi, 1971, pp. 185-6) and Mythily Shivaraman, (*loc cit*) cite increases in landless labourers and unemployed.

32 See Hamza Alavi, 'Imperialism, Old and New', *The Socialist Register*, 1964, Monthly Review Press, 1964, pp. 104-26; and A.K. Bagchi, *loc cit*, for characteristics of neo-imperialism in India since Independence and for comparisons and contrasts with the period of British rule. Alavi's later essay, 'The State in Postcolonial Societies: Pakistan and Bangladesh', in Gough and Sharma, eds, *op cit*, pp. 145-73, is also in many respects highly relevant to India.

33 See, eg, 'Bangladesh Maoists', *Frontier*, Calcutta, January 16, 1973, pp. 16-17.

34 E.J. Hobsbawm, 'Primitive Rebels', Manchester University Press, 1959, pp. 13-29; 'Bandits', The Trinity Press, London, 1969, pp. 13-23; and 'Social Bandits: Reply (to Blok)' in *Comparative Studies in Society and History*, Vol. 14, No. 4, September 1972, pp. 503-5.

35 Aberle, *op cit*, pp. 316, 318 and 322-3, for discussion of transformative movements.

36 For discussions of relative deprivation, see Aberle, *op cit*, pp. 326-9; and Aberle, 'A Note on Relative Deprivation Theory as Applied to Millenarian and other Cult Movements', in Sylvia L. Thrupp, ed, 'Millennial Dreams in Action', Mouton, The Hague, 1962, pp. 209-14.

37 Norman Cohn 'The Pursuit of the Millennium', Secker and Warburg, London, 1957, pp. 307-14.

38 S.B. Chaudhuri, *op cit*, 1955, pp. 16, 60, 61, *et passim*.

39 These revolts were those of (1) the Kallar of Madura 1710-84; (2) the Rajas of Dhalbhum, 1769-74; (3) the Chuar tribe of Midnapore, 1799; (4) a chief in Sylhet, 1787; (5) a dispossessed zamindar in Sylhet 1799; (6) Vizier Ali in Banaras and Gorakhpur 1799; (7) the Raja Vizieram Rauze in Vizagapatam, 1794; (8) the Maratha Dhundia Wagh in Mysore, 1799-1800; (9) the Pazhassi or 'Pyche' Raja in North Malabar, 1796-1805; (10) the *poligars* of Bellary, Anantapur, Cuddapah and Kurnool, 1803-5; (11) the *poligars* of Tinnevelly, 1901; (12) the *poligars* of North Arcot, 1803-5; (13) Velu Thampi, the Prime Minister of Travancore, 1808-9; (14) the heirs of the Desai of Kittur, 1824; (15) the Bhils of Khandesh, 1818-31; the Bhils of Malwa, 1846; (17) the Khonds of Orissa, 1846; (18) the Santhals of Bihar, 1855-6; (19) an ex-chief, Gopal Singh of Bundelkhand, 1802-12; (20) the chiefs of forts in Aligarh, 1817; (21)

the Paiks and Khonds of Cuttack, 1817-8; (22) the Gujars of Sindhia, 1824; (23) the Kols, Hos, and Mundas of Chota Nagpur, 1831-2; (24) the Bhumij and Chuar of Manbhum, 1832; (25) the Khasis of Assam, 1829-58; (26) the Garos of Assam, 1852, 1857, and 1872; (27) the Syntengs of Assam, 1860 and 1862; (28) the Mers of Merwara, 1820; and (29) the 'Sepoy Mutiny' in north and central India, 1857-8. For the Kallar, see W. Francis, *op cit*, pp. 66, 88-91; for the Garos and Syntengs, Stephen Fuchs, *op cit*, pp. 111, 115, 126; and for the Mutiny, Chaudhuri, *op cit*, 1957. The other rebellions are reported in Chaudhuri, *op cit*, 1955. L. Natarajan includes further information on the Santal revolt of 1855-6 in 'Peasant Uprisings in India,' 1850-1900, People's Publishing House, Bombay, 1953.

40 See Benoy Ghosh, 'Prepolitical Rebellions in Bengal', *Frontier* Calcutta, Vol. 5, Nos. 27-9, October 14, 1972, pp. 9-14, for a recent account of the Chuar and Santhal rebellions.

41 The Moplah revolt of 1857, for example, was influenced by the belief that the British would soon be driven out of India by the northern rebels (W. Logan, 'Malabar'. Vol. 1. Government Press, Madras, 1951, p. 576).

42 Chaudhuri *op cit*, 1957, p. 269.

43 Hobsbawm, *op cit*, 1959, p. 58.

44 Norman Cohn, 'Medieval Millenarism: Its Bearing on the Comparative Study of Millenarian Movements', in Sylvia L. Thrupp, ed, *op cit*, 1962, p. 43.

45 Peter Worsley, 'The Trumpet Shall Sound', Schocken Books, New York 1968, p. 224.

46 Cohn, *loc cit*, p. 32.

47 Fuchs notes 14 characteristics of the movements he calls messianic. They are: intense dissatisfaction with socio-economic conditions, emotional unrest with hysterical symptoms, a charismatic leader, the leader's demand for implicit faith and obedience, his demand for a radical change of life or for destruction of property, rejection of established authority and a call for rebellion, threat of severe punishment of traitors and opponents, the remembrance of a 'Golden Age' at the beginning of mankind's career, revivalism or renewed interest in traditional religion, nativism or the conscious attempt to restore selected aspects of traditional culture and to reject alien elements, vitalism or the desire for alien gifts from heaven, syncretism or indiscriminate adoption of various traits in the oppressors' culture, eschatologism or the expectation of world renewal after a worldwide catastrophe, and millenarianism or chiliasm, the hope or expectation of a paradise on earth. (See Fuchs, *op cit*, pp. 1-15.).

48 The fullest account of the Moplah revolts up to the mid-1880s is contained in Logan, *op cit*, pp. 554-94. See also C.A. Innes, *Gazetteer of the Malabar District*, Madras Government Press. 1908, pp. 82-9.

49 Fuchs records a movement among the Pankas of Raipur an untouchable caste of weavers and village artisans; the messiah thought that a deity had entered him and preached that good men's crops would grow without sowing; when his following grew large and the revenue fell off he was arrested in 1860 (Fuchs, *op cit*, p. 106.).

50 Cf Aberle, *op cit*, 1962, pp. 209-10.

51 Fuchs, *op cit*, pp. 134 *et seq*.

52 Logan, *op cit*, p. 567.

53 Fuchs, *op cit*, pp. 218-21.

54 Fuchs, *op cit*, pp. 28-34.

55 Fuchs, *op cit*, pp. 240-3. The fifth classically millenarian movement was that of a Hindu messiah in Badawar, Patiala state, in the early nineteenth century who

believed that he was Kalki, the last of the incarnations of Vishnu, the inaugurator of a happy and virtuous Hindu millennium. He announced that on an appointed day he would overturn the foreign government and set up his kingdom. He was arrested and his followers disappeared. Fuchs points out that Vaishnavism, Shaivism, Jainism and Buddhism, all contain millenarian mythologies—Vaishnavism that of Kalki, Shaivism of the 26 or 28 incarnations of Shiva each ushering in an age of liberation from evil, Jainism in the coming period of 63 saints whose saving qualities are similar to those to the Vishnu *avatars*, and Buddhism with its belief in the Buddha Maitreya, a future saviour of the world (Fuchs, *op cit*, pp. x-xi, and for the Patiala movement, p. 178).

56 Logan *op cit*, pp. 558-9.
57 There have been at least three massacres of political prisoners, chiefly members of the Communist Party of India (Marxist-Leninist) since mid-1970. In particular on November 26, 1971, police admitted that six 'Naxalites' had been beaten to death with clubs and 237 wounded; according to some reports, however, up to 50 were murdered and many of the injured, at the time of reporting, hovered between life and death (*Frontier*, Calcutta, December 4, 1971; and *Le Monde*, Paris, November 30, 1971).
58 For a brief account and bibliography see 'Thug', *Encyclopaedia Britannica*, 1958, Volume 21, p. 1095.
59 Fuchs, *op cit*, pp. 109-11.
60 Chaudhuri, 1955, *op cit*, p. 152.
61 Fuchs, *op cit*, pp. 71-72.
62 Francis, *op cit*, pp. 88-93.
63 Fuchs, *op cit*, p. 71.
64 E.J. Hobsbawm. 'Social Bandits: Reply (to Blok)', *Comparative Studies in Society and History*. Volume 14, Number 4, September 1972, p. 504.
65 Stewart N. Gordon argues that Thuggee bands were employed by Maratha chiefs in the late eighteenth century in Malwa in order to provide them with a non-local source of revenue from plundering far afield during a period of competition in small state formation and to pay for European-style artillery and infantry (Gordon, 'Scarf and Sword: Thugs, Marauders and State-formation in 18th Century Malwa', *The Indian Economic and Social History Review*, Volume 6, Number 4, December 1969, pp. 403-29).
66 Vasudeo Balvant Phadke, the Maratha Brahman religious leader who believed himself an incarnation of Shivaji Maharaj, recruited Ramoshi bandits in 1879 and with them carried out robberies and attacks on police stations to obtain supplies with which he hoped to build an army and drive out the British. He was disillusioned, however, by the fact that the Ramoshis looted for their own benefit, and so he turned instead to the Dhangar shepherd caste and to the Kolis, who joined him because they believed they had been unjustly deprived of a large part of their cultivated land (Fuchs, *op cit*, pp. 228-33).
67 Francis, *op cit*, pp. 91-2.
68 Chaudhuri, *op cit*, 1955, pp. 66-7.
69 Chaudhuri, *op cit*, 1955, p. 109.
70 Logan, *op cit*, p. 584.
71 Six of the revolts took place before the Mutiny, and are described by Chaudhuri, *op cit*, 1955, sections 3, 4, 31, 43 and 45.
72 Chaudhuri *op cit*, 1955, pp. 65-7.
73 Chaudhuri, *op cit*, 1955, pp. 175-6.
74 Chaudhuri, *op cit*, 1955, pp. 171-2.
75 Menon, *op cit*, p. 179.

76 Chaudhuri, *op cit*, 1955, p. 61.
77 The leader, Dirjinarain pleaded for the life of Gaurmohan the first agent, at some risk to his own, because Gaurmohan was a Brahman and Brahmans were exempt from execution by traditional law. The peasants, however, insisted on killing him.
78 In 'The Myth of the Deccan Riots', *Modern Asian Studies*, November 1972, Neil Charlesworth has argued that the extent of the uprising was much overestimated in current and subsequent reports. His argument does not seem convincing in the light of data cited by Natarajan and other writers.
79 The Khilafat movement was begun to protest against Britain's removing various Middle Eastern territories from the control of Turkey in violation of promises made by Lloyd George during the First World War.
80 See Kathleen Gough, 'Indian Nationalism and Ethnic Freedom', in David Bidney, ed, 'The Concept of Freedom in Anthropology', Mouton, 1963, pp. 170-207, for further discussion.
81 See Hamza Alavi, 'Peasants and Revolution', *Socialist Register*, 1965 edited by Ralph Miliband, Monthly Review Press, 1965, for accounts of the Tebhaga and Telengana revolts. See also Mohan Ram, 'The Telengana Peasant Armed Struggle, 1946-51', *Economic and Political Weekly*, Volume Number 23, June 9, 1973, pp. 1025-32.
82 See John F. Muehl, 'Interview with India', John Day, New York, 1950, pp. 249-92.
83 See E.M.S. Namboodiripad, 'Kerala Yesterday, Today and Tomorrow', pp. 193, 196.
84 For all of these actions see Mohan Ram, 'Maoism in India', Delhi, Vikas, 1971, pp. 38-163. See also Mohan Ram, 'Five Years After Naxalbari', *Economic and Political Weekly* Volume 7, Numbers 31-3, Special Number, August 1972, pp. 1471-6.
85 For differences in ideology and strategy among the Communist Party of India, the Communist Party of India (Marxist), the Communist Party of India (Marxist-Leninist) and the Andhra Pradesh Revolutionary Communist Committee, see Mohan Ram, 'The Communist Movement in India', *Bulletin of Concerned Asian Scholars*, Volume 4, Number 1, Winter 1972, pp. 32-42.
86 The Cominform intervened in 1951 to induce the Communist Party of India to abandon armed struggle (Ram, *loc cit*, 1972, p. 34).
87 The movement originally started by the Kacha Naga religious leader Jadonang in 1929 and carried on intermittently by his woman disciple Gaidillu into the 1960s seems in particular to have been a forerunner of the Naga nationalist movement, although confined to one tribe, and much smaller in scale (see Fuchs, *op cit*, pp. 147-56).
88 By the time of the Tebhaga rebellion the zamindar or landlord retained rights to only a small proportion of the produce and the jotedar or occupying tenant received most of the surplus. By the time of the Naxalbari revolt the zamindars had been removed and the jotedars were the landlords.
89 Hamza Alavi, *loc cit*.
90 Kanu Sanyal, 'Report on the Peasant Movement in the Terai Region', *Liberation*, Volume 2, Number 1, November 1968. For the circumstances surrounding the Naxalbari rebellion and for the attitude taken towards it of the Communist Party of India (Marxist) which was then in power in a coalition government in West Bengal, see *People's Democracy*, weekly organ of the CPI (M), Volume 3, Numbers 23-30, 1967. See also Mohan Ram, *op cit*, 1971, pp. 38-71.
91 Mohan Ram, *op cit*, 1971, pp. 165-9.

92 Mohan Ram, *loc cit*, 1972, p. 42.
93 Mohan Ram, *op cit*, 1971, pp. 136-63; *loc cit*, 1972, p. 41.
94 *Frontier*, Volume 5, Number 30, November 4, 1973, pp. 15-6.
95 Several massacres of Naxalites and supposed Naxalite supporters have been conducted in the streets by police or gangs of hired hoodlums, notably one in Baranagar on August 12, 1971, when about 1,000 goons, under police protection, rampaged over an area of two square miles and killed 150 Naxalites and their sympathisers *(Frontier*, August 21, 1971, p. 1, and September 18, 1971, p. 10). Using police figures, which in some cases are known to be much too low, it has been estimated that 1,788 members of the CPI (ML) were killed outside the jails in West Bengal between March 1970 and August 1971, and 42 (unofficially, 172) inside the jails in Midnapore, Berhampore, Alipore, Dum Dum and Howrah (*Frontier*, Volume 5, Number 40, January 13, 1973, pp. 3-4.) In the same period, 368 members of the Communist Party of India (Marxist) were reported to have been killed outside the jails, but some of these are alleged to have been people who had recently left the CPI (M) for the CPI (ML). Nine members of other political parties, including the ruling Congress party, were killed in this period and 66 police, businessmen, moneylenders, landlords and others. In November, 1973, a trial began at Parvathipuram in Andhra Pradesh involving 68 leaders of the Communist Party of India (Marxist-Leninist) and 38 of the Andhra Pradesh Revolutionary Communist Committee, perhaps the largest trial of Communist revolutionaries in history. The trial continues at the time of writing (May 1974). About 45,000 other revolutionaries or alleged revolutionaries are still in jails in India, many of them under the legal classification of criminals rather than of political prisoners. Many have been held for four or more years without being brought to trial.
96 See Hamza Alavi, *loc cit*, 1965.
97 On March 1, 1971, the Government of India sent about 10,000 paramilitary personnel into the districts of Warangal, Khammam and Karimnagar in Andhra Pradesh and subdued the revolutionary struggle there. Something similar to the Vietnamese strategic hamlet plan has been attempted in Srikakulam district, people of scattered villages being herded together in camps at three mile intervals so that food supplies to the guerillas are cut off. No civilians are allowed out after dusk. Some 50,000 tribes people were still confined in these hamlets in April 1974. (See Mohan Ram, *loc cit*, 1972, p. 42, *Frontier*, Volume 5, January 27, 1973, p. 8; and *Economic and Political Weekly*, Volume 9, Number 17, April 27, 1974, p. 666.).

PART II
Agrarian Struggles In The 19th Century

Introduction

(1)

THE SEVEN ARTICLES in this section provide detailed descriptions of some of the powerful tribal, tenant and peasant uprisings which took place in various parts of India in the second half of the nineteenth century. Further, they provide an idea as to how rural India was being qualitatively transformed under the impact of the economic, political, juridical and administrative measures adopted by the British rulers.

The British ushered in a qualitatively new set of property relations by making land a *commodity*, thereby giving a mortal blow to the peculiar feudal relations prevailing in the countryside. This new type of proprietory relations were called the *zamindari* and *ryotwari* systems. Under the former, vast tracts of land comprising of districts, talukas, villages and even large tribal areas were made over to zamindars by the British as private property. In ryotwari areas, every peasant within the village was transformed into a proprietor of a specific piece of land, thereby freeing him from all customary and earlier legal obligations which prevented him from transfering his proprietory or possession rights in the market to any bidder.

The British introduced a new policy of revenue assessment, revenue payment and revenue collection—the prime source of income for the new rulers. The assessment was based on the potential productivity of land. Payment was to be made by the individual assessee, the new zamindar or ryot (proprietors) and not by the village community as a whole, on the basis of a proportion of share of the total produce. Further, it had to be paid in cash and not in kind as in the pre-British period. The necessity for cash ushered in a process of sale, mortgage, transfer of proprietory rights, assets and crops all of which made the alienation of land a powerful feature in the peasant's life. This led to a dependence on the moneylender and trader who could give money in advance to pay the revenue in cash. The transformation of land, assets and crops into commodities involved a legal system and an administrative machinery and induced the moneylenders, traders, richer landlords and men of means to advance money in lieu of various types of hypothecation. These developments created in the zamindari areas a chain of sometimes fifty to hundred intermediaries between the chief zamindar, owning villages and estates comprising thousands of acres of land, and the actual cultivators, who were reduced to the status of share croppers, tenants and even landless labours bound to the land with the status of almost semi-slaves. It also generated a fierce competition for security of tenure and of occupancy rights between various categories of tenants like, *jotedars*, *bargdars* and a host of others. It also created a chain of contractors, farmers (including even Europeans), moneylenders, traders and others who leased the land from the zamindars to grow particular types of crops like, jute, indigo, tea, etc.

In ryotwari area, a process of pauperization, proletarianization and fragmentation of land set in with assets and crops passing into the hands of usurers, traders and richer farmers creating a peculiar type of stratification involving various categories of groups related to the land in different ways.

The new tenure system deprived the tribal population of their communal rights over forests and lands, forcing them to give up many vital activities which were customary rights and essential for day-to-day living. They were brought under a new bourgeois legal, property and administrative set-up which uprooted them from their own patterns of justice based on a different set of norms and values. British policies encouraged an influx of zamindars, their representatives, forest contractors, traders, moneylenders, administrators, and educationists (predominantly missionaries) into the tribal areas. These sections of people exploited the tribals with the political and juridical backing of alien Government. Vast sections of tribal people were transformed into landless labourers, and bonded serfs, who were economically and socially dependent on the various categories of people described above. This had a devastating effect on every aspect of tribal life; there was no functional alternative to compensate for the loss of security and institutional safeguards in the economic, social and cultural matrix. This was an all-India process, operating unevenly.

In course of time the tribals were reduced to such a state that they had no other way of existence, but to resort to activities which the Government labelled 'criminal'. The British Government branded entire tribes as criminal tribes and isolated them in certain areas, almost similar to vast concentration camps, where they were kept like beasts in reserved forests or sanctuaries under the terror of the British administration and the social and moral supervision of the missionaries.

(2)

We have represented this background in brief for a number of reasons: (1) to make intelligible the framework within which the struggles described in the following pages were fought. It may be added that the participants in the struggles were not conscious of this framework. (2) To point out how the major historians, both representing British apologists and the nationalist bourgeois and petty bourgeois interests, either view these struggles as unhealthy reactions causing law and order problems, or as misguided reactions causing splits and diversions within the nationalist movement. (3) To clear the confusion created after Independence by a dominant group of marxists that in the rural areas feudalism is the prevailing mode of production. (4) To highlight the fact that a proper understanding of the agrarian problem in the post 1947 period can be possible only if it is grasped that the British introduced a bourgeois judicio-administrative and economic framework by transforming land into a commodity and demanding revenue in cash the British rulers changed the Indian countryside by bringing it within the framework of the world capitalist system. The phenomena of indentured labour, plantation labour and forced cultivation of various cash crops, though occurring within the share cropping or tenant system does not imply feudalism but is a system of a qualitatively different nature—the result of land being transformed into a commodity.

(3)

The first selection in this part, 'The Santhal Insurrection of 1855-56', is a brief, but vivid account of an episode representative of similar revolts which took place all over the country. Indian history during the British period is replete with such struggles. Unfortunately, very little attention has been paid to them. The selection describes the capacities and techniques of struggles used by the tribal people and the brutal methods used by the rulers to suppress them ruthlessly. It also shows the emergence of a new problem: the need for a leadership which could view these struggles in the context of the larger socio-economic and political matrix and evolve strategies on that basis. The present selection also raises a very important point which has acquired acute poignancy after Independence. Can the basic problems of the tribal population be solved within the 'exploitative capitalist social system' even after the withdrawal of the British rulers? Of course, L. Natarajan does not clearly pose this issue in his study. However, subsequent tribal struggles all over India beginning with the Nagas, Mizos, Gonds, Bhils, Warlis, Naiks, Sovarias and others reveal the need to examine this problem from this angle.

(4)

The second selection, 'Indigo Cultivators' Strike—1860', unfolds another aspect of the impact of British policies in rural India. The cultivation of certain commercial crops were required to be developed and expanded to satisfy the needs of the international trade as well as to meet the requirements of the growing industries in Britain. Tea, jute, cotton, indigo, sugar and a few other items became vital. The British evolved an elaborate technique of either procuring slave or indentured labour to provide the work force to cultivate such crops not merely in India but in various occupied territories which they captured and brought under their control. Marx has described some aspects of this phenomena in his classic section in Capital, Vol.I, on 'Primitive Accumulation'.

This phenomenon of indentured labour took various forms which still remain relatively unstudied. In India, it initially took the form of buying off or leasing the lands from the zamindars by the British traders, retired officials or trained slave drivers from USA. It also took place in the form of occupying sparsely populated tribal areas, where either specifically new crops like tea and others were grown, or the cultivation of crops like indigo, jute, etc., were expanded. These European planters adopted cruel and perverse methods to force the cultivators to grow these crops at the cost of food crops so essential for daily consumption. They broke up the self-subsistent village economies and reduced the cultivators to a semi-serf condition subjecting them to various types of social and personal oppression. Though the tools and techniques of production were the same, though the relations between the owners, plantation owners, or owners of the cultivated land did not take the form of wage labour, the objective of production and the legal framework within which the production was carried on were capitalist. It had all the characteristics of a new type of exploitation and oppression, which though reminiscent of slavery and serfdom, were linked to and a part of the growing world-wide capitalist system and therefore qualitatively different.

(5)

'Maratha Uprisings: 1875', is reproduced next to highlight the impact of British agrarian strategies in ryotwari areas. The payment of revenue in cash, the assessment of revenue on the basis of potential productivity of land, and the periodical reassessments made the peasants more and more dependent on the moneylenders, traders and other financiers. The moneylenders and traders utilised this opportunity to put the peasants under their bondage and generated, as indicated, a process of sub-division, fragmentation, pauperization and proletarianization. The struggle against the high land revenue assessment as well as the struggle against the usurers became the main features of the struggles in the ryotwari areas.

This selection helps us to search for the phenomenon of 'primitive accumulation' in various parts of the country practiced by other communities who later on became the powerful sections of the capitalist class after Independence.

(6)

The fourth selection, 'Conclusion' from Natarajan's book, is provided to disclose the manner in which eminent Marxists of the united Communist Party of India, just after Independence, assessed the forces generated by the British rulers and the reactions of the tribals, indigo cultivators and indebted peasants in the ryotwari areas to these forces. Natarajan's piece is to my knowledge, one of the first systematic appraisals of the 'role of peasant revolts' in the context of British agrarian policies and their consequences on the rural population. It also makes generalizations which show how the academic scholarship emerging after Independence and coming under the influence of British and American imperialist ideologies began to ignore the study of the process of revolutionary modernization' launched during the British period among the exploited strata and revealed in the series of gigantic struggles unleashed by them which threatened the capitalist development initiated by the Indian bourgeoisie.

Natarajan's 'Conclusion' is also included to highlight how the peasantry and their role and activities during the British period require to be analysed in a different manner for a correct assessment.

(7)

'Unrest in Andhra Pradesh' provides details about an area where a series of revolts have taken place during the last two hundred years, including the recent Naxalite uprising. It gives a clue to the fact that similar conditions generated by the British economic, political and cultural policies, produced revolts in all parts of the country, thus helping us to clear some misconceptions which lead to treating every revolt as a unique case.

It also shows how the persistence of certain socio-economic structural conditions will always perpetuate the climate for revolts and rebellions, whether the rulers are foreign or Indian.

(8)

The sixth and seventh selections 'Peasant Struggles in Pabna' and 'Agrarian Disturbances in Eastern and Central Bengal in the late 19th century', draw attention to a type of development in the zamindari area which has hitherto been ignored. Here, it was a conflict between the Zamindars and the various strata of tenants which emerged as a consequence of the permanent zamindari settlement.

The operation of the zamindari system introduced during the late 18th century in the course of the first half of the 19th century had created a chain of tenants, sub-tenants, and share croppers, who were being transformed into excessively poor tenants without resources or very meagre resources operating on tiny pieces of land. In many cases they were transformed into the status of agricultural labourers. The zamindari system, with the permanent settlement also inaugurated a process whereby the zamindars themselves sold portion's of their vast estates to augment their wealth, sometimes to their own collectors of revenue or to merchants and moneylenders who extracted various types of illegal exactions and services with the help of brutal terrorist methods which even led to evictions.

These legal and extra-legal practices caused a gigantic ferment among the tenants. The British administrators, realizing its threat to peace and security as well as its effect on agrarian production processes (especially on the production of commercial crops like, jute, indigo, etc.) passed the rent Act of 1859 which ensured occupancy rights to certain sections of the tenants and also prevented the zamindars from enhancing their rent claims arbitrarily. This Act introduced a new feature in landlord-tenant relationship viz. restrictions on the absolute proprietary rights of big zamindars, recognizing occupancy rights of tenants and also restricting, at least theoretically and judicially the arbitrary rights of zamindars to enhance their revenue rates as well as to demand various types of illegal dues and services. This Act is one of the earliest of the series of Acts passed by the British rulers, to mitigate the injustice which found expression in the unrests and agitations launched by the oppressed and the exploited tenants. This Act opened up for the tenants, sub-tenants, share-croppers and evicted peasants a legal way to prevent the zamindars and their agents from perpetrating legally disapproved exactions. While this advantage was enjoyed predominently by substantial tenants, who in course of time themselves became owners of the land, the other sections of the peasantry could only secure a certain measure of protection and temporary relief. The Act also opened up an avenue to form associations and organizations, to ventilate grievances, to awaken various sections of the tenants to their rights, to distinguish between legal and illegal acts of landlords and their representatives and to demand redress both against irregular practices of zamindars as well as to rectify the laws which were either ambiguous or highly unjust. Professor Kalyan Kumar Sengupta, in these two articles provides a very vivid picture of the various devices adopted by the zamindars to counteract, violate and bypass the Act.

The articles also give a glimpse of the emergence of new types of associations, which espoused the cause of the tenants and which launched an organized legal battle to rectify immediate grievances and some of the illegal practices.

7 The Santhal Insurrection: 1855-56

L. Natarajan

> *'We shall see how much twine could the Daroga procure, so as to fasten all the peaceful Santhals whom the wicked Daroga wanted to send up.'*
>
> —Answer from Gocho, one of the Santhal leaders to the police Daroga Mahesh Lal Datta.

THE SANTHALS were a quiet unassuming people who worked under primitive agricultural conditions. Sir George Campbell paid tribute to them as being 'most industrious and even skilful clearers of the jungle and reclaimers of the soil'.[1] With the establishment of the Permanent Zamindari Settlement (1793), the lands which they had cultivated for centuries were overnight turned over to the zamindars. With this followed pressing demands for increased rents. The Santhals found these new arrangements disturbing. Being peace-loving by nature, they started retreating from the districts of Cuttack, Dhalbhum, Manbhum, Barabhum, Chhotanagpur, Palamau, Hazaribagh, Midnapur, Bankura and Birbhum.[2] Hounded from their homelands, with great industry they cleared the forests in the plains skirting the Rajmahal Hills and, bringing large tracts of land under cultivation, started life anew. At that time this area was called Daman-e-Koh.

Sir George Campbell described their situation thus:

'They fairly think the land is his who first tilled it. If pressed beyond that they would rather retreat further into the woods and make new reclamations in places where they would not be molested. Unfortunately, however, they have reached extreme limits of retreat, and now find themselves on the borders of the plains of the Ganges at the very place where the competition for land is keenest and where rack-rents are screwed up to the highest pitch.'[3]

Their peaceful existence in the new settlements was not to remain for long undisturbed. The same class of zamindars who had hounded

---

Reproduced from *Peasant Uprisings In India (1850-1900)*, by L. Natarajan, People's Publishing House Ltd., Bombay, 1953.

them out of their lands in their former districts was to harass them again soon. As long as the forest lands were not cleared, the zamindars kept themselves away. However, once the land was made suitable for cultivation, they were not slow in coming up to claim proprietorship of the soil and demand rents. 'Greedy Zamindars', reported the Calcutta Review of 1856, 'living near the borders of the Daman had begun for some time to cast a wistful eye on their lands.' It cited a typical example:

'Gangadhar is an influential Zamindar. The border of his Tuppeh touches the boundary pillars of the Daman; within the pillars, Manick Santhal has a lovely spot of corn-land which he has nourished with frugal care; he has paid his rent for it for five years. Gangadhar can by no means claim it, for even his own ancestor has signed the plot away. As, however, Manick has paid six annas per mensem, he (Gangadhar) thinks no harm of levying on him the 'lenient' sum of six rupees in consideration of the fact that he will thenceforth be relieved of his exactions for that year!'[4]

Mr W.C. Taylor, Assistant Commissioner at Sreekand wrote to Mr A.R. Thompson, Deputy Commissioner at Naya Dumkha that the Rajahs of Maheshpur and Pakur were hated by the Santhals because they granted leases of Santhal villages to non-Santhal Bengali zamindars and moneylenders.[5]

A contemporary writer in the Calcutta Review described the situation in these words:

'Zamindars, the police, the revenue and court alas have exercised a combined system of extortions, oppressive exactions, forcible dispossession of property, abuse and personal violence and a variety of petty tyrannies upon the timid and yielding Santhals. Usurious interest on loans of money ranging from 50 to 500 per cent; false measures at the haut (weekly market) and the market; wilful and uncharitable trespass by the rich by means of their untethered cattle, tattoos (small ponies), ponies and even elephants, on the growing crops of the poorer race; and such like illegalities have been prevalent. Even a demand by individuals from the Santhals of security for good conduct is a thing not unknown; embarrassing pledges for debt also formed another mode of oppression.'[6]

Thus, besides the zamindars, there were the moneylenders too.

The rates of interest as described above, were incredibly high. The Santhal, wrote the Calcutta Review, 'saw his crops, his cattle, even himself and family appropriated for debt which (though) ten times paid, remained an incubus upon him still.'[7]

Seeing the opportunity of good trade and profitable money-lending, many moira and bania families from the districts of Burdwan and Birbhum, and Bhojpuri and Bhatia families from Shahabad, Chaprah, Betiah and Arrah had migrated to the Santhal areas. Barahait, 'the capital town of the hills' was reported in 1851 to be 'a substantial village with a large population and about fifty families of Bengali traders'; two markets were held there every week. The Santhals brought their produce to Barahait where the traders bought it at 'a price far below its true value.'[8] Large quantities of rice, bora, mustard and several other oilseeds were carried on bullock carts by the merchants to Jangipur on the Bhagirathi. From there on, they were sent to Murshidabad and Calcutta. 'Much of the mustard was exported to England.'

On top of this, there was also oppression from Europeans employed in railroad construction. The Calcutta Review of 1856 cites cases of 'forced abduction of two Santhal women, and even murder and some unjust acts of oppression as taking kids, fowls, etc., without payment on the part of the Europeans employed on the line of the railroad.'[9]

The oppression by the zamindars, the moneylenders, traders and Europeans and the government officers had inflicted great sufferings on the Santhal peasantry. The peacefulness of the Santhals was taken for timidity. The extent of oppression was intensified as time went by. All this was causing great discontent. The Pakur Record of the Calcutta Review of 1856 indicated that in 1854, some time before the actual start of the insurrection, the village committees of the Santhals 'seem to have begun in right earnest to cogitate what might be the proper course for them to pursue'. When finally they took the road to open insurrection, it was forced on them by a 'long course of oppression silently and patiently submitted to by those unsophisticated people'. As far as the government was concerned, it had learned nothing from earlier Santhal uprisings in 1811, 1820 and 1831.

Warnings of the seething discontent were given by the events in 1854. After consultation among themselves, the leading Santhals began by robbing the mahajans and the zamindars of their ill-earned wealth. In the opinion of a contemporary writer in the Calcutta Review, 'these were well-merited reprisals for their unprovoked cruelties'. According to a detailed account by Digambar Chakravarthy, a pleader of Pakur, the moiras and dikus (the Santhals called the Bengalis by these names), were frightened by the secret meetings of the Santhals under the leadership of Bir Singh of Sasan in Lachimpur. Among the other participants in these meetings, were Bir Manjhi of Boiro, Kaoleh Pharmanik of Sindree and Doman Manjhi of Hatbandha. The mahajans and the local officials sought the assistance of Rani Ksemasundari, the zamindar of Ambah Paragana (Pakur Raj). Babu Jagbandhu Roy, her Diwan, summoned Bir Singh to the Zamindari Kacheri. A heavy fine was imposed on him and he 'was mercilessly beaten with shoes before his followers.'[10]

The feelings of the Santhal peasantry were forcefully expressed by Santhal Gocho when he was unjustly harassed by the Daroga Mahesh Lal Datta. Gocho declared challengingly:

'We shall see how much twine could the Daroga procure so as to fasten all the peaceful Santhals whom the wicked Daroga wanted to be sent up.'[11]

This was the warning of the coming storm. However, the apparent calm prevailing at the close of 1854 was taken to have been caused by cowardice on the part of the Santhals.

The repressive measures instituted by Mahesh Lal Daroga only added fuel to the fire. Early in 1855, nearly six to seven thousand Santhals from Birbhum, Bankura, Chhotanagpur and Hazaribagh assembled for the purpose of avenging the punishment inflicted on their comrades in the last year. They complained that 'their comrades had been punished while nothing had been done to the Mahajans whose exactions had compelled them to take the law into their own hands.'[12]

The decisions of this meeting were circulated to all the other Santhals by the symbol of a sal tree, which is still used as a sign of unity and for the purpose of passing the word around. As a result, a large gathering of over 10,000 Santhals representing 400 villages met at Bhagnadihi on the night of June 30, 1855. It was decided that the time had come for the Santhals to rise as one man and get rid of the control exercised by their oppressors. On the instructions of the meeting, 'letters were then written by Kirta, Bhadoo, Sunno and Sidhu, addressed to Government, to the Commissioner, Collector and Magistrate of Birbhum, to the Darogas of Thanahs Dighee and Rajmahal and to several zamindars and others'. To the zamindars, they issued a clear ultimatum calling for 'replies within fifteen days'.[13]

In their letters, the Santhal leaders declared their solid determination to get rid of the oppressions by the zamindars and the mahajans and to 'take possession of the country and set up a Government of their own'.[14] Nobody cared to answer their letters.

Although the government remained deaf to the Santhals' letters, other non-Santhals resident in the area threw their support behind the Santhal peasantry. The extent of this support is evident from a letter which the Commissioner of Bhagalpur wrote to the Secretary to the Government of Bengal on July 28, 1855:

'From all accounts it appears that the Santhals are led on and incited to acts of oppression by the gowallahs (milkmen), telis (oilmen) and other castes who supply them with intelligence, beat their drums, direct their proceedings and act as their spies. These people as well as the lohars (blacksmiths) who make their arrows and axes ought to meet with condign punishment and be speedily included in any proclamation which Government may see fit to issue against the rebels.'[15]

Thus, with hope in their hearts, a song on their lips and bows and arrows in their hands, the Santhal peasants raised the flag of open armed insurrection against the unholy trinity of their oppressors—the zamindars, the mahajans and the government.

Daroga Mahesh Lal Datta, who had been so ruthless toward the Santhal leaders in 1854, became their immediate objective. With his usual arrogance, the Daroga advised them 'to disperse quietly and cultivate their fields so that they might be able to pay their rents'.[16] This last minute concern of the Daroga for the payment of rents was too much for the Santhals to stomach. After chopping off the Daroga's head, the Santhals proceeded to Barahait.

Seeing the strong demonstration of the outraged Santhals, the zamindar's agents, moneylenders and traders, took to their heels. The insurgents were not slow to consolidate their early gains. Establishing full control over the area between Borio and Colgong, they started moving towards Bhagalpur and Rajmahal.

The Government, still officially expressing innocent surprise at the insurrection, was making large-scale preparations to suppress it. All available police and military forces were being alerted for immediate action. Orders were also issued to the zamindars and darogas of the neighbouring paraganas to aid in suppressing the insurrection.

The insurrection was spreading rapidly. Mr Barnes, an indigo planter at Colgong, wrote to the Commissioner of Bhagalpur on July 1, 1855 that there was a general uprising in his area and called for government assistance. Major F.W. Burroughs was dispatched to Colgong after the insurgents had left the place. His letter of July 11, to the Commissioner of Bhagalpur indicates clearly the lines on which the Santhal fighting was being directed. He wrote: 'We hear that the insurgents move about in very small parties but on their drums sounding they assemble in parties of 10,000 men each.'

Like all popular insurrections, the technique of guerilla fighting and assembled battalions was combined by the insurgents. The appearance of the Santhal insurgents on the Indian arena was a novel experience. Here were the first people's armies, composed of rebellious peasants marching against their oppressors. It is a supreme tribute to their organization and voluntary discipline that, without any previous military training, such large numbers of persons, exceeding 10,000, assembled and disassembled at a very short warning.

Postal and railway communications between Bhagalpur and Rajmahal were completely severed. The insurgents were in control of the area lying between the two cities. The high road between Pirpainti and Sakriguli was in the insurgents' hands. Some persons who had escaped from Pirpainti later reported that the insurgents loudly proclaimed 'that the Company's rule is at an end; the regime of their Subah has commenced'.

Major Burroughs was ordered to Pirpainti. Roundly defeated in a serious encounter near Pirpainti at about 2 p.m. on July 16, 1855, he escaped leaving more than 25 soldiers and half a dozen officers dead on the battlefield. 'The rebels,' he reported later, 'stood their ground firmly and shot not only with hand-bows but with bows which they used with their feet, sitting on the ground to pull them and fought also with a kind of battle-axe.'

The 40th Regiment N.I. headed by Major Shuckburgh, and the Hill Rangers and the 7th Regiment N.I. commanded by Lt. Fajan, were rushed into the battle. Railway operations had completely stopped. The Government's panic was 'intense'. The situation was entirely out of control.

Martial law was declared on July 19. The proclamation stated that the insurrection had by now 'assumed all the characteristics of a rebellion', and sanctioned 'the destruction of the rebels found in arms' and offered large rewards for the apprehension of the leaders: for the 'principal chief Rs. 10,000; for each of the Dewans (supposed to be about 3 or 4 in number) Rs. 5,000, and for each of the minor chiefs of the Pergunnah Rs. 1,000.' The military was empowered 'to take all the measures considered necessary for the extirpation of the rebels.'

With this began the most brutal suppression of the rebellion. In spite of the brutality, the insurrection was spreading to Godda, Pakur, Maheshpur, Murshidabad and Birbhum. Isree Bhakt, Tilak Bhakt and Thootha Bhakhta of Litiparu—who, despite their names indicating meek religious devotion, were 'notorious even amongst the Bhakts for devising and exercising inhuman cruelties on the debtors'—paid for their crimes with their lives.

Now the Santhal forces were being helped by 'a large number of low-caste dikus' (non-Santhals). With their ranks thus reinforced by a brotherly bond which cut across all lines of castes and religions, they marched to Sangrampur and from there on, under the combined leadership of Sidbu, Kanhu, Chand and Bhairab, laid siege to Pakur. After three days they captured it. Dindyal Roy, the richest moneylender of the place, being a corpulent man could not escape. His servant Jagannath Sirdar, who was being kept in virtual slavery, caught him and brought him before the Santhals. There Jagannath, to avenge his life-long slavery, lopped off Dindyal Roy's limbs bit by bit with a tangi axe, exclaiming: 'With those fingers you counted your interest and ill-begotten wealth! With this hand you snatched away food from the mouths of the hungry poor!'

Dindyal's head was taken to the nearby temple of Siva Chakrapaniswar and placed in a niche for all oppressors to see.

The Government was now counter-attacking with full force. Captain Francis with the 13th Regiment, Lieutenant Loskart with the 7th Regiment, Lieutenant-Colonel Liptrap with the

42nd Regiment engaged the Santhals in battle. A guard of one thousand Garhawalis at a monthly charge of Rs. 3050 was hired 'to watch the passes of the district.' The zamindars and the indigo-planters also threw their resources on the side of the government.

Many of the zamindars in the Bhagalpur and neighbouring districts lent their elephants for service with the different detachments operating over the battle-front. They expressed their willingness 'to receive no hire', but preferred to lend the elephants to the government only desiring that they should be 'well-fed and taken care of during the period of their employment'. The Nawab Nazim of Murshidabad, too, supplied 'a train of elephants at his personal expense'. 'The troops engaged against the insurgents', wrote the Commissioner of Burdwan on September 27, 'were supplied with funds by the European indigo-planters'.

With all the forces thus assembled, the Government moved with ruthlessness to suppress the insurrection. Captain Sherwill moved the 40th Regiment into action and during a tour following July 29, 'destroyed twelve Santhal villages'. Major Shuckburgh started in a south-eastern direction to Deadeh and then turned north-east through Khonerah and round the hills to Lohundia 'destroying fifteen Santhal villages by the way and clearing that part of the country of the rebels'. On the afternoon of July 29, Major Burroughs sent Lieutenant Gorden with a detachment 'to destroy the Santhal villages of Munhan and Munkatro' and the next day Lieutenant Rubie 'made a detour to the North-west and destroyed the villages of Bhuggya, Titereah, Buskudar, Rangokitta, Hurrialia and Bockai'. In all 36 Santhal villages were destroyed.

The Rajmahal Hills were drenched with the blood of the fighting Santhal peasantry. In the face of this annihilation of their villages, the Santhal peasants stood like granite rocks of courage defending their homes and hearths. Typical of their heroism is the narration given by L.S.S. O'Malley of one encounter.

'They showed the most reckless courage, never knowing when they were beaten and refusing to surrender. On one occasion, forty-five Santhals took refuge in a mud hut which they held against the Sepoys. Volley after volley was fired into it, and before each volley quarter was offered. Each time the Santhals replied with a discharge of arrows. At last, when their fire ceased, the Sepoys entered the hut and found only one old man was left alive. A sepoy called on him to surrender, whereupon the old man rushed upon him and cut him down with his battle-axe.'[17]

Despite the murderous repression, the Santhal insurgents, even by the middle of August, 'were still estimated to exceed 30,000 men' in arms. Many of them were proceeding towards Monghyr 'into the village of Mulheapur'. The Commissioner of Bhagalpur, reviewing the government operations, wrote on August 11, to W.I. Tucker, Magistrate of Monghyr; 'They have as yet shown no signs of submission to Government, but are on the contrary openly at war with our troops'.

No repressive measure was regarded too drastic to be tried against the Santhals. Finally, in August, Mr A.C. Bidwell, Commissioner of the Nadia Division, was appointed Special Commissioner to carry out 'the measures necessary for the entire suppression of the insurrection'.

Despite their unflinching heroism, the Santhal's were facing a hopeless task. The rest of India was quiet and the entire army of a mighty empire was moving against them. The number of troops engaged against them ran into tens of thousands. 'A number of outposts,' wrote K. Datta, 'sometimes consisting of twelve to fourteen thousand men drove away the insurgents from the open country.'

The apologists of this criminal suppression by the government loudly proclaimed the 'inhuman cruelty' displayed by the Santhals and justified the harsh punitive measures employed against them. One of them, L.S.S. O'Malley writes:

'The insurrection proved them capable of inhuman cruelty. When a Mahajan fell into their hands, they first cut off his feet with the taunt that was four annas in the rupee; then hacked off his legs to make up eight annas; then cut his body in two to make up twelve annas and finally lopped off his head, yelling out in chorus that he had full payment of sixteen annas in the rupee.'[18]

Compare this pent up vengeance against the moneylenders, erupting with volcanic fury from the anger repressed for decades, with what the government did.

The account of the insurrection in Balfour's Encyclopaedia of India is a classic understatement: 'The insurrection was not suppressed without bloodshed'. With a cold-bloodedness which only imperialist ruthlessness is capable of, the account concluded: '—indeed, half their numbers perished'.[19]

This means that out of a total of thirty to fifty thousand insurgents, fifteen to twenty-five thousand were murdered before the insurrection was finally suppressed. During those memorable days of July and August, the Rajmahal Hills surely saw an unprecedented blood-bath.

Kanhu and other leaders of the insurrection were captured by the third week of February 1856 near Operbandhoh, north-east of Jamatra and were executed. Evidently not satisfied with the murder of fifteen to twenty-five thousand Santhals, the Editors of the Friends of India and the Calcutta Review, asked for harsher punishments for those who were left alive.

The Editor of the Friends of India wrote:

'It is only by striking terror into these blood-thirsty savages, who have respected neither age nor sex, that we can hope to quell this insurrection. It is necessary to avenge the outrages committed, and to protect the cultivators of the plain (sic) from a repetition of them. The Santhals believe that they can enjoy the luxury of blood and plunder for a month without a certainty of retribution. It is absolutely necessary that this impression should be removed, or obliterated, if Government would not in these districts sit on bayonet points. To achieve this end, the retribution must be complete, leaving no calculation of chances for future rioters; so striking that none may fail to know and understand; and so tremendous that people may know their lives and happiness are not held of light account. It is to Pegu that we would convey the Santhals, not one or two of the ring-leaders, but the entire population of the infected districts. India has not arrived at the point where armed rebellion can be treated with the contemptuous forebearance with which the English Ministry can pardon a knot of Chartists or banish a gang of Irish patriots. Let the Santhals' punishment be entrusted to a special Commission as was done in Canada in 1838. Or even if this expedient be too arbitrary, let the village be fined in an amount almost equal to the plunder retained, and the sum distributed among the sufferers. To secure the punishment of the race, and restore the prestige of British authority the mass of the Santhals should not remain unpunished.'

The unanimous voice of the outraged humanity of the Santhals demanded peace and protection against their oppressors. The imperialists, however, wanted more blood-letting, more punishment, more desolation.

Large numbers of the Santhal peasants were taken hostages and prisoners. K. Datta mentions that 'there are two big files of cases of Santhal prisoners in the Record Office of the Deputy Commissioner of the Santhal Paraganas.'[20] All these still remain unexamined. We do not know how many in all were tried and what severe sentences they had to undergo. However, one folder from these files has come to light. It shows that the Commissioner of the Santhal Paraganas tried at one time a batch of 253 prisoners from 52 different villages. Of them three were released and two turned approvers during the trial. Amongst the 248 prisoners tried, there were 46 boys of ages ranging from 9 to 10 years, 'who were', according to the official version, given stripes of rattan after the manner of school discipline.' Others were sentenced to long-term imprisonments varying from seven to forteen years.

Witnesses against the prisoners were hard to obtain. This indicates the support they had among the population. The special Commissioner, A.C. Bidwell, pointed out in his letter to the Lieutenant-Governor of Bengal that though he was in favour of 'speedy trials', he was beset by difficulties in the matter of 'procuring the attendance of witnesses'.

The Great Santhal Insurrection was thus cruelly suppressed. This was not the end of the oppressions against the Santhals, or in point of fact, against peasants in other parts of India. On the contrary, the oppression was intensified. And yet, the Santhal Insurrection was highly successful in one important aspect. The Santhal area, which had up to then been administratively broken up and merged into the neighbouring districts, was now reorganized into a separate entity known as the Santhal Paraganas. The Santhals had thus succeeded in forcing recognition of their special status as a national minority.

The din of the actual battles of the Insurrection has died down. But its echoes have kept on vibrating through the years, growing louder and louder as more peasants from various places joined the fight against zamindari oppression. The clarion call that summoned the Santhals to battle on that fateful night of June 30, 1855 at Bagnadihi was to be heard in other parts of the country at the time of the Indigo Strike of 1860, the Pabna and Bogra Uprising of 1872, the Maratha Peasant Rising in Poona and Ahmednagar in 1875-6. It was finally to merge in the massive demand of the peasantry all over the country for an end to the oppression of the zamindars and moneylenders. The Santhal blood has etched this slogan in letters, bold and large.

Glory to the immortal Santhals, who raised this slogan and showed the path to battle! The banner of militant struggle has since then passed from hand to hand over the length and the breadth of India.

References

1 Abhay Charan Das, *The Indian Ryot*, (Calcutta, 1881), pp. 564-5.
2 Captain Walter Sherwell, *Journal of the Asiatic Society of Bengal*, 1851.
3 A.C. Das, *op. cit.*, pp. 564-5.
4 *Calcutta Review*, 1856, pp. 238-40.
5 Kalinkar Datta, *The Santhal Insurrection of 1855-57*, (Calcutta, 1940), p. 7.
6 *Calcutta Review*, 1856.
7 *Calcutta Review*, 1860.
8 *Journal of the Asiatic Society of Bengal, 1851*, pp. 566, 574-6.
9 Datta, *op. cit.*, p. 8.
10 L.S.S. O'Malley, *Bengal, Bihar and Orissa* (1917), p 255.
11 Datta, *op. cit.*, p. 12.
12 *Ibid.*, p. 12.
13 Letter from the Commissioner of Bhagalpur to the Secretary of the Government of Bengal, dated July 9, 1855. Cited by Datta, *op. cit.*, p. 14.
14 *Ibid.*, pp. 15-16.
15 *Calcutta Review*, 1856.
16 Datta, *op. cit.*, p. 16
17 Most of the details regarding the actual events during the Insurrection are taken from Datta, *op. cit.*,
18 L.S.S. O'Malley, *op. cit.*, pp. 193-4.
19 Balfour's *Encyclopaedia of India, III*, p. 527.
20 Datta, *op. cit.*, pp. 67-8.

8 Indigo Cultivators' Strike—1860

L. Natarajan

'Let there be profit or let there be loss. I will die sooner than cultivate indigo. No, I won't cultivate indigo for any one on any account,' Dinu Mandal of Mozumpore, factory Dalalnagar, Thana Damuhuda, to the Indigo Commission (1860).

—Questions 1165-7 in Minutes of Evidence.

CENTURIES before the modern chemical industry began producing artificial bluing dyes, Indian cultivators had been growing a plant called indigo which yielded the dye necessary for bluing cotton cloth. With the growth of the modern textile industry in Great Britain in the late eighteenth and early nineteenth centuries, there was a great expansion in the demand for this dye. Indigo trade became a rich source of high profits for the East India Company in India. However, its cultivation was too limited to meet the growing needs of the British textile industry. Retired officers of the East India Company, and young upstarts, who had previously been slave drivers in America, therefore, decided to acquire lands from native zamindars in Bihar and Bengal and extend the cultivation of this crop on a large-scale as a plantation industry. Tenants were forced to grow indigo under a system of great oppression.

The opposition from the cultivators to this serfdom was so great that the Governor-General in Council was forced to issue a circular as early as July 13, 1810 stating:

'The attention of the Government has recently been attracted, in a particular manner to abuses and oppressions committed by Europeans, who are established as indigo planters in various parts of the country.... The facts however, which have recently been established against some individuals of that class before the magistrate and the Supreme Court of Judicature, are of so flagrant a nature that the Governor-General in Council considers

Reproduced from L. Natarajan, (1953), *op. cit.*

it an act of indispensable duty to adopt such measures as appear to him, under existing circumstances, best calculated to prevent the repetition of offences equally injurious to the English character, and to the peace and happiness of our native subjects.'[1]
The circular charged the planters with these grave offences:

'1 Acts of violence, which, although they amount not in the legal sense of the word to murder, have occasioned the death of the natives.

'2 Illegal detention of natives in confinement, especially in stocks, with a view to recovery of balances alleged to be due from them or for other causes.

'3 Assembling in a tumultuary manner the people attached to their respective factories and others and engaging in violent affrays with other indigo planters.

'4 Illicit infliction of punishment by means of rattan or otherwise on the cultivators or other natives.'

This concern by a callous alien government about the wrong-doings of the planters is not difficult to understand when it is realized that, faced with deadly wars with the Marathas, Tipu, and the French in India and with Napoleon in Europe, the British under Lord Minto were interested in maintaining a facade of peaceful intentions and avoiding serious popular disturbances.

That this pious declaration of the Government was only formal and for the record is evident from the fact that nothing more was done to prevent the oppression. As a result, during the course of the next forty years, local monopolies and acquisition of zamindaris by European planters were extended a great deal. With this, the oppression of the cultivators was all the more intensified.

The sale of indigo was highly profitable to the planters. However, the terms under which the peasants had to grow indigo involved great losses for them. It was necessary therefore to compel the cultivators to grow indigo in place of other crops.

Even the Lieutenant-Governor of Bengal was forced to admit in his Minute on the Report of the Indigo Commission that:

'Rejecting all extreme cases, and giving indigo the benefit of all doubts, I cannot put the absolute loss to the ryot at a low average, reckoning the net loss on the cultivation of indigo at the highest price now allowed and the loss of the net profit the ryot would make by any other ordinary crop at the market price, at less than seven rupees a beegah, equivalent at least to seven times the rent of the land.'[2]

No wonder the cultivator had to be forced to grow a crop under terms which were so unprofitable to himself. The nature of the oppression was clearly expressed in a letter written by A. Sconce, Judge of Nadia, to the Secretary of the Bengal Government on April 20, 1854. The letter, *inter alia*, stated that the tenants were forced to cultivate indigo and not anything else in the fields chosen by the planters; every two and a half bighas of land were considered by planters as only one bigha; not content with this, the planters took away two bundles of indigo for one; the tenants' crops were wantonly destroyed by the planters, their households harried, their houses burnt, and their cattle carried off as plunder or drowned. Mr Sconce, as District Judge in Nadia, was concerned over the growing opposition from the tenants to this brutal oppression. He requested that the Government appoint a commission to investigate the whole system of indigo cultivation.[3] It goes without saying that his request was turned down. The Government had not yet gone through the experience of the Santhal Insurrection of 1855-6.

In the meantime, the excesses committed by the planters continued to increase in intensity. From village after village and district after district, petitions were sent to the Government to intervene. Typical is this petition from the inhabitants of Nadia to the Lieutenant-Governor of Bengal on January 16, 1860:

'That your petitioners being severely oppressed by certain proceedings on the part of certain planters in the district of Nuddea and having unfortunately met with no redress or protection from district authorities, respectfully appeal to your honour for the same.

'That on the 28th October 1859 Boroo Mundle and Chunder Biswas, ryots of your petitioners' village, were by force carried away by armed people belonging to the factory, and they have not been since heard of.... That their complaints before the magistrate were dismissed (although proved on local investigation) on the ground that the functionary had no authority to interfere in such cases. That these efforts made by your petitioners to obtain justice have infuriated the planters and on 2nd December Anund Sirdar of Gobindpore was carried off. Subsequently, again, on the 8th instant Oojul Mullah, and Patan Shaikh were carried away from Soneprokooreah: Six other ryots of Soneprokooreah have also been carried off....'4

Planters, some of whom were former slave-drivers in America, were repeating their brutal performance in India.

The names of the persons so brutally carried away by the planters testify that Hindu and Muslim tenants stood shoulder to shoulder against the planters' oppression.

A. Grote, Commissioner of the Nadia Division in his Third Weekly Report (March 10-17, 1860) to the Secretary of the Government of Bengal indicated the mood of the peasantry. He stated:

'I have this week visited the Damoorhoodah subdivision. The general impression is that the ryots are much more determined here not to sow. The agitation is much stronger and evidently better organized.'[5]

Indignation was spreading all over the indigo-growing districts. Peasants' resistance was growing in Nadia, Barasat and Pabna. In place of mute protests, the peasants were getting together and taking action on a mass scale. In April 1860, all the cultivators of the Barasat sub-division undertook what was probably the first great general strike in the history of the Indian peasantry. They declared themselves against the oppression of the planters and refused to sow any indigo. The planters were in panic. In a memorial submitted in April 1861 to Sir Charles Wood, Secretary of State for India, D. Mackintey, Chairman of the Landholders and Commercial Association of British India, declared that

'the state of the mofussil had now (July 1860) become one of entire confusion. The debtors were not content with repudiating their debts and contracts, but they even combined to drive their creditors and employers out of the country, and thus to get rid of all Europeans in the province, to retain the property they had seized and to cancel all debts and obligations due to Europeans.'[6]

Havildar Sheebho Khan, commanding the Second Bengal Police Battalion, was at Neesanpore factory in the Pabna district on April 10, 1860. In a letter, describing the events that followed, he wrote:

'In the morning we got ready and marched to a village called Peeraree. We were almost immediately surrounded by about 2000 men armed with spears, bows and lathees; they came on and wounded the magistrate's horse with a spear. It is stated that the rioters were men from 52 villages; one man was conspicuous amongst them, from which direction there was some firing.'[7]

Here we see that the peasants were not only content with declaring a general strike. The very fact that over 2000 persons, drawn from 52 villages collected at one point ready for action indicates the extent of active unity and organization they had succeeded in building up.

This was a unique event in the history of the Indian peasantry. Indigo cultivators in the large districts of Pabna and Nadia and in the Barasat subdivision had declared the first general strike which soon spread to Jessore, Khulna, Rajshahi, Dacca, Maldah and Dinajpur, encompassing most of Bengal. Even before the start of the Indian working-class movement, even before the birth of Mahatma Gandhi, the peasants in these districts had taken to the path of general strike. That the indigo cultivators from these districts, separated by so many miles, undertook this united action testifies to the intensity of united support they had. If the area over which the strike spread, and the number of peasants participating in it are taken into consideration, it surpasses the campaigns led by Mahatma Gandhi at Champaran, Kaira and Bardoli.*

Planters had experienced scattered opposition from the peasants before and were prepared in their own brutal way, tried and tested through decades, to meet it. Organized opposition on a mass scale, however, was never anticipated by them. They were frantic when faced with the immense unity and strength of the peasants' opposition. A. Forbes, Acting Secretary to the Indigo Planters' Association, wrote to A.R. Young, Secretary to the Government of Bengal, warning him that 'a general rebellion throughout lower Bengal is, in my opinion, inevitable, unless strict and decided measures are without delay taken by the Government to put it down.' The planter slave-drivers, who had relied upto then on their brutal power, were now paralysed. 'The dissatisfaction,' Mr Young added, 'is entirely out of the planters' power to quell without the aid of the Government.'[8]

Here were the British planters calling for help against the wrath

---

* Bardoli campaign was, accurately speaking, led by Sardar Vallabhai Patel.

of an angered peasantry. The Government, however, was not to be easily moved to rush troops against such peasant determination and unity. The memories of the great Santhal Insurrection of 1855-6 were too fresh in their minds. Barely four years had passed since then. Nor could they easily forget the mass support which the peasants had given to the Rebellion of 1857.

There were other factors, too. The brutality of the indigo planters was so obviously indefensible that the peasantry had succeeded in winning wide support from other sections of the population, such as the urban middle class and even some of the missionaries. Harishchandra Mukhopadhyaya, Girish Chandra Basu, Dinabandhu Mitra, Sisir Kumar Ghosh, the founder of the 'Amrita Bazar Patrika', and many other well-known intellectuals took up the grievances of the peasantry and widely publicized them in the local press. Dinabandhu Mitra wrote a highly popular play 'Nil Darpan' exposing the oppression and injustice of the planters in Mollahati.

The extent of popular support to the indigo cultivators' struggle was so immense that even some of the missionaries were moved to express sympathy with it. One of them, Reverend James Long, published a widely circulated pamphlet in Bengali called 'The Oppression of the Indigo Planters' and supported the demands of the peasantry.[9]

Of all these factors, however, the consideration which influenced the Government most with regard to the measures to be taken against the peasantry was the haunting fear of the great Santhal Insurrection. It is clear how one mass uprising influences the course and the outcome of another. Instead of sending troops to break the general strike and quell the uprising, the Government announced the appointment of a commission to investigate the whole system of indigo cultivation.

The strong fears of the Government were expressed in the most unequivocal words by a person no less than J.P. Grant, Lieutenant-Governor of Bengal in his 'Minute on the Report of the Indigo Commission.' Answering those who criticised the government for not taking stronger measures to suppress the uprising, he stated:

'If anyone thinks that such a demonstration of strong feeling by hundreds of thousands of people, as we have just witnessed in Bengal, has no meaning of greater importance than an ordinary commercial question concerning a particular dye, such a person, in my opinion, is fatally mistaken in the signs of the times.' To this he added that people who have 'any responsibility for the tranquillity of the country, and the strength of the British Government within it' should consider this with great attention.[10]

He warned in unmistakable terms that,

'no human power exerted in defiance of the law, in support of the (indigo plantation) system, could have upheld it much longer; and that if the Government had disregarded justice and policy so far as to make the attempt, it would have been speedily punished by a great agrarian rising, the destructive effects of which upon European and other capital, no man can calculate.'[11]

These were not empty words on the part of the Lieutenant-Governor. He himself had observed at first hand the extent of the peasant resistance during a trip he made by boat through the river Gadui, a branch of the Padma. On hearing of his trip, tens of thousands of peasants lined the banks of the Gadui calling on him to come ashore and hear their grievances. When the peasants gave him their word of honour that he would not be molested, he ordered his steamer ashore and consulted with the peasant leaders. He had to promise them on the spot that everything in his power would be done to relieve their grievances.

Faced with such solid unity and immovable determination of the peasantry and haunted by the fear of another great agrarian uprising, the government was compelled to issue a proclamation in the form of instructions from the Hon. Ashley Eden, Chief Magistrate at Kalawah sub-division. The proclamation was also printed and published in Bengali. It read:

'You will perceive that the course laid down for the police in indigo disputes is to protect the ryot in the possession of his lands, on which he is at liberty to sow any crop he likes, without any interference on the part of the planter or any one else. The planter is not at liberty, under pretext of having promised to sow indigo for him, to enter forcibly upon the land of the ryot. Such promises can only be produced against the ryot in the civil court, and the magisterial authorities have nothing to do with them, for there must be two parties to a promise; and it is possible that the ryots, whose promises or contracts are admitted, may still have many irresistible pleas to avoid the consequence the planters insist upon them.'[12]

This was a complete victory for the indigo cultivators. As a result of the strike, indigo cultivation was largely forced out of these districts to Bihar and Uttar Pradesh.

The commercial interests of the planters were important. But certainly not more important than the future of the British Government in India!

The investigations carried on by the Indigo Commission are most revealing. The Commission's Report on the strength, determination and forthrightness of the indigo cultivators who were called before it as witnesses is so eloquent that it is better to quote it in full here. They reported:

'The dislike to this particular kind of cultivation was so strongly manifested and appeared to be so deeply seated that we could not mistake the reality of the feeling. It is not easy to possess those who have not witnessed the demeanour and heard the language of the ryot, as we have done, with a just appreciation of this intense dislike. Ryots of different concerns, at miles distance from each other, have expressed to us the same idea in language, clear, emphatic and pointed and striking as coming from the mouths of persons in their rank of life, namely, that indigo and its attendant evils had been the bane of their lives.'[13]

Witness after witness appeared before the Indigo Commission and in clear and determined words testified to their intense hatred of the system of indigo cultivation. Repeatedly, the Commission asked them about the terms on which they would be willing to sow indigo in future. Dinu Mandal of Mozumpore, Thana Damuhuda, Factory Dalalnagar was emphatic in his answer. 'Let there be profit or let there be loss,' he told the Commission, 'I will die sooner than cultivate indigo'.

But supposing a person in whose justice you had confidence asked you to sow indigo, the Commission inquired of Kulin Mandal of Kangrapore, Thana Mirpore, near Factory Nundanpore. 'I would sow indigo for nobody, not even for my father and mother,' was Kulin Mandal's immediate answer.

Jurdan Mandal, a Muslim cultivator from Ramkistopore, Thana Mirpore near Katuli concern replied: 'I have lost everything by indigo. I would rather be killed than sow indigo.' Panju Mullah of Arpara, Thana Hardi of Nadia district was equally bitter:

'I would rather be killed with bullets and have my throat cut than sow indigo.'[14]

The intensity of popular feeling against the indigo planters is evident from the testimony of Reverend James Long of the Church Missionary Society in Calcutta. He was a regular reader of the vernacular press which frequently dealt with the subject of the planters' oppression. Even in Calcutta, he said, the missionary preachers were constantly pestered with the question:

'Why do you not tell your countrymen, the indigo planters, to be less oppressive? Go, preach them first.'[15]

Thus we see that the indigo cultivators' strike was a powerful mass movement which generated a wide popular support from the intellectuals and some of the missionaries. The support for the planters, however, was to come from somewhat unexpected quarters. The planters, in their Memorial to the Secretary of State for India, quoted statements from two well-known Indians, Raja Ram Mohan Roy and Dwarkanath Tagore, extolling the virtues of the indigo planters and the plantation system. Raja Ram Mohan Roy was quoted to have remarked:

'As to the indigo planters, I beg to observe that I have travelled through several districts in Bengal and Bihar, and I found the natives residing in the neighbourhood of indigo plantations, evidently better clothed and better conditioned than those who lived at a distance from such a station.... There may be some partial injury done by indigo planters, but on the whole, they have performed more good to the generality of the natives of this country, than any other class of Europeans, whether in or out of service.'[16]

In view of the fact that the Indigo Commission could not find a single cultivator who would have a kind word to say about the indigo planters, it would surely come as a great surprise to many that the well-known reformer, Raja Ram Mohan Roy, was so far removed from the people of his country and so much attached to the Europeans that he had to make such a pitiful attempt to defend a system that was so universally condemned.

Dwarkanath Tagore's remarks in this connection are more revealing. He stated:

'I have found that the cultivation of indigo and the residence of Europeans have considerably benefited the community at large, the zamindars becoming wealthy and prosperous, the ryots materially improved in their condition and possessing many more comforts than the generality of my countrymen where indigo cultivation and manufacture are not carried on.... I do not make these statements merely from hearsay, but from personal observations and experience.'[18]

He went on to cite the example of prosperity on his estate which before the introduction of the indigo cultivation 'did not yield a sufficient income to pay the Government assessment', but which now 'gives me handsome profit'. Many of his relatives and friends now 'are receiving a large income from their estates'.[17] Undoubtedly Dwarkanath Tagore's praise of indigo cultivation was solidly based on the enlarged income he himself received from it. What was good for Tagore, must have been good for the cultivators too! He belonged to the planters' class and no wonder he defended his own class interests.

The sharp contrast between the testimony of the indigo cultivators on the one hand and the certificates of good behaviour given to the planters by Raja Ram Mohan Roy and Dwarkanath Tagore indicate vividly the gulf that divided these so-called reformers and the masses of the people at that time. How far removed were they from the pressing problems of the people!

Indian historians, while showering praises of Raja Ram Mohan Roy and Dwarkanath Tagore, have completely neglected to analyse this aspect of their opinions and activities. No wonder then that most of them have been silent on the glorious struggle waged by the indigo cultivators; if they mention it at all, it is only in the form of a brief contemptuous reference under the heading, 'Indigo Riots.'

No different has been the attitude of the historians of the Indian national movement. While playing up the Champaran Satyagraha led by Mahatma Gandhi in 1917-8, they completely ignore the glorious Indigo Strike of 1860. Through the magic of non-cooperation, Pattabhi Sitaramayya assures us, 'the grievances which leaders of the day and the Government (could do nothing about) for a hundred years were thus in a few months removed.'[18] Sitaramayya writes of the potency of this 'new weapon' of non-cooperation tried for the first time in the history of India. Nowhere does he mention that as far as the indigo cultivators were concerned, there was nothing new in non-cooperation. Nearly sixty years before the Champaran Satyagraha, they had used it on a much vaster scale and with much greater effectiveness. The support that Mahatma Gandhi was able to get from the cultivators in Champaran was in fact, in no small measure, due to the unforgettable memories of the first strike by the indigo cultivators. But the official historian of the Congress would not even refer to these facts least they restore to the peasants of Bengal the richly deserved credit of having launched the first large-scale non-cooperation movement, in the form of a complete strike, in modern Indian history.

References

1. *Indigo Cultivation in Bengal*, Parliamentary Papers, (1861), Vol. XLV, pp. 70-1.
2. *Ibid.*, p. 77.
3. *Ibid.*, pp. 6-7.
4. Parliamentary Papers, (1861), Vol. XLIV, pp. 171-2.
5. *Ibid.*, p. 241.
6. Parliamentary Papers, (1861), Vol. XLV, pp. 5-6.
7. Parliamentary Papers, Vol. XLIV, p. 309.
8. *Ibid.*, p. 195.
9. Cited by Abhay Charan Das, *The Indian Ryot* (Calcutta, 1881), pp. 294-5. The pamphlet contained songs which were sung far and wide among the peasants and were set to music.
10. Parliamentary Papers, Vol. XLV, p. 78.
11. *Ibid.*, Vol. XLV, p. 75.
12. *Ibid.*, Vol. XLV, p. 4.
13. *Ibid.*, Vol. XLV, para 131; pp. xxxiii-iii
14. *Ibid.*, Vol. XLIV, Question Numbers, 1165-7, 1250, 1262 **and 3214; pp. 65, 69,** 70, 204; also see Question Numbers, 918, 1248-9, **1165, 1351, 3214, 3230**
15. *Ibid.*, Vol. XLIV. Question Number 1625, p. 95.
16. *Ibid.*, Vol. XLV, p. 27
17. *Ibid.*
18. B. Pattabhi Sitaramayya, *History of the Indian National Congress*, (Bombay, 1946), p. 140.

9 Maratha Uprising: 1875

L. Natarajan

'If the example of these villagers be followed everywhere, and the unanimity of the people secured, the pauperized state of our country will certainly disappear soon.'

—Letter to the Editor of Dynan Chaksu (January 27, 1875) relating the events in village Kardeh of Sirur Taluka.

THE CONDITIONS which led to the agrarian uprising in the Poona and Ahmednagar districts were in the main typical of conditions in the entire ryotwari area. The Commission which was later appointed to inquire into the uprising admitted that the,

'condition of the villagers was such that even if Supa (where the uprising began) had not taken the initiative, some other place would have doubtless done so. The combustible elements were everywhere ready; design, or mistake or accident would have surely supplied the spark to ignite them.'[1]

The main concern of the East India Company administrators was to obtain a steady flow of large revenue from the land. At the time of the land settlements, therefore, the assessment imposed on the cultivators was excessive. Moreover, it had to be paid in cash and without respect to the crop conditions. As early as 1850, Sir G. Wingate had drawn attention to this fact. 'There can be little doubt', he wrote, 'that the over-estimate of the capabilities of the Deccan, formed and acted upon by an early collector, drained the country of its agricultural capital.' The Deccan Riots Commission, too, agreed that the exorbitant assessment was based on 'an exaggerated estimate of the peasants' capabilities'.[2]

Famines and scarcity were by no means infrequent. But rain or no rain, the government demands had to be satisfied. There were also difficulties caused by fluctuating prices. Under the circumstances, the farmers, to save their land from forfeiture and public

Reproduced from L. Natarajan, *op. cit.*

auction by the government for failure to pay revenue demands, had to turn to the moneylenders.

Before this, the moneylender was no more than a humble village servant, mainly a village accountant or a small shopkeeper. Now, with land offered as a security and with a government ever ready to grant his claims against the peasant, the moneylender assumed a highly important role. If the peasant repaid the loan, he would benefit from a high rate of interest; if the loan was not repaid he would get the peasants' land through a government decree. No wonder in a business where there never was a chance of loss, the moneylenders prospered rapidly.

Sir G. Wingate, with a deep knowledge of the working of the British land settlements and of the civil courts, had drawn attention to such a development nearly a quarter of a century earlier. He warned:

'The facilities which the law affords for the realization of debt have expanded credit to a most hurtful extent.... All grades of people are thus falling under the curse of debt, and should the present course of affairs continue, it must arrive that the greater part of the realized property of the community will be transferred to a small moneyed class, which will become disproportionately wealthy by the impoverishment of the rest of the people. No greater misfortune can befall any nation than this, by which many are made miserable in order that the few may be pampered. And yet this is the inevitable tendency of the existing relations between debtor and creditor in our Presidency.'[3]

Sir G. Wingate had correctly forecast the course of events. Peasants' indebtedness was mounting. With it was also rising the number of civil suits to take possession of the peasants' land. In the course of fourteen years, the number of civil suits increased seven to eight fold.

Number of Civil Suits about Land: 1851-65

	1851	1861	1865
Ahmednagar	98	318	689
Poona	75	282	632

Once the farmer's land was mortgaged, it was practically lost. The Commission stated 'that the instances of redemption of mortgages are almost unknown; a mortgage is equivalent to a transfer of the ryot's title.'⁴

Mr Invararity, the Revenue Commissioner, submitted to the Government in 1858 a report from Mr Tytler, the Collector of Ahmednagar, 'who was well known as an earnest and competent officer'. The report stated:

'The aid given by our courts is all on the side of the Marwari, who alone knows how to turn that aid to his own advantage. The position of the litigants is not, therefore, simply of debtor and creditor; it is the fraudulent Marwari, backed by civil courts, versus the helpless ryot, signing any bond without even a true knowledge of its contents and powerless to oppose any decree that may be passed. This matter keeps up a constant irritating sore throughout the society and the whole onus is thrown by the people on the civil courts.... The question is one of vital importance both to the Government and the people. Even the passive society of the East cannot bear so great a burden without making from time to time convulsive efforts to shake it off. The efforts must increase in frequency and strength.'⁵

The entire legal apparatus of the Government was thus in favour of the moneylenders and against the peasants.

Since the strong warning from the Revenue Commissioner was in a formal report, the Government had to take note of it. So the Governor-in-Council passed the following resolution:

'His Lordship in Council entertains no doubt of the fact that the labouring classes of the native community suffer enormous injustice from the want of protection by law from the extortionate practices of the moneylenders. He believes that our civil courts have become hateful to the masses of our Indian subjects from being made the instruments of almost incredible rapacity of usurious capitalists. Nothing can be more calculated to give rise to widespread discontent and disaffection to the British Government than the practical working of the present laws. The attention of the legislative council on the subject should be requested, and a copy of the Revenue Commissioner's letter forwarded for their consideration.'⁶

One would imagine that after such an outburst of 'self-criticism', immediate steps must have been taken to make the laws more favourable to the peasants. However, nothing of the kind happened.

As the Commission almost drily remarked: 'The subject was then for a time dropped.'

Nearly twelve years later, official attention was again focused on the subject. In 1870, the Revenue Commissioner of the Northern Division, sounding a menacing warning to the indifferent Government, reminded it

> 'that the Santhal rebellion arose out of the things precisely similar to that now existing in the west of Khandesh, and that though no indications of an approaching outbreak may have presented themselves here, neither did the Santhals give a word of warning before they burst over the plains of Beerbhum with an army of thirty thousand strong to avenge themselves on the usurers who had robbed and enslaved them under the tacit sanction of law.'[7]

A mountain might have moved, but not the Government of Bombay, especially in matters concerning the wellbeing of the people.

Meanwhile the conditions of the farmers were deteriorating rapidly. Cotton prices which had sky-rocketed during the American Civil War in the sixties had fallen into a deep slump. Together with this, all other agricultural prices had started to fall rapidly. There was a general agricultural depression. Farmers' cash incomes suffered a disastrous blow. To add to this there was a major famine in 1876.

Land revenue, which even in prosperous years was an unbearably heavy burden, now became impossible to pay. The rigidity of the revenue system was so notorious that the Deccan Riots Commission ridiculed it with a popular story:

> 'A man, it was said, desired to ford a river, and inquired the depth at various distances across; in some places the stream would be over his head, at another point but ankle deep, and so forth. Finding the average to be within his depth, he attempted to cross, and of course drowned.'[8]

Crops or no crops, high prices or low prices, the demands of the government had to be met! Now even the moneylenders were afraid that if the government proceeded first against the peasant and took away his land for payment of arrears of revenue, they would be unable to recover their debts. So there were more law suits, more decrees and an endless chain of dispossession of farmers' lands.

Nearly one-third of the cultivators was reported to be suffering under heavy indebtedness. This, according to the Deccan Riots Commission, meant certain transfer of their lands.

Peasants were bitter. They were yet unaware of the full workings of the system which was oppressing them. While they had misgivings about the government, they had no doubts about the role of the moneylenders. Debts were mounting; decrees were being handed out against them; their houses and lands were passing into the hands of the moneylenders right before their own eyes. There was no end in sight. Experience had shown that no relief was to be expected.

Enraged at the loss of their lands, the peasants of Poona and Ahmednagar districts let loose their accumulated anger against the bonds, documents, deeds and decrees which the moneylenders held against them.

The first warning of the approaching peasant uprising in these two districts was given in December 1874 by the events at the village Kardeh in Sirur Taluka.

Marwari Kalooram was the chief moneylender in Kardeh. He instituted a suit against Baba Saheb Deshmukh, one of the cultivators in Kardeh, and obtained a decree against him from the court at Talegaon. Deshmukh's house was put on auction and Marwari Kalooram purchased it himself for Rs. 150. Not content with this, he started pulling down the house and asked Baba Saheb Deshmukh to evacuate it. Baba Saheb requested Kalooram not to pull down the house and promised to repay his debts and pay rent for the house while he occupied it. But Kalooram would listen to none of this and continued the harassment.

Baba Saheb was now quite upset. He called together the villagers, all of whom had some grudge against the Marwari moneylenders. They resolved that as the moneylenders Kalooram, Sachiram, Pratap and Shivram were intent on ruining them, they should have nothing to do with them. The water-carriers, barners and even the house servants of the moneylenders joined the village in this boycott. The villagers opened a grocery shop for their needs. The moneylenders were isolated and decided to run away to Sirur. It was now the cultivators' turn. They would not let them go. There was nobody to drive their loaded carts. It was only with police protection that they were able to escape to Sirur.[9]

The moneylenders and officers may not have realized the full significance of this incident at Kardeh. However, the peasants in various villages were busy consulting with each other and preparing plans for future action. May 12, was the bazar day at Supa, Bhimthari Taluka. As usual, hundreds of peasants came there ostensibly to make their periodic purchases. However, plans were already laid for steps to be taken against the moneylenders. This was certainly the most fitting 'welcome' that the Maratha peasantry had planned for the visit of the Prince of Wales.

As the Deccan Riots Commission, later appointed to investigate the causes of the uprisings, observed:

'The object of the rioters was in every case to obtain and destroy the bonds, decrees, etc. in the possession of their creditors; when they were peaceably given up to the assembled mob, there was usually nothing further done. When the moneylender refused or shut himself up, violence was used to frighten him into a surrender or to get possession of the papers.'[10]

Within twenty-four hours of the uprising at Supa, there were similar incidents at Kheirgaon, situated fourteen miles away. The fodder stacks of the chief moneylender were burnt down as a warning and he was forced to surrender the bonds, deeds and decrees which were burnt in an open fire in the village square.

In a few days, similar occurrences took place in four other villages in Bhimthari Taluka. The flame lit by the peasant uprising at Supa was spreading like wild fire. Many villages of the neighbouring districts of Indapur and Purandhar soon joined in the fight.

Marwari and Gujarati moneylenders were running away from the countryside. At Vavra in Sirur Taluka, the moneylender refused to give up his documents. Only a serious threat to his life forced him to surrender them. Incidentally, only two years earlier, his uncle had been murdered by debtors in the same village. Other villages, including Kardeh, joined in the conflagration. At Damreh, a moneylender had his leg broken and was saved from death by the peasants massed outside his burning house.

While these uprisings were going on in Poona District, similar outbreaks were also occurring in the neighbouring talukas of

Ahmednagar District. During a fortnight following the first signal given at Supa on May 12, there were uprisings in Shrigonda, Parner, Nagar and Karjat Talukas.

While the peasants in their desperation were trying to undo the past injustices of the moneylenders by burning their documents, the Government lost no time in moving against them. The Government, which in quarter of a century had not once lifted its finger to help the peasants despite repeated urges and warnings from its own officers, suddenly burst forth into repressive activity, thus justifying the peasants' earlier suspicions "that the Government approved of the proceedings" of the moneylenders.[11]

All available police forces were sent into action to restore 'law and order'. But they were helpless against the mass of the aroused peasantry. Soon troops had to be moved in. A detachment of infantry was sent to Supa. The Poona Horse, stationed at Sirur, was ordered into action. Another detachment was moved to Shrigonda. Punitive police and military posts on a large scale were established and collective fines were levied on villages to meet the expenses. Arrests on an unprecedented mass scale were carried on. In just a fortnight, 559 persons from Poona District and 392 from Ahmednagar District were arrested.[12] The alien government let loose the full force of its repressive machinery against the unprepared and defenceless peasantry which was only trying to settle accounts with the moneylenders in a united but a rather moderate way.

By the first week of June, the punitive measures imposed by the Government were successful in repressing the uprisings. Yet the smouldering fire still kept on bursting out in to the open. On June 15, there was again some upsurge at Mundhali in Bhimthari Taluka. The peasants in Nimbut of the same taluka seized the documents of the moneylender and cut off the nose of the official who had come to enforce a decree of the civil court on June 22.[13]

The mood of the peasantry is clear from the Report of the Deccan Riots Commission. The recurrence of outbreaks in Bhimthari during June and July showed 'that the warning conveyed by the long catalogue of convictions and punishments, and the imposition of punitive police posts had not extinguished, but only repressed, the violent temper of the cultivators.'[14]

The echoes of the peasant uprisings in Poona and Ahmednagar

travelled far and wide. The news of the uprising 'had no doubt reached all parts of the country' and the cultivators in Kukrur, a hundred miles away from the nearest point of the Poona District, were not slow in starting a similar movement against the Gujarati moneylenders. Over one hundred farmers attacked the house of a moneylender, 'collected all papers and accounts which they found in the house, destroyed them and dispersed.'[15]

The active phase of the uprising in Poona and Ahmednagar lasted only three weeks. The peasants, unprepared as they were to withstand the onslaught of terrific repression by the Government, had no alternative but to abandon active struggle. Only through such bitter struggles were they to learn the lesson that the Government was the protector of the moneylenders and the landlords.

The short duration of the struggle should in no way detract from the immense popular support which it had generated among the masses of the people. It was almost impossible for the Government to obtain 'trustworthy evidence against' the participants in the uprising.[16]

Despite the serious grudges the peasants had against the moneylenders, the moderation they showed toward the person of the moneylenders was a supreme example of self-restraint on the one hand and of the wide popular support they had on the other. This was not a general rebellion against the oppressive moneylenders and government. The main purpose of the movement was 'to accomplish a very definite and practical objective, namely, the disarming of the enemy by taking his weapons (bonds and accounts), and for this purpose mere demonstration of force was usually sufficient.'[17] Behind this simple objective was the immature understanding that the destruction of these bonds and other pieces of paper would end the tyranny of the moneylenders. Only through the experience of such struggles were the peasants to learn that a complete redressal of their grievances could not be attained without overcoming the power of the Government, which provided the sanction and the effective force behind the claims of the moneylenders.

The speed and the ruthlessness with which the Government suppressed the uprising is evident from the number of arrests made. Within the course of just a fortnight, nearly a thousand peasants were arrested in the two districts with a total population of only 16 lakhs.

To understand the significance of this figure, it may be noted that the number of persons arrested at the peak of the first non-cooperation movement (early 1922) was 30,000; during the ten months of the second non-cooperation movement (upto the Gandhi-Irwin Pact in March, 1931), the number of persons sentenced was 60,000 according to official reports and 90,000 according to Congress sources.[18] If the long duration and the total of 250 districts over which the non-cooperation movements spread are taken into consideration, it may come as a surprise that the incidence of persons arrested during the peasant uprising in Poona and Ahmednagar Districts in 1875 was in point of fact greater than in the biggest non-cooperation movement launched by the Indian National Congress.

The ashes of the bonds burnt during this uprising were in course of time to spread all over the country, reinforcing one of the strongest demands of the Indian peasantry: cancellation of the peasants' debts.

Although the Government, through the sheer exercise of its repressive machinery, was able to suppress the uprising it had a lasting effect on the future of the Indian peasantry. It succeeded in breaking to some extent the shell of masterly inactivity into which the British rulers had withdrawn when it came to enacting legislation protecting the peasants' interests. The introduction of the Deccan Agriculturists' Relief Act of 1879, placing some restrictions on the alienation of the peasants' lands and restraining usury, was the direct result of the forceful assertion by the Maratha peasantry of its demands.

Some may wonder why the peasants, instead of being grateful to the moneylenders for helping them to tide over their difficulties, were so hostile to them. The Commission itself was concerned with this and the moneylenders appeared before it as the innocent unjustly hurt. 'It is only when indebtedness is attended with circumstances, which,' the Commission observed, 'produce in the mind of the debtor a sense of hardship, of unfair treatment, of being oppressed and having no redress, that a feeling of hostility is aroused such as led, in the present instance, to actual violence.'[19]

The moneylenders were not like poor widows kindly loaning

pennies to needy neighbours from the saving of a lifetime. They were rapacious usurers, who, in return for their support of an alien government, were given the licence of looting the peasantry. Naturally they were the immediate object of the wrath of the angered peasantry.

There is another question of contemporary importance which was quite categorically answered during the Poona and Ahmednagar uprisings. Many have attributed the peasant's debts to his extravagant expenditure on marriage, funerals, festivals and such other occasions. Others, less jealous of the peasant's 'indulgence', advanced his inefficiency and laziness as an explanation. The Commission carried out a thorough on-the-spot investigation and examined the whole question in great detail. Its conclusion on this score is so important even today that it deserves to be cited in full.

'The results of the Commission's investigations show that undue prominence has been given to the expenditure on marriage and other festivals as a cause of the ryots' indebtedness. The expenditure on such occasions may undoubtedly be called extravagant when compared with the ryots' means, but the occasions occur seldom, and probably in a course of years the total sum spent in this way by any ryot is not larger than a man in his position is justified in spending on social and domestic pleasures. The expenditure forms an item of some importance in the debit side of his account; by itself it rarely appears as the nucleus of his indebtedness. The sums usually spent on these occasions have probably been over-estimated, or the operation of other causes in producing debt have been overlooked by officers who have attributed the ryots' burdens so largely to this cause. This oversight would indeed be a natural consequence of the fact that it is only on marriages or similar occasions that the expenditure by a kunbi comes under observation. The amount spent by a kunbi of average circumstances on a (marriage)...is from Rs. 50 to 75, a sum which by itself, even at 24 per cent interest, could be repaid without much difficulty if his average margin of profit was not forestalled by other debt, and he were treated with fairness and moderation by his sowkar. The constantly recurring small items of debt for food and other necessities, for seed, for bullocks, for the Government assessment do more to swell the indebtedness of a ryot than an occasional marriage.'[20]

The Commission went even further and condemned the whole revenue system as the cause of peasants' indebtedness. It concluded: 'It is evident that a revenue system which levies from the cultivators of a district...the same amount yearly without regard to the out-turn of the season, must of necessity lead to borrowing. In bad years, the ryot must borrow. The necessity remains even when the assessment is fixed far below the standard of a fair season, for his creditor would not allow him to retain the savings of a good year even if he were prudent enough to desire to do so.'[21]

References

1. Report of the Deccan Ryots Commission, (Parliamentary Papers, Vol. LVIII, 1878), p. 2; for the purpose of brevity, it shall be referred to as *The Report*. The word 'riot' reveals the contempt with which the peasant uprisings have been characterized in official records.
2. *Ibid.*, p. 10.
3. *Ibid.*, p. 16.
4. *Ibid., paras* 70-7.
5. *Ibid.*, p. 16.
6. *Ibid.*, pp. 16-7.
7. S.S. Thornburn, *Mussalmans and the Moneylenders in the Punjab*, (London, 1884), p. 64.
8. *The Report*, p. 24.
9. Letter from a traveller to the Editor of *Dynan Chaksu*, dated January 27, 1875; cited by *The Report*, p. 1.
10. *Ibid.*, p. 2.
11. *Ibid.*, p. 3.
12. *Ibid.*
13. *Ibid.*
14. *Ibid.*
15. *Ibid.*
16. *Ibid.*
17. *Ibid.*, p. 4
18. Pattabhi Sitaramayya, *History of the Indian National Congress*, II, p. 876.
19. *The Report*, p. 33.
20. *Ibid.*, p. 20.
21. *Ibid.*, p. 21.

10 Conclusion

L. Natarajan

A NUMBER of highly significant facts emerge from the brief outline of some of the peasant uprisings during the second half of the nineteenth century.

1 It shows that the Indian peasants have a proud, militant heritage. Each new uprising focused attention on the foremost demands of the Indian peasantry: particularly, the end of zamindari and moneylending oppression. The uprisings not only added living reality to these demands but helped establish them as the very core of the peasants' long-cherished aspirations. So long as these aspirations remain unfulfilled, the peasant struggles will go on.

2 Each struggle enriched the peasants' consciousness and raised it to a higher and more mature level. It was only through these bitter struggles that the peasants were to learn that the real force behind the zamindars and the moneylenders, their immediate enemies, was the organized power of the Government; that the Government, instead of being a neutral in the strife, was a direct supporter of their oppressor.

The courage and unflinching heroism with which these peasants raised the banner of militant struggle, at a time when political parties were unknown in India, testified to the reality of their grievances and their steadfast determination to put an end to their oppression. More than that, it also exposes the malice and gross ignorance of those who today rush to brand the peasants' struggle as a creation of foreign agents. No foreign agents did or could rouse the Santhals, the indigo cultivators, the Maratha peasants or the Moplahs to such heroic struggles.

3 Even with all the limitations of the sporadic and spontaneous nature of their struggles, theirs were no mean achievements. As a result of the Santhal Insurrection, the Santhal Paraganas were

Reproduced from L. Natarajan, *op. cit.*

organized as a separate entity, thus forcing recognition of their special status as a national minority. Those who conceive of the Santhals as 'aboriginals' and believe that the Santhals' salvation lies only in their assimilation into their more 'cultured' Bengali and Bihari neighbours should realize how hollow are their claims of superiority.

The Indigo Cultivators' Strike succeeded in reasserting the peasant's right to sow the crops he chose and in forcing the indigo planters out from Pabna, Bogra and Barasat to Champaran and other parts of India. The peasants in these districts did not have to go through the terrible experience of the Champaran indigo cultivators in the early 20th century when the planters passed on the losses of a ruined industry to the peasants.

The Maratha Peasant Uprising forced the imperialist rulers to undertake the first legislation offering some protection to the peasants against usury and transfer of their lands. The Deccan Agriculturists Relief Act of 1879 was a direct result of the uprising.

The peasants waged battles every inch of the way and their partial victories, were wrung out of the unwilling hands of their oppressors.

One must also remember that the massive fights put up by the peasantry had shaken the confidence of the British in their ability to hold on to their dominion in India. A.O. Hume had seen the voluminous evidence of the seething discontent in the country and was aware that nothing could be more disastrous for British rule than the possibility of a merging together of these potent undercurrents of popular opposition. Something had to be done and that something was the founding of the Indian National Congress. In a memorandum found in his papers, Hume wrote:

'The evidence convinced me... that we were in imminent danger of a terrible outbreak. I was shown seven large volumes... containing a large number of entries... all arranged according to districts, sub-districts, sub-divisions, and the cities, towns and villages... from over thirty thousand different reporters—all going to show that these poor men were pervaded with a sense of hopelessness of the existing state of affairs, that they were convinced that they would starve and die, and that they wanted to do something. They were going to do something, and stand by each other, and that something meant violence....

It was considered also that everywhere the small bands would begin to coalesce into large ones, like drops of water on a leaf... and that very soon after the bands obtained formidable proportions, a certain small number of the educated classes, at the time desperately, perhaps unreasonably, bitter against the Government would join the movement, assume here and there the lead, give the outbreak cohesion, and direct it as a national revolt.' (Sir William Wedderburn, A.O. Hume, *Father of the Indian National Congress*, (1913), pp. 80-1.).

The fear of the spreading popular discontent and especially the stubborn struggles waged by the rebellious peasantry sent Hume rushing to Dufferin, the Viceroy of India at that time, with his plan for the creation of the Indian National Congress. According to the plan, the Congress was to draw into its fold the discontented intelligentsia and to perform the role of a loyal opposition. Haunted by the spectre of a mass uprising, they were thus trying to foreclose the possibility of a real national rebellion emerging out of the merger of these two currents—the peasant uprisings and the agitation by the intellectuals.

Thus, it was the militant peasantry, and not the mild-mannered and soft-spoken gentry who pompously constituted themselves into the Indian National Congress in 1885, that voiced the people's grievances and waged struggles to remove them. What greater tribute could be paid to the real extent of the achievements of these uprisings than the fact that they were responsible for the creation of the Congress, thus placing their indelible impression on the future history of India. No wonder the Congress remained a body of pitiful speechmakers till the end of the First World War when it realized the necessity of drawing in the peasantry.

4 Although these uprisings were spontaneous and sporadic, the forms of struggle created by them have a deep historical meaning even today. Witness the last-ditch battles waged by the Santhals in 1855; the massive strike by the indigo peasants in 1860 and the burning of the moneylenders' bonds, deeds, documents and decrees by the Maratha peasantry in 1875. All these foreshadowed the form in which peasant discontent is finding its expression in modern India.

5 While the uprisings indicate a considerable amount of planning and organization during their course, they were on the whole

spontaneous outbursts of the peasants' discontent against their exploitation. When their grievances were aggravated to unbearable proportions, due to a local famine, price decline, excessive repression, forced auction of their lands or some such factors, they hit back with heroic fury. In the face of the odds against them, however, they could not hold out for long. The peasants' understanding of their opponents was immature and their ability to create, continue and widen peasant organizations was limited. The uprisings, therefore, were sporadic and spontaneous. They could not create the basis for an ever-growing organized peasant struggle which could lead to the complete realization of their aspirations.

These uprisings, however, were the necessary dress-rehearsals of the future struggles of the Indian peasantry.

11 Unrest In Andhra Pradesh

V. Raghavaiah

UNREST AMONG THE TRIBAL people of Andhra Pradesh is not a matter of yesterday or today. It has been raising its aggrieved and ugly head now and then in the past 167 years. It is now also active in the Agency Areas of Andhra Pradesh stretching out in a half-moon pattern its agitated arms, indicating a deep seated anguish, resulting from dashed hopes, broken promises and frustrated aspirations. The tribes in this part of the country live both in the plains as well as in the hills and the jungles. While many tribes of the plains are nomadic, landless, homeless and primitive, those in the Agency Areas have their lands alienated, meagre properties heavily mortgaged, and their health irretrievably shattered, owing to the relentless attacks of malaria, year after year, sapping their energy and thwarting all efforts at better living conditions and purposeful lives....

Most of the South Indian tribes, including the 33 different tribes of Andhra Pradesh, are pre-Dravidian and to some extent share Negroid features. Ecologists assert that the early and the middle palaeolithic civilisation of pre-historic times flourished in the districts of Kurnool, Guntur and Nellore in Andhra Pradesh.

Andhra Pradesh is a large State occupying a fourth place in the Indian Union and covering an area of 106,286 sq. miles, with a scheduled population of 13,24,368 most of whom live in the Agency parts of the State which roughly covers 29,683 sq. miles. In addition to these Agency tribes, Andhra Pradesh has a nomadic ex-criminal and unscheduled population of six more lakhs of tribals who can be classified as primitive. The scheduled tribes form 3.68 per cent of the total population of Andhra Pradesh of 3,59,83,447. The numerically largest groups inhabiting both plains and Agency areas are Gonds, Koyas, Hill Reddis, Savaras, Bagatas, Valmikis, Yerukalas and Yanadis, as well as smaller

Reproduced from V. Raghavaiah, *op. cit.* pp. 27-34.

groups like Ronas, Kattunaikars and Bhils. Nearly 52.6 per cent of the total tribal population of Andhra Pradesh consists of Koyas, Yanadis, Yerukulas and Gonds. While Gonds are confined to the district of Adilabad bordering on Madhya Pradesh, Koyas are found in all the Agency districts. Gonds, Koyas, Bagatas and Valmikis are more advanced than Khonds, Savaras, Hill Reddis and Kolams. The Agency tribes inhabit parts of the main districts as mentioned in the following table based on the 1961 Census report:

District	Extent in sq. miles	No. of tribal villages
(1) Sirkakulam	1303.04	462
(2) Visakhapatnam	6671.36	1565
(3) East Godavari	6637.70	699
(4) West Godavari	1492.56	105
(5) Khammam	6647.53	888
(6) Warangal	980.76	152
(7) Adilabad	4534.35	415
(8) Mahaboobnagar	1415.63	60
	29682.93	4346

It is mostly in the first four districts that tribals revolts have been occurring, though in Adilabad a sporadic uprising of the Gonds led by Bhimu was summarily put down by the British. Some of the revolts took place during the rule of the British East India Company. The main seat and stronghold of the recent as well as the current 'Naxalite' uprisings is the Srikakulam district which borders on Orissa State, separated only by a long chain of low hills which have been thoughtfully selected by the English-educated Naxalite leaders from Visakhapatnam and East and West Godavari districts for their strategic and logistic facilities. Rebels pursued by the police found a cosy home in the caves and dugouts of these hills access to which is somewhat difficult. Moreover they could easily slip into Orissa....

Tribal revolts in Andhra Pradesh erupted on four occasions. Though the immediate causes were somewhat different, the basic factors that contributed the powder for the guns were on all occasions the same. The first of the revolts led by Rambhoopati took place in 1802-3, now popularly known as the Rampa Fithuri (rebellion), named after Rampa near Chodavaram. The Rampa country is the area covered by the Chodavaram taluk of the East Godavari district of Andhra Pradesh. The second revolt around 1879 led by Chandrayya, Sambayya, Thammandora and Ambul Reddi spread over 5,000 sq. miles in the Rampa country. The third uprising took place in 1922-4 under the leadership of the saint-patriot hero Shri Alluri Sreerama Raju who was murdered, after his voluntary surrender on May 7, 1924, at Koyyur on the orders of a British Major, Goodall, against all canons of justice, national or international. The fourth revolt is continuing since the last two years in the district of Srikakulam, under the guidance of educated pro-Chinese extreme Communists, known as Naxalites, who have taken their name after a village called Naxalbari in the Darjeeling district of West Bengal, where the first outburst took place....

The first two rebellions were due to disputes relating to succession to the Muttadari estates. The Muttadars were petty tribal chiefs who were appointed by the British East India Company's minions for keeping peace and collecting a very nominal land revenue from the tribal people more as a symbol of overall authority of the Company's Government, rather than as a source of revenue to the State. Taking ample advantage of even this limited authority, the Muttadars used all questionable and violent methods to terrorise the poor Koya and Konda Reddi tenants and effect several illegal and unconscionable exactions from the helpless and hapless tribal farmers.

The Revolt of 1879-80

For nearly two centuries the British were in possession of the Northern Circars including the Rampa country, though in Chodavaram Taluk containing the Rampa area, no regular collection of land revenue was enforced till the end of the 19th century. During the period of the cession of the above country to the British, Rampa was ruled by an independent zamindar, recognised by the Reddis as their feudal lord or Mansabdar. During the revenue collection of 1802-3 no settlement was done for Rampa. Ram Bhupati, the Mansabdar seized some villages which were under British control, but was soon repulsed and forced to acknowledge the Company's sovereignty. In 1813, an agreement was reached between the two by which the Company restored the above villages to him free of rent (Peshkash) on condition that he maintained peace in this restless land. Ram Bhupati subleased these villages to his subordinate hill chiefs called Muttadars, on an annual payment of Rs. 8,750. After his death his daughter succeeded to his estate though on a hot contest by Ram Bhupati's illegitimate son, she surrendered the property to him. The Muttadars accepted him on condition that he reduced the total rent to Rs 1,000 in 1848. He first agreed to do so but later broke his promise and began to rackrent the Muttadars and make illegal exactions which the hill Reddy Muttadars and the tribal people refused to pay. In addition to this, free drawing of toddy by the tribals was obstructed by the Mansabdar and several types of taxes which were unknown before were invented and levied. The tribals and their Muttadari tribal leaders got vexed with litigation in the civil courts and finally the call to revolt was given as the zamindar obtained *ex-parte* decrees and attached the property of the tribals through the courts at Rajamahendravaram. Cattle and property worth Rs 100 were attached to realise a debt of only Rs 5. All the attached goods were taken away with the police helping the Mansabdar and the Courts decreeing for him. This left no alternative to the tribals except to revolt and they did it in right earnest perhaps knowing full well the consequences thereof.

The first outbreak of the rebellion occurred in March 1879 when the tribals captured 6 policemen under Thammandora's leadership near Boduluru, 22 miles from Chodavaram, kept them in custody for several days and finally took them to Kodigandi where a head constable and one constable were kept tied under a tamarind tree. Thammandora himself severed their heads as a sacrifice to the Goddess in the presence of 200 tribesmen. The rebels then attacked the Chodavaram police station and reduced to ashes the station at Addatigala. Soon the Rampa country was ablaze and the rebellion assumed serious proportions.

The disturbances spread to Golugonda hills in Visakhapatnam in April and to Rekapalli country in Bhadrachalam in July. Here the immediate cause of the revolt was the sudden increase by the Madras Government of the assessment of Podu lands by three times while it was only four annas an acre hitherto. Further, the ryots were excluded from certain areas and a tax was newly levied on the felling of certain varieties of trees. The fight with the tribals who could penetrate unseen into the jungles and launch surprise attacks—the manner of guerilla warfare avoiding direct confrontation—made the task of the Government troops very difficult. Towards the end of 1879 the Government despatched from Madras, 6 regiments of the Madras Infantry, 2 Companies of Sappers and Miners, a Squadron Cavalry, one wing of Infantry, besides several hundreds of Police. The war with the tribal insurgents lasted till November 1880.

12 Peasant Struggle in Pabna, 1873
Its Legalistic Character

Kalyan Kumar Sengupta

I

AN OBSCURE *parganah*, Yusufshahi, situated in the Serajgunge sub-division of the district of Pabna[1] became in 1873, the scene of a powerful agrarian movement. This movement, conducted by a well organised agrarian league[2] created the conditions for the launching of similar agrarian movements in other parts of Eastern and Central Bengal[3] in the decade which preceded the enactment of the Bengal Tenancy Act of 1885.

The basic cause of this agrarian unrest was the persistent attempts of the local landlords to do away with the right of occupancy of a new class of ryots, the occupancy ryots, who had been browbeaten into existence by the Bengal Rent Act X of 1859[4]. The agrarian movement in Pabna and other areas of Eastern and Central Bengal, was moreover, basically, a movement of the substantial section of this type of tenantry who saw in the newly conferred occupancy right, a position of greater social responsibility for them in the rural society and more effective share in land control. In fact, this conflict between the zamindars and the richer tenants marked the beginning of a long struggle in rural Bengal which culminated, through the enactment of various tenancy legislations, in the consolidation of the socio-economic position of the substantial tenantry. In the 20th Century, these well-to-do peasants, as *jotedars*, themselves became the exploiters of the share-croppers, known in Bengal, as *adhiyars* and the *burgadars*.[5]

The primary aim of this movement of the substantial tenantry was to defend and consolidate the occupancy status gained by the Act X of 1859. Other sections of peasantry—the non-occupancy

Reproduced from *Nineteenth Century Studies*, Calcutta Vol. I No. 3, July 1973, pp. 328-40.

ryots, the under-tenants of the occupancy ryots, the share-croppers and the agricultural labourers—participated in the movement fairly willingly since the zamindar was supposed to be the common enemy of all.[6] However, the specific problems and the grievances of a large majority of the peasant population consisting of the share-croppers and the agricultural workers never came in for serious consideration at any stage.

This agrarian movement in the district of Pabna, rarely degenerated into a *jacquerie*. The tenantry on the contrary displaying a remarkable sense of discipline fought the principal landlords of Pabna, the Tagores, the Pakrasis, the Sanyals, the Banerjees and the Bhaduris, in the civil courts.

However, scholars like Binay Chaudhuri and Suprokash Ray have failed to take into consideration this particular aspect of the character of the movement.[7] On the contrary by underlining the violent character of the movement they have uncritically accepted the contemporary landlord press bias regarding the Pabna tenantry.[8] The present paper seeks to emphasise this point and tries to show that the legalistic passive character of tenant resistance was one of the novel features of this important agrarian movement.

II

As the movement of the occupancy ryots of Pabna gradually spread throughout the district, the Bengal landlords apprehended that a further extension of the movement would adversely affect the position of the landlord class as a whole. It was feared that the Government would eventually be forced to review the entire question of landlord-tenant relationship—a review which might ultimately lead to a further amendment of the rent law in the interest of the tenantry. Consequently the pro-landlord enthusiasts in the city of Calcutta made a conscious attempt to confuse the issues. A deliberate effort was made to create an impression that the Pabna movement was not an agrarian movement at all but a movement organised by men who wanted to use the peasants to further their selfish interests.[9] There was thus a persistent clamour that law and order had practically ceased to exist in Pabna where the ryots were committing all sorts of atrocities.

Thus Dwijendranath Tagore, poet and musician, one of the famous cultural figures of 19th Century Bengal,[10] drew the attention of the Lieutenant-Governor of Bengal to the acts of wanton violence committed by the Pabna peasantry upon the 'inoffensive people'.[11] Tagore's complaint was corroborated by a group of Pabna *mukteers*, the agents of the local landlords, who in a petition to the Government painted a livid picture of mob-violence in the district.[12] The *Hindoo Patriot* as well as the *Amrita Bazar Patrika* also sent from Pabna highly coloured accounts of wanton plunder, rape and arson committed by the enraged peasantry. The *Hindoo Patriot* wrote: 'The contagion rapidly spread in the Pubna district in the quarters very near Shahazadpore. Its first fury had to be borne by the residents of Gopalnagar where respectable men were plundered, their females insulted and their homesteads burnt down to ashes in broad daylight.... Then occurred a series of plundering raids throughout that part of the Pubna district which lies between Gopalnagar on the north-east and Padma near Goalondo on the south... villages after villages were mercilessly plundered and subjugated.... In this way, village after village was, as was styled by them, brought to "subjection" till this dangerous mob of ruffians, frenzied freebooters and ignorant credulous peasants overran nearly the whole of Shahazadpore *chowkee*, spreading all sorts of rumours regarding the Government aid which they were sure of getting.'[13] The special correspondent of the *Amrita Bazar Patrika* also sent from Pabna almost an identical report.[14] 'The whole subdivision of Serajgunge in Pabna is in a state of dread of excitement. Thousands of ryots have combined together and risen against their Zamindars, plundering and devastating everything in their way. The life, property and honour of the people are in imminent danger.' This then was the crux of the landlord position and shows clearly enough that the Chaudhuri-Ray position is really an uncritical acceptance of landlord press bias.

III

The enquiry conducted by the Government which followed the publication of these reports in the pro-landlord Calcutta press established, however, that most of them were either maliciously false or deliberately exaggerated.[15] This was confirmed by the results of the Pabna trials which showed that the ryots arrested on charges of rioting or plunder were either acquitted or let off with light punishments.[16] Most of the influential newspapers also thought that the reports of mob-violence circulated by the agents of the landlords were grossly exaggerated since the outrages committed by the ryots were remarkably few.[17] The *Bengalee* thus wrote on August 9, 1873: 'After carefully suppressing everything favourable to the ryots and unfavourable to the Zamindars, after charging the ryots with rape and other outrages on females never committed by them, the *Amrita Bazar Patrika* sheds some crocodile tears over the fate of the wretches who have been sent to prison for their misdeeds. Lest it should be thought that our contemporary by his unscrupulous advocacy of the landlord had descended to the level of the famous Sampson Brass, he apostrophies the ryots in the following strain: "O poor! misguided deluded men, how you have been befooled by Mr Nolan".' The *Friend of India* reported on July 17, 1873: 'Pubna continues quiet. The peasant as resolute as ever against exaction, is no less determined to keep within the law.' The *Pioneer* stated on July 15, 1873: 'It is to be hoped that some attention will be given to the real grievances of the cultivators. The native newspapers which are almost entirely under the influence of the Zamindars have been publishing ludicrously exaggerated accounts of "outrages" that have been perpetrated by the ryots. According to these truthful historians, an epidemic of rape and murder has fastened upon the ryots of Pubna. The facts officially reported, however, reveal a very different tale. Two or three houses have been burned, a few more have been gutted and some persons have been moderately beaten. No one excuses this illegal violence but the glib falsehoods of the native press make it necessary that it should be accurately reported.' The opinions of these responsible and influential newspapers representing respectively, the progressive middle class Bengalees, the Christian missionaries and the English officials, thus unmistakably underlined the fact, that the pro-landlord press represented by the *Hindoo Patriot* and the *Amrita Bazar Patrika* did not accurately report the facts pertaining to the agrarian movement in Pabna. This will be more clear if we analyse the nature of the various incidents which took place in Pabna during this period of agrarian unrest.

IV

The first serious incident in the Sadar sub-division had taken place at Gopalnagar and Faridpore on the 27th June, 1873 when an attack was made on the estate of the local landlords, the Mazumdars, where extra police under an inspector had to be sent. On June 28, large bands of men had collected at Dhuboori (Nakalia) and manhandled two constables in whose custody were some recovered stolen articles. In the meanwhile a large crowd of about a thousand men attacked the Mathura Police Station and the Post Office presumably to assault the Officer-in-Charge, but they left subsequently without doing any harm.[18] The principal objective of the rioters, it appeared to the Magistrates, was to recover some stolen property seized by the officer. At Shagurkandi where the rioters, some twelve hundred men, had attacked one Govinda Dutta's house on June 30, the damage was considerable and according to W.V.G. Tayler, the District Magistrate, who visited the spot, the attitude of the rioters was 'most malicious'. It is significant that none of these very serious cases were in any way connected with the rent question. The Gopalnagar and the Shagurkandi incidents were caused by old zamindari quarrels[19] while the Nakalia episode was the result of some private ill-feeling between some of the rioters and the complainants. The complaint however, fell through for lack of evidence.[20]

In Serajgunje sub-division, where the movement had originally started, practically the entire countryside supported the tenantry.[21] At Sallop, an illegal assembly had taken place and a number of unionist ryots went in a threatening manner to some villages which had not hitherto joined the movement. Assemblage of ryots had also taken place at Ullahparah where buffalo horns were blown at night to cause terror and intimidation. According to Inspector Krishna Sundar, who was sent to the affected areas by the Sub-Divisional Officer of Serajgunge, P. Nolan, the agents of the zamindars had evacuated from the out-lying *cutcheries*,[22] though no serious riot had taken place.[23] At Mowpore, where all the ryots had joined the combination there was not a single case of violence.[24] At Shahazadpore, there was a general panic and scare among the zamindars but the only serious outrage was committed upon the ryots of Sagtolla by the ryots of Nakalia to force the former to join the combination. This incident was a very complex one. A piece of land belonged to the Pakrasis, the zamindars of Sthal, who had let it on a three years' lease to two Muhammedans residing at Nakalia for a sum of two annas in excess of the old rent. The lessees proceeded to demand four annas beyond the old rent upon which Sagtollah broke with them and went over to the zamindars. After the agrarian movement had commenced the lessees posed as the champions of the ryots against the zamindar; but Sagtolla persistently refused to join the combination. As a result, the two lessees organised and planned an attack upon the village which had taken place when they themselves were absent and in course of which many houses were plundered.[25] This was an exceptional case where the league was misused for the purpose of intimidation. According to Nolan, this outrage was committed for two distinct contrary reasons. The lessees, who planned it, were excited against the cultivators because they would not consent to an enhancement and, the ryots who executed the design because they would not join the league.[26] At Jamirta there were several cases of plunder and according to the Tagores, the zamindars of the village, two women were ravished. Nolan, however, found on enquiry that the reports were very much exagerrated and the incidents were connected not with the agrarian movement but with an old private dispute between the Pakrasis and the Tagores. Nolan thus recorded in his diary of the 4th July, 1873: 'This is an instance of the way in which occurrences of an ordinary nature got up very likely by the Zamindars themselves are mis-represented as glaring outrages proving the anarchy of the country.'[27]

At Gopalpore village, a serious dispute concerning the proprietory right of the village had been going on for three years between Brojo Bhaduri and Ishan Ray (who was also the principal leader of the league) the lessees of five Hindu widows. The dispute however assumed a new character with the outbreak of the agrarian movement as one of the contestants was also a leader of the unionists. On the 3rd July, 1873, a clash between the rival parties, resulted in gun shot injuries to two ryots belonging to Ishan Ray's camp. This outrage was also not even remotely connected with the agrarian movement, but the landlords had taken advantage of the prevailing excitement to obtain men to fight in their long-standing private quarrels.[28] At Jamirta *char* there were two cases of looting of sheds of which one was proved false. The incident was a trivial one and was not connected with the rent dispute.[29] Though in some cases the news of the league caused old rivalries to be revived for the purposes of private interest, these cases were marginal to the agrarian question and the question of tenant right. But it must be granted that the news of the formation of the league did bring these old rivalries out into the open.

V

Basically therefore, the Pabna movement was a non-violent agrarian rising. Instances of violence were rare since the peasant leaders did not take the law into their own hands and actually advised the ryots to keep themselves within the bounds of law.[30] In fact in parts of Yusufshahi *parganah* where the influence of Ishan Chandra Ray was greatest and most direct, namely Ullahparah, Doulatpore and Shahazadpore, all in the Serajgunje Sub-division, the movement was accompanied with the least excesses and carried on in a legal manner. Whereas in the Sadar Sub-division of Pabna, where he was least known, and where his influence was hardly felt, there had been far more plundering and the rioting.[31]

Illegal violence, however, never formed an essential part of the agrarian union.[32] In many instances the rioting and plundering, which was supposed to have its origin in the bad feeling of the ryots, had been proved to have been instigated by some zamindars against neighbouring landlords, against whom they had a grudge; and then the movement was unfairly saddled with the whole responsibility of disturbances for which it was only partially responsible.[33] At the worst the breaches of peace by the *bona fide* tenants were rare, presenting a significant contrast to the outrages of the Zamindars. The cases of violent crime apart from occurring in conflicts between the followers of rival landlords were also due to the criminal class who took advantage of the excitement.[34] These bad characters were definitely responsible for violence in certain areas.[35] Even then the outrages committed by these bad characters fell short of the outrages habitually perpetrated by the zamindars of the district.[36]

The unionists thus strictly confined themselves within the bounds of law since their organisation according to E.W. Molony, the Commissioner of Rajshahi Division, was 'essentially defensive and dangerous only incidentally'.[37] Nolan felt that the ryots who commenced the movement combined to defend property and the interest they possessed in their holdings as occupancy ryots against present and future litigation.[38] It is also significant that in spite of the class feeling prevailing in the Yusufshahi *parganah*, during this period, the zamindars themselves were not molested, the roads and ferries were not beset and the zamindars' agents could freely come to the Magistrates to lodge complaints or to present their petitions.[39] In fact, Nolan, who extensively toured the countryside when the excitement was at its height, found that most of the disturbed villages (Sataintolla, Mowpore, Shahazadpore and Jamirta) though determined to resist the extortionate demands of the zamindars were at the same time maintaining perfect peace and order.[40] This fact clearly emphasised the legalistic character of the movement.[41] Thus, none was killed or seriously injured, and there was no significant damage to property, even when the miasma of class-hatred was spreading throughout the district.[42] The Pabna peasants, in fact, did not imitate the crimes of their landlords taking all the vengeance that makes a *jacquerie*, and their movement never showed any tendency to graviate towards the criminal courts.[43] This led Sir William Hunter to remark: 'They have [the rural population] fought with keen persistence but with a few ebullitions of violence the struggle between the landlords and tenants and are conducting before our eyes an agrarian revolution by the course of law'.[44] Indeed it was 'an agrarian revolution by due course of law'.

References

1. A district in Bangladesh, lying at the south-eastern corner of Rajshahi division. Originally it formed part of the great district of Rajshahi but became a separate district in 1832.
2. *See*: K.K. Sen Gupta, 'The Agrarian League of Pabna, 1873,' *Indian Economic and Social History Review*, vol. 7, no. 2, June 1970. pp. 253-69.
3. *See*: K.K. Sen Gupta, 'Agrarian disturbances in eastern and central Bengal in the late 19th century', *Indian Economic and Social History Review*, vol. 8, no. 2, June 1971. pp. 192-212.
4. This point has been elaborately discussed in my two articles mentioned above.
5. *See*: Sunil Sen, *Agrarian struggle in Bengal, 1946-47*, New Delhi, P.P.H., 1972. Sen describes in this book the *tebhaga* movement of the bargadars in Bengal on the eve of independence.
6. *Ibid*. p. 82. Sen writes: 'So long as the abolition of zamindary system is the main point at stake, the interests of all these categories of the peasantry are the same. Once this is achieved different categories of the peasantry are likely to be motivated by different aims and ambitions.'

7   Binay Chaudhuri, 'Agrarian economy and agrarian relations in Bengal, 1859-85', in N.K. Sinha, ed. *History of Bengal*, Calcutta, C.U., 1967. pp. 288-92.
    Suprokash Ray, *Bharater krishak vidroha o ganatantrik sangram*, Calcutta, Vidyodaya, 1966. Chapter on Serajgunge rebellion.
8   Chaudhuri, *op. cit.* p. 228. In describing the situation in Pabna in 1874-75, Chaudhuri writes: 'In Pabna itself the tension was far from resolved. The number of *overt hostilities*, involving loss of life and property decreased entirely because of strong police measures' (italics mine). In criminal law an overt act is an open act done in pursuance and manifestation of a criminal design. Quite obviously Chaudhuri blieves that the agrarian movement in Pabna was a violent manifestation of criminal design.
    Ray *op. cit.*
    Suprokash Ray also emphasises the lawlessness of the Pabna ryots.
9   *Hindoo Patriot*, July 14, 1873.
10 Eldest son of Maharshi Debendranath Tagore, the proprietor of the Tagore estate in Pabna.
11 *Bengal Judicial (Police) Proceedings* (hereafter BJPP), File 448, no. 37, July 1873.
12 *Ibid.*, no. 44, July 1873.
13 *Hindoo Patriot*, July 14, 1873.
14 Quoted in *Hindoo Patriot*, June 30, 1873.
15 P. Nolan. Letter to Gayler, no. 321, para 11.
    In BJPP. File 448, nos. 111-13, July 1873.
16 BJPP. File 448, nos. 78-9, August 18, 1873.
17 *Indian Daily News* as quoted in *Bengalee*, July 19, 1873.
    Bengalee, August 9, 1873.
    The Spectator as quoted in *Bengalee*, September 27, 1873.
    Friend of India, July 17, 1873, *and* July 24, 1873.
    Englishman, July 5, 1873, *and* July 12, 1873.
    Pioneer, July 8, 1873, *and* July 15, 1873.
    Indian Mirror as quoted in *Pioneer*, July 10, 1873.
    Indian Observer, July 12, 1873.
    Compbell. Letter to Argyll, dated July 8, 1873. *In:*
    Argyll papers, item 8 (N.A.I. microfilms, reel 316).
18 BJPP. File 448, nos. 111-13, July, 1873.
19 *Ibid.*
20 *Ibid.*, nos. 78-9, August 1873.
21 *Ibid.*, nos. 111-13, July 1873.
22 A zamindar's office.
23 *Op. cit.*, no. 112, July 1873.
24 Nolan's diary, dt. July 8, 1873. in: BJPP. File 448.
25 *Ibid.*, no. 112, July 1873.
26 *Ibid.*
27 *Ibid.*
28 *Ibid.*
29 *Ibid.*, nos. 78-9, July 1873.
30 *Pioneer*, August 4, 1873.
31 *Ibid.*
32 *Pioneer*, July 29, 1873.
33 *Pioneer*, July 28, 1873.
34 *Friend of India*, July 24, 1873.
    Indian Daily News wrote: 'The disturbances were never of the essence of the movement but the acts of a number of professional clubmen and thieves joined

by the more foolish and ignorant villagers. They were almost entirely confined to the south of the Parasagur and Burral rivers which divide Pabna district into two equal halves. The genuine rent union originated in and still hardly exists out of the northern division. Where it prevails, it includes nearly all the villages which were recently been subjected to enhancement of rent or from which an enhancement has been demanded this year. The ryots in these parts are perfectly peaceful and show no signs of regret for the step they have taken. They are measuring their lands with the Collectors' standard pole and when this work is completed they profess to be prepared to deposit the rent which they acknowledge due to the Munsiff or to pay it to the zamindars if the latter are willing to accept it.' Quoted in *Bengalee*, July 19, 1873.

See also: C.E. Buckland. *Bengal Under the Lieutenant-Governors;* Vol. 1. Calcutta, S.K. Lahiri, 1901. p. 545.

35 Nolan's diary, BJPP. File 448, nos. 111-13, July 1873.
Bengalee, July 26, 1873.
Friend of India, July 17, 1873.
Pioneer, July 29, 1873.
Sadharani, Kartick 18, 1280 B.S. (November 2, 1873).
36 *Pioneer*, July 29, 1873.
37 *Op. cit.*, no. 40, July 1873.
38 P. Nolan. Letter to Taytor, dt. July 1, 1873, BJPP, File 448, nos. 111-13, July 1873.
39 BJPP. File. 448.
40 Nolan's diary, BJPP, File 448.
41 *Friend of India*, July 31, 1873, and August 14, 1873.
42 BJPP. File 448, nos. 78-9, August 1873.
43 *Pioneer*, July 8, 1873; *Friend of India*, July 24, 1873.
44 W.W. Hunter. *Statistical Account of Bengal*. Vol. 9. 1875. Preface.
The facts stated above clearly shows that Hunter was *not* 'over simplifying the situation' as stated by P. Sinha. *See*: P. Sinha, *Nineteenth century Bengal*. Calcutta, Firma K.L., 1965. p. 25.

13 Agrarian Disturbances In 19th Century Bengal

Kalyan Kumar Sengupta

THE DECADE which preceded the enactment of the Bengal Tenancy Act VIII of 1885 was an important period in the history of agrarian relations in Eastern and Central Bengal. It saw a perceptible change in the relations between the landlords and the tenants, a change which almost inevitably produced widespread agrarian conflicts in the region.

The forerunner of these disturbances was the agrarian conflict in the district of Pabna in 1873. It was a protest of the occupancy ryots of the district against the conscious and systematic attempts of the landlords to do away with the occupancy title granted to a large number of cultivators by the Rent Act X of 1859. This resistance of the Pabna peasantry had assumed in course of time, the character of an organised and legalistic agrarian upsurge under the aegis of a powerful agrarian league which controlled and directed the movement from its base at Serajgunje, the prosperous jute mart of Eastern Bengal.

The movement in Pabna though it did not succeed in ending landlord exploitation in the district, nevertheless greatly restricted the landlords' absolute power in estate management. By emphasising the basically unstable nature of landlord-tenant relationships the distrubances in Pabna inspired agrarian movements in other parts of Eastern and Central Bengal which soon took the character of a widespread peasant protest against the concept of high-landlordism.[1]

This paper seeks to establish a historical link between the Pabna revolt and the peasant disturbances in Dacca, Mymensingh, Tripura, Backergunje, Faridpore, Rajshahi and Bograh: to analyse the causes of these conflicts, to examine the methods of peasant resistance and to offer an explanation for the absence of agrarian tensions in the neighbouring districts of Rangpore, Noakhali and Chittagong.

I The Basic Causes of the Conflicts

According to some contemporary vernacular newspapers these conflicts in Eastern Bengal were caused, partly by the arrogant temper of the ryots themselves, partly by the conduct of the social reformers, partly by the Lieutenant-Governor of Bengal, George Campbell's pro-ryot policy, partly by the course of legislation, partly by the faulty legal system, partly by the intrigues of 'wicked men' and partly the increase of luxury among the people.[2] The Joint-Magistrate of Dacca, J.G. Charles in his report to the government in 1873, also mentioned certain specific causes of the conflicts.[3] According to him (a) the growing independence of the ryots, (which was caused by the increasing knowledge of their legal rights and marked increase of wealth, during the past few years, by supplying them with the means of fighting for their rights in the civil courts) and (b) the decline in the influence of the landlords (owing to a strict application of the criminal law) actually precipitated a crisis in the relations between the landlords and the tenants.

Apart from over-simplifying the complex problem of landlord-tenant relationship, these sources thus deliberately propagated the myth that the prosperity of the ryots of Eastern Bengal was an important factor which contributed to the growth of agrarian tensions in Eastern and Central Bengal. In fact, most of the local magistrates who were in charge of the disturbed districts in this period of unrest, maintained that the prosperity of the East Bengal ryots was one of the primary reasons which facilitated the rapid growth of agrarian leagues.[4] This generalization however did not correspond to reality. The majority of the cultivators of East Bengal, barring a few richer ryots (who were to be found in every village) generally lived from hand to mouth in the late nineteenth century. A large number of them were also involved in debts from which they found it hard to get out in their lifetime.[5] In fact the correct index of a ryot's economic position, was the extent of his holding in his possession. The statistics of the ryoti holdings compiled from the Road Cess returns by the government showed that in the districts of Dacca, Tripura and Faridpur about three-fourth of the ryoti holdings did not exceed five bighas of land, the money value of which was only Rs 61.8 as. with which a ryot not only maintained his family but also paid his rent.[6] An average ryot of East Bengal in the late 19th century was therefore not rich by any standards. His poverty, rather than his prosperity, indeed induced him to resist the extortions by the landlords.

The fundamental cause of the friction in East Bengal was the landlords' persistent refusal to recognise tenant right which even the law of the country partially accepted. The landlords had taken their stand on what Dr. Binoy Chowdhury has called the doctrine of high-landlordism.[7] This concept was, however, clearly, incompatible with the spirit of the Act X of 1859 which had recognised the concept of occupancy right. Not unnaturally, a large number of East Bengal landlords made deliberate attempts during 1837-85 to destroy this newly acquired right of the peasantry. The contemporary district officers, the leading members of the Bench as well as the influential vernacular newspapers of the time fully corroborated this fact. According to a district officer who knew both Bengal and Behar, all proprietors and tenure-holders wished to see the existing law changed since they desired two things, the limitation or destruction of occupancy rights and increased facilities for enhancing rents.[8] In Chittagong Division according to the Commissioner, most landlords during this period were taking precautions against allowing their ryots to obtain occupancy rights.[9] A petition from the ryots of Attia Sub-Division of the Mymensingh District alleged that the landlords were busy sending their *lathiyals* and dependents from village to village to take leases for limited period from the ryots.[10] In Parganah Sherpore situated in the Jamalpore Sub-Division of the district of Mymensingh there was a general tendency on the part of the landlords to take *kabuliyats* for limited periods in order to prevent the accrual of occupancy.[11] In Dacca, according to a District Officer, as long as the ryots paid their rents their tenancies were not interfered with unless the landlord was anxious to prevent their acquiring a right of occupancy.[12] In Faridpur, in the years which preceded the enactment of the Tenancy Act of 1885, the landlords had issued hundreds of temporary leases for purposes of preventing the acquisition of rights of occupancy under the new law.[13] In Madaripur Sub-Division of this district in particular, the landlords did not recognise the occupancy right of their peasants and persistently refused to give them written leases.[14] The Sub-Divisional Officer, Sirajgunge, Peter Nolan believed that occupancy rights were being very rapidly extinguished in Eastern Bengal.[15] This was also the considered opinion of Justice O'Kinealy, a member of the Rent Law Commission (1879).[16] A leading contemporary vernacular journal *Sadharani* wrote in 1875 that the East Bengal landlords were continually seeking means of preventing their tenantry from acquiring occupancy rights.[17] The leading landlords, too, openly expressed their feelings against the concept of occupancy right. The British Indian Association, the official forum of the Bengal landlords, declared in its report for 1878 that the provisions of the Rent Law of 1859, concerning the occupancy rights being opposed to the rights of the zamindars were highly 'objectionable'.[18] A prominent Bengal zamindar of the time, Joykrishna Mukherjee of Uttarpara in a letter addressed to the *Friend of India*, expressed his views against the concept of occupancy right. He wrote; 'The law and the courts have vested mere squatters on the land with rights of occupancy ...The most meagre evidence adduced by the ryots to support a claim for right of occupancy...has been held sufficient to prove their case'.[19]

One of the principal aims of high-landlordism in Eastern and Central Bengal in between the two Rent Acts of 1859 and 1885 was therefore, the destruction of the rights of occupancy of a large number of cultivators. The ruthlessness with which some of the East Bengal landlords sought to fulfil this objective brought about a sharp change in the relations between the landlords and tenants, and planted the seeds of mutual discord and animosity which directly led to combined peasant resistance in many East Bengal districts.

Since the doctrine of high-landlordism also assumed the inherent right of the landlords as the sole proprietors of the land so enhance the ryots' rents, the enhancement of rent became almost a universal problem throughout East Bengal in the period under review. The problem had become particularly acute in Munshigunje Sub-Division[20] and Utrashpur Estate[21] in the district of Dacca. In the rest of the district during 1876-85, the landlords wanting to participate in what they considered the increased value of the produce of the land persistently demanded enhanced rents and illegal cesses.[22] Consequently, the civil courts in Dacca became flooded with rent suits.[23] In the district of Mymensingh, the rent problem had become particularly acute in Attea,[24] Pakhuriah,[25] Parganah Mymensingh,[26] Kheliajori[27], Hussainshahi,[28] Naraindhar,[29] Kagmari,[30] Atharabari,[31] Tangail and Jamalpur,[32] and Hussainpore and Alapsingh.[33] The enhancement of rent by the zamindars also created agrarian tensions in the district of Faridpore particularly in Madaripur Sub-Division[34] and in the large estates of Mr David of Dacca,[35] Rani Rangini Chowdhury of Narail[36] and Raja Shyama Sankar Chowdhury of Teota.[37]

In Backergunje, too, the absentee landlords always looked for opportunities to enhance the rents of their ryots and did not as a rule display any positive feeling of goodwill for their tenantry.[38] In areas like Bamna,[39] Shingkhali, and Ulania[40] and Dakhin Shabazpur[41] the enhancement of rent by the landlords caused frictions between them and their tenants which considerably strained the relations between the two classes. In fact since 1880-85, the Backergunje landlords instituted a large number of enhancement suits against their ryots.[42] This only helped to widen the gulf which separated the two classes. The problem was also very much acute during 1875-85 practically throughout Tripura where the landlords in addition to enhanced rent generally demanded illegal cesses of various sorts.[43] In the district of Bograh in Central Bengal, the enhancement problem was particularly acute in the estates which were leased out to the new *Patnidars* who in order to recoup themselves for the high premium they had paid demanded rents at exorbitant rates. [44] In this particular district as well as in the neighbouring district of Rajshahi, the enhancement problem baffled solution since 1881 when there was a marked tendency on the part of the landlords to extort from the ryots as much as they could before the proposed Rent Act came into operation.[45] Consequently there was a spate of rent suits in these two districts.[46]

Thus we see that the demands for rents at exorbitant rates was one of the basic causes of friction between the landlords and the tenants in most districts of Eastern and Central Bengal in the decade preceding the enactment of the Bengal Tenancy Act of 1885. The provisions of the Rent Act X of 1859 which conferred occupancy title on all cultivators of 12 years' standing also considerably restricted the landlords' powers to raise the rents of the occupancy ryots. Consequently with a few exceptions, the enhancement of rent of the occupancy ryots in Eastern and Central Bengal was part of a deliberate policy of the landlords to annihilate the occupancy rights which recognised the tenants' right to pay rents at fair rate.

The doctrine of high-landlordism also assumed the landlords complete freedom in the management of their estates. Naturally the zamindars of Eastern and Central Bengal who practised this doctrine did not generally keep themselves within the bounds of the existing tenant law which did not allow them such unrestricted freedom. Consequently in most districts of Eastern and Central Bengal, the adoption of various extra legal methods by the majority of the landlords for the enforcement of their claims not only strained their relations with the tenantry but also planted the seeds of widespread agrarian discontent. Thus in the district of Mymensingh the landlords were in the habit of levying cesses in excess of the road cess[47] (imposed in 1871). There was also a general tendency on the part of the landlords to credit the current collections to the old arrears of rent.[48] Apart from this, certain landlords of Madaripur and Backergunje persistently refused to give written leases and receipts to their tenantry even after obtaining the rent due,[49] while others demanded *kabuliyats* in which the ryots were asked to incorporate the illegal cesses.[50] Certain landlords of Dacca, moreover, in a bid to weaken the morale of the ryots sought to lure the leading tenants by offering them leases on very easy terms. The plan of operations was simple: when a village had gone on strike, the landlords used to single out a few of the leading ryots and win them over to his side with a measuring pole greater than that used in the village or he threw in a few *bighas* or *hoojoori* or some other fancy name. These men then went to the court ready to swear anything against the men on strike.[51]

It is thus clearly evident that in almost all the districts of East Bengal where agrarian disturbances took place during the seventh and the eighth decades of the 19th century the landlords invariably sought to apply the doctrine of high-landlordism and challenged in consequence the newly acquired occupancy rights of the cultivators by illegally raising their rents and by applying various extra legal coercive methods for the enforcement of their demands. The nature of landlord extortion was thus practically the same everywhere in East Bengal.

The challenge of high-landlordism inevitably produced sharp tenant responses in various districts of Eastern and Central Bengal. The tenantry in these areas protested not only against one element of oppression namely illegal rents but against the doctrine of high-landlordism which rejected the very idea of tenant right. Thus in Eastern and Central Bengal, the struggle between the landlords and the tenants tended to assume the character of a conflict between the two mutually contradictory concepts of high-landlordism and tenant right.

II The Methods of Peasant Resistance in Eastern and Central Bengal

The occupancy ryots of Eastern and Central Bengal met the challenge of high-landlordism by forming agrarian combinations. Consequently the methods of peasant resistance in these areas tended to have a more or less uniform pattern, very much similar to those adopted by the Pabna ryots, in 1873. Moreover since the character of landlord exploitation was practically similar throughout Eastern and Central Bengal the combined resistance of the tenantry, represented not the ephemeral discontent of a particular local peasant group but a general protest against the concept of high-landlordism, notwithstanding the fact that these agrarian combinations had no common organisational base.

During the years 1870-85 agrarian combinations thus sprang up in different areas of Dacca, Mymensingh, Tripura, Backergunje, Faridpore, Bograh and Rajshahi; the regions where, as we have seen, the landlords were systematically enforcing the doctrine of high-landlordism.

In the district of Dacca, the tenantry, invariably resisted the high-rent demands by forming agrarian leagues.[52] As a matter of fact, there was a general inclination on the part of the ryots to decline any communications whatever with their landlords except through the medium of the civil courts,[53] a fact which unmistakably pointed to the uneasy relationship which existed between the two classes.

The symptoms of this growing ill feeling between the landlords and the tenants first manifested itself since 1870-71 in Munshigunje Sub-Division round an area of alluvial formation on the Meghna, an area which constituted about one-eighth of the Munshigunje *thanah*.[54] This region was mostly inhabited by the Muhammedan tenantry among whom the *Faraizies* had an extensive following.[55]

The localities to which this particular movement had extended were the recent alluvial formations: Satgon, Borogaon and Turkeer Char; the old alluvial formations: Jawar Bhuber Char and Jawar Gajaria, and the high mainland areas: Jawar Abdullahpur, Jawar Hyderabaj, Jawar Panchashar and Jawar Shirajbaj.[56] The agrarian leagues which came into existence in these areas had the support of about 10,000 to 15,000 ryots who generally offered passive resistance and on the whole the movement was marked by a respect for the law except where the landlords had been the first to employ force to coerce their ryots to submit to their terms.[57]

Gradually the movement of the tenantry spread to a wider area and by 1874 the disputes between the landlords and the tenants in the Utrashpur estate, formerly the property of the indigo planter J.P. Wise assumed a very serious character when the ryots of this estate combined against the new purchasers of the property.[58] In this particular estate the unionist ryots on many occasions forced some of the ryots to join the union against their will. This was possible because the popular feelings against the landlords were too strong.[59] Though the leaders of the league at first doggedly refused to come to terms with the zamindars, the Commissioner of the Dacca Division at last succeeded in settling the matters by arbitration.[60] Similar measures taken by the District Superintendent of Police prevented clashes between the landlords and the tenants in Munshigunje where also peasant combinations were very much active.[61] In the extensive estates of Kalinarayan Roy of Bhawal also agrarian combinations came into existence but the disputes were settled amicably though not without difficulty by the local government officials.[62]

Though no cases of aggravated land disputes were reported during the years 1876-85,[63] there was however no real concord in many estates. Consequently the Civil Courts became filled with rent suits.[64] Thus throughout this period there was hardly any abatement of the tensions in spite of the outward quiet and the local officials felt that the 'stillness might any moment be broken'.[65]

In Mymensingh, since 1873 the ryots were beginning to feel their own strength and were ready to repel force by force.[66] Thus in this district too, the tenantry protested not only against the enhancement of rent but also against the attempts of the landlords to destroy the occupancy rights of the cultivators. This became strikingly clear in 1873 when land riots broke out in the Mirzapur village in the Attea Sub-Division,[67] Parganah Pakhuria,[68] Parganah Mymensingh,[69] Kheliajori and Hussainshahi Parganah.[70] In none of these instances however the disputes were carried to the extremes.[71] In spite of the early dissolution of the Hussainshahi combination in 1875 the relations between the landlords and the tenants were far from cordial since the Kheliajori combination was still doggedly carrying on its passive resistance along with brisk litigation at the headquarters.[72] One positive effect of this ill feeling was the more frequent exchange of *pattahs* and *kabuliyats* which both the parties were required to produce in the civil courts in justification of their respective claims.[73] Notwithstanding these tensions the local government officials succeeded in settling some of the disputes out of court and the zamindars, expecting an act for the speedy realisation of arrears also remained quiet. Thus throughout the year 1877 there was an outward quiet, even though the ryots were not paying the rents.[74]

The enhancement question was however not permanently solved; it was merely postponed.[75] This became clear when new areas like Naraindhar,[76] Kagmari,[77] and Atharabari[78] in Parganah Hussainpore were affected by land disputes. In the Atharabari estates, the tenants formed a union to resist the demands of the landlord Mohini Chandra Roy and declined to give him any *kabuliyat*.[79] The agrarian league in Hussainpore Parganah tended to become violent in the beginning but later on resorted to passive resistance.[80]

As the year 1882 drew to a close, agrarian combinations were being formed everywhere in Mymensingh. These unions became particularly strong in the Parganahs Hussainpore, Mymensingh, Alapsingh and Kagmari.[81] Gradually the conflict spread to wider areas and by 1884, Tangail and Jamalpore sub-divisions were affected.[82] In these areas the combined tenantry refused to give written *kabuliyats* to their zamindars since they apprehended that the execution of such *kabuliyats* would result in the destruction of their occupancy rights.[83]

In Faridpore, the ryots by forming agrarian leagues, passively resisted throughout this period the demand for high rent, the attempts to destroy the occupancy rights and illegal coercion. In Madaripore where the ill-feeling between the two parties had appeared very acute since 1874, the agrarian combinations led by the *faraizis* steadfastly opposed the landlords who systematically tried to destroy the tenants' occupancy right by refusing to give them written leases.[84] In Parganah Dhuldi of this Sub-Division in particular, the landlords were not on good terms with the tenantry.[85] The former wanted the latter to cultivate indigo and to pay a cess called *bain khajna*, a fee upon every pot placed upon the fire for the purpose of manufacturing molasses. The ryots objected to both these demands. The zamindars also instituted a number of suits for arrears of rent and though no decided action had been taken on either side,[86] the relations between the two parties were marked by an utter lack of cordiality.[87]

The relations between the landlords and the tenants in other parts of the district were also full of tensions. On many occasions the servants and the agents of the leading zamindars, Mr David of Dacca, Rani Rangini Chowdhurani of Narail and Raja Shyamashankar Chowdhury of Teota fomented certain riot cases some of which ended in loss of life.[88] The ryots too, on many occasions turned violent and tried to meet force by force. The murder in 1875 of Purna Chandra Roy, a zamindar who demanded illegal cesses is an instance in point.[89]

In Backergunje the years between 1873 and 1879 were marked by widespread discontent of the Muhammedan tenantry as a result of which riots and affrays were taking place practically in all the estates. In this district the tenant protest was directed against the enhancement of rent, the imposition of *abwabs* and the attempts to destroy the occupancy right. Naturally agrarian combinations came into existence in all the estates where landlord oppressions were particularly glaring.[90] In fact the Lieutenant-Governor of Bengal, Sir Richard Temple, did not feel very happy as to the prospects of affairs in that deltaic region in spite of the reassuring reports sent by the local officials.[91] The events in Backergunje fully justified Sir Richard's apprehensions. In 1879 the ryots of the estates of Bamna and Singhkhali combined against their respective zamindars.[92] Agrarian combinations also became active in Mehdigunje in 1880 under the leadership of Noa Meah, the son of the *faraizi* Didoo Meah of Faridpore.[93] In 1881, the Ulania zamindars also came face to face with a powerful agrarian combination.[94] In 1884 the discontent spread to Dakhin Shahabazpur where the combined tenantry opposed the landlords who usually collected from the tenantry on account of the road cess, an amount which far exceeded the actual government demand and imposed in addition certain illegal cesses.[95]

In Tripura, the tenants were quick to take up the challenge of the landlords by forming agrarian leagues. Since they were capable of organising such combinations at the slightest notice, the landlords gradually found it more convenient to resort to the civil courts rather than to coercive measures.[96] But the spirit of combination to resist the landlords' demands even in the civil courts was spreading among the tenantry and gradually it meant active and passive resistance to the execution of decrees of the civil court as a result of which the landlords often hesistated to enforce the decrees obtained by them.[97]

In *thanah* Chaugalnaya, at first, these conflicts became particularly serious and threatened to disturb the peace of the entire region during 1872-3.[98] The original owner of the estate was the Raja of Hill-Tipperah who had given it out from time to time in a number of farming leases for short periods to the officers of his army who agreed to pay rents at exorbitant rates.[99] These farms were in some cases underlet at a still higher rental. Naturally the new lease holders demanded from the actual cultivators exorbitant rents which at once led to misunderstandings and to disturbances.[100] The ryots 'carried the war into the enemies' country' by combining to resist the farmers' demands.[101] Taking advantage of the absence of collection papers they entered into a league to pay no rents whatever and to attack and drive away the farmers and their collectors whenever they appeared on the scene.[102]

The unionists had a peculiar way of intimidating the minority into joining the union. If any ryot was bold enough to withstand the league he received a solemn warning. A bundle of straw shaped like a torch was placed in front of his house, an action which signified that if he continued to hold out his house would be burnt.[103] By this and other means a very large body of ryots had combined into a powerful union for the purpose of resisting the landlords in every way.

Gradually the movement spread throughout Chaugalnaya *Parganah* and areas like Khandul, *Julai* Chandernagore, Ruthnagore, Jugatpore, and *Julai* Gangapur became particularly affected by this resistance movement.[104] The revolt of the Chaugalnaya ryots encouraged the tenantry in other areas to combine against their landlords. In 1873, the ryots of Patoriah *Parganah*, an estate belonging to Raja Satyananda Ghoshal of Bhukailash in Kidderpore, whose family had brought waste lands in this region since the time of the *Dewani* administration in 1765,[105] had combined and stopped the payment of rent.[106] The movement gradually spread to Dihin Kangsoo and Gangamandal *Parganah*, the property of Raja Kamal Krishna where the ryots formed similar combinations.[107] In 1874, an agrarian league came into existence in *thanah* Thollah.[108] By 1875, the resistance movement spread to the northern part of the Brahmanbaria Sub-Division where the ryots formed a league and put up organised opposition to the landlord's demands.[109] Thus practically all Tripura was convulsed by agrarian disturbances during the period 1873-9 and by 1880-1 it appeared that in Tripura at least the zamindars were hardly able to hold their own against the ryots.[110]

In Bograh, the ryots, had become acquainted both with their right and with their strength and had learnt that they enjoyed the sympathy of the government. Thus they were growing less and less disposed to comply with the demands of their landlords.[111] This invariably led to the growth of the peasants' unions in the estates where the landlords appeared oppressive.

The flames of the Pabna revolt had hardly died down when smoke was rising in Bograh.[112] The estate of the Raja of Dighapatia was the first to become the scene of an acute conflict in 1873 when the ryots of Nowkhila *Parganah* who were praying for a reduction of rent for the past few years began to combine against the landlord.[113] Though during the years 1874-80 Bograh remained outwardly quiet the combinations of the ryots in different estates were fully active in preventing the landlords from demanding anything beyond what was legally due.[114] They were quick to resist the extortionate demands through their combinations in the estates of the Raja of Dighapatia and A.S. Chawdhuri.[115] In *Parganah* Jaffarshahi the relations were particularly unsatisfactory in the estates of Kali Kishore Ray Chawdhury and Bisweswari Devi.[116]

In Rajshahi too, there was a general tendency on the part of the ryots to combine against their landlords in the same way as the ryots of Pabna did.[117] In fact throughout the year 1873 when Pabna was convulsed by serious agrarian disturbances, Rajshahi remained in a state of tension.[118] Yet barring a serious outrage committed by the ryots of Kumashambhir,[119] no serious land riots had taken place in the district though it appeared that the feeling which began to show itself in 1873 had not altogether died out.[120] The district remained more or less quiet during the next few years but since 1881 the relations between the two classes once again deteriorated because the landlords from this time onwards began to serve enhancement notices in large numbers.[121] This, not unnaturally caused widespread discontent amongst the tenantry which found expression in the combined movement launched by them against their landlords in Meercha Deear [122] as well as in the estates of the indigo planters, M/s. Robert Watson Company and Raja of Dhubulhati.[123]

III Why Certain Districts in Eastern and Central Bengal Remained Free from Agrarian Disturbances

Chittagong, Noakhali and Rangpore, however, saw little of these agrarian disturbances even during this period of acute tensions in the rest of Eastern and Central Bengal. This was principally owing to the peculiar system of land control prevailing in these areas. In Chittagong and Noakhali the interest in land and wealth were more evenly distributed among the people than in any other districts of lower Bengal.[124] Chittagong in particular, was a land of prosperous middlemen who possessed an influence often not wielded by the proprietors.[125] The landlords of Chittagong were mostly in debt and therefore were incapable of exerting an influence either for good or evil.[126] They were, with few exceptions, the same class of men who would be tenants in other districts because in this district the settlement was made with the tenants and consequently there were hardly any proprietors of a village or whole *parganah* as elsewhere.[127] The owner of an estate in this district was most frequently a man who owned a multitude of small interests in a number of others estates.[128] Thus there was no distinct class of zamindars as compared with the tenants. All were tenants quite as much as Zamindars.[129] Besides, the landlords had parted with most of their rights by granting perpetual leases to a very large extent and the rents of such tenants were always regularly paid.[130] The persons who obtained perpetual leases might have some difficulties with his ryots but he in his turn also granted perpetual leases and often possessed sufficient local influence to enforce his claims.[131]

In Noakhali too, the zamindars seldom dealt directly with the tenantry but sublet to *talookders* who again sub-let to inferior tenants.[132] The very occupancy ryots under the title *howlader* claimed where it suited him to be a middleman and as a matter of fact had tenants of various degrees paying rents to him. The result of this arrangement was that each tenant was but little inferior in position and wealth to the man immediately above him and no bitter class feeling existed among them.[133] In the district of Rangpore however, the operation of a totally different phenomenon prevented any clashes between the landlords and the tenants. In this district land being at a premium the landlords were entirely at the mercy of the tenants and that there was no need therefore for the tenants to combine against the landlords because in case of any oppression, they could always move to the next landlord's estates where they were always welcome.[134]

IV Conclusions

Thus we see that in the districts where the landlords did not or could not apply the doctrine of high-landlordism, the ryots were not inclined to combine against the former. But in the districts where the landlords had taken their stand on this doctrine, the tenantry invariably put up combined resistance against the zamindars.

In all the areas where the struggle for the redefinition of the respective rights of the landlords and the tenants was going on the nature of landlord oppression was practically the same. Like the Pabna landlords the zamindars of Eastern and Central Bengal also sought to destroy the occupancy rights, raised the rents, demanded illegal cesses and applied illegal coercive measures to enforce their demands. This led the *Pioneer's* special correspondent to remark: 'It is not only in Pabna where the ryots have found courage to protest that the cultivating classes require to be protected from the rapacity of the landlords. All Bengal is suffering from the political disease which the government has undertaken to cure in Serajgunje'.[135]

The methods of peasant resistance in all these areas also bore a striking resemblance to those adopted by the Pabna ryots. In fact, according to the *Bengalee*[136] messengers from Pabna actually went to Dacca and Tripura in 1873 where their example was immediately followed. Consequently, in the districts where agrarian combinations came into being, the ryots following in the footsteps of the Pabna ryots refused to give *kabuliyats* to the landlords, resisted the imposition of illegal cesses and prevented the zamindars from consolidating the rents and the *abwabs* and refused to pay the enhanced rents.

The Pabna episode was therefore not an event *per se*; rather it was the symptom of a general ill-feeling existing between the landlords and the tenants in serveral districts of which Pabna was one. In other words the revolt of Pabna was not a fortuitous occurrence. Properly considered, that conflict had reference to the respective rights of the landlords and the tenants. In the rest of Eastern and Central Bengal too, the agrarian conflicts were caused by the landlords' attempts to superimpose the concept of high-landlordism on the concept of tenant right. Consequently, the movement which started in Pabna unmistakably took the character of an extensive protest of the occupaney ryots against the concept of high-landlordism practically throughout Eastern and Central Bengal in the decade which followed the Pabna uprising.

References

1   For details see my article 'The Agrarian League of Pabna'. *Indian Economic & Social History Review*, Vol. VII, No. 2, June, 1970, pp. 153-269.
2   *Hindu Hitaishini*, May 15, 1875, *Sadharani*, February 28, 1875, *Bharat Sanskarak*, March 15, *Dacca Prakash*, Feb. 28, 1875 (R.N.P.).
3   Misc. Colln. 14, Nos. 26-7, paras 20/21, B.L.R.P., Jan., 1874.
4   Divisional Report, Rajshahi, 1867-8, B.G.P., Aug., 1868, para 6, *ibid* for Dacca, 1873-4, para 26, B.G.P., Nov., 1874, *ibid*, 1874-5, para 34, B.G.P., Sept., 1875, *ibid*, 1875-6, para 34, B.G.P., Aug., 1876, *ibid*, 1876-7, B.G.P., Sept., 1877, *ibid*, 1877-8, paras 18,20,22,24, B.G.P., Sept., 1878, *ibid*, 1880-1, para 26, B.G.P., Aug., 1881.
5   *Statistical Reporter*, June, 1876, p. 5, P.C. Roy. *Rent Question In Bengal*, Calcutta 1881, pp. 246-52.
6   *Ibid*.
7   B. Chowdhury, in N.K. Sinha (ed.) *History of Bengal*, Calcutta 1967, pp. 268-9.

8. *Bengal Government Report* on the Tenancy Bill, Vol. I, p. 11, Calcutta, 1883.
9. Despatch No. 6, dt. 21st March, 1882, Viceroy to the Secy. of State, Para 54, Quoted by P.C. Roy *op. cit.*, pp. 124-37.
10. *Ibid.*
11. Divisional Report, Dacca for 1884-5, File 31/3/4, B.G.P., December, 1885.
12. Despatch No. 6, dt. 21st March, 1882, Viceroy to the Secretary of State, Para 54. *loc. cit.*
13. *Ibid.*
14. Divisional Report, Dacca for 1875-6, File 129/1/2, B.G.P., Sept., 1876.
15. Despatch No. 6, dt. 21st March, 1882, *loc. cit.*
16. *Ibid.*
17. *Sadharani, Aug. 22,1875.*
18. The Progs. of the British Indian Association's 27th Annual General Meeting, dt. 7th June, 1879, the Report for 1878.
19. Joykrishna Mukherjee's letter entitled 'Ryots & Zamindars', cf. *Friend of India* Oct. 16, 1873.
20. Misc. colln. 14, Nos. 26/27, B.L.R.P., Jan., 1874, N. K. Sinha (ed.) *op. cit.*, p. 288.
21. Divisional Report, Dacca for 1874-5. File 13/11/12, para 27, B.G.P., Aug., 1875, N.K. Sinha (ed.) *op. cit.*, p. 288.
22. *Ibid* for 1876-7, File 153-1-4, B.G.P., Sept., 1877.
23. *Ibid.*
24. *Ibid* for 1873-4., File 5/32/33, B.G.P., Nov., 1874.
25. *Ibid.*
26. *Ibid.*
27. *Ibid* for 1874-5, File 13/112, B.G.P., Sept., 1875.
28. *Ibid.*
29. *Ibid* for 1878-9, File 87/5/6, B.G.P., Nov., 1879.
30. *Ibid.*
31. *Ibid* for 1879-80, File 38/20/26, B.G.P., Aug., 1880.
32. *Ibid* for 1884-5, File 31/3/4, B.G.P., Dec., 1885.
33. *Ibid* for 1882-3, File 49/34, B.G.P. Nov., 1883.
34. *Ibid* for 1875-6, File 129/1/2. B.G.P., Sept., 1876.
35. *Ibid* for 1881-2, File 118/1/2, B.G.P., Oct., 1882.
36. *Ibid.*
37. *Ibid.*
38. *Ibid* for 1873-4, File 5/32/33, B.G.P., Nov., 1874, *ibid* for 1880-1, File 120/1/2, B.G.P., Sept., 1881.
39. *Ibid* for 1879-80, File 38/20/26, B.G.P., Aug., 1880.
40. *Ibid* for 1882-3, File 49/3/4/, B.G.P., Aug., 1883.
41. *Ibid* for 1884-5, File 31/3/4, B.G.P., Dec., 1885.
42. The number of enhancement suits instituted in Backergunje during 1880-5: 1880-1—59; 1881-2—53; 1883-4—109; 1884-5—155.
    SOURCE—Divisional Reports, Dacca for these years.
43. Divisional Report, Chittagong for 1874-5, File 128/1, B.G.P., Aug., 1875.
44. Divisional Report, Rajshahi, for the years 1872-3, File 1/72/75, B.G.P., Oct., 1873, Para 122.
45. Cf. Divisional Report, Rajshahi for the years 1880-1, 1881-2, 1882-3, 1883-4.

46 Rent suits instituted 1880-84:

	In Rajshahi,		In Bograh
1880	— 1179	1880	— 476
1881	— 1335	1881	— 694
1882	— 1366	1882	— 913
1883	— 1978	1883	— 860
1884	— 1853	1884	— 1083

47 Divisional Report, Dacca for 1875-6, File 129/1/2, B.G.P., Sept., 1876.
48 *Ibid* for 1884-5, File 31/3/4, B.G.P., Dec., 1885.
49 *Ibid* for 1879-80, File 38/20/26, B.G.P., Aug., 1880. *Ibid* for 1885-6, File 21/7/8, B.G.P. Oct., 1886.
50 *Ibid* for 1874-5, File 13/11/12, B.G.P., Sept., 1875. *Ibid* for 1882-3, File 49/3/4, B.G.P., Nov., 1833.
51 *Ibid* for 1872-3, File 1/52-54, B.G.P., Sept., 1873.
52 *Ibid* for 1873-4, File 5/32/33, B.G.P., Nov., 1874.
53 *Ibid.*
54 Misc. Colln. 14, Nos. 26/27, B.L.R.P., Jan., 1874, N.K. Sinha (ed.) *op. cit.*, p. 288.
55 *Ibid.*
56 *Ibid.*, Appendix B, *Hindu Hitaishini*, Aug. 16, 1873 (R.N.P.).
57 *Ibid.*, para 37.
58 Divisional Report, Dacca for 1874-5, File 13/11/12, para 27, B.G.P., 1875, N.K. Sinha (ed.) *op. cit.*, p. 288.
59 *Ibid.*
60 *Ibid.*, paras 28-9.
61 *Ibid.*, para 30
62 *Ibid.*, *Friend of India*, Aug. 14, 1873, *Amrita Bazar Patrika* quoted in *Friend of India*, Aug. 28, 1873, *Hindoo Patriot*, Sept. 22, 1873.
63 Cf. Divisional Reports of Dacca for these years.
64 Divisional Report, Dacca, 1876-7, File 153/1-4, B.G.P., Sept. 1877.
65 *Ibid.*
66 Divisional Report, Dacca, 1873-4, File 5/32/33, B.G.P., Nov. 1874.
67 *Ibid.*
68 *Ibid.*
69 *Ibid.*
70 Divisional Report, Dacca, 1874-5, File 13/112, B.G.P., Sept., 1875.
71 *Ibid.*
72 *Ibid* for 1875-6, *loc. cit.*
73 *Ibid* for 1876-7, *loc.* cit.
74 *Ibid* for 1877-8, File 110/1/11, B.G.P., Sept., 1878.
75 Resolution of the Lt. Governor, dt. 21st Sept., 1877, File 153/5, B.G.P., Sept., 1877-9, para 27.
76 Divisional Report, Dacca, 1878-9, File 87/5/6, B.G.P., Nov. 1879.
77 *Ibid.*
78 *Ibid* for 1879-80, File 38/20/26, B.G.P., Aug., 1880.
79 *Ibid.*
80 *Ibid* for 1880-1, File 120/1/2, B.G.P., Aug., 1881.
81 *Ibid* for 1882-3, File 49/3/4, B.G.P., Nov., 1883.
82 *Ibid.* for 1884-5, File 31/3/4, B.G.P., Dec., 1885.
83 *Ibid.*

84 *Ibid* for 1875-6, File 129/1/2, B.G.P., Sept., 1876, Barisal *Bartabaha*, Aug., 26, 1874, (R.N.P.).
85 *Ibid* for 1874-5, File 13/1/1/12, B.G.P., Sept. 1875, para 32.
86 *Ibid*.
87 *Ibid* for 1875-6, File 129/1/2, B.G.P., Sept., 1876.
88 *Ibid* for 1881-2, File 118/1/2, B.G.P., 1882.
89 *Ibid* for 1875-6, *loc. cit.*
90 *Hita Sadhini* (Barisal), Aug. 11, 1874, (R.N.P.).
91 Resolution of the Lt. Governor on the Dacca Report for 1874-5, File 132/2, B.G.P., Sept., 1875, Para 11.
92 Divisional Report, Dacca for 1879-80, File 38/20/26, B.G.P., Aug., 1880.
93 *Ibid* for 1880-1, File 120/1/2, B.G.P., Aug., 1881.
94 *Ibid* for 1882-3, File 49/3/4, B.G.P., Aug., 1883.
95 *Ibid* for 1884-5, File 31/3-4, B.G.P., Dec., 1885.
96 Divisional Report, Chittagong, 1881-2, File 113/1/2, B.G.P., Oct., 1882.
97 *Ibid*.
98 Mangies, Commissioner, Chittagong to Bengal, dt. 2nd Jan., 1875, File 56/11/12, B.J.P.P., April, 1875.
99 *Ibid*.
100 *Ibid*.
101 *Ibid*.
102 *Ibid*.
103 The Magistrate, Mr N.S. Alexander's, Report dt. the 10th Dec., 1874, *ibid*.
104 *Ibid*. These villages were possibly inhabited by the Muslim weavers since the term *Julai* roughly corresponds to the Bengali word *Jolah* which means a muslim weaver.
105 W.K. Firminger (ed.), *Letter Copy Book of the Resident at the Durbar of Murshidabad on Gokul Ghoshal's Lease of Waste Lands*. I am grateful to Dr Barun De for this reference.
106 *Hindoo Hitaishini*, Aug., 16, 1873 (R.N.P.), *Friend of India*, Aug. 14. 1873.
107 *Ibid*.
108 Divisional Report, Chittagong, 1874-5, File 128/1, B.G.P., Aug., 1875.
109 *Ibid*., Dacca for 1875-6, File 129/2/2, B.G.P., Sept., 1876.
110 *Ibid*., Chittagong for 1880-1, File 34/4/5, B.G.P., Aug., 1881, para 84.
111 District Report Bograh, 1872-3, dt. 30th June, 1873, cf. Divisional Report Rajshahi, 1872-3, File 1/72/75, B.G.P., Oct., 1873.
112 Mis. colln. 14, No. I, B.R.L.P., Jan., 1874, *Friend of India*. Aug. 28, 1873. *The Englishman*, Sept. 2, 1873.
113 *Gram Barṭa Prakashika*, Sept., 13, 1873 (R.N.P.).
114 Cf. Divisional Reports, Rajshahi for these years.
115 *Ibid* for 1881-2, File 124/1/2, B.G.P., Oct., 1882.
116 *Ibid*.
117 *Educational Gazette*, Nov. 7 and 14, 1873, *Samachar Sudhabarshan*, Dec. 13, 1873 (R.N.P.).
118 Police File 448, No. 8. B.J.P.P., July, 1873.
119 *Ibid*.
120 *Ibid*.
121 *Ibid*.
122 Divisional Report, Rajshahi, 1882-3, File 18/2/26, B.G.P., Oct., 1883.
123 *Ibid* for 1884-5, File 22/1, B.G.P., Jan., 1886.
124 *Ibid* for Chittagong, 1875-6, para 27, File 26/1/2, B.G.P., Sept., 1876.

125 *Ibid.*
126 *Ibid* for 1876-7, para 155, File 1561/1, B.G.P., Oct., 1877.
127 *Ibid* for 1880-1, para 83, File 34/4/5, B.G.P., Aug., 1881.
128 *Ibid.*
129 *Ibid.*
130 *Ibid* for 1875-6, para 138, File 126/1/2, B.G.P., Sept., 1876, N.K. Sinha (ed.) *op. cit.*, pp., 310-314.
131 *Ibid.*
132 *Ibid* for 1881-2, File 113/1/2, para 136, B.G.P., Oct., 1882, N.K. Sinha (ed.) *op. cit.*, p. 312.
133 *Ibid.*
134 Divisional Report, Rajshahi, 1880-1, para $38\frac{1}{2}$, File 67/3, B.G.P., July, 1881.
135 The *Pioneer*, July, 1873.
136 The *Bengalee*, Sept. 27, 1873.

Abbreviations

B.G.P.	— Bengal General Proceedings	(West Bengal State Archieves)
B.L.R.P.	— Bengal Land Revenue Proceedings	(-Do-)
B.J.P.P.	— Bengal Judicial Police Proceedings	(-Do-)
R.N.P.	— Report on Native Press	(-Do-)

PART III
Agrarian Struggles In The Early 20th Century

Introduction

(1)

THE TWO SELECTIONS from Sukhbir Choudhary's *Peasants and Workers Movement in India* are valuable for as they describe a new category of struggles which emerged in the countryside during the first two and a half decades of the twentieth century.

The period during which the peasant struggles took a qualitatively new turn saw a number of tumultuous national and international developments. During this phase the nationalist movement gathered momentum in India, enveloping a larger and larger strata of society. Broadly, the period could be divided into three major phases in the context of Indian society; (a) the period from 1901 upto 1913; (b) from 1914–18 during which Indian society was drawn into World War I by the British, and (c) the period from 1919 to 1923, wherein Indian society and polity became entangled in the first phase of post-world war readjustments. This came as a consequence of the weakening of British Imperialism (though victorious in war), and the emergence of the new Socialist state—a result of the great October Socialist Revolution which took place in Czarist Russia. The October Revolution inaugurated a new epoch in the history of mankind, particularly generating a new type of awakening and hope in the people of the colonial and semi-colonial countries.

The first decade of the twentieth century began in India with the rapid development of objective and subjective situations for various classes. In this period the nationalist movement gathered momentum, enveloping a wide strata of the population including the peasantry.

The terrible famines of the last decade of the 19th century described vividly in various publications, particularly in the work of Bhatia, had a shattering effect on the life of the peasantry and also on the urban population in the context of the new measures adopted by the British.

The growing unemployment among educated middle classes and urban youth, the realization that Western white colonialists are not invincible, was demonstrated by Japan's defeat of Russia, and the impact of the first powerful insurrectionary upheaval in Czarist Russia in 1905 generated among the colonial bourgeois and the middle classes a new courage to offer resistance to the imperialist masters. In India, the strategy adopted by the British Rulers to use communalism to divide Hindu and Muslim upper and middle strata by adopting the principle of communal electorate and the partition of Bengal, generated a new level of indignation and awareness. The policy of concession, counterpoise and coercion adopted by the British, as revealed in the technique of giving pacificatory constitutional reforms (Morley-Minto Reforms), partition and withdrawal of partition of Bengal, and the ruthless policy of coercion as revealed in repression of Swadeshi, Boycott, Anti-partition and other movements launched by the militant wing of Indian National Congress, pushed the Indian people into a new phase of their political development.

During the second decade the Indian people were enmeshed in the First World War. While involvement in the war assisted the growth of certain industries and strengthened a section of the Indian capitalist class, the British put as many obstacles as possible in the path of this development. The war had a damaging effect on the overall economy and the living conditions of the masses of the Indian people. The ruthless policies adopted by the British against anti-war movements, aggravated the situation in the country. The working people in urban and rural areas suffered heavily as a consequence of the effects of the war on the Indian economy and society. The war also exposed the Indian masses to larger international politico-economic developments and generated a vague but new awakening about larger issues, national and international. It also evoked hopes among people that a new epoch may emerge, a new political regime may be installed which would redeem their grievances and usher in a new phase in their existence. Under the impact of wars and revolutions taking place on a global scale, a revolution of rising expectations and hope for improvement took root among various strata and they began to assert themselves more prominently. The Nationalist forces launched some movements for Constitutional Reforms, Responsible Government and Home Rule and agitated for the same, carrying the message to rural areas in the form of opposition to recruitment for the war and the collection of war funds. The anti-British sentiment deepened, and reached out to more and more layers of the peasantry, who now saw the oppression and exploitation by their own local landlords, zamindars and moneylenders as rooted in the British raj and its policies to support and buttress local exploitation. A social climate for an all-India anti-Imperialist nationalist militant struggle to overthrow British rule was created during this period which burst out on a gigantic scale during the third phase of this period—from 1918 to 1923.

The period from 1918 to 1923, has been crucial from many points of view. The post-war disillusionment among various strata of Indian society, the strategy of coercion, concession and counterpoise adopted by the British, the explosive situation created by economic aftermath of the World War I, the powerful impact of the revolutionary movements, successful or unsuccessful in various countries, the disillusionment with hypocritic democratic pretentions of the Imperialist nations, the immense appeal of the Bolshevik Revolution and heroic and successful resistance against imperialist intervention to subvert Soviet Russia, and the widespread discontent that enveloped various strata of Indian society, exploded into some of the most powerful struggles of workers, peasants and urban population in India, giving a new tone to Indian politics. It manifested itself in the active intervention of the masses in political struggles.

On a national scale, the call given by the Nationalist leaders for struggles against Jallianwallah Bagh massacre, Anti-Rowlatt Act agitation, boycotts, hartals, strikes, culminating into non-cooperation and civil disobedience movements brought a new awakening among and participation by masses, lifting the spontaneous partial and local struggles into wider, conscious, nationalist, anti-imperialist struggles.

During this period the Indian National Congress emerged as a mass organization spreading its influence among the masses. Mahatma Gandhi emerged as the astute and the most farsighted leader of the Indian bourgeoisie. He experimented with various approaches to both politicize and also to regulate the mass and class movements. He unleashed various movements, withdrew them when he got frightened by the possibilities of these unleashed forces getting out of control and leaping into mighty revolutionary class struggles affecting both the imperialist masters and the local exploiters. Mahatma Gandhi also elaborated during this period astute organizational devices to prepare a chain of leaders to organize workers and peasants in a manner which would harness their energy and direct these energies into particular types of movements that would be reformist, economic, non-violent and based on the principle of class collaboration, which was founded upon a theory of the exploiting classes functioning as 'trustees' of the people. However, it should be recognized that conscious unleashing of movements by Gandhi and the Indian National Congress did raise the consciousness of the peasants and workers and they could view their problems in a wider nationalist perspective.

The withdrawal of the movement by Mahatma Gandhi after the Chaurichaura incident, created tremendous discontent among the intelligentsia, as well as among sections of peasants and the working class, leading to the emergence of various political currents, which now actively and consciously evolved various political platforms and modes of struggles. This phenomenon which initiated the emergence of various political parties, class organizations and tendencies within the Indian National Congress, become the major theatre of Indian history during the subsequent period, described in Part IV onwards.

(2)

The first selection 'Early Struggles—1905-18' provides a picture of the peasant struggles not described so far by scholars in a comprehensive manner. It covers the following categories of struggles.

1 Peasants opposition to subscribe to the war fund or to be recruited for war as a response to Home Rule Agitation launched by Tilak and Annie Besant and also by Liakat Husain through his agitation against the Government's move to ask people to join the Bengal Regiment. Liakat Husain was arrested and prosecuted under rule 23 of the Defence of India (Consolidation) Rules 1915.

This movement took many forms; desertion of villages by the lower strata to avoid forcible recruitment; desertion from training camps by those who were already recruited; withdrawal of applications or non-appearance of youths at war recruitment centres; agitation in the form of appeals, protests against internment of Mrs Annie Besant, Messrs. Arundale and Wadia; refusal to contribute to war loans; subscribing to the funds of Home Rule Leagues or joining them.

This aspect highlighted by Sukhbir Choudhary requires closer and more detailed inquiries for getting a rounded picture of the peasant struggles during the war period. It also reveals how nationalist leaders started approaching the rural population to involve them in larger, political, anti-British struggles.

2 Sukhbir Choudhary, also describes the major peasant struggles led by Mahatma Gandhi, who returned to India from South Africa. Initially he undertook to help the British war efforts by participating in a recruitment drive launched by the British. However, he subsequently groped for a strategy of struggles to pressurize the British to rectify certain wrongs. The author describes the Champaran struggle against the British Indigo Planters in Bihar and the Satyagraha struggles of the peasant proprietors—the rich and the poor in Gujarat against revenue collection carried on by the British administrators inspite of scarcity conditions prevailing in certain parts of that area. From now onwards, representatives of the bourgeoisie, and the pettie bourgeoisie, realized the necessity of approaching the peasantry, agitating among them, taking up specific issues for struggles, either to redress their grievances, build up an organization, training cadres to represent the various sections of the peasantry, adopting various techniques of struggles, and encouraging only certain methods while discouraging others. These struggles also reveal how a number of educated urban sons and daughters of the bourgeois, the landlords, and the professional and salaried classes, began going to the rural areas to agitate, to educate, and to organize movements to redress the grievances and also to harness their energies for larger national movements. It also reveals how the Indian National Congress acquired roots in the rural area, and deepened its base and gave active direction to the peasant struggles in a particular manner.

3 The struggles described in these selections also draw attention to certain important features of the emerging shape of the peasant struggles which deserve careful attention to grasp the dialectics of class struggles in rural India. These features can be enumerated as below:

(a) Mahatma Gandhi emerges as the towering strategist evolving various types of nationalist pressure movements involving workers, peasants and middle classes launched in the interests of the Indian bourgeoisie.

(b) He works out detailed techniques and forms of struggles, issues around which struggles maybe organized, with an organizational set up, necessary for elaborating, guiding and withdrawing the struggles.

(c) He clearly formulates and the Indian National Congress accepts as its policy the major premises on which the peasantry was to be organized for the nationalist movement.

(i) The principle of *Compensation* as a basis for transfer of ownership of land, (it included even lands acquired by fraud, oppression, coercion and disposed of in the distressed conditions of the peasants and further not cultivated by owners). Even owners who used the ownership title to appropriate the surplus value from tillers on the basis of ownership of land and other assets, were to be compensated.

(ii) The exploited or oppressed strata were to remain strictly within the bounds of non-violence, and to adopt only non-coercive pressure on the oppressing and exploiting proprietory groups to change their heart, and thereby to pursuade them to concede to the demands.

(iii) To organize specific sections of the peasantry around issues directly linked with British Rule. For instance issues like Land revenue, famine relief, certain categories of taxes, canal and salt taxes oppression by the bureaucratic apparatus of the British Rulers, or pressing for enacting certain types of Acts or for proper implementation of the Acts:

(iv) To avoid as far as possible struggles by exploited strata of the peasantry, like poor peasants comprised of tenants, sub-tenants, share croppers, landless labourers, and tribal poor, against native exploiting classes like landlords, zamindars, money-lenders, traders, and richer farmers. To avoid and oppose a revolutionary militant path of overthrowing Foreign Rule by evolving struggles of expoited strata which could become the basis of organs of new administration in a free India.

(3)

The second selection 'Post-war Awakening (1919-21)' is reproduced as it deals with the third phase of the crucial period embodied in this part.

During this period India becomes the theatre of the first nation-wide organized movement against Imperialism. It takes the form of protest against Rowlatt Acts, Jallianwallah Bagh massacre, and launching of non-cooperation, civil disobedience and Khilafat movements against constitutional reforms proposed by the British rulers in the form of Montague-Chelmsford Reform Act. During this period a widespread movement of workers, peasants, and middle classes burst out in various parts of the country, which in the context of political calls given by the Indian National Congress under the leadership of Mahatma Gandhi acquired gigantic proportions. As mentioned earlier the post war international developments including the Great Socialist Revolution in Czarist Russia also created a deep impact on the Indian people.

Sukhbir Choudhary tries here to capture the flavour of this gigantic international and national development. He further describes in vivid details the entry of rural masses as active participants in larger national movements.

The selection highlights the following facets of agrarian struggles which emerged during this brief but stormy phase of Indian social history.

It gives a detailed account of the peasant struggles in the United Provinces; Moplah Revolt in Malabar, Peasant agitation in Bengal, and no-tax campaign in Guntur. The selection also gives an account of an independent peasant struggle which emerged in U.P. under the leadership of a band of leaders emerging from the lower classes and castes of the peasantry, famous as Ekka Movement after Mahatma Gandhi withdrew his NCO and civil disobedience movements and generated a deep frustration among the peasantry.

The selection while narrating the agrarian struggles in the U.P. Zamindari area provides glimpses into various aspects of the struggles such as;

(i) The awakened tenants and poor farmers, spontaneously as well as under the impact of the message and organization evolved for developing Non-Cooperation Movement in rural areas, acquire self-confidence, militancy, and courage. They seized hoarded grains and other objects. They took possession of godowns and shops of the zamindars, traders and shopkeepers, and defied police and even military repression organized by the British in the name of maintaining 'law and order'.

(ii) Descriptions of how poor tenants, agricultural labourers,

share-croppers and other sections of rural poor, generally joined the Indian National Congress and deepened its influence on various strata of Indian population both in urban and rural areas. The INC tried to link economic and immediate grievances of various strata to larger political nationalist movement. They gheraoed and took possession of police chowkies, and even surrounded local courts to release the arrested leaders from jails or police chowkies, or prevent their false trials in the Courts.

(iii) The emergence of a new kind of unity among the fighting peasants transcending caste and communal barriers, throwing up a category of active leadership from the lower strata organizing these movements.

(iv) Conscious, politically motivated movements of the rural-poor towards towns and cities, taking various form such as ticketless travelling in trains to attend meetings and participate in agitations, processions and struggles, to halt unjust trials of their leaders or even to free their arrested comrades and leaders.

The article also draws attention to certain important aspects of the growing links between the larger national movement and the peasant struggles. Emergence of a new leadership in the form of politically oriented group of young and educated from urban areas, large number of whom were dedicated and oriented to work among the peasantry. These educated urban cadres, started going to rural areas, began to form Kisan organizations, held meetings, launched agitations, processions, and demonstrations, carried on propaganda and pamphleteering work, called upon the peasantry to oppose illegal dues of Zamindars, moneylenders, traders, organized movements legal and even extra-legal but constitutional to redress their grievances, and also spread the message of Non-Cooperation and Civil Disobedience against British Rule. These educated groups also through press and other means of propanganda broadcast the developments in rural areas to larger areas and thereby taking these issues to all India forums.

The article also points out another important phenomenon. As a result of leadership in Champaran and Gujarat peasant struggles, as well as leadership in Anti-Rowlatt Act movement, Gandhi's name, his slogan of Charakha (spinning Wheel), strategy of Satyagraha, civil disobedience and non-Cooperation as techniques of redressal of wrong, acquired a symbolic significance for the new urge of defiance and struggle among the peasantry. Gandhi acquired a peculiar charisma and the exploited and the oppressed strata believed that Gandhi was their new messiah and interpreted his call for fighting injustice as a call to them to launch struggles—peaceful and militant even on class lines. They organized massive movements against local exploiters and oppressors, and the oppressive British laws, police and military apparatus protecting them. They interpreted (their subsequent disillusionment apart) the call of non-cooperation, civil disobedience, satyagraha and militant struggle against their local exploiters and local authorities as a call for carrying and deepening the struggles on class struggle lines.

This selection has tried to show how the Chauri Chaura episode and its aftermath in the form of withdrawal of non-cooperation movement by Gandhi and the Indian National Congress became a watershed in the history of the peasant movements in India. It further highlights the heroism, militancy and readiness to struggle exhibited by rural poor which struck terror in the hearts of the propertied classes in India. The display of courage and defiance exhibited by the peasantry against British repression and the ingenuity shown by the fighting peasantry in evolving peculiar types of organizations raised the spectre of 'Soviets of peasants'. British Rulers are baffled and taken aback by the fierce resistance offered by the peasants even against their police and military forces.

Gandhi, crystalized his strategy of a non-revolutionary path of opposition against the British rule to pressurize it to grant reforms including Swaraj after realizing the revolutionary, heroic potentiality of the peasantry, sensing and fearing that this militancy and heroism exhibited by the poorer peasants, tenants, agricultural labourers and ruined artisans may develop into bitter class struggle against local exploiters and thereby transforming nationalist pressure movement against British rule into an alternative anti-Imperialist freedom movement based on the Revolutionary path of class struggle under the leadership of proletarian ideology slowly coming to India on the 'wings of Bolshevism'.

Gandhi withdrew the movement, got a resolution passed in the Indian National Congress wherein the central principles of the nature of struggles and the basic strategy of agrarian movements under Indian bourgeois leadership were formulated. Sukhbir

Choudhary by reproducing the resolutions and statements of Gandhiji and the Indian National Congress indicates these principles and strategies: the principle of Trusteeship, the principle of Compensation as a basis of acquiring property and not confiscation, the principle that 'legitimate dues' of zamindars, moneylenders, traders and other proprietory classes should be paid by tenants, share croppers and indebted peasants, the principle that exploited and oppressed strata should adopt non-violence in their struggle. The same Gandhi who did not mind recruiting soldiers for the British army during the First World War, and who also never clearly denounced the violence inherent in the state as an institution, was the chief architect of these principles.

The description of the post-Chauri Chaura *Ekka* Movement in UP after disillusionment with the Indian National Congress, points out how the lower caste and the lower classes of rural India, evolved militant, well organized and heroic struggles, and projected local leadership for local struggles, revealed the need for a larger perspective as well as an appropriate theoretically armed leadership and programme.

(4)

The two selections reproduced here deserve closer attention for another reason. They expose the class bias, and hollowness of the establishment scholarship which thrives on irrelevant surveys of village communities, on the assumption that Indian peasantry is traditional, change resistant, non-enterprizing, soaked in caste prejudices, steeped in superstition and incapable of actions transcending caste and village boundaries. It also invites attention to the fact the Indian bourgeoisie and its astute leadership headed by Gandhiji did evolve a strategy of involving the peasantry in the larger nationalist movement and that these efforts of the bourgeois leaders did unleash a number of movements which generated a new climate in the countryside enabling the peasantry to take to larger national and international issues and lift their local, sectional struggles into larger national and class struggles.

14 Early Struggles (1905-18)

Sukhbir Choudhary

The First World War and Peasants

IT IS TRUE that a large number of people living in the villages joined the British Army when the first world war broke out. They became mercenaries to defend an imperialist structure not because they were loyal to the system but because of economic and social compulsions. It is also a fact that people subscribed to the war fund. But there is also the other side of the picture which had been kept hidden from public notice so far. Digging the confidential records of the government of that period in the National Archives has resulted in revealing some very interesting developments.

At certain places the villagers were forbidden to subscribe to the war fund. Writing on 19 May 1917 the district magistrate of Satara in the Bombay presidency reported that he had recently had an interview with a number of villagers, who informed him that a party of four members of Tilak's Home Rule League had visited their village, delivered lectures on Home Rule and induced several villagers to sign the roll of the League. The villagers informed the district magistrate that the visitors had advised them not to subscribe to the war loan because government was not for them and they would lose their money and to Tilak, who was going to England to ask for Home Rule. The British government, they said, would soon come to an end and Home Rule would be established.[1]

At certain places the colonial police and authorities used high-handed measures which created an impression that villagers would be forcibly recruited. When the district magistrate of Dacca visited a village on tour in October 1917, a rumour went round that he was going to take off all ablebodied labourers in his launch. The night before he arrived all the lower class men of the village disappeared and stayed away till he had gone. It was also reported that in another village in the Bakerganj district a drum was kept handy

Reproduced from *Peasants' and Workers' Movement in India 1905-1929* by Sukhbir Choudhary, People's Publishing House, New Delhi. 1971, pp. 23-40.

in the house of some influential villagers in order to raise an alarm should any police officer try to enlist recruits. In the Mymensingh district three duffadars were prosecuted for taking bribes for promising to save people from being forcibly recruited for the Labour Corps.[2]

Liakat Husain, the famous Calcutta agitator, made a violent speech at Dacca in the middle of October 1917 in which he is reported to have used most offensive language regarding persons joining the Bengali Regiment and to have said that no one should join until government altered its internment policy. He was arrested and was prosecuted under rule 23 of the Defence of India (Consolidation) Rules, 1915.[3]

Those recruited in Gujarat and sent to the Meerut cantonment for training were reported to have deserted.[4]

Enrolment in the Indian Defence Force was quite slow. In Malabar it was estimated that the total number for the district might not ultimately go beyond 250.[5] In Guntur district the collector referred to recruiting being opposed by the local Home Rule politicians but serving as a healthy counter-excitement with many of the younger men. That the same measure of enthusiasm did not prevail everywhere was evident from the fact that in Tanjore many of the youth who were under the influence of Mrs Besant's eloquence, though they had applications to join the forces, either did not appear at all or definitely withdrew, while in South Arcot, nearly half the original applicants had failed to put in a personal appearance in response to the notices sent them. Again in Chingleput one candidate specifically withdrew his application with reference to the interment of Mrs Besant and Messrs Arundale and Wadia, writing that he did not "care to add to the strength of a government that is stupid and mischievous enough to use the powers it has to strike down the best and foremost of us, the most innocent and law-abiding in the country".[6]

Likewise the volunteering for the Indian Defence Force in the Central Provinces was still not catching on. The Chief Commissioner in his speech at the closing session of the Legislative Council held on 16 October 1917 referred to the poor response made by the people of this province to the call for volunteers, but it was to be feared that no advice would be of any effect, as the people to whom volunteering should have appealed were showing no sign of any desire to come forward, the fact of the matter being that service of the kind required was distasteful to the illiterate classes. Even the entreaties of the extremist leaders fell on deaf ears, when a campaign for enrolment of volunteers was started by the latter.[7]

At certain places even the promises to subscribe to the war loan were not fulfilled. A striking discrepancy was reported from South Kanara in Madras Presidency, where it is stated that the actual subscriptions totalled only Rs. 1.73 lakhs as against promises to the aggregate amount of Rs. 4.27 lakhs[8].

Recruitment was slack in Alipore, while 120 convicts from the Trichinopoly Central Jail entrained for Bombay.[9]

The Champaran Struggle

At about this time Gandhiji returned from South Africa. He made the experiment of non-cooperation on a miniature scale by leading the peasant struggles in Champaran (Bihar) and Kheda (Gujarat). No doubt these struggles were carried out in a reformist way. No doubt Gandhiji stuck to his fixed determination to keep the local and circumscribed character of these struggles. It is also a fact that a broadbased agrarian programme was not placed by Gandhiji before the peasants. Still, it has to be recognised that here one comes across, for the first time, the nationalist organising the peasantry as a class against British feudal lords and the imperialist government and carrying out a struggle on their economic demands. All this demonstrated the probability of a broad organised peasant struggle. These demonstrations filled the urban intellectuals with enthusiasm.

The struggle of the peasants in Champaran launched in 1917-8 was a manifestation of peasants' consciousness and thereby of an opposition to the European planters who resorted to illegal and inhuman methods of indigo cultivation at a cost which by no canons of justice could be called an adequate remuneration for the labour done by them. Besides, the struggle also reflected the spirit of revolt against the exactions, oppression and annoyance to which the poor indigo cultivators were exposed at the hands of the factory servants employed by European planters could run an indigo business with great profit by forcible cultivation and low cost labour. In his report submitted for the perusal of Mr Maude, the Chief Secretary to the Government of Bihar, on 12 May 1917, Mahatma

Gandhi stated all these grievances of the Champaran peasantry:

'Indigo...may now be defined as an obligation presumed to attach to the ryot's holding...under coercion. It is inconceivable that the ryots would agree to an enormous perpetual increase in their rents against freedom from liability to grow indigo for a temporary period, which freedom they were strenuously fighting to secure and honourably expecting... Under the tinkathia system the ryot has been obliged to give his best land for the landlord's crops; in some cases the land in front of his house has been so used, he has been obliged to give his best time and energy also to it, so that very little time has been left to him for growing his own crops—his means of livelihood... Inadequate wages have been paid to the ryots...and even boys of tender age have been made to work against their will... There can be no doubt that the latter (planters) have inherited a vicious system. They with their trained minds and superior position have rendered it to an exact science, so that the ryots would not only have been unable to raise their heads above water but would have sunk deeper still had not the government granted some protection. But that protection has been meagre and provokingly slow and has often come too late to be appreciated by the ryots.'[10]

This report by Gandhiji was severely criticized by the editor of the Madras Mail. Defending Gandhiji against the criticism made in that paper, H.S.L. Polak wrote a letter to the editor of the newspaper. In the course of his letter he said:

'You are likely shortly to have a severe shock and your vaunted knowledge will be immensely enlarged when you come to know the contents of the preliminary report just submitted privately by Mr Gandhi to the Bihar government. Had Mr Gandhi been the indiscreet professional agitator that you suggest him to be, India would now be aflame from end to end and an angry demand would be put forth from every platform in the country to put an end to the horror that has disgraced your countrymen and mine for many years in Bihar.'[11]

D.G. Tendulkar also wrote:

'The tale of woes of Indian ryots, forced to plant indigo by the British planters, forms one of the blackest chapters in the annals of colonial exploitation. Not a chest of indigo reached England without being stained with human blood.'[12]

Though outwardly the struggle was against the European planters, from within it was also a reflection of their dissatisfaction against the ruling class which had racial ties with the planters. For the sake of the planters the British bureaucracy was alleged to display a strong bias in disposing of their petitions filed against the European planters to get justice. In protest Gandhiji had written:

'I have entered upon my mission in the hope that they as Englishmen born to enjoy the fullest personal liberty and freedom will not fail to rise to their status and will not be grudging the ryots the same measure of liberty and freedom.'[13]

The peasants of Champaran were led and organised by the intelligentsia. The most prominent organisers besides Mahatma Gandhi were Dr Rajendra Prasad, Brij Kishore Prasad, Muzharul-Haq and a number of other people belonging to the intelligentsia. Gone were the days when the peasant movements could remain confined to limited and local economic aims or could end in fiasco without achieving any tangible results. No longer could they be characterised now as spasmodic bickerings culminating in generating more confusion and disorder. Neither was the struggle of the peasant an isolated phenomenon, nor were the intelligentsia disinterested witnesses to the whole show. The realization of the interdependence of each other paved the way for not leaving the peasantry alone to face the organised oppression of a politically and financially powerful alien feudal community, and finally to suffer the consequences of the agonising episode. Supporting the cause of the peasantry in his presidential address at the annual conference of the Bihar Provincial Congress Committee held on 10 April 1914 Babu Brij Kishore drew the attention of the assembled delegates towards the dichotomy:

'Whatever good the planters might have done, their dealings with the ryots have brought about a serious agrarian situation and they have resulted in a considerable suffering and misery to the poor and defenceless villagers. It is well known that the ryots' allegations against the planters, which have been held by the courts to be generally well-founded, are to the effect that they are bound to execute illegal sathas by methods of coercion including the institution of vexatious cases; that fines and cesses are unlawfully realised from them and they are ill-treated if they attempt in the least to refuse compliance with the orders of the planters... I warn the government that there are rocks ahead and they had better look out.'

In the same address he urged the provincial government to appoint an enquiry committee composed of official and non-official individuals to investigate the entire problem and thus to redress the grievances of the tenants.[14]

Next year in 1915 the provincial conference of the Bihar Congress Committee passed a resolution demanding an inquiry committee to redress the hardships of the peasantry in Champaran. Nand Kishore Lal, the president of the conference, also referred to the strained relations between the planters and the ryots.[15] A few months afterwards Babu Brij Kishore moved a resolution in Bihar Legislative Council in May 1915 in which he again urged the authorities concerned to comply with his demand of the appointment of a mixed committee.[16] The contents of this resolution were more or less the same as that moved by him later in the 1916 Congress session at Lucknow. However, the provincial government refused to comply with his request.

At the 1916 Lucknow session of the Indian National Congress the delegates assembled took up the cause of the Champaran peasantry for the first time in its history. They listened to the grievances of the tenants. Raj Kumar Shukla who had borne the brunt of the indigo planters' oppression and who, in the words of Gandhiji, was 'filled with a passion to wash away the stain of indigo for the thousands who were suffering',[17] delivered a moving speech at the session. The following resolution was proposed and unanimously carried out on the second day of the session:

'The Congress most respectfully urges on the government the desirability of appointing a mixed committee of officials and non-officials to inquire into the causes of agrarian trouble and the strained relations between the indigo ryots and the European planters in North Bihar and to suggest remedies therefor.'[18]

After returning from Lucknow Raj Kumar Shukla wrote the following letter to Mahatma Gandhi on 27 February 1917:

'In a corner of India, the inhabitants of this place (Champaran), who have the proud privilege of being under the comfortably cool shade of British umbrella, are leading their lives like animals suffering from all kinds of miseries.'[19]

On 17 January 1917 the Pratap Press of Kanpur printed a leaflet, entitled Prarthana.[20] A few months later was organised the actual struggle. Associating themselves with the struggle the intelligentsia were ready to face all its consequences. In a letter written to the district magistrate of Champaran, W.B. Heycock, on 14 May 1917 Mahatma Gandhi stated emphatically:

'The desire of the planters generally is that my friends and I should not carry on our work. I can only say that nothing but physical force from the government or an absolute guarantee that the admitted or provable wrongs of the ryots are to stop for ever can possibly remove us from the district. What I have seen of the condition of the ryots is sufficient to convince me that if we withdraw at this stage, we would stand condemned before man and God and, what is most important of all, we would never be able to forgive ourselves... The determination to secure freedom for the ryots from the yoke that is wearing them down is inflexible.'[21]

Gandhiji, who was acting in this matter entirely in accordance with the advice of the provincial leaders, had no intention of giving up his investigation. In fact he had written for assistance from Bombay. In the Bombay Presidency young men were being asked to volunteer to assist Gandhiji. They were told that they would be paid for the work out of funds placed by patriotic individuals at Gandhiji's disposal. It is said in a confidential report of the Central Intelligence Department that Gandhiji was at one time anxious to extend his investigations to the whole field of relations between the zamindars and their tenants. It is well known that the disabilities of the tenants were by no means confined to the indigo plantations owned by Europeans. But the local politicians of vested interest could not afford to set the local landlords against themselves, and that was the reason why Gandhiji's investigations were so restricted.[22]

Resuming the study of the struggle, it may safely be stated that no less significant was the contribution of the peasants themselves. Actually, they were the main elements of the movement, for whose sustenance the agitation was organised. In fact they were in the struggle since its very inception in the latter half of the nineteenth century. In the absence of the mitigation of their sufferings to any extent or in any form their smouldering dissatisfaction frequently found expression in violent protest in 1907-8. The peasants at the Sathi Factory and other neighbouring factories stopped the cultivation of indigo and organised an agitation. To quell it 19 persons were convicted in November 1908. Nearly 200 prisoners awaited trial at Motihari under different charges, including assaulting the alien planters, and arson.

On their refusal to pay the excessive revenues others were also tortured. Among the methods adopted were setting Dhangars and Doms, the low caste people, on the high caste tenants besides the policemen tying them down and beating them, and putting logs of wood on their chest. In another method of torture the hands were put underneath the leg and tied to the neck, the leg being raised. If the peasants did not pay even then, they were brought to the factories. They were forced to embrace a neem tree with both their hands tied together, and set upon by policemen. On such occasions the indigo planter used to be present on the scene. On the other hand, the red ants on the tree would bite the man tied to the tree, but he could do nothing as his hands were tied.[23] Still other coercive measures adopted against the tenants were the impounding of their cattle, the stopping of their wells, compelling the Chamars to cease to render their services to the tenants and the forcible taking of thumb impressions. Besides the spasmodic violent activities against the feudal planters they went on filing petition after petition to the governmental authorities in order to get their grievances redressed, e.g. to prevent the exaction of higher rents from them, and to stop the forcible cultivation of indigo without adequate payment for the same and to prevent the forcible execution of the indigo sathas.[24]

When their struggle took place in April 1917, the statements of more than 8,000 tenants from about 850 villages in Champaran against 60 factories of the European planters were recorded under the supervision of Mahatma Gandhi. Dr Rajendra Prasad has provided a graphic eyewitness account of the active participation of the peasants:

'The statements of tenants continued to be recorded the whole day. There was such a continuous stream of these tenants that there was not a minute's break between 6.30 a.m. and 6.30 p.m. Many had to stay overnight and still their statements could not be recorded the next day.'[25]

The continuous recording of these statements for many days showed the growth of a new political consciousness in the peasantry.

The presence of the intelligentsia amidst them generated more and more confidence in the validity of their case. They became bold enough to defy the authority of the European planters. Fearlessly, they complained against Mr Lewis in his presence. They had realised that if they lacked boldness this time in presenting their valid grievances, their future would be doomed for ever. Observing this change in the attitude of the peasantry Dr Rajendra Prasad wrote:

'It was an extraordinary thing for Champaran. Who could have said before Mahatmaji's visit that the tenant of Champaran, who used to conceal himself at the very sight of the factory jamadar, who used to suffer all kinds of disgrace and oppression silently for fear of more and more oppression coming if he complained about it, would in this way accuse the factory manager and the subdivisional magistrate in their very faces. We were all much struck by this change.'[26]

Mahatma Gandhi himself wrote later in this Autobiography about this political awakening: 'It was an ocular demonstration to them (governmental authorities) of the fact that their authority was shaken. The people had for the moment lost fear of punishment and yielded obedience to the power of love which their new friend exercised.'[27]

The legitimacy of peasants' demands was recognised when the Inquiry Committee composed of official and non-official members submitted its recommendation. The outstanding features of the recommendation were that tinkathia was to be abolished, and sarahbashi was to be reduced by 20 to 26 per cent in various factories. The tenants were allowed to hold their lands free from any obligation to grow indigo. Proper arrangements to prevent unnecessary litigation between the peasants and the planters were promised by the authorities.

The victory of this peasant movement became a foregone conclusion on the very day when on 29 November 1917 Mr Maude introduced the Champaran Agrarian Bill in the Legislative Council of Bihar and Orissa. During the course of his address to the House Mr Maude stated most emphatically:

'History for fifty years and more has been building up a case for drastic action by government and that the findings of the recent committee... have merely set the keystone in the case for interference. The tinkathia system has outlived its day and must perforce disappear... The sooner it disappears from off the face of the country the better it will be.'[28]

The peasant movement reached its final stage of success when the Champaran Agrarian Act was approved and assented to by the Governor-General of India on 1 May 1918.

The success in the struggle generated a new confidence among the peasants in the invincibility of their power. They began to equate their struggle to a movement against oppression. This political consciousness led them to gradually integrate their struggle with the political movement started by Mahatma Gandhi a few years later. The significance of the contribution made by them for the growth of nationalism in India can be gauged from the following observation made by Dr Rajendra Prasad:

'At that time the Home Rule agitation was at its height in India. When we used to ask Mahatmaji to let Champaran also join that movement, he used to tell us that the work that was being done in Champaran was the work which will be able to establish Home Rule. At that time the country did not perhaps realise the importance of the work, nor did we who were there too do. But today when we look back upon the methods of work pursued there and consider the history of the national struggle... then we can see that the great movement of today is only an edition of the work in Champaran on an immensely vaster scale.'[29]

Appraising the contribution of the Champaran struggle to the development of nationalism, E.M.S. Namboodiripad writes:

'... despite stiff opposition by the European planters and their protectors in the bureaucracy, Gandhiji and his comrades were able to bring the struggle to a successful conclusion. This, therefore, may be said to be the first dress rehearsal of that type of national struggle which Gandhiji was subsequently to lead on more than one occasion. Here was a movement in which a band of selfless individuals from the middle and upper classes identified themselves with and roused the common people against the powers-that-be in order to secure some well-defined demands.'[30]

Kheda Struggle

The alignment of the intelligentsia and peasantry again manifested itself in March 1919 when the Kheda Satyagraha was launched under the leadership of Mahatma Gandhi, Sardar Vallabhbhai Patel, Indulal Yajnik, N.M. Joshi, Shanker Lal Pareekh and several others. Like at Champaran, the Intelligentsia seized another opportunity to acclaim itself a better champion and more sincere benefactor of the mass of the peasantry than the alien bureaucracy, against whose arbitrary assessment of land revenue the movement had commenced. Incidentally, the Kheda campaign compelled the educated public workers to establish contact with the actual life of the peasantry. They learnt to identify themselves with the latter and their capacity for sacrifice increased. While persons like Amrit Lal Thakkar, N.M. Joshi and G.K. Deodhar inquired into the conditions approaching famine owing to a largescale failure of crops, on the non-official level, eminent personalities like Vithalbhai Patel raised the issue in the Bombay Legislative Council and waited upon the Governor in deputation more than once.

The Gujarat Sabha submitted petitions and telegrams to the highest governing authorities of the province. In their inquiries and deputations, the leaders of the movement emphasised persistently that the peasantry of the locality was fairly justified in demanding the suspension of the revenue assessment for the year, according to the rules of the Government Revenue Department, which conditioned its non-payment if the crop was below four annas in case of national calamity, or any other such unforeseen devastation. But the officials maintained that the crop could easily be assessed over four annas, and also considered the popular demand for arbitration not justified. On the refusal of the authorities to accept the demand of the peasantry Mahatma Gandhi exhorted the partidars to resort to satyagraha. On the eve of launching their movement more than 2,000 participants solemnly declared in a public pledge:

'...the government has not acceded to our prayer. Therefore, we the undersigned, hereby solemnly declare, that we shall not of our accord pay to the government the full or the remaining revenue for the year. We shall let the government take whatever legal steps it may think fit, and gladly suffer the consequences of our nonpayment. We shall rather let our lands be forfeited, than that by voluntary payment we should allow our case to be considered false or should compromise our self-respect. Should the government, however, agree to suspend collection of the second instalment of the assessment throughout the district, such amongst us as are in a position to pay will pay up the whole or the balance of the revenue that may be due. The reason why those who are able to pay still withold payment is that if they pay up, the poorer ryots may in a panic sell their cattle or incur debts to pay their dues and thereby bring suffering upon themselves. In these circumstances, we feel that for the sake of the poor, it is the duty even of those who can afford to pay to withhold payment of their assessment.'[31]

In this movement too the intelligentsia played not an insignificant role in seeking to 'rid the agriculturists of their fear by making them realise that the officials were not the masters, but the servants of the people, in as much as they received their salaries from the tax payer'.[32] In fact they provided an anti-imperialist bias to every struggle that the peasants had to wage in order to free themselves from imperialist impositions and machinations. The countrywide campaign was organised with nationalism as its dynamic and economic pressure.

On pursuing the novel technique of the removal of the opium crop from a field wrongly attached many people were arrested and tried. The inauguration of the trial attracted huge crowds of peasants to the court. After being convicted the satyagrahis were escorted to the jail by the people in procession. 'The Kheda Satyagraha marks', wrote Mahtma Gandhi, 'the beginning of an awakening among the peasants of Gujarat, the beginning of their true political education.... Public life in Gujarat became instilled with a new energy and a new vigour. The patidar peasant came to an unforgettable consciousness of high strength. The lesson was indelibly imprinted on the public mind that the salvation of the people depends upon themselves, upon their capacity for suffering and sacrifice.'[33]

This active demonstration of political consciousness by the peasantry and the intelligentsia was interpreted by the alien bureaucracy as a designed motive for threatening the stability of the British regime in the war when it was at its critical and climactic point. The regime threatened to adopt coercive measures to silence the growing consciousness of the peasantry by confiscating the peasants' land. In reply to this arbitrary interpretation of the peasants' motives by the bureaucracy, Mahatma Gandhi wrote on 15 April 1919:

'The commissioner has invited a crisis. And he has made such a fetish of it that he armed himself beforehand with a letter from Lord Willingdon to the effect that even he should not interfere with the commissioner's decision. He brings in the war to defend his position and abjures the ryots and me to desist from our cause at this time of the peril to the empire. But I venture to suggest the commissioner's attitude constitutes a peril far greater than the German peril, and I am serving the empire in trying to deliver it from this peril from within. There is no mistaking the fact that India is waking up from its long sleep. The ryots do not need to be literate to appreciate their rights and their duties. They have but to realise their invulnerable power and no government, however strong, can stand against their will. The Kheda ryots are solving an imperial problem of the first magnitude in India. They will show that it is impossible to govern without their consent. War cannot be permitted to give a licence to the officials to exact obedience to their orders, even though the ryots may consider them to be unreasonable and unjust.'[34]

Such an emphatic reply by Mahatma Gandhi on the one hand strengthened the agitation and inspired the peasant satyagrahis to agitate with geater vigour and enthusiasm to redeem their grievances, and on the other hand antagonised the bureaucracy, which had remained so far unchallenged by any active anti-bureaucracy demonstration. To counter the surge of the developing consciousness among the mass of peasantry and its unswerving attitude, the bureaucracy asserted its previous decision to resort to coercion. The officials auctioned the peasants' cattle and confiscated from their houses whatever movable property they could lay hands on. Notices of fines and penalties were issued to the 'seditious' peasants and their standing crops in the fields were attached. Despite these repressive measures the majority of the peasant agitators remained stubborn in their struggle. The movement ended only when the officials accepted the peasants' demands. The agreement arrived at between the officials and the representatives of the peasants laid down that the well-to-do patidars would pay up the rents and the poorer ones would be granted remissions.

The acceptance of the peasants' demands brought a new awakening among the peasantry. The struggle brought home to them that their complete emancipation from injustice and exploitation would not take place so long as their country did not achieve complete independence. The bureaucracy appeared to these people no longer their well-wisher but only an agent of the alien regime.

Peasants Demand Swaraj

The establishment of the closer alliance between the peasantry and the nationalist-minded intelligentsia and the success achieved in the peasant movements repudiated the theory so far held that only the upper classes, intellectuals and professionals mattered in the growth of nationalism, that the ideals and aspirations of and the endeavours and struggles launched by the mass of peasantry could easily be set aside and ignored. Simultaneously, the mass of the peasantry also came to realise that their struggle against feudal exploitation had better chances of success if it was organised under the guidance of the nationalist-minded intelligentsia which could channel it on rational lines as it acquired knowledge through the system of modern education. Secondly, the intelligent section of the peasantry also came to realise that the end of the feudal exploitation would not come so long as the alien domination in India would continue. The development of this outlook gradually made this class also the champion of self-rule which was being already advocated by the intelligentsia.

The realisation by the either class of each others' strength and affinity of their interests promoted their further alignment in December 1918 when nearly 700 peasant delegates from around the Delhi area attended the Congress session of that year and collaborated along with the delegates of the intelligentsia in the demand of self-rule. Speaking in Hindi on the same issue Chaudhary Peeru Singh (tenant delegate) stated:

'It is said that only the educated people sat together to demand swaraj. It is not so. We also demand it. I have said "demand" accidentally', we want to get swaraj, we are not beggars... Our brethren have sacrificed themselves in Europe for which they are being praised all over the world. I am a Jat and a cultivator and a resident of the district which has supplied twenty-one thousand recruits. We are all with Pandit Malaviya. We want that we should manage our own affairs. But you will never get swaraj till you carry the cultivators with you.[35]

References

1. Home (Pol.) Department, Government of India, June 1917, File No. 438-41. p. 18.
2. Home (Pol.) Department, Government of India, October 1917, File No. 2, p. 10.
3. Ibid.
4. Ibid., p. 2.
5. Ibid.
6. Ibid., p. 20
7. Ibid., p. 2
8. Ibid.
9. *The Collected Works of Mahatma Gandhi*, The Publications Division, Government of India, 1964, Vol. XIII, p. 385.
10. Home (Pol.) Department, Government of India, 1917, File No. 438-41, p. 4.
11. D.G. Tendulkar, n. 10, p. 1.
12. Ibid., pp. 65-6.
13. Rajendra Prasad, *Champaran and Mahatma Gandhi*, Delhi, 1955, pp. 63-5.
14. Ibid., pp. 66-7.
15. Ibid., p. 67.
16. *The Story of My Experiments with Truth*, Ahmedabad, 1926, p. 494.
17. *Report 1916*, p. 68. Also see Rajendra Prasad, p. 80.
18. *Freedom Movement in Bihar*, Government of Bihar, 1957, Vol. I, p. 194.
19. For detailed study see *ibid.*, pp. 188-91.
20. Cited by Rajendra Prasad, *Satyagraha in Champaran*, Ahmedabad, Navjivan Publishing House, 1949, 2nd ed., p. 201. Also see The Collected Works of Mahatma Gandhi, n. 61, p. 395.
21. Home (Pol.) Department, Government of India, June 1917, File No. 438-41, p. 4.
    'The Bihar Labour Enquiry which Gandhiji had been conducting has the full support of the party in Calcutta. It was proposed that Gandhiji should be asked to undertake a similar investigation in connection with the grievances of the labourers at the collieries in Bengal. Materials in this connection were being collected and as soon as Gandhiji was able to finish his work in Bihar he was to be asked to extend his labours to the Bengal coalfields', (Ibid., p. 8).
22. Freedom Movement in Bihar, *op. cit.*, n. 70, p. 544.
23. For further study of some of the petitions filed by the tenants see Rajendra Prasad, *Satyagraha in Champaran*, *op. cit.*, pp. 29-31.
24. Ibid., p. 121.
25. Ibid., p. 141.
26. Mahatma Gandhi, n. 2, p. 303.
27. Rajendra Prasad, *Satyagraha in Champaran*, Appendix A, n. 72. For further study see also Rajendra Prasad, *Mahatma Gandhi and Bihar*, Bombay, Hind Kitabs Ltd, 1949; B.B. Misra, *Mahatma Gandhi's Movement in Champaran*, Government of Bihar, Secretariat Press, 1963; and Dr K.K. Datta, *Writings and Speeches of Gandhiji Relating to Bihar, 1917 to 1947*, Government of Bihar, 1960.
28. Ibid., pp. vii-ix.
29. E.M.S. Namboodiripad, *The Mahatma and the Ism*, People's Publishing House, 1958, pp. 20-1.
30. For text see Gandhi Smarak Nidhi Papers.

31 M.K. Gandhi, *The Story of My Experiments with Truth*, Ahmedabad, Navjivan Publishing House, 1945, fourth ed., p. 534.
32 *Ibid.*, 538.
33 Text of the letter preserved in Gandhi Smarak Nidhi, New Delhi.
34 Report of the Special Session of the Indian National Congress Held in Delhi, 1918, p. 116.

15 Post-war Awakening (1919-21)

Sukhbir Choudhary

Contribution of Gandhiji

GANDHIJI'S MISSION to Champaran in 1917 and his organisation of a labour strike in the Ahmedabad textile mills in 1918 were no less significant a contribution to the growth of mass awakening. It may be recalled that the work of Gandhiji had culminated for the first time in the success of the peasantry and the labouring class against their oppressors, viz the English indigo-planters and the Indian industrial bourgeoisie. The news of his success had spread like wild fire in urban and rural centres and had reached the exploited masses—Hindus as well as Muslims.

Non-Cooperation

About this very time, when the exploited classes had grown aware of the havoc wrought by British imperialism and by the local and foreign exploiters and landlords, there appeared the non-cooperation movement.

It is an undeniable fact that the exploited masses of India not only actively participated in all the boycott programmes of Gandhiji (without whose cooperation the movement would have fizzled out) but also organised their distinctive struggles simultaneously to get their most acute grievances redressed. It will not be out of context to provide the readers with some glimpses of these mass struggles.

First Phase of Peasants' Movement

Although peasant unrest was universal and peasant risings were increasingly frequent at this time, the fury and unrest of the kisans spent itself in isolated actions of vendetta and violence against individual moneylenders and feudal lords.[1] It was only from the

Reproduced from, *Peasants' and Workers' Movement in India, (1905-1929)*, by Sukhbir Choudhary, People's Publishing House, New Delhi. 1971. pp. 73-114.

last phase of the first world war onwards that peasant unrest, especially in the form of the Champaran and Kheda struggles, advanced at a speed without any previous parallel, and, during the non-cooperation and Khilafat movements, it acquired more and more a radical character. In the annual session of the Indian National Congress at Amritsar in December 1919, the class demands of the peasantry were put forward for the first time for adoption in the national programme. A secret report of the British government recorded that the resolutions submitted by the Kisan Sabha to the Amritsar National Congress in December 1919 were as follows:
(a) That peasants all over India should be declared the actual owners of the soil they cultivate;
(b) That peasants should be subjected to tax, but not to rent; and
(c) That in the provinces, where the zamindari tenure prevails, the ownership of lands lent to the tenant should be bought up and given over to the tenants.
Commenting on these demands the Director of the Intelligence Bureau communicated to his superior: 'Russian pro-Bolshevik practice, in the matter of division of land, would appeal to him (the Indian peasant) very much.'[2]

Peasant Movement in Rae Bareilly and Fyzabad Districts in the United Provinces

The first big centre of the peasant movement was the United Provinces (now known as Uttar Pradesh), where the agrarian situation was truly appalling. The British conquerors had introduced the most oppressive form of the zamindari system. Under the new regulations large tracts of cultivated lands, pasture lands, forests and irrigational schemes were permanently declared as the property of landlords. The majority of the cultivators were thus reduced to the status of serfs and tenants without any rights. They were thus left to the mercy of landlords and moneylenders who cruelly exploited them.[3] According to the report of the Royal Commission of Agriculture, there was far more pauperism in the United Provinces than in other Indian provinces. In the postwar years the wages of the agricultural workers fluctuated between 1.5 and 4 annas a day, whereas in the Punjab at that time 12 annas a day was the usual wages.[4] Jawaharlal Nehru concurred with these facts when he wrote:

'The progressive pauperism of the peasantry had been going on for a long time. What had happened to bring matters to a head and rouse up the countryside? Economic conditions, of course, but these conditions were similar all over Oudh ... Oudh ... was, and is, the land of taluqdars—the "Barons of Oudh" they call themselves—and the zamindari system at its worst flourished there. The exactions of the landlords were becoming unbearable and the number of landless labourers was growing.'[5]

Referring to the parasitic class character of these landlords, Nehru said:

'The taluqdars and the big zamindars, the lords of the land, the "natural leaders of the people", as they are proud of calling themselves, had been the spoilt children of the British government, but that government had succeeded, by the special education and upbringing it provided or failed to provide for them, in reducing them, as a class, to a state of complete intellectual impotence. They did nothing at all for their tenancy such as landlords in other countries have to some little extent often done, and became complete parasites on the land and the people. Their chief activity lay in endeavouring to placate the local officials, without whose favour they could not exist for long, and demanding ceaselessly a protection of their special interests and privileges ... They have not even the virtues of an aristocracy. As a class they are physically and intellectually degenerate and have outlived their day; they will continue only so long as an external power like the British government props them up.'[6]

In his telegram sent to the Secretary of State for India on 13 January 1921, the Viceroy recognised that the Tenancy Act favouring the interests of the taluqdars admittedly needed amendment and that genuine discontent of the tenants with the working of the existing law was the main reason for the success attained by the non-cooperators. He added that the opposition of the taluqdars in the past had made the amendment of Tenancy Law difficult, but that the need for concession had now probably been brought home to them.[7]

Even in the summary report on the peasant disturbances prepared by the Government of India in the light of the information provided by the UP government it was admitted that the agrarian population ... has legitimate grievances. They (government) consider the difficulties of the problem are social and economic rather than political and are considering the amendment of Oudh Rent Act.[8]

The fairly broad network of railways and important centres of cotton textile industry and woollen industry in the province could not provide relief by way of alternative employment to the tenants. Deplorable conditions of underemployment and poverty caused starvation; then there were terrible epidemics which spread like wild fire and turned the province into a permanent breeding-ground of those diseases.[9] The failure of the harvest, culminating in widespread famine in 1920–21, deteriorated the situation further.

Being utterly tired of their economic and social background, the peasants of Rae Bareilly and Fyzabad districts began to think in terms of a rebellion on the pattern of the liberation struggle waged by their predecessors in 1857. Their smouldering fury burst into flame during the nationwide movement of non-cooperation in 1920–21 throughout the country.

In the meantime, one Ramchandra who was originally from Maharashtra had drifted to the districts of Oudh. While he wandered about reciting Tulsidas's Ramayana, he listened to the grievances of peasants. He possessed remarkable powers of organization. He taught them to assemble periodically for a discussion of their own problems, and thus created a feeling of solidarity among them. Off and on big mass gatherings were held, and this produced a sense of power. 'Sita Ram' was a traditional and common way of greeting in the area, but he invested it with the significance of a war slogan. 'Having organised the peasantry to some extent he made,' writes Jawaharlal Nehru, 'all manners of promises to them, vague and nebulous but full of hope for them.'[10]

At this time Nehru also joined the kisan movement. He paid frequent visits to the villages and watched the kisan movement grow in strength. 'The downtrodden kisan began to gain', he wrote, "a new confidence in himself and walked straighter with head held up. His fear of landlords' agents and the police lessened, and when there was an ejectment from a holding no other kisan would make an offer for that land.'[11] Though outwardly there appeared a lull, it was a lull before the storm. Nehru's enquiries showed that agrarian upheavals were leading to jacqueries. The peasants of part of Oudh in those days were 'desperate and at white heat,'[12] and 'a mere spark would have lighted a flame'.[13]

The foundation-stone of the coming struggle was laid by an ordinary peasant who went up to a taluqdar as he was sitting in his own house in the midst of his well-wishers, and slapped him on the face for being immoral in his conduct towards his wife.[14]

Such physical assaults on the parasitic class of taluqdars led to the growth of a new spirit of defiance among the peasants. They were told to defy British rule itself which had imposed these barons of feudalism on them. This defiance of British rule manifested itself in the form of peasants travelling by train in large numbers without tickets, especially when they had to attend their periodical mass meetings in which sixty to seventy thousand persons used to participate. It was difficult to control them and bring them to book. They openly defied the railway authorities, telling them that the old days were gone.[15]

The crisis came to a head towards the close of 1920, when a few peasant leaders were arrested for some minor offence. They were to be tried in a town called Pratabgarh, but on the occasion of the trial a huge concourse of peasants filled the court compound. Thousands lined the route to the prison where the accused leaders had been lodged. The judicial officer thought it expedient to postpone the trial to the next day. But the crowd went on increasing and besieged the prison, so to speak. The peasant could easily carry on for a few days on a handful of parched gram. Finally the peasant leaders were freed. 'For the kisans this was a big triumph', says Nehru, 'and they began to think that they could always have their way by weight of numbers alone. To the government this position was intolerable.'[16]

In the beginning of January 1921 the peasants revolted enmasse against their taluqdars in the south of the Rae Bareilly district. The Deputy Commissioner received reports to the effect that a large crowd of villagers, numbering several thousands, was on the rampage moving from one estate to another in tehsil Dalmau and destroying crops on the sir (personal cultivation) land of the taluqdars.

On 2 January 1921, the crops (tilled by the peasants) in the fields of Sardar Nihal Singh, a taluqdar, whose family had acquired these vast landed interests by its dubious role in the First War of National Independence in 1857, were destroyed at Aundu by a large crowd of peasants.[17]

On 3 January 1921, crops owned by another national traitor and taluqdar, Thakur Ram Pratab Singh, were destroyed in the village of Chichauli. The taluqdar estimated the damage at Rs. 8,000. On 4 January, another farm at the same place of the same taluqdar was totally despoiled. A godown was forced open and its contents looted, causing a loss of more than Rs. 5,000.[18]

On 5 January 1921, a mob of about a thousand peasants attacked one Rup Singh, a henchman of a taluqdar called Thakurain Sheoraj Kunwar, looted his textile merchandise in the Rustampur bazaar, and also took away various other kinds of property, including his gun, from his quarters in the courtyard of the Thakurain. Still another landlord, Tribhuwan Bahadur Singh of Chandanian, was besieged in his house by a mob of about three thousand peasants led by one Baba Janaki Das. Some gold rings and coins are alleged to have been extorted from the taluqdar. Fortunately for him the Deputy Commissioner and the Superintendent of Police arrived there in time accompanied by a harassed land-lord, Sardar Nihal Singh, at the nick of time, and rescued him. Three peasant leaders were arrested on the spot.[19]

On 6 January Sardar Nihal Singh's store and zilladar's office were destroyed by a band of about one hundred men at Anti. A crowd of about one hundred and fifty peasants looted the bazaar at Mau, the property of the Raja of Tiloi. Sardar Birpal Singh's store at Khurenti was also looted by about five hundred peasants. At Dih, on the Tiloi estate, the houses of two moneylenders, contemptuously known as Badri Banya and Musammat Durajiya, were looted by a party of about two hundred. The houses of two more moneylenders, Sarju Banya and Mussamat Sadni, were looted in Jagdishpur by a group of about two hundred men.[20] On the same day a large band of peasants planned to attack and loot the bazaar at Munshiganj, about two miles south of Rae Bareilly. The attack at Munshiganj did not materialise as the place was protected by a sufficient number of armed police. But a large mob, about four thousand strong, attacked the Fursatganj bazaar where the subdivisional magistrate was present with armed policemen.

In his confidential report submitted to the Deputy Commissioner of Rae Bareilly, the magistrate said that when he arrived in the bazaar, he found that a mob of three to four hundred men, most of whom were armed with lathis, lances and even axes, had gathered in the centre of the bazaar, shouting, 'Mahatma Gandhi ki Jai', and 'Shaukat Ali, Muhammad Ali ki Jai'. Some of the leaders of the mob were approached and reasoned with. Their names were Ram Avtar and Ram Narain of village Pura Kalu and Ausan Brahman of village Potni. They complained about the dearness of grain and cloth and about the high handedness of the taluqdars and zamindars. They said that unless these grievances were redressed, they would 'not be satisfied, and would not return to their houses, and would do all in their power'.[21]

In his usual way the officer asked the peasant leaders to address petitions to the Deputy Commissioner. The peasants were not satisfied with this routine reply. In the meantime, they were joined by others who came in their thousands from the nearby villages. They all rushed into the bazaar, formed themselves into a procession and repeated the slogans already cited. Their number was continually swelling. Commenting on the tension, the subdivisional magistrate wrote:

'I told them to preserve order in the bazaar and retire, but they were so overpowered with excitement that nobody paid any heed to us. Sometimes they said that banias (traders) have made heavy profits, we should avenge ourselves on them. Sometimes they complained about the dearness of the grain and cloth and said that all shopkeepers should at once be ordered to sell cloth at four annas per yard and flour at eight seers per rupee, otherwise they will not be pacified but plunder the people and burn the houses. For about two hours I with some other men continued to reason with the mob but their excitement was growing and their numbers swelling. In my opinion the mob swelled to about eight or ten thousand and rushed into some houses and shops. They broke open the lock and began to plunder and riot. To prevent them from plundering and rioting I with the guard reached at once near the shops. But as soon as we reached there the mob rushed in upon us shouting 'jai', 'jai' and crying, 'Kill them, burn them and take away their guns'. Some persons of the village and of other villages who were with us and tried to reason with the mob were also attacked. They attacked us with brick-bats and lathis, lances and axes and engaged in 'marpit'. Scores of brick-bats and lathis were thrown at us all. One of them threw a piece of wood at me, which missing my head and fell on my breast, otherwise I would have been severely hurt. They began to rob a few houses ... I ordered the guard to fix their bayonets and to open their cartridge bundles. They had no effect on the crowd; on the contrary they began to make fun of us. Eventually I ordered the guard to fire in the air in order that the mob might disperse. But the mob raised a cry, 'Take away their guns; they are but few and can do nothing.'[22]

At this time one of the peasants aimed his axe at the sub-divisional magistrate whom he believed to be an obstacle in the execution of their plan. The magistrate immediately ordered the guard to fire. It was reported that four men were killed and two wounded. An additional force of armed police and mounted soldiers was despatched from Lucknow by train on 6 January 1921. Several arrests were made.[23]

Certain further developments took place on 7 January and on the days that followed.[34] Some peasant leaders like Baba Janaki Das had been arrested in connection with the agitation. They had been lodged in the local jail. Being full of the success they had won at Pratabgarh and the tactics that they had been adopted, the kisans marched to the town of Rae Bareilly for a mass demonstration. On 7 January they surrounded the jail en masse and demanded the release of the kisan leaders. But this time the authorities had made up their minds not to yield. Additional mounted police and the military had been brought. They forcibly drove the peasants back with the butts of their lances across the river. But near Munshiganj the retreating mob was sufficiently enforced and augmented by a peasant procession coming towards the city. The crowd at this time was about ten thousand strong. The crowd again demanded the release of their leaders. But the Deputy Commissioner admonished the crowd and said that their leader Ram Chandra, Baba Janaki Das and Baba Ram Ghulâm were not in the Rae Bareilly jail. They had already been transferred to Lucknow, he said, and they would not be released in any case.[25] This attitude of the officer angered the peasants. A bitter scuffle ensued. The police sowars opened fire, killing and wounding many and trampling others under the hooves of their horses.[26] The peasants retaliated with stones, kankars, and lathis. Several of the mounted police were severely injured and two unhorsed.²⁷ Nehru, who also reached there in the meantime, provides the following eye-witness account of the situation:

> 'As I reached the river, sounds of firing could be heard from the other side. I was stopped at the bridge ... We found that men had been killed in the firing. The kisans had refused to disperse or to go back ... They refused to take their orders from men they did not trust. Someone actually suggested to the Magistrate to wait for me a little but he refused. He could not permit an agitator to succeed where he had failed. That is not the way of foreign governments depending on prestige.'²⁸

Nehru held a meeting of the peasants and tried to assuage their fear and lessen their excitement. 'It was rather an unusual situation with firing going on their brethren within a stone's throw across a little stream ... But the meeting ... took away the edge from the kisans' fear', writes Nehru.²⁹

In thousands the peasants were arrested and sent to prison.³⁰ This repression only served to infuriate the peasants. On 7 January 1921, in addition to the serious disturbances at Munshiganj, cloth merchants at Bawanpur were robbed by a party of about sixty men. The houses of Swaymbar Singh and Lalta Prasad were looted by some three hundred men at Bimiaon on the Tiloi estate. Plans had been prepared to loot several important bazaars at Jais and other places. Capperganj bazaar was to be looted on 8 January 1921. But these plans came to nothing because of government vigilance. A deputy magistrate, Nasrulla by name, dispersed several crowds in this way for days together.³¹ Alarmed by this peasant revolt, the Chief Secretary to the Government of the United Provinces, G.B. Lambert, reported to the Secretary to the Government of India, Home Department, 13 January 1921:

> 'The southern portion of the Rae Bareilly district was in a very disturbed state and rapidly approaching anarchy. Serious crimes amounting to decoity began to occur in alarming numbers.'³²

Reporting the gravity of the situation, the Commissioner of Lucknow, who formerly served in Rae Bareilly district as Deputy Commissioner, and who had thus had personal experience of the district, stated:

> 'The situation at that time was extremely serious. The ignorant

peasantry had been persuaded by perambulating agitators that not only the taluqdars but the British Raj would shortly cease to exist and that under the beneficent rule of Mr Gandhi they would enter on a golden age of prosperity in which they would be able to buy good cloth at 0.4.0. a yard and other necessities of life at similar cheap rates.'[33]

A correspondent of *The Pioneer*, in his report on the Rae Bareilly disturbances telegraphed to the London press, said that peasant 'Soviets'[34] had been established all over the area controlled by rebel peasants. On reading these accounts, the Secretary of State for India was greatly alarmed. On 12 January, he wired the Viceroy:

'Yesterday's and today's newspapers are full of accounts with scare headlines and terrific posters of agrarian riots in Rae Bareilly and Sultanpur districts beginning apparently from January 4th. It is stated that the trouble is spreading, that civil and police authorities are quite unable to cope with it, that the rioters have a certain amount of justice in their cause, and that the suppression by landowners of "Soviets" among tenants is one of the reasons for disturbances. I am once again wholly without news. Please telegraph an account of these incidents. Clear the line: what is present situation and what are your anticipations and how far Gandhi is connected with them.'[35]

On 13 January 1921. the Viceroy stated in his reply that the agitation which had been carried on amongst villagers had been largely, if not solely, the work of noncooperators, though there was no information to show how far the movement had been directly inspired or controlled by Mahatma Gandhi himself. The Viceroy also anticipated[36] the possibility of similar disturbances breaking out in other parts of Oudh.

On 18 January 1921 the Secretary of State despatched another telegram to the Viceroy, in which he asked the latter to realise the embarrassing position caused by his inability to speak with authority on the events in India or to appraise the extensive danger posed by the movements which had been reported. For example, he added, he had never heard of the existence of the 'Soviets' referred to in the report telegraphed by the correspondent of *The Pioneer*, and did not know the correct information to answer to those who were naturally anxious to know more about them.[37]

Meanwhile, according to the telegrams of the Indian News-agency and the Chief Secretary to the Government of the United Provinces, agrarian disturbances involving much damage to property again broke out in the police circles of Baskhari and Jehangirganj in Tanda tehsil of the Fyzabad district on 13 and 14 January 1921.

It may not be inappropriate to recall that the majority of the villages were under zamindars or proprietors. The kisan sabha movement was very well organised in this area. Its principal supporters and adherents were the small tenants or low-caste labourers employed by the Brahmin zamindars. On 12 January 1921, a public meeting was held by the kisan sabha, in which the low-caste serfs and tenants were persuaded not to work for the old wages for their zamindar employers. They were also exhorted to organise a strike. An attack on the zamindars of Bankara was also urged. They were told that it was the wish of Mahatma Gandhi that they should loot. They willingly and readily consented to carry out this behest, amidst sky-rending slogans of 'Mahatma Gandhi ki Jai'.[38] They were also told that British raj was coming to an end and that Gandhi raj was about to dawn.[39]

The success of this first operation inspired further action. On the following day (13 January), therefore, large bands of tenants, consisting mainly of Chamars, Luniars and Ahirs, assembled and proceeded to loot and plunder 'every person of substance'.[40] The zamindars could not offer any resistance as the peasant bands came in overwhelming numbers. Each band is believed to have consisted of about five thousand men. For two days—on 13 and 14 January—the looting continued in some thirty villages. In some villages only the grain-stores were looted, whereas in others the looting was thorough. Many of the houses were completely sacked and the zamindars lost almost all their household possessions. Even doors and mill-stones were carried off. In some instances the clothes and ornaments of women were taken away. Even the tutors of landlords' children were plundered. Much of the loot carried away was hidden, burnt or thrown into the wells. In all, the losses were put down at over two lakhs of rupees.

On the first day, the movement was largely directed against particular zamindars, but after that the object was loot, pure and simple. The primary object of looting were houses of zamindars; but bannias (moneylenders), sunars (goldsmiths) and patwaries (village revenue officers), who were considered the henchmen of zamindars, were also not spared. With the passage of every hour the mobs grew in strength, and were followed by crowds of women to carry off the plunder. The armed constabulary, led by the Deputy Commissioner and the Superintendent of Police, arrived in search of the peasants, who had already dispersed after fulfilling their jobs. A few arrests were effected at the time of carrying off plunder. Cart-loads of loot were recovered.

According to an official source, in all 346 persons were arrested.[41] Intimidated by the police, some local people assisted them at first in combing jungles in which the peasants, officially described as 'dacoits', were believed to have taken refuge. With the arrival of some of the leaders of the kisan sabha, however, the local people withdrew their support to the police in their search for the rebel peasants.

On 19 January 1921 two peasant leaders were assaulted and beaten by a zamindar family whose women-folk had had their clothes stripped off by some hooligans at the time of plunder. One of the assaulted leaders thereupon addressed a meeting in the bazaar in which he implied that he had been beaten at the instance of the police and summoned a meeting for the next day at Baskhari. The other declared his dharna (intention of sitting) at the thana until the police apologised. The Deputy Commissioner prohibited the meeting fixed for the following day. But the peasants defied the order and on the morning of 20 January 1921 they assembled in large numbers at Baskhari. The police could not disperse them because of their overwhelming number. Large bodies of peasants from nearby Akbarpur also came to attend the meeting. It was obvious that the police could not disperse them. The crowd was generally well behaved and refused to leave except on orders from their leader.

The situation was saved as a result of an offer from the leader to send the people back to their homes in return for an undertaking by the government to inquire into the alleged assault. The result of the inquiry was to be announced at a subsequent meeting to be held at Akbarpur on 27 January 1921. All the same, at the time of the inquiry, there was a hot altercation. The peasant leader lost his temper and struck certain persons who he believed were the cause of his dishonour.

On 27 January 1921 the public meeting was held at Akbarpur

as announced. A strong police force was present on the spot to terrorise the peasants.

Shortly afterwards there occurred a riot at the Goshainganj railway station. Two constables deputed to attend a meeting at Baskhari were beaten. Thereupon thirteen persons were arrested. A number of papers belonging to the leader of the kisan sabha were recovered. These were mostly petitions to Mahatma Gandhi relating to agrarian grievances.[42]

On 17 January 1921 the Chief Secretary to the Government of the United Provinces sent the following despatch: 'The agrarian position in Oudh is still unsettled. The early revision of the Oudh Rent Act (34 years' old) is necessary.'[43]

According to a telegram sent on 24 January 1921 by the Chief Secretary to the Government of the United Provinces to the Home Secretary, serious riots occurred in village Sahgaon, Panchagaon, and Thana Bachhrawan in the Rae Bareilly district, as a result of agrarian discontent.[44] According to the version of the Deputy Commissioner, the peasants had turned loose the local zamindar's cattle upon his sugarcane field. The police arrived at the spot to disperse the peasants and to defend the landlord. But it was a market day and a large number of peasants had assembled in a meeting to voice their grievances. They were advised by their leaders, Ramavtar and Salik, to bring to an end the obsolete system of zamindari. It would appear that the police present on the sport considered the speeches objectionable and tried to intervene. This resulted in a scuffle. While the police opened fire, the peasants attacked the police with lathis and spears. One constable was killed by a lathi blow which smashed the back of his skull. Some other constables tried to escape, but the crowd chased them. Two of them were beaten down and left for dead with severe wounds in the head and other injuries.[45]

On 29 January 1921 a mob held up a train in order to rescue a peasant leader who had been arrested.[46]

In order to silence the fury of their masters in London and keep themselves in their good books, the English bureaucrats adopted very severe measures to crush the upsurge. Firstly, they ridiculed its progressive character. Secondly, they tried to demoralise the arrested peasants in various questionable ways. Thirdly, they took severe punitive measures. In fact, official reports for 1919–23 described most of the peasant movements in the United Provinces as the operations of exclusive bands of 'dacoits',[47] though the compilers of the reports had to admit that these 'dacoits' attacked only the propertied classes like feudal lords and traders, attacked the police, and were generally supported by the agrarian population. The report for 1920 stated that in 1919 there were repeated clashes between the police and 'robber bands'. Simultaneously it pointed out that the difficulty in combating the 'dacoits' was that 'it was absolutely impossible to find anybody who would stand witness against them'.[48]

In the course of disorders in different parts of the Rae Bareilly district, according to official sources, 1,024 persons were arrested. 108 men alleged to have been active in the Fursatganj disturbance were given severe punishment.[49] A few kisans were put in custody at the police station. The sub-inspector of police was not present at that time. The kisans reaching there shouted 'Gandhiji ki Jai'. In the meantime a few high officers reached there and ordered them to shout 'Sarkar ki Jai' and 'Gandhi ki Chhai' (May destruction attend upon Gandhi). The kisans refused to do so. These officers, therefore, began to insult and humiliate them in different ways. There-upon an advocate, who had suspended his practice in pursuance of the noncooperation movement, said to the thanedar: 'Are you not ashamed of your actions? How ungrateful you are? Your life is only in the hands of God. These men who have been locked up and who are patiently submitting to all your abuses say it is only Gandhi who is withholding them from committing violence. And you abuse him!'[50]

Outside the jail there began a reign of terror for every prominent peasant worker or member of a panchayat. The colonial authorities were determined to crush the peasant upsurge. Hand-spinning on charkha had spread among the peasantry. The charkha had, therefore, become the symbol of revolt. All those who spun got into trouble. The charkhas were confiscated and burnt.[51]

As regards the punitive measures, in the daily Independent (Allahabad) of 11 and 12 January 1921, there appeared statements such as 'troops have been pouring into Rae Bareilly only to exhibit their capacity of shooting well', 'casualties inflicted on the unarmed kisans must be appalling', 'infliction of reckless violence altogether uncalled for', '190 shots were fired', etc.⁵² Commenting in an editorial entitled 'The Kisan Crisis' on 11 January 1921, the newspaper continued:

> 'Surely the military and police could have avoided infliction of reckless violence which is altogether uncalled for. We thought that the government of Sir Harcourt Butler was not much in love with O'Dwyerian carelessness for human lives. But the havoc which was wrought in Rae Bareilly will call for an answer ... If the kisan had paid the local bureaucracy in the same coin, in the name of "peace and safety" it could have inflicted greater atrocities. So far there is no knowing whether the district officer and the machines of militarism will exercise a much needed self-restraint.'⁵³

In another article, entitled 'New Era in Rae Bareilly' in the same issue:

> 'Rae Bareilly, which is distinguished for taluqdar tyranny as many other districts in Oudh, has been given a taste of military violence ... A few superfluous kisan lives never matter to the unscrupulous men clothed in authority.'
>
> 'Apparently Mr. Sheriff thinks that his duty begins and ends by using his uncontrolled power on behalf of the taluqdars of Rae Bareilly. Taluqdar tyranny like the bureaucratic terrorism is bad enough—but when the two combine the mischief becomes rampant.'⁵⁴

'The Government of the United Provinces will no doubt consider whether any action is desirable as regards these articles', wrote S.P. O'Donnell, Secretary to the Government of India, Home Department, to G.B. Lambert, Chief Secretary to the Government of the United Provinces.⁵⁵ And subsequently the action was taken. Not only was its security forfeited, its editor was also imprisoned.

Peasant Movement in Sultanpur

In the beginning of March 1921, yet another peasant disturbance broke out in Sultanpur, an eastern district of the United Provinces. Not bothering much about the genuine grievances of the peasantry, the colonial authorities embarked upon a policy of repression. Not only were the peasants arrested in large numbers, but they were also maltreated and beaten and harassed in a manner which could by no canons of justice be upheld. Vehemently opposing this attitude of the authorities, 'Independent' of Allahabad wrote (editorial) on 6 March 1921:

'It is excessively painful to inform the general public how the government has planned the destruction of the noble and sacred movement of the kisans in this district. Police and zamindars have been backed and encouraged by the government and they work as right and left hands of government's oppression. The oppression is so great that it is beyond easy description ... When a person is arrested, he is very mercilessly beaten until he is senseless or unless he promises to make his statements just as the police desire. (In accordance with the "plans" of government it is the obvious innuendo.)'[56]

Further Uprising in Rae Bareilly

Another disturbance ending in loss of life occurred in the Rae Bareilly district on 20 March 1921. The facts are as follows. Four peasant leaders who had been making inflammatory speeches announced that they would hold a large meeting and make speeches at Karhaiya in the Salon tehsil on 20 March 1921, which was the day of the weekly market. Orders were issued by the authorities prohibiting speeches at the meeting and for the arrest of all the four leaders. The sub-inspector of Salon, accompanied by another sub-inspector and five armed policemen, went to Karhaiya on 20 March 1921 and arrested Brijpal Singh and Jhanku Singh, two of the four leaders referred to above. In the process of arrest the police were attacked by the assembled peasants who rescued the prisoners in spite of the fact that the police fired on them. The crowd drove back the police who retreated firing and took shelter in a house of one Thakurain Jadunath Kaur. They were besieged by the crowd who tried to break into the house, but were repulsed by the fire of the police. Two of the chasers were killed and five wounded.

In the scuffle one constable succeeded in escaping through a window at the back and went off to Salon. The tehsildar of Salon sent a message by car to the Deputy Commissioner. The latter, accompanied by the Superintendent of Police, some other subordinate officials and 28 armed police, arrived in time to rescue the besieged party which would otherwise have been ultimately overpowered and probably killed. The peasant leaders had in fact openly expressed their intention to raze the house to the ground and kill the constables. The crowd assembled at the spot was several thousand strong. It was ordered to disperse. But nobody moved. In fact the crowd assumed an attitude of defiance. Inflammatory speeches were made by the leaders. There were shouts of 'Mahatma Gandhi ki Jai'. This went on throughout the night. The leaders were alleged to have told the crowd that Mahatma Gandhi would arrive in the morning. The peasants many of whom were armed with spears under the direction of their leader Brijpal Singh, an ex-sepoy in the Ninth Bhopal Infantry, posted groups of men all around the house and picketed the roads.

In the meantime a force of one defadar and ten sowars of the mounted police which had arrived at the village in the morning was held up on the road. It, however, eventually succeeded in evading the pickets and reached the taluqdar's house. The rebels also used carts to block the road. There was a scuffle when the police pounced upon the peasant assembly and tried to disperse it. Brijpal Singh was arrested in the fray. When the Deputy Commissioner and the Superintendent of Police tried to arrest Jhanku Singh, he struggled and called to the crowd to rescue him. And the crowd made a rush, surrounded the two officers and separated them from the main body of the mounted police. At this a police constable fired and tried to save the lives of the officers. In the confusion that followed, Jhanku Singh managed to break away but was soon recaptured. To defend the leader the mob again attacked the police which opened fire. Some were killed and hundreds were wounded.[57]

According to government sources there occurred another bloody disturbance next day (on 23 March 1921). The Prevention of Seditious Meetings Act was extended to disturbed area.

The Governor in Council reviewed the disturbances and decided to post additional police in the locality and to make the inhabitants pay the cost of maintaining it. He also decided to prosecute the leaders. The use of spears and swords was prohibited in the four districts of Rae Bareilly, Pratabgarh, Fyzabad and Sultanpur for a considerable period.[58]

Giving his approval to these repressive steps of the provincial government, the Home Secretary to the Government of India, C.W. Gwynne remarked on 24 March 1921:

'We must agree. The recommendation is made by the Government of the United Provinces including the ministers and it would be madness to resist them ... (though the) result of yesterday's debate (in the Assembly) renders the application of extraordinary laws more difficult than at present, we still could not tell the United Provinces we did not agree with their proposal because the members of the Assembly disliked the policy. The prime duty to maintain law and order cannot be superseded by a resolution of the Assembly.'[59]

Detailing all these repressive steps the Government of the United Provinces issued a press communique which was answered by the newspaper 'Independent' on 25 March 1921. The style shows that no person other than Jawaharlal Nehru could have written the answer. It remarked:

'The preliminary stages of the inauguration of bureaucratic repression in this district (of Oudh) have already been prominently noticed in your columns towards the fag end of February. Its development since has marked the systematic administration of still stronger, hotter and Napoleonic doses of repression until now it presents a terrible tale of terrorism, harassment and persecution ... It has now passed from the domain of conjecture to that of hard reality that Mr. Ibbeston will leave no stone unturned in strangling the panchayats and throttling the kisan movement.'[60]

The repressive measures further provoked the peasantry. On the night of 17-18 April 1921 the Rae Bareilly Collectorate was partially destroyed by fire. To frighten the peasants of Rae Bareilly district a squadron of the 28th Cavalry made a route-march of the week's duration through the south of the district. Dispositions had been made which would place additional armed and mounted police at points where their present was most needed to display the might of British imperialism. Reserves totalling about 600 men had been concentrated at important strategic centres. Thousands of armed policemen and mounted police had been drawn off from the more secure districts for this purpose.[61]

Political Conferences

Efforts were made to secure a demonstration of cultivators at the meetings of the Allahabad district conference, held on 10 and 11 May 1921. Peasants from the Oudh taluk attended in large numbers. The function assumed importance from the fact that it was made to coincide with the marriage of Pandit Motilal Nehru's daughter, Swarup Rani (later Mrs. Vijaylakshmi Pandit). All the prominent political leaders were present on the occasion and their presence was made the occasion of an ambitious political demonstration. The meetings were fully reported in all sections of the press. The District Commissioner reported, 'a great deal of panic on both sides, the city being full of probable arrests (of the Ali brothers) and of action by troops, and the Anglo-Indian and Indian Christian community much alarmed about the alleged intention to attack them on the 10th (May 1921).'[62]

According to official sources, one special feature of the conference was the attempt to strengthen the hold of non-cooperators on the kisan sabhas, particularly in the Oudh districts which had been proclaimed under the Seditious Meetings Act. The campaign opened with the distribution of a leaflet addressed to cultivators and signed by Pandit Motilal Nehru. In Pratabgarh district they were distributed among peasants by some youths who were promptly dealt with under Section 108 of the Criminal Procedure Code. According to the local press, the young men were criminally assaulted and tortured by the police. This enraged the politically advanced sections of the society. The daily newspaper 'Independent' promptly wrote an editorial on 12 May 1921 severely criticising the unwanted behaviour of the police. It said:

'Lord Reading has been denouncing violence, and quite rightly too. We do not want any favour of Lord Reading as Viceroy but he happens to be a bencher of the Middle Temple and we know he is a gentleman who is interested in fair dealing. We believe that he will recoil from the crude violence of an ill-mannered policeman. May we, therefore, present him with the incident which is reported from Sultanpur? It is a piece of sheer bullying and torture to which only a wild animal would resort (God forgive us if we do injustice to dumb animals). It is idle to speak of the wickedness of violence in this province as long as the man who commits violence happens to be a government official. We are convinced of the futility of such a procedure. The districts in Oudh have been handed over to the torture. Unspeakable things have been done and more will be done.

No discrimination can save men from the violence of government; neither age nor youth nor station will be respected. But we thank all the Gods that the brave lads who have been put to the torture have refused to bend the knee to the torturer or to the tyrant.'[63]

Next day Jawaharlal Nehru himself proceeded to distribute the leaflet. But the government did not dare to take any action against him. The leaflet was immediately proscribed. It was followed by attempts to organise a big mass meeting of peasants at Allahabad.

Information of a serious agrarian disturbance in a village in the Allahabad district on 22 May 1921 was published in the local newspapers. It resulted in a serious tension between Muslim zamindars and the villagers who were mostly Hindus. The clash did not, however, take a communal colour. The usual causes of dispute were not confined to the particular village in which the disturbance occurred, but were like an epidemic and common to a number of villages in the vicinity. The Fortnightly Report of the Government of the United Provinces for the second half of May 1921 blamed local non-cooperators who, according to officials, 'usually hurry to the scenes of such disorders like vultures'.[64] Significant of the times was also the widespread nature of the incendiary campaign carried out in the forests of Kumaon and Garhwal. According to a government communique issued on 29 May 1921, 50 to 75 per cent of the forest area was burnt down. Admitting that the damage was serious, the communique held that incendiarism was due to 'irresponsible people infected with the non-cooperation doctrine'. It added that 'the grazing interests of the hill zamindars suffer too much from forest fires for it to be likely that they were in any way involved.'[65]

The agrarian trouble continued unabated for months together in the United Provinces. 'There was a quick response,' wrote G.M. Lambert, Chief Secretary to the Government of the United Provinces on 4 June 1921 to C.W. Gwynne, Deputy Secretary to the Government of India, Home Department, 'to the agitators' appeal based on special agrarian grievances.'[66]

These peasant conferences and movements along with the other activities of the non-cooperation movement played a historic role in undermining British power and prestige. In his telegram dated 13 May 1921 the Chief Secretary to the Government of the United Provinces reported to the Home Department in Delhi that the 'situation is steadily deteriorating; confidence in power of government growing less; officers are losing heart; and the belief that lives of Europeans are in danger is growing.'[67] On 9 June 1921 the Viceroy telegraphed to the Secretary of State about the United Provinces that here was 'little sign of return to settled peace.'[68]

Salient Features of the Peasant Movement in the United Provinces

The peasant movement in the United Provinces had a number of characteristic features. It was the most mature and organised action of the Indian peasantry during this period. Appraising the dynamic character of the movement *The Times* (London) wrote on 6 March 1922:

'Formerly the tenants crushed by requisitions of all kinds were in no condition to effectively express their protest, but in connection with the recent political awakening of the masses they bagan to put up a fight for their rights.'

The class nature of the movement was very clearly defined. Unlike the peasant movements in other provinces, religion was kept completely out of the picture.

Heavy exploitation by the landlords and the fact that the majority of the peasants in the United Provinces were Hindus also played a certain role. In the course of the movement caste differences faded into the background. The acknowledged leaders of the peasants in Oudh generally came from the lower castes.

This movement against the feudal barons who were in league with colonialist rulers obviously assumed an anti-imperialist character and on many an occasion got mixed up with the anti-British demonstrations going on in the urban areas. The peasants actively supported the political agitations of the city people, and the latter responded by giving their active support to the peasant movements. Sometimes they even led these movements. It is self-evident from the report submitted on 14 January 1921 by the Deputy Commissioner of Rae Bareilly to the Chief Secretary to the Government of the United Provinces. He stated:

'The non-cooperators finding their efforts to stir up trouble among students and the general public unsuccessful had to look round for some more promising field for their operations. They failed to influence the general public and students to any extent, because these had no real grievances. They had succeeded in stirring up the cultivators of Oudh to a state of considerable excitement, because the cultivators have in many cases considerable grievances against the landlords ... What the kisans are interested in is their own condition and in particular nazrana and ejectments.'[69]

A resolution setting forth their version of the peasant disturbances was issued by the Government of the United Provinces. It alleged that the 'local agitators had exploited the feeling against 'coolie labour.' It also added that there had been some increase in extremist activity since the return of the Congress delegates from Nagpur. It alleged that school masters, chaukidars and students showed signs of restiveness. With the first two classes the trouble principally was economic. But the students were 'being made cat's paw agitators as in other cases,' it declared.[70]

The peasant upsurge in the United Provinces, as in other parts of India, merged with the nation wide anti-imperialist struggle, producing a very tense situation throughout the country. The British rulers were compelled to pay considerable attention to these revolts. In a report of the military command responsible for suppressing them, it was admitted that the movement was very serious and '... endangered the basis of the traditional land tenure system and administration'.[71] To put an end to the movement the authorities started making concessions to the Oudh tenants. Pretending that they considered the complaints of the peasants against the landlords justified to some extent, the government arranged a special investigation into the collection of rents in Oudh. It enacted the 'Rent Act for Oudh, 1921'. Under the new Act tenants were recognised as permanent and they received the right of owning the land for life.[72] But the majority of the Oudh peasants were temporary tenants and subtenants. They did not come under this category and the landlords continued to exploit them mercilessly and to evict them from the land. Later the authorities had to admit in an official memorandum that the new Act left much to be desired.[73]

By introducing the Act of 1921 the authorities were trying to improve the position of the wealthy tenants. They hoped, on the one hand, to create a new foothold in the villages and on the other, to retard the rapid decline in agriculture. Owing to the half-heartedness of the Act, however, neither of these aims was achieved. The

The Moplah Revolt

Towards the beginning of the middle of 1921 there arose a mighty, unprecedented upsurge by the Moplahs in Malabar. For a considerable length of time British rule was completely wiped out from the region and an independent Khilafat kingdom was established. Though the main grievances of the Moplahs were related to agrarian discontent, in the absence of a scientific, rational and secular leadership, the movement passed into the hands of reactionary, outmoded and orthodox priests and divines. In their traditional, conventional way these divines perverted the dynamic character of the upsurge into a communal strife by forcible conversion of a considerable number of Hindus. The consequences of such short-sighted action could easily be foreseen.[74] Isolated morally from the rest of Hindu India and surrounded on all sides by the overwhelmingly superior and technically better-equipped imperialist forces which blocked all routes of arms supply, the Moplahs could not sustain their resistance for long. The Moplah casualties were quite heavy.[75] More than 3,000 died; several thousand more were wounded.[76] Among the fifty thousand who surrendered there were also the ruler of the Khilafat kingdom,[77] Kunhahmad Haji, and six of his lieutenants. They were shot on 20 January 1921.

Contrary to the principles preached by the non-cooperators, the rebels had turned to armed struggle against the imperialists and their henchmen, the landlords. The attitude of the Indian National Congress towards the Moplah revolt was different from that adopted towards the Akali movement. The Congress Working Committee convened a special meeting to discuss the Moplah question and expressed deep sorrow at the violent methods adopted by the insurgents. The committee indicated that the people on the Malabar coast had misunderstood the message of the Congress and the Khilafat Committee, which as the committee pointed out that the government report had exaggerated the harm caused by the Moplah rising and under-estimated the cruelty of the authorities, 'in the name of peace and order.'[78]

The Moplah upsurge, a link in the chain of the anti-colonial agitations of the masses during the postwar years, was of very great significance, not for the peasants alone, but for the national liberation movement as a whole. Notwithstanding its drawbacks it magnificently demonstrated the will of the peasantry to struggle for its rights.

Role of the Peasantry in Bengal

The peasant movement at this period was not confined only to the United Provinces and Malabar. There were struggles in the other provinces too. The first move towards capturing the sympathy of the peasantry on the lines of non-cooperation organised by the leaders of the first nationwide anti-British movement may be said to have taken place in February 1921 in Bengal. Even before the Nagpur Congress it had apparently been realised that if success was to be achieved in this direction something more concrete was required to work upon than the wrongs done to the Punjab and the Khilafat, and, accordingly, proposals were made to ryots in December 1920 for the formation of national unions for the purchase and sale of all local produce without the agency of middlemen. A raiyat association had been in existence since 1913 and this was probably a move to capture its organisation. Nothing further was done, however, until the launching of the Jute boycott campaign in February 1921.

The real motive behind the boycott of jute was undoubtedly the desire to catch the indignation of the ryot. It explained to the peasants that the reduction of jute acreage meant more land for raising foodgrains or cotton. In some places the ryots were told that this was the wish of the government. In Mymensingh the district Congress Committee went to the length of issuing a pamphlet on growing cotton in place of jute. This scheme was said to have been drawn up in consultation with the Agricultural Department. By these and similar means cultivators in Barisal were made to restrict jute cultivation to one-quarter of the previous year. At Harirampur, in the Dacca district, the area was restricted to a little more than half an acre under threat of social boycott, and the price of jute seed accordingly went down from $2\frac{1}{2}$ to 16 seers a rupee. Whereas at Kaokhali, cultivators were still sceptical, the crop was ploughed up by 'strike' students. This kind of boycott made considerable progress in April 1921 and in no case was any complaint lodged in the court. The one result of this agitation was to make cultivators think of other methods in which they might improve their position and prepare the way for the no-tax and no-rent movement which afterwards appeared in eastern Bengal.[79] Finally, the Ahmedabad session of the Congress and the Khilafat Committee paved the way for a full civil disobedience movement.

The Intelligence Bureau of the government admitted that the events of the first quarter of 1922 had confirmed the fear that the peasant movement had got beyond the control of the leaders of Bengal. It was clearly known that in the interior the authority of the Bengal National leaders amounted to nothing, and even that of the District Committees was rapidly lost in a 'great wave of lawlessness, which swept over' the affected area of eastern and western Bengal.[80] The policy of civil disobedience had never been accepted by the Provincial Congress Committee and the Khilafat Committee, and there was no systematic inauguration of it in any definite area, but the rural areas of the province were clearly drifting towards it. The report of the Intelligence Bureau declared that the spirit of violence and the contempt for authority which had begun to show themselves were not due to the bourgeois leaders but to the masses.[81]

The situation in Tippera had for some time given room for anxiety to the authorities. In this area the rural police had ceased work since November. No taxes were being paid, and no agricultural rents could be collected, whether by the government or by private landlords. Effforts to execute distress warrants and criminal processes were thwarted by assaults on the officers concerned. When armed police was sent to make arrests, the villages were found to be empty. It was remarked by the local intelligence that the agitation was due entirely to Muslims, although it was not communal in character. The peasants, according to it, were simply out to assert themselves. A similar situation prevailed in other areas of East Bengal. People had been told that their subscription to the Swarajya Fund would exempt them from all future taxation, and they literally believed it.[82]

No-Tax Campaign in Guntur

In Guntur district a civil disobedience campaign was engineered by the local non-cooperators against the advice of Mahatma Gandhi. The first move in this campaign was the refusal to pay taxes. There was no open violence but village officers in considerable numbers tendered their resignations. Those who showed themselves willing to take their places were intimidated. The government decided to impose punitive measures on a group of eighteen villages in which the movement was most advanced. When the police proved helpless, four armoured cars and a body of Indian Infantry were sent to the district for a show of force. The refusal to pay taxes continued throughout the month of January. Out of a total revenue of Rs. 14.75 lakhs, the government could collect hardly Rs. 3.5 lakhs. The special staff sent to carry out the processes for revenue recovery met with passive obstruction everywhere, volunteers being at hand in every village to see that they were given no help or information, though there was no active resistance to the service of demands or to the restraint or attachment of property.

In addition to the Paddanandipadu firka, which was the centre of the movement for nonpayment of taxes, there were various isolated villages in Guntur district which had become affected with a general spirit of defiance to British imperialism. The revenue collection in the district up to 23 February 1922 amounted to a mere Rs. 32.5 lakhs, out of a total demand for the whole year of Rs. 58.75 lakhs.[83]

Faith in Gandhian Leadership Shaken

In the course of the peasant movement there occurred certain incidents which led to the shaking of the peasants' faith in Gandhian leadership. As already pointed out, at the behest of some one that it was the wish of **Mahatma Gandhi** that they should plunder the local landlord's house, **the peasants** turned violent in Fayzabad district. Later when **Jawaharlal Nehru** came to know about the episode, he went to the **village concerned**, called a meeting of the peasants, admonished them **for the** so called 'shame' which they had brought on their cause, **and called** upon the so called 'guilty' persons to confess publicly by **raising** their hands.

This sort of strict Gandhian morality was all right for the prominent followers of the **Mahatma,** as they enjoyed considerable influence not only among the **general public** but also among officials. But it was quite different in **the case** of the poor peasants. Many of them were contemptuously characterised as habitual criminal offenders or absconders by the bureaucracy. Public confession by about two dozen poor peasants of their guilt in the presence of numerous police officials who were present at the meeting as reporters meant certain trouble for them. As a result of this adventure of Nehru, which he himself later on regretted, a number of poor peasants were exposed to long terms of imprisonment, torture, and other kinds of oppression. For the bureaucracy this was too good a chance to be missed. Full advantage of the occasion was taken by it to crush the agrarian movement in the district concerned. According to Nehru himself, over a thousand arrests were made. He writes: 'The district gaol was overcrowded, and the trial went on for the best part of a year. Many died in prison during the trial. Many others received long sentences... Some of them, boys and young men, spending their youth in prison.'[84]

As the movement in the United Provinces practised violence and was directed against private property, the National Congress leadership not only refused to support it but adopted a definitely negative attitude. Earlier, in 1921, while discussing this movement, the Congress had, in its address to the peasants stressed:

'...that they must not use sticks and knives...must not plunder the estates, the peasants must win the stone-hard hearts of their enemies by their kindness and love. The attempt to achieve their aims by refusing to pay the lawful rent of the landlord or refuse to fulfil their conscription duty to him may be looked upon as an immoral act.'[85]

These directives were, of course, quite impressive as far as the trained volunteer corps were concerned. To apply them to persons who had been exploited since their birth by the oppressive economic and social structure imposed by British imperialism was just meaningless. The peasants were no longer in a position to tolerate oppression silently. Their patience had been stretched to such an extent that they were left with no alternative except to do or die, 'marta kya no karta'. An incident relating to such a psychological case occurred on the eve of the preparations being made by Mahatma Gandhi to inaugurate his civil disobedience campaign at Bardoli.

Chauri Chaura and Afterwards

The bazaar at Chauri Chaura (Gorakhpur district of the United Provinces) had been for some time the scene of vigorous picketing.

Foreign cloth was totally excluded from sale and the liquor shops had no customers. This was resented and resisted by the local landlord, the owner of the bazaar. On 1 February the local police officer, notorious for his short temper, was alleged to have visited the bazaar with a police force and to have beaten some of the volunteers and peasants engaged in the picketing.

This provocative behaviour of the police officer led all the volunteers of the surrounding villages to assemble at one place on 4 February. They marched in a big crowd to the police station. There the volunteers and peasants, it is said, wanted to know why the subinspector had beaten them, expressed their determination to picket the bazaar that day, and asked the police to prevent them from doing so, if they dared. Some neutrals acted as peace-makers and managed to pacify the angry procession, which then moved on. Some stragglers who stayed behind were roughly handled and abused by the constables. They hit back with brick-bats. A scuffle ensued. The constables opened fire and killed a few. The rest cried out for help.

The main procession then returned in a fury. All the twentyone constables at the police station, along with the young son of the subinspector were overpowered and both the station and the men in it were set on fire. All of them died. Those who tried to run out of the station were caught, beaten, soaked in kerosene, and hacked to pieces. The mangled bodies were thrown into the raging fire. In the meantime the railway communication between Chauri Chaura and Gorakhpur were cut off. The centuries-old oppression and humiliation had forced the Chauri Chaura peasants to express their indignation in violence against the administrative apparatus of colonial oppressions. In its appeal issued on 14 March 1923, the Executive Committee of the Communist International appeared to be right in its sarcastic evaluation that the 'only crime' of these Indian peasants was 'their hunger', because in that unbearable hunger they were forced to contribute too much to the waging of the 'war for democracy' during 1914-8.[86]

The news of this violence on a minor scale shocked the bourgeois leaders and resulted in the suspension of the civil disobedience movement.

A close scrutiny of the columns of the journal Young India of February 1922 shows clearly the most startling fact that it was

Madan Mohan Malaviya and M.R. Jayakar, the two Rasputins of India, that exercised their most unhealthy influence upon Mahatma Gandhi. Like the Russian Rasputin, who was an apostle of arch reaction and who proved fatal and detrimental to the growth of a healthy and progressive Russia, both Malaviya and Jayakar presented a very dismal picture of a bloodthirsty India coming up if violent incidents like that of Chauri Chaura were further permitted to occur. Whatever may be the fact, they prevailed upon Mahatma Gandhi and pressed him to suspend the great anti-imperialist movement.[87] And Gandhiji did likewise.

Besides the suspension of the movement, the Congress Working Committee at Bardoli took note of the complaints having been brought to their notice that ryots were not paying rents to the zamindars. The working Committee advised Congress workers and organisations to inform the ryots that such withholding of rents was contrary to the resolutions of the Congress, and that it was injurious to the 'best interests of the country'. The Working Committee also lost no time in assuring the zamindars that the Congress movements in no way intended to attack their legal rights and, that even where ryots had grievances, the committee desired that redress should be brought by mutual consultations and by the usual recourse to arbitrations.[88]

The Bardoli decision had cast a deep gloom over the peasant movement. Whatever might be faith that Gandhiji had reposed in the divine revelations of his inner voice, a large number of villagers could not blindly follow him. To them it became clear that non-violent non-cooperation was not a type of action which would annihilate the imperialist state structure, but one which was meant to pressurise the colonial rulers into coming to an understanding with the Congress.

They pointed out that the much-talked of dislike for violence, however, was nothing but the obvious fear of the bourgeoisie that once the masses enter the sphere of political action with their own technique of struggle, the movement would cross the limits set by it. That is why the Mahatma, who did not hesitate for a moment to call for 'twenty recruits from every village' to be offered as cannon fodder in imperialism's bloody war, shuddered at some minor incidents of bloodshed which occurred when the masses joined the sphere of action as an organised political force.

The critics asked why, when the Mahatma himself had no doubt that the police in Chauri Chaura 'had given much provocation' and that it was due to this provocation that the mob had set fire to the police station and murdered the constables, he was not prepared to condone this 'mob violence'. Was it not clear to him, they asked, that once the peasants had been made to revolt and brought into action, such clashes between them and the upholders of colonial rule would be inevitable? To try to escape from bloodshed and violence through metaphysical casuistry was the negation of real politik.

It is interesting to recall here that aroused by the call of Gandhiji: young militants like S.A. Dange, E.M.S. Namboodiripad and a host of others joined the anti-imperialist movement and cheerfully had gone to prison. But the debacle of 1922 terribly disappointed them. They said good-bye to Gandhian leadership and organised shortly afterwards a new militant Marxist organisation. Ridiculing the Gandhian technique of independence, S.A. Dange wrote:

'So Gandhism requires a change in human nature or purification, which in due course will destroy the necessity of the present system of life. Destroy vanity, love of show and there will be no necessity to engage wage-earning slaves to produce silks and luxuries. Destroy fear and love of power, wars will stop, and militarisms and governments will melt. Destroy the devil within man and the outside nature of incongruities will die out. Lenin might as well answer to this: "Destroy the Universe and God himself, who is the cause of all this, and everything will stop; a madman's reasoning; an impossibility.'[89]

Likewise M. Singaravelu Chettiar was very critical of Gandhiji's attitude. He complained that the Congressmen had not acted up to the Bardoli Resolution of starting a civil disobedience movement. 'It has been a disaster', he added, 'to have postponed the movement after Chauri Chaura'. He also regretted that the Congress had failed to take up the workers of India in the cause of swaraj. He concluded his argument by stating: 'We have suffered miserably for our errors and mistakes.'[90]

Criticizing the Bardoli decision, E.M.S. Namboodiripad was to write years later:

'Gandhiji's reaction was characteristic of the man and the

movement which he was to lead for nearly three decades. Far from being inspired by the tremendous response of the masses to his call for non-cooperation with the "satanic government", he was alarmed at the lack of what he called "that nonviolent and truthful atmosphere which alone can justify mass civil disobedience".'

'He was alarmed at first during the Rowlatt Act agitation when "I retraced my steps, called it a Himalayan miscalculation, humbled myself before God and man, and stopped not merely mass civil disobedience but even my own, which I knew was intended to be civil and nonviolent."

'It was, however, not till the Chauri-Chaura incident of 1922 (which he called his "bitterest humiliation") that he came to realise that the mass civil disobedience, which he had visualised, and for which he was preparing, could often go completely beyond his control. He then decided to suspend the civil disobedience movement.'[91]

The Bardoli Working Committee resolutions suspending every activity of an offensive nature and recommending social work to achieve self-purification and national education, chilled the enthusiasm of the whole of the militant wing within the national liberation movement. 'The Udaya' (Amraoti) of 21 February 1922 observed:

'The resolutions...have, indeed, sounded the death-knell of the current politics in India... This altered form of the Congress runs counter to the chief aim of the body, viz, devotion to Indian politics... The nation is sure to receive a serious political setback for about quarter of a century. Further, if the non-cooperation movement was primarily started to cut off our cooperation with the Britishers and paralyse the existing system of British administration in India, it has now ended in advising the people to promote and emphasise unity among all classes and races (even Europeans and Indians, etc.) and cultivate mutual good will. Thus the movement has now completely eschewed politics and become one of self-purification. What a conflict between the definitions and scope of non-cooperation!'[92]

'The Maharashtra' (Nagpur) of 22 February 1922 observed:

'It is high time for Mahatmaji's friends and admirers to speak out their mind candidly in India's interest.'[93]

Papers like 'Rajasthan Kesari' (Wardha) became increasingly convinced of the impracticability of the Gandhian programme. In an editorial the paper said:

'...while vehemently condemning the idea of altering the present programme (we believe) that any alterations in the current national programme, especially at a time when the country is passing through a period of storm and stress, will mean nothing but treachery towards those who have already gone to jails in the cause of the country.'[94]

Five years later, on the occasion of the Madras session of the Congress, Jawaharlal Nehru, who presided over the meeting of the Republican Congress held in the Congress pandal on 28 December 1927, complained:

'Since the failure of the non-cooperation movement the Congress had been drifting to middle class or Babu politics and was losing the support of the masses... It was important for them to form some kind of an organisation which would keep the National Congress up to the mark and also prepare the country, not only in a republican ideal, but also in a right republican ideal.'[95]

After the imprisonment of Gandhiji, a Civil Disobedience Enquiry Committee was established to investigate whether the country was prepared for a fresh struggle or not. The masses were jubilant and expected that a new call would come from the committee to continue the national liberation movement. But they were disappointed when the committee decided not to renew the call. 'Rajasthan Kesari', in its leading article on the report of the Committee on 26 November 1922, remarked:

'The committee has by its recommendation not only damped the courage of the country, but has also exhibited that the nation woefully lacks in leaders consistent in their views, conduct and ideals'[96]

New Peasant Movement

The vacillating conduct of the Congress leaders which culminated in the betrayal of the masses led to the growth of independent peasant movements in various parts of the country. For instance, the peasant movement in Oudh produced its own leaders and put forward its own demands which radically differed from those of the Indian National Congress. The new organisation of the Union of Peasants against Landlords became popular and was known as Eka.[97] Its leaders were two peasants, Passi Madari[98] and Sahreb.[99] They both came from the lower castes.

The founding of this organization considerably strengthened the peasant movement in the United Provinces. The official report of the colonial authorities for 1922-3 stated that although 'the number of dacoits (i.e. the revolting peasants) even in 1921 was almost unprecedentedly high, the first six months of 1922 showed nearly double the number of cases reported during the last six months of 1921'.[100]

Under the leadership of the Eka union, the peasants put forward demands which were in the interests of wide sections of the rural population—the poorest and the middle tenants and partly of those who owned land. This can be seen from the programme of the union as published in 'The Indian Daily News' of 10 March 1922. It called on the peasants to refuse to leave the fields when they were unlawfully appropriated, to pay only the fixed rent, to demand a receipt for every payment, to do no work for the landlords without adequate payments, to use the water from the ponds free of charge, to allow their live-stock to graze in forests and on other lands, etc.[101]

The Eka programme showed that its leadership consisted of representatives of the tenants, but it did not put forward any demands for radical changes in the system of land tenure. This displayed the narrow outlook of its leaders. But the movement went beyond the framework developed by the Eka platform. In February and March 1922 it developed into a vigorous peasant warfare.

At the beginning of 1922, over a hundred peasants in the Hardoi district (north-east of Lucknow) armed themselves with lathis and stones and attacked the houses of the zamindars. The police were called and they opened fire on the peasants. The peasants resisted stubbornly and suffered serious losses. According to 'The Times' of London, many were killed. Several days after these events the Eka Union organised meetings in the Bara Banki (east of Lucknow) district. The speakers openly advocated the expulsion of the British and called for the killing of the chief of the district.[102]

The authorities took all steps to localise and suppress the movement. Reinforcements of mechanised infantry were sent to Oudh. Lorryloads of troops and cavalry detachments moved about all over the province. Mass arrests were made and the courts were kept busy from morning till night.

The movement, however, had its weaknesses. The peasant revolts were not united. The Eka movement covered only a few of the Oudh districts. The platform of the peasants was not clearly formulated. It did not go beyond the demand that the arbitrariness of the landlords should be curbed, and it failed to advance the slogan for the abolition of landlordism. The peasants were practically unarmed and could not put up strong resistance for long against the police who were armed to the teeth. All this made it possible for the government to round up all the leaders and suppress the Eka movement and also crush the peasant movement in other districts of the United Provinces.

References

1. The widely known peasants' upsurges in the latter half of the nineteenth century were the Santhal rebellion of 1855 and the Deccan riots of 1875.
2. *Bolshevism in India*, Report by the Director, Intelligence Bureau, Home Department, Proceedings, January 1921.
3. It is worth noting that the total rural indebtedness of undivided India in 1921 was estimated between Rs 500 crores and Rs 550 crores by a British civilian in the Punjab, M.L. Darling. (See H.D. Malaviya, *Land Reforms in India*, New Delhi, 1954, p. 49.) With the passage of time the amount went on increasing. It amounted to Rs 900 crores in 1930 according to the Central Banking Enquiry Committee Report; the rates of interest than ranged up to 300 per cent. In the United Provinces the total indebtedness up to 1930 was, according to the UP Banking Enquiry Committee Report, Rs 125 crores. In undivided Bengal the extent of rural indebtedness increased from Rs 100 crores in 1930 to Rs 150 crores in 1944-45 according to the Ishaque Report of the Government of Bengal. (Cited by Bhowani Sen, *Indian Land System and Land Reforms*, People's Publishing House, Delhi, 1955, pp. 23-4.)
4. *Documents of the Royal Commission on Agriculture in India*, Vol. 1, 1935, p. 206 (one anna = 6.25 paise now).
5. Jawaharlal Nehru, *An Autobiography*, Allied Publishers, New Delhi, 1962, pp. 52-3.
6. *Ibid.*, p. 58.
7. *Disturbance in the Rae Bareilly and Fyzabad Districts*, Home (Pol.) Department, Proceedings February 1921, File Nos. 195-216-A, p. 10.
8. *Ibid.*, p. 7.
9. For further study see V.V. Balabushevich and A.M. Dyakov, ed., *A Contemporary History of India*, People's Publishing House, New Delhi, 1964, p. 79.
10. Nehru, *op. cit.*, p. 53.
11. *Ibid.*, p. 57.

12 *Ibid.*, p. 59.
13 *Ibid.*
14 Instance quoted by Nehru, *op. cit.*
15 *Ibid.*
16 *Ibid.*, p. 60.
17 *Disturbance in Rae Bareilly and Fyzabad Districts*, *op. cit.*, p. 11.
18 *Ibid.*
19 *Ibid.*, p. 11.
20 *Ibid.*
21 *Ibid.*, 22.
22 *Ibid.*, pp. 22-3.
23 *Ibid.*, p. 8.
24 See the telegram No. 21-F, dated Lucknow, 7 January 1921, from the Chief Secretary to the Government of the United Provinces, Home (Pol.) Department, *op. cit.*, p. 8.
25 *Ibid.*, p. 8.
26 Telegram No. 41-E, dated Lucknow, 9 January 1921, *Ibid.*, p. 8.
27 *Ibid.*, p. 9.
28 Nehru, *Ibid.*, pp. 60-1.
29 *Ibid.*, p. 60.
30 Telegram No. 41-E, dated Lucknow, 9 January 1921, *Ibid*, p. 9.
31 *Ibid.*, pp. 11-2.
32 *Ibid.*, p. 11.
33 *Ibid.*, p. 12.
34 *Ibid.*, p. 3.
35 *Ibid.*, p. 9.
36 Telegram No. 36, dated 13 January 1921, from Viceroy to the Secretary of State, Home (Pol.) Department, pp. 9-10.
37 *Ibid.*, p. 13.
38 Nehru, *op. cit.*, p. 61.
39 Home (Pol.) Department, *op. cit.* No. 17, p. 20.
40 *Ibid.*, p. 15.
41 *Ibid.*, p. 19.
42 *Ibid.*, p. 19.
43 *Ibid.*, p. 12.
44 *Ibid.*, pp. 16-7.
45 *Ibid.*, p. 17.
46 *Ibid.*, p. 22.
47 It is interesting to remember that one of the kisan leaders, Baba Ram Ghulam, was contemptuously characterized as a 'registered criminal pasi'. Likewise other leaders were 'also really men of bad character in disguise. The garb of a fakir is, of course, very commonly adopted by a criminal', thus stated J.C. Faunthorpe, Commissioner, Lucknow Division, in his report sent to the Government of United Provinces on 18 January 1921. (*Ibid.*, p. 30.)
48 *India in 1920*, Government of India, Delhi, 1920, p. 181.
49 *Disturbances in the Rae Bareilly*, *op. cit.*, p. 21.
50 Home (Pol.) Department, Government of India, File No. 11, 1921, p. 34.
51 Nehru, *op. cit.* p. 61.
52 *Disturbances in the Rae Bareilly...*, *op. cit.*, p. 1.
53 Home (Pol.) Department, Government of India, File No. 112, 1922, serial nos. 1-8, p. 25.
54 *Ibid.*, p. 26.

55. *Disturbances in the Rae Bareilly...*, *op. cit.*, p. 12.
56. Home(Pol.) Department, *op. cit*, n. 53, p. 27.
57. Account based on the telegram sent on 22 March 1921s by the Chief Secretary to the Government of the United Provinces, Home (Pol.) Department, Government of India, Proceedings, March 1921, File Nos. 334-9, pp. 3-4.
58. See the semiofficial letter from G.B. Lambert, Chief Secretary to the Government of the United Provinces, to the Home Secretary dated 24 March 1921, *Ibid.*, p. 2.
59. Riots in Rae Bareilly District: Application of the Prevention of Seditious Meetings Act, 1911, to the Districts of Pratabgarh, Rae Bareilly, Sultanpur and Fyzabad in the United Provinces; *Ibid.*, p. 1.
60. Home (Pol.) Department, *op. cit.*, n. 53, p. 27.
61. Report on the Political Situation in India during Fortnight Ending 30 April 1921, Home (Pol.) Department, Government of India, Proceedings, June 1921, File No. 13, p. 35.
62. *Ibid.*, File No. 63, p. 13.
63. *Ibid.*, p. 41.
64. *Ibid.*, File No. 46, p. 13.
65. *Ibid.*
66. *Ibid.*, p. 14.
67. *op. cit.*, n. 62, pp. 1-2.
68. *op. cit.*, n. 64, p. 31.
69. *Disturbances in the Rae Bareilly...*, *op. cit.*, p. 27.
70. *Ibid.*, pp. 19-20.
71. Quoted in S.N.A. Jafri, *History and State of Landlords and Tenants in the United Provinces*, Allahabad, 1922, p. 181.
72. *Ibid.*
73. Memorandum Submitted by the Government of the United Provinces to the Indian Statutory Commission, London, 1930, p. 77.
74. For further study see author's monograph *Political Background of Indian Nationalism* (1919-31), Vol. I.
75. *Ibid.*
76. See *The Life of Nationalities*, Moscow, 1922, No. 1/7, p. 12.
77. E.M.S. Namboodiripad, *A Short History of the Peasant Movement in Kerala*, Bombay, 1943, p. 7.
78. The Indian Congress, 1920-23: A Collection of Resolutions Passed at the Annual Sessions of the National Congress, Allahabad, AICC, 1924, p. 119. Also see the Report of the Thirty sixth Indian National Congress Held at Ahmedabad on 27 December 1921, p. 48.
79. P.C. Bamford, *Histories of Noncooperation and Khilafat Movement*, Home (Pol.) Department, Government of India, File No. 185, 1925, p. 73.
80. *Ibid.*, 81.
81. *Ibid.*
82. *Ibid.*, 82.
83. *Ibid.*, p. 145.
84. Nehru, *op. cit.*, pp. 61-2.
85. Cited from the preface written by R. Ulyanovsky to the book: M.K. Gandhi, *My Life*, Moscow, 1934, p. 19.
86. J. Degras (ed.), *The Communist International (1919-43)*, *Documents, II*, Oxford University Press, 1960, p. 13.
87. In later years both these communalist leaders continued to exercise their evil

influence upon Gandhiji. At the time of approval of the Nehru Report, Jayakar and a host of others thwarted all attempts to achieve a timely and pragmatic solution of the communal question. Shortly afterwards at the Second Round Table Conference in 1931, Malaviya blocked the emergence of Gandhiji as the undisputed leader of the Hindus and Muslims.

88 Home (Pol.) Department, Government of India, File No. 489, 1922, p. 34.
89 S.A. Dange, *Gandhi vs. Lenin*, Bombay, Liberty Literature Co., 1921, pp. 33-4.
90 Report of the Gaya Session of the Indian National Congress, 1922, p. 118.
91 E.M.S. Namboodiripad, *The Mahatma and the Ism*, People's Publishing House, 1958, p. 30.
92 Brambord, *op. cit.* p. 63.
93 *Ibid.*, 64.
94 *Ibid.*
95 *The Indian Quarterly Register*, Calcutta, Vol. II, July-December, 1927.
96 Brambord, *op. cit.*, p. 64.
97 *India in 1921*, An annual Report Exhibiting the Conditions of India, Government of India Press, p. 100.
98 See *The Times*, London, 13 March 1922.
99 *The Life of Nationalities*, Moscow, 1922, No. 14/149, p. 14.
100 *Statement Exhibiting the Conditions of India during the year 1922-3*, Government of India Press, p. 78.
101 See V. Moskalyov, The National Revolutionary Movement in India in 1919-22, *Historical Journal*, Moscow, 1940, No. 2, p. 85.
102 See *The Times*, London, 1 March 1922.

PART IV
Agrarian Struggles In The Twenties And Thirties

PART IV

Introduction

(1)

PART IV CONTAINS four selections. It covers peasant struggles during a crucial period in Indian history starting with the withdrawal of the non-cooperation movement in 1921-2 and ending with India's involvement in the World War II. The four selections included in this part attempt to illustrate four different types of peasant struggles emerging in India.

The first selection 'Sreerama Raju's Uprising 1922-4 describes in vivid detail the mighty uprising of the tribal population in Andhra Pradesh against the imposition of forced labour introduced by the British bureaucracy to build roads and other construction works in the forest and hills inhabited by the tribal population. Unlike the tribal revolts described earlier, wherein the exploited tribals under the leadership of charismatic tribal leaders launched their struggles against moneylenders, forest contractors, zamindars and others, this struggle was a direct confrontation with the Government. This struggle was led by a leader who under the influence of the Gandhian approach of constructive reformist work and the spirit of non-cooperation and civil disobedience, settled in a tribal area. Moved by the horrible plight of the tribal population he was soon disillusioned with Government policies. Initially he adopted the Gandhian method of non-cooperation and civil disobedience but was compelled by force of circumstance to lead one of the most bitter, fierce and heroic armed struggles of the tribal population against the British.

Sreerama Raju's own evolution, his own involvement and leadership of the uprising, his method of struggle, the strategy of his warfare, the selectivity in choosing the foes to be attacked, and the various tactics as well as limitations of manoeuvres in the battlefield, reveal a number of features of tribal struggles which were subsequently to become general and more pronounced. This struggle also revealed some of the major limitations which tribal revolts were to experience if they were to be carried out without the support of the larger non-tribal population and also without the backing of the proletariat, which though small in number to a great extent controlled the modern means of transport and communication and could prevent the rulers from augmenting their armed forces and supplying armaments necessary to quell the revolts.

The article clearly points out the following important trends of development.

1. The intense exploitation and oppression of tribal population was linked up with the colonial-capitalist matrix which was evolved during the British period, revealing the law of uneven and combined development of capitalism generated by the British.

2. The exploiters and oppressors were foreigners, Indian and even a small section of the local tribal beneficiaries.

The response of tribal people was to initiate struggles which became increasingly better organized under the influence of the ideologies of class struggles in particular and Marxism in general.

3. The overwhelming majority of the tribal population were transformed into landless labourers, share croppers, serfs or bonded labourers chained to forest contractors, moneylenders, traders and a small section of absentee landlords as a result of the operation of laws of the market and the money economy.

4. The struggle of the tribal population therefore, either takes on the forms of a separatist movement, for autonomous regions or states if the leadership does not take to class struggle, or increasingly becomes a part of the class struggle which develops into a wider movement of agrarian revolution under the leadership of Marxist parties.

5. The movements of the tribal population always transcended the limits of non-violence imposed by Gandhian leadership, even compelling some of the middle class leaders to break through Gandhian-bourgeois formulas and adopt the path of revolutionary class struggles.

(2)

The second article is selected from one of the most important 'forgotten' books on India. It is a report of a committee appointed in Britain, under the chairmanship of Bertrand Russell to objectively assess the situation in India which developed as a consequence of the second nationalist movement described as Civil Disobedience Movement launched in 1930 under the leadership of Mahatma Gandhi. This movement passed through two phases the Salt Satyagraha and Gandhi's famous Dandi March was the beginning of the first phase of the Civil Disobedience Movement and continued till the Round Table Conference with Gandhi participating there as the representative of the Congress, and subsequently suspending it on the basis of agreement or truce with the British. The second phase began with the failure of the Round Table Conference and the return of Gandhi and subsequently his arrest by the British who then placed the country under the Ordinance Raj. This phase of the movement was more or less spontaneous—though in the spirit of Civil Disobedience. The Commission visited India to study the situation, toured the country, met and interviewed a large number of governmental and other agencies and individuals and submitted the report on the *Condition of India* to the British public.

The selection reproduced here describes how the British launched a wave of repression in village India and how the rural population faced that terror in the process of conducting a struggle in the form of No Tax, No Rent and Civil Disobedience to the laws framed by the British Government.

The article shows:

1. How Gandhi and the Indian National Congress evolved strategies, forms and types of struggles to deepen the disaffection against British rule within a reformist framework and without permitting the peasants to initiate class struggle against the local exploiters.

2. How Gandhi and the Indian National Congress restricted the call to a specific, limited strata, unlike the larger call given during 1921 days of non-cooperation.

3. How the Congress under guidance of Gandhi first unleashed movements and then regulated them by restricting their scope. Whenever the British showed willingness to negotiate with the Indian bourgeoisie to inaugurate some constitutional reforms such movements were formally withdrawn. It reveals how the leadership was keen on adopting a policy of negotiation with the foreign rulers to secure as much as possible in the transfer and sharing of power. Thus the mass movements were used more and more as instruments of pressure to strengthen their bargaining position.

4. The article also reveals how the British adopted an astute policy of concession, counterpoise and coercion in handling the Indian situation. However, while carrying on diplomatic maneouvres to sustain the policy of negotiations with various sections of the Indian propertied classes and political parties, the rulers adopted brutally repressive measures to terrorize the masses both in rural and urban areas.

5. The article also reveals how even the limited calls given by Gandhi and the Indian National Congress unleashed gigantic political ferment among the peasantry, deepened the anti-imperialist consciousness in various strata of rural India and linked the rural masses with the larger nationalist anti-British movement. It also reveals that the peasant struggles once launched, took rapid strides and transcended limits imposed by the Gandhian leadership. It was crying for a more dynamic, more militant and more revolutionary leadership capable of providing programmes strategies and tactics which would orient the energies of the exploited strata on revolutionary, uncompromising, lines of class struggle.

6. The selection is included here to rectify an error which is committed by a number of Marxist scholars, particularly after Independence, who try to either belittle the role of the Indian National Congress and particularly Gandhi in unleashing peasant struggles and stimulating a nationalist consciousness among the rural population. In their zeal to emphasize the comprador pro-feudal, pro-imperialist and collaborationist nature of the Indian proprietory classes, they ignore the oppositionist role of the Indian capitalist class and its party. They also forget that the Indian National Congress representing the Indian bourgeoisie, from its infancy, had a particular philosophy and programme of involving the peasantry in its anti-British struggle. They forget that after the emergence of Gandhi as the leader of the Indian National Congress this programme became more crystalized, and fairly consistent, leading to an elaborate organizational framework, comprized of institutional structures, cadres and their training on reformist economic, cultural, educational lines. Day to day political programmes which involved the specific strata of the peasantry in the movements launched by the Indian National Congress, prevented the peasantry from organizing struggles that would have transcended the limits of reformism and taking to revolutionary militant class struggles.

A section of Marxist scholars have also ignored the fact that the Gandhian strategy included many programmes which took up the issues of securing relief to the poor peasantry, the tenants, share croppers and the exploited tribals as well as specially aggrieved strata like the untouchables and the artisans of lower classes. Further, some of the reformist pressure movements were launched against the local exploiters, not to destroy the exploiting classes but to extract from them some reforms and concessions. These facts should not be ignored. They help us to evaluate properly the way in which the Indian National Congress and Gandhi played a specific and important role in launching a number of struggles among the peasantry and thereby deepening the hold of the Indian National Congress in the countryside.

7. It is necessary for a proper understanding of Indian history, to grasp how the Indian bourgeoisie and its leadership headed by Gandhi developed a philosophy and worked its programme of action and strategy evolving other levels of leadership and organizations. It is true that this philosophy and strategy was basically capitalist in the context of the needs of the bourgeoisie in a backward country—wanting not to smash semi-feudal and feudal relations prevailing in the country, but definitely to mend, curb, and ultimately to recondition them in a certain manner. They did this without unleashing forces which might destroy their own class existence, and which would help capitalist development in the country after power is transferred to them.

8. It should also be recognized that by pointing out that the grievances of the masses could be removed only if British political control was eliminated, the Indian National Congress suceeded in linking up the immediate demands to political demands and enabled various exploited strata to lift their consciousness from immediate local grievances to politico-structural causes, which subsequently helped them to see their problems in the context of larger issues of Socialism and Capitalism

Thus, even within Congress two currents emerged; one represented by the orthodox and reformist Gandhians comprising the constitutionalists and the leaders of reformist economic and political movements, and the other represented by a pettie bourgeois wing increasingly being attracted to Marxism, socialism and the policy of pursuing class struggles, as revealed in the growth of Socialist and radical movements, developing youth, Kisan and worker's organizations and struggles against the local exploiters. This category of leadership attempted to interpret the technique of civil disobedience and non-cooperation evolved by Gandhi as a particular technique of struggle suitable for developing class struggles in India, and viewed the Indian National Congress as a movement rather than a party of the bourgeoisie.

Though the present selection does not consciously highlight these aspects, it does point out to the fact that the nationalist movement under bourgeois leadership did generate political conciousness and political movements among the peasants.

(3)

The third selection, 'Agrarian Movements in Bengal and Bihar, 1919-39' by Binay Bhushan Chaudhuri, is 'an attempt to study such actions of one of the groups, the peasantry of Bengal and Bihar in the period between 1919-39—their aspirations and struggles in the context of particular economic and political developments, the interaction of their "social radicalism" with the mainstream of the nationalist movement, and the extent of their success'.

The article discusses the following aspects of this peasant movement. He begins with a criticism of the entire scholarly tradition which underestimates and ignores the extent of peasant movements in India, by pointing out how peasant movements have been a constant feature throughout British rule from its inception. Chaudhuri's characterization, that peasant organizations and peasant struggles suffered from certain major limitations deserves notice. Peasant movements according to him were spontaneous and arose mainly out of particular grievances. The peasant associations which emerged were mostly in the nature of local groups. They were generally dissolved as soon as the issues round which the movement burst out had been resolved. Furthermore, according to him, by relating the peasants' grievances to some fundamental social and economic institutions the programme of action of the rebel peasants provided the rebels with broad perspectives for their movement. Chaudhuri states that the representatives of the zamindars, unnecessarily and wrongly attributed radicalism to some educated middle class elements who tried to organize the peasants for eliminating some immediate grievance. Chaudhury also asserts that 'the nationalist movement led by Congress had in its early phase an elaborate agrarian programme, but, could not provide an appropriate philosophy' for a broad based peasant movement. His evaluation that some Congressmen occasionally took part in peasant struggles and were accidentally involved in the peasant movement, by pointing to Gandhi's participation in the Champaran struggle and by quoting from Jawaharlal Nehru's impressions about the character of the Indian National Congress and its activities prior to Gandhi's intervention, requires a closer examination because the reality of the situation does not warrant such a conclusion.

It is unfortunate that Chaudhuri is unable to see the philosophy worked out by Gandhi through his experiments with the peasant struggles in Champaran, Borsad, Kheda, and elsewhere and his elaborate strategy and tactics of reaching out to the masses by evolving organizations and by starting training centres for the leadership to work among the peasantry. His chain of Ashrams and other organizations attempted to reach out to the peasants by providing them relief from their day to day economic and social hardships. Chaudhuri also forgets how the Indian National Congress launched a number of struggles for rectifying day to day grievances, and through fasting, satyagrahas, civil disobedience movements, put moral pressure on local exploiting classes, and also educating and involving them in the non-violent pressure movements against the British.

Chaudhuri, while giving illustrations and evidence for such approaches, hesitates to draw logical conclusions from his own observations. For instance, as pointed out in an earlier article by Sukhbir Choudhury as well as the article reproduced in the present section from the *Report on India* by the Bertrand Russell Committee, the role of Gandhi and the nationalist movement in involving the peasantry in the political struggles and thereby politicizing them and awakening them cannot be denied. Chaudhuri is unable to see the profound significance of the struggles launched in the United Provinces against the Oudh Talukdari System compelling the Government to pass the Oudh Tenancy Act, by winning over an upper section of the tenants against the zamindars and Talukdars. Similarly he does not see the significance of the Tenancy Act of

1885—a consequence of the Patna uprising, wherein a class of upper tenants and jotedars, get certain privileges and security thus creating further insecurity for bargdars, and share croppers belonging to the lower strata of tenants. The increasing support which the Indian National Congress secured from the upper sections of the tenants helped it to spread its influence in rural areas. This section of tenants enabled the Congress to launch some reformist pressure movements against zamindars, either to bring them to 'change their hearts' or to raise the slogan of removing the intermediaries and abolishing zamindari through a takeover of lands not cultivated by them by paying compensation.

Similarly Chaudhuri underestimates the strategy of Gandhi in his withdrawal of the non-cooperation movement after Chauri Chaura. In fact, as indicated earlier, withdrawal of non-cooperation movement under the pretext of the Chauri Chaura incidents became a model for the strategies to be adopted later by Gandhi and the Indian National Congress in involving the peasantry in the larger national movement.

Similarly, Chaudhuri does not take note of the various movements which sprang up in the country attempting to transcend the limits laid down by the Indian National Congress. The Ekka movement, movements in Andhra Pradesh, in Malabar and other places reveal how gradually a new, more militant current of peasant movements searching for alternative paths of agrarian as well as anti-imperialist movement, were emerging through a realization of the significance of Marxism in providing the possible alternative.

The article provides a brief but very illuminating account of the spread of Marxist ideas among the peasants, particularly in zamindari areas. It indicates how after the non-cooperation movement, the bourgeois leadership did not penetrate deeper into the lower strata of tenants, and was afraid to start any militant pressure movements of bargdars and lower strata of the cultivators and share croppers.

Chaudhuri goes on to provide an excellent picture of the spread of Marxist ideas crystalizing very soon in the formation of the Peasants and Workers Party (1926-8). He tells us how the Party developed a Marxist world outlook, and how the party was formed as an alternative to the Congress approach for developing nationalist movement to secure freedom. It is interesting to note that

The Peasants and Worker's Party formulated its programme which was 'Complete Independence from British imperialism and democratic organization of society involving the nationalization of key industries and appropriation of land without compensation'. This programme was in contrast with the one formulated by the Indian National Congress which still stood for Dominion Status within the empire and upheld the principles of private property in industry and trade. The Congress also stood for the payment of compensation for securing land from the zamindars and did not favour the abolition of zamindari.

Chaudhuri gives a vivid account of how the Party proposed militant programmes for action and developed working class, peasant and youth organizations to organize such movements. He also gives an idea of how journals, leaflets and other types of literature were prepared in regional languages to spread those ideas.

He describes the rise of the Workers and Peasants' Party and points out its historic significance as a symbol of an emerging revolutionary Marxist alternative to the Indian National Congress, providing a new philosophy, programme, strategy and tactics for a peasant movement.

But Chaudhury, ignores the question of how this party operated in the background of a vascillating Commintern dominated by the Communist Party of the Soviet Union under the finally triumphant Stalinist leadership, shaping the major shifts in positions taken by the Indian Communist Party. He also does not mention the crucial developments which took place in India during 1923 and 1933, compelling Congress to pass a resolution on complete Independence at Lahore session and then subsequently launching the Civil Disobedience Movement beginning with Dandi March by Gandhiji. He also does not reveal how as a consequence of the spread of Marxist ideas and activities of the Marxist groups, a powerful working class movement developed, leading to one of the longest and disciplined, militant textile workers' strikes in Bombay, the launching of Kanpur and Meerut Conspiracy Cases and also the rise of a revolutionary terrorist movement started by Bhagat Singh, Chandra Sekhar Azad and others, which subsequently came under the influence of Marxism, and provided a group of cadres to various marxist groups in the country.

Chaudhuri also does not indicate the emergence of the Congress Socialist section which brought together the younger and radical elements within the Congress and launched more militant peasant movements under the influence of Marxism.

However, after describing the emergence of the Peasants and Workers' Party, he switches over to the description of the development of objective conditions, particularly the impact of the great economic crisis of 1929-33 extending upto almost 1936-7 in India, which created a fertile ground for the spread of militant peasant movements as well as the spread of Marxist ideas within the movement.

Chaudhury's description and portrayal of the rise of Kisan Sabhas, culminating in an all-India Kisan Sabha, is valuable. His description of the peasant struggles launched under the conscious direction of Kisan Sabhas in Bihar and Bengal, is extremely vivid and gives a glimpse of a new, more radical alternative to the peasant organisations operating in rural areas under the inspiration of the Gandhian class collaborationist, reformist approach. Chaudhuri reports with remarkable clarity how Kisan Sabhas launched various struggles in Bengal and Bihar and how the Congress leadership became alarmed at this growth particularly after the withdrawal of the civil disobedience movement. The Indian National Congress developed a hostile attitude towards this emerging alternative and tried in various ways to weaken its influence within its own structure and finally curb its growth as an alternative force in rural areas. His account of the growth of Swami Sahajanand Saraswati, from an idealist and deep humanist into a leader of all-India stature, building up a powerful peasant movement particularly in Bihar under the influence of Marxist ideas of class struggle is highly instructive. His brief reference to the all-India Kisan Sabha's experiences of its weakening strength which came as a consequence of its reliance on an upper section of tenants and peasants also deserves careful attention. It raises a highly significant question as to what factors led to such a distortion in the movement and organization basically inspired by Marxist ideas. Chaudhuri also carefully notes how different regional communal political parties also tried to influence and lead peasant struggles. He points out how these parties used communal sentiments of the poor tenants and share-croppers. This phenomenon, he observes, was quite prevalent in many areas of Bengal where the tenants and share-croppers belonged to the Muslim community and the landlords happened to be upper caste Hindus.

(4)

The fourth selection, 'The Damodar Canal Tax Movement' by Buddhadeb Bhattacharyya in collaboration with Dipak Kumar Das and Tarun Kumar Bannerjee is presented here to provide a detailed description of a particular type of movement which developed as a protest against a governmental measure directly affecting every section of a rural community.

Indian social scientists, generally speaking, have not paid much attention to a proper appraisal of the function of rains, rivers and irrigation through the canals, tanks, and wells in the life of the rural population in particular and Indian society in general. The importance of dams as means of taming flooding rivers, checking floods and ensuring water supply to the fields particularly during the periods of scarcity or drought has not adequately been appreciated.

The art of taming rivers, regulating their water and preventing its waste or preserving it for supply in case of drought, has played a significant role in Indian history. For a long time the British neglected this function. This neglect was also partly responsible for famines. But from the beginning of this century and more particularly after World War I, the British Government endeavoured to build canals and dams to assure a certain amount of water supply in case of drought and also to prevent the further decay of agriculture which affected their revenue from land. The Government also took steps in this direction to ensure the safety of the roads, railways and other means of transport and communication built by them. This was deemed essential for the movement of troops, administrative personnel, goods, labour, and also to ensure law and order in the country. Such steps were absolutely essential for the collection of revenue and taxes and to provide for the smooth flow of trade.

However, the financial burden involved in building and dams and maintaining canals was generally passed on to the rural population through various categories of taxes imposed in the name of betterment levies and taxes. Sometimes, Acts in the name of regional or state development, like the Bengal Development Act, were passed and people were asked to pay a development tax.

These policies of regulation of rivers and building of canals acquired a special significance in a number of areas, particularly in Punjab, U.P., Bihar, Bengal and Sind. The British government undertook such measures, though spasmodically and insufficiently and for different purposes, in different parts of the country. However, the impact of these measures was felt by all sections of the rural community and extended to other areas of life in the country sometimes directly and sometimes indirectly. The burden of taxes fell on all strata of society, but its impact varied from one class to another. Precisely for this reason the struggles organized by the different sections of the rural community differed in methods and objectives. The burden of these taxes was felt much more by the poorer section of the peasantry as compared to the upper section of the peasantry. The upper section wanted to create a basis of compromise with the government after launching a struggle, whereas the exploited strata of the peasantry wanted to continue the struggle till the total withdrawal of these tax measures.

Such struggles emerged more significantly from the twenties and acquired greater and greater importance in India, not only during the British period, but also after Independence. Struggles against the state, which imposed various kinds of taxes for providing canals and dams for irrigation and realized betterment levies in the name of developmental programmes, grew sharper from the twenties and became more intense after Independence. The State imposed heavier financial burdens on the lower strata of peasantry to such an extent that in most of the cases they could not even take advantage of these facilities.

Prof. Buddhadeb Bhattacharyya's selection acquires importance for a number of reasons

1 It gives a meticulously detailed account of various strategies adopted by the government and the various associations which were involved actively in the struggle against the government.

2 It also familiarizes us with various categories of organizations, and associations trying to develop movements, and thus gives us an idea of how in rural areas a number of associations—national, provincial, regional, secular, communal—were operating and shaping peasant struggles. It also indicates how the phenomenon

of provincial autonomy and the demands of electoral politics at state legislature level and at the level of ministry formation were important political factors. These factors have a direct link with the different types of activities going on in rural areas in which different political parties and groups are engaged. The only objective of these parties and groups is to gain influence among the peasantry for electoral success.

3 It also acquaints us with the important individuals and leaders who were to play significant roles in providing leadership to the future political movements in Bengal.

4 It gives an intimate account of how in the course of struggles, different groups representing different classes of peasantry, acquire prominence and leadership, how they hesitate to go beyond a particular level, how they withdraw and subsequently compromise with the government.

5 It also gives some idea of the complexity of political stances which different political parties took in two different situations: one when they secured a majority in the assembly and formed ministries, and the other when they were forced to be in opposition.

6 It also indicates how a proper comprehension of the politicization of the peasantry and various other classes within rural areas, requires an understanding of the interplay of various political forces and associations, and their links with different strata of rural and urban communities.

The pattern discernible is one which has continued to this day; the peasantry (the lower strata) is organized for partial demands as a pressure group for the advantage of the upper strata and then dispensed with when the limited aim of securing political position or some economic benefit of the latter is ensured.

This article though valuable in a number of ways, would have gained in depth if it had examined the class strategies involved in the actions of various organizations and parties.

The article should have pointed out why the Congress, and the Kisan Sabha under the leadership of the Communist Party behaved as they did at the end of the struggle. It should have pointed out how the underlying strategies behind this behaviour had far reaching implications in terms of shaping the future movements of the peasantry during the World War and post independence periods.

Inspite of the limitations mentioned above, this selection is highly important for drawing our attention to a struggle over an issue which is of vital significance. We believe a number of struggles must have developed in other parts of the country around this issue. The need of the hour is to record them systematically.

16 Sreerama Raju's Uprising—
—1922-24:

V. Raghavaiah

THE THIRD REVOLT of the Andhra Pradesh tribals against their Indian exploiters and incidentally against the armed forces of the British Government, took place in 1922 and lasted till March 7th, 1924 on which day the saint warrior Alluri Seerama Raju was brutally murdered under the orders of an uncivilised brute, one Major Goodall, by his equally unscrupulous Jemadar of the East Coast Special Police, Kunchu Menon. This was perhaps the longest war waged on the Indian soil between Indian freedom fighters and their alien exploiters—the British. The leaders of the freedom struggle were Shri Alluri Sreerama Raju, a Kshatriya youngman from Mogallu in the district of West Godavari. The immediate cause of the uprising was the extraction of free forced labour from the tribal people of the Andhra Agency for constructing a highway penetrating thick jungles and across low hills from Narsipatnam to Chintapalli. A Tahsildar, by name Bastion, well-known for his tenacity and roughness, was posted to implement this rather hard work. Bastion soon realised that he could not justify his appointment without taking stringent measures to secure local labourers for doing the road work. He began to insist on forced labour from the Koyas who lost no time in resisting the demands. Force was employed by Bastion and this worsened the situation further. He attached the plough cattle of the tribals, stopped the inflow of foodstuffs from outside for the use of the people and took recourse to violent methods for achieving his objects.

By this time, Sreerama Raju who gave up his high school studies and took to a life of meditation and prayer when he was only eighteen years old, had arrived in these woods and was living like a hermit in one of the tribal villages. As he evinced much interest in the well-being of the simple, unsophisticated Koya people, the latter sought

Reproduced from 'Tribal Revolts' by V. Raghavaiah *op. cit.* pp. 35-50.

his help in escaping from the exactions of the unscrupulous road builder.

Those were the days of non-cooperation and civil disobedience, preached by Mahatma Gandhi. The saint from Mogallu cited Gandhiji's preachings and asked them to non-cooperate, with the result that his advice was immediately accepted and word was passed from one end to the other of the A.P. Agency to resist all demands on their labour. The British authorities who were struggling hard to suppress Mahatmaji's country-wide agitation scented greater dangers in allowing a tribal revolt to have its way in the Agency areas, in view of the previous experiences the British had had in the Rampa country, as well as in the Santhal Parganas and from the Birsites in Bihar. The revolt which was already in the blood of the Koya and the Konda Reddy burst forth and the entire Agency country from one end to the other was ablaze with insurrection. The record below briefly shows the march of events as they took place from day to day as well as the repercussions the struggle had on the alien rulers who were ill-advised by their panic-stricken Indian employees.

Sreerama Raju was a student of yoga and astrology and he was not interested in the material prospects, having been dedicated to the life of a recluse and a seeker of Divine grace. He hardly deserved the appellation of 'bandit and malcontent' attributed by the Government officials. He was generous to a fault and listened to the grievances of the simple Koya men and women, with remarkable patience and purposeful sympathy. He was a votary of non-violence and was keen on following the Gandhian path, even in solving the tribals' grievances and facing a ruthless enemy. It may be even said that when he took up the leadership of the Koyas he least imagined that the agitation would develop into such huge proportions that would involve the entire Agency tribal world from Bhadrachalam to Parvatheepuram, and would last for over two years, despite the combined military and police forces drawn from all the adjacent States and the Frontier Rifles to boot. In fact, the agitation led by the Raju did not take a violent turn till the latter stages of the agitation, when he could not control the thousands that flocked to fight under his banner, from taking to retaliatory methods to meeting the brutal assaults and insults of despicable armed men.

It is clear from the official records that at no time had Raju wielded the weapon and released a bullet or an arrow against the intruding forces. He is reported to have strictly instructed his followers not to take even a single Indian combatant's life, but inflict punishment only upon the foreign enemy. His instructions were so meticulously followed that when a combined force of Indians and Europeans was moving along the serpentine mountain paths, his followers would let go the Indian part of the fighting line unattacked but aim only at the European sergeants and commanders. His attacks on the police situations showed a remarkable self-control, for as soon as Raju's force were spotted, the police would surrender their arms and retreat to safety. This may be due to a spate of rumours believed by his followers as well as his Indian opponents, that the Raju possessed magical powers which would turn bullets into water and that the persons of Raju and his followers were immune to danger, a belief curiously shared in all the numerous struggles of the tribesmen against the Britishers throughout India. It may also be due to a patriotic reverence the Indian constable had for the saint-leader, that no resistance was offered in any one of the numerous encounters the Raju had with the Government officers and police stations.

To characterise the Raju's struggle for freedom as 'not so much a popular rising' and to state that his movement had only sporadic support, is to close one's eyes to the immense suffering endured for over two years continuously, by a hundred thousand forest folk at the hands of the vicious Malabar special police, noted for their unbridled curelty, and the Assam Rifles and to ignore the long-standing and deeply-rooted discontent the exploited Koyas and Reddis were forced to entertain against the non-tribal money-lenders and their own Muttadars.

The following day-to-day events that occurred during the two-year-old struggle may give a fairly accurate pen-picture of the Raju's famous fight, from the pen of the celebrated historian and scholar, Sri M. Venkatarangaiah Garu of Hyderabad:

'Raju was born in 1897. He visualised the Agency struggle as a political movement to first rid the Agency of the British rule by resorting to guerilla warfare, on the lines of the great Maharashtra hero-ruler, Sri Chatrapati Sivaji Maharaja, and later extend the movement throughout the country. Raju was interested from his boyhood in riding, and medicinal herbs, and was a keen student and believer in the science of Astrology and Yoga. At the age of 18 he became a Sanyasi, wandered in the hills of the Agency and acquired the ability to tame wild animals. He soon gained the confidence and admiration of the tribal people who credited him with magical powers.

'Sri Raju joined the Non-cooperation Movement of 1921, organised Village Panchayats, was placed under police surveillance by the Government authorities, but later secured relaxation from the surveillance and freedom of movement and then wanted to visit Nepal. He was never a believer in non-violence, though he was a scrupulously austere vegetarian, and had never been known or seen wielding a weapon, though some attributed this to him in the last days of the struggle. Even if it were true, it must have been a measure of defence against the British forces. He was convinced that to achieve freedom from a foreign rule he had no other alternative except to choose the path of violence.

'Sri Raju worked upon the usually well-known grievances of the people against forest authorities. Namely, the restrictions placed by the forest officials on the wasteful cultivation of 'Podu', the slash and burn method by the tribals which even now constitutes a chief factor of tribal discontent; the forest rules and restrictions which are still an eye sore for the tribal people as well as farmers inhabiting villages bordering on Reserved forests, throughout the country; the high-handed misbehaviour of one, Bastion, the then Tahsildar of Gudem, who was provoking the tribals every day by enforcing free forced labour on them for constructing the Narsipatnam-Chintapalli Agency road. It is the opinion of the British officials that "Raju had the courage and influence to work on this combustible material".'

2 -8-1922—Chintapalli Police Station raid:
300 strong, Raju raided the Chintapalli Police Station. The attack yielded 11 guns, 1,390 rounds of ammunition, 5 swords and 14 bayonets.

23-8-1922—K.D. Pet Police Station raid:
He gave advance warning to the Krishnadevipet Police Station and surrounded it. The police surrendered and all left the station and fled before the Raju's arrival.

Rajavommangi Police Station raid:

Some resistance was offered here by the police force. Raju's force overpowered the police. This raid was undertaken by Raju to release Veerayya Dora, who earlier in 1918 took part in an uprising against the Government, known as the Lagurayi rebellion, and was arrested and imprisoned but escaped and was re-arrested. Raju rescued him in his onslaught and there after Veerayya became his right hand supporter in the entire freedom struggle.

In this raid Raju's forces seized 8 carbines, 825 bald cartridges. About the same time Gam Gantam Dora and Gam Mallu Dora also became his able lieutenants.

Raju now extended his operations to other Agency parts and gathered more men and arms and built up a system of able espionage and propaganda. He employed able and elusive couriers to convey messages across the jungles from place to place. Their activities were so carefully concealed that they wrung admiration from the British forces.

The Government retaliated by posting Keene, Dawson, Saunders and Scott Coward at Narsipatnam, Addatigala, Krishnadevipeta and Chintapalli as their headquarters to quell the revolt.

Raju's victories

First encounter: ongeri Ghat was the first place where Raju routed the Government forces and celebrated his first victory on 3-9-1922.

A second clash: occurred on the same day between the Raju's forces and those of Tremenhere in the course of which Tremenhere was seriously wounded. Sri Raju's forces were commandeering their supplies from Koya villages.

A third clash: occurred between the two forces while the Raju was engaged in the worship of 'Kali' at Dharakonda when the special police party tried to attack him but failed. This incident endowed Raju with divine powers and raised his esteem in the eyes of the tribals.

The fourth encounter: occurred at Damanapalli Ghat. The battle raged fiercely here. While the police were descending the ghats four miles long, Raju ambushed them, only after allowing the Indian police to pass through unhurt. He then attacked the rear section consisting of Europeans. In this fight, Rayter and Scott who were commanding the regiment were both shot dead and four other policemen killed. Six (303) rifles and several cartridges and bayonets were seized.

The fifth battle took place down the hill and the police were repulsed according to the Agency Commissioner's report. This battle changed the method of the attack as Raju's men were employing guerilla tactics, which were more successful in this particular terrain.

Despite three notorious man-eaters prowling around and the equally tenacious armed police engaged in combing operations, Raju's forces were more than a match for the military who, with their heavy equipment, could not cope with the quick movements and the unfamiliar tracks used by Sri Raju's soldiers. The Commissioner's report stated: 'The Raju had better spies than our men, the hide and seek tactics were all in their favour. The strategy adopted by Raju is indeed far superior.'

At this stage the Agency Commissioner in charge of the operations realised the inadequacy of the special police and urgently appealed for military aid as well as the Malabar Special Police force. Emphasis was laid by him on being on the defence and not get lost on foraging moves, as Raju had better advantages in the wooded country than the Government forces.

The sixth encounter: took place on 29th and 30th September 1922, Raju's men raided Turamamidi and Lakkavarapupeta and captured the Sub-Inspector of Police. The Commissioner proceeds with the following description about Raju in that incident:

'Raju was sitting on a cot surrounded by seventy men with an automatic pistol by his side. The captured Sub-Inspector was warned not to repeat his spying activities and let off. The S.I. prostrated before Raju when questioned by him about the movements of one, Pathi, whom Raju vowed to kill...'

The seventh encounter: took place on 12-10-1922 when Raju attacked for the seventh time the Government forces at Addatigala and Rampachodavaram. The police retreated. At Chodavaram Raju sent for the Tahsildar and expressed regret that he was handicapped in shooting the British troopers as they were usually mixed up and accompanied by the Indian soldiers. He did not want to take away the lives of Indians even by accident.

18-10-1922: Mr Bracken, the Collector, in his report remarked: 'The situation was pretty serious, this must tell seriously on the prestige of the Government.'

21-10-1922: 'N.C.Os. (Non-cooperators) were sympathising with Raju. The attacks at Addatigala and Rampachodavaram told on our prestige.'

The Commanding Officer's remarks were as follows:

'The Raju's Intelligence Department is very able. All that we receive from our intelligence force is only false news set aflot by Raju to mislead us. His military movements are very intelligently planned. His camps are always carefully chosen, easy for escape if attacked.'

3-11-1922: Makavaram: The Raju captured Nityananda Patnaik, a Sub-Inspector and released him.

17-11-1922: Chapartipalem and Rampolu were raided by the Raju's forces.

29-11-1922: 'We have learnt some lessons,' said the Commander.

30-11-1922: Anantasagaram and Velagapadu were raided by Raju.

The eighth encounter: took place on 6-12-1922. This is the first setback for the Raju. The rebels were surprised at Peddagaddapalem. The engagement between the two lasted for one hour. Raju was wounded and escaped. The following arms were seized from the Raju: nine Police muskets, two 303 rifles, 748 rounds of ammunition, 17 bayonets, six Police swords, Raju's bed and kit and miscellaneous articles.

The ninth encounter: (Raju's second reverse) on the same day. These two disasters occurring on the same day lost Raju his influence, though not his popularity, as claimed by the Commander of the Government forces. On the head of Raju, a price of Rs 1,500/–; against the Gam brothers, Rs 1,000 each; against Veerayya, Rs 1,000; and for each of the other rebel leaders, Rs 50/– each were announced and for some months there after, Raju's movements were not known. The freedom fighters moved farther into the inaccessible jungle recesses like Peddavalasa, Gudem, Dhara Konda, Gurthedu. Every attempt was made to demoralise Raju's forces. Government Commanding Officer commenced several measures to destroy their morale and even surreptitiously supplied them through obliging intermediaries large quantities of intoxicants and drinks.

4-2-1923: The Commanding Officer made the following remarks: 'No rebel movements known from Kiravu to Gudem. It is getting impossible to obtain information about Raju, and those harbouring him.'

Bracken then ordered the prosecution of several village officers for harbouring Raju and suppressing information about his movements.

16-2-1923: Police captured 4 rebels.

March 1923: Government concluded that all villages below the ghats had deserted the Raju and there was no likelihood of rejoining him. They also resolved to send back the Malabar Police, wireless, and mule transport, the intelligence squad, and the medical outfit and decided to retain 300 police only.

Raiding of Anantagiri near Lagurayi which encouraged Raju to re-commence his activities.

The tenth clash: on 18-4-1923: Raju appeared at Annavaram Police Station suddenly. No arms were recovered as they were removed by the Deputy Tahsildar. A Sub-Inspector of Police and Postmaster took Raju to their houses; women washed his feet and sprinkled the water on their heads.

The eleventh raid: occurred at Sankhavaram. A similar reception was given to the Raju here also. The Government levied a collective fine of Rs 4,000/- on this village. The Government concluded that the support to Raju was once again growing as strong as before. The Raju's men collected supplies from the people.

The twelfth clash: Gantam Dora appeared at Koyyuru, captured the Sub-Inspector and Deputy Tahsildar, beat them and released them. He also burnt the forest rest house. He also narrated the misdeeds of Bastion. He said, 'I aimed my gun at Onjeri ghat against Bastion but narrowly missed him, fortunately for him. Either he should die or I should die.' He then prostrated before the Brahmin Tahsildar as a mark of respect.

15-6-1923: Kondakambedu and Malkangiri: Raju summoned the Tahsildar and gave him an idea of his plans.

Raju wore a turban, long shirt and knickers—all of red coloured khaddar. He had stockings and boots also. He had a flowing beard and was followed by Aggi Raju (probably alias for Pericherla Suryanarayana Raju of Kumudavalli), lieutenant of the Raju. He also wore red khaddar.

Raju always spoke in Telugu. He praised Gandhiji and vowed to continue his campaign till Swaraj was established. The Tahsildar's statement stated, 'Raju bragged of bullet-proof powers. He selected auspicious days based on astrology for his fights. He wanted to visit Rajahmundry and recruit forces and to get help from Punjab.'

21-6-1923: The Raju visited Avulu and carried two spies with him. Raju built a concealed military camp 58 yards from the Government post near Gudem to be used whenever occasion demanded.

14-8-1923: Raju visited several villages and collected rice and provisions for his army.

The thirteenth encounter: 2-9-1923: Raju attacked but he retreated. The punitive police withdrew in September.

17-9-1923 & 18-9-1923: Gam Mallu Dora was captured at Nadimpalem while hiding in a bamboo paddy container on an attack. Mallu Dora was the most dangerous hero among the Raju's lieutenants.

The fourteenth encounter: 20-9-1923: Raju attacked Gangaraju Madugula.

The fifteenth clash: 22-9-1923: Raju visited Paderu, raided it and moved towards Padua.

14-10-1923: Raju camped at Tokarayi.

It is clear from the above narration of events as corroborated by the State records, that from the beginning the struggle of the Raju was an unequal fight. Once again the bow quailed before the bullet. It was indeed impossible for the impoverished, semi-starving, simple Koyas to fight a long-drawn battle with the well-organised, richly-fed, powerfully-armed, numerous forces of the British Government. Owing to a complete encirclement of the Agency forces by the military, cutting off all the communications between the tribals and non-tribal people of the State, obstruction caused to all supplies of food and materials into the Agency, the tribals were reduced to misery and starvation. The few guns they snatched from the police stations had no ammunition. The loss of the few battles by the Raju towards the end of September 1923 dispelled the till now unshaken belief in the magical powers of the Raju to ward off a disaster. The simple tribal men and women got panicky in the face of mounting disasters. They had killed every available domesticated animal for sustaining their life, and at last a stage came when they lost all their offensive and had to be content with a defensive hiding which naturally demoralised them. The capture of leaders one by one, and the wounding of the great Raju quickly lowered their morale. Having scented this plight of the tribals, the Government forces got emboldened to make more raids into the tribal hamlets and molest men and women, destroy their crops and inflict untold miseries on them. This resulted in streams of men and women heading to the Raju for advice and encouragement and shelter. Even Raju got unnerved, not due to fear for his life, but owing to his sorrow at the plight of his followers. In a moment of desperation and supreme sacrifice, the noble Raju thought that he could stop the rout and bring relief to thousands of his followers by surrendering himself to the enemy and bring an end to the struggle.

With this object in view, Raju after offering his prayers, with a small cane in his hand, wended his way along the course of narrow hill stream towards Koyyuru, the roadside headquarters of Major Goodall. Being an educated and highly cultured noble man, the Raju thought that he would be meted out the same treatment as was due to a prisoner of war and least expected that he would be murdered most unceremoniously and cruelly in cold blood. As it was already daylight, Goodall's Jemadar of the East Coast Special Police, arrested him and produced him before his Major at village Mampa. By that time a large gathering of the neighbouring villages was on the scene. An altercation ensued between Raju, now a handcuffed prisoner standing against the roadside tamarind tree and Major Goodall chuckling over what he thought was a windfall, for which he was striving his best all these months. It is learnt that in the course of this wordy battle, the Major was rude and insulted Raju and was getting ready to shoot him, whereupon the latter remonstrated that he was a prisoner of war and that the Major had no right to kill him. He wanted to be produced before Mr. Bracken who was the Collector or the Commanding Officer, so that he might be legally dealt with. Goodall taunted him that he was not going to provide him an opportunity to try his luck in law courts and drew out his pistol threatening to shoot Raju. On second thoughts he directed Kunchu Menon to shoot Raju, which order was carried out immediately. Thus ended the life of a great man whose unparalleled patriotism and intense devotion to the suffering humanity had led him to unprecedented martyrdom.

Yendu Padal, an associate of Raju was killed on 26-5-24, by two villagers. On 7-6-24, Gantam Dora, right hand man of Raju lost his life in a skirmish with the police. By September 1924, the revolt was all over.

The Andhra Provincial Congress Committee dropped a resolution glorifying the Raju's leadership and exploits as smacking of approval of violence.

In the Madras Legislative Council a demand was made for ascertaining the causes of the tribal revolt. Sri C.R. Reddy pleaded (as a member of the said Council prior to Raju's death) for putting down the 'fithuri' (revolt) first and embark upon the enquiry thereafter. All the speakers demanded the suppression of the revolt but also condemned the violence and excesses of the police authorities against the tribal people.

The revolt under Srirama Raju's leadership is similar to the previous revolts of Santals, Mundas, Gonds and Bhils in that all of them were provoked by genuine grievances against Government officials who were unimaginative and wooden. All the three were major revolts in which thousands of tribals took part actively and staked their all for securing freedom from official interference and oppression. In all these revolts the leaders paid the extreme penalty of death. All the leaders were quite selfless and gave their all for the emancipation of their fellow tribesmen. In all these uprisings supernatural powers were claimed by the leaders so as to act as powerful stimulants in inspiring their followers and not for selfish aggrandisement. The after effects of all these revolts were crushing and disastrous to the defeated tribals. Coming to points of contrast the Santal, Munda, Gond and Bhil revolts were sparked off by agrarian grievances caused by money-lenders and petty Muttadari Zamindars while the immediate cause of the Raju-led revolt was the enforcement of forced labour which the tribals resented. The prior Rampa revolt of the Reddis was purely dynastic in nature, in which the tribals played only a secondary part. The leader of the 1922-4 revolt was a non-tribal person of high prestige while the leaders of the Santals and Mundas were ordinary tribals, whose transparent sincerity and spirit of self-sacrifice were the sole motivating forces in attracting to the banner of revolt, thousands of followers from almost every corner of their respective tribal lands. As conceded by even his own opponents, Raju was a leader of great organising calibre, skilful strategy and commanding talent while the same cannot be said of Birsa Bhagwan, the Munda leader, Kanu and Sidu, leaders of the Santals, though on that account the latter were not even a whit behind Raju in patriotism, purity of character and courage in facing danger at great personal risk. Munda, Santal, Bhil, and Gond insurrections were short-lived and much simpler than the two year-old continuous struggle of the Raju, which kept the British army successfully at bay. The battle fronts of the Koyas and Reddis were located in steep ravines, narrow winding mountain paths and thick jungles and fought in the guerilla patterns in the jungle terrain, unlike the fights of the Santals and Mundas, who tried to fight pitched battles with their opponents.

As a direct result of all those struggles costly lessons were learnt by the foreign rulers and the result was a grant of special treatment to the Agency people for development, as a compensatory measure for past neglect and a realisation on the part of the authorities that the tribal required a protective approach rather than a mere administrative one. This led to the separation of tribal legislation and tribal welfare from the Central and the State Legislatures, State Courts and State Cabinet authority and placing the same in the hands of the State Governors, who could make laws or regulations to suit the well-being of tribals and be responsible to none except the President of India.

17 Village Repression by British Rulers

Report of India League Delegation in 1932

'...Upon the whole, the police have acted splendidly. They have acted often under the greatest provocation. They have acted against tremendous odds at great risk to their own lives and to the lives of their own families, and they have acted, speaking generally, with admirable restraint and conspicuous moderation.'

(Sir Samuel Hoare, Parliamentary Debates, 29th February, 1932.)

'Hereafter the Members of the Legislative Assembly, especially those who live in villages, will be at the mercy of the village officers and village *chaprasis*.... Hereafter, we, M.L.A.'s, will have to play to the tune of these village officers, and hereafter, we M.L.A.'s will have to keep the village officers in good humour lest we should come under the provisions of this clause. Not only we have to humour the village officer, but also his relatives and any member of his family.... By this enactment what the Government are going to do is to terrorise Indians and to terrorise our souls. Government talks of terrorism in India, but who are the real terrorists in this country? It is the Government who are the real terrorists in this country.'

(Uppi Saheb Bahadur, M.L.A. (Moslem), Legislative Assembly Debates, 24th November, 1932.)

(1) What the Peasant Thinks

THE AVOWED PURPOSE of the Ordinance rule is 'to prove that Civil Disobedience cannot succeed against the organised resources of the State.'[1] In actual operation, the vast powers given to the executive and Police and Revenue officials have been used on a large scale, and with little restraint, against masses of the people. Its aim, and its effect, after many months of continuous repression, has been to terrorise the villager either into submission or into sullen discontent. In the village, the struggle between Government and Congress is more acute than in the town and city, it affects a larger percentage of people, in any given area, and it is more grim.

Reproduced from *Conditions in India*, Report of India League Delegation, 1932, (Chairman Bertrand Russell). pp. 352-84

In cities like Bombay or Ahmedabad, while both resistance and repression have been determined, large sections of the people are still outside the ranks of the actual combatants. In the village, however, owing to its more homogeneous character, its village sense, and the character of Ordinance and Police methods, the village as a whole is terrorised, suppressed or fighting. Some features of Ordinance rule and Police excesses and their results are similar to what obtains in the urban areas, and we do not propose to multiply instances of such.

Principal Features

Among the items that, in our view, merit special attention and are discussed in the successive sections of this chapter are:

(a) Village Opinion.
(b) Village Resistance.
(c and d) Punitive measures and excesses.
The Consequences of the Repression.

Men and women have allowed their ancestral lands to be pillaged and sequestrated, their houses looted and their furniture to be broken up, when a formal apology or some indication that they were opposed to Congress would have obviated all this and in addition brought them material advantages.

Bardoli

The villages have persisted in their resistance. Bardoli is a typical instance. The Government point to it as a success. Mr. Clee, of the Bombay Government, who did not appear to share the facile assumption that 'Congress is crushed,' pointed to Bardoli and said rents are coming in. The Collector of Surat claims a success in that he has collected revenue in Gandhi's own Bardoli. It is true that in 1932 Government collected revenue from the *Taluka*. We shook off our police shadows when we went into the villages of the *Taluka* and saw things for ourselves.

Bardoli has maintained its resistance for over a decade. During this period it has seen repression of the worst kind. Once, when the issues involved were investigated by Government, the findings justified the position taken by the villagers and Government revenue policy was found to be in the wrong. To-day, part of its lands have been sold to outside capitalists, who have bought them for ridiculous prices. They are, of course, the Government's men, not villagers.

Some of the inhabitants have left the village rather than pay. There are still others who have allowed themselves to be reduced to beggary rather than yield. Houses remain sealed, and crops, as at Ras, cannot be reaped.

The Village and Politics

The Simon Commission expressed the view that 'while abstract political ideas may leave him (the villager) unaffected, the personality of a leader, such as Mr. Gandhi, will make a great appeal.' The Commission also says that 'the politically minded in India are only a tiny minority, but they may be able to sway masses of men in the countryside.'

The assertions are true in a measure. The masses are behind the politically-minded, but we did not find them apathetic to the great issues before the country. They were illiterate but by no means unintelligent, or unreceptive to ideas. The awakening in the villages is no doubt to a great extent due to personalities like Gandhi, Abdul Ghaffar Khan, Vallabhai Patel, Purshottamdas Tandon, Jawaharlal Nehru, Kellapan, and others. But these men have made their appeal on the basis of ideas and facts. Not all of them have an all-India or international reputation, nor are all of them reputed for the saintliness that Mr. Gandhi has.

We tested for ourselves in a number of places the extent to which the villager has appreciated the issues, and understood the causes, in the pursuit of which his property and person is being subjected to losses and risks. In a Madras village, we spent quite a long time in questions and cross-examination of villagers, individually and in a gathering, and in talking with the village official. We found that the economic and social issues were very live ones. We heard about poverty, taxation, foreign exploitation, neglect of education and all the other factors that are at the back of India's resistance. We found out that the villagers knew what the Congress stood for, and also that they had no illusion about the enormity of the task before the country. They knew it would mean suffering, perhaps for a long time.

Swaraj

We went on to talk about *Swaraj* and why they wanted it. We suggested in great detail that their conditions would be better if they had more schools, roads and other facilities, if their taxes were lightened, and that to win *Swaraj* was merely a political business. We expected this to go down and to be told that the material improvements we suggested were all that they really wanted. Instead, an old man who was a working agriculturist himself, told us that *Swaraj* was a matter of self-respect, freedom, and self-power.[2] Also he felt quite sure that without 'self-power' the conditions which we had mentioned would not be obtained.

Economic Issues

In Allahabad the peasantry, who showed us their crops, which they said were 'all grass and no grain this year,' knew how, ultimately, the economic plight was connected with politics. We were pointedly asked, in a village near Allahabad, why rents of landlords should be collected by a policeman, and whether a body of people who did not fight obtained anything for themselves. It was also a revelation to us that the Indian peasantry, who are so dependent on the monsoon and the bounty of nature, who still cultivate their land and order their lives on ideas and views which are intertwined with their Faiths, now thought in terms of improvement by social effort. The Indian peasant does not now think that the causes of famine and drought are beyond remedy, though perhaps he does not know just what that remedy is and how it should be applied.

Some Statements

An aged partly blind lady,[3] who lives with her daughter in a thatched hut, formerly a neighbour's cowshed, discussed *Swaraj* with us. Her lands have been confiscated; she, however, refused to run away from the village. She said:

'I am happy that the land has gone. We are still for Congress. Mahatmaji has ordered us not to pay taxes. I cannot be on both sides (Government and Congress). Congress is for making us independent. We do not want to live under this Government. If the others, the men of this village, wear bangles,[4] what am I to?[5]

Koholo Raghala, a *Chodra*, a hill tribe similar to the *Bhills*, spoke to us about Congress and the Mahatma. Raghala wears *khaddar*, is a Congressite, and has given up drink. The Mahatma, he said, lived in his hut, seven years ago. Other Congressmen also have lived in his hut on several occasions. He said: 'To me a Congressman is a Gandhi man. That is all I know. I want to do what Gandhi says, but the memories of beating restrain me.'

We discussed Civil Disobedience and the non-payment of taxes with a no-taxer, Isuharabhai Mundas, aged 60, of Sunav (Kaira District). He said:

'The Government is entitled to taxes, but why do they put Mahatmaji in jail?'

We followed up the remarks with a number of questions, which he answered. We reproduce them here, as they tend to show the extent to which the villagers appreciate the issues involved. Isuharabhai Mundas was not a specially selected witness, but one from a crowd. He was not a specially sophisticated individual, but an average Gujerati farmer.

Question: If Gandhiji breaks the law, what else can any government do?

Answer: But there are too many laws. Government is both a trader and a ruler. That is not good. It must be one or the other.

Q.: If you encourage boys to break laws, will it not lead to difficulties when *Swaraj* comes?

A.: But this Government is bad. Monkeys destroyed the Lanka of Ravana, but not the Ayodhya of Rama. This Government is bad. It is bad because the people get no bread under this Government. Everything belongs to it and nothing is ours.

Q.: If the Government remits 75 per cent of the land revenue and opens hospitals and provides for all comforts for villagers, will you be satisfied?

A.: This Government cannot be trusted. They will again do the same thing as now.

Q.: But will you have a bad *Swaraj* Government or a good British rule?

A.: If there is *Swaraj*, in any case all our money will remain here with our brothers, if not with us. But now they take everything to *Vilayat* (England).

Ras

In Ras, where all the cultivable land has been taken from the villagers, as they are no-taxers, and part of it confiscated, and the

'Congress House' seized, the women told us 'every house is a Congress House.' They also asserted with emphasis that they would not give in till the freedom of India was won.[6]

The village view of the Police is that they are an oppressive force, and in our own experience there was not one village which looked on the police as a force that protected the people.

Kareli
'We do not want a *thana* at all.'
'The police are here not to protect but to beat us.'

These statements, made to us by villagers at Kareli in the presence of Head Constable Ahmed Mian, might be taken as expressing the general view. They added that some years ago there was fear of dacoity, and the village undertook its own defence. There are only two persons in the village with licences for firearms, and they are 'Government men.' The police have never been attacked, and the Head Constable confirmed the statement that the people were peaceful.

(II) The Village and Civil Disobedience

The Civil Disobedience programme in the villages, and the methods of resistance employed, are of a two-fold character, indicative, at once, both of the causes of the Indian unrest and its present objectives. On the agrarian side, rural India adopted the non-payment of agricultural rents and taxes; and on the political side it carried out the general Congress programme of boycott and disobedience of law, both of which were practised with loyal adherence to the doctrine of non-violence. Villages, nearer the forest areas, also included the breach of the Forest Laws as a part of their programme. The defiance of law is usually symbolic, and there is no attempt to create disorder.

The Awakening in the Villages

The moral support given by villagers to the Congress, and to the national movement generally, is a marked feature of the political situation in India. Much of the rural awakening has begun to find orientation and leadership in the village itself, while the methods of Congress organisation, and the attitude of the volunteers, makes the village a significant item and not merely useful ballast. The village is also conscious of the issues involved, and it understands the main features and consequences of the activities and the risks involved. Loyalty to the Congress is spontaneous, and the official story of paid volunteers and Congress intimidation is unfounded. The best reminder of this loyalty of the masses is seen in the total failure of the *Aman Sabhas*, 'Loyalty Leagues,' and officially organised meetings and conferences. These ventures are not merely viewed sceptically, but laughed at. In the United Provinces the Government has made very sustained efforts and harnessed to it the support of landlords, loyal Indians, school teachers and officials. But the Congress is still, in the people's estimate, their organisation. Another piece of evidence is the sacrifices which the villager makes. The Government view is that the Congress was exploiting the economic situation and fomenting discontent. The situation in the United Provinces, where the peasantry had organised themselves, was regarded as grave, and the Government looked upon the action of the Congress in organising the peasants as a hostile act and as a preparation for 'war.'

Official View of Present Trouble

During the Truce period the Congress endeavoured to act as intermediary between Government and the people, and the exposition of Congress policy, and its interpretation of the Truce, amounted in the Government's view to preparation for hostilities. The Government case in this respect has been set forth in 'East India (Emergency Measures), 1932. Cmd. 4014.'

Pundit Jawaharlal and Vallabhai Patel, who were the main leaders of Congress when Mahatma Gandhi was in London, and their lieutenants are charged by Government with campaigning in preparation for a renewal of Disobedience, and in evidence of its allegation it cites Congress statements, as, for instance, extracts from the All-India Congress Committee's circular, dated 10th March,[7] signed by Jawaharlal Nehru:

> 'It is vitally necessary that you should take immediate steps to consolidate the position gained by the Congress during the last year and to strengthen it still further. The immediate action to be taken is to send out our workers, those who have been discharged from jails and others, to the villages to explain exactly

what has been done in Delhi, further to see that there is no harassment or oppression of any kind in the rural areas.

'If we now establish firmly definite centres of work and activity in rural areas we shall strengthen our organisation and prepare the people for any contingency that might arise. I need not tell you that the provisional settlement at Delhi means a truce only and no final peace. That peace can only come when we have gained our objective in its entirety.'

The Government also argues that 'by the middle of April (1931) the Congress was pursuing a definite policy, the objects of which were:

(a) To consolidate and extend Congress influence in rural areas in preparation 'for any contingency that might arise,' the settlement being regarded as a truce only;

(b) To intervene between Government and landowners in regard to the payment of land revenue and between the landlord and the tenant in regard to the payment of rent; and in effect to carry on with an ultimate political purpose, under the cloak of the relief of economic distress, a campaign against the payment of land revenue and rent;

(c) To establish institutions parallel to those of Government where conditions were favourable.

The Charge

The gravamen of the official charge is that the Congress was acting as an intermediary between Government and the people. Referring to a manifesto issued by Mr. Gandhi, which was sent to Sir Malcolm Hailey, the Governor of the United Provinces, beforehand, it says:

'But the chief mischief of the manifesto lay in its assumption that Congress was an authority competent to decide what rents should or should not be paid, to adjudicate disputes between landlords and tenants, and to receive complaints against the former lodged by the latter.'

The Government also took exception to what it alleged is the Congress attitude to the landlord, and in his address to the Legislative Council, on July 20th, Sir Malcolm Hailey said:

'Tenants, already troubled by the economic distress, were told that landlords are parasites, that their only hope for the future is in a peasants' and workers' republic which will abolish landlords, and that landlords who resist Congress now will be "swept beyond the seven seas." Again I refrain from applying an epithet to this line of action. Once more: when certain newspapers are allowed to tell the world that landlords habitually perpetrate nameless horrors on tenants, that in order to force the payment of rents they have habitually been burning villages, maiming peasants, and raping their women, then clearly there is something far beyond a mere desire to find a remedy for the economic distress of tenants. Once more I refrain from applying any epithet to this attempt to spread class hatred through the countryside.'

The Ordinances

As has been pointed out in Chapter III, the situation had gone from bad to worse, and Ordinances were promulgated in the United Provinces on the 14th December.[8]

The Congress side do not deny, nor have they attempted to conceal, the fact that it regards itself as the representative of the people, and particularly of the peasantry. It, however, denies that it violated the terms of the Truce or that it incited the people to violence.

The main centre of the agrarian movement is the United Provinces, but it spread to every Province. Ordinances, promulgated for all India, were brought into operation, and the provisions of the ordinary law, notably the Forest Laws, were pressed into service on a mass scale.

With the promulgation of the Ordinances and the termination of the Irwin-Gandhi Truce, the no-rent and no-tax campaign was definitely adopted by Congress as part of the Civil Disobedience programme.[9] The Congress organisation, which had ramifications in thousands of villages, received instructions from the All-India Congress Committee about the items of Civil Disobedience that were permitted to be practised. The adoption of particular items and plans were left to the local and Provincial committees. Refusal to pay rents and taxes, which in normal times would be matters for the courts, were now dealt with under Ordinance procedure.

The Agrarian Issues

Under the system which obtains in India in some areas, the Government is the landowner. In Gujerat, for instance, we were told all land is owned by the Government, from whom the cultivator holds it. When rents were withheld from the Government, attachments of movable and immovable property were effected, and in areas and cases where resistance was particularly strong seizures and confiscations took place. The tenants who were thus displaced have held their lands for generations, and in all but Revenue Law it is their land, for which they pay Government certain dues. Confiscation, therefore, in their view is a form of political reprisal. The official argument, which was explained to us by a District Collector, is that the tenant holds the land on condition of payment of rent, and if he refuses the payment his right to hold lapses, and it is open for the Government to take the land and do what it likes with it.

Use of Political Weapons

While the rent and tax strike was in progress, Civil Disobedience villages sought to intensify their resistance to the Government by the adoption of political weapons also. Village officials, particularly in Gujerat, resigned, orders about meetings and processions were defied, and Congress volunteers courted arrests. The Government met both the economic and the political protest in the same way as in the first half of 1932. It extended to the landlord all the protection it could give, and where rents were payable to the landlord it made these dues 'notified liabilities' under the Ordinances, failure to pay which would be dealt with under Ordinance procedure. Thus the collection of landlords' arrears became no longer a matter for the civil courts, but a political issue. In the debate on the Ordinance Bill in the Assembly, Sir Harry Haig drew attention to this as an argument in support of the Bill.

Armed policemen, whom we saw in the villages, watched and dealt with political activity, and along with revenue officials engaged themselves in rent collection. In the carrying out of its policy, however, the conduct of the Police and the Executive does not show that what was aimed at was the realisation of arrears of revenues.

The No-Tax Campaign

The no-tax campaign was pursued on a mass scale in the Allahabad and Rae Bareilly districts of the United Provinces, in the Kaira and Surat districts of Gujerat, in the Canarese districts of the Bombay Presidency, in certain areas of Bengal, such as Contai, Midnapore, and Tamluk, in Bihar, and in the North-West Frontier Province. In the rest of India, this item of the Civil Disobedience programme was not widely adopted, and where it obtained it was a matter of individual rather than mass disobedience.

We visited villages in all these areas and made close investigations. The campaign was still in progress everywhere except in the United Provinces.[10] Gujerat, Bengal, and the North-West Frontier Province had suffered the most. In the villages in these areas Government servants resigned their posts and cultivators allowed their land to be seized. The extent of the movement may be gauged from the following figures taken from a number that we collected. In the United Provinces, in the district of Cawnpore, in one Tashil alone 209 summonses had been issued, 298 attachments made, and 44 auctions had taken place.

In *Ankola Taluk* (Bombay Presidency), out of 40 major villages, 26 had taken up the campaign in the first six months of 1932, and 11 out of 63 village officials had resigned.

In *Ras*, 16 police encampments, in which were posted parties of armed police pickets, encircled the whole cultivated area. Out of 2,600 acres, 500 acres had been confiscated and sold and 900 acres seized but not sold at the time we were there.

In *Sisri* (Karwar District), 19 persons withheld payment of first instalment in 1932, over a hundred withheld the second instalment, and 210 attachments were made.

At *Siddapur* (Canarese), 233 persons withheld payment of first instalment and 450 of the second instalment; 200 attachments were made.

In the *Broach* District, 370 acres of land in Jambusur taluka and 245 in Uber had been confiscated.

In the Bengal Council the Revenue Member stated that 261 estates had been sold for not paying the September instalment of the Land Revenue.

In the *Kaira* District about 800 attachments had been made in the first seven months of 1932.

These instances, which are taken at random from different parts of the no-tax areas, indicate the extent of the no-tax movement.

The Government measures included:
1. Proclaiming that landlord rents may be recovered as land revenue.
2. Police camps.
3. Special attachment officers.
4. Blockading of villages.
5. Prohibiting reaping of crops.

Apart from these measures as sanctioned law, as under the Ordinances, the police terrorised the villages, and landlords took the law into their own hands and smashed up tenants' houses, and took their property with the aid of the police.

Police Camps

Punitive police, for which the villagers had to pay, were stationed in many areas. Police camps were built round the crops to prevent tenants reaping their crops. In Ras we saw crops rotting in the fields. In some places, police had mowed the corn, while in others it had been impossible to do this, where local labour was usually not available for reaping confiscated crops, and the police imported outside labour. In some areas the tenants set fire to the crop rather than allow it to be reaped by others. The police encampments, with the armed pickets, gave the place the appearance of areas under occupation.

Attachment of property, usually a revenue process, has now become a police job. The police raided the villages, beat the foremost resisters, seized livestock, fodder, foodstuff, from them, pulled down parts of houses, and none of these can be questioned in a court of law even if Congress people decide to fight actions in court. Police officials told us that they were being put on a revenue job, while the revenue officials said that the police were responsible for the trouble. The Revenue officials, however, are heads of the police as well, and in any case, under the Ordinances, the police are the officials who count, in fact.

Blockading of Villages

Villages were blockaded, to round up people, and as a particularly noxious form of coercion. In the Gujerat districts the police made a practice of blockading villages for twenty-four hours or more. It is the residential part of the village which is thus besieged, and the object is to prevent people from going out into the fields for their natural functions. This might be a piece of unauthorised police tyranny, but blockading, of which we have given instances, in our chapter on the North-West Frontier Province, is part of recognised police policy for coercion of villages.

Kuslabhai Hathibhai stated that on the 16th January and 21st February his village was blockaded from five in the morning till eleven at night, and no one was allowed to go out into the fields or to fetch water.

Sir Purshottamdas Thakurdas, a member of the Round Table Conference, also told us of cases of such blockading of which he had knowledge.

Prohibition of Reaping of Crops

The land seized after the sowing was guarded by the police, and the tenant was not allowed to sow his crop if he was a no-taxer. In Sylhet, Assam, we saw in the village of Bhanubil acres of such crops. The tenants had cultivated the land. The landowner, however, claimed that the crops were his and the tenants had been ordered not to reap the crops. We inquired what would happen to the crop, and the answer was that it is a tradition among peasants that if they do not reap the crops which they have sown, no one else will. We understand that no labour would be available for the harvest in the village if the landlord decided to reap the corn. In similar cases crops had been set on fire by peasants.

Dayabhai Jhaveribhai, of Amod village, is the tenant of the wife of Poonambhai Shankarbhai, of the same village. The lady is a no-taxer, and Shankarbhai had already suffered imprisonment because he manages his no-taxer wife's estate. Dayabhai, the tenant, paid his land revenue, when his buffaloes were attached, and he had paid all his dues to the landlord as well. The next instalment of land revenue fell due on January 5, 1933. Dayabhai had been served with a notice (about October, 1932, when we were there) not to remove his crops unless he gave security for taxes due from his landlord. He said that the crop was already overripe and would be useless in a week.

(III) Punitive Measures and Results

Among punitive measures and excesses[11] to which rural India was subject should be mentioned:
  (1) Attachments.
  (2) Looting and pillage (by landlords and Government agents).
  (3) Intimidation and humiliation   Women.
                                                 Neighbours.
                                                 Civil resisters.
  (4) Attacks on constructive work.
  (5) Punitive police and taxes.

Attachments

The Ordinances have, as has been already noted, made landlords' rents recoverable in the same way as the Government's taxes. Apart from direct seizure and confiscation of lands, attachment of movable and immovable property and livestock, and their sale for ridiculous prices, have taken place on a large scale. In this process the law of the country has been disregarded in several ways.

Illegal Seizures?

Plough animals, Agricultural implements and Seed are not liable to attachment in lieu of debts and arrears of rents or taxes. It is a principle accepted by law, since the deprivation of these 'tools' of his craft renders the agriculturist incapable of earning his sustenance and of paying his debts.

In the present campaign, animals, implements and stock have been seized and sold for nominal prices, or destroyed.

Peasants' houses have been sealed by the police; we saw a number of these, and not only movable property, but detachable parts of houses, such as doors, window shutters, galvanised iron roofing and even bricks from the walls have been taken away.

(1) *Ramabai Butcha Bai*, aged about 60, of Bochasan, Borsad Taluka, the wife of a blind man, made a statement to us. Her son,

aged 24, was in jail, and so eight out of her ten acres of land could not be cultivated. Her buffalo was attached for land revenue. She had bought it for Rs. 100 on instalment payments. Only the first instalment had been paid. She is now in debt for the balance, though she no longer possesses the animal.

(2) *Mangalabhai Vajhibhai* was released on 'parole' on the 14th January, and ordered to report to the police and not to enter the village. He obeyed the order, and his wife, Dahi Bhen, who was a Congress worker, was angry. The lady had been fined Rs. 100 and sentenced to six months' imprisonment for her activities. The police took away two sets of doors, a cradle, corrugated iron roofing, spinning wheels and other property.

(3) *Ishwarbhai Mundas*, of Sunav village, aged 60, owed Rs. 8 in taxes. All his movable property, estimated at Rs. 200, was attached in January, when he was away in the fields and no one was in the house. His wife and children were visiting in the next village. After a month a demand for taxes was made, and he refused to pay. He was then sentenced to three months' imprisonment and fined Rs. 50. In the fourth month the police went to his family house and attached the buffalo, whereupon his brother paid Rs. 20 for tax, Government costs, fees, etc. The next day the police again went to this brother's house and demanded the fine of Rs. 50, and threatened to take away the buffalo. He was then released. None of the movable property originally taken has been returned.

(4) *Mothibhai Hathibhai*, a no-taxer of Sunav, owed Rs. 6 in taxes. His tobacco crop, worth Rs. 250, was attached, and he received nothing from the sale of it, nor any receipt of any kind. He heard from the headman that the crop was sold for Rs. 11.

(5) *R. Nadhabhai Kaldas*, aged 65, of Gana village, told us a story of torture.[12] The revenue due from him was Rs. 15 and *Thakavi* (loan) Rs. 10. He had been manhandled by the police, and finally they were forcing him to touch the battery of a motor car when another man out of pity offered to pay the revenue. The Government had already taken Rs. 200 worth of property, which had not been

refunded. He stated that he refused to pay because the Government had put Mahatma Gandhi in jail.

(6) *Chathurbhai Baijabhai* owned 13 acres of family land. He and the family ran away with three buffaloes when a police party arrived. The police entered their houses and broke up cooking vessels and household articles, etc. They destroyed the hayrick and took possession of agricultural implements.

The Government had attached and sold his crop, which he said was worth at least Rs. 70. It was bought by the Head Constable Allabux Hussain, for Rs. 5, in May, 1932. His whole property is worth Rs. 16,000. He had reaped the rest of his crop. He owed Rs. 125 in revenue.

Sipahi Lal, of Karma village, U.P., stated that he was unable to pay his rent. His land was taken without notice. He continued to cultivate the land and was accused of trespass and fined Rs. 100. He was unable to pay and therefore was sent to prison. His four bullocks and one cart were then attached and sold. He had 20 acres of land and was in difficulty only on what was due from a plot of $3\frac{1}{2}$ acres. As he had only two bullocks left, he was unable to cultivate his land properly.

Paramufty Village, United Provinces—We came across a number of instances where people were unable to pay land revenue, some of them women, who had sold everything they had and found it impossible to feed their starving babies and children.

One peasant stated that he had 20 bighas of land and had to pay Rs. 175 per year in taxes. He owned five bullocks, one cow and six calves. He had a wife and four children. His brothers' widows and their children made the joint family of fourteen members. All his property, including the cattle and five mango trees, had been attached.

A widow with three sons, of whom the eldest was ten, said that she owned four bighas of land; but all of it had been attached, and she had been turned off the land, and she and her children were actually starving. They had had nothing to eat for the 'last two days' (28th September, 1932).

In *Karchana*, about 14 miles out of Allahabad, the crops had failed. Peasants had been unable to pay revenue dues. Buffaloes worth over Rs. 50 had been attached and sold for about Rs. 5. The people were starving.

We also saw in the villages of the North-West Frontier Province the results of wholesale attachments, both in the homes of the poor and the comparatively well-to-do. We have referred to instances in the chapter on the Frontier Province.

In Abdul Ghaffar Khan's[13] own house we saw that all the furniture had been taken away, in lieu of land revenue; the Khan himself is in jail, without trial.

Looting and Pillage

Where punitive police are stationed, entering of houses, taking away of goods, looting and destruction take place as part of Police *Raj*, according to the evidence we received and the results that we saw. In the villages, mainly in Gujerat, looting has followed in the wake of tax collection.

Houses Entered

We went into a large number of houses in the Gujerat villages and saw the destruction that had been wrought. Utensils and furniture had been broken up where they had not actually been taken away. In Ras and Bochasan we saw house after house, in which the huge earthen jars, in which grain is stored, were broken up. These are part of the peasants' stock, and they have been in possession of these families for generations. It was stated to us that armed police had entered and broken up things with the butt ends of their rifles, *lathis*, or anything else they could lay hands on. Beds, food, etc., had also been taken away in villages in Bengal, the North-West Frontier Province, and Gujerat. We have the particulars of a number of instances, some of which we give below.

In one village alone (in Borsad Taluka), out of 800 houses about 200 had been entered by the police. In Ras, there was hardly a house which the police had not entered and looted.

Ishvarbhai Mundas, of Sunav, whose statement about attachments of property we have already cited, stated to us in cross-examination that 'the police resident in Sunav usually buy their things from the shops in that village or from Petlad (the next village), but when attachments are made they take things not only for the Government but for themselves, and they take what they like.'

Khusalbhai Hathibhai made a statement[14] that about 'fifty policemen who were brought from Anand by Revenue Officer Manilal

Gandabhai were posted at every corner in the village and practically all the houses were entered. They broke up water pots, big jars, and boxes, and beat people, several of whom were aged men.

Gangaben, wife of Chathrubhai Baijubhai, aged 26, stated[15] that the police and the *Mamlatdar* asked her to say where she had hidden money. The police, armed with rifles, went to her house. She was asked to show the buffaloes. The *Mamlatdar* took away ornaments from the house.

(Her husband's lands, which she said were worth Rs. 20,000, have been confiscated and sold for Rs. 200. They were bought by Abdul Ahmed, who does not belong to the village.)

Elephants to Destroy Houses

We saw the results of some of the looting and destruction in Bhanubil, in Sylhet. The village is about ten or twelve miles from the nearest road, and there is not even a cart track to reach it. We travelled on an elephant, which negotiated the muddy fields and numbers of little rivulets which had to be crossed.

The village belongs to a Zamindar, who is alleged to have increased the rent from $13\frac{1}{2}$ annas to Rs. 2.80.[16] The tenants refused to pay, and the Zamindar got a decree of ejectment. Armed Gurkhas and constables, headed by a Superintendent of Police, helped in the ejection of the tenants. The Zamindar brought his elephants and pulled down the houses, which were razed to the ground and all the property trampled on. Over fifty houses were thus destroyed.

We met one of the victimised families. Lapoi Devi, whose husband was in jail, told us that these elephants were brought out and three houses which belonged to her family, all in the same compound, were destroyed. The rent due originally was Rs. 20. It had been enhanced. The houses are estimated to be worth Rs. 680. The Superintendent of Police was present. Representations were made to the Government before the incident; the answer was that it would not interfere.

The rents were not paid, Lapoi Devi told us, because they could not afford the enhanced amount. Their lands were taken away, but they were cultivating them, all the same, without permission. She also said that there were many people similarly victimised.

They were given no opportunity of removing their belongings. They now live in huts, which they have built on the Zamindar's land without permission. The Zamindar and the police, she said, took away their cattle, and she was not sure that they would be allowed to reap the crop they had sown, as they were trespassers.

Her father, Bijendanath Sharma, and her uncle, Harimohan Sharma, were arrested, one for being a member of an unlawful assembly and the other for trespass, for building the house in which she now lived.

'The police,' she said, 'even now come into our houses and take away our utensils, grain, bedding and clothes. The Sub-Divisional officer visits the house and abuses us from a distance.'

In Bengal, as in the North-West Frontier Province, police pillage has reached excesses comparable only to conditions under military occupation in times of war.

Cases Cited in the Assembly

Mr S.C. Mitra cited[17] in the Assembly cases,[18] and produced documents and photographs in evidence. The details could not be published in the press owing to the Press Law. We quote some extracts:

'In the house of Mahendra Nath Jana, of Dalimba Chauk, Sutahata Police Station, all his movable properties were looted, and even the image of the goddess "Laxmi Devi" was thrown away from its place. The other is about the occurrence of the house of Jogendra Nath Kalsa, of Dundipur, on the 22nd September, 1932 Here the District Magistrate, Mr Burge, and the Sub-Divisional Officer, Mr Richardson, were also present when the police destroyed their granary. and spoilt the paddy collected there.

'This is the photograph of that place (shown). Here is another case where, in the village of Bar-Basudebpur, in the house of Brojalal Kniti, the Bhagwat-Geeta was torn to pieces and put into the boiling *handi*, and the man was beaten. This is the statement, and this is the photograph, which will indicate how these things are done.... I am giving you the date at the very time— September last. In the village of Hadia, in the house of Kartick Chundar Das, the punitive police burnt the teakwood furniture and burnt the doors and windows. In the same village, in the house of Pran Krishna Das, they entered the temple and stole ornaments even from the body of the image of the family god.

I particularly give these instances to show that in Eastern countries people are very sensitive when their religious sentiments are hurt in this way, so that the mighty Government at Simla also should know how the day-to-day administration is being carried on under the Ordinances that are now going to be made law....

'There are numbers of pictures taken. I am now showing the House a few only to prove that we do not draw these pictures from our mere imagination. Here is another case where, on the 24th September, 1932, in the house of Bihari Lal Maiti, for a tax of Rs. 24.9, 320 maunds of paddy were taken away in the absence of male members. Then this is another picture of a place where Swadeshi *Khadi* is sold, and they have destroyed all these things. Of course, they may have a special grudge against the Swadeshi-wallahs. This is the photograph of the house of Ajit Kumar Maiti, of Dari-Bera, where the doors and windows have all been taken away, and property destroyed. Here is the photograph of a place of the house of Rakhal Chandra Samanta, of Hadi, where the corrugated tin shed has been destroyed. Here is a picture of a house belonging to Gora Chand Kaisher, of Dundipur village, where the cottage has been destroyed and all the thatched roofs have been brought down....

'Here is a photograph of a place where all the trees, banana trees, were cut, etc. How all these things are necessary for the realisation of a tax one can easily imagine. Here, on the 24th September, 1932, at about one o'clock, the second officer of the Thana, Dhirendra Nath Chatterjee went to the house of Sukuma Maiti for collecting the tax, but he destroyed his thatched house and his walls. This is another picture of a house of Keshab Chandra Mandal, of Dundipur, where all the ceilings have been destroyed. How the destruction of property or the ducking of a man in the tank helps the realisation of punitive tax has got to be explained. This is another picture of a stationery shop belonging to Nagendra Nath Das, where the entire property was destroyed. Now, this is the picture of a pharmacy where all the medicine bottles have been thrown out and destroyed.'[19]

Intimidation and Humiliation

The presence of troops in the villages of Bengal is one of the more glaring instances of mass intimidation. Sieges of villages by police and threats to women and those giving hospitality to Congressmen, collective fines, and action against the neighbours of persons arrested, are other forms.

Some Cases

At *Kareli*, villagers stated to us that those who gave shelter to non-cooperators were beaten. Villagers who took food and water to women non-co-operators were also maltreated. The police sealed the doors of the temple, where the non-cooperators were staying. Villagers removed the doors. They were charged with theft. They were acquitted after six months, but had been beaten severely. Some cases were treated in the Government hospital at Broach.

Soma Shankar stated that on the 18th September he was stripped naked by the police in the *Chora*.

Bahji Bawa, aged 14, also stated that he was stripped of his clothes and beaten by Constable Mahomed Mustafa. Sub-Inspector Bapu Bhai took out his knife and threatened to cut off his genital organs.

Jetha Bhai, aged 19, made a similar statement, that P.C. Mahomed Mustafa stripped him naked.

P.C. Mahomed Mustafa was present when Jetha Bhai made this statement, and we asked him if it was true. He said: 'It was not I who stripped the boy naked; the Sub-Inspector did it.' On second thoughts, he added: 'Nobody stripped him naked. A search was made of everybody.'

We asked, 'What kind of a search: for weapons? These people, with so few clothes, can be searched without taking off their clothes.' Mustafa made no reply.

Village of Gujera.—One hundred and fifty people were arrested at a Taluka conference on the 18th September. Forty were taken upstairs one by one and beaten. Six were severely injured, others were given blows on the face and body. Fifteen were stripped naked. Inspector Khambatta and Sub-Inspector Bapu Bhai were concerned in the beatings, but the former was not present when the stripping took place.

Desai Pursotam, aged 35, cultivator of Kareli, stated that Sub-Inspector Bapu Bhai slapped him and kicked him with nailed boots till he fainted. He was taken the next day to Jambasur lock-up for two nights. He was then bleeding from the intestines. He was convicted for six months, and was in the jail hospital for three days. The doctor sent him to the hospital after examining the injuries. He was on a barley water diet for some days.

Bahmatpur, Monghyr District. The women came in large numbers to tell us of abuses and insults which they received at the hands of the police. Some of them, though very poor, had been called on to pay punitive taxes; Dhane Masomat, a widow, had been taxed Rs. 2, though she earns her living as an agricultural labourer on two or four annas a day, when she obtains work.

Dhansi Sahu, a labourer without land, had been ordered to pay Rs. 38. He had an aged sick wife and four children. The police entered his house, beat him, on the day we were in the place (23rd September, 1932). The old man said: 'We have no weapons, but we cannot bear this.'

In *Jahman* Village (Punjab), women alleged attempts by the police to dishonour them. One lady said that her door had been broken open many times, and if there was a prosecution of the police she would be willing to give evidence.

A Pro-Government Group

In the same village we met the pro-Government party—a group who told us that we had heard only one side. They said to us: 'We thought it our duty to help the British Government, so we gave the police milk, etc.'

There were nine of them present, and they said there were thirty or forty others. They were Sikhs and Mohammedans. Bhuj Singh, the spokesman, said: 'None of us had to pay punitive taxes. We were exempt. We do not want self-government. We always pray for the gracious Government.'

Indecent Attacks?

Attempts at indecent assault on boy prisoners were alleged in several reports made to us. We took a very full statement in one case,[20] which is in our possession.

The use of filthy language to young women and aged men, who take part in Civil Disobedience, was alleged in statements all over the country. Indian women, who are to-day in the Congress fight, have been accustomed to sheltered lives, and this form of coarseness is intended to frighten them away. It was accompanied, in some cases, by violence, and in others by taking them out of their towns or villages to distant and lonely places and leaving them stranded there.

Jinabhai Jijibhai, aged 56, of Porda, Borsad Taluka, stated to us that he was arrested by British police in Baroda State territory, where he and other villagers had gone, because there was plague in Porda. His hands were tied behind his back, and he was taken to Sunav lock-up at night.

Sub-Inspector Mejha, and Head Constable Chiman, used filthy and insulting language about his mother and sister. He was beaten. The Head Constable used more filthy language and dragged him towards the wall, and said that he was 'going to give him *Swaraj*,' and putting his hands on the man's shoulders pounded him against the wall. Mr Jijibhai was then subjected to more filthy abuse. We asked him to tell us what it was, but he said, 'I am an old man and would not like to repeat it.' He was then shown the statement made by a boy who had alleged that the police attempted an unnatural offence on him, and the old man said that the language was of the same kind.

Khusalbhai Hathibhai stated that his daughter-in-law, Dahi Bhen, was surrounded by the police, who called at the house when he was in the field and beat her with sticks.

Women Insulted

Rami Nathabhai Kaidas, aged 65, stated that he was taken to the village office, and his shirt and cap removed by force. The police entered the house, took utensils and other movables, threatened his daughter-in-law, who was ill in bed, with beating, and asked for her ornaments. The *Mamlatdar* (Magistrate) Manibhai Gandabhai took her out of the house, locked it up and took the keys away. His son was also brought to the village office. They were taken to the field after an hour. In the field they were stripped of all their clothes, and they were made to bend and touch their toes. Two police with sticks were on either side, and whenever they tried to stand up they were given blows by the *Mamlatdar*.

Gangaben, the wife of the owner of the field, was then brought by the village police to see them in that condition. She was questioned about her husband and ordered to look at the naked men.

The old man said he was kicked with nailed boots, at intervals, violently. (Scars of nail marks were visible on his back.)

Gangaben, the wife of Chaturbhai Bhajibhai, aged 26, who it was alleged in the previous statement, was insulted and intimidated, was then examined by us.

She confirmed the story and also said that the *Mamlatdar* used foul language.

Forced Labour

Shivabhai Jagabhai, aged 50, a barber, stated:

'On the night of the 5th February (1932), when I was asleep, the police came and knocked on my door with big sticks. I was ordered to come down, which I did. I was dragged out and beaten with a *lathi* on my back and with hands on my head and face. I was bleeding. With the next blow on the head I fainted. My mother, who was eighty years of age, cried out, "Don't kill my son!"

'The police went to her bed and beat her. She died after about a month. I was taken to the village office along with another barber and beaten again.

'We were asked to do work for the Circle Inspector, two clerks, and the second-class Magistrate. *Bagar* (forced labour) for two days had been demanded of us both. We refused. That was our offence. We have always paid our land revenue and we are not connected with the Congress.'

Koiolo Raghala, [21] of the *Chodra* (aboriginal,) tribe made a statement to us of terrorisation.

'In last April or May (1932), the police stopped a procession, after beating all the volunteers. Sub-Inspector and constables came to me at nine o'clock at night. They fell on me, the Sub-Inspector beat me with his cane and the Head Constable with a *lathi*. The others also beat me. This continued for over half-an-hour. I was taken to the police office at Marvi and compelled to prostrate. I was threatened with death if I entertained Congress people any more.'

He also stated that police officers were forcing people to sell lottery tickets, and threatening to attach lands if sufficient were not sold.

Maghanbhai Ranchojai, aged 22, Khoti by caste (aborigine), of Karadi village, and *Ukhabhai Panchibhai*, also a Khoti, made statements of terrorisation and beating.

IV Attacks on Constructive Work

Constructive work carried on by Congress, its allied organisations, and other independent bodies, has suffered under Ordinance rule in several ways, which include[22]:

(1) Direct and deliberate attacks on organisations and individuals.
(2) Deprivation of leadership as a result of arrests, etc.
(3) The state of fear and suspicion created by Police and Ordinance *Raj*.
(4) Police excesses and action taken by over-zealous officials.
(5) Attacks made under misapprehension of the nature of the institutions concerned.
(6) Stoppage of funds.

Direct Attacks

Many Congress *Ashrams*, which have scrupulously refrained from politics, have been broken up or closed down by the police. One of the worst instances that we saw was in Sitanagaram, in the Telugu area, where the building was under police occupation, and the looms and doors, which had been wantonly smashed, were being eaten by white ants. With the breaking up of that *Ashram* much medical, educational, and cottage industries work, for which it was the centre, had been destroyed. The destruction of looms and smashing of other property is no doubt legal, because no action taken under the Ordinances can be called into question in a court of law, and no officer can be held responsible for his conduct. But the wanton destruction, the result of which we witnessed, is, in our opinion, one of the most eloquent comments on Police *Raj*.

All over India, such centres, including schools, have been seized and broken up. If the Government holds that they are run by men whose sympathies are with Congress, and should therefore be closed, they should have seized Mr Gandhi's *Ashram* at Ahmedabad. Policy here, as elsewhere, is haphazard, and left to the man on the spot, who, in these regrettable instances, appears to mistake aggressiveness for zeal.

In another Gandhi *Ashram* in South India, at Thiruchengodu, there was a doctor whom the settlement had sent for training in the treatment of leprosy. The gentleman returned to his duties to find that he was served with a restraint order, severely curtailing his movements in the villages in which he had to work. As a leprosy doctor for the settlement he became useless, and as a man he felt the order a humiliation, and he disobeyed it. He was sent to prison, and lepers go untended.

Government policy has also added to the misery of some of the peasantry in certain areas, as in the villages of the United Provinces, where the repression has resulted in the breaking up of the spinners' organisations to some extent.

Leadership

The constructive work in the Indian village has largely centred round the Congress volunteer, who is now either barred from the village or is in prison. Organisation, and the sense of village consciousness, which their work inculcated, is now arrested, or, where it is still virile, is canalised in civil resistance. Anyone attempting similar work is taking a great risk.[23]

Fear and Suspicion

Police action against *Khaddar* in different parts, and the surveillance that is exercised, have struck terror into rural areas. Where repression has been severe, as in the Surat District, the Government have crushed the people, so that few are left to take the risk of doing anything that will bring the police on their trail. Ordinances, and police conduct, preclude any safeguards which appeals to law or the assertion of rights may be expected to provide.

Police Zeal

It is probably true that in some instances higher officials are either ignorant of, or have not sanctioned, some of the measures which the police practise. They probably are not responsible for the persecution of well-meaning men or for restricting their movements. The actual state of affairs is that anyone is liable to arrest and any kind of activity is suspect.

Cases of Misapprehension

Mr S.C. Mitra quoted in the Assembly[24] a case in which, on the 28th September, 1932, the police destroyed the Co-operative Bank's accounts and the ploughs in the house of Purna Chandra Das, of the village of Hadia, in Bengal.

Mr N.M. Joshi[25] referred to the case of a colleague of his, Mr Thakkar, of the Servants of India Society:

'After the Civil Disobedience movement was started and several Congressmen were sent to jail, Mr Thakkar was given a small sum by a gentleman in order that the wives and children of Congressmen who had gone to jail should not die of starvation. Only a few days ago, one of the District Magistrates in Gujerat called Mr Thakkar in order to bully him and browbeat him. He asked whether he was supplying funds to the wives and children of the people who had gone to jail. Now, Mr President, I want to ask this question: Why should an officer object to anyone relieving the distress of the wives and children of Congressmen? I can understand Government putting the Congressmen in jail, but certainly it is not according to the rules of any civilised warfare that a combatant should desire that the wives and children of his opponents should die of starvation....

'You have given so much power that if a man does anything which the officer does not like, he calls him to his office and asks him not to do it. This is not the only thing. You ask your officers —here I am not talking of the petty officers, but of the higher officers—not only to defeat the Congress but to crush and uproot the Congress.'

Professor Joshi,[26] a trustee of the Bhagini Seva Mandir, of Poona, told us of the case of his organisation. It has six trustees, three of them Congressmen and three members of the Servants of India Society. One of the bodies connected with Congress was a tenant in its buildings. To avoid difficulties, the trustees terminated the lease. Nonetheless, the police asked for an undertaking that the *Mandir* would not enter upon unlawful activities. Undertaking was not given. Policemen were posted at the gates.

Funds

People are afraid of subscribing to any organisation which may be suspected by some policeman or stated to be under suspicion. Good causes are thus deprived of their resources, which are essential to their work. Also, as in the case of the Gujerat Sabha, funds are sequestered without justification.[27]

Punitive Police and Taxes.

Additional police forces have been quartered in a number of villages in several Provinces in India. In the no-tax areas of Bombay, Bihar, Madras, the United Provinces, the Punjab, and Bengal, the terrorist areas of Bengal, and the Red Shirt villages of the North-West Frontier Province, such Forces have been quartered.

Punitive Police

The Punitive Police are, as far as we saw, and ascertained, armed. They are quasi-military in character and usually the members of the Force do not belong to the Province in which they are quartered. Official reports, to some of which we have referred, have pointed to the bad discipline and organisation of certain sections, at least, of this force. Among the people the punitive and special police have a thoroughly bad reputation. They are comparable to military detachments of occupation in a martial law area.

In Bengal, punitive police have been stationed in certain areas where those wanted for terrorist outrages are believed to be at large. The view taken is that the village is conniving at terrorism, and without local assistance it would be impossible for the offenders to be in hiding.

Fines

The cost of the force is met, at least in part, by the levying of fines, which, we understood, were collected by the police themselves and not by the Revenue Department. Those who criticise the stationing of punitive police ask whether the people are to be penalised and taxed because they are not able to perform the task in which the Police Department have failed, namely, tracking down terrorists.

The levying of fines is left to local discretion. In the terrorist areas it is the Hindu population who are as a rule fined, though they are in a minority. This discrimination has canvassed for the Government the support of Conservative Moslems.[28]

The punitive police posted in the other areas are either as a punishment for, or to deal with the difficulties created by, the no-rent campaign.

The Government's Case.

The general Government case for the imposition of such fines is, perhaps, best stated in the following extract, which we have taken from a *communique* issued by the Bihar Government on the 28th May:

'The Local Government are not in a position to keep so considerable a force of police detached from their ordinary duties, but on the other hand, in view of the sustained and deliberate defiance of the villagers, in spite of many warnings, it is unsafe to leave the village unpoliced. The Local Government has accordingly declared that the village is in a disturbed and dangerous state, and that a force of additional police will be employed in it for a year at the expense of the inhabitants.

'Exemptions will be granted to those who have kept themselves aloof from the movement.'

Authority to Quarter Punitive Police

The actual imposition of these forces may be in exercise of the power conferred by emergency legislation like the Bengal Ordinances or the Emergency Powers Ordinance, or under the Police Act.

We were informed that the posting of such punitive forces is a matter within the discretion of the Local Government but Indian opinion holds that the terms 'Local Government' and 'Local Official' are in fact interchangeable in matters of administration.[29] A proclamation is issued, and the specified area is made responsible for its maintenance. We print below the copy of a proclamation which would help to explain the procedure and the character of the arrangement:

June 1, 1932.

PROCLAMATION

The 26th May, 1932.
No. 312. P.R.

In exercise of the powers conferred on him by Section 15 of the Police Act, 1861 (V. of 1861), as amended by Act VIII. of 1895, the Governor-in-Council declares that the conduct of the inhabitants of the area specified below within the jurisdiction of the Lakhisarai Police Station, in the District of Monghyr, has rendered it expedient to increase the number of police by the appointment of an additional force consisting of one Deputy Superintendent of Police, one Inspector, two Sub-Inspectors, eight Havaldars and one hundred armed constables, to be quartered in the said villages, at the cost of the inhabitants thereof, subject to any orders which may be passed exempting any person, or class or section of the inhabitants. This proclamation shall remain in force for a period of one year with effect from 1st June, 1932.

2. The above proclamation shall apply to the whole of the village named in column 2 below.

Thana No. 1.   Name of Village.
187.
　　　　　　　　　　　Barahiya including three tolas, viz., Chuharchak, Tajpur and Bodhnagar, English (Barhiya).

By Order of the Governor in Council.
　　　　　　　　　　　　　　　P.C. Tallents,
　　　　　　　　Offg. Chief Secretary to Government.

Police 'Garrisons'

Some of the worst police atrocities in India are the work of the Special Police Forces, as different from the Regular Force. They, unlike the Regular Force, have no houses in the areas in which they are stationed, and are rather like a garrison, indifferent to and ignorant of the sentiments of the community in which they live. They lack the discipline which longer service and the performance of duties, other than coercive, give to the members of the Regular Force. Roughnecks are recruited to the Force as a deliberate policy, while the task which they are set would affect the *morale* of even disciplined men.

(1) Looting and pillage.
(2) Outrages on women.
(3) Intimidation and violence.

Looting by Punitive Police

Houses have been entered and property smashed. We have already referred to some of these. In Madhkaul, a small village, we saw some of the results of the conduct of the punitive police. Granaries had been looted, women insulted, bayonets thrust into kitchen pots and vessels. In the village we saw a store which had been wrecked. The kerosene oil in the store had been poured over the stores of rice and pulses. The villagers, through their spokesman, told us a story of wrecking and looting.

Sabuj Mishra, a cultivator, whose house had been looted, told us that his cash box had been broken open and the family ornaments taken away. We asked him whether he had reported this robbery to any officials, and he said that he reported the wrecking and looting of the house to the Sub-Divisional Officer, an Indian, who replied, 'Don't come to me with your complaints. I am not going to hear of these things. Pay your taxes.'

Shops had also been looted, and we discovered, from the information we gathered, that complaints had sometimes been made to officials, but it was little use, as the police did what they liked and the regular officials had little control over them.

We asked the old villager who had acted as spokesman whether he thought that the police were acting lawfully. His answer was: 'Our throats are being cut by the servants of a Government which says it is the law, and you ask if it is just! The Moghals never did this.'

In the next village, Sheohar, we learned that the trouble, which was the cause of the firing which led to the posting of the punitive police, was started by police agents. No proper inquiry was made.

Terrorisation

From the statements and information in our possession, we could give instance after instance of the terrorising activities of the police garrison, which is what the punitive police resembles.

They levy blackmail, and rob women, visiting the area, of their jewels.

The punitive fines must be paid, if the officials say it must be paid, whether one can afford or not, or whether one is Congress or not.

At *Sheohar*, Sobhai, a Moslem, told us the story of his daughter, a married woman, who, while cutting corn in the field, was rushed at by the punitive police and violated.

At *Midnapore*, we saw people who had received wounds at the hands of the punitive police. In Tamluk, Bengal, Pathans, Punjabis, and Gurkhas have been planted all over the district. The people had been beaten, robbed, fired on, and tortured and made to pay for the very force that was responsible for these acts.[30]

What we have said of the punitive police may, perhaps, leave the erroneous impression that they are a band of guerillas who take the law into their own hands, and that higher officials are not aware of what is being done. Guerillas they may be; they may take the law into their own hands, but it is still 'law' in India. They, however, act under orders, which, as the villagers say everywhere, are 'Smash everything.'

People Defend Themselves

In some areas, like Tamluk, people are developing a form of defence against official terrorism. When the punitive police approach the village, the women blow a conch shell as a warning, and the cultivators take their wives and daughters away to the depths of jungle swamps. At the time of our visit, women in the villages of the Tamluk District had taken to sleeping in the fields, out of fear of night raids of their houses by the punitive police.

Under the punitive exactions and persecution people are fleeing from the villages. Press reports, which we saw in India at the time, stated that from the villages of Sijbena, Rajarampur, Shivramnagar, and several others, people had left their homes and the Union Board were therefore not able to raise the taxes.

Shortly after our visit to Tamluk, we saw the following press report about a raid:

'On the 10th instant (September), Punitive Police surrounded the village Keorakhali, in Sutahata, P.S., in order to realise punitive tax. The villagers began to vacate their homes. The wife of Sj Upendra Nath Das, of Hadia, who was in an advanced stage of pregnancy and was running away, stumbled and fainted. She was taken care of and removed to Basanchak, where she expired after two hours. Another lady of Keorakhali, with her sucking baby of five months was fleeing away. She had to cross a marshy land. There her baby slipped from her arms. She searched for the baby for some time till she got it back alive.'

Exactions

The fines, as we have stated, are attached by the police. Illiterate villagers are not always able to ascertain what is due and what is receipted for, as the copies of receipts below will show:

KACHA (TEMPORARY) RECEIPT

Received *Rs.* 6 *annas* 15 (6/15)[31] *only*. 77. Dhisendralal Rakhit, c/o Ramchandra Rakohit, of Amuchia, as Punitive Police tax.

(Sd.) A.C. Biswas.
Dhorala Subthana.
29/6/32.

PUCCA RECEIPT
Govt. of Bengal. A855380.
No. 6.
Dated 3/7/1932.
Received from 77. Dhircudralal Rakshit. 87. Ram Chandra Rakshit, of Amuchia, through a/c Dhorala, *Rs.* 5 *annas* 3 *only.* Credited to P. Tax.

Suryya Gupta.[32]
A.S.I

References

1 Sir Samuel Hoare in the House of Commons. (Hansard, Vol. 267, No. 120.)
2 He used the words *Swathanthriya* and *Swashakti*, which mean freedom and self-power. This was in a Telugu village.
3 At Khojhpardi, in Bardoli.
4 This expression means, 'If they are cowards.' She was referring to those who had submitted to terrorisation. Her own menfolk had refused to surrender. This village had been cowed down by terrorism. People were tired of fighting. They were still opposed to the Government but were afraid even to talk.
5
6 We have described the conditions in Ras later in this chapter.
7 The Congress was at that time assisting in the collection of Revenue as a result of the Irwin-Gandhi agreement. The agreement did not preclude Congress organisation in the villages, and, indeed, in view of its being intermediary between peasants and the Government its organisation work was a natural consequence.
8 Mr Gandhi was in London at the time.
9 *Cf.* Chapter III. Congress resolution, January, 1932.
10 In the United Provinces the drastic operation of the Ordinances, preventing workers from going into the villages, the arrest of all workers in the villages, and the severe handling of demonstrators in the villages, was followed by concessions to the villages. We were told that the Government, after delivering its blow against the Congress, made greater remissions, in many cases, than were demanded by Congress at truce time as a means to maintain peaceful relations.
11 We have referred in this section mainly to classes of instances, to which attention has not already been drawn in the chapter on Police *Raj* in Action.
12 Cf. p. 299

13 This was denied in part by the official spokesman in the Legislature. The statement here refers to what we have seen ourselves, and we therefore print despite the denial.
14 The statement was made to us at Sunav. The additional police were brought from Anand. We are not certain whether the village referred to is Sunav or one of the neighbouring villages. The entry in our notes is indistinct.
15 The parts of the statement dealing with Intimidation appear on p. 375.
16 We are not sure whether the enhancement was uniform for all lands in the village. Under the permanent revenue settlement, the Zamindar's taxes to the Government cannot be enhanced, and, as an absentee landlord, he does nothing for the land or the tenants.
17 Assembly Debates, Vol. VII., No. 5.
18 Most of the incidents took place while we were in India.
19 The debates in the Provincial Councils and the Assembly on the Ordinances and the Ordinance Bill and the questions and answers on administration are replete with instances of police terrorism.
20 There are several sworn statements in the Katyu (non-official) Jail Committee of the United Provinces, whose report we have used in writing the chapter on Jails.
21 He belongs to a tribe like the Bhills. Mr Gandhi stayed in his hut some years ago.
22 We have dealt with these in other chapters, where we have discussed the constructive programme.
23 Under Section 51 of the Emergency Powers Ordinance and now corresponding provisions in the 'Ordinance Act.'
24 Assembly Debates, Vol. VII., No. 5.
25 Assembly Debates, Vol. V., No. 9.
26 Not Mr N.M. Joshi, mentioned above.
27 We have already referred to Government policy in relation to Swadeshi and the 'Buy Indian' movement, both as officially stated and as in actual fact.
28 Mr Abdul Matin Chaudhury, speaking in the Legislature on the 3rd December, 1932, said: 'Under these Ordinances, the Frontier Mussulmans have been terrorised; the Red Shirt movement has been crushed; the Ahrars have been suppressed; the Moslem Press has been throttled; and even in this Imperial City of Delhi, under the very nose of the Government of India, the sanctity of the Moslem mosque was violated. Wherever the Mussulmans have shown any sign of life, activity or vigour, they have been put down with an iron hand, and there is nothing to be surprised at in this, because when you give this autocratic power to the irresponsible executive it is bound to be abused.'
29 In Stuart times one of the items against which the early champions of British liberty fought was the 'billeting of soldiers.'
30 Lieut.-Colonel Arthur Osborn, D.S.O., in his book, *Must England Lose India?* quotes an official who told him: 'I give you my word that after some of my punitive police have been stationed in a village for a few days the spirit of the toughest of the political agitators is broken.' Lieut.-Colonel Osborn inquired, 'How?' 'Well, they will help themselves to everything. Within twenty-four hours there will not be a virgin or a four-anna piece left in that village.'
31 Italics ours. Note the difference in the amounts.
32 The name on our copy is not very clear.

18 Agrarian Movements in Bengal and Bihar, 1919-39

Binay Bhushan Chaudhuri

THIS PAPER is an attempt to study such actions of one of the groups, the peasantry of Bengal and Bihar in the period between 1919 and 1939—their aspirations and struggles in the context of particular economic and political developments, the interaction of their 'social radicalism' and the mainstream of the nationalist movement, and the extent of their success.

Peasant movements were, however, by no means an entirely new development in the period under review. In fact, the strength and extent of such movements before have been greatly underestimated.[1] Combined peasant resistance could be traced right from the beginning of British rule. It became increasingly strong in the second half of the 19th century, particularly in Bengal. The revolt of the Pabna peasants in 1873, sparked off a series of similar revolts in other districts. The resistance was most widespread during the period of the controversy over the Bengal Tenancy Bill (1879-85), which was finally enacted in 1885. The Bill aroused in the peasants extravagant expectations, and they construed it as a moral approval of their stand by the Government. All sorts of rumours were circulating: the despotic power of zamindars would soon be gone forever, and with it the scare of enhancement of rent; the rent-rate would be reduced everywhere and legislation would deprive zamindars of all powers to enhance it. As long as the peasants had nothing to hope for, they remained tame. Hope now made rebels of them.

The Bihar peasants also rebelled from time to time, though such uprisings were mostly confined to the indigo cultivators and the tribal people.

Reproduced from '*Socialism in India*', (ed.), B.R. Nanda, Vikas Publications, Delhi 1972, pp. 190-229.

I

The novel features of the peasant movement in the period under review mainly relate to its organization. Peasant associations (Kisan Sabhas) were created nearly in every district under a unified command. Certain strata of the peasantry which previously remained largely inactive or aloof, increasingly participated in the kisan movement. Moreover, the initiative of the peasants now remained sustained over a much longer period than before.

The peasant organizations which already existed were far from adequate for building up a sustained movement. The peasant associations were mostly local groups, because the peasant rebellions arose mainly out of particular local grievances. Some movements did spread outside the localities. The rebellion in Pabna, for instance, encouraged similar rebellions in the neighbouring districts. The movement pertaining to the Bengal Tenancy Bill was also fairly widespread. But here also the organizational base was very weak. In the first case, the rebels of Pabna had only tenuous links with their followers in other districts, such as transmission of inflammatory messages by the emissaries from Pabna. The basis of the second movement was identical hopes shared by a large section of the peasantry. With the growing disenchantment of the peasants over the Bill, the movement soon petered out.

A far more serious shortcoming was the absence of what may be called a philosophy behind the programme of action of the rebel peasants, which, by relating the peasants' grievances to some fundamental social and economic institutions, could provide the rebels with a broad perspective for their movement. The main concern of the peasants was the removal of some specific immediate grievances. The criterion of judging what particular set of conditions properly constituted a grievance was whether the existing law approved or disapproved of such conditions. For instance, the asking by zamindars of a larger quantum of rent irrespective of form or occasion, constituted a grievance where the law disapproved of it. The abruptness with which such demands were made by the zamindars made them all the more galling to the peasants. The acceptance by the peasants of this criterion, naturally imposed serious restraints on their movements, from the very beginning. This meant that they did not question those institutions the working of which added to their grievances. The removal of such grievances, therefore, deprived the movement of the basic impulse which could sustain it over a long period.

It was once thought that the participation of a section of the intelligentsia in the movement of the peasants, which was a particularly striking phenomenon during the agitation over the Bengal Tenancy Bill (1879-85), gave the movement a radical tone. Jatindra Mohun Tagore, Secretary, British Indian Association (an organization dominated by zamindars) explained the social roots of this alleged radicalism and its nature thus:

'They have neither status nor stake in society, and to attain the one or the other or both, they resort to various kinds of agitations, social, religious, reformatory and so on.... They are for the most part East Bengal men, joined by some English-returned natives, who also hail from that part of the country. Many of them have seen something or read still more of the doings of the Irish agitators, and with a natural love of emulation and a highly ambitious mind, they would fain try their chance in the socialist line to eke out, if possible, a living, or create a position for themselves by following in the footsteps of their European examplars.... They go to the ryots, pretend to be their friends, sow seeds of dissension between them and the zamindars, and thus set class against class.... In their pretended zeal in the interests of the ryots they had, two years ago, nearly brought the country to a blaze by inciting agrarian insurrection.... The Bengal Tenancy Bill... has proved a powerful weapon in their hands for setting class against class.'[2]

Such a characterization of their plans of action was far from correct. It was not enough that some of them had radical faiths. In fact the peasant movement was not appreciably affected by such faiths, and they scarely left any trace after the Tenancy Bill agitation had died out.

The nationalist movement led by the Congress had in its early phase an elaborate agrarian programme, but could not provide an appropriate 'philosophy' for a broad-based peasant movement. The Congress agrarian programme was mostly confined to a critical analysis of the British land revenue administration in India. The British land revenue policy, a feature of which was believed to be a drive for the maximization of land revenue, was denounced by the Congress as one of the most vital causes of India's poverty, since the high revenue demand was thought to be the biggest single drain on the surplus generated in the agricultural sector, thus keeping the accumulation of capital at a frightfully low level and making the peasant economy increasingly vulnerable to occasional failures of crops. Arguing from this premise, the Congress concluded that a demand for the fixation of the land revenue would help to resolve the crisis in the nation's economy. Hence its plea for the extension of the permanent settlement of the Bengal type to other parts of India. The support for the Bengal model however did not necessarily imply a support for the particular zamindari system of Bengal, with which the permanent settlement was associated from its beginning.

Curiously enough, the Congress accepted the zamindari system for granted, and tended to ignore the fact that most of the zamindars were mere parasites living off the labours of peasants, and that the numerous exactions on their part did constitute a factor in the impoverishment of the peasantry.

Some Congress leaders occasionally took part in the peasants' struggle, but the fact was that sometimes they were drawn into it in spite of themselves and this participation was not part of any commitment by the Congress as an organization to the struggle. We can take Gandhiji's defence of the interests of the indigo cultivators of Champaran (1917) as an illustration. The Congress had nothing to do with the movement. In fact, as Gandhiji wrote, it was practically unknown in those parts. His confessions are revealing:

> I did not then know the name, much less the geographical position, of Champaran, and I had hardly any notion of indigo plantations. I had seen packets of indigo, but little dreamed that it was grown and manufactured in Champaran at great hardship to thousands of agriculturists.[3]

To Gandhiji, however, the indigo system appeared as an isolated instance of an unjust system, and not as a part of a wider institutional set-up. Moreover, he was cautious not to give the movement a political colour. His stand was justifiable once we assume the correctness of his understanding and characterization of the indigo system and of the aims of his movement, i.e. to reform the indigo system for the time being and not to destroy it.[4]

The first significant contacts of Jawaharlal Nehru with the peasantry too were quite fortuitous. 'I was thrown,' he tells us, 'almost without any will of my own, into contact with the peasantry.'[5] This is explicable once we keep in mind the particular aims of the Congress at the time, and also the nature of the social groups whose interests the realization of such aims would have promoted. What Nehru wrote of the kind of politics he had been engaged in, till 1919-20, largely applies to the politics of the dominant Congress leadership at the time:

> My politics had been those of my class, the bourgeoisie. Indeed all vocal politics then were those of the middle classes, and Moderate and Extremist alike represented them and, in different keys, sought their betterment. The Moderate represented especially the handful of the upper middle class who had on the whole prospered under British rule and wanted no sudden changes which might endanger their present position and interests. They had close relations with the British Government and the big landlord class. The Extremist represented also the lower ranks of the middle class. The industrial workers, their number swollen up by the war, were only locally organized in some places and had little influence. The peasantry were a blind, poverty-stricken suffering mass, resigned to their miserable fate and sat upon and exploited by all who came in contact with them—the Government, landlords, money-lenders, petty officials, police, lawyers, priests.[6]

II

It was in the period under review that we find the gradual emergence of a strong peasant movement equipped with the philosophy of a kind which enabled it to transcend peculiarly local limits. Such a movement, however, cannot be traced from the beginning of this period. A great upsurge did occur among the peasantry in 1920-21, primarily as a consequence of the Non-Cooperation movement. For the first time after the widespread agitation against the partition of Bengal (1905), the nationalist leadership sought to draw the masses into the nationalist movement. This by itself could not move the peasants much. The Congress leadership did not intend it either. But the Non-Cooperation movement created an atmosphere which was favourable to the growth of an independent peasant movement. The scope of the Non-Cooperators' programme tended to widen, and included at one time agitation against the payment of choukidari (village police) tax and land revenue. Examples of non-payment of land revenue to the Government by the peasants (where such a system of direct payment prevailed) undoubtedly encouraged similar evasions of payment of rent to zamindars. It is also probable that some local leaders having radical faiths and acting on their own judgement irrespective of Congress leadership had a hand in the peasant agitations, which gradually grew to an alarming extent.[7]

With the calling off of the Non-Cooperation movement, the main impulse behind the peasant agitations quickly disappeared. Even if the former movement had continued it is doubtful whether the Congress leadership could have for long ignored the implications of the growing peasant movement for the nationalist movement. Though the Congress wanted the peasants to participate in the nationalist movement the emphasis throughout was on how to strengthen it through such participations. If the peasants through an independent movement of their own threatened to be a divisive force in it then the Congress would have preferred doing without them. The resolution of the Congress Working Committee at Bardoli (12 February 1922) was bitterly critical not only of the occurrence of violence in the movement, but also of any independent peasant movement inevitably developing into a kind of 'No Rent' movement:

> The Working Committee advises Congress workers and organizations to inform the peasants that withholding of rent payment to the zamindars is contrary to the Congress resolutions and injurious to the best interests of the country. The Working Committee assures the zamindars that the Congress movement is in no way intended to attack their legal rights, and that even where the ryots have grievances, the Committee desires that redress be sought by mutual consultation and arbitration.

As a result the peasant movement suffered a great set-back. However, peasants got opportunities to renew their activities when the Government brought a Bill in 1923 for amending the Bengal Tenancy Act of 1885. The changes that were contemplated were many, but the one that created quite a stir at the time related to the sharecroppers, bargadars, who constituted a considerable group. They had neither legal rights, nor in most cases any customary rights in the lands they cultivated. The zamindars or the richer peasants whose lands the bargadars cultivated could evict them without much ceremony. The Government contemplated conferring on them the status of 'occupancy ryots,' a group enjoying special legal protection in regard to the tenure of their holdings and the level of their rent. This daring move created much enthusiasm among the bargadars. They formed, for the first time, their own associations in various places. But their enthusiasm was not enough to create a strong movement for which they needed active co-operation of other social groups. This was mostly wanting. On the other hand the zamindars and the substantial peasants whose interests were threatened by the Bill opposed it strongly. Several newspapers and journals which used to uphold their point of view also joined the protest. So did the members of the Swaraj Party and, of course, the representatives of the zamindars in the Legislative Council. Moreover, some zamindars and richer peasants fearing that some revolutionary measures would soon be adopted, hastened to evict their bargadars, in a desperate attempt to save as much as possible before the worst came to the worst, even though this rash step resulted in an appreciable contraction of cultivation. This opposition persuaded the Government to leave bargadars and landowners to themselves.

III

The formation of the Workers' and Peasants' Party (1926-28), constituted a turning point in the history of the growth of the peasant movement, particularly in Bengal. Its origin and programme was thus described by the Defence Counsel at the Meerut Conspiracy Case:

> Its world outlook was Marxian, and it applied Marxian principles to its study of the contemporary political situation and the social and economic organization in India. The background of the formation of the party was the result of a growing feeling that the way the Congress had been leading the country's struggle for freedom was wrong. The Congress, the founders of the Party felt, misunderstood the class character of the groups hostile to this struggle, and this had resulted in weakening the struggle.

The Principles and Policy of the Party says:
The chief exploiting interests were British imperialism, Indian capitalists, landlords and princes, and there were no chances of any serious divisions among the ruling classes, and they jointly exploited the large masses of workers and peasants.

The Congress was not sufficiently aware of this. The members of the Workers' and Peasants' Party felt indignant at the way the Congress had been used for their own purposes by the landlords and capitalists. The collapse of the Non-cooperation Movement and the experience of the Swarajists in the Assembly had convinced them that the programme based on the co-operation of the exploiting classes, who were themselves in part a creation of an alien rule, was not enough to achieve national liberation. They decided that the dynamic force of a mass movement should be the sole basis of national struggle.

The Programme of the Party was 'complete national independence from British imperialism and a democratic organization of society involving the nationalization of key industries and appropriation of land without any compensation.' For achieving this the Party 'decided to establish contacts with all anti-imperialists organizations and work among all politically revolutionary social strata.' To increase the momentum of the mass movement it was decided to establish mass organizations and organize mass demonstrations and mass non-payment of taxes and rent and general strike.

The Party preached these ideals in Bengal through two Bengali journals, Langal (Plough) and Ganavani (Voice of the People). Here was a plan of integrating an independent peasant movement with the general anti-imperialist struggle.

It is not known whether Marxian ideas influenced the leaders of the peasant movement before the October Revolution in Russia. There is no doubt that such ideas quickly spread in Bengal after the Revolution. The reports of the Intelligence Branch of the Political Department of the Government of Bengal suggest that by 1920 the circulation of 'Bolshevik' literature was large enough to attract the attention of the Government. A number of leading journals of the time (like the Samhati, Atma-sakti, Samkha, Bijli, Dhumketu and Dainik Basumati) show how deeply the revolution had moved a sizeable section of the Bengali intelligentsia. The stir created by it soon reached even the rural masses. The ideas that attracted them most were in fact simplified versions of the Marxian concepts of social struggle. The educated members of society, with whom rural masses presumably came into contact, taught them that the zamindars were mostly responsible for their poverty and misery, and that the destruction of the zamindari system would bring them prosperity and happiness. What had happened in Russia was presented as a prototype of the things to come in Bengal after the elimination of the tyrannical zamindars. Lenin represented to them the ideal type of leader to lead them to such a goal. Rathindra Nath Tagore, son of the poet Rabindra Nath Tagore, visited their estates in East Bengal a few years after the first world war. At that time he met a number of peasants who were inspired by such faiths. Once when he was discussing with a group of peasants how best to improve agriculture, a fairly old peasant intervened and talked disparagingly of the nationalist leaders. According to him, they talked big but were completely ineffective when it came to concrete action. He concluded his discourse thus: 'Were there such a man as Lenin in the country, everything would be put right.'[8] The poet Tagore himself saw when he visited some parts of Eastern Bengal in 1926, how 'innumerable' local literary journals were propagating a cult of violence directed against zamindars and money-lenders.[9]

The influence of the Marxian ideas was thus gradually spreading. The formation of the Workers' and Peasants' Party was, however, a significant point in the process. Instead of various agencies scattered over the country, including a number of literary journals which had seldom any consistent social and political philosophy, an organized group (in addition to one or two more) now took upon itself the propagation of Marxian ideas and it formed a nucleus for the growth of independent peasant associations.

One finds here the vital role of ideas in building up the base of a peasant movement. It is, however, doubtful whether a 'philosophy' alone could produce, let alone sustain it. Without the presence of objective political and economic conditions, the new ideas would have soon lost their force. Such conditions emerged mainly as a result of the economic depression of the thirties. Awadheswar Prasad Singh, Secretary to the Bihar Provincial

Kisan Sabha, emphasized the point in 1938: 'The Kisan movement as developed today is the direct outcome of the objective situation intensified by the agricultural crisis.'[10]

Fluctuations in the prices of agricultural produces occurred in Bengal and Bihar. Changes in the state of crops, either a shortfall in the production or a bumper harvest in the context of a more or less fixed market, reacted sharply on the prices. Two other characteristics of a predominantly peasant economy, particularly of its monetized sector, also account for such variations—the tendency of the output of primary products to be inelastic and the fluctuating demand for such products.[11]

When depression set in, the prices slumped. In the period between 1929 and 1935 a fall by 60 per cent to 70 per cent was a common phenomenon in many districts of Bengal and Bihar. There was a steep fall in the prices of jute, which was the most important cash crop of the peasants in many districts. The crash came abruptly. Since the beginning of the 20th century, the jute prices showed a steady rise, aggregating to about 150 per cent in the period between 1900 and 1929. The peak year was 1925, when the prices shot to Rs. 16 per maund. In 1933 the harvest prices fell as low as a little over Rs. 3/–. It was remarkable that for the first time since 1900 there came about an organized move for restricting jute cultivation.[12]

The extent of the fall in the prices was not however entirely unprecedented. What was particularly striking was the duration of the depression and its universality. The steep fall in the prices was of course a disaster for the peasants, but their recovery from its effects would have been easier if the disaster had not continued beyond a single year. It lasted for about eight years. Moreover, the depression affected not only one or two agricultural produces, but all the produces at the same time. Previously this was scarecely the case, so that the loss from one crop was at least partly made up by the gains from another crop. Where, for instance, the conditions of soil and climate made the cultivation of jute possible, a slump in the prices of rice resulting mostly from a bumper harvest led the peasantry to increase the cultivation of jute. Similarly, a fall in the prices of jute, so much so that its cultivation scarcely repaid the producers, led them to abandon it for the time being and to concentrate on rice. The well-known phenomenon of the interchangeability of rice and jute thus partly resulted from the movement of their relative prices.

The depression suddenly aggravated all the ills from which the peasants had long been suffering. Where their income was derived almost entirely from the sale of their crops, the consequences are not hard to realize. The burden of their normal unavoidable financial obligations suddenly increased, since they had to part with a far larger quantity of their produce than before to meet their old obligations. The upward movement of rent during the long spell of high prices of nearly two decades and a half, particularly since 1905, made the rent obligations heavy indeed. Rents were not automatically reduced when the depression had set in, at least not proportionately to the fall in the prices. Arrears of rent thus tended to accumulate, leading in several cases to eviction of the peasants. Where the commutation of produce rent into money rent had taken place on a considerable scale during the period of the high prices, the distress of the peasants was naturally far greater, since the system of produce rent imposed a much heavier burden on the peasants in terms of the quantity of produce they had to surrender to the zamindars. It is, however, wrong to suppose, as Dr Walter Hauser did,[13] that the kisan movement in Bihar was mostly confined to the regions where the system of produce rent prevailed. The intensity of the distress resulting from the depression, varied of course from region to region, but it was severe enough to produce deep discontent in the peasants which resulted in kisan movements. That was why in Bengal proper where the system of produce rent was confined to small regions the kisan movement was no less widespread or intense. This was partly because of the fact that rent formed a small part of the total financial obligations of the peasants. In fact, their debt obligations were also quite heavy, and indeed exceeded the rent obligations in several places. Even where the peasants had not incurred fresh debts, the falling prices by themselves made the debt obligations still heavier.

The depression with all its consequences seemed to reinforce the Marxian class analysis. The poverty and misery of the peasantry which the depression had suddenly brought to the surface, were attributed to the particular class composition or society, which according to the Marxists was mainly determined by the fact that the law had invested in the class of zamindars property right in the land. Elimination of this poverty and building up the base of a new peasant economy therefore necessitated the destruction of the zamindari system. For this the peasants had to organize themselves and fight the system out.

In view of the magnitude of the economic crisis produced by the depression, it seems surprising that it was only in 1936 that the abolition of the system was formally stated as one of the basic aims of the kisan movement.

This formed a strikingly new feature of the peasant movement. Even earlier, peasant agitations had occasionally led to a complete suspension of rent payment. This, however, did not result from any doubts on the part of the rebel peasants as to the propriety or legality of the institution of zamindari, but from a dead-lock created by the resolve of the peasant community not to pay rent exceeding a certain rate which the zamindars on their part had found unacceptable. The warring groups soon found a way out, and rent payment became normal. The aim of eliminating the zamindari system was indeed revolutionary. This inevitably meant that the struggle would not end with the mere removal of some particular grievances. Independent peasant movements in several places gradually came to be influenced by ideas derived mainly from the Marxian philosophy. This transformation can be clearly traced in Bihar.[14]

It was a deep compassion for the wretched peasantry, a basically humanitarianism that first led Swami Sahajanand and others to try to organize them around some specific demands. Being nationalists they had no doubt whatsoever, in the beginning, about the priority of the nationalist movement, and did not hesitate to subordinate the kisan agitation to it. However they gradually outgrew their belief that this subordination would eventually do real good to the peasants. This happened as a result of ideological influences.

It is significant to note that in the long period between 1920, the year in which he took a leading part in the Non-cooperation movement in Bihar, and 1927, when he first began to take a keen interest in the problems of the peasantry, Swami Sahajanand seemed to have been completely unaware of the existence of a distinctively peasant question. This was partly due to the fact that after the movement of the indigo peasants in Champaran a peasant movement worth its name was virtually non-existent in

Bihar. With the abrupt withdrawal by Gandhiji of the Non-Cooperation movement, the Swamiji, like a number of Congress leaders of Bihar at the time, became actively associated with an organization of the prominent zamindars belonging to the Bhumiar Caste—Bhumiar Brahmin Sabha. He was asked by the Bhumiar zamindars to establish at Bihta in Patna district, an ashram mainly for the purpose of giving their children lessons in Sanskrit. The ashram came into existence in 1927.

It was in the zamindari estates around the ashram that he had his first contacts with the peasants. He understood some of the worst features of the zamindari system, including the system of forced labour, begar, and thus gradually realized the need for an independent organization of the peasants. In 1929 the Bihar Provincial Kisan Sabha was set up with the co-operation of the major Congress leaders. To begin with, he conceived of the kisan movement 'in the spirit of a reformist.... At that time I did not know what revolution was, nor did I understand its import.... What we had in our mind was to do some good to peasants by exerting constitutional pressure and getting their grievances redressed.'

Even this 'reformist' movement could not be reconciled with the nationalist movement. When the Congress started the Civil Disobedience Movement, the Swamiji promptly suspended the kisan agitation since he feared an independent kisan agitation would tend to 'weaken our struggle for freedom.'

A large number of peasants did participate in the Congress movement, but the utter indifference of the Congress leadership to the grievances of the peasants shocked the Swamiji. Peasants in numerous places, as in Gaya under the leadership of Sri Jadunandan Sharma, a close associate of the Swamiji, sent numerous petitions to the Congress Agrarian Committee (1931), explaining such grievances. The Committee, however, had scarcely anything new to say.

The disillusionment with the Congress leadership alone was not enough to make a radical peasant leader of the Swamiji. He also needed a social philosophy, and his close association with the leaders of the Congress Socialist Party soon provided him with one. The Programme adopted by the Party in October 1934 particularly impressed him. It included, among other things, transfer of all power to the producing masses, elimination of zamindars and 'all other classes of exploiters without compensation' and redistribution of land to the peasants. The Swamiji's radicalism can in fact be dated back to 1934 when he started thinking in terms of abolition of the zamindari system. Initially, however, he feared that this stand would alienate a considerable number of supporters from the Kisan Sabha, particularly the small landholders. Such doubts were soon overcome. The manifesto of the Bihar Provincial Kisan Sabha (11 July 1936) outlined some of the Sabha's 'basic' demands. These included abolition of the zamindari system, the creation of a system of land tenure where peasants could own land and the provision of 'gainful employment' to the landless.

Similar Kisan Sabhas were gradually formed in other parts of the country. Such sabhas, however did not for long remain isolated from their counterparts. The first session of the All-India Kisan Sabha with Swami Sahajanand as the President, was held on 11 April 1936. The 'Manifesto of Demands of the Kisans of India' adopted by the All-India Kisan Sabha Committee (21 August 1936) formulated the 'main object' and the 'main task' of the Kisan movement. The 'object' was—'complete freedom from economic exploitation and achievement of full economic and political power for peasants and workers and all other exploited classes.' The 'task' was—'organization of peasants to fight for their immediate political and economic demands in order to prepare them for emancipation from every form of exploitation,' and this was to be done through 'active participation in the national struggle for independence.'

IV

The Kisan Sabha was not, however, the only organization of the peasants at the time. In Bengal the Muslim League sought to 'wean away' the peasants from the influence of the Kisan Sabha. The League feared that increasing activities of the Kisan Sabhas among the Muslim peasants would endear the Congress to them and thus eventually result in weakening the League's hold over them. To prevent the Muslim peasants from attending the session of the All-India Kisan Sabha at Comilla (in Eastern Bengal, May 1938), the League members went to the extent of scattering pages from the Koran on the main road to the Conference, believing that the Muslim peasants would not be bold enough to trample on them.

The success of the League was only partial. Whatever success it had, was largely attributable to the particular composition of the Bengal peasantry. The majority of them were Muslims, while their zamindars were mostly Hindus. The League, professing to defend the interests of the Muslim community, succeeded to a certain extent in influencing the Muslim peasants by playing on their religious sentiments. It, however, did not set up any separate peasant organization.[15]

The Krishak Proja Party, another organization working among the peasants in Bengal, had a much wider influence on the peasantry, though it was mostly confined to the richer section of the Muslim peasantry. The proclaimed aims of the Party gave it the look of a radical peasant organization. The Party's programme advocated the abolition of zamindari as also the elimination of the host of intermediaries between the state and the actual peasant cultivators. It stood for a 'permanent peasant proprietary system of land' where 'all proprietors of land will be the actual cultivators,' and would pay a fixed tax, not rent or revenue to the state.

The differences between the Krishak Proja Party and the Kisan Sabhas were, however, fundamental. The former conceived of the peasant movement primarily as an economic movement, unrelated to the struggle for the country's freedom. To the latter, the peasant movement formed a vital part of the freedom struggle, since the zamindari system, which the movement aimed to destroy, was propped up by British rule. Moreover, the Krishak Proja Party had serious reservations about the way the Kisan Sabhas had been leading the peasant movement, and strongly disapproved of any class struggle of the Kisan Sabha style, which necessarily involved some violence at a certain stage. This was how two leaders of the Proja Party felt over the question. Qazi Imam Husain remarked:

'The distinction between the kisan movement in the United Provinces... and the Proja movement of Bengal is remarkable in the fact that the former one is a little aggressive, inclined towards socialism... while the latter is purely economic, parliamentary in its demand and is averse to violence.'[16]

The worsening situation in regard to rural indebtedness which reduced several small owner-peasants to the status of agricultural labourers provoked N. Azizul Haque, another Proja leader, who remarked:

'The process has to be stopped if a univeral agrarian unrest with its disastrous repercussions on the province as a whole has to be avoided. The average Bengal agriculturist is much too conservative, spiritual and resigned to his fate to be easily amenable to socialistic and communistic preachings. But a province with a vast mass of landless labourers as one of the features of its rural economy has within it the seeds of real danger. Dictatorship of the proletariat is a very comprehensive phrase and may be twisted and distorted to appeal to the sentiments of the aggrieved and suffering classes. Release the cultivator from the bonds of indebtedness, help him to make agriculture pay and the country will be saved from some of the dangers of communism.'[17]

The Proja leaders, naturally, wanted the peasants to keep away from mass movements. The initiative of the peasants inevitably languished under such circumstances, and often the leaders acted on behalf of the peasants. Through the provincial Legislatures they put pressure on the Government for the adoption of particular measures for redressing some of the grievances of the peasants. The peasants were mainly supposed to elect them to the legislature. The Proja movement was aptly described by Qazi Imam Husain as being 'parliamentary in methods.' Such a movement could do little harm to the radical kisan agitation.

V

The ultimate aim of the Kisan movement was, as we have noted earlier, 'complete freedom from economic exploitation and achievement of full economic and political power for peasants and workers and all other exploited classes.' The achievement of political power for peasants was part of the larger question of the country's political freedom. And until political freedom was achieved the Kisan movement aimed mainly at the destruction of the zamindari system. The demand for abolition of the zamindari system came from various other quarters also. The assumption that this abolition would have a big role to play in the economic regeneration of Bengal was so widespread that an enquiry into its feasibility formed one of the terms of reference of the newly set-up Bengal Land Revenue Commission (November 1938). The Kisan Sabhas did not, however, leave the question to the Commission. It launched a countrywide agitation to press its demands. The Commission in fact recommended the abolition of the zamindari system.

The immediate programme of the Kisan Sabhas had various aspects. The struggle for the reduction of rent and debts was by far the most important.

The Civil Disobedience movement had already created among the peasants a spirit of defiance against their zamindars. Some zamindars of the Tamluk sub-division of Midnapur, for instance, were threatened by their tenants that 'they would not any longer receive the customary services of the labourers, barbers, dhobis (washerman) etc.'[18] The Depression made reduction of rent an increasingly urgent question for the peasants. And with the increasing strength of the Kisan movement, the struggle for such reductions soon developed into a virtual 'no rent' movement. By 1932, the spread of the movement was alarming enough to call for the adoption of preventive measures by the Government. In the worst-affected districts like Noakhali and Tippera, the Government promulgated Ordinance No 111 of 1932 under which any person who instigates directly or otherwise any person or class of persons not to pay rent was made liable to six months' imprisonment. Notices under Section 144 of the Criminal Procedure Code were issued by the Sub-divisional Officers prohibiting meetings organized by the Krishak Sabhas. A common slogan of the peasants in many parts of Bihar was 'Malguzari lo ge kaise, danda hamara zindabad' (How could our rents be realized? Long live our cudgels).

The militant peasants could not, however, be tamed. In fact, several developments between 1934 and 1939 tended to harden their attitude. The anti-money-lender legislation of the period was one such development. Initially it had a modest scope and aimed at curbing mostly the non-Bengali money-lenders, particularly the itinerant Pathans and Kabulis. More stringent measures were taken in 1936. By the Bengal Agricultural Debtors Act, the Government imposed ceilings on interest rates and set up arbitration Boards (called Debt Settlement Boards) empowered to write off a portion of agricultural debts. The existing debts were thus considerably reduced. The peasants however were reluctant to pay even the reduced debts. The result was a virtual moratorium on the payment of debts in many places.

The question of rent was outside the purview of the Act, but an idea increasingly gained ground among the peasants that the Act applied to payment of rent as well. This naturally strengthened the 'no-rent' campaign. Complaints of the zamindars on this score became nearly universal,[19] and the Government admitted that they were well-founded.[20]

The peasants were encouraged in this by the 'electioneering speeches' in 1937. The new Act of 1935 greatly increased the size of the electorate, and during the first election held under the Act (1937) the candidates made big promises to the peasants with a view to getting their votes. Townend, then Commissioner of the Burdwan Division observed:

'This tendency to refuse rents undoubtedly has its origin in the irresponsible electioneering speeches made by candidates of all parties who sought election to the legislature.... To get the cultivators' vote they spoke as if the interests of the cultivators alone would be considered in future. There was talk of the abolition of the Permanent Settlement, which was understood to mean the abolition of all tenures, and everything possible was done to arouse discontent and to inflate expectations.'[21]

Such expectations further arose as a result of the countrywide agitation in 1937 and 1938 over the amendment of the Bengal Tenancy Act. Some provisions of the Bill, debated in the provincial legislature in April 1937, were quite favourable to the peasants.

The Bengal Provincial Kisan Sabha launched an agitation demanding the resignation of the Coalition ministry if it failed to pass the Bill. (The Act was passed in August 1938). An official report noted that partly as a result of this there occurred 'a general change in the ideas of the tenants regarding their own rights in the land.'[22]

The organization of the Kisan Sabha vastly improved at the same time. This was due to the fact that a number of political workers who relied till then on 'terrorist methods' increasingly lost faith in their efficacy and were attracted by the Marxian ideas relating to class struggle and organization of industrial workers and agricultural labourers. The terrorist activities appreciably declined by 1935. A police report of the year records:

'A fresh wave of revolutionary activity is gathering momentum. A large number of the terrorists are involved in this new movement, which is closely connected with communism and the methods adopted by the Russian revolutionaries. Terrorists have already realized that a revolution cannot be brought about by terrorism alone. It does not produce the social and economic chaos which is the necessary preliminary to a violent revolution. Vigorous propaganda on these lines is going on in many quarters... among students, industrial workers and agricultural labourers.'[23]

This trend was not later reversed. Another police report of 1938 says:

'Information in the possession of the Government shows beyond a shadow of doubt that a large proportion of the ex-terrorists and revolutionaries... are obsessed in varying degrees by theories of communism.... These doctrines are being assiduously propagated among youths and students, labourers and peasants.... The influence of prominent communists is visible in practically every organization.'[24]

The release, by the end of 1938, of most of the persons detained under Regulation III of 1818, the Bengal Criminal Law Amendment Act of 1930, and the Bengal Suppression of Terrorists Outrages Act of 1932, resulted in bringing a new vigour to the kisan sabha and similar other 'mass' organizations.[25] The Mymensingh Landholders' Association despairingly told the Land Revenue Commission in 1939 that 'the leadership of rural areas has fallen into unworthy hands, and the result is going to be chaos, confusion and communism.' By 'unworthy hands' the Association meant 'socialists, who are a class of educated landless people having no stake in the country.'[26] The Bengal Land Revenue Commission had to admit that the growth of a 'no-rent mentality among the raiyats had threatened the stability and security of the land system as a whole.'[27]

A similar resistance was organized against money-lenders. In fact the no-rent movement and the anti-money-lender movement progressed side by side. In Noakhali, for instance, prior to the launching of a no-rent campaign, anonymous notices were reported to have been received by several money-lenders threatening them with execution if they failed to return the bonds.[28] A meeting in

Noakhali of the representatives of the Joint Stock Banks and Loan Offices on January 4, 1932 'viewed with alarm the present situation arising out of the propaganda carried on by some agitators throughout the district instigating people for non-payment of all rents, debts and other dues.'[29] A resolution passed at another meeting in the district held on the same day urged the money-lenders 'to exempt debtors from all interests and to accept the principal only in 20 instalments in view of the present economic crisis.'[30] A police report of 1934 attributed the increase in 'dacoity' in Tippera and Noakhali 'to the activities of the krishak samities which are secret organizations whose main object was to loot wealthy money-lenders and destroy their documents.'[31]

When the Congress formed the ministry in Bihar (1937), the Kisan Sabha persuaded it to intervene on behalf of the peasants. The measures of the Congress, however, disappointed the kisan leaders. At the 1937 session of the All-India Kisan Sabha, it was resolved that, if by December 1937 the Congress had failed to adopt more effective measures, 'the peasants should be entitled to declare a moratorium themselves and further to boycott any legal machinery set up for reducing or negotiating debts and take all the concerted measures they might deem fit to promote the object in view.'[32]

The Kisan Sabhas also succeeded to some extent in organizing the sharecroppers (bargadars). The bargadari system was in many places part of the larger question of rural indebtedness. Small owner-peasants, unable to repay accumulating debts, gradually lost their lands to money-lenders. The latter, not considering it worthwhile to cultivate such lands themselves, let them out to the expropriated peasants. These peasants continued to cultivate them agreeing to surrender half the gross produce to their creditors.

The bargadars were not a docile group. There are several instances of combined resistance by them particularly in the 1920's. This resistance owed much to the hopes aroused in them by a move on the part of the Government for a better legal definition of their rights on land. Towards the end of 1924, the Muslim bargadars of the Manikganj subdivision of Dacca district collectively decided to 'boycott the Sabha community,' to which their creditors mostly belonged, 'on the ground that members of the caste ill-treat their servants, charge interest at exorbitant rates and foreclose on their debtors' lands.' Despite its apparent 'religious tinge,' the movement was 'fundamentally economic—a case of peasant versus capitalists,' as an official report put it.³³ The movement gradually spread to other parts of Dacca and to Mymensingh, and continued upto 1930.³⁴ In 1929, in some parts of Jessore the bargadars demanded two-thirds of the crop as their share. The zamindars disagreed with their demands with the result that cultivation was stopped. As a consequence the area under cultivation shrank considerably.³⁵

The Depression further aggravated the plight of bargadars. The high level of rent, usually half the gross produce, was by itself enough to reduce them to dire poverty. Their distress increased in the context of a steep fall in the prices of agricultural produce. At the same time, the number of bargadars went on increasing, primarily because more owner-peasants lost their lands to moneylenders. The anti-money-lender measures of the Government, like reducing the debts of the peasants, gave them some relief. This was, however, temporary, and before long the peasantry realized the adverse effects of these measures. Scared by such measures, the creditors refused to lend any money at all. Rural credit was nearly frozen as a result. But since the peasants in the grip of the depression could scarcely do without borrowing, they eventually agreed to borrow on more stringent conditions than before. Curiously enough, though the size of indebtedness actually diminished in the late 1930's, the number of distress sales of peasants' holdings largely increased. The Bengal Land Revenue Commission estimated the size of the barga cultivation in 1939 at more than 20 per cent of the total cultivation.

The influence of the Kisan Sabhas among the sharecroppers was mainly visible in some districts in northern and eastern Bengal. In northern Bengal, the main centre of their activities was the district of Dinajpur where their primary concern was the problem of the adhiyars, the local name for sharecroppers. The adhi system was quite extensive, and about 25 per cent of the cultivation in the south and west of the district was done by the adhiyars.³⁶ They were indebted to the landowners, jotedars, as they had a precarious tenure in the lands they cultivated. Indeed, such was their 'precarious position' that 'instances have been found where the threat of withholding adhi settlement has been used to force surrender in social quarrels'.[37]

The adhiyars had tamely accepted their fate without a protest till the Kisan Sabhas appeared on the scene. The Kisan Sabhas found it very difficult to break this inertia. But once roused from indifference they seldom relapsed into it thereafter. The struggle of the adhiyars developed mainly over two demands. The first related to the question of the place where the crops would be stored before division. Previously the place used to be the khamar (own place) of the jotedars. This gave the jotedars opportunity for intrigues, and it often happened that the adhyar's share dwindled to insignificance, because they claimed much of it on one pretext or another. The adhiyars now demanded that the place for storing the crop should be of their choice. The second demand related to the rates of interest charged on the grain-loans made by the jotedars. The adhiyars could scarcely do without such loans, since their stock of grain used to be insufficient. The rate of interest used to be about 50 per cent. They now refused to pay more than 25 per cent. If the grain lent was exclusively seedgrain, they were reluctant to pay any interest.

The struggle began in 1939 and gradually intensified. Even severe police repression on the Kisan leaders could not suppress it. The jotedars eventually came to a compromise, mainly as a result of the intervention of the Magistrate. The settlement of the main points of dispute was now left to a Board (panchayat) composed of members chosen by both adhiyars and jotedars.

In eastern Bengal, the main area of the Kisan Sabha activities among the sharecroppers was the pargana Susang, in the district of Mymensingh, inhabited largely by tribes, including the Hajangs and Garos. The Kisan movement, beginning in 1938, was aimed against the most widely prevailing system of rent payment—the tanka system. Under it a fixed portion of the produce had to be paid as rent, whatever the produce. The movement partly succeeded. The tanka system was not formally abolished, but the Hajangs were given the option of paying their rent in kind or cash. This was no small gain, in view of the tendency of the agricultural prices to rise since 1939.

In 1939 the Kisan Sabha sought to organize a larger movement in northern Bengal. It demanded an increase in the share of the bargadar from one-half to two-thirds. The movement did not catch on. However, it was the beginning of the tebhaga movement, which started in 1946.

The Kisan Sabha was aware that such reforms were only partial solutions of the problem of bargadars. To the Sabha the real solution was the abolition of the barga tenure altogether and the eventual conversion of bargadars into occupancy ryots, defined and protected by law. While struggling for the reforms the Sabha never lost sight of this ultimate goal. It is quite likely that the arguments of the Bengal Land Revenue Commission (1940), in favour of abolition of the barga system were influenced by the constant preachings of the Kisan Sabha.

In Bihar the Kisan Sabhas had another grim battle to fight to stop evictions of peasants by zamindars from the so-called bakhast land. These lands were the zamindars' 'own' lands, distinguishable from the lands cultivated and owned by the peasants. The origin of the bakhast land can be traced to the dispossession by zamindars of the owner-peasants on grounds of non-payment of rent. The formal dispossession, however, rarely resulted in the change of cultivators. Evictions on a considerable scale began in 1937. The zamindars were provoked largely by the agitation at the time over the amendment of the Tenancy Bill. They feared that the amended Act would confer on the cultivators the status of occupancy ryots, which in fact was precisely one of the demands of the Kisan Movement.

The Kisan Movement was aimed both at restoring to the owner-peasants the lands they had lost and preventing the evictions from the bakhast lands. The measures of the Congress ministry in regard to the first question disappointed the kisan leaders. These measures provided for the restoration of all lands, in respect of which the rent was enchanced or commuted into cash in the years between 1911 and 1937, and also of the lands sold in the years between 1929 and 1937. They, however, did not apply in cases where the zamindar was exempted from the payment of agricultural income-tax and where the land had already been settled with other tenants 'in good faith.' Thus only a small portion of the bakhast land was affected.

Far more difficult was the problem arising out of the evictions from the bakhast land. The Kisan Sabhas organized satyagrahas by the evicted peasants—thereby preventing others from cultivating the land. This resulted often in violent clashes. Such clashes were most numerous in Barhayiatal in Monghyr district, a place mostly inhabited by the low-caste Dhanuks. The Kisan Sabha had a strong hold there, having led in 1936 a fight against begari (unpaid labour). The All-India Kisan Sabha observed the 'Bihar Kisan Day' on 18 October 1937 as a mark of protest against severe police repression on the satyagrahis.[38]

Another problem which the Bihar Kisan Sabha had to face was that of the sugarcane growers. The peasants cultivated sugarcane with or without advances from the sugar mills. With decreasing demand for sugar, the demand of the sugar mills for sugarcane suddenly fell. Earlier in similar circumstances the sugarcane growers could partly make up for the loss by pressing the sugarcane themselves and making molasses and gur. Now that the market for gur also shrank, the producers had no other alternative but to accept whatever prices the sugar mills had offered. The Kisan Sabha organized a movement for securing higher prices. In 1933, it asked the producer not to enter into contracts with the mills except through the newly set-up Provincial Sugarcane Sabha. The Kisan Sabha contended that in face of combined opposition by the sugarcane growers the mill-owners would eventually prefer paying higher prices to shutting their mills for want of sugarcane. Similar agitations on a much larger scale took place in 1935 in the Dinajpur subdivision. The Sugar Factories Control Act passed by the Congress ministry fixed a minimum price for sugarcane. In fact this did not help the producers. The Kisan Sabha soon found that 'the minimum has invariably become the maximum, as millers have never thought it fit to pay even a pie more than the minimum price fixed by the Government.' The Kisan Sabha's success was only partial in respect of this problem.

In the context of the falling prices of agricultural produce, the rates fixed on the basis of the pre-depression prices for the use of the canal water in the Sone canal area in Sahabad and in the Damodar Canal area in Burdwan became extremely iniquitous for the peasants using water for canals. A significant aspect of the Kisan Sabha activities was a fight for a reduction in the water-rates. The peasants won a complete victory in the **Damodar canal** area.

VI

The peasantry in Bengal and Bihar was not at all a homogeneous group. This again posed problems for the Kisan Sabha. The strategy of the Kisan movement in its early phase does not seem to have been influenced very much by the heterogeneous nature of the peasantry. The earliest constitutional document of the Bihar Kisan Sabha (1929), defined a peasant as anyone whose primary source of livelihood was agriculture. The more elaborate constitution of the Sabha (1936) said essentially the same thing.[39] The Sabha ignored the different aspects of production in agriculture. In fact agriculture provided means of livelihood to different groups in different ways.

It was in the introduction to the Hindi edition of the Manifesto of the Bihar Kisan Sabha (1936), that Swami Sahajanand for the first time considered an agricultural labourer as a peasant. He said: 'A peasant is known as a Grihasta, a person who earns his livelihood by cultivation and agriculture, be he a petty landlord, ryot or labourer working on wages for ploughing fields.'

A separate organization of agricultural labourers was not however considered necessary: 'The Kisan Sabha does not desire that by creating a separate organization of agricultural labourers any strife should be let loose between them and landlords and ryots, nor should the latter oppress agricultural labourers.'[40] At the 1937 session of the Bihar Provincial Kisan Sabha at Niyamatpur in Gaya district (15 July 1937), Sahajanand said: 'The interests of the agricultural labourers and the Kisan are the same'.[41]

The ideas of the Kisan leaders gradually changed, presumably because of a better understanding on their part of the then existing agrarian structure. At the first session of the Mymensingh District Krishak Samiti (24 February 1938) the President Muzaffar Ahmed classified the peasants into four groups: (a) those who tilled other men's lands; (b) those who tilled their own lands and also other men's lands, because their own holdings were not large enough for their subsistence; (c) those who had lands just enough for them, and (d) those who had enough land and got it cultivated by hired labour. Ahmed felt that the last group should not join the Kisan movement, and that its strength should come from the first three groups.[42] The Secretary of the Bihar Provincial Kisan Sabha, Awadheshwar Prasad Singh, also thought alike, though he thought that the Depression had tended to blur the distinction between a large number of owner-peasants and agricultural labourers.[43]

Gradually the emphasis further changed, and the Bihar Kisan Sabha under the leadership of Swami Sahajanand tended more and more to rely on the 'lowest strata of the peasantry' as the backbone of the Kisan movement. He said in 1944:

'It is they, the semi-proletarians or the agricultural labourers who have very little land, or no land at all, and the petty cultivators who anyhow squeeze a most meagre living out of the land they cultivate...who are the kisans of our thinking...and who make and must constitute the Kisan Sabha ultimately.'[44]

It seems, however, that the Kisan Sabha's success was only partial in bringing the 'lowest strata of the peasantry' into the Kisan movement as a permanent force. An enquiry made in 1939 by the Bengal Provincial Kisan Sabha into the nature of the composition of the membership of the Sabha in the Kishoreganj subdivision of Dacca showed that 'the majority were raiyats, and a smaller number were under-raiyats and bargadars.'[45] Swami Sahajanand admitted that even as late as 1944 it was 'really the middle and big cultivators...(who were) for the most part with the Kisan Sabha.' He even suspected that the 'middle and big cultivators' were 'using the Kisan Sabha for their own benefit and gain.'[46]

VII

The thirties in which the Kisan movement came into existence and became a powerful force in rural Bengal and Bihar was also the period of great advances in the nation's struggle for freedom led by the Congress. For the sake of convenience the present study of these relations is confined to Bihar. Apart from other reasons, the evaluation by the Kisan Sabha of the performance of the Congress ministry in Bihar, particularly in regard to the peasant question, was a decisive factor that influenced the attitude of the Sabha to the Congress.

The relations were at first quite cordial. This was partly due to the nature of the Kisan leadership. Most of the Kisan leaders in the early phase of the Kisan Movement were also actively connected with the Congress. They believed that by drawing the peasants into the freedom struggle they were only strengthening the Congress organization. They were naturally averse to doing anything which would result in weakening the Congress. Indeed, where the Kisan Movement was thought to be a division force in the nationalist movement, the Kisan leaders promptly called it off.[47]

At the same time, the Kisan leaders had no doubt about the need for an independent organization of the peasants. This was not because of any assumption that by its very structure and composition the Congress would necessarily be hostile to the peasants, but because of a feeling that the Congress was too preoccupied with political questions to take interest in a distinctively peasant question. 'The Congress included in its fold various interests,' but such diverse interests did not at first appear irreconcilable to the Kisan leaders. On the contrary, they believed that the Congress could be made a real Kisan organization. In fact they justified an independent Kisan organization precisely on the ground that the pressure put on the Congress by it through a broadbased Kisan Movement could prevent the domination of the Congress by vested interests hostile to the Kisan.

This optimism gradually disappeared. During the Civil Disobedience movement, the Kisan leaders did much to draw the peasants into it and went to the extent of calling off an independent movement of the Kisans out of a fear that the former might suffer, only eventually to find the Congress utterly indifferent to the woes of the Kisans. The Kisan leaders gradually started doubting the earnestness of the Congress in this regard. Such doubts developed into a positive mistrust after the Congress Ministry had begun to function (August 1937).

The Bihar Kisan Sabha had serious reservations about the acceptance of office by the Congress. The Bihar Provincial Kisan Council at a meeting on 24 February 1937, with Swami Sahajanand in the chair opposed it on the ground that 'the Government of India Act was brought with a view to entrenching the vested interests in power and making the imperialist grip stronger.'[48]

However, when the Congress finally decided to form the government, the Kisan Sabha did not in any way seek to undermine it. On the contrary, the Sabha decided to make use of it, as far as possible for promoting the peasants' cause. It tried to convince the government of the urgency of the peasant question by organizing big peasant rallies. The Kisan leaders, for instance, asked the peasants throughout Bihar to muster strength before the Legislative Assembly on 23 August 1937, the opening day of the Assembly. The Kisan leaders thus exhorted the peasants on the occasion:

'Constant agitation should be made...so that you can be free from rural indebtedness, imposition of numerous taxes, and oppressions of many a person. It is you, tillers of the soil, who have chosen your representatives in the Assembly, and it is you who shall draw their attention to your needs and wants.... Your fight has reached a critical stage, and it is time for you to keep alert.... Simply saying that the Congress is now the Government will not take you anywhere.'[49]

The peasants responded warmly. Twenty thousand peasants gathered near the Assembly shouting the slogans: 'Give us water, we are thirsty; give us bread, we are hungry; remit all our agricultural loans; down with zamindars and save us from oppression.'[50] The Kisan demonstration was unprecedented in the history of Bihar.

The Kisan leaders evidently expected much of the new government, and sought to persuade the Congress to make a firm commitment to the defence of the peasants' interest. The Bihar Provincial Kisan Council, at a meeting held on 4 November, 1937 said: 'There are numerous interests which are opposed to the interest of the Kisans, but the responsibility of the Congress is towards the exploited and the downtrodden rather than towards the privileged and vested interests.'[51]

The performance of the Congress Ministry disappointed the Kisan leaders although some of its measures undoubtedly helped the peasantry.[52] Rent was reduced by about 25 per cent, on an average. Peasants' holdings were made transferable without the prior consent of zamindars, and the salami that was previously payable to them at the time of such transfers was greatly reduced. Sales by zamindars of the entire holdings of peasants on grounds of non-payment of due rent were made illegal. Zamindars could sell only a part of the holdings, which was enough for the realization of the arrears of rent. The Ministry persuaded the zamindars to agree not only to a reduction of the cash rent, but also of the share of the crop.

The Kisan leaders however expected much more. The problem of rural indebtedness remained as chronic as before. The Congress ministry did very little towards solving the bakhast land question. A meeting of the All India Kisan Committee in Calcutta on 27 October 1937, expressed 'strong dissatisfaction with the piecemeal, superficial and perfunctory manner in which the Congress ministries have dealt with only some of the problems affecting the Kisans.'[53] The kisan leaders in fact wanted the Congress to establish a kind of Kisan raj. 'Kisan raj kaem ho' (a kisan regime would soon be coming) was one of the popular slogans with the Kisan demonstrators.[54] This involved confiscation of the zamindar estates and the distribution of the lands thus acquired among the landless.

The Congress ministry found the Kisan slogans much too radical for their taste, and made no bones about it. The Prime Minister Srikrishna Sinha once observed: 'If lands are taken without compensation, volcanic eruption will be sure to follow.'[55] The Kisan leaders sought to explain the failure of the Congress ministry in terms of class interests. 'All the fights of the Congress,' said Swami Sahajanand at a Kisan rally at Siwan on 26 November 1938, 'had been fought by the masses, whilst the capitalists and landlords sided with the imperialist forces. Zamindars and capitalists seeing that they had no hope from the imperialists, were now joining the Congress and monopolizing it.'[56] According to the Kisan leaders the failure of the Congress ministry was due to the structural weakness of the Congress movement. Pandit Jadunandan Sarma observed:

'Unfortunately, politics have so far dominated the Congress.... The masses have so far been kept in a mere state of emotional exaltation, and the Congress has always tried to reconcile the irreconcilable interests in its attempts to keep intact its national character.... The masses who staked their all have not been allowed to ventilate their genuine grievances against their exploitation by Indian feudalism and rising capitalism. It is time for the leaders to realize that the exploiters and the exploited cannot be benefited at one and the same time. It is high time for them to realize the absurdities of the position that there cannot be compromise between landlords and tenants.'[57]

Swami Sahajanand stressed the point at the Comilla session of the All-India Kisan Conference (May 1938):

'It is dangerous to agree that the Congress is a Kisan organization.... I do not want that the Congress should be a Kisan organization in name only. I want it, if ever, to be so in its ideology.... I want that the Congress should reflect the class interests of the Kisans and cease to be dominated by the those who fatten on the exploitation of the Kisans.'[58]

The Congress could not for long afford to ignore such criticisms. The criticism that the interests of the Kisans were not safe in their hands and aspersions at their moral integrity[59] incensed the Congress leaders. The Congress also reproved the Kisan Movement for its being prone to violence. Gandhiji went to the extent of saying that such a movement 'would be something like fascism.' Reforming the land system, the Congress believed, did not at all necessitate violence.[60]

In December 1937, the Congress took the decision forbidding Congressmen from participating in the Kisan Sabha activities. The Saran District Congress Committee on 7 December 1937, asked Swami Sahajanand to suspend his proposed tour in Saran district, since it feared 'his presence might lead to unrest among the Kisans and tenants.'[61] The Congress members were asked 'not to attend or organize or help in organizing Kisan Sabha meetings to be addressed by Swami Sahajanand.' Other district committees soon followed suit. The Bihar Provincial Congress Committee formally approved of the ban of 14 December 1937. In justification of their action they said that the propaganda of the Sabha 'has been responsible for producing a poisonous atmosphere.... Attacks are being made on the principle of Ahimsa which is the cherished creed of the Congress. An atmosphere is developing in certain parts of the province which, it is apprehended, is likely to do much harm to the country and put obstacles in the way of the country's march toward freedom.'[62] Prominent Congress leaders toured different parts of the province and sought to explain Congress' stand towards the Kisans. In his two-day tour in Saran in April 1938, Vallabhbhai Patel asked them not to be misled by

'what is inspired by western ideas and also by the Red Flag, which is the symbol of violence and against the culture and tradition of India.... Comrade Lenin was not born in this country and we do not want a Lenin here. We want Gandhi and Ramachandra. Those who preach class hatred are enemies of the country.[63]

Misunderstanding between the Congress and the Kisan Sabha thus tended to increase. At the Gaya session of the All India Kisan Conference (9-10 April, 1939) radical Kisan leaders like Swami Sahajanand wanted a complete breach with the Congress. Moderate opinions, however, ultimately prevailed, and the formal breach did not occur.

VIII

During the period under review, unlike the earlier period, the Kisan Movement was sure of its ground from the point of definition of aims and also of organization. The Kisan leaders sought to build an appropriate organization, though it remained, admittedly, an imperfect one.[64]

However, the elements of weakness in the Kisan Movement should not be overlooked. In view of the Depression and the aggravation by it of the manifold evils of the agrarian society, the movement would have been stronger. Barrington Moore found the Indian peasants far less rebellious than the Chinese peasants, and attributed the phenomenon partly to the particular character of the nationalist leadership in India. 'The character of nationalist leaders imparted to their movement a quietist twist that helped to damp down what revolutionary tendencies there were among the peasants.'[65] The point is debatable. The disapproval by the Congress of the particular form of the Kisan agitation in Bengal and Bihar has been noted. The Congress occasionally succeeded in drawing the peasantry into the nationalist movement, but it did not lead any appropriate peasant organization. It had failed not only to keep up their enthusiasm, but also alienated them when 'violence' on the part of the peasants, as the Congress understood the word at the time sometimes led it to call off the nationalist movement. Indeed, the Kisan Movement developed in spite of the adverse reactions of the Congress leadership. Such reactions, therefore, could not be a real source of weakness of the Kisan Movement.

Moore was aware of the 'the huge size and appalling misery of India's rural proletariat,'[66] but he pointed out that tension of the kind that one would, under the circumstances, assume to have built up in the rural society, was largely nonexistent. According to him apart from the fact that 'many' of the agricultural labourers were 'tied to the prevailing system through possession of a tiny plot of land,'[67] the caste system provided a niche for landless labourers and tied them into the division of labour within the village, while its sanctions depended for their operation less directly on the existence of property.[68] Moreover, 'the system of caste did enforce hierarchical submission. Make a man feel humble by a thousand daily acts and he will behave in a humble way. The traditional etiquette of caste was no mere excrescence; it had definite political consequences.'[69]

A 'very high correlation between caste ranking and superior and inferior rights to land'[70] was undoubtedly a significant feature of the land system in Bengal and Bihar. But how did the caste system, involving as it did a system of sanctions, correct the imbalance in the rural society resulting from the reduction of a sizeable sanction of owner-peasants to the status of agricultural labourers? Could it just sanction away such a reality? The caste system could not surely provide employment for the dislocated group. The relative infrequency of rebellions by the agricultural labourers need not be related to the 'submissiveness' enforced by the caste system. They hesitated to rebel, partly because they were not sure of the results of such rebellions.

For the sources of weakness in the Kisan Movement we must therefore look elsewhere. The Kisan Sabha had a formal organizational structure, but, as Hauser puts it, 'It is more accurately characterized as a movement than an organization as such. Its primary instruments were numerous meetings, the rallies and annual sessions.'[71] The number of formal members seems impressive (250,000 in Bihar in 1938 and 50,000 in Bengal in 1939), but the organization largely depended on a small group of dedicated workers. It, therefore, sometimes failed to cope with the task of organizing large movements.

Another source of weakness can be attributed to the particular agrarian relations in Bengal and Bihar. The Depression created for the peasantry an extremely difficult situation, but the class relations did not admit of any adjustment, though whether the Indian caste system made the process any easier, as Gunnar Myrdal thinks,[72] is an open question. The zamindars were not a particularly rapacious tribe enforcing their rent demands regardless of whatever had happened to the peasantry. The steep fall in the prices made the old level of rent grossly iniquitous to the peasants, but, in fact, many of them just defaulted without necessarily provoking 'legal actions' on the part of the zamindars. Rent arrears and also arrears of debt tended to accumulate. Zamindars had the legal power to evict them and money-lenders to force the payment in various ways. But many of them did not go as far as they could. The forbearance of the zamindars was not entirely a matter of kindness for the afflicted peasantry. They realized that as long as the Depression continued, changing peasants for the cultivation of their lands would not be of much use. Moreover, where the majority of the peasant community defaulted, other legal steps short of eviction were seldom more effective, particularly because the legal process was tardy as well as costly.

The elements of weakness in the Kisan movement also partly resulted from the particular composition of the peasant community itself. It is wrong to describe a village in Bengal and Bihar as one 'composed entirely mass of poor tenants united in opposition to the absentee landlords and their agents.' The peasant community was not a homogeneous group. It was a complex structure composed of elements which were sometimes naturally hostile. The Kisan Sabha, therefore, found it difficult to organize all the groups in a united movement. For instance, where bargadars were employed by richer peasants, as was often the case, the Kisan Sabha, fighting with the former, risked alienating the latter, which had backed them once in their fight against zamindars. In Bihar, Swami Sahajanand was shocked to find how big occupancy ryots had largely succeeded in turning the Kisan Sabha into an instrument for promoting their own interests. This was the reason for the increasing emphasis afterwards on the need to bring the agricultural labourers and 'the lowest strata of the peasantry' into the Kisan Movement.

Where bargadars or agricultural labourers were involved, the Kisan Sabha sometimes failed to attract them largely because of their fear that by opposing their employers they risked losing their tiny plots of land, which were their only means of subsistence. Such fears, as we have seen earlier, were not baseless. This was the reason why the settlement officers carrying on survey and settlement work often failed to persuade a sizeable section of the bargadars to declare their status, so that this could be included in the settlement records. Such was the hold of their employers over them that many bargadars altogether denied that they had cultivated lands on a crop-sharing basis.

IX

The Kisan Movement began to decline towards the end of the period under review particularly in Bihar. Hauser attributed it partly to the tactical mistake of the Kisan Sabha leadership dominated by the personality of Swami Sahajanand and partly to a series of developments which tended to reduce the misery of the peasants.

'The Kisan Sabha was a strong movement of agitation. It was not organized structurally because of the impatient and articulate leadership which Swami Sahajanand provided. He was a Swami who sought change, a charismatic revolutionary. So long as he maintained that attitude within the framework of the nationalism which sustained all political activity in India during this period, the movement was effective. When he was attracted to ideological politics of the anti-national Left, he and the movement he had created found no support among the peasants of Bihar.'[73]

According to Hauser, the new legislative measures reducing the rents in the south Bihar districts between 1937 and 1940, and the improved price situation of the war period, were responsible for diminishing the distress of the peasants.

Hauser's view with regard to the responsibility of Sahajanand for the decline of the Kisan Movement seems to be of doubtful validity. The main strength of the movement lay not in its appeal to nationalist sentiments, but in its particular stand on the basic grievances of the peasantry. It may, however, be true that the Swamiji's increasing inclination towards the 'Left' in the country's politics alienated a number of persons actively connected with the leadership of the Kisan Movement. The rank and file of the peasants do not seem to have been much affected by the alleged political bias of the Swamiji.

The tendency of the prices to rise since the end of 1938, particularly since the beginning of the second world war, undoubtedly helped the peasantry in making a recovery from the effects of the long Depression. So did the measures reducing the rent burdens. Needless to say, these were temporary reliefs. The basic maladjustment in the peasant economy and agrarian society persisted. In fact, certain developments made this still worse, particularly the drying up of rural credit as a result of the legislative measures designed for reducing rural debts. We have seen how more peasants lost their land as a result. The famine of 1943 left the peasant economy in ruins. The background for a wider Kisan agitation was thus formed. It began soon after the end of the war and became stronger year after year.

References

1 I have elsewhere made a detailed study of the peasant movement in Bengal and Bihar in the second half of the 19th century. 'Agrarian economy and agrarian relations in Bengal, 1859-1885' (unpublished Oxford D. Phil dissertation, 1968), Ch. 5
2 Private correspondence of Ripon with persons in India, 1883, Vol. 1; Letter No. 335; Tagore wrote the letter to Bayley, Member of the Viceroy's Council, and it was enclosed in Bayley's letter to the Private Secretary to the Viceroy, 5 June, 1883.
3 M.K. Gandhi, *An Autobiography* (Ahmedabad, 1945) Part V, Ch. 12.
4 'I had decided that nothing should be done in the name of the Congress.... For the name of the Congress was the bête noire of the Government and their controllers—the planters.... Therefore we had decided not to mention the name of the Congress and not to acquaint the peasants with the organization called the Congress.' (*Ibid*, Ch. 14).
5 *Ibid*., Ch. 8.
6 Jawaharlal Nehru, *An Autobiography* (Calcutta, 1962), p. 48.
7 This was how some of the local journals reacted:—
Tippera Guide, Comilla, (24 January 1922): 'The spirit of non-cooperation has spread into the lower stratum of society. The non-cooperation movement has assumed threatening proportions and the storm of unrest is blowing over the villages.'

Harald, Dacca (9 February 1922): 'If the proportion of private owners of land be taken to be 10 per cent, it would be much more in Eastern Bengal, then the campaign of non-payment of taxes would at once mean a fight between this 10 per cent, on one side and the 90 per cent on the other. On the one side will be skill, resource and accumulated strength and on the other shall be numbers to swamp the other side. There will be set in the country a regular civil war.' *Atma Sakti*, Calcutta (5 April 1922): 'A social revolution without political freedom will be injurious to a dependent country.... Who will deny that if the ire of the masses is once roused against social oppressions, etc., to which they have been subjected for centuries, it will consume the whole community like a volcanic eruption.'

8   Rathindra Nath Tagore, *Pitri Smriti* (Reminiscences of my Father).
9   'Raiyater Katha' (About the Peasants) in *Collected Works*, (Centenary Edition), Vol. 13, pp. 345-6.
10 *Amrita Bazar Patrika*, 26 April 1938, Report on the Second Session of the Gaya District Kisan Conference, held on 23-4 April 1938.
11 Discussions on the point are innumerable. Here is a good summary: 'The output of primary products tends to be inelastic, which means that it does not change very much in response to changes in the price. This is essentially a matter of time-periods. The output of manufactured goods can often be increased quite quickly by putting in new plant and equipment, or simply by working overtime; but it takes a long time to grow more rubber trees or sink a new copper mine. Similarly, the output of manufactured goods can be reduced by laying men off; but coffee trees or cotton plants will go on producing regardless. Moreover, the demand for primary producing fluctuates much more than the demand for manufactured goods, precisely because it is known that a shortage will not result in much extra production, so that people will react to any hint of a shortage by intensive stock-piling; and similarly, when the threat of a shortage disappears, will live off their stocks and thus drastically reduce their demand for what is currently being produced.' Big variations in price inevitably result from a combination of these two circumstances. (Michael Stewart, *Keynes and After*, a Pelican Original, pp. 260-1).
12 Report of the Bengal Jute Enquiry Committee, 1934; Vol. 1, Majority Report, Para 13.
13 Walter Hauser, '*The Bihar Provincial Kisan Sabha, 1929-42; A Study of an Indian Peasant Movement*' (unpublished Ph.D. Thesis, the University of Chicago, 1961). I have used a copy in microfilm kept in the Nehru Memorial Museum and Library, New Delhi.
14 *Ibid*.
15 The Muslim League leaders, unlike the wahabi and ferazee leaders working among the peasantry in Bengal in the 19th century, were not in the least influenced by the social radicalism of Islam.
16 Qazi Imam Husain, 'Nature of the Proja Movement in Bengal,' in *Amrita Bazar Patrika*, 31 March 1937.
17 M. Azizul Huque, *The Man Behind the Plough*, pp. 151-2.
18 Bengal Land Revenue Administration Report, 1930-31, para 38.
19 Bengal Land Revenue Commission (also called the Floud Commission) heard these complaints day after day. The Jessore Landholders' Association said: 'The Bengal Agricultural Debtors Act has supplied additional impetus and strength to the agrarian agitation and no-rent campaign, and has caused an all-round suspension of rent.... It has engineered a class war and an all-round

communist spirit' (Volume IV of the Commission's Report, p. 67). One of the popular slogans was: 'Rent is payable when able, land belongs to those who plough.' According to the Khulna Landholders' Association: 'The ignorant mass has been over-encouraged to think that they can avoid all sorts of payment by taking resort to the law' (ibid., p. 95). The Maldah Landholders' Association remarked: 'By the passing of the Act an impression has been firmly rooted in the minds of the agriculturists that they have been released from all liabilities of payments of debts as well as rents' (Ibid, p. 111). Equally categorical was the observation of the Bengal Landholders' Association: 'Tempers have been roused to such a pitch by incessant preaching of class hatred and zamindar-baiting in particular that cool reasoning can no longer be expected.... The impression is now common that all debts and even arrears of rent can be wiped out by executive order or legislation.' (Vol. III, pp. 84 and 107).

20 Bengal Land Revenue Administration Report, 1938-39, para 39.
21 Report of the Floud Commission, III, 423.
22 Bengal Land Revenue Administration Report, 1937-38, para 38.
23 Bengal Police Administration Report, 1935, para 32.
24 Bengal Police Administration Report, 1938, para 32.
25 Bengal Police Administration Report, 1939, para 32.
26 Report of the Land Revenue Commission, IV, pp. 286 and 314.
27 Report, I, para 88.
28 *Amrita Bazar Patrika*, 5 April 1932.
29 *Ibid.*, 8 January 1932.
30 *Ibid.*, 7 January 1932.
31 Bengal Police Administration Report, 1934, para 31.
32 *Amrita Bazar Patrika*, 18 November 1937.
33 Bengal Land Revenue Administration Report, 1923-24, para 2.
34 *Ibid.*, 1925, para 35. *Ibid.*, 1927-28, para 35. *Ibid.*, 1929-30, para 38.
35 *Ibid.*, 1928-29, para 2 and 38.
36 F.O. Bell, *Dinajpur Survey and Settlement Report*, 1934-40, para 20.
37 *Ibid.*
38 *Amrita Bazar Patrika*, 16 November 1937. 'Agrarian trouble in Barhayiatlal' A statement by Karyanand Sarma, Secretary, Monghyr District Kisan Sabha, 15 November 1937.
39 Hauser, n. 13, Ch. 1.
40 *Ibid.*
41 *Amrita Bazar Patrika*, 18 July 1937.
42 *Amrita Bazar Patrika*, 27 February 1938.
43 *Amrita Bazar Patrika*, 26 April 1938.
44 Hauser, n. 13, Ch. 1.
45 Oral Evidence of the Bengal Provincial Kisan Sabha before the Floud Commission, 22 March 1939. Report of the Floud Commission, Vol. IV, p. 62.
46 Hauser, n. 13, Ch. 1.
47 Swami Sahajanand, for instance, did it once during the Civil Disobedience movement.
48 *Amrita Bazar Patrika*, 27 February 1937.
49 *Ibid.*, 20 August 1937.
50 *Ibid.*, 24 August 1937.
51 *Ibid.*, 6 November 1937.
52 For details see Rajendra Prasad, *Autobiography* (Hindi), New Delhi, 1955, pp. 454-9.

53 *Amrita Bazar Patrika*, 30 October 1937.
54 *Ibid.*, 12 January 1938.
55 *Ibid.*, 30 January 1938.
56 *Ibid.*, 29 November 1938.
57 *Amrita Bazar Patrika*, 23 January 1938.
58 *Ibid.*, 15 May 1938.
59 Congressmen with khaddar and their Gandhi caps were compared to Sadhus who with their tilaks and other marks cheated the people. Rajendra Prasad's statement on 11 January 1938, *Amrita Bazar Patrika*, 12 January 1938.
60 Gandhian notion of eventual change of heart of the property owners greatly influenced them. He said: 'I want them (zamindars and ruling chiefs) to outgrow their greed and sense of possession, and to come down in spite of their wealth to the level of those who earn their bread by labour.' *Economic and Industrial Life*, I, 119. In the *Harijan* of 23 April 1938, he remarked that if the zamindars did not change, 'they will die a natural death.'
61 *Amrita Bazar Patrika*, 9 December 1937.
62 *Amrita Bazar Patrika*, 16 December 1937.
63 *Ibid.*, 10 April 1938.
64 The presence of these two features also distinguished the Kisan movement from the radical millenarian peasant movements in several parts of the world, of which much has been written. The essence of the millenarianism was 'the hope of a complete and radical change in the world which will be reflected in the millennium, a world shorn of all its present deficiencies.' (E.J. Hobsbawm, *Primitive Rebels*, Ch. 4). This hope gave the movement a tremendous force. However, they shared 'a fundamental vagueness about the actual way in which the new society will be brought about,' and a notable thing about them was their indifference to the question of organization. 'Its (the movement's) followers are not makers of revolution. They expect it to make itself, by divine revelation, by an announcement from on high, by a miracle—they expect it to happen somehow. The part of the people before the change is to gather together... to undertake certain virtual measures against the movement of decision and change, or to purify themselves, shedding the dross of the bad world of the present so as to be able to enter the new world in shining purity'. (*Ibid.*).
65 Barrington Moore, *Social Origins of Dictatorship and Democracy*, p. 378.
66 *Ibid.*, p. 455.
67 *Ibid.*
68 *Ibid.*, p. 213.
69 *Ibid.*, p. 383.
70 Gunnar Myrdal, *Asian Drama* Vol. II, (London, 1968), p. 1059. For some evidence on the point see Benoy Chaudhuri, 'Agrarian economy and agrarian relations in Bengal 1859-85,' in *History of Bengal*, 1757-1905 (published by the University of Calcutta), pp. 315-16 and 321-22.
71 Hauser, n. 13, p. 87.
72 Myrdal, n. 70, p. 1061. He writes: 'A social environment in which high status is accorded to abstinence from physical work encourages adjustments by the more privileged strata to relieve at least the direct distress of the dispossessed.'
73 Hauser, n. 13, p. 156.

19 Damodar Canal Tax Movement

Buddhadeva Bhattacharyya
with
Tarun Kumar Bannerjee and Dipak Kumar Das

I

IN THE LATE 1930s serious popular discontent gathered force in the canal areas of the river Damodar over the question of the Bengal Development Act and the levy imposed thereunder. A movement crystallized and awakened the unsophisticated village-folk of Burdwan. To understand its nature it is necessary to go deep into the history of the Damodar Canal.

Till the close of the 18th century the river Damodar had been connected, on either side, with a number of spill-channels, streams and watercourses and had served the purpose of irrigation in the whole of the Burdwan zamindary. A cess called 'poolbundy'[1] was levied on the ryots of the riparian areas to meet the cost of repair and maintenance of the banks of the river. When the Burdwan Raj was relieved of its responsibilities and liabilities to maintain the poolbundy works at the end of the 18th century, the Government admitted its obligation to keep the watercourses, spill-channels, streams, dykes, pools, tanks and their embankments, etc. in a proper state. Eventually, however, the Government was found to have failed to keep its promise and worked in the opposite direction. After taking over the poolbundy works, it thoroughly strengthened the left embankment and made it watertight. As a result its innumerable spill-channels were closed, and subsequently, the zamindars and tenants, according to Sir William Willcocks, made numerous secret breaches through the embankment. In the period between 1856-9 the Government cut off 20 miles of embankment on the right side of the Damodar with a view to protecting

Reproduced from *Satyagrahas in Bengal. 1921-9*, Minerva Associates, (Publications), Calcutta, 1977.

the E.I. Railways and the G.T. Road and left the right embankment unrepaired. All this accelerated the silting up of the river bed, reduced the sectional area, and indirectly caused the death of the live channels. Sir William Willcocks called them satanic chains of the Damodar which doomed the once healthy and prosperous tract to malaria and dire poverty.[2]

To fulfil a part of its obligation and to compensate the people of Burdwan and Hooghly the Government opened the Eden Canal in 1881 and the Damodar Canal in 1933. The Damodar Canal Project as sanctioned by the Secretary of State in 1921 was intended to irrigate nearly 200,000 acres of rice-producing area every year (140,000 acres according to a press report) in 379 villages. The canal was expected to supply water to the Eden Canal also for irrigation of at least 24,000 acres in addition to the area then supplied by the Eden Canal. The expenditure to be incurred for the purpose was estimated to be about Rs. 73 lakhs, but the actual cost rose up to about 1 crore of rupees and a quarter. The construction of the canal started by 1926-7 and the new canal began supplying water for irrigation in May 1932, but it was formally opened at Rondia headworks, some 30 miles away from Burdwan, by the Governor of Bengal on 22 September 1933. It was practically completed in 1935-36. Then the area served by it stood at 134,464 acres extending over 297 villages.[3]

II

After the formal inauguration of the canal the Government began to think of realizing a part of the capital expenditure by imposing a canal tax on the ryots who derived benefit from the canal. At first it wanted to collect the canal tax through a lease system by appointing *mukhia* in each village. The tax being heavy the ryots refused to execute any lease to get the canal water. As a result, the Government thought it proper to impose a compulsory levy by means of a suitable legislation.[4] With that end in view on 18 February 1935 Khwaja Nazimuddin, Minister-in-charge of Irrigation, introduced the Bengal Development Bill, 1935 which provided for the improvement of land in Bengal and imposition of a levy in respect of increased profit resulting from improvement works constructed by the Government.[5]

As the Bill referred to above became the cause of a bitter popular struggle against governmental high-handedness it is necessary for us to acquaint ourselves with the object, nature and scope of the aforesaid bill. The object of the bill, according to the Minister introducing the Bill, was to tide over the financial difficulty which prevented the Government from taking up works undoubtedly necessary for the prosperity of the province and to enable complex and far-reaching schemes of improvement to be undertaken with the knowledge that so far from being a burden on the provincial resources they would prove remunerative. In accordance with the spirit of the Bill, the cost of the schemes financed by the Government out of loan-funds should be met by means of tax levied at a flat rate on the total area benefited and provisions for appointment and realization should be made as elastic as possible. The principle was that the Government should be entitled to recover a portion of the increased profits which accrued to private individuals and companies from land of any description, whether used for agriculture or not, owing to works undertaken at the cost of the State and which they would not have otherwise enjoyed. The principle was applicable to areas where schemes for the improvement had only recently been carried into effect, as well as to areas where such schemes were to be undertaken in future.[6]

As regards the nature and scope of the Bill, the Minister said that when the Government had improved the outturn of land it should be allowed to take back for itself at least half of the net increase. In his opinion, it was a fair proposition: 'I shall give you a rupee if you give me back eight annas.' The Bill, it was argued, would not only compel the ryots to pay up to half of their increased profits, but also would enable them to make increased profits by taking advantage of the improvements. The Minister in justification of his stand said that during years of normal rainfall the people did not take the canal water, rather they treated the irrigation canal as an insurance against a failure of the monsoon. It was impossible, he said, to finance irrigation works by recoveries only in years when the monsoon failed, and if the people regarded the irrigation works as an insurance they ought to pay every year for that insurance. It was not unreasonable, he argued, that the people who possessed lands were under a moral obligation to society to develop these lands in the best possible way; and in the malarious tracts of the delta when anyone refused to take advantage of flood irrigation he was actually encouraging malaria or not helping in its eradication. He emphasized that if individuals were allowed to act in accordance with their sweet will, the schemes simply would not work. That was why the Bill proposed that if any man indulged in the luxury of keeping land underdeveloped, he should at any rate pay as the man who co-operated in the improvement by cultivating his land. In his opinion it could hardly be regarded as a harsh measure. Further, he observed that not more than half the net increase in outturn was the maximum levy to be imposed under the Bill. As the yield of the lands varied, there would have to be a full inquiry before the rate of any improvement levy was fixed, and the idea would be to fix it at such a rate as to leave the prayer substantially better off. The improvement levy would not be a tax in the ordinary sense, but so far as it could be called a tax, it would be 'what the Government is looking for—a tax that would not hurt anybody but benefit everybody.' He admitted that the Bill did not specify the classes of persons who would be liable to pay the improvement levy; it left this to be determined by rule. There was a risk in such an attempt of allowing certain persons to escape their obligation to pay under the proposed Act and of causing hardship to persons who had had no real benefit from improvement. So it was intended to determine after a full inquiry, when any area was taken up for improvement levy, what particular classes in it ought to be assessed. The improvement levy was to be paid out of the profits due to the improvement and so it should be paid by persons who get the benefit. As regards the question of assessment, he observed that the Government wanted to estimate the average outturn before and after improvement. As regards the period for which an assessment would hold good, he said that it would be convenient alike to the Government and to the assessees if the rate did not vary too often; but until the conditions returned to normal the rate might have to be revised (according to fluctuations in prices) at comparatively short intervals, perhaps every year. The questions of assessment and revision were to be left to a process of trial and error and to be governed by rules. Another most important feature of the Bill was the provision that the civil court should not interfere. The Government feared that a court might, at any stage, on some nice point of law declare some action illegal and throw the whole, or a large part, of the cost of a scheme of improvement upon the provincial revenues. There was also a risk that it might pass orders which could paralyse administration and be fatal to an improvement scheme. These were the problems facing the province; and it was therefore necessary to steer clear of these difficulties by providing for special appeal authorities to deal with all disputes which might arise in connexion with the scheme. Hence the Government asked for wide and drastic powers. The non-interference by civil courts, the rule-making power, the assessment by executive authority and the refusal to recognize as a matter of course the right to compensation were some of the provisions of the Bill which some members of the Legislature opposed.[7] The Bengal Development Bill was, however, finally passed on 3 October 1935.

Even a cursory reading of the Bengal Development Act, 1935 would suggest that though certain provisions of the Act were sugar-coated, it was, in essence, detrimental to the interests of the poor cultivators. The difficulties facing the Government as regards the costs of construction, maintenance and establishment of the Damodar Canal were attempted to be overcome by bringing the canal area under the operation of the above-mentioned Act. Within the area notified as benefited by the canal, water was supplied, though no application was made under section 74 of the Bengal Irrigation Act and the Government imposed a levy at the rate of Rs 5-8-0 per acre per year irrespective of the benefits derived or likely to be derived from the irrigation facilities of the canal.[8]

III

The primary motive behind the canal tax agitation was, of course, political. It was aimed at stimulating resistance against the colonial rule. Secondarily, the movement was based on the grievances of the local peasantry burdened with a heavy rate of improvement levy. The Bengal Development Act, 1935 and the tax rate imposed thereunder—these two being clearly interlinked—together sowed the seeds of agitation and disaffection among the cultivators of the canal area.[9]

Shortly after the Bengal Development Bill was proposed, the

drastic provisions of the Bill stirred the members of the Burdwan Bar Association and other literate people of the town. Later when a heavy burden of tax was imposed under the enactment it had a crushing effect on the already famished peasantry. The National Congress was then lying low in the district. The illiterate rural masses are wont to attribute their miseries to an unkindly providence. To rouse the inert and sluggish peasantry and to give some relief to their mute and inglorious life half a dozen members of the Bar came forward. They formed an association, namely the Burdwan District Raiyats' Association, with D.P. Chaudhuri and Balai Chand Mukhopadhyay as President and Secretary respectively, to fight the regressive measures as embodied in the aforementioned Act and to agitate against the canal tax.[10]

In the initial phase the Burdwan District Raiyats' Association organized a meeting on 27 July 1935 in the Burdwan Town Hall in protest against the Bengal Development Bill which was yet to be adopted as an enactment by the Legislature. The meeting was presided over by Sir Nalini Ranjan Chattopadhyay. Sir Bijoy Prasad Sinha Roy, while delivering his speech, said that 'we have assembled here to criticize this Bill, not to protest against it.' Then Abdus Sattar, Secretary, District Congress Committee, opposed Sir Bijoy Prasad and said that 'we have assembled here to protest against the Bill, not only to criticize it.' He emphasized that the Bill must be revoked. Sriharsa Mukhopadhyay, President of the reception committee for the meeting, supported Abdus Sattar and voiced the opposition of the general masses towards the Bill.[11]

When the Government enacted the Bill in October, 1935 in utter disregard of public opinion, the Raiyat's Association decided to hold public meetings and publish pamphlets explaining to the people the motive of the Government and the effect of the legislation.[12]

On 20 December 1935 a mass meeting attended by the peasants of about 500 villages of the Damodar Canal area was held under the auspices of the Raiyats' Association at Bangsagopal Hall with Md. Yasin in the chair. The meeting adopted a number of resolutions repudiating the figures regarding estimates of the produce of lands in the pre-canal and post-canal days and protesting against improper application of the Development Act and the rules framed thereunder. The meeting also decided to send copies of the resolutions to the District Magistrate, Burdwan, the Member, Board of Revenue, the Member-in-charge of the Irrigation Development, Bengal, and to the Governor of Bengal.[13]

Three months earlier the Congress had started its election campaign in Burdwan. Though the Congress had not yet formed any separate organization exclusively meant for the canal tax agitation, the Congress leaders discussed canal tax issues at several election meetings with an eye to the ensuing election. The campaign continued till the end of January 1937. The Congress propaganda no doubt helped the people of the canal area to form a definite opinion about the Bengal Development Act and the tax imposed in accordance with its provisions.[14]

The Raiyats' Association organized another meeting which was presided over by Netai Gupta and addressed by Jadabendra Nath Panja at Sodya on 31 January 1937. It is interesting to note that this was attended by the members of the Krishak Samiti.[15]

By the beginning of February the agriculturists of the canal area were seriously affected on account of the enforcement of the Development Act. The Government started harassing poor cultivators for the realization of the canal tax and began to recover the arrears of taxes by notice of demand, certificate procedure and the like.[16]

As regards the grievances of the cultivators in the Damodar Canal area an informal discussion took place on 10 February in the Burdwan Raj Palace with the Maharaja in the chair. Besides the two Kumars the following gentlemen attended on invitation: Durga Pada Chaudhuri, Balai Chand Mukhopadhyay, Prafulla Kumar Panja, Mahadeva Roy, Lakshman Kumar Chattopadhyay, Helaram Chattopadhyay, Secretary, Krishak Samiti, Maulavi Golam Mortuza and S.N. Batabyal. The President and the Secretary of the Burdwan District Raiyats' Association described in detail how the improper application and missuse of the Bengal Development Act, 1935 by the officials concerned had caused great hardship to the ryots who had failed to get any relief even on repeated representations to the Government authorities. Further, they pointed out that the imposition of the development tax at the rate of Rs 5-8-0 per acre had badly hit the tax-payer. Thereafter the Maharaja suggested that a public protest meeting should be held with Maharaj Kumar Uday Chand Mahatab as president to formulate the grievances of the ryots in the form of resolutions and place them before the Government for consideration. The Kumar would meet such officers as he might think necessary in order to get their grievances redressed and would propose in the provincial Assembly such amendments to the Bengal Development Act, 1935 or table such resolutions as might be necessary for the purpose. In the meantime, the Maharaja urged, the present gentlemen should send through him a formal representation to the District Magistrate of Burdwan for the purpose of mitigating the rigours of the executive proceedings for the realization of the arrears of the canal rates.[17]

On 14 February 1937 about one thousand representatives of the cultivators of the Damodar Canal area attended a conference held at the Town Hall Maidan under the presidentship of Niharendu Dutta Mazumdar to decide their future course of action in view of the Government demand of Rs 5-8-0 per acre as development tax. The president referred in his speech to the miserable condition of the peasantry in India and the crushing burden of taxes on their shoulders. He characterized the canal tax as exorbitant and unjust and urged for unity among all sections of the people to give vent to their feeling and to make their demands effectively felt by the Government.[18] The resolutions passed at the conference were as follows: That in the opinion of the conference the principles underlying the Bengal Development Act and sections thereunder were arbitrary, opposed to the interests of the *prajas* and *krishaks* in general in the sense that they had been placed outside the jurisdiction of the civil court so that the application of the Act might make the executive officers all-powerful and give them absolute, arbitrary and unfettered authority which was sure to be used to oppress the ryots; that an estimate of the surplus produce of lands in the Damodar Canal area made by the officials of the Irrigation Department was devoid of logic and was not based on facts; that the amount of paddy produced in the canal area did not admit of a taxable surplus after the deductions for payment of rent to the zamindar and expenditure on cultivation; that the conference recorded strong protest against the remarks made by the Collector of Burdwan that the cultivators were ready to pay at $\frac{1}{4}$ rate of the canal tax, and that the Government be requested to appoint a committee of enquiry to investigate how the Eden and the Damodar Canal might be best utilized for the benefit of the local people.[19]

On 24 February 1937 a meeting attended by about three thousand people was held at Bhatar bazaar under the auspices of the Raiyats' Association. This meeting too resolved to fight the canal tax.[20]

By the end of the month the working of the canal system embittered the people at large and a vast number of villagers of the non-canal areas submitted petitions to the canal authorities requesting the latter not to extend branch canals to their areas.[21] It was also learnt that about 40,000 certificates had even been prepared for the realization of the canal dues.[22]

On the first day of March 1937 the Raiyats' Association organized another meeting of the cultivators of the canal area at the Town Hall Maidan under the presidentship of Maharaj Kumar Uday Chand Mahatab. The Maharaj Kumar said that though there might be differences of opinion as regards the utility of the canal, there could not be any doubt as to the fact that the canal rate was excessive. He urged the cultivators to send petititons to the Divisional Commissioner praying suspension of the issue of certificates and assured the audience that he would support their cause so long as they would fight through legal means. Then Bankim Mukhopadhyay, an important leader of the Communist Party of India, said that they did not want to adopt any illegal course, but at the same time the Government should proceed in a legal way; if the Government remained obstinate and intractable and did not submit to people's legitimate demands, the people must surely be prepared for a bitter fight. The meeting resolved that since there had been no development, and no increased outturn of lands situated in the Damodar Canal area, no improvement levy as such could be imposed under the Bengal Development Act, 1935; that the improvement levy had been fixed solely with reference to heavy and extravagant capital expenditure and costs, etc. incurred by the Government in the construction and maintenance of the said canal without any regard to the paying capacity of the agriculturists and actual benefit, if any, derived by them; that the improvement levy as assessed by the Government was totally illegal, unjust, unreasonable and contrary to facts and opposed to natural justice; that the scheme and provisions of the Bengal Development Act were too drastic and arbitrary and were prejudical to the interests of the peasants and cultivators in general inasmuch as the Act made no provision for considering the objections or grievances of the cultivators in respect of their liabilities and amount of assessment, and moreover, by shutting out the jurisdiction of the civil court, the Act had placed the entire canal administration under the control of a few executive officials of the Government; that with a view to redressing the above grievances of the people, the scheme, principle and the provisions of the Bengal Development Act ought to be thoroughly revised and recast as early as possible and the newly elected members of the Bengal Legislature advised accordingly to urge for early amendment of the Act.[23]

Apart from the meetings organized by the local organizations, the citizens of Calcutta convened a meeting at Albert Hall on 9 May 1937 under the presidentship of Santosh Kumar Bose MLA. The meeting unanimously demanded a joint enquiry committee consisting of official and non-official members to probe the grievances of the cultivators of the canal areas in the districts of Burdwan and Hooghly regarding the imposition of canal taxes under the B.D. Act and urged that pending the report of the enquiry committee the realization of arrears of canal tax by the Government by means of attachment or otherwise be kept in abeyance. In his speech Santosh Kumar Bose emphasized that for a proper understanding of the situation arising out of the Government's efforts for realizing canal dues it was necessary to look at the question in its proper perspective. It was true that the Government had spent a huge sum of money for the construction of the canal. But it arbitrarily decided to impose a levy at an exorbitant rate upon all lands commanded by the canal, irrespective of any consideration of the actual benefit derived or likely to be derived from the canal water by the cultivators. It was suggested by many that the method of flood irrigation was necessary for improving the productive power of the land and also useful in coping with malaria. But the Government refused to take all those suggestions into consideration and tried to throw the whole burden of the tax on the shoulders of the tenants whose paying capacity had already been strained to the limit. The speaker demanded that an impartial inquiry should be made and alternative methods of assessment be explored. Meanwhile, he said, the order for realization of the arrears of canal tax should be revoked. Pramatha Nath Bandyopadhyay MLA, Sukumar Dutta MLA and Bankim Mukhopadhyay also addressed the audience and demanded an immediate inquiry into the grievances of the peasants. Among others present were Kamal Krishna Roy MLA, Hemanta Kumar Bose, Mahendra Chandra Sen, Balai Chand Mukhopadhyay, Sailendra Nath Roy, Panchanan Bose, Satindra Mitra, Abdus Sattar, Dasarathi Tah, Basantalal Murarka and Kalipada Mukhopadhyay. The meeting unanimously resolved that the imposition of the levy under the B.D. Act at the high rate of Rs. 5-8-0 per acre irrespective of the benefit derived or likely to be derived was inequitable, unjust and oppressive and caused hardship to the poor peasantry of the canal area.[24]

Meanwhile with the intensification of people's agitation against the canal tax the Government officials at the local level began to resort to repressive measures like the issue of certificates and attachment of movable properties for the realization of arrears. According to a report dated 24 April 1937, a large number of certificates were issued for the realization of arrears of tax in the canal area, and seven cows and calves of Gostha Muchi of Samsore were attached and kept in the village pound. It was also learnt that movable properties of the inhabitants of Bhatar, Palar, Natun Gram, etc. were liable to be attached as thirty days had expired from the date of issue of the certificates.[25] The officials of the Canal Development also attached and seized one calf, one bullock, two buffaloes and five cows for the realization of Rs 133-6-0 from Panchanon Maitra and Dharmadas Maitra of the villages of Mahuagram and kept the attached animals in the municipal pound. But these repressive measures failed to cow the aggrieved peasantry and break their morale.[26]

In the middle of May 1937 the Burdwan Districk Krishak Conference was held at Ghuskara under the presidentship of Muzaffar Ahmad. The conference lent its support to the resolutions passed at the meeting of the representatives of the cultivators and tenants of the Damodar Canal area at the Burdwan Town Hall Maidan under presidentship of Niharendu Dutta Mazumdar MLA on 14 February 1937 and also to those adopted in a meeting called by the Raiyats' Association at the same place on 1 March 1937 under the presidentship of Maharaj Kumar Uday Chand Mahatab MLA. It expressed its deep resentment at the forcible collection of taxes, assessed on the basis of wrong data by Government servants, by issuing certificates, attaching movables, etc. and applying the old repressive policies, and drew the attention of the Government to the fact that the dissatisfaction amongst the cultivators was growing more and more serious and urged it to immediately appoint a non-official enquiry committee, reduce the assessed tax and remit the unrealized tax in proportion to the tax so reduced.[27]

In the foregoing paragraphs we have referred to the proceedings of the several meetings organized mainly by the Burdwan District Raiyats' Association. Apart from these, a kisan conference presided over by Niharendu Dutta Mazumdar was held on 13 June in the district of Burdwan. The conference dealt with the canal tax movement.[28] Further, the first meeting of the All India Kisan Committee, held on 14 July at Niramatpur in Gaya district (Bihar) endorsed the criticisms levelled against the Bengal Development Act by the local peasantry which were supported by the Bengal Kisan Conference. It strongly condemned the action of the Government in repressing the peasantry of the villages adjacent to the canal area, the wholesale attachment of the properties of the defaulters and the delay in settling the issue.[29]

Besides, Balai Chand Mukhopadhyay, Secretary of the Raiyats' Association, issued statements from time to time drawing the attention of the members of the Bengal Legislature as well as of the Ministers to the serious situation created by the imposition of the 'improvement levy' in the canal area and demanding an open inquiry into the actual state of things. The Government, on the other hand, characterized in its communique's those meetings and deliberations as 'mischievous machinations of designing agitators from Calcutta.'[30]

The Burdwan District Congress, which had so long kept quiet or had not actively intervened, took up the matter seriously only in the middle of 1937. Jadabendranath Panja, in accordance with the resolutions of the District Congress Committee, appointed an enquiry committee on 9 June 1937. The committee first met in Calcutta on 12 June and it was decided that it would inquire how far the Damodar Canal was helpful to the people concerned for the purpose of irrigation and whether the assessment was just and the ryots were in a position to pay for the benefit, if any, derived from the canal. J.N. Bose was appointed President, Priya Ranjan Sen, Secretary and Hemanta Kumar Dutta, Assistant Secretary of the committee.[31]

On 25 June, for the first time, at the invitation of Maharaja Srish Chandra Nandy, Minister-in-charge of Communications and Works, a representation was made on behalf of the cultivators of the Damodar Canal area by Abdul Hashem MLA, Balai Chand Mukhopadhyay, Radhagobinda Hati, Advocate, Maulavi Fakir Mandal and others. The deputation pointed out that the Damodar Canal had done some good to the people but the Government should reduce the rate of the canal tax; otherwise Burdwan would turn into a 'second Midnapore'. (The reference is here to the Contai Union Board Boycott movement.—B.B.) The Minister gave them a patient hearing for three hours and promised to give early relief to the cultivators of the canal area.[32] However, the Canal Kar Pratikar Samiti[33] held that the members of the deputation were pro-establishment and hence could not truly represent the interests of the suffering peasants. It observed that the resolutions adopted in the meetings at the Burdwan Town Hall on 14 February and 1 March should be taken as their charter of demands.[34]

Realizing the gravity of the situation the Government issued a press communique on the Damodar Canal issue which was published on 10 August 1937. The communiqué refuted the allegations of the agitators that the increase in the value of outturn had been overestimated and was not so much as to justify the charge of Rs. 5-8-0 per acre. Referring to Townend Report dated 10 March 1937 it defended the methods employed in estimating the pre-canal and post-canal yields and in fixing the rate of assessment. It said that the Government accepted the principle of assessment under the Bengal Development Act as scientific and was satisfied that the charge of Rs. 5-8-0 which was as a rule much less than half the value of the excess produce due to irrigation, was fair and equitable. It, however, admitted that much hardship was caused to the cultivators as the assessment for 1934-5 was made very late and the rates had, therefore, to be paid in the following year. In order to give some relief, it said, the Government had decided to grant a remission of four annas in the rupees on the demand for the year 1936-7.[35]

On 16 August Balai Chand Mukhopadhyay once again issued

a statement refuting the arguments put forward by the Government in its defence in the above-mentioned press note. He tried to draw the attention of the members of both the houses of the Legislature to the utter helplessness of the poor cultivators of the canal areas who on several occasions prayed, but in vain, to all the powers that be, ranging from the canal *zamadar* and the District Magistrate to their Excellencies, the Viceroy and the Governor and the Hon'able Ministers. He once more appealed to the members of the said legislative bodies to compel the Government to hold an open inquiry into the matter.[36]

In response to these appeals Pramatha Nath Bandyopadhyay moved two cut motions in the Bengal Legislative Assembly on 28 August to discuss the appalling conditions of the people living in the canal areas. He said that the canal project was intended to serve two purposes—one of supplying water to the area under irrigation and the other of fighting malaria. The canal was also expected to distribute 'liquid gold' all round. But its actual operation belied all those hopes and expectations. True, the canal project cost the Government of Bengal a sum of Rs. 124 lakhs and the Government of India raised a loan at a high rate of interest to meet the capital expenditure. But, Pramatha Nath Bandyopadhyay said, Sir Otto Niemeyer's report[37] enabled the Government of Bengal to liquidate all those obligations to the Government of India with certain exceptions and so far as the capital which was borrowed from the Government of India and the interest charge on that capital were concerned, they had been written off. Therefore, he observed, the plain position was that under section 12 of the B.D. Act the people of the locality were bound to pay levy only for the maintenance, establishment and the repair charges of the canal area. Thus, even for fiscal purposes, he said, it was not necessary to continue the levy at the rate of Rs. 5-8-0 per acre in the canal area. He maintained that it was an intolerable burden on the peasantry. He refused to regard the question as a local one because Mr Townend said that the Damodar Canal area was the testing ground for the whole of Bengal. For all these reasons, he said, the question should receive serious consideration from the Government, the area should be surveyed and the grievances of the peasantry carefully ascertained. He requested the Ministers concerned to visit the area and settle the issue so as to alleviate the distress of the canal area. Then the Maharaj Kumar of Burdwan intervening in the debate said that though the Government had proposed to give some concessions to the people for paying up their arrears the actual trouble remained there. He suggested that the Irrigation Minister should at his earliest convenience visit the area, hear the grievances direct from the people and try to come to some sort of settlement. He also demanded that no further expansion of the Damodar Canal should be undertaken until proper inquiry was made and the present question of levy settled. Thereafter Banku Bihari Mandal spoke in support of the motion. He said that the oppression perpetrated by the certificate officials for the realization of the canal rate had become so much severe that the Damodar Canal was 'now...a menace' to the people of Burdwan. He urged the Minister-in-charge of Irrigation to consider the case of the cultivators, reduce the tax and extend the time for the payment of arrears of taxes As regards the appointment of the enquiry committee he said that it should consist of non-official members along with some members of the Cabinet. Among others who supported the cut motion moved by P.N. Bandyopadhyay were Al-Haj Maulana, Dr Sanaullah, Adwaita Kumar Majhi, Abul Hashem and Bankim Mukhopadhyay. Thereafter F.C. Brasher spoke on behalf of the European group and opposed the motion. In reply Maharaja Srish Chandra Nandy of Cossimbazar, Minister-in-charge of Irrigation, assured the House that the Government had decided to appoint an enquiry committee with the Premier as its Chairman to examine the Damodar Canal issue in all its aspects and submit a report at the earliest opportunity. Premier A.K. Fazl-ul-Huq admitted in his speech that there had been a widespread agitation in the canal area against the B.D. Act and the tax-rate imposed under the same. Since the question was a complicated one, he observed, nothing could be done except by appointing a committee to investigate the matter. As regards the personnel of the committee, he assured the House that the Government would consult the leaders of various groups before it came to a final decision. At last the motion was withdrawn in view of the assurance given by the Premier.[38]

On 31 August 1937 about 1,000 cultivators from the villages of Sodya, Simpra, Korori, Saligram, Chakundi, Bora, Hatgobindapur, Bongram, Palsa, Nabastha, Bhodhpur, Begut, Kuchut,

Faridpur, Bakalsa, Bararuntia, Jarui, Ataghat, Tajpur, Sukur and twenty other villages of the Damodar Canal area arrived in the town and entered the court compound to impress upon the collector the fact that they were unable to pay the canal tax at the present rate and the arrears thereof. As he was not present, the cultivators approached the Sadar Subdivisional Officer and urged him to contradict the Government communiqué on increased outturn. The Subdivisional officer, while regretting his inability to do so, assured that he would place before the Government through the Collector their demands regarding reduction of the canal tax, suspension of certificate orders pending the publication of the report of the enquiry committee and inclusion of a sufficient number of their representatives in that committee. The cultivators then met the Revenue Officer and requested him to stop executing certificates till the next harvest. The Revenue officer said that he could defer it up to September 30 after which a fresh order from the Government was required for suspending the execution till the next harvest. Afterwards the cultivators went out in a procession shouting different slogans along several thoroughfares of the town.[39]

During the next two months no fruitful attempt was made to settle the canal issue except a few statements and counter-statements by the Government and the Congress Committee.[40] It was on 11 November 1937 that a conference regarding the Damodar Canal dispute was held at the Writers' Building and attended by Sir B.P. Sinha Roy, Maharaja Srish Chandra Nandy, Maharaj Kumar U.C. Mahatab MLA, Adwaita Kumar Majhi MLA and some other gentlemen from Burdwan. Sir B.P. Sinha Roy said that he would like to have a fresh discussion with the gentlemen present with a view to arriving at a solution of the problem. He was ready to conduct a fresh crop-cutting experiment in such a manner as would win support from all quarters. In this experiment, he said, four villages from each union would be selected and the lands classified before crop-cutting in the presence of the villagers. The only object of this experiment would be to find out the actual increase in outturn. He agreed to accept the pre-canal yield as six maunds per *bigha* and hoped that the people would not refuse to pay 50 per cent of the average increase in outturn. Then Balai Chand Mukhopadhyay said that the cost of cultivation actually left no margin of profit to the cultivators to pay the canal tax.

He also observed that the Government was trying to make profit instead of doing any good to the cultivators and since the Government had been still persisting in applying the B.D. Act, it was useless to discuss the matter any further. He asserted that the pre-canal yield was not less than eight maunds per *bigha* on average. At this stage Maharaja Srish Chandra Nandy brusquely remarked that the cultivators might be heavily indebted, but the Government was not concerned with their miseries. Thereafter Sir Bijoy Prasad requested the representatives of the cultivators to ask the people of the canal area to pay off the canal tax. In reply Sri Kumar Mitra said that they could not ask the people to do so unless the Government gave them substantial relief immediately. At last Sir Bijoy Prasad and Maharaja Nandy assured them that they would soon visit the canal area to make an on-the-spot study of the situation.[41]

On 25 November Maharaja Srish Chandra Nandy and Sir Bijoy Prasad came to Burdwan and went to a village, about 17 miles away from the town, where they met about 6,000 agriculturists and discussed with them the Damodar Canal issue in detail. The local people complained of the high rate of canal tax which, they said, they were not in a position to pay because of the fall in the prices of agricultural produce. But they intimated their willingness to pay a reasonable rate. They all accepted the suggestion of the Ministers relating to a fresh crop-cutting experiment to determine the actual outturn and agreed to co-operate with the local officials to make the experiment a success. The Ministers asked them to make a part payment of the arrears of taxes pending the crop-cutting experiment and final decision regarding the canal tax, so that they might not have to pay a heavy sum at a time. The Ministers said that the part payment might be made at a lower rate to be shortly announced by the Government and necessary adjustment would be made against next year's payment. The Ministers also assured that the crop-cutting experiment would be conducted in their presence and with their help. Later the Ministers visited Galsi and met 7,000 people and held a discussion on the same line.[42]

Balai Chand Mukhopadhyay said in a statement on behalf of the Raiyats' Association on 6 December that the Government, instead of determining the average yield of pre-canal days from the pre-canal settlement records, old registered deeds and decrees of civil courts, had this time quite arbitrarily assumed the average of pre-canal yield to be six maunds per *bigha*. The Government by proposing a new crop-cutting experiment following a curious method of chance lottery in the classification of lands and making this experiment on the current year's crop, would be taking advantage of an exceptionally good year of bumper harvest. He regarded it as a matter of regret that the authorities of the Revenue and Irrigation Departments, instead of making an earnest endeavour to arrive at an honourable settlement, appeared to be confusing the real issue.[43] The same day an almost similar statement was issued by Jadabendranath Panja, President, Burdwan District Congress Committee.[44]

It was reported on 16 December that the Government after dragging its feet for a long time had, in pursuance of the assurance given in the last session of the Bengal Legislative Assembly, appointed an enquiry committee with Mriganka Bhusan Roy, Revenue Officer, as Secretary.[45] The first meeting of the newly appointed Damodar Canal Enquiry Committee was held on 15 December, Sir B.P. Sinha Roy presiding in the absence of the Premier. During the long discussion it was pointed out that because of the irrigational facilities the canal areas were yielding a crop which was 50 per cent more than the amount the cultivators used to get in the pre-canal days and hence the rate was to be fixed on the basis of that increased outturn. The Government was, however, prepared to consider the question in all its aspects and ready to fix the rate at Rs 3 per acre. But the Government had to accept Townend Report as the basis of calculation although by its own admission it had no intention to regard the said report as infallible. One of the members of the committee asserted that the levy should be imposed only to meet the maintenance, establishment and repair charges for the canal, since the capital expenditure incurred for the construction of the canal had been paid off by the Government of India on the latter's acceptance of Otto Niemeyer's Report. However, it was finally decided that a few sites would be selected and the committee would visit those places in order to ascertain facts and figures.[46]

On 17 December Balai Chand Mukhopadhyay made a statement on behalf of the Raiyats' Association. Referring to the official enquiry committee and its first conference he said that the task of the committee would be difficult and hazardous in view of its restricted and undefined scope and terms of reference. He resented the Ministers' decision to stick to their previous stand and their refusal to consider whether the cultivators had actual capacity to pay the high rate of canal tax or not.[47]

In the last week of December the Government announced its decision relating to *ad interim* relief. A press note issued on 23 December said that it might take some time for the enquiry committee 'to submit its report and for Government to consider it and to reach a decision thereon. To prevent an accumulation of arrears, it has been decided by Government that three-fourths of the demand should be collected now as an 'ad interim' measure pending their final decision on the subject. As the demand has already been reduced from Rs. 5-8-0 to Rs. 4-2-0 per acre by the grant of a rebate of 25 per cent, the collection be made at the rate of Rs. 3 per acre which approximates to three-fourths of the demand after deducting the rebate.' The communiqué further added that '...the above concession and the rebate will be admissible to those who pay up their dues by the end of February, 1938.'[48]

The Government decision to give some 'ad interim relief' to the cultivators of the canal area was criticized by Balai Chand Mukhopadhyay and Jadabendranath Panja. Their point was that when the Government had decided to hold an inquiry and start fresh crop-cutting experiment, it should not urge the cultivators to pay the arrears of canal tax at the rate of Rs. 3 by the month of February 1938 pending the report of the enquiry committee. The Government should await the report of the said committee and concede the demands of the agriculturists.[49]

By the first week of January 1938 the Damodar Canal authorities were reported to have finished their crop-cutting experiments. Balai Chand Mukhopadhyay lodged his protest against the irregular and unreliable methods and procedures adopted by the authorities concerned in the matter. He said that crops of several plots of land were cut and measurement thereof taken by Government officials without letting the respective owners or cultivators know anything about the matter. The final measurement or weighting was not done in the presence of local men. Hence, he observed, the aggrieved cultivators could not have any confidence in the experiments made in such a perfunctory and surreptitious way and the data or figures collected by such wrong and improper devices could not be relied upon for a fair and correct estimate of the increased outturn.[50]

On 29 January twelve of the eighteen members of the Damodar Canal Enquiry Committee including Sir B.P. Sinha Roy, Maharaja Srish Chandra Nandy, J.N. Bose, B.B. Mandal, A. Majhi, Maulavi A. Hashem and Maulavi N. Ahmed visited Khana junction, about 12 miles west of the Burdwan town. There Sir B.P. Sinha Roy addressed about 1,000 people and explained to them the purpose of their visit. Jadabendra Nath Panja, President, District Congress Committee and a resident of the area, submitted a memorial on behalf of the local cultivators. The members of the enquiry committee then went to a village, Balgona, where Chandra Sekhar Konar submitted on behalf of 2,000 cultivators a memorial similar to that of Mr Panja. Netaipada Gupta of Saligram placed before the members of the enquiry committee an account of the production of the last five years (1339 B.S. to 1344 B.S.) to show that the cultivators earned no profit from the canal. The memorial submitted by the inhabitants of the villages affected by the improvement levy may be summarized as follows.

'... There is no increase in the outturn of paddy owing to irrigation from the canal.... The crop-cutting experiment at the last harvest season was vitiated by the fact (i) that the lands were not classified according to the quality of the soil (ii) that the plots in which crop-cutting operations were held were not selected in the presence of the villagers concerned, (iii) that crop-cutting was mostly made without notice to the owner of the field and in his absence, (iv) that in some cases crops were cut from a larger area than the standard one of 11 × 9 ft. and (v) that no allowance was made for the boundary ridges (*ayils*) of the fields and the inevitable wastages of the produce in reaping, stocking, carrying and storing the paddy. At least one sixteenth should be deducted from gross produce for the last item.' The memorial also said that 'the total cost of the construction of the canal was met by the loan from the Government of India. With the inauguration of the provincial autonomy, on the basis of Sir Otto Niemeyer's Report, the Government of India remitted the loan, thereby exempting the Bengal Government from the payment of the cost of construction. The Government now can demand at the utmost the most reasonable maximum cost of maintaining the canal in proper condition.' But, the memorial continued, '...the whole cost of maintaining the canal cannot be equitably charged upon the impoverished peasants alone, inasmuch as one of the objects of the Damodar Canal is to mitigate the strength of the flood, which may even endanger the city of Calcutta. Having regard to those facts, the East Indian Railway, the Grand Trunk Road, Burdwan-Katwa Ligh Railway, the Bengal Nagpur Railway, the city of Calcutta, towns and other vested interests which are benefited...should be made to contribute to the cost.' The memorialists admitted that the 'only benefit the peasants derive from the canal is some sort of insurance against the uncertainty of rains—against drought which occurs occasionally at an interval of 7 or 8 years.' The memorialists, therefore, prayed that 'the Committee may be pleased to recommend to the Government of Bengal... that the agriculturists holding not more than two acres of land may be exempted from the levy; that the minimum rate may be levied upon your Memorialists adjudged by your Committee on due consideration of facts set forth in the memorial; that arrears outstanding may be adjusted to the altered rate; and that steps may be taken to have proper drainage for the low lands so as to save them from utter ruin.'[51]

To the said committee Kiron Chandra Dutt submitted a separate memorandum since he could not agree to the points contained in the memorial of Jadabendra Nath Panja. He made out seven points in his memorandum: 'No development tax should be levied on Burdwan people even if they have got benefit by the Damodar Canal or even if their lands have improved. The estimate of the "increased outturn" of land in the Damodar Canal area is... arbitrary and too high. The supply of water is not regular and scientific and great mischief is being done; comparatively lower 1st class Sali lands are becoming waterlogged and the high lands do not get water—no water is available where it is necessary and it is supplied where there is superfluity of it. Owing to the defect in the system the quantity of silt carried in the canal water is negligible whereas on the other hand quantity of sand is so large that sand carried by the canal water deteriorate them. There has been no improvement at present. The cultivators at present in the canal area have no taxable surplus after defraying their necessary costs and they have no paying capacity and the authorities while assessing overlooked the economic condition of the cultivators and considered only the heavy expenditure of the department; and the system is expensive out of all proportion. The procedure of assessment in the Act is not according to the fixed principles of public finance and opposed to the interests of the peasants.'[52]

On 4 February 1938 a meeting of the official enquiry committee was held in Sir B.P. Sinha Roy's room in the Assembly House, Calcutta. After considering the facts and figures collected from the cultivators the committee arrived at the conclusion that the average increased outturn per acre was four maunds of paddy and six *pans* of straw. Sir B.P. Sinha Roy said that the cultivators were getting Rs. 6 as profit per acre and hence they should pay Rs. 3 as improvement levy. However, he said that the cost of maintenance of the canal system was Rs. 320,000 per annum, and unless Rs. 2-10-0 was paid to the Government as tax per acre to enable it to meet the establishment costs, it would not be possible to allow 15 per cent remission for fields which became waterlogged and those which did not receive adequate supply of water. It was learnt that P.N. Bandyopadhyay and Maulavi Abdul Hashem could not accept the figures supplied by the Government about the results of crop-cutting experiment.[53] Abdul Hashem later submitted a note of dissent and upheld the arguments as contained in Kiron Chandra Dutt's memorandum.

Both Jadabendra Nath Panja and Balai Chand Mukhopadhyay later protested against the decision of the Government to fix the canal tax at Rs. 2-10-0 per acre. Mr Mukhopadhyay said that the cultivators were agreeable to pay Rs. 1-8-0 per acre for the only benefit they derived from the canal as a drought insurance. He asked the people not to lose heart but to take a bold stand and resolutely assert their rights against the arbitrary decision of the Government.[54]

On 14 February a big meeting was held at the Burdwan Town Hall Maidan under the presidentship of Umapada Roy of Sodya. In their speeches Sukumar Bandyopadhyay, Sambhunath Konar, Chandra Sekhar Konar, Pramatha Nath Bandyopadhyay and Aswini Kumar Mandal explained the attitude of the Bengal Government towards the canal tax agitation and exhorted all to stand united and fight back every unjust move of the Government.[55]

The Congress Canal Levy Enquiry Committee finalised its report by the end of February. On examination of the pre-canal accounts of agricultural produce, settlement records, decrees of *bhag chas* suits in law courts, results of crop-cutting experiments, quinquennial reports, figures available from other governmental publications and records and the evidence collected from the peasants, the committee came to the conclusion that 'the Damodar Canal has not, to any appreciable extent, increased the productivity of the area served by it.... The yield per acre was about 24 maunds before the canal and the same is the average even after the canal.' The Report admitted: 'There is, however, a general consensus of opinion that the canal is really useful in years of drought. Therefore, if any levy can at all be imposed on the cultivators of the canal area, it can only be on the basis of drought insurance benefit.' But the committee held that 'On the whole... for the purpose of levy on the ground of drought insurance, we may proceed on the basis that there is drought in one year in course of six years, and that once in six years there is half failure of crop. It further pointed out that the benefit might, therefore, be calculated at half the full crop i.e., twelve maunds of paddy per acre. Distributed over six years, it came upto 2 maunds of paddy per acre, half of which might be charged for according to the Development Act Rules. Therefore, the Report said, 'the levy per year then amounts to the price of one maund of paddy and one maund (*sic*) of straw, the price being calculated according to the current rates each year in January. But in view of the fact that a large number of assessees are owners of holding not exceeding one acre, and also that the cost of cultivation in relation to the falling price of paddy is disproportionately high along with the high rent the cultivator has to pay, the Committee thinks it desirable that such cultivators (with holding not exceeding one acre) should be exempted from the levy.' The committee admitted no question of realizing the capital expenditure for the canal, because the Government of India exempted the Government of Bengal from repaying the capital borrowed from the former in accordance with Sir Otto Niemeyer's report. It only considered the question of running expenses for the canal. On this point the Report said: 'The levy which we are now recommending (viz. the price of one maund of paddy and one maund (*sic*) of straw per acre in January which in the present year comes to about Re. 1 and 8 as.) may not be sufficient for the purpose. But it is quite obvious from the history of the Damodar Canal project that the canal was never meant for irrigation purpose alone. It was intended 'inter alia' that the canal should protect the railways, the Grand Trunk Road, the Burdwan town, the port of Calcutta etc. by moderating the strength of the Damodar flood.' The Report, therefore, recommended: '...there are important beneficiaries other than the cultivators of the canal area. In all fairness and justice, if more money has to be raised for the purposes of maintaining the Damodar Canal, Government should look to those beneficiaries for making good the deficiency, if any, rather than overtax the poor cultivators for benefit which may in a sense be said to be problematical.'[56]

In the second week of May the Government issued a communiqué on the modification of canal rates. It said: 'After due consideration Government have accepted the recommendations of the Committee and reduced the rate for the levy under the Bengal Development Act for the years 1936-7 and 1937-8 to Rs 2-9-0 per acre to afford the cultivators some relief on account of the present low price of paddy and to enable them more readily to pay off the accumulated arrears of the levy.... In view of the very great misconception prevalent in the area commanded by the Damodar Canal regarding the imposition of compulsory levy under the Bengal Development Act, Government have decided to reintroduce the system of voluntary irrigation through leases under the Bengal Irrigation Act. On account of the prevailing low price of agricultural produce the rates of the kinds of leases have been modified.... The chief reduction is in the rate for an annual lease which is now Rs. 4 per acre instead of Rs. 4-8.'[57]

A few days before the publication of the above press note, Balai Chand Mukhopadhyay called the decision of the Government on the modification of canal rates anomalous and inscrutable. He condemned the 'shop-keeper's policy' adopted by the Government. Instead of giving any relief to the famished peasantry, said Mukhopadhyay, the Government had poured ridicule on their helpless condition.[58] Jadabendra Nath Panja also blamed the Government decision to collect the canal tax at a rate absolutely beyond the paying capacity of the peasants.[59]

From the middle of May through the next two months several

protest meetings were organized in villages like Hatgobindapur, Galsi, Mandalgram, Karuri, Kulgarh, Kuchut-Dharmarajtala, Belgram, Baroshibtala, Uragram etc. Those meetings were addressed by Jadabendra Nath Panja, Bankim Mukhopadhyay, Abdus Sattar, Sasthi Das Chaudhuri, Manas Gobinda Ghatak, Abdullah Rasul, Pramatha Nath Bandyopadhyay, Sachindradas Adhikari, Chandra Sekhar Konar, Helaram Chatterjee, Dasarathi Tah, Mahendra Khan, Jahed Ali, Gobinda Dutta, Ashutosh Hazra, Mahaprasad Konar, Narayan Mandal, Balai Deb Sharma, Golam Mahabul, Nakul Chandra Dutta, Aja Kumar Kesh, Balai Chandra Haldar, Kartik Chandra Ghosh, Choudhury Ali Saheb, Phelaram Mandal and others. They all exhorted the people of the canal area not to bow down to the Government decision and take canal water by signing lease deeds at a high rate. They urged the people to carry on their agitation until their legitimate demands were fulfilled.[60]

The Government, on the other hand, since the publication of the press note in which it declared its decision to reduce the improvement or rather the compulsory levy to Rs 2-9-0, had kept quiet and hoped that the people would happily agree to its decision and pay up their arrears. The local peasants, however, considered the Government decision arbitrary and refused to sign lease forms. At last the Government broke the dreadful silence and began to issue certificate notices for the realization of arrears of taxes. In consequence, it was reported in October 1938, the peasants of the canal area had marched on foot to the office of the District Collector to lodge their complaints against the coercive measures adopted by the canal authority.[61]

By the beginning of the following year the Government had started attaching movable properties of the defaulters of the canal area. On 12 January 1939 eight attached cows of the village of Kadra had been kept in the village pound of Ausha. The peasants divided in several groups had been trying to resist the attachment operations. The local cultivators were determined to launch a satyagraha movement and continue their agitation till all their demands were fulfilled. On the other hand, the Government had decided to send a large contingent of Gurkha soldiers and deploy them on patrol duty in order to bring the situation under control.[62]

Within a month the satyagraha movement began to take shape.

In a statement Manoranjan Hazra, member, Bengal Provincial Congress Committee and Kisan Sabha, appealed to the people of Bengal for help. He said that for several months the people of the canal area had been vigorously protesting against the imposition of a high rate of canal tax and, at present, finding to their exasperation that the Government had miserably failed to fulfil the demands of the poor peasantry, they had resorted to satyagraha.[63]

According to a report dated 15 February, Rabi Majumdar, Secretary, Volunteers' Division of Bengal Provincial Kisan Sabha, said that at Aushagram a satyagraha camp had been set up to conduct the campaign in a peaceful and non-violent way. About fifty satyagrahis had been keeping watch on the pound by turns so that the police authorities could not take out the attached cattle to put the same on auction. He also reported that seventeen thousand certificates had so far been issued and a huge posse of soldiers had been kept ready. But even in the face of all the repressive measures the satyagrahis remained undaunted in spirit and unflinching in determination. The cultivators had expressed their readiness to pay the canal tax at the rate of Rs 1-8-0. But they were determined to resist any move of the Government to collect the tax at a higher rate. The peasant women, under the leadership of Nanibala Samanta, took an active part in the movement.[64]

Bankim Mukhopadhyay observed in a statement that the Government had promulgated section 7 Cr. P.C. and ordered the police to attach movable properties of the defaulters. On 15 February, he said, a procession of peasants was scheduled to be taken out, but the local authorities prohibited it under section 144. In the face of this provocation the peasant leaders decided to postpone the holding of the procession.[65]

On 16 February Pramatha Nath Bandyopadhyay moved an adjournment motion in the Legislative Assembly to discuss the serious situation arising out of the notification No. 656 P, dated the 10th February, 1939, of the Government of Bengal, extending the provision of section VII of the Criminal Law Amendment Act of 1932 to the whole of Burdwan district, excluding Asansol subdivision, and the promulgation on 13 February of section 144 Cr. P.C. in certain parts of the district. In the said notification the Government stated that 'the arrears in that area come up to about Rs 642,000 and the collections amounted to less than Rs 32,000 only. The result has been practically a stoppage of all collections and ... that the stoppage in the collection has been due to political agitation of an undesirable type involving the boycott of officials. It is for this reason that Government have been obliged to despatch armed police and motor lorries and buses for the purpose of removing properties attached of the tenantry who are either unable or unwilling to pay. They have also promulgated section 144 prohibiting public meetings and they have called in (*sic*) their assistance section 7 of the Criminal Law (Amendment) Act of 1932.' Pramatha Nath Bandyopadhyay requested the Minister concerned to put a halt to the 'policy of terrorization' and settle the dispute with the tenantry.[66]

An emergency meeting of the executive committee of the Burdwan District Congress Committee held on 19 February adopted a resolution strongly condemning the Government policy of letting loose repression on the people of the district. The meeting demanded immediate release of all persons arrested in this connexion and repeal of all repressive measures. In another resolution it protested against the false propaganda carried on by the Government that the Congress had started a no-tax campaign. The meeting also reiterated its stand on the canal tax issue and urged the people to pay their arrears.[67]

On 21 February eighteen volunteers were arrested from the Ausha satyagraha camp.[68] Arrests were also made in other parts of the canal area and a reign of terror prevailed.[69]

Till the middle of 1939 the satyagraha movement continued unabated and the police could not demoralize the illiterate masses of the canal area. However, even such a heroic and long-protracted struggle failed to compel the Government to reduce the tax to Rs 1-8-0. As a result the people subsequently accepted the Government rate of Rs 2-9-0[70] and paid the arrears. The Government, on its part, released the convicted persons and thus ended the movement.

IV

An attempt will be made here to make an analytical review of the organizations which actively participated in the movement and their differences regarding the formulation of the demands of the peasantry and the methods they followed in the course of the movement.

It is on record that the Burdwan District Raiyats' Association first plunged into the agitation and took up the issue in right earnest. The reason was that the pleaders and advocates who were doyens of the Association had landed interests in the canal area and naturally they got alarmed about the possible financial drain when the Government decided to impose a heavy burden of compulsory levy on the ryots of the canal area.[71] They admitted the utility of the canal and never decried the scheme as such. What they wanted to achieve through their agitation by means of 'appeals' and 'prayers' was to persuade the Government to reduce the canal tax to a rate within the paying capacity of the ryots. The Association, at the initial stage, tried to 'keep aloof from the Congress for fear of government repression' which, it thought, 'would scare away the peasants from uniting for a common cause.'[72] The Raiyats' Association held several public meetings at the Burdwan Town Hall Maidan and in different villages of the canal area. The members of the Association established contact with the masses through direct personal approach and propaganda by means of publishing pamphlets and booklets and also by issuing appeals and statements in newspapers. With a view to attracting their attention to the grievances of the peasants they visited the members of the Legislature and furnished them with facts and figures.[73]

The Congress actively joined the movement after its defeat in the elections,[74] and stood by the side of the peasants till its acceptance of the modified rate of canal tax fixed by the Government. The Congress first appointed an enquiry committee on 9 June 1937 to investigate the grievances of the ryots arising out of the canal levy. The Congress Enquiry Committee took the trouble of going to the rural areas for an on-the-spot-study. The committee submitted its report in the first week of March 1938. In accordnace with the report the Congress advised the cultivators to accept the canal as a drought insurance and to pay one maund of paddy and one *pan* of straw per acre.[75] Moreover, the Congress organized meetings and demonstrations and its leaders issued appeals to the Government for reduction of the canal rate and published statements on several occasions in newspapers either ventilating the grievances of the local cultivators or refuting Government communiqués which always defended the canal scheme and the rate imposed under it. Further, the Congress MLAs moved cut motions compelling the Government to appoint an enquiry committee to investigate the canal issue. The Congress Working Committee during its session in Calcutta from 26 October to 1 November 1937 adopted resolutions sympathizing with the Damodar Canal tax agitation.[76] The Bishnupur Conference of the Provincial Congress Committee also expressed its full sympathy with the canal tax movement.[77] On 28 May 1938 Subhas Chandra Bose came to Burdwan and next day he discussed the canal tax issue with the local workers of his party and urged them to see to it that the peasants did not sign the lease forms. He also asked them to launch a vigorous movement against the unjust tax imposed on the poor cultivators.[78] Not only did the Congress Working Committee and its leaders sympathize with and lend support to the canal tax agitation, its other wings too supported cause of the local peasants. The Burdwan District Krishak Conference which was held in the first week of June 1938 in the village of Kasipur under the presidentship of Prafulla Chandra Sen of Arambagh condemned the Government policy of imposing compulsory betterment levy on the poor peasants. The conference resolved that the canal tax should not be more than Rs 1-8-0 and the peasants with small landholding be exempted from payment of canal tax.[79]

Nevertheless, from the material at our disposal, we can safely observe that the Congress did not urge the local people to launch any satyagraha movement or no-tax campaign against the Government when the latter had refused to accept the rate recommended by it. Finally, when the Government in utter disregard of the popular sentiment intensified repression, the Congress only issued statements in protest and its MLAs appealed to the Government for an early settlement of the dispute, and strangely enough it denied any connexion with the satyagraha movement and advised the people to pay the arrears at the rate fixed by the Government.

The Krishak Samiti[80] which mainly conducted the satyagraha movement differed both from the Raiyats' Association and the Congress both in respect of the issues and the goal of the movement. Before we dwell on those points, we should add a few words on the justification behind 'its co-operation with the Congress'.[81]

The members of the Krishak Samiti constituted the 'left wing' of the Congress. They tried to press the canal issue on the Congress leadership soon after the Congress defeat in the election and persuaded it to form a joint platform.[82] As the two differed from each other in their political convictions and moorings the organizational progress of the newly formed Canal Kar Pratikar Samiti suffered to a great extent. On many occasions the left-wing Congressmen and the Communists had to fall in with the Congress leadership, because they wanted to pursue a policy of 'united front'[83] with the Congress with a view to giving the latter a 'national revolutionary orientation'[84] and to widen their mass base through it. However, in the middle of 1938 the Congress-Krishak Samiti alliance broke down on account of intransigence of both the parties.[85]

The Communists or the leaders of the Krishak Samiti formulated the issues of the movement in a slightly different way. To quote one of them: 'The Burdwan Canal Tax Movement was based on the stand that availability of irrigation was to be there as a matter of course. As a matter of fact, it was claimed that there had been an irrigation system prevailing when the British established their regime. If the system broke down, it was maintained that such breakdown was due to the failings of the administration and the landlords in commission and omission. So whatever irrigation arrangement was being made was a belated compensation and a meagre compensation at that for damages that had already been done. Hence no levy was due from the raiyats.'[87] But the Congress Enquiry Committee considered the canal useful as a drought insurance and its report did not say a single word on the damage done to the peasants by the administration. For that reason, the Congress Enquiry Committee could fix the canal rate equal to the price of one maund of paddy and one *pan* of straw—which was then Rs 1-8-0. But it was not unknown to the members of the said committee that the price of paddy fluctuated, and if the price rose up the peasants were to pay more. The Krishak Samiti understood the real implication of the Congress decision and declared that it was ready to accept the rate of Rs 1-8-0 but would not accept any rate in terms of agricultural produce as suggested by the Congress and reiterated this stand in several meetings.[87] When members of the Krishak Samiti found to their utter consternation that the Government would not budge an inch from its decision of Rs 2-9-0 and the Congress had tactly accepted the rate, they started satyagraha movement.[88] They asked the people to surrender their movable goods on demand by the executive officials for collection of arrears. They exhorted the people to refuse payment at the rate of Rs 2-9-0. Their volunteers kept vigil on the pound guards so that they could not get out from the villages with the attached animals and goods to put them on auction. They even foiled the Government officials' attempt to sell the attached articles by auction by giving 'no-bid' calls.[89]

V

Now we will deal with the attitude of the Government and the measures it adopted to curb the movement and the people's reaction to them.

It becomes obvious from our chronological narration of the events of the movement that the Damodar Canal tax agitation was present in a nascent form even when the Bengal Development Act was not finally passed. At the initial stage the Government did not attach any importance to the movement and, accordingly, refrained from taking any stern measures against the agitators. Several meetings took place in Burdwan to register the protest of the ryots against the Bill till its final passage in October 1936. When in the beginning of 1936 the vast area adjacent to the Damodar Canal was notified as benefited and improved by the canal and a rate of Rs 5-8-0 per acre was fixed, the Burdwan District Raiyats' Association came to the fore and initiated a movement against the application of the drastic provisions of the Bengal Development Act to the canal area. They organized meetings, published pamphlets and contacted peasants to express their resentment against the high rate of canal tax. From the last quarter of 1936 till the end of January 1937 the Congress was busy with the election campaign and, side by side with its propaganda in election meetings, the Congress leaders tried to explain to the peasantry the far-reaching implications of the Development Act and urged the people to agitate against the imposition of compulsory 'improvement' levy. On February 13 the Congress appointed the Damodar Canal Levy Enquiry Committee to probe the grievances of the raiyats and fix an equitable rate of tax. Now these hectic activities of the Raiyats' Association and the Congress made the Government realize the gravity of the situation. Accordingly, it arranged to send ministers and officials to the affected areas to mobilize the support of the local people in favour of the Development Act and the canal scheme. Meanwhile the Krishak Samiti joined the movement and began to co-operate with the Congress. As a result the movement gained added strength and momentum. In the Bengal Legislative Assembly the Premier and the Minister of Communications gave an assurance to form an enquiry committee after a cut motion was tabled by a Congress MLA on behalf of the people of the canal area. The local peasants submitted several memoranda to the Ministers for the redress of their grievances. The Government earlier announced a 25 per cent. rebate and was now compelled to reduce the tax to Rs. 3-0-0. After a good deal of vacillation it also appointed an enquiry committee which soon began to work, though not in a satisfactory manner. By the first week of March 1938 the Congress Enquiry Committee published its report and recommended a levy equal to the price of the one maund of paddy and one *pan* of straw per acre. Later, the official Enquiry Committee fixed the improvement levy at the rate of Rs. 2-9-0 per acre. But this partial fulfilment of the demand of the poor peasants could not dissuade them from launching a satyagraha movement even against the reduced rate. They refused to sign lease forms and pay the modified rate. The villagers happily parted with their possessions when attached and refused to participate in the subsequent auction. Once a cobbler's cow was attached in Bhattar. Under the leadership of the Krishak Samiti nearly five to six thousand peasants encircled the area so that the Government officials could not go out of the villages with the attached goods. Nine cows belonging to a Brahmin of the village Kandra (Sadar P.S. Burdwan) were attached and taken to a village named Aula situated in the Nabastha area for sale. Thousands of peasants intercepted the Government party with the cows, set up camps and started satyagraha. The peasants boycotted the canal officials. The volunteers organized picketing. The Government, on its part, unleashed repression. Section VII of the Bengal Criminal Law Amendment Act of 1932 (otherwise known as Anderson Act or the Black Act) was enforced in Burdwan district, and section 144

Cr. P.C. promulgated everywhere. On 14 February 1939 about fifteen to twenty thousand peasants under the leadership of the Krishak Samiti assembled from all sides to enter the town of Burdwan to violate section 144 in protest against the policy of attachment. In the face of the Government's provocative measures and the lukewarm attitude of the Congress, the Krishak Samiti controlled the peasants and sent them back home in a disciplined way. That night eleven lorry loads of the military personnel raided the village of Aushagram. They marched inside the village singing the tune of an infantry band. They beat the villagers and collected money from them. The attached cows were brought under military escort to the Burdwan Revenue office for auction. The peasant volunteers picketed before the office. The local executive officials issued seventeen thousand certificates in all and indiscriminately attached movable properties of the defaulters and put them on auction. The volunteers who organized picketing and resistance were arrested and sentenced to six months' imprisonment under clause 7(2) of the B.C.L. Act. Even in the face of these repressive measures the satyagraha workers continued their agitation till the middle of 1939 when the movement fizzled out for reasons more than one.[90]

VI

Before we conclude we may divide the Damodar Canal Tax Movement into two stages. The first stage started with the introduction of the Bengal Development Act and the imposition of the compulsory canal levy of Rs. 5-8-0 thereunder. The next stage began with the launching of the satyagraha movement by the Krishak Samiti. In so far as the aim of the Raiyats' Association and also of the Congress was to compel the Government to reduce the canal rate to an acceptable minimum, the movement was successful in the first stage. The Government was forced to institute an inquiry, modify the canal rate, withdraw the levy and reintroduce the lease system. But since it was the goal of the Krishak Samiti in the second stage to bring down the canal rate to Rs. 1-8-0 it was, no doubt, a failure. The failure may be partially attributed to the fact that though the Congress urged the people not to sign the lease form for taking canal water at the rate of Rs. 2-9-0 for a few months and condemned the repressive measures of the Government, it did not provide any organizational support to the satyagraha movement. Its lukewarm attitude and half-hearted participation in the later stage damped the spirit of the local people. The left wing, on the other hand, stuck to their decision even when they realized that they had no sufficient mass base to carry on the movement without the Congress support. However, the Burdwan Canal Movement considered as a whole was partially successful.[91] It goes to the credit of the organizers of the satyagraha movement that they set in motion the politically inert peasants and taught them to remain alert, even when engaged in a movement, about the leadership which was often guided by its own class interests. Finally, it must be recorded that the Communists, while committed to an ideology of their own, adopted the non-violent technique of satyagraha, for it proved the most effective weapon in a particular historical context.

References

1. 'The charge of cleaning the tanks and canals, the repairs of their banks, those of rivers and causeways is known under the denomination of *Poolbundy*.' *Fifth Report*, vol. II, p. 98, cited in the Memorandum submitted by Kiron Chandra Dutt p. 5.
2. Sir William Willcocks, *Lectures on the Ancient System of Irrigation in Bengal and its Application to Modern Problem*, pp. 23-4. See also the Memorandum submitted to the Damodar Canal Enquiry Committee by Kiron Chandra Dutt of Burdwan on the 29th January, 1938; the Humble Memorial of the Peoples of the Trans-Damodar Area for Relief Measures.
3. *Report of the Damodar Canal Levy Enquiry Committee*, Burdwan District Congress Committee, 1939, pp. 2-3. Though we have accepted the figures as contained in the said Report, they are not similar to those given by the Government in Townend Report and the Press Notes published in *Amrita Bazar Patrika*, 7.9.37, 14(3) and *Hindusthan Standard*, 12.5.38, 5(6-7).
   Mr H.P.V. Townend was the Rural Development Commissioner, Bengal.
4. Interview with Hemanta Kumar Dutta, 21.11.71.
5. Nripendra Nath Mitra (ed.), *Indian Annual Register*, 1935, I (Jan.—June),176.
6. Statement of Objects and Reasons, *The Calcutta Gazette*, Part IV, 14 February, 1935, p. 49.
7. *Proceedings in Council*, XLV, 7 March, 1935, 79-90, cited in the *Bengal Acts*, pp. 951-6.
8. See note no. 4.

9 Interview with Niharendu Dutta Mazumdar, 27.10.72.
10 Interview with Durgapada Chaudhuri, 22.11.71. See also note no. 4.
11 Interview with Santosh Mandal, 4.11.71. See also *Vardhaman Varta* (a local Bengali weekly), 17.7.39.
12 See note no. 4.
13 Proceedings of different meetings and conferences were made available to us by Mr Kiron Chandra Dutt.
14 *Vardhaman Varta*, 17.7.39. Also interview with Santosh Kumar Mandal.
15 *Vardhaman Varta*, 17.7.39.
16 *Advance*, 12.2.37, 13(4); 14.2.37, 13(4).
17 *Ibid.*, 12.2.37, 13(4); 13.2.37, 7(1).
18 *Ibid.*, 19.2.37, 13(4-5).
19 Resolutions adopted by the peasants' conference. See note no. 13. See also *Advance*, 19.2.37, 13(4-5) and *Congress Socialist*, II(17), 1.5.37, 21(1-2).
20 *Vardhaman Varta*, 17.7.39.
21 *Advance*, 3.3.37, 13(5).
22 *Ibid.*, 4.3.37, 15(1).
23 From the proceedings of the meeting held on 1 March 1937. See note no. 13. See also note no. 22.
24 *Amrita Bazar Patrika*, 10.5.37, 2(7)
25 *Advance*, 29.4.37, 12(2); *Amrita Bazar Patrika*, 27.4.37, 13(4).
26 *Advance*, 15.5.37, 12(1).
27 From the proceedings of the Burdwan District Krishak Conference. See note no. 13. See also *Vardhaman Varta*, 17.7.39.
28 *Congress Socialist*, II(25), 26.6.37, 22(2).
29 N.G. Ranga (ed.), *Kisan Hand Book*, pp. 33-4.
Later also the AIKC in its Tripura meeting held on 7-8 March 1939 'greeted the Kisans of the Damodar Canal area of Burdwan district (Bengal) in their heroic struggle against the excessive canal tax imposed on them in the face of police and military terror, and wished it complete success.'-M.A. Pasul, *A History of the All India Kisan Sabha*, p. 48.
30 *Amrita Bazar Patrika*, 9.4.37, 12(4); *Advance*, 14.4.37, 13(3).
31 The committee consisted of the following members: Jatindranath Bose MLA, Atul Chandra Gupta Advocate, Pramatha Nath Bandyopadhyay Bar-at-law, Dr Prafulla Chandra Ghose, Jadabendranath Panja, President, Burdwan District Congress Committee, Priya Ranjan Sen, Lecturer, Calcutta University and Mr Hemanta Kumar Dutta Pleader, Burdwan. See *Advance*, 11.6.37, 6(4); 13.6.37, 10(5) and *Report of the Demodar Canal Levy Enquiry Committee*, 2.
32 *Amrita Bazar Patrika*, 15.6.37, 7(1).
33 A decision was arrived at in a meeting held in the village of Sodya to form a Canal Kar Pratikar Samiti with all sorts of people and groups affected by the imposition of the canal rate. However, a dispute cropped up as to the nature and composition of the organization. The Communists and the Krishak Samiti workers who represented the leftward tendency within the Congress held that the doors of the organization should be thrown open to all who were agreed to fight for the cause of the affected peasantry irrespective of their political conviction and party affiliation. The District Congress leadership, on the other hand, insisted on its control over the organization and demanded that the Samiti should owe allegiance to the Congress and be affiliated to it. A convention to chalk out the programme of the Canal Kar Pratikar samiti of the Congress was called at the Bangshagopal Town Hall Maidan. The Communists and the Krishak Samiti

workers had to agree to the Congress proposals and enrolled themselves in large numbers as members of the Congress-sponsored Kanal Kar Pratikar Samiti. As many as fifteen committees were formed under the leadership of the District Krishak Samiti and Communist workers. Three other committees owing allegiance to the official Congress leadership were also formed.—Interview with Syed Sahedullah, 16.2.72.

34 *Advance*, 13.6.37, 10(5).
35 *Amrita Bazar Patrika*, 10.8.37, 10(5-6).
36 *Ibid.*, 24.8.37, 8(7); *Advance*, 19.8.37, 11(2-3).
37 The Government of India Act, 1935 provided for a scheme of federal finance. Certain heads of revenue were made entirely federal. Certain others were made entirely provincial and a few other heads of revenue were made partly federal and partly provincial. A fourth category of taxes was to be administered by the Federal Government, but the proceeds were to be transferred to the provinces, subject to surcharges for federal purposes in cases of emergency.
Sir Otto Niemeyer was appointed by the Secretary of State to recommend the proper distribution of the proceeds of a share of the income-tax and of the export duty on jute to the provinces, as also the subventions to be paid to the different provinces. His recommendations were adopted by an Order-in-Council. In accordance with the recommendation of Sir Otto Niemeyer, the debts due from the provinces to the centre were consolidated or cancelled, either wholly or in part, and the balances held by the Central Government were decentralized. See Pramatha Nath Banerjee, *A Study of Indian Economics* pp. 262-3.
This Pramatha Nath Banerjee was the Minto Professor of Economics of Calcutta University and was not the same person as Pramatha Nath Bandyopadhyay referred to in the text.
38 *Extracts from Bengal Legislative Assembly Proceedings*, Second Session LI, 3-4, 20.8.37—30.9.37, 721-37. See also *Advance*, 29.8.37, 9(1-2).
39 *Advance*, 2.9.37, 5(5).
40 *Amrita Bazar Patrika*, 7.9.37, 14(3); 9.9.37, 6(4); *Advance*, 10.9.37, 12(2).
41 *Hindusthan Stadard*, 12.11.37, 5(3); *Advance*, 18.11.37, 12(4). For the reaction of the District Congress Committee, see *Advance*, 26.11.37, 12(2).
42 *Amrita Bazar Patrika*, 27.11.37, 10(6).
43 *Advance*, 8.12.37, 11(3).
44 *Ibid.*, 9.12.37, 8(5); *Hindusthan Standard*, 9.12.37, 13(2).
45 The committee consisted of the following members: the Hon'ble Abdul Kasem Fazl-ul-Haq, Premier, the Hon'ble Nalini Ranjan Sarkar, Minister of Finance, the Hon'ble B.P. Sinha Roy, Minister of Revenue, the Hon'ble Maharaja Srish Chandra Nandy, Minister of Communications and Works, the Collector of Burdwan, Nizamuddin Ahmed MLA, Jatindra Nath Basu MLA, Maharaj Kumar Uday Chand Mahatab MLA, P.N. Banerjee MLA, Adwaita Kumar Majhi MLA, Banku Behari Mandal MLA, Maulavi Abdul Hashem MLA, Maulavi Md. Abdul Rashid MLA, Maulavi Abdul Quasem MLA, Khan Behadur Alfazuddin Ahmed MLA, Khan Sahib Maulavi S. Abdur Rauf MLA, Maulavi Abdul Wahab Khan MLA, Mr David Hendry MLA, See *Amrita Bazar Patrika*, 16.12.37, 2(7). The report of this committee was not published.
46 *Hindusthan Standard*, 17.12.37, 5(7).
47 *Advance*, 20.12.37, 12(5).
48 *Hindusthan Standard*, 24.12.37, 5(7).
49 *Ibid.*, 31.12.37, 13(4); 6.1.38, 13(3); *Amrita Bazar Patrika*, 31.12.37, 10(3); *Advance* 2.1.38, 2(5), 7.1.38, 6(5) and *Ananda Bazar Patrika*, 6.1.38, 11(7).

50 *Advance*, 5.1.38, 8(3)
51 *Hindusthan Standard*, 1.2.38, 13(6-7); *Ananda Bazar Patrika*, 31.1.38, 5(6-7) and *Advance*, 1.2.38, 9(4).
52 Memorandum submitted by Kiron Chandra Dutt of Burdwan on the 29th January, 1938, 1.
53 *Hindusthan Standard*, 8.2.38, 13(5).
54 *Hindusthan Standard*, 10.2.38, 13(3); 13.2.38, 15(2).
55 *Ibid.*, 16.2.38, 13(4).
56 *Report of the Damodar Canal Levy Enquiry Committee*, 8-10. See also *Hindusthan Standard*, 4.3.38, 4(6); 11.3.38, 6(2-3); 12.3.38, 6(2-3); *Advance*, 5.3.38, 6(4) and *Amrita Bazar Patrika*, 4.3.38, 10(2).
57 *Hindusthan Standard*, 12.5.38, 5(6-7); *Vardhaman Varta*, 9.5.38, 1 & 3.
58 *Advance*, 28.4.38, 6(7); *Hindusthan Standard*, 28.4.38, 4(4).
59 *Vardhaman Varta*, 2.5.38, 1 & 2; *Hindusthan Standard*, 14.5.38, 3(7) and *Advance*, 15.5.38, 8(5).
60 *Vardhaman Varta*, 23.5.38; 6.6.38, 4; 20.6.38, 3; 4.7.38, 1 & 2; 11.7.38, 2.
61 *Ibid.*, 24.10.38, 4.
62 *Ibid.*, 13.2.39, 4.
63 *Jugantar*, 14.2.39, 4(1).
64 *Ibid.*, 15.2.39, 7(6-7).
65 *Ibid.*, 16.2.39, 4(5).
66 *Extracts from Bengal Legislative Assembly Proceedings*, LIV(1-2), Sixth Session, 15.2.39—7.3.39, 99-103.
67 *Vardhaman Varta*, 27.2.39, 3.
68 *Ibid.*, 27.2.39, 2.
69 *Ibid.*, 6.3.39, 4-5; 27.3.39; 3.4.39; 10.4.39.
70 *Ibid.*, 4.12.39.
71 Interview with Santosh Mandal; Helaram Chattopadhyay and Sivaprasad Dutta (3.11.71).
72 Interview with Durga Pada Choudhuri.
73 See note no. 4.
74 Interviews with Santosh Kumar Mandal; Syed Shahedullah.
75 *Report of the Damodar Canal levy Enquiry Committee*, 10.
76 *Indian Annual Register*, 1937, II, 326.
77 *Ananda Bazar Patrika*, 28.1.38, 13(4).
78 *Vardhaman Varta*, 6.6.38, 1 & 3.
79 *Advance*, 8.6.38, 8(4); *Vardhaman Varta*, 4.7.38, 2.
80 The Burdwan District Krishak Samiti was formed in a meeting held in May 1933 at Hatgobindapur under the presidentship of Dr Bhupendra Nath Dutta. Helaram Chattopadhyay was the Secretary of the Samiti. See M.A. Rasul, *Krishak Sabhar Itihas*, 79-80.
81 Interviews with Helaram Chattopadhyay and Sivaprasad Dutt; Syed Shahedullah.
82 See note no. 75.
83 Interview with Syed Sahedullah.
    For an analysis of the CPI's policy of United Front with the Congress, see Gene D. Overstreet and Marshal Windmiller, *Communism in India*, pp. 166-70; L.P. Sinha, *The Left Wing in India*, pp. 418-26 and M.R. Masani, *The Communist Party of India*, pp. 59-66.
84 See note no. 9.
85 *Vardhaman Varta*, 17.7.39.
86 Interview with Syed Shahedullah.

87 Interview with Helaram Chattopadhyay and Sivaprasad Dutt.
88 Cp. "The Congress leaders who had been carrying on the agitation felt that, *with their present strength of organization*, it would be wise to strike the bargain at that point. The pressure of the Government for the realization of water-rates was great, and there were also signs of wavering and indecision among the peasants, for the latter did not belong to one class, but ranged from a fairly prosperous section to those who possessed no land. If a settlement could be arrived at this point, it would at least lead to *a sense of success* among those who had tried to resist. A consultation was held in the Congress office, when the senior members pleaded for acceptance of the Government offer. The younger Leftists were however determined to stick to the lowest demand. Eventually the negotiations failed." (italics in original). See Nirmal Kumar Bose *Lectures on Gandhism*, p. 27.
89 Interviews with Santosh Mandal; Helaram Chattopadhyay and Sivaprasad Dutt; Niharendu Dutta Mazumdar; and Syed Shahedullah.
90 Interviews with Helaram Chattopadhyay and Sivaprasad Dutt; and Santosh Mandal. See also Md. Abdullah Rasul, *Rasul, Krishak Sabhar Itihas*, pp. 79-80.
91 Dr Binay Bhushan Chaudhuri, however, holds a different view: 'The peasants won a *complete* victory in the Damodar Canal area.' (emphasis added). See his 'Agrarian Movements in Bengal and Bihar, 1919-1939,' in B.R. Nanda (ed.), *Socialism in India*. p. 217.

PART V
Agrarian Struggles on the Eve of British Withdrawal

Introduction

(1)

THE SELECTIONS reproduced in this part are extremely important for a number of reasons. They deal with peasant and tribal struggles during the World War and the post-war periods which have not yet been adequately examined by Indian scholarship.

A section of 'established' scholarship attempts to glorify the strategy adopted by the leadership of the Congress viz. Gandhi, Jawaharlal Nehru, Sardar Patel and others in working out the transfer of power. They highlight their skill in preventing the emergence of a gigantic civil war, and in adroitly managing to withdraw the mass movement launched by the people under the slogan 'Quit India'. These articles point out how the leadership of the Indian National Congress accepted the caretaker Interim Ministry after conducting post-war elections on the basis of limited franchise given under 1935 Act, and describe the skill used in drafting the Constitution of India, through a Constituent Assembly, worked out an ad hoc basis. They also point out the skills used in pressurising the British and the legal talent displayed by the leaders of the Indian National Congress in preventing the British diplomats from using Native States as a force to balkanize the Indian sub-continent, and the skills used to persuade, coerce or outwit some of the Princes of the feudal states from making further 'mischief, and finally to work out their merger with the Indian Union.

Received scholarship, however, never explains why the Congress Party accepted an unprincipled partition of India on communal lines. It never explains why the creative, mass upsurge, which took place in India during the war and immediate post-war periods was not systematically organized to evolve a strategy of counteracting the machination of the British or the communal diplomacy of the Muslim League. It never highlights how during the 'Quit India' upheaval and after, workers, peasants, middle classes and the people living in the feudal states showed unparalleled heroism and readiness to launch struggles, partly organized but mainly spontaneous to paralyze the administration in many areas of the country. They also do not provide an adequate account of the mighty upheavals which shook the police, army, navy, airforce, and which if properly guided in the context of mass discontent and upheaval, would have led to a new stage of anti-imperialist struggle.

The Congress could have avoided the partition of India, prevented the spread of communal frenzy in the country, halted one of the most hideous crimes of the uprooting of millions of people from their homelands, and ushered in a totally different phase of the freedom movement. It never explains why the Congress created the climate for Quit India Movement, but never actively prepared itself and the masses to organize that struggle in a proper form and why they at the time of carrying on negotiations with the British, disowned the responsibility of the movement by declaring it a spontaneous mass reaction to the 'Leonine Violence' of the British. It also does not explain why the leadership of the Congress which did not mind participating in the violent, brutal, cruel war in the name of 'Defence of Democracy' was so delicately and fearfully afraid of the revolutionary force used by the masses to overthrow British rule, and the supporters of the British rule in the country.

The overwhelming majority of the scholarly fraternity broadly supporting the actions of National Congress have been reluctant to present an objective account of the war period and immediate post-war strategies and tactics of the party which came to power. They do not explain why the Congress government after coming to power as a care-taker Ministry at the centre and also after the transfer of power in the Indian Union, became so furious and ruthless in suppressing all struggles launched by the exploited strata.

A systematic record of the various types of upheavals, and struggles which took place in rural and urban India, including feudal states, resulting in some areas and districts of various states in a paralysis of the administration, and even in the formation for sometime of alternate popular administrations, described variously in different parts such as *Patri Sarkar* (in Maharashtra), has become necessary to properly account for the role of the masses and the mass struggles in weakening British rule. It has become necessary also to analyze the class character of the national leadership which utilized, circumvented and prevented these movements from taking to revolutionary, democratic and militant anti-imperialist struggles.

It is no accident that even during the twenty five years of Independence a full length account of workers, peasants, tribal and states people's struggles faithfully recording even their occurrences in a proper chronological and issue-wise basis has not been worked out by historians and social scientists. Even an exhaustive descriptive picture of the history of these movements during the British period or even the war and post-war periods prior to British withdrawal has still to be written. Marxist scholarship too has failed to provide a dialectical, all sided picture of the developments during the war and immediate post-war periods in India. It provides better information about the peasants' and workers' movement in the country as compared to the dominant anti-Marxist, pro-Congress scholarship, but their treatment of these struggles exhibits a certain one sidedness, which suits their changing party positions.

They have given us some interesting accounts of the peasant struggles which were spontaneous, and militant, and which provided violent resistance to British repression, or zamindari or shahukari oppression backed by the British sword. They also provide a selective but useful account of some struggles launched by the tribals, share-croppers, and others in zamindari areas between the World Wars. However, they consciously or unconsciously avoid providing information about the struggles launched by the Indian National Congress, or pettie bourgeois militants inside and outside the Indian National Congress, who helped to develop and at times themselves adopted militant mass and even class struggles. They also ignore the movements launched by the social democratic Congress Socialist and other parties and groups, as well as by those Marxist groups and parties who emerged independently or broke away from the CPI. They do not examine these movements which they opposed due to sudden shifts in their lines dictated by changes in the policies adopted by the Communist Party of the Soviet Union under Stalin. This scholarship is silent over the mighty peasant movements unleashed during the Non-Cooperation Movement of 1919-21, or peasant movements which were taking place from 1929-33 (the period of the Civil Disobedience Movement), and also between 1941-5 under the impulse of the 'Quit-India' slogan. Further they do not explain how the CPI instead of participating and deepening the movements launched by the nationalists in the thirties and during the war period after

1941, opposed them and thereby harmed the cause of the movements, on the one hand by preventing them from developing into more militant, anti-imperialist class struggles and on the other hand by making Marxism appear as basically anti-national and an alien instrument of the Communist Party of the Soviet Union. They do not point out how they in the name of supporting the anti-fascist war of the allies, isolated themselves from the sweep of peasants, workers, state's peoples and the tribal people of the country, even actively opposed them, and reduced their activities to some agitation for economic concessions or anti-feudal agitation which would not obstruct the war efforts. They also do not clearly describe the mighty sweep of peasant uprisings which unnerved the Congress leadership and which if lead by a party of the proletariat, would have helped to evolve a powerful political leadership, an alternative possible to the Indian National Congress, and would have resisted and probably prevented the Indian National Congress from back-door unprincipled horse trading with the British and the Muslim League, culminating in the partition of India.

(2)

Section I in this part contains two selections providing a very rich and vivid account of a mighty peasant struggle known as the Tebhaga Movement in Bengal.

The reproduction from Sunil Sen's writings (one of the architects of Tebhaga Movement) is a narrative written in a lively dramatic style giving an intimate picture of the background, the objective matrix, and the unfolding of the Tebhaga Movement in its two phases. It provides a useful though brief account of the growth of the Kisan Sabha, the changing attitude of the Commintern which shaped the strategy of the Communists in India with regard to linking the peasant struggles with larger national struggles. It gives us a valuable insight into the spread of the Kisan Sabha in Bengal. It further provides a backdrop to the situation which led to the agitation of 'Tebhaga Chai' pointing out how the agitation involved lower stratum of tenants, such as bargadars, adhiars and others and was a struggle not merely against zamindars, but also against a section of rich peasants, (both new owners and permanent rich tenants) who benefited from legislation following the Pabna revolt and described as jotedars to distinguish them from old zamindars.)

In Bengal, agricultural labourers, share croppers, poor peasants in the form of tenants of various categories, now become the driving force against jotedars, zamindars, moneylenders, traders, and the British bureaucracy. This section of landlords, jotedars, traders and moneylenders provided opposition to British rule and high landlordism and stood for the elimination of the zamindari system. This struggle had the support of either the Congress or the Muslim League who favoured the principle of compensation, and pressed for a reformist opposition to the British rule. However, these classes were deeply hostile to the agricultural labourers, share croppers known as bargadars, adhiars and poorer peasants existing either as independent farmers or as tenants. The Tebhaga struggle represents a movement demanding a right to two thirds of the share of produce and putting the crops after harvest in the enclosures of the tenants rather than in the enclosures of the jotedars or landlords. This movement was essentially an economic struggle, but took a political form when it had to confront and battle the jotedars and the political apparatus of the state.

Sunil Sen points out how Shurawardy introduced the Bargardar's Bill to take legal note of this confrontation and to show a consideration for these rent-paying tenants.

Sen portrays the heroic struggle against police-jotedar repression in fascinating detail highlighting various forms of struggles in depth.

The second article in the section by Krishnakant Sarkar deals with an area called Kakdwip in Bengal. Sarkar has specially prepared the article for this volume. It deals with the rise, growth and conclusion of the Tebhaga Movement as it developed in an area not covered by Sunil Sen. The peasant struggles that took place in this area are not commonly known. Krishnakant Sarkar gives a very vivid account of the history of the area, the land tenure systems operating there, the class stratification which emerged there during the British period, the nature of the exploitation and oppression which was carried on in this area, and the conditions of sharecroppers in the context of larger socio-economic problems confronting this relatively unknown area in the Sunderbans of Bengal. The value of Sarkar's article lies in the fact that it concretely indicates the gains of Kakdwip Tebhaga movement in a number of significant ways. It also points out how such struggles, while not being permitted to go beyond particular limits, were also taken note of by the Indian bourgeois state, particularly the regional state, to curb and soften feudal and semifeudal conditions and pave the way for creating conditions favourable for rich farmers, jotedars and others, by curbing and restricting the feudal forms of exploitation. It also points out how these struggles launched by the Communist Party and the Kisan Sabha led by the Communist Party were essentially fought on economic demands, and had no plan for linking them to the larger political processes taking place in the country.

(3)

The three selections in Section 2 of this part deal with a peasant-tribal movement, which in its extensiveness, duration, intensity and conscious direction was one of the most significant struggles launched by the peasantry in India during the last phase of British rule in India.

The Telangana peasant struggle beginning with 1946 and lasting upto 1951 is in one sense a unique struggle fought by the peasantry in India.

1 It was launched in the territory of Nizam State, one of the biggest feudal states in India, with peasantry and population overwhelmingly Hindus and tribals, and an aristocracy, administrative bureaucracy and the feudal chieftains springing from the Muslim upper strata. The Nizam's state spread across territories of many linguistic groups, more particularly Andhras, Karnataks, Maharashtrians and others. It had Urdu as its administrative language. The Nizam, himself was the largest landowner in the state. The Nizam, the landowing classes and the bureaucracy had imposed many and varied types of taxes, legal and customary, feudal, semi-feudal exactions, and levies on various sections of the population. The Nizam, utilized the British strategy of giving the feudal states an option of either a merger or as independent sovereign states, without merging with the new Indian Union or State of Pakistan.

The strategy and tactic adopted with regard to the problems posed by the Nizam state, showed the strength and weaknesses of various political parties which were trying to shape the future of post-British India. In fact the struggle in Nizam State, culminating with its merger into the Indian Union and dividing its territories into future linguistic states of India, especially Andhra State and the state of Maharashtra, the intense movements to bifurcate Andhra State into two—Andhra and Telangana States deserves a more careful study.

2 The Telangana struggle in the Nizam State, developed under unique objective and subjective—local and international—contexts. The rapid rise of the Communist leadership in the struggle, its link with the states people movement launched under the leadership of the Praja Mandal headed by the Congress, Arya Samaj, and other political currents, its links with Vishal Andhra Movement, linking the movement with other belts of Andhra Pradesh, the intense exploitation and oppression of landlords, moneylenders, traders and Nizam officials, the deliberate launching of an armed organization on communal lines in the form of Razakars by the Nizam to terrorize the Hindu population—including traders, merchants, farmers, poorer peasants and tenants, deserves a study in depth.

The Indian National Congress, heading the caretaker interim government at the centre, and working out the plans for a divided India, evolved its pattern of cajoling or coercing the rulers of states to merge with India. It adopted a special stance with the Nizam, initially showing even readiness to keep the state intact if the Nizam agreed to shed certain powers and vested them with the Indian Union.

The interpretation and relevance of the Telangana struggle, the role of various parties, the relation of the phase of that struggle to national development, the impact of the changing policies of the Soviet Communist Party, the zigzags of the Communist line in India and in Telangana, the switch over of the Communist Party in 1951 by winding up the Telangana struggle and taking to parliamentary electoral politics, and contesting the first General Elections—all these have become topics of acrimonious debates and discussions, even among the different Communist parties which have emerged after the great split in the united Communist Party.

The three articles selected here provide a kaleidoscopic picture of this significant movement launched by the Communist Party of India.

Dhanagare's article is reproduced here because it is one of the few compact, comprehensive analysis and evaluations of the social origins of peasant insurrection in Telangana (1946-51). It not only provides a matrix within which the Telangana struggle started, developed and was wound up, but also examines some of the important issues raised by various thinkers with regard to the role of various classes, and particularly the role of rich farmers, and middle peasantry as the crucial axis of peasant struggles.

The second selection on Telangana by C.Rajeshwar Rao, is extremely useful for a number of reasons: (a) It provides a vivid account of post-war situation as it affected the Nizam State. It tells us how the CPI unit in Telangana along with the Party unit in Marathawada was organizing various sections of the population, viz. workers, students, women peasants and others and thus was becoming a significant political force in Hyderabad. (b) It shows how after the end of the War basic changes were taking place in the international scene. (c) It refers to anti-imperialist national liberation movements and national liberation wars which began raging in the colonized countries of Asia, Africa and Latin America, but does not refer to the role Communist's played in opposing such struggles in a number of countries, because of their policy of supporting the War. (d) It does not explain how the Communist Party of India, during the entire period of 1941 to 1945 had opposed the Quit India Movement, lost the opportunity of taking leadership not merely in few pockets of the country but to the anti-imperialist wave which enveloped the whole country. (e) He refers to the transfer of power as a mere neo-colonialist move, which according to him did not succeed, without explaining why he makes both the statements in such a summary fashion. He does not want to refer to the Quit India Movement, the heroic battles of States' People Movements, the strikes of workers, and resistance movements by urban and rural people during war period. (f) He also does not want to refer to the parliamentary politics adopted by CPI just after the Second World War when interim elections were organized on old limited electoral basis to form state legislatures and an interim caretaker government at the Centre, and the change in line as a consequence of a shift in Soviet policy, described as the

'Zednoff Line', and subsequently criticized as left adventurism by the CPI itself.

Rajeshwar Rao then provides an interesting, clear but controversial summing up of the lessons of Telangana for post-Independence India. His conclusions very explicitly admit that the aim of the CPI was only to realize anti-feudal, bourgeois political-economic aspirations and the Telangana movement was essentially a movement with limited objectives. Rajeshwar Rao does not discuss the movement in the context of the larger matrix wherein a gigantic game of transfer of power was being played in India.

The next selection by P.Sundaraiya is from the book *Telangana Peoples Struggle and its Lessons*.

The purpose of publishing this work twenty years after the withdrawal of the Telangana Struggle on October 21 1951, is to provide an authentic narration of the origin, development and withdrawal of the struggle, as no such narration even in outline is available. It was also written to counteract tons of literature produced by avowed enemies and detractors of this great movement denouncing the struggle as Communist 'violence, banditry and anarchy'. It sums up the impressive record of achievements and gains to the credit of the peasant uprising. It also highlights Sundaraiya's version of other gains, viz. 'pushing the question of agrarian revolution to the forefront', compelling the unwilling hands of the Congress to embark upon various agrarian reforms, and Vinobha Bhave to launch the Bhoodan Movement.

According to Sundaraiya, the Telangana struggle indirectly forced the pace of states' reorganization on linguistic basis, thereby helping the democratic demand of linguistic nationalists for separate statehood. The author emphasizes the contribution this struggle made to national, democratic and agrarian problems confronting India after the withdrawal of British rule. He further proudly proclaims how the Communist Party, which led Telangana struggle, along with numerous other struggles in Kerala, Bengal and other places between 1946 and 1948, emerged as the single biggest opposition group in the first parliament following the 1952 general elections.

However, according to Sundaraiya, the single biggest contribution made by the Telangana peasant revolt to the Communist movement in India was in bringing to the forefront 'almost all the basic theoretical and ideological questions concerning the strategy and tactics of the Indian People's Democratic Revolution for correct and scientific answers and realistic and practical solutions'. He also asserts that the Communist Party of India (Marxist) after prolonged inner-party struggle 'arrived at a fairly correct political line with satisfactory answers to most of the problems posed'.

The author also feels that the germ of the future split in Communist Party of India were laid during the Telangana struggle, particularly during the Second phase of the Telangana struggle.

Section two of the essay provides a very detailed picture of the socio-political background of Hyderabad State which enables the readers to properly comprehend the matrix within which the Telangana struggle emerged and grew. In this section, Sundaraiya also analyses the larger political stances of various political parties, with regard to World War II particularly during its first phase when Soviet Union was not attacked, as a result of the Hitler-Stalin pact and the Second phase when Hitler launched an offensive against the Soviet Union. Sundaraiya confidently asserts that the changes in the line adopted by CPI with regard to their attitude towards the war effort—from opposition to support of British rule—was justified.

In section three of the essay the author gives one of the most detailed and lively accounts of the Communist movement in Andhra, and Telangana. This part of the selection is valuable as it gives a rare and brilliant portrayal of the actual struggles of the peasantry under the leadership of the Communist Party. This section has to be carefully studied as it is one of the few elaborate descriptions of the peasantry in action, as well as glimpses of how the Communist Party spread its influence and exhibited a heroic stance which endeared it to the lower strata of the population.

Section four explains under what conditions the Communist Party was forced to give a call for the withdrawal of the struggle.

(4)

The last selection in Part V reproduced from *Revolt of the Varlis* by S.V. Parulekar, describes the struggles which were launched in Dahanu and Umbergaon Talukas of Thana District by a tribal population in Western India, just a few miles away from Bombay. This booklet is a rare account of the awakening of Varlis against their intense exploitation and oppression by forest contractors, moneylenders, rich farmers and landlords with the backing and support of the British bureaucracy. The selection portrays in detail how the liberation movement of Varlis started in May 1945, when they raised their red banner under the leadership of the Kisan Sabha against their serf-like exploitation.

Parulekar discusses the struggle of the Varlis, after providing the socio-economic matrix under which the Varlis were exploited and oppressed. Though Parulekar himself participated in these struggles, he describes these struggles as an observer, and not as a propagandist of the Communist Party.

The selection describes how Varlis were brought close to the Kisan Sabha, how they were convinced about the cause the Kisan Sabha held, how the Kisan Sabha adopted various approaches to reach out to Varlis, educate them, awaken them and prepare them for struggles. The selection also highlights the heroism, determination and astute understanding exhibited by Varlis while carrying on their struggles against local exploiters and the British repressive apparatus. By giving a pen-picture of a conference at Mahalaxmi, Parulekar provides an understanding of the molecular processes that builds up a movement.

The description of a strike of Varlis regarding the rate of cutting grass which also lead to the strikes and struggles on other issues against timber merchants in the forest also throws light on different types of issues on which struggles developed in the tribal belts.

The relevance of this selection lies in the fact that this struggle inaugurated a set of social currents in this area and also became the focal point to try out various types of experiments in areas of social and economic welfare, carried out by the post-independence government as well as the reformist social service wings of the Congress and other bourgeois and petti-bourgeois parties. It also became a laboratory to test the veracity of different conceptions of revolutions such as National and Peoples' Democratic Revolutions, and the two-stage theory of revolution as formulated by various Communist Parties.

(5)

The six selections reproduced in this part are extremely significant for a proper understanding of the role of the peasantry and its various classes in shaping Indian history.

1 They point out that the peasantry by itself cannot project an

independent political national party. They have the support of the parties of the bourgeois, petti-bourgeois or the proletariat and have been politicized by these parties.

2 While exhibiting great ability to carry on mighty battles if properly lead, they also point out how their energies could be misdirected if wrong leadership is provided.

3 They reveal how the Indian National Congress and the Muslim League were consciously pursuing a strategy of pressure and bargain to inherit the British State apparatus and were not interested in evolving a genuinely new alternative State apparatus. They were aware from the beginning that any revolutionary path of overthrowing British Imperialism, by involving exploited classes would result in the exploited masses breaking the dams of bourgeois-feudal framework and effect a socialist overthrow of the proprietory classes in India.

4 The six selections also reveal how the Communist Party during war and post-war period had no clear policy of an alternate strategy for securing Independence. In fact during the entire war period, when the Indian National Congress was elaborating a strategy of securing Independence, on the basis of pressure cum negotiation, and also based on occupying key positions after World War II, the Communist Party had hardly any programme to prepare an alternative.

5 The Communist Party during the war period strictly adhered to opposing any movement to overthrow British Rule, and even endeavoured to see that the wheels of Government were not disturbed by opposition forces. Even during the post-war crucial initial years, when the Communist Party's line was to sharpen some of the struggles of workers, peasants', tribals, and middle classes, it was essentially on immediate economic or short term anti-feudal political demands as could be seen in the issues involved in Tebhaga, Telangana and Varli revolts. In fact, it appears that conceptions, subsequently projected like the two stage theory of revolution either via National Democratic, or People's Democratic to Socialist Revolutions, were absent during the entire war and immediate post-war period. Projecting these notions in the Telangana struggle, as formulated by CPI, CPI(M), and even CPI(ML) and their various factions, is an afterthought to justify the subsequent policies.

6 The struggles launched by the Communist Party of India, in Tebhaga, Telangana, and among the Varlis, reveals the readiness of the masses to develop and deepen the struggles, to participate in battles against both native and foreign exploiters, to evolve great ingenuity in working out tactics for conducting a variety of strategies during battles and even to establish local Soviet-council type alternate administrative mechanisms to conduct their local rule. These struggles also indicate the changing role of the various classes in rural areas during their different phases and finally the role of agrarian proletarian, share-croppers, or very poor peasants, who constituted the bulk of rural population as the stable lasting and crucial category to carry the agrarian revolution to its conclusion only if it was led by the proletariat and the revolutionary party of the proletariat. These struggles also reveal clearly that the Communist Party of India, did not provide that leadership, nor was the Communist Party theoretically prepared for it. It had no conception of an alternate strategy for the seizure of power.

20 The Kisan Sabha

Sunil Sen

ALTHOUGH JACQUERIE FLARED UP in parts of Bengal in the nineteenth century these hardly made much impact on the national movement. The early Congress took no notice of the kisan. In the tumultuous days of the swadeshi there was hardly any attempt to build up peasant unions. In Russia the Narodniks, clad in peasants' clothes, went to the village to live among peasants and hoped to bring about a revolution with their help. The revolutionaries in India relied on middle-class youth and foreign arms to liberate the country. It was in the Gandhi era that the peasants were drawn into the political movement, notably in Bihar and modern Uttar Pradesh; peasants learnt the strength of collective action at Champaran and Gujarat, Tamluk and Contai. By 1935 peasant unions had been formed in Bihar, Uttar Pradesh, Andhra, Malabar, Gujarat, Punjab and Bengal. Yet there was no central organisation or any organised peasant movement in India.

We will briefly review the early history of the Kisan Sabha. It seems that the Congress Socialist Party and some nonparty individuals took a leading part in the formation of the Kisan Sabha. Professor Ranga writes that the South Indian Federation of Peasants and Workers convened an All-India Peasants' and Workers' Conference in October 1935. The Bihar kisan leaders, however, issued a statement opposing the formation of an all-India organisation; they had a feeling that the conference was being organised by moderate elements who would impose a liberal programme on the kisans. Professor Ranga and Kamala Devi Chattopadhyaya went ahead with the preparations of the conference which was in fact held in Madras and appointed an organising committee, with Professor Ranga as secretary, to get in touch with provincial organisations. On behalf of Bihar kisan leaders Jayaprakash Narayan, leader of the newly-formed Congress socialist Party, had a meeting with the Madras leaders and it was agreed

Reproduced from *Agrarian Struggle in Bengal, 1946-47*, by Sunil Sen, People's Publishing House, New Delhi, Chapter 2, pp. 16-32.

that a more representative conference would be convened in Meerut in January, 1936. The Meerut conference decided to hold an All-India Kisan Congress at Lucknow in April, 1936 at the time of the annual session of the National Congress.[1]

Although the Communist Party was formally banned in 1934 it took a leading part in the formation of the Kisan Sabha. At this stage it would be worth while to briefly review the programme of the Communist Party which was to establish its leadership in Kisan Sabha in the years to come. At the seventh congress of the Communist International (1935) 'left sectarianism' of Indian communists came in for severe criticism. In the words of Wang Ming: 'Our comrades in India have suffered for a long time from left sectarian errors; they did not participate in all the mass demonstrations organised by the National Congress or organisations affiliated to it. At the same time, Indian communists did not possess sufficient forces independently to organise a powerful and mass anti-imperialist movement'.[2] The seventh congress gave the call of united front and participation of Indian communists in the anti-imperialist movement headed by 'national reformists'. In March, 1936, R.P. Dutt and Ben Bradley, leaders of the British Communist Party, published a thesis in Labour Monthly. In this thesis entitled. 'The Anti-imperialist People's Front in India' Dutt and Bradley sought to work out the policy implications of the Comintern resolution. The salient points of the thesis may be summed up. In the first place, the Congress had achieved 'a gigantic task' in uniting the diverse elements seeking national liberation; it could play 'a great part and a foremost part in the work of creating the anti-imperialist people's front'. Secondly, the leadership of the Congress was described as bourgeois leadership 'whose interests often conflict with the interests of the masses and with the interests of the national struggle'. Thirdly, the mass organisations of workers and peasants that were outside the Congress must be drawn in it either by collective affiliation or united front agreement; the working class could play increasingly the role of vanguard within such a broad anti-imperialist people's front. Fourthly, the demand for a constituent assembly would be the central rallying slogan which could be a mass mobilising force in the present stage of the national struggle. Fifthly, the establishment of unity with all leftwing elements within the Congress on the basis of a common minimum programme was to be the immediate task which would be a prelude to the united front of all anti-imperialist forces.[3] It may be noted that Dutt developed the main formulations in this thesis with a mass of facts and statistical material in India Today which remains his major work.

As decided at Meerut the All-India Kisan Congress (which later changed its name to All-India Kisan Sabha) met at Lucknow on 11 April, 1936. Swami Sahajananda Saraswati, the Bihar kisan leader, was the president of the session. The congress elected an All-India Kisan Committee in which socialists, communists and congressmen were represented. The manifesto adopted at the congress declared that 'the object of the kisan movement is to secure complete freedom from economic exploitation and the achievement of full economic and political power to the peasants and workers and other exploited classes'; peasants to fight for their immediate political and economic demands in order to prepare them for their emancipation from every form of political exploitation'. The fundamental demands centred on abolition of zamindari and vesting of land in the tillers; the minimum demands included moratoriam on debts, abolition of land revenue and rent from uneconomic holdings, reduction of revenue and rent, licensing of moneylenders, minimum wages for agricultural workers, fair price for sugarcane and commercial crops, irrigation facilities, gradual income-tax, death duty and inheritance tax on landlords and merchants.[4]

Evidently the Kisan Sabha sought to reconcile the interests of all categories of peasants—from the rich peasant to landless labour—and unite them on a common platform; the preservation of peasant unity seemed to be the overriding consideration. The emphasis was on immediate demands which could be realised, so that it could appeal to the broad masses of peasants. First September was to be observed as Kisan Day to popularise peasants' demands. It was also decided to publish a weekly journal called 'Kisan Bulletin' with Indulal Yajnik, the Gujarat kisan leader, as the editor. The Kisan Bulletin, which was regularly published, helped to give a direction to the kisan movement in the formative phase.

The formation of the All-India Kisan Sabha opened a new period of peasant movement. It branched out in the provinces.

In Bengal the communists took the lead in organising the Provincial Kisan Sabha which held the first session at Bankura in March 1937; it had then only 11,080 members. Within a year Kisan Sabha branches were formed in most districts. The Bengal Provincial Kisan Sabha held annual conferences with elected delegates from primary or village level kisan sabhas, and it became a regular practice to end the conference with a mass rally which was considered to be as important as the delegates' session. The list of members of the Provincial Kisan Committee showed that they came mostly from urban middle class; some intellectuals joined the Kisan Sabha, notably Dr Bhupendranath Datta, brother of Swami Vivekananda, Satyendranath Majumdar, eminent journalist, and Gopal Haldar, novelist and journalist; there was not a single peasant in the committee.[5]

It will be necessary to tell the story of the district level committees which maintained direct contact with the broad masses of peasants. How did Kisan Sabha workers go to the grassroots and bring peasants within the organisation? What was the form of kisan movement? How did Kisan Sabha workers train peasant cadres? To what extent were they successful in uniting peasants who remained divided by religion and caste? We will take up the example of Dinajpur district, a strong base of the Kisan Sabha, to seek an answer to these questions. With the material available we can deal with these complex matters only particularly; but even an examination of the bare outlines may be helpful.

Dinajpur, a North Bengal district, figures prominently in official records mainly because it was one of the big zamindaris of Bengal since the days of Murshid Quli. Buchanan-Hamilton has told us that in the first decade of the present century adhi system developed in the district; the adhiars were settled mainly in unreclaimed lands in border areas. Over the years the barga system became widespread; the jotedars were mostly Rajbansi and Muslim; few were caste Hindus. The census figures of 1931 show that Muslims comprised 53 per cent of the population, and Rajbansis 20 per cent. Who are the Rajbansis? There is a legend that the Rajbansis were the descendants of the kshatriyas who fled away to escape wrath of Parasuram. According to Risee, ethnically Rajbansis, Paliyas and Koches are the same. This is confirmed by Mr Bell: 'Formerly they (Rajbansis) were known as Paliyas. Officially in the census they were listed as Rajbansi kshatriyas.... The Koch, Rajbansi and Paliyas are really the three names of the same thing'.[7] The great majority of the Rajbansis were poor peasants and adhiars; some were rapacious jotedars who owned between 300 and 500 acres of land. Unlike absentee landlords the jotedars lived in the village and dominated rural life, and treated adhiars as their serfs. The adhiars felt helpless before the powerful jotedars and turned instinctively to the Kisan Sabha as the hope of the future. It was among the Rajbansis that the Kisan Sabha found its earliest recruits.

The Kisan Sabha was founded in Dinajpur in 1938 by a small group of ex-detenus who had accepted Marxism in jail and left the Congress. Bibhuti Guha, a university graduate, came out of jail in 1937 and chose Dinajpur, his home district, as the field of his political activity. He contacted Kali Sarkar, his old comrade in Anusilan Samity who lived in Phulbari and had some land. Sarkar became a full-time functionary and moved in the villages, held baithaks and trained kisan cadres. In Dinajpur town there was a small group of left congressmen vaguely inclined towards Marxism; the members of this group, Sushil Sen, Ajit Ray, Janardan Bhattacharya, joined the Communist Party. Thus was formed the nucleus of the Communist Party which built up the Kisan Sabha in Dinajpur.

The Kisan Sabha branched out in villages. Bibhuti Guha writes that in eighteen months 30 village committees were formed, and the Kisan Sabha held 250 meetings, distributed sixty thousand leaflets and enrolled 4,000 members. When flood and famine devastated Thakurgaon subdivision the Kisan Sabha adopting Gandhian technique, perhaps unconsciously, organised a satyagraha in the court of the subdivisional officer; the police tried to disperse the peasants who refused to leave and stayed on until late at night the SDO gave way and promised to supply agricultural loan.

Led by Haji Muhammed Danesh and Satyen Ray the Kisan Sabha also organised relief work. Haji Danesh, a graduate of Aligarh University, a lawyer by profession, was a nationalist Muslim and the president of the Sub-divisional Congress Committee. Danesh who came from a peasant family was a remarkable personality; he loved the peasants and was loved by them. The

Kisan Sabha found in him an able leader and an excellent speaker. Although son of a rich jotedar Satyen Ray, a graduate, moved in Thukurgaon villages, addressed meetings in Rajbansi dialect, and was quickly accepted by the peasants as their leader.

Meanwhile some peasants had emerged as local leaders: Rajen Singh, a rich peasant of Balia village, Atwari police station; Ramlal Singh and Pathal Singh, two poor peasants who lived in Rajen's village; Benode Das, a middle peasant who lived in the vicinity of Thakurgaon town. They were the first batch of kisan cadres who drew hundreds of kisans within the fold of the Kisan Sabha. In fact as the Kisan Sabha grew kisan cadres multiplied, and they came increasingly from middle peasants and poor peasants. It was the job of kisan cadres to arrange baithaks, organise public meetings, distribute leaflets, enrol members and volunteers.

The Kisan Sabha took up simple demands which could be realised and did not provoke a big clash with jotedars or the government. What developed as a popular movement not only in Dinajpur but also in neighbouring Jalpaiguri and Rangpur districts was the campaign against hat tola or levy exacted by landowners from poor peasants who came to the hats or weekly markets to sell a few seers of paddy or rice or vegetables. The volunteers marched in weekly markets and fairs and called upon peasants not to pay tola; sometimes landowners came to a compromise and exempted peasants from paying tola. Another popular issue was lowering of interest rates changed by jotedars for karja or paddy loans from adhiars. Land to the tiller was certainly the central slogan which was however used for propaganda, not for immediate action, agrarian revolution still lay in the future.

It was not smooth sailing for the Kisan Sabha. Apart from police harassment it was faced with the formidable opposition of the Muslim League and the Kshatriya Samity. Invariably the Muslim League tried to incite religious fanaticism of Muslim peasants against Hindu landowners. The vicious propaganda of the maulavis was countered by Haji Danesh who, as a devoted Mussulman, was held in high esteem by the Muslims. The propaganda of the Muslim League achieved limited success; class demands of Muslim peasants seemed to have a stronger appeal than communal propaganda. It deserves mention that there was not a single incident of communal riot in this district between 1938 and 1947. We will presently see that Muslim peasants joined in large numbers the Tebhaga struggle of 1946-7. It has become a ritual to emphasise caste differences. The fate of Kshatriya Samity therefore deserves particular mention. It tried to wean away the Rajbansis who were told that the Kisan Sabha was dominated by Hindu bhadralok. But the Kshatriya Samity had no economic programme, and mere appeal to caste had little effect on poor Rajbansi peasants; in fact, the candidates put up by this caste organisation were trounced in the 1946 election when Rupnarayan won as a candidate supported by the Kisan Sabha.[8]

We have concentrated on Dinajpur to illustrate the pattern of activity of a district kisan sabha. In most districts the leaders were drawn from former revolutionaries who had accepted Marxism in jail: Benoy Chaudhuri, Hare Krishna Konar (Burdwan); Bhupal Panda, Mohini Mandal, Deben Das (Midnapur); Provash Ray (24-Parganas); Moni Singh (Mymensingh); Krishnabinode Ray, Sukumar Mitra (Jessore); Sachin Bose, Bishnu Chatterjee (Khulna); Dinesh Lahiri, Sudhir Mukherjee, Mohi Bagchi (Rangpur).[9] It is noteworthy that very few intellectuals joined the Kisan Sabha. In 1938-9 the Bengal Provincial Kisan Sabha had only 50,000 members. Surely the Kisan Sabha was developing but slowly. The emphasis everywhere was on partial demands. It is reasonable to ask if the Kisan Sabha formulated any agrarian programme. In 1939 the Bengal Provincial Kisan Sabha submitted a memorandum[10] to the Land Revenue Commission (also called Floud Commission after its chairman, Sir Francis Floud) appointed by the Fazlul Haq ministry in November 1938. Since this memorandum constituted the first serious treatment of the agrarian question it deserves particular notice. Excerpts from this memorandum are reproduced below:

"The government of Bengal consists predominantly of landlords whose primary purpose ... is to maintain the status quo. That such a government should feel obliged to consider either the revision or the abolition of the permanent settlement only goes to prove the reality of economic collapse and danger of political upheaval.

'... it is the permanent settlement which is responsible for the present deplorable condition of our cultivators. In the minds of the oppressed cultivator it is this system which perpetually strives through its various agents, the landlord, the moneylender and the police, to drive him off the land.

'... the number of rent-receivers increased during the decade 1921-31 by about 62 per cent; this is simply an increase in the number of intermediaries between the zamindar and the cultivator. The process was started immediately after the framing of the permanent settlement; with the inability or the unwillingness of the zamindars to manage their own estates it gathered speed as new lands were brought under cultivation; it became a mad race during the period of the general rise in prices when rents were systematically raised on all sides under the provisions of the tenancy act, and the margin of profit between rents and revenue grew wider, and now, in the last few years, it has become a frantic scramble on the part of usurers and petty professional middle-class men to buy their way into the rent-receiving class.

'Not only has agriculture in the province failed to utilise the advance of science to increase its productivity, not only have no improvements in the land or in the mode of farming been made, but we actually see that the productivity of the land per acre has decreased with the fragmentation of holdings.

'Payment of rents in kind is fairly frequent in Bengal.

'The class of sharecroppers known in Bengal most widely as bargadars (also adhiars, bhagchasi, etc.) are not strictly speaking in the eyes of the law tenants at all. They have no tenure, no permanent right in the land they till, but only a temporary or oral lease. In practice there are cases in which the landlord allows the bargadar to cultivate the same strips of land for several years in succession, but one more often finds that the lease is only made for one year and often not committed to writing.

'Amongst other reasons encouraging the growth of sharecropping, we may notice the growth of a new type of landlord—the moneylender-cum-landlord ... the investment of capital in land is more attractive to him under present conditions than investment in industrial concerns.

'Rent must go. In place of rent we must have the agricultural tax. Like the income-tax agricultural tax must be graded.

'If the law recognises democratically elected peasant committees and appoints these committees with the functions of gathering taxes and disbursing grants, loans, etc. from the state, the whole problem is simply, cheaply and realistically solved.

'The ownership of land by landlords is clearly incompatible with our scheme above, and so to us inadmissible. The only two alternatives are (a) state ownership and (b) peasant ownership. The argument in favour of state ownership with annual leases to the peasantry is that it is of advantage from the point of view of centralised land reform. But such a system would be more open to influences of corruption. In view of this danger, and in view also of the opinion of the overwhelming majority of the cultivators themselves, we would advocate the transfer of full rights of property to the individual cultivators.

'But really it is no solution of his poverty. The average cultivator has not the money to buy seed.

'Reclaimed land should be state-owned and worked by agricultural labourers.'

In this memorandum, surely a memorable document, the emphasis was on abolition of zamindari which correspondend to the interests of all categories of peasants. No specific demand for bargadars was formulated. Instead of nationalisation of land, peasant ownership was the declared objective, although it was conceded that it was 'no solution to his poverty'. The need to develop the large unit of cultivation in the form of collective farm was not even the long-term goal; only reclaimed land was to be state-owned. This programme, formulated in 1939, was to remain basically unaltered in subsequent years.

The political orientation of the Kisan Sabha became increasingly marked as war-clouds began to gather in Europe. Since its inception it had declared its solidarity with the Congress movement for independence. But landlord-dominated congress committees proved to be hostile, and opposed the separate existence of the Kisan Sabha; the proposal of 'collective affiliation' of peasant unions, though backed by Nehru, was rejected by the Congress. On the question of united front between Congress and Kisan Sabha there were sharp differences among leading functionaries of Kisan Sabha. It was argued, for instance, that the Congress did not want unity; there could be no unity between exploiters and exploited; national front was therefore a chimera. In a leading article published in 'National Front' on the eve of the Gaya session of the All-India Kisan Sabha held in April, 1939, P.C. Joshi, the then general secretary of Communist Party of India, defended the united front policy:

'... it is necessary in every case to consciously work to get the active cooperation of the local Congress Committee and thus to transform every kisan struggle into a people's struggle, and thus build from below national unity. The division is between imperialism on the one hand and the entire people on the other, the greatest class struggle today is our national struggle, the main organ of our struggle is the National Congress. Any course that takes the kisan away from this straight course separates him from the people, takes him away from the anti-imperialist struggle. It is the Congress-kisan unity which will move the Congress itself forward.'[11]

The differences within the Kisan Sabha were resolved, at least on the theoretical level, at Gaya. It was the period of 'the gathering storm'; anti-imperialist united front was the need of the hour.

Within a few months of the Gaya session came the 'phoney war'. Linlithgow, the Viceroy 'with almost a rock's lack of awareness', as Nehru put it, took no notice of the Congress offer of cooperation in the war effort, and the Congress ministries resigned in October in protest. Repression was let loose on the democratic movement, the main target being the communists. It seems that in the face of this repression the kisan movement beat a retreat and tried to regroup its forces; only in two North Bengal districts, Jalpaiguri and Dinajpur, kisan struggle assumed a popular character. The most striking feature of the kisan struggle was mass participation of Rajbansi bargadars. It ushered in a new period of kisan movement. No longer was it confined to middle peasants. The demands raised by the bargadars were simple: right to stack paddy in their khamar, and reduction of interest rates of karja. The Kisan Sabha formed a volunteer corps, and the volunteers waving the Red Flag marched from village to village. As the adhiars started stacking the paddy in their khamar the jotedars got panicky and pressurised the government for action. Invariably the police came to the help of the jotedars, and several clashes, minor in nature, occurred. In Jalpaiguri the movement was suppressed, but it continued in Dinajpur, and spread rapidly in the entire Thakurgaon subdivision. Ramlal Singh and Pathal Singh of Balia village emerged as local leaders; they were middle peasants who assumed the leadership of the adhiars' struggle. Some petty landowners who had earlier joined the Kisan Sabha now left it and became hostile. The movement gathered momentum, and Satyen Ray toyed with the idea of forming 'soviets'. Then came severe repression; it was easy for the police to suppress the movement which remained confined to a subdivision of one district. Yet the social tension between jotedars and adhiars began to grow and erupted in the Tebhaga struggle in the same Thakurgaon subdivision in 1946.

In the autumn of 1940 Gandhiji launched 'individual' civil disobedience movement in which selected individuals were to shout antiwar slogan and court arrest. Vinoba Bhave, who later became the leader of bhoodan movement, was the first satyagrahi to offer himself for arrest. In Bengal the whole campaign was a tame affair with little popular enthusiasm. What was the Mahatma's motivation is not clear, but the assessment of the government is revealed in a secret report: 'The immediate and local effect was good; it put an end to the sort of agrarian discontent that Nehru had been endeavouring to stir up'.[13] It is a fact that 'individual' civil disobedience movement and kisan struggle did not merge in a common anti-imperialist struggle. Although there were about 14,000 detainees by the spring of 1941 the movement petered out.

In 1940 the kisan movement was virtually driven underground; several leading functionaries in the districts evaded vigilant police hunt and went to the village and remained sunk among the peasants. In Dinajpur there was considerable demoralisation after the collapse of the adhiar movement; Satyen Ray left Thakurgaon; most of the functionaries were interned in Dinajpur town; several kisan cadres were in jail. Abani Lahiri, a student leader of Calcutta, went underground and dressed like a peasant moved from village to village in Thakurgaon. To his great surprise the kisan cadres gave him shelter, worked as couriers, distributed leaflets. Ajit Ray, a district leader, joined him and made Thakurgaon his headquarters; communists came from other districts: Mohi Bagchi and Jiban De from Rangpur, Basanta Chatterjee from Malda and Subodh Sen from Dacca.[14]

The pattern was the same in other districts. In Jalpaiguri Naresh Chakravarty, a local student leader who had just obtained the Bachelor of Law degree, went underground, and worked among the peasants in Debiganj police station. Charu Majumdar (now the famous Naxalbari leader) was then a student, the only son of his father who was the president of Siliguri Congress Committee. From Siliguri Charu came to Jalpaiguri, went underground, and became a full-time functionary of the Kisan Sabha.

The Kisan Sabha characterised the war as anti-fascist and declared its solidarity with the Soviet Union. But the slogan of 'resist Japan' hardly made any sense to the peasants who had not heard of Japan or Germany. Furthermore, the war was being conducted not by a national government. In February 1942 Swami Sahajananda, president of All-India Kisan Sabha, issued a policy statement: 'This war can effectively be converted into an Indian people's war only when it is fought under the leadership of a national government'.[15]

But this approach was not acceptable to the socialists or nationalists. The Congress under Gandhiji's leadership chose to adopt, despite Nehru's opposition, a policy of non-cooperation with the war effort; this policy culminated in the 'Quit India' resolution and the August movement. In September 1942 Professor Ranga (now a Swatantra stalwart) left the Kisan Sabha; he was followed by Indulal Yajnik next year. Although Swami Sahajananda still remained the president, he began to waver and finally chose to leave the Sabha in 1945. With Swamiji's exit the Sabha ceased to be a multiparty organisation only communists remained in the field.

Despite the split and initial setback the Kisan Sabha remained with the people. In July 1942 the ban on the Communist Party was lifted; leading functionaries emerged from underground and made the best use of legal existence. The experience of the underground period was not lost; they remained sunk in the peasants, carried on relief work, formed food committees and dharmagoals, unearthed hoarded stocks, and undertook 'grow more food' campaign. Class struggle on which they had concentrated in the proceeding period went *imperceptibly* into the background; this was offset by organisational consolidation. Political classes were held at the village level which helped to remould the outlook of peasant cadres. About one thousand full-time functionaries worked in the districts; the membership of the Kisan Sabha in Bengal increased from 178,000 in 1944 to 255,000 in 1945.[17] The Kisan Sabha was on the eve of the great Tebhaga struggle.

References

1. N.G. Ranga, *Kisans and Congress, op. cit.* pp. 60-1.
2. Report of the Seventh Congress of Communist International, 1935.
3. R. Palme Dutt and Ben Bradley, 'The Anti-imperialist People's Front', *Labour Monthly*, March, 1936.
4. L.P. Sinha, *The Left Wing In India*, 1919-47, pp. 391-3; Dr. Sinha gives a connected account of the growth of All-India Kisan Sabha between 1936 and 1940; also Gene D. Overstreet and M. Windmiller, *Communism in India*, p. 384.
5. For the list of members of the Bengal Provincial Kisan Committee, see A. Rasul, *Krishak Sabhar Itihash* (in Bengali) which brings the story up to 1967.
6. (Footnotes follow original numbering, and have been left blank where extracts have been ommited.—Ed.)
7. The typical Rajbansi has a short broad figure, with flat nose and thick lips, the eyes are long and narrow, the cheek bones high; they speak a local dialect of Bengali, generally use loin cloth, claim to be Hindus; they are found in North Bengal districts: Jalpaiguri, Dinajpur, Rangpur, Malda, Cooch Behar and Darjeeling (only Siliguri subdivision); they are poor and mostly illiterate. For an account of the Rajbansis see C.C. Sanyal, 'The Rajbansis of North Bengal', *Asiatic Society of Bengal*. 1965.
8. B. Guha, 'Dinajpur Kisans Marching Ahead', *National Front*, 13 August 1939. Much of the material has been obtained from interview with B. Guha, A. Lahiri, S. Sen and A. Ray.
  Bibhuti Guha was secretary of Dinajpur District Kisan Sabha in 1938-39.
  Sushil Sen was secretary of Dinajpur District Committee of CPI, 1942-47. Sen, son of a local lawyer, obtained the degree of B.A. from Rajshahi College, worked for some time as a school teacher, joined the CPI in 1938.
  Ajit Ray, born in a middle-class family, was one of the builders of Kisan Sabha in Dinajpur.
9. Hare Krishna Konar, born in Raina, Burdwan, in 1915, son of a rice trader, grandson of a rich peasant, joined the Congress movement while a student in Bangabasi College, came in contact with revolutionaries (Hooghli Yugantar Group), was arrested and sent to the Andamans in 1933, joined the CPI in 1938 and worked as a full-time functionary among Burdwan peasants.
  Provash Ray, born in 1907 in Burul, 24-Parganas, son of a businessman, joined the Congress movement in 1920s, came in contact with Chittagong group of revolutionaries, remained in jail from 1931 to 1936, was elected secretary of 24-Parganas District Congress Committee in 1939, and simultaneously worked among peasants.
  Bhupal Panda, son of Brojomohan Vidyaratna, a Brahmin pandit and a small landowner, joined a revolutionary group, the Bengal Volunteers, while a college student, was arrested and sent to the Andamans, joined the Communist Party in 1938.
  Mohini Mandal, also a revolutionary, joined the Communist Party in 1938, and was one of the builders of Kisan Sabha in Midnapur.
  Deben Das was active in the Congress movement and joined the Communist Party in 1938.
  Krishnabinode Ray, born in 1903 in a middle-class family in Jessore, obtained the degree of Bachelor of Laws, joined a revolutionary group (Jessore-Khulna

Youth Association) linked with Anusilan, became a leading lawyer in Jessore, joined the Communist Party in 1934 after the collapse of the civil disobedience movement, was a member of the All-India Congress Committee in 1936, 1938, 1939, and was elected President of Bengal Provincial Kisan Sabha in 1946.
Dinesh Lahiri, born in a landowner's family, was active in the Congress movement, joined the Kisan Sabha in 1938, and was one of the builders of Kisan Sabha in Rangpur.
Mohi Bagchi joined the Yugantar group, accepted Marxism in jail, went underground in 1939-40, and worked among the peasants in Dinajpur and Rangpur.
Sudhir Mukherjee, also a revolutionary, accepted Marxism in jail and joined the Communist Party unit in Rangpur.
Sachin Bose and Bishnu Chatterjee, revolutionaries in their youth, accepted Marxism in jail, and founded the Kisan Sabha in Khulna in 1938.
Moni Singh, born in Calcutta in 1901, was connected with Anusilan, arrested and interned in Susang, his native village, and turned to kisan movement in 1936.

10 'Memorandum' by the Bengal Provincial Kisan Sabha, 27B, Gangadhar Babu Lane, Calcutta, 1939. Abani Lahiri told the present writer that this document was mainly drafted by Rebati Burman, secretary, research department of BPKS, in 1936-9. Burman was born in a talukdar family in Kishoreganj. Mymensingh. See for full text: 'Report of the Land Revenue Commission, Bengal, Vol. 6, pp. 3-61'.
11 P.C. Joshi, 'Kisan Movement: Review and Tasks', *National Front*, 2 April, 1939. Joshi gives a short review of kisan movement between 1936 and 1938.
12 ....
13 *History of Civil Disobedience Movement*, 1940-41 (Government of India, unpublished), quoted in M. Brecher, *Nehru: A. Political Biography*, p. 135.
14 Interviews with A. Lahiri, A. Ray, S. Ganguli.
15 *People's War*, 14 January 1945. Sahjananda's appeal to Congressmen is published in full.
16 ....
17 '*People's War*, 15 April, 1945. The membership of AIKS rose from 553,000 in 1944 to 825,000 in 1945; also see A. Rasul, *op. cit.*, pp. 139, 140.

21 Tebhaga Chai

Sunil Sen

THE SITUATION took a radical turn in February 1946. There was a popular upheaval in Calcutta on the occasion of Rashid Ali Day; for three days Calcutta witnessed mighty demonstrations, in which students took a prominent part, demanding release of Abdur Rashid, an INA prisoner to whom clemency was refused.[5] Almost simultaneously there started the rising of the ratings of the Royal Indian Navy. On 18 February the revolt of the ratings began in Bombay; it quickly spread to Karachi and Madras, Responding to the call of the Central Naval Strike Committee the industrial workers of Bombay, led by the Communist Party, observed hartal and came out in the streets. For three days (21-23 February) Bombay was in the vortex of an upheaval; British troops were called in, and shootings took a toll of 250 lives. Indeed, as the Central Naval Strike Committee declared in a manifesto: 'For the first time the blood of men in the services and of men in the streets flowed together in a common cause'. Finally, on 23 February under the pressure of Vallabhbhai Patel the Central Naval Strike Committee decided to surrender.[6]

Yet, apparently, there was all quiet on the agrarian front; peasants did not rise in struggle in this tumultuous period. The reasons are not clear. It seems that peasants were watching events and waiting for the harvesting season which was the normal period of bargadars' struggle.

Meanwhile the national situation was taking an ominous turn. Neither the nationalists nor the left could understand how deep communalism had penetrated in the country. In the absence of an agrarian movement it was relatively easy for the vested interests, backed by powerful political leaders, to spread the poison of communalism.

Communal riot appeared to be the dominant feature of Indian politics; democratic movement was in shambles.

Reproduced from '*Agrarian Struggle in Bengal, 1946-7*', by Sunil Sen, *op. cit.*, pp. 34-46.

In this grim background Bengal Provincial Kisan Sabha gave the call for Tebhaga struggle in September 1946. It was a demand for two-thirds share of the crop for bargadars, a demand recommended by the Land Revenue Commission, 1940. The kisan leaders addressed public meetings that were not always largely attended, and leaflets written in very simple language were distributed; demonstrations followed in some villages with such slogans as 'Inqilab Zindabad!, Nij Kholane Dhan Tolo! (Stack paddy in your khamar), Tebhaga Chai! (We want tebhaga)'. The Kisan Sabha enrolled volunteers who marched across the villages, shouting slogans and distributing leaflets. The time for action came in the harvesting season, and the first clash between peasants and the police that heralded the bargadar revolt occurred in Atwari police station in Dinajpur district.

As we have already noted, Dinajpur was a stronghold of the Kisan Sabha. In 1939 the adhiars had launched a struggle that ended in defeat. The kisan movement recovered between 1940 and 1945. In March 1946 Rupnarayan was elected to the Legislative Assembly. In November the Kisan Sabha began preparations for the tebhaga struggle. Sushil Sen went to Rampur village in Atwari police station to start the movement. Presumably, Rampur was expected to serve as an example to other villages. The Kisan Sabha which was centred in Rampur had established village level committees throughout Atwari; it was a centre of the adhiar struggle of 1939. The leaders of this struggle, Ramlal Sing, Pathal Sing, Rajen Sing, came from contiguous Balia village. Bhaben Sing, Ramlal's grandson, and Naba Sing, Pathal's son, represented the new generation of kisan cadres. Sushil Sen held a baithak attended by about one hundred kisan cadres, and the decision of launching the struggle was taken.

On the following morning when the volunteers went to cut the paddy in the land of Phuljari, a bargadar, the police came and arrested Sen. This had no deterrent or restraining effect; next morning the peasants went to cut paddy in the same village. Again the police came, and as they started beating the peasants, Dipsari, a young Rajbansi widow, waving a lathi rushed to them and the volunteers armed with lathis followed her.

There was a clash and the police beat a retreat; things had certainly changed since 1939. The news of the clash spread and there was a temporary lull.[11]

Soon after this incident, leading functionaries of the district met in a hurriedly convened meeting in Thakurgaon town. There could be no mistake about the mood of the masses manifested in the Atwari clash. It was decided that leading functionaries would immediately go into hiding to evade arrest and guide the movement. The slogans remained unchanged; the general directive was to stack the paddy in bargadar's khamar. Bibhuti Guha, Ajit Ray, Sushil Sen (who had just been released on bail), Gurudas Talukdar, Sunil Sen, Janardan Bhattacharya, Basanta Chatterjee, Kali Sarkar, Sudhir Samajpati went underground to take charge of the zones marked out for them. Haji Danesh was to remain in Thakurgaon town; his main assignment was to draw in Muslim peasants. Sachindu Chakravarty, Hrishikesh Bhattacharya and Satyabrata Chakravarty took charge of Dinajpur town.[12] The initial leadership of the movement came from the Kisan Sabha; with the spontaneous support of bargadars it soon gathered momentum. What would be the future course of the movement was unpredictable, but the leading functionaries boldly decided to take the plunge.

From their hideouts the leaders moved from village to village, held evening baithaks which lasted till midnight, and sought to give a direction to the developing movement. The bargadars' response was overwhelming and spontaneous. Within a fortnight the movement spread to 22 out of 30 police stations in the district; it was particularly intense in Thakurgaon sub-division. Several thousand peasants enrolled as volunteers. The peasants of one village were called upon to assist those of another, not by beat of drums but by shouting 'Inqilab'. The carrying of lathis was compulsory for volunteers; bands of lathials had been an institution maintained by zamindars; now the volunteers became 'lathials' of the Kisan Sabha.

The special correspondent of *The Statesman* gives an eye-witness account of the movement in its early phase: 'Dumb through past centuries, he is today transformed by the shout of a slogan. It is inspiring to see him marching across a field with his fellows, each man shouldering a lathi like a rifle, with a red flag at the head of the procession. It is sinister to hear them greet each other in the silence of bamboo groves with clenched left fists raised to foreheads and a whispered "Inqilab Comrade".

'The carrying of lathis is apparently compulsory. "The party requires that we carry the Red Flag and lathis", one peasant who looked like an aboriginal told me. "It is a sign of our solidarity". By the party he meant his peasant organisation, the membership fee for which is an anna. A townsman sympathiser declared: "To people who have been downtrodden for generations the lathi gives courage". They are not above using them despite their vehement deprecation of violence'.[13]

Thakurgaon was once again the centre of the movement. As the movement spread to distant villages it became physically impossible for the few middle-class leaders to keep track of it, and they relied invariably on kisan cadres. These cadres fixed up shelters for underground leaders, acted as couriers, held baithaks and maintained contact with peasant masses. Some of them emerged as local leaders, and went underground as they were wanted by the police. Rajen Sing, whom we have already mentioned, though a rich peasant, did not hesitate to join the movement. In Atwari police station the movement was led by Avaran Sing, middleaged, sober, taciturn, who owned about 5 bighas of land, and Bhaben Sing, young, energetic, restless, who never said 'no' to any assignment, however risky. In Baliadingi the undisputed leader was Kamparam Sing, a middleaged man of indomitable courage, short and stout, a middle peasant who gave away his life's savings to the Communist Party, and became a full-time functionary. Doma Sing was another leader, handsome and cheerful, also a middle peasant, whose entire family joined the Kisan Sabha. From the same locality came Pastaram Sing, a poor peasant, who became a full-time worker, left home with his wife Jaymani to work in Rani-sankail as the local peasants urged Gurudas Talukdar to send a leader to guide them. Jaymani, tall and pock-marked, learned to read and write, and emerged as a leader of Rajbansi women. As the story proceeds we will hear of brave Rajbansi women who led the men in resisting police attack.

Meanwhile the movement had spread to Rajbansi villages in adjoining Rangpur and Jalpaiguri districts. The pattern of the movement was the same. The bargadars took the crop to their khamar (instead of jotedar's); volunteers shouldering lathis marched across villages with the familiar slogans: 'Inqilab Zindabad', 'Tebhaga Chai'. There was spontaneous response from the bargadars, and the movement rapidly spread from village to village. Anticipating police offensive middle-class leaders took no risk and went underground. In Jalpaiguri the movement was confined to three police stations: Debiganj, Boda and Pachagarh. In Debiganj an old Rajbansi widow, affectionately called 'old mother', took the lead. As the men vacillated, 'old mother' took out a procession of women and started cutting the paddy. Then the men came to the field and joined the women in cutting the crop. In Boda the leader was Madhab Datta, an old kisan leader; three peasant cadres, Bachcha Munsi, Indramohon and Radhamohon Burman, played a leading role. Radhamohon, a middle peasant, was a popular leader who polled 9,000 votes in the 1946 election and lost by a small margin. Charu Majumdar had his first experience of leading a kisan struggle at Pachagarh; how and whether this experience ultimately led him to choose the 'Naxalbari path' is not known. Charu was assisted by Dulal Ghosh and Biren Pal, two middle-class cadres. In Debiganj a young middle-class cadre came to guide the movement—he was Samar Ganguli, who was to become the leader of the tribal movement in the Duars in the subsequent period.[14]

In Rangpur the movement remained confined to Nilphamari subdivision which was severely hit by the great famine of 1943. As in Thakurgaon the bargadars, mainly Rajbansi and Muslim, were concentrated in this subdivision. Within a month the movement spread to six police stations—the leadership was taken by Mohi Bagchi, Moni Krishna Sen and Mantu Majumdar who went underground to evade arrest and guide the movement. Hundreds of volunteers went to the field and removed the crop to bargadars' khamar. In the second week of January there was a clash. Some Muslim jotedars of Dimla, armed with guns raided the house of a bargadar to snatch away the crop. The peasants, led by Bachcha Muhammed and Tatnarayan Ray, resisted the attack, the jotedars fired on the peasants; Tatnarayan was killed and Bachcha severely wounded. The news of Tatnarayan's death spread like wild fire and about 3,000 peasants, armed with lathis and spears assembled in the villages. Since the jotedar was a Muslim the leaders persuaded the peasants, who were in a militant mood, not to attack his house; they were afraid that attack on a Muslim jotedar could spark off a communal riot. The peasants put the jotedar under social boycott and held a demonstration that marched through the villages to Nilphamari town. The jotedars fled the village and bided their time.[15]

The Tebhaga struggle was no longer confined to North Bengal districts; it spread to Mymensingh and Midnapur districts. In Mymensingh in East Bengal the struggle was intense in Kishoreganj subdivision. The peasants were mostly Muslim and tribal, and zamindars and talukdars Hindu and Muslim. Despite the attempts of the Muslim League to rouse communal passions there was remarkable solidarity of Hindu and Muslim peasants.

Almost simultaneously the Hajongs in Susang started the tanka movement. On 8 December about 5,000 Hajongs held a demonstration demanding reduction of tanka rent and its conversion into money-rent. Like adhi, tanka was produce-rent which a tenant had to pay in a quantity fixed by the landowners, even if the crop failed due to drought or heavy rains; the expenses of cultivation were borne by the tenant; like the bargadar the tanka tenant had no tenancy right and could be evicted by the landowner. In 1937 the Kisan Sabha started a movement for reduction of tanka-rent. Apart from Hajongs the Muslims formed a large portion of tanka tenants, and the movement first started among Muslim peasants of Desal village in Susang. Moni Sing, originally a trade union worker in Calcutta, and for a long time a prisoner under the Bengal Criminal Law Amendment Act, came to Mymensingh, his home district, remained sunk among the Hajongs, and organised them in the Kisan Sabha after his release from the detention camp. There was Lalit Sarkar, a popular Hajong leader, who had joined the Congress movement in 1920s and 1930s, and was drawn in the Kisan Sabha in 1937-8. On the crest of the tanka movement the Kisan Sabha spread in this area, and several Hajong cadres, trained by the Kisan Sabha came to the fore. The influence of Kisan Sabha considerably increased when tanka-rent was reduced by Fazlul Haq ministry in 1938.

The Statesman published a special article on 25 March, 1947 that gives a fairly objective background of the tanka movement in 1946-7:

'Agrarian unrest in Mymensingh differs in cause and extent from the unrest in the districts in Dinajpur, Jalpaiguri and Rangpur. In these places, its effects are confined to 'pockets' or 'former communist strongholds' as some prefer to call them; in Mymensingh it is spread throughout a 50 mile long, ten mile wide belt south of the Garo hills.

'Nobody seems to know much about the history of the Hajongs except that once they were head hunters, offered human sacrifice, and were guilty of unspeakable crimes in their tribal wars.... The Hajongs, it appears, belong to Kachari group of tribes who gave Cachar its name, held a warlike tradition and were once a ruling people of Assam.... They exhibit no proportionate hostility towards "foreigner" who came to their country and set new standard of exploitation of man by man. The tribes people, whatever other vices they practised, did not know about greed for land until "foreigners" arrived and proceeded to trick the owner out of it. It was not until 1923 that this belt was declared a partially excluded area. By the thirties 50 per cent of Hajongs had lost their land while other tribes like the Hodis had been more thoroughly fleeced. In 1938, following tribal agitation, the government ordered a revisional settlement and hundreds of thousands of rupees worth of land was restored to its rightful owners.

'Another reform was the reduction of tanka ... after the revision it is said to average about a quarter of the crop and the man who pays it is a tenant. Tanka, unlike adhi rent, now has the sanction of law, not custom alone.

'The present agitation to convert tanka into much lower money-rent seeks to give to the peasant benefit of the postwar level of agricultural prices and to make the eviction of tenant more difficult. Money-rent has another advantage for the cultivator. If there is a dispute and the landlord refuses to accept his rent the rent can be deposited at the thana, if it is in money. But if it is in kind he cannot do so for lack of storage facilities and is liable for interest.

'Hajongs are in the fore of this struggle for change but they know nothing about the tactics of agitation and this is where the communists come in. The communist hold on the Hajongs is remarkable. It is stated to date back to the outbreak of the Far East war and the Congress movement of 1942, when communists stepped into the shoes of that incarcerated party and basked in a sort of official favour.

'The communist approach to the tanka problem is simple. It was the peasant who cleared the land of the jungle, his labours bring forth the crop; but it is the landlord who takes all the profit ...

their critics say that they gave away plots to Hajongs and bid them cut wood from forest preserves. They are even charged with trading on the religious susceptibilities of the Hajongs by telling them 'join us and we will take water from your hands'. There were too the usual promises of the coming of a 'Hajong raj".'[17]

In the entire northern Mymensingh comprising Netrokona, Sadar and Jamalpur subdivisions the tanka movement rapidly spread. The peasants took the crop to their houses and refused to pay tanka until their demands were fulfilled; it was directed not against the jotedar but the zamindar of Susang. The leading figure was Moni Sing. In face of mammoth demonstrations of Hajong peasants, landowners and even missionaries who worked in this area for years evacuated their families to towns. Although Hajongs were in the fore of the movement there was no incident of tribal clash between them and Garos. There is no evidence to prove that Hajongs resorted to violence or coerced other tribes; in fact the movement was perfectly peaceful in the beginning, and took a violent turn only towards the end of January 1947. In vain they hoped for government intervention in reducing tanka-rent and converting it into money-rent, and the nationalist press, inexplicably enough, remained silent until the peasant-police clash in January.

The Tebhaga struggle also spread to some pockets in Midnapur, a stronghold of the Congress since 1920. It was in this district that the 1942 August movement assumed a popular character. In Tamluk a 'national government' was formed which was in existence from 17 December, 1942 to 8 August 1944. The hero of Tamluk movement was Ajoy Mukherjee. Matangini Hazra, an old woman who held the national flag in her grip when bullets were flying, called upon the troops to join the freedom movement, and was killed by a bullet, had become a legend.[18]

Although the Kisan Sabha was formed in this district in 1938 it remained weak; in the 1946 election Bhupal Panda was defeated by the Congress candidate. But in December the peasants responded to the call of the Kisan Sabha despite the opposition of landlord-dominated Congress Committee. The bargadars were mostly scheduled caste or tribal or Mahisya. As in other districts the movement was spontaneous and rapidly spread in Mahisadal, Sutahata and Nandigram; hundreds of peasants, men and women, enrolled as volunteers. Following the tradition of the Congress movement women joined the Tebhaga struggle in large numbers. Bimala Mandal, a young woman who came of a middle-peasant family, emerged as a local leader. There was Bhupal Panda, veteran kisan leader, who was assisted by Ananta Maji, a young student of B.Sc. honours class in Midnapur College, who came of a peasant family, gave up studies, and became a full-time worker of the Communist Party.[19] Ranjit Sukul with a group of students moved in the villages of Nandigram and popularised the Tebhaga demand.

On 4 January 1947 the police opened fire on a peasant demonstration in Talpukur village in Chirirbandar in Dinajpur district, killing Sibram, a Santal landless peasant, and Samiruddin, also a landless peasant, on the spot.

Chirirbandar, only six miles from Dinajpur town, was a new base of the Kisan Sabha; the bargadars, Rajbansi, Santal and Muslim, comprised a large section of the rural population. Sachindu Chakravarty, a local communist leader, lawyer by profession, held some public meetings in this area. There was spontaneous response from the bargadars who started removing paddy from the field to their khamar. The local leader was Sudhir Samajpati, a young middle-class cadre who had joined the Communist Party through student movement. Madhu Burman, a poor Rajbansi peasant, who had recently joined the Kisan Sabha, went underground, held baithaks in villages and maintained contact with the Dinajpur town unit. The jotedars lodged charges of 'paddy looting', and on 2 January Sachindu Chakravarty was arrested from the Bar Library in Dinajpur town. On 4 January the police party came to Talpukur village to execute arrest warrants. As the police party entered the village about 400 peasants gathered and a quarrel started. There is no sufficient evidence to establish that the move was violent; it appears that the Santal peasants fought with bows and arrows when the police started shooting. Sibram and Samiruddin fell dead; the bullets were flying; suddenly a Santal peasant rushed towards the police party and pierced his arrow into the abdomen of a policeman who died in hospital. It cannot be definitely established whether this man was Sibram or someone else who managed to escape. Pohatu Burman, a poor Rajbansi peasant, was wounded, and his right leg had to be amputed. Several peasants received bullet injuries. The People's Relief Committee rushed medical aid to the village, and Dr B.K. Basu personally attended peasants who received bullet injuries.[21] What was a striking feature of the Chirirbandar incident was Muslim peasants' participation; in fact, one Muslim peasant was killed and several were wounded. After the firing there was a temporary lull; but the movement had gathered momentum and spread to neighbouring villages. The police could not arrest Sudhir and Madhu who remained in hiding and continued to guide the movement.

On 6 January Torab Ali, the district magistrate, called a conference of jotedars and adhiars at Thakurgaon town to evolve a compromise formula, and sent invitations to Haji Danesh and Sunil Sen. A pandal was erected in the court compound, and jotedars came from all parts of the district. A big demonstration organised by the Kisan Sabha marched to Thakurgaon. Sen, who was underground, accepted Torab Ali's invitation and reached Thakurgaon at midnight on 5 January. Danesh came to meet him on the following morning. A courier brought a message from Bidhuti Guha to the effect that there could be a settlement only on one condition: Tebhaga must be conceded. Sen and Danesh decided not to attend the conference. There was no chance that jotedars would concede Tebhaga. The Chirirbandar firing rankled the peasants. If they accepted any compromise formula the peasants would not relish it. They had no right to take a decision over the heads of peasants. Sen went straight to the maidan where the peasants had assembled, and in his speech reiterated the tebhaga demand and condemned Chirirbandar firing. Torab Ali, accompanied by a police force, came to the maidan and stood silently as Sen addressed the peasants. The peasants, shouldering lathis, formed into a procession and marched through the streets of Thakurgaon. The jotedars watched them from a distance. The beautifully decorated pandal looked like 'a banquet hall deserted'.

Torab Ali kept his word; he did not order the police to arrest Sunil Sen which could have precipitated a clash. Months later Arun Guha, prominent Congress leader, wrote in Amrita Bazar Patrika: 'It is also a puzzle to us even now that a leader of that particular political party, while in hiding, could come and address an open meeting at Thakurgaon and yet was not apprehended'.[22] The fact is that the police did search for Sen when the sun set. But the bird had flown.

References

1 ....
2 ....
3 ....
4 ....
5 H. Mukerjee, *'The Gentle Colossus'*, 1964, p. 103; Professor Mukerjee gives a fascinating account of this tumultuous period.
6 R.P. Dutt, *India Today*, 1947; pp. 471-4; Dutt severely castigates the national leadership: 'The upper class leadership of the Congress and Moslem League found themselves in opposition to the mass movement and aligned with British imperialism as the representative of law and order against the people' (p. 474). Dr Majumdar refers to this event in just one paragraph, see R.C. Majumdar, *op. cit.*, pp. 752-3.
7 ....
8 ....
9 ....
10 ....
11 Interview with Sushil Sen. The present writer had been to Atwari exactly one day after the clash. Dipsari had a daughter and lived in the house of her husband's brother, Tejnath Sing, an old member of the party who owned about 15 bighas of land.
12 This writer was present in this meeting.
13 'Peasant Unrest in North Bengal', *The Statesman*, 19 March, 1947.
14 Interview with Samar Ganguli; also *People's Age*, 22 December, 1946.
15 Interview with Mohi Bagchi; also Satyen Sen, Gram Banglar Pathe Pathe (in Bengali), Dacca, 1970. Sen, a journalist of Bangladesh, writes a moving account of this incident; Gholam Quddus who went to Dimla to cover the Tebhaga story for *Swadhinata* also writes on it in *Sambodhan*, Calcutta, 1969.
16 ....
17 'Tribal Unrest in North East Bengal', *The Statesman*, 25 March 1947; A. Rasul, *op. cit.*, pp. 107-9; Pramatha Gupta, *Mukti Yuddhye Adibasi* (in Bengali), 1964. Gupta was active in kisan movement in Mymensingh district between 1938 and 1950. Altab Ali, 'Moni Sing', *Saptaha*, 14 August 1970; in this biographical sketch Ali gives a brief account of tanka movement.
18 R.C. Majumdar, *op. cit.*, pp. 653-55. 5.
19 Ananta Majhi's note; interview with Bhupal Panda. Sukul later worked as a school teacher and was murdered by jotedars during the land movement in 1970.
20 ....
21 Swadhinata, 5 January 1947; Amrita Bazar Patrika, 22 January 1947; Sachindu Chakravarty's note on the incident; A. Rasul, *op. cit.*, p. 157. Rupnarayan Ray gives a different story in his assembly speech on 18 February 1947: the police put Samiruddin under arrest and shot him dead without any provocation from the peasants, and this infuriated the peasants; see 'Assembly Proceedings, Bengal Legislative Assembly', Vol. 72, No. 1, 1947. Dr B.K. Basu of the People's Relief Committee was a member of the Congress Medical Mission to China and lived for some years in Yenan, 'red base' of the Chinese communists.
22 A.C. Guha, 'Lessons of Dinajpur', *Amrita Bazar Patrika*, 15 April 1947. Guha rose to be a Minister in the Union Cabinet.

22 The Bargadars Bill

Sunil Sen

IT WAS ONLY after a period of acute agrarian unrest that the government took any notice of the peasants' demands. The Rent Act of 1859 and the Indigo Commission of 1860 came in the wake of the "Blue Mutiny"; the Bengal Tenancy Act of 1885 was passed after the Pabna peasant revolt had flared up in 1872-3 and spread to Bogra district. What was Suhrawardy's motivation in bringing the Bargadars Bill is not clear. The Bill was shelved, and Jyoti Basu, leader of the communist group in the Legislative Assembly, accused the Muslim League ministry of 'playing up to the gallery' when they drafted the bill.[1] Yet the positive effects of the bill cannot be underestimated. No such legislation seeking to ameliorate the condition of rent-paying tenants was undertaken by the Congress ministries between 1937 and 1939. The fact cannot be denied that rent-paying tenants remained unnoticed over the years. It was after independence that the Congress ministry passed the West Bengal Bargadars Act in 1950, whose provisions were bodily taken from this bill.

The provisions of the Bargadars Bill may be summarized. In the case in which the jotedar supplied 'the plough-cattle, plough and any other agricultural instruments and any manure', the bargadar would get half of the produce of such land. If the jotedar did not supply these inputs, the bargadar would retain two-thirds share. There were some provisions on the division of seed. If the seed was supplied by the jotedar, it would be delivered to him by the bargadar. If the seed was supplied by the bargadar, it would be retained by him. If the seed was supplied partly by the jotedar and partly by the bargadar, it would be divided between them in the proportion in which the seed was supplied by them. Although the declared objective of the bill was to stop evictions, wide scope

---

Reproduced from *Agrarian Struggle in Bengal, 1946-7*, by Sunil Sen, *op. cit.*, pp. 47-56.

was left for the jotedar to evict bargadars. The bill provided that the jotedar could evict a bargadar if he wanted 'to cultivate the land himself or with the aid of the members of his family'. There were also other provisions, equally prejudicial to the bargadar. For instance, he could be evicted if 'there has been any misuse of the land', or if he 'has failed to cultivate the land properly', or if he 'has failed to deliver to the owner such share of the produce as he is bound, subject to the provisions of this Act, by any express or implied agreement with the owner to deliver to such owner'.[2]

Yet the Bargadars Bill, with all its limitations, gave an impetus to the tebhaga struggle. The jotedars could no longer say that the tebhaga demand was illegal. The news spread that two-thirds share for the bargadar had been conceded by the government. One may recall the effects of the famous parwana of Ashley Eden, published by Hem Chandra Kar, a deputy magistrate, in August 1859. As the knowledge of this parwana spread, the raiyats of Barasat refused to sow indigo, and their example was followed by the raiyats of other districts.[3] Similarly, the knowledge of the Bargadars Bill, which gave legal sanction to tebhaga demand, gave new heart to the vast number of bargadars who had so long remained neutral, passive and hesitant. In fact there was the extension of the movement to new villages where the Kisan Sabha did not exist. Some of the heroic peasant struggles occurred not in the old bases of the Kisan Sabha, but in these new villages, and the struggles were led not by veteran cadres, who mostly remained in the background, but by new cadres who came to the fore in the wake of the movement.

Meanwhile the first phase of the struggle was almost over; the adhiars had stacked the paddy in their khamar, instead of jotedar's. Now the struggle entered a new phase. In villages where the Kisan Sabha had no base the adhiars had stored the paddy in jotedar's stacks. As the news of the Bargadars Bill spread they thought that they should also act to reap the fruits of victory, and they started, sometimes without the sanction of the Kisan Sabha, removing paddy already stored in the jotedar's stacks to their khamars. It was a spontaneous movement which assumed a mass character in Dinajpur and Jalpaiguri. The movement was not always concentrated against the landowners; adhiars refused to distinguish between large and small landowners, and argued that small jotedars also should concede tebhaga that had received legal sanction in the Bargadars Bill. Inevitably new social tension was created, and with it new complications. In the earlier period social tension was primarily confined to large landowners and the bulk of poor peasants; now its area extended to small landowners and rural middle class. It would however be fatuous to think that these elements had been taking a neutral position; on the contrary, they generally maintained a hostile attitude, and their sympathies lay with large landowners.

The jotedars who had fled the village were biding their time, and showed their sharp cunning when opportunity came. They suddenly became very active, formed jotedar samity, raised funds, and began to put pressure on the government. Suhrawardy referred in his assembly speech to 'the flood of telegrams which have been pouring in from these areas complaining of looting from the houses of various jotedars'.[5] The special correspondent of The Statesman who toured North Bengal districts made some interesting comments: 'Some adhiars went further; they removed new paddy already stored in the jotedar's stacks to their own for their shareout. It was an attempt to alter custom by force, but it is doubtful if it amounted to a criminal breach of the law, and observer wise in the ways of the country say it is an exaggeration to describe it as "looting". But the jotedars, wise also in these matters, lodged charges of dacoity'.[6] The jotedars constituted a formidable pressure group, and exerted considerable influence on the Congress and the Muslim League. It seems that the government yielded to the pressure campaign, and sent armed police force to the villages to arrest peasants and their leaders.

We will now briefly describe how this movement took shape and focus attention on some major incidents. Pastaram and his wife Jaymani, whom we have already mentioned, had been working in Ranisankail, a new base of the Kisan Sabha. Anil Chakravartty, a middle-class cadre, came to Ranisankail to help Pastaram. In this police station the movement mainly took the form of removing paddy stored in jotedars' stacks to bargadars' khamar. The jotedars filed cases of 'paddy looting'. On 2 February as the police came to arrest some peasants, they were surrounded by Kisan Sabha volunteers led by Bhandani, a young Rajbansi girl, who had recently joined the Kisan Sabha along with her husband. She snatched away the gun from the daroga who was overpowered and confined in a house, and Bhandani kept watch throughout the night. On the instructions of Gurudas Talukdar the daroga was released next morning. Two days later he came with a large police force, arrested several peasants and let loose a reign of terror. There was no resistance. Pastaram, Jaymani and Bhandani, however, managed to evade arrest.[7] Along with Jaymani, Bhandani continued to work among Rajbansi women, gave shelter to underground cadres, remained loyal to the Kisan Sabha when some old cadres got cold feet in face of repression.

We have referred to police firing in Chirirbandar in Sadar subdivision. From Chirirbandar the movement had spread to Parbatipur and Nababganj. But Balurghat subdivision remained quiet. It was a strong base of the Congress. During the 1942 August movement several thousand people, mostly from rural areas, formed a procession under the leadership of the local Congress leader, Saroj Ranjan Chatterjee, besieged Balurghat town, cut telegraph wires, burnt the court building and took control of the town. Although Congress leaders were put in jail in 1942, their influence in Balurghat was undiminished. In the face of the opposition of the local Congress Committee the Kisan Sabha could not make much headway in this subdivision. But the situation took a radical turn towards the end of January. The peasants started removing paddy from jotedars' stacks to their khamar. The leadership of this movement was taken by the Mohanto family of Patiram. Krishnadas Mohanto who belonged to bairagi community came from Burdwan and settled in Patiram, and had about 30 acres of land. He joined the Congress movement in the 1920s and 1930s. His son, Nani Das, a revolutionary belonging to Yugantar group, was sent to the Andamans where he came in contact with communists and accepted Marxism. After the collapse of the 1942 August movement the Mohanto family joined the Communist Party, and Nani Das became a full-time functionary of the party. In the first week of February the movement became widespread in the adjoining villages of Patiram; the most notable incident occurred in 'Sinha Cutchery' where Gobinda Sinha, a rich jotedar, used his gun to disperse the peasants who had gathered to remove the paddy from his cutchery. The peasants did not disperse, and removed the paddy to their khamar.[8] This incident culminated in the Khanpur armed clash to which we will presently refer.

In Boda, Pachagarh and Debiganj in Jalpaiguri district the first phase of the movement was over in mid-January. The jotedars mostly fled the village; the bargadars started threshing and sent notice to the jotedars to take their one-third share. At this stage there started a new movement, popularly called kholan bhanga, in which bargadars began removing the paddy from jotedars' stacks to their khamar. As in Dinajpur, jotedars lodged charges of 'looting' and 'dacoity', and the police was sent to arrest peasants. This new movement became widespread and intense in the Duars where tribals, much more militant than Rajbansis, pressed forward, and were joined by tea-garden labourers, also mostly tribals. In fact, a marked feature of the Duars movement was an upsurge among tribals. Although the immediate issue was tebhaga, the forces of an agrarian revolt had been gathering in this region for a long time. The upsurge among the tribals merged with the general upsurge among the peasantry in the postwar period, revealing the same features of spontaneity and militancy. The communists sought to lead this tribal upsurge and achieved lasting success. The tribal peasants were organised in Kisan Sabha, and tea-garden labourers in trade unions, and there was the awakening of the tribals to a new life and to active struggle to realise their aspirations.

We will briefly describe the social condition of the Duars so that we may comprehend why and how the tribal upsurge developed in the situation. Covered with dense forest the Duars was drawn into contact with the modern world as tea gardens began to be established by European planters. The possibility of the growth of the tea industry in India opened with the passing of the Charter Act of 1833; British investors evinced great interest in this industry; in fact, tea companies headed the list of sterling companies which were registered between 1874 and 1904. The first garden in Cachar was opened in 1855; the industry spread to the Tarai in 1862 and the Duars in 1874. Within eight years 47 tea gardens were opened in the Duars; the number rose to 235 in 1901; in 1941 there were 189 tea gardens employing 141,387 labourers, of which about five thousand were temporary labourers. Roads were built and small trade centres sprang up. Along with the opening of tea gardens, the settlement of land for cultivation progressed rapidly;

lands were reclaimed mostly by the tribals; and Rajbansi cultivators came from Rangpur and Cooch Behar. The Bengal Duars Railway was constructed in 1893, and a railway workshop was opened at Domohini employing nearly 1,000 labourers. During the period 1901-11 cultivation made rapid progress in the Alipur Duars, mainly because rents were low and the land was fertile. The Dam Dim-Oldabari-Bagrakot railway was opened in 1901-2, and the Mal-Madarihat line in 1901-3. By 1921 most of the land which was not taken up by tea or remained reserved forest was brought under cultivation. Despite the fact that death-rate due to malaria was very high, there was a constant stream of immigration in the Alipur Duars during the decade 1931-41. In 1931-3 several miles of railway line were opened connecting Domohini with Barneshghat. During the second world war Alipur Duars sprang into sudden importance, and air strips were built all over the Duars and Alipur Duars sub-division[9].

The Santals and Oraons constituted the bulk of the peasant population; the Santals came from that part of Bihar and West Bengal which is drained by the Damodar and Kasai rivers, and the Oraons from Chotanagpur. It occurred to landowners that the waste land might be reclaimed if Santals were imported and settled in this region. The experiment proved such a success that the influx continued; the Santals were followed by Oraons from Chotanagpur. In fact, this is the history of land reclamation not only in the Duars but also in Dinajpur, Malada, Midnapur, Bankura, Birbhum and the Sundarbans. O'Malley, census superintendent of 1911, gives the following account of their social life:

'The system of tribal government among the Santals is closely bound up with the communal system. Its unit is the village, at the head of which is the Santal headman or manjhi. He is essential to Santal life, every public sacrifice, ceremony and festival requiring his presence.

'The manjhi summons the villagers when any question arises affecting their common interests, or when a villager has complained to him and a communal judgement is required. The meeting is called a panchayat or in Santali More-hor (literally five men), a term which probably originally signified the headman and the four other village officials. The latter are ex-officio members, and the panchayat also includes any adult male belonging to the village.

If there is dispute between Santals belonging to different villages, the people of villages meet together to decide the case. If they cannot arrive at a conclusion, or if one or both of the parties are dissatisfied with their findings, a reference is made to a full bench consisting of a parganait (who is the head of a group of villages), the village headman of the group and other influential men in the neighbourhood. As the manjhi has an assistant in the village, so the parganait has an assistant in his circle called the desh-manjhi.

'Every village has its council place (the manjhi than) where panchayats are held and petty disputes are settled. The panchayat also disposes of more serious questions, such as disputes about marriage and inheritance. Questions of a serious importance are referred to a panchayat consisting of the neighbouring manjhis under the control of the parganait.

'The tribal hunt is the one occasion in the year when the Santals act as a united tribe, all local units and official being then subordinated to the tribal session. It is a common hunt to which people are summoned by an official called dihri, who acts as priest and hunt master. The summons is sent by a sal branch being circulated. In the evening, when the hunt is over, the people meet in council. Here the manjhis and parganaits are, if necessary, brought to justice; and if anyone has to be excommunicated, his case is dealt with. Any matter, great or small, may be brought forward by anyone; if the case cannot be finally decided then, it is kept in abeyance till next year's hunt'[10].

What is relevant to this study is the fact that the Santals and Oraons became organised in trade unions and the Kisan Sabha; they were led and guided not by manjhis or village elders but by the leaders of trade unions and Kisan Sabha who were mostly drawn from Hindu middle class; instead of panchayats the trade unions and the Kisan Sabha won their confidence and stood by them as they rose in struggle to win partial economic demands.

Over the years the lands they had reclaimed passed into the hands of landowners, who were mostly Muslim, while they had passed into the army of bargadars and agricultural labour. They were inducted by a landowner to reclaim a waste. They were usually exempted from rent for the first year or two, and thereafter assessed to a produce-rent for the next few years. As the land was reclaimed and its fertility restored by good husbandry, the landowner began to be anxious to evict him and settle it with tenants willing to pay enhanced rents. In fact, the bargadars in the Duars were the original owner-cultivators who had been dispossessed of their lands by various means by the jotedar-cum-mahajan. It was the same story in other districts. The discontent of the Santals was revealed, as in a flash, in the Santal insurrection of 1855-6; it had been crushed, but not for good. Numerous disturbances, minor in nature, occurred throughout the nineteenth century and continued in the present century.

References

1. Speech by Jyoti Basu, 12 March 1947, Assembly Proceedings, Vol. 72, No. 2.
2. *The Calcutta Gazette Extraordinary*, 22 January 1947. The bill is published in full.
3. Blair B. Kling, *The Blue Mutiny*, 1966, p. 63. Kling writes: 'A regular league was formed against indigo cultivation, oaths were subscribed to by both Hindus and Mussalmans'.
4. ....
5. Suhrawardy's speech in Bengal Assembly on 28 February, 1947, Assembly Proceedings, Vol. 72, No. 1.
6. 'Peasant Unrest in North Bengal', *The Statesman*, 19 March 1947. The special correspondent blames the communists for encouraging this form of movement: 'But the communists seem to have paid little consideration to tactics.... It is they apparently who were behind the seizure of paddy that brought the police in on the side of the jotedars..... Most of the 'looting' took place in Dinajpur district where there were consequently five peasant-police clashes'.
7. *Swadhinata*, 4 February 1947. Jaymani and Bhandani attended the state conference of the Communist Party in September-October, 1947.
8. Note of Sushil Sen.
9. For an account of tea industry, see S.K. Sen, *Studies in Economic Policy and Development of India, 1848-1926*, 1966, pp. 51, 52.
10. L.S.S. O'Malley, Census Report, 1911; Bell, settlement officer in Dinajpur in 1934-40, writes that their houses, built of mud, are usually neat-looking; the women help the men in agricultural work, and enjoy almost equal status with them in social life, see J.C. Sen Gupta, West Dinajpur, 1965, p. 72.
11. ....
12. ....

23 The Dilemma

Sunil Sen

WHEN THE TEBHAGA STRUGGLE began in November 1946, Calcutta was quiet. The democratic movement had suffered a severe setback after the great Calcutta killing in August. Months passed before the democratic movement showed signs of revival. On 7 January 1947 the Mahatma started his famous 'one night one village tour' in riot-stricken Noakhali. Citizens' committees were formed in Calcutta. On 8 January the Tramway Workers' Union with a recorded membership of 8,000 served strike notice demanding a rise in the basic wage from 20 to 40 rupees. The historic strike which was to last 85 days actually began on 21st January. It was a complete strike which involved 8,000 tramway men[1] and heralded a revival of the working-class movement. By 26 January about 30,000 workers including clerical employees and industrial workers in Howrah, Lilloah, Shalimar, Kamarhati, Palta and Kushtia were on strike[2]. Yet the working class movement, compared to the July days, remained weak.

Meanwhile the students were fighting a real battle in the streets of Calcutta. On 21 January the Bengal Provincial Students' Federation, a leftwing student organisation affiliated to All-India Students' Federation, gave a call to observe Vietnam Day. A mammoth demonstration was brought out to express solidarity with the struggle of Vietnam for independence as the French went ahead with their machinations to reconquer the old Indochinese empire, machinations which were to receive a crushing blow at Dien Bien Phu. The police fired five times on the students' demonstration; one student was killed, 19 received bullet wounds, 50 were injured and about 200 students were arrested.[3] To protest against the police firing the Bengal Provincial Trade Union Congress called a general strike next day. On 22 January Calcutta was in flames. Barricades

Reproduced from *Agrarian Struggle in Bengal, 1946–7*, by Sunil Sen, *op. cit.*, pp. 58–62, pp. 65–8.

were erected; street battles were fought; students were joined by workers and urban middle class. The Suhrawardy ministry let loose an orgy of repression; the police, according to official report, opened fire on three occasions; four persons received bullet injuries, and 70 people were arrested.[4] No wonder people talked of 'the miracle of Calcutta'. No trace seemed to remain of communal bitterness. The student unrest spread to Mymensingh. On 22 January the students brought out a demonstration to protest against police firing on Calcutta students. As the demonstration entered the court compound, the police opened fire; Amalendu Ghosh, a school student, was killed on the spot, Anita Bose, a girl student of the degree class, received bullet wounds. This incident sparked off serious disturbances. Government buildings were set on fire; train services to and from Mymensingh were disrupted; there was a complete hartal in Mymensingh town.[5] Never before Mymensingh had witnessed such an upheaval in which students played the leading role.

Almost simultaneously the Hajong movement in Susang reached its climax. On 21 January a muharrior (collector employed by the landowner) was attacked by Hajong peasants as the carts carrying paddy collected from Garos were being wilfully driven over standing crops, but he escaped unhurt. On 31 January the police went to Bahertali, a village four miles from Susang, to arrest some Hajongs and their leaders. They raped two Hajong girls and dragged away Saraswati who cried for help. Rasimani, a middle-aged widow, leader of women volunteers, armed with a dagger, chased the police; she was followed by Surendra Sarkar, young Hajong cadre and several Hajong volunteers. There was a real battle on the banks of the Someswari river. Rasimani and Surendra were killed. But the Hajong volunteers continued to fight with bows and arrows and spears and the police were routed; two policemen were killed and their rifles taken away.[6]

On hearing the news of the Bahertali battle, demonstrations were held in several villages. After Chirirbandar this was the second incident in which policemen were killed. The Chirirbandar firing was followed by the Bargadars Bill; after the Bahertali firing there was severe repression. The government sent detachment of Eastern Frontier Rifles to suppress the Hajong unrest.

The *Amrita Bazar Patrika* also reported the Bahertali incident:

'On January 31 a clash took place at Bahertali between the police and the aboriginals in which two police men and a number of Hajongs were killed due to police firing. More police then entered the area and the Hajongs are believed to have retreated to the interior, leaving their property and paddy behind. From Bahertali the police are reported to be advancing, but no details are available. Reports of lawlessness have likewise been received from the Sherpur side of communist-led aboriginals who are said to be withholding rent in paddy'.[8]

The agrarian movement had indeed reached a crucial stage and several questions had come to the fore. It was now becoming clear that the government was not serious in passing the Bargadars Bill, but had embarked on repressive policy. Threshing had begun in Dinajpur, Jalpaiguri and Rangpur, but the jotedars, with their sharp cunning, were not at all keen to take their share which remained stacked in bargadars' khamar. What should the peasants do when the police would come to the village to arrest them and snatch away their paddy? To resist or not to resist police repression —this was the question which confronted the Kisan Sabha. A decision had become imperative. Should the peasants, who were in hiding, surrender or evade arrest? What would be the form of peasant resistance? What should they do with the paddy that remained stacked in their khamar? The spontaneous phase of the movement was over. In face of police repression the peasants, particularly Muslim peasants, were showing signs of vacillation. Only the Hajongs and Santals remained as militant as ever, but they comprised a small section of the rural population.

It seems that on these questions there was no clarity. In its meeting held in the second week of January 1947 the Provincial Kisan Council admitted its failure to work out 'the forms of struggle' and to strengthen the volunteer corps; the council decided to set up 'Councils of Action' in villages and to train volunteers.[9] In mid-February the Dinajpur District Committee of the Communist Party of India met to review the new situation. Despite warrants of arrest against them, most of the district leaders managed to attend this meeting held in a village about ten miles from Thakurgaon. The police had got the information that 'a special training camp would be held, and that Ananta Sing was coming from Calcutta as 'the instructor'. How and by whom this information was leaked to the police is not known. It was unanimously decided to postpone 'the training camp', and Abani Lahiri rushed to Thakurgaon town to send Ananta Sing, who had in fact arrived at Setabganj, back to Calcutta. Next morning Bhowani Sen, the then secretary of the Bengal Committee of the CPI, reached the village via Rangpur, and heartily endorsed the decision.[10] The idea of 'special training camp' was nipped in the bud; it was not to be revived during the entire phase of the tebhaga struggle.

What would be the tactical line and the forms of struggle in the new phase of the movement? The development of the movement in different regions was extremely uneven. In East Thakurgaon, for instance, the bargadars were threshing the paddy, although jotedars did not turn up to take their share. In the case of small owners who were sometimes cadres of the Kisan Sabha, the question of sharing out was amicably settled through a series of baithaks. In West Thakurgaon the bargadars did not undertake threshing despite prodding from leaders, mainly because jotedars did not come to take their share. Fear of eviction had led a small section of the bargadars, mainly Muslim, to surrender their paddy to the jotedars. In Balurgat subdivision the kholan bhanga movement was continuing. The middle peasants remained firm, but rich peasants were generally taking a hostile attitude. The urban middle class was positively hostile. Bhowani Sen put forward a new tactical line which he later elaborated in an article published in Swadhinata. His main contention seemed to be that the Kisan Sabha should now proceed to build a broader movement for the abolition of zamindari; the rallying slogan should be: land to the tiller.[11] It was a rational approach; the League ministry was also thinking of bringing a comprehensive bill for the abolition of zamindari, and the movement of the Kisan Sabha could rouse all categories of peasants against zamindari system. But under existing circumstances the slogan appeared like running after the will-o'-the-wisp. The essential pre-condition for building a broader movement was success in the continuing tebhaga struggle which was faced with severe police repression. If the government succeeded in crushing the movement there would be great demoralisation among the peasants. The immediate question therefore was if and how to resist police repression. There was no directive on this question and the movement was allowed to drift. Perhaps there was the lingering hope that the League ministry could yet be forced by public pressure to pass the Bargadars Bill.

The news of police firing at Khanpur and Thumnia became known everywhere. The Kisan Sabha unit in East Thakurgaon took the decision to hold a demonstration in Thakurgaon town to protest against police firing on the peasants. It seems that the leaders still hoped that protest demonstrations could influence government policy. There could be no other justification for holding this demonstration. Surely they did not hope that the Thakurgaon middle class which took a consistently hostile attitude to the tebhaga struggle would welcome the peasants. On the afternoon of 25 February several thousand peasants marched to Thakurgaon with the familiar slogan, 'Tebhaga Chai'. The police had already taken positions in the maidan. The procession was declared illegal; Rani Mitra and Bina Guha who had come from Dinajpur town to address the peasants were served with externment order. As the peasants began to disperse the police suddenly opened fire. The demonstration was perfectly peaceful; the peasants had come not to fight, but to hold a demonstration. Two Rajbansi peasants and Hiramon Muhammad, a poor Muslim peasant, were killed on the spot. Two Santal peasants received bullet injuries and died in hospital. Niamat, a local leader whom we have already mentioned, was wounded and his leg had to be amputated. There was hardly any reaction in Thakurgaon town; the urban middle class did not think it necessary to hold a protest meeting.[19]

Dusk had fallen when the news of Thakurgaon firing reached the villages. Rumour spread that many peasants had been killed. Hundreds of peasant cadres and volunteers rushed to Bibhuti Guha and Ajit Ray who had organised this demonstration. They demanded arms. How could they fight with lathis the police armed with guns'. What should they do now? The leaders racked their brains but could not give any answer. There was no question of resisting police attack with lathis. It was now clear that the police would shoot the peasants if there was any resistance. Retreat was the only course left. The morale of the peasants slumped, and the movement which reached new heights in Thakurgaon rapidly disintegrated.[20]

On 27 February Jyoti Basu in his assembly speech held 'the governor and the bureaucracy' as mainly responsible for sabotaging the Bargadars Bill: 'The policy of the ministry has been to ditto the action of the governor and the bureaucracy and to surrender to the vested interests .... and give way to the zamindars and jotedars on the countryside. For instance, we find that the Bargadars Bill has been thrown to the winds and successfully sabotaged. And I am sure the abolition of the zamindari system will not come about'.[21] This was the first time that a spokesman of the Communist Party publicly declared that the Bargadars Bill had been shelved.

On 26 February the *Swadhinata* published a secret circular of the Bengal government with elaborate instructions to district officers to suppress the agrarian struggle'.[22] On 28 February Saheed Suhrawardy made a long statement in the assembly which was devoted to the theme that 'lawlessness' had to be suppressed with whatever means the government had at its disposal. There was no reference to the Bargadars Bill in the whole statement. Inflated accounts of 'parallel trial courts', 'committees of action', 'volunteer corps' were fabricated to justify repression. We will quote extracts from this statement which historians are likely to pounce upon as 'primary source material':

'... there is not merely a general wave of unrest but of lawlessness and defiance of authority .... The unrest has also spread among the cultivators, fortunately in a few restricted areas, where it has taken the form of tebhaga movement, in others, of nonpayment of tanka-rent and in still others of catching fish without authorisation from beels or nonpayment of chowkidari-tax and of agricultural loans. In some places such agitation is accompanied with violence. Persons have been advised to resist arrest in spite of warrants legally issued by a court of law and to rescue persons arrested and to attack police, if necessary, to intimidating others into accepting their demand, to remove crops by force from the fields and sometimes from the houses of jotedars. Parallel trial courts have been set up and persons are brought under confinement and are convicted for opposing the movement. Personal indignities are inflicted and punishment awarded. Lands are being cultivated by force, in cases side by side with jotedars. Committees of action, volunteer corps, propaganda leaflets, secret shelters have been organised. Badges and lathis have been issued and the volunteers are taught to drill and parade. It is a matter of greatest regret to the government that innocent and law-abiding cultivators have fallen a prey to this agitation and have resorted to such steps as made it incumbent on our forces of law and order to use force against force .... Fortunately as I have stated it is confined only to a few areas of Dinajpur, Mymensingh and Jalpaiguri, although some slight rumblings can be heard elsewhere.

'Between the 7th and 17th February, 14 cases of paddy looting were reported in two unions of Balurghat thana .... This looting which has been done more or less on a mass scale in Dinajpur was a result of constant propaganda inculcating a spirit of lawlessness and definace. On the 16th of February warrant of arrest legally issued by a court of law could be executed only against three persons. Further arrests were made impossible without the interference of the armed force'.

Suhrawardy then referred to Khanpur and Thumnia incidents in Dinajpur which we have described. He continued commenting on Mymensingh upsurge;

'On the 21st January a large number of Hajongs attacked the muharrior of Susang when he was bringing home paddy which he collected from the Garos. He extricated himself with difficulty from the place. 14 Hajongs were arrested although a clash was averted as 2,000 Hajongs well-armed came to the scene. On 22nd January Hajongs trespassed into Durgapur thana. On the 26th January as many as 4,000 trespassed into the compound. They broke the fencing, damaged the telegraph wire and set fire to postal documents. On 30 January a meeting was held when it was decided to resist the police. Two incidents occurred at Bahertali when a police party arrived to execute warrants; they were chased with bows and arrows and other weapons. Two armed constables were speared to death .... Communist leaflets had been discovered in remotest villages. In some villages large stocks of tankapaddy and a number of spears, lathis and bows were discovered. As soon as the headquarters of the agitators were searched they left their villages and took to the hills.

'On 5 February a body of Hajongs were holding demonstration at Nalitabari when at the instance of the district magistrate propaganda leaflets were dropped from an aeroplane ... Reports indicated that communists were still active in certain areas in Shèrpur and Jamalpur subdivisions. Only one section of the Hajongs was now giving trouble'.

The concluding paragraph was significant: 'We are on the eve of independence. We should proceed steadily and constitutionally along the path of independence so that we might be in a position to reap its fruits'.[23]

Indeed, a turning point had come. Peaceful transfer of power was in the offing. At this point agrarian unrest appeared to be the only obstacle in their path and had to be smothered. The Bargadars Bill was buried. Scared by the sweep of the agrarian struggle the Muslim League leaders chose to be representatives of law and order, and sought to crush the movement with wholesale violence.

References

1 *The Statesman*, 22 January 1947.
2 *Ibid.*, 26 January 1947.
3 *Ibid.*, 22 January 1947.
4 *Ibid.*, 23 January 1947.
5 *Ibid.*, 24 January 1947.
6 P. Gupta, *op. cit.* In his assembly speech Suhrawardy suppressed the fact that the police raped two Hajong girls.
7 ....
8 *Amrita Bazar Patrika*, 5 February 1947. It was reported that the movement was intense in Haluaghat, Nalitabari and Sherpur; aeroplanes were seen flying over the area.
9 A. Rasul, *op. cit*, p. 157.
10 The present writer attended this meeting; of the district leaders Gurudas Talukdar and Kali Sarkar could not come.
11 *Swadhinata*, 15 February 1947.
12 ....
13 ....
14 ....
15 ....
16 ....
17 ....
18 ....
19 Ajit Ray's note; interview with B. Guha; *Amrita Bazar Patrika*, 26 February 1947.
20 Interview with B. Guha.
21 Assembly Proceedings, Vol. 72, No. 1.
22 *Swadhinata*, 26 February 1947; *Amrita Bazar Patrika*, 1 March 1947.
23 Assembly Proceedings, Vol. 72, No. 1.

24 Kakdwip Tebhaga Movement

Krishnakant Sarkar

I

YOKED TO a defective socio-economic system, ('Lotdari' system) which reduced them to tragic non-entities, the peasants of Kakdwip rose in revolt against their traditional oppressors in a bid to establish their right to live. It began as a movement of petition and protest. But the main movement, Tebhaga, and the formulation of its demand did not originate from below. It was not confined to the area and did not start until the Communist Party came into the picture. At the initial stage, the peasants could not think that their demand, Tebhaga, would ultimately be met.[1] 'The famous Kakdwip movement began', observes Mr K.B. Ray, the then President of Bengal Provincial Kisan Sabha, 'not as an independent and spontaneous action but as a part of All Bengal Tebhaga Movement sponsored by Bengal Provincial Kisan Sabha'.[2] The main objective of Tebhaga movement was to establish 'Tebhaga' principle i.e. two-thirds share of the produce for the share-cropping cultivators instead of customary half.

When the Tebhaga movement in Kakdwip broke out in 1946, very few knew about the condition of its people and of the nature of this region. Although Kakdwip is only fifty miles to the south of Calcutta the region as a part of the Sundarbans was very backward and almost inaccessible from administrative centres. Mr Kangsari Halder, the famous leader of this movement, says, 'It would not be wrong to say that before Tebhaga, the region was unknown to the Civilized World'.[3] And observing from administrative point of view, a member of the Bengal Legislative Assembly pointed out '... it seems to be that the people of this region are not under the British rule'.

As has been said earlier, the Kakdwip peasants did not move of their own, they were actually brought into the vortex of the movement by the Communist Organizers. From this one should

This article was especially written for this volume.

not come to the over-simplified conclusion that Kakdwip movement was Communist engineered one. The objective conditions were ripe enough for the movement to take a long plunge.

II

The Kakdwip area as a part of the Sundarbans of 24 Parganas district was excluded from the Permanent Settlement of 1793. The British rulers provided temporary settlement, a lease-holding system for the region. The remarkable feature of this system was that big lots of forest land were leased out to private individuals for a term of 99 years or 40 years as provided by the Grant rules of 1853 and 1879 respectively. The lease-holders, known as lotdars, were held responsible for reclamation of their lots step by step which had to be completed at the expiration of some specific years failing which they would be liable to forego all rights and interests theirin.[5] Reclamation began at the end of the last century. But it was not so easy to reclaim such big lots. Consequently, most lotdars had sublet some portions of their grants to other individuals who were called 'chakdars'. Being entitled with the rights and obligations of lotdars, the chakdars were equally held responsible to facilitate *Hat* (market), *Gola* (barn), *Ganj* (habitation) and *raiyoti* settlement.[6] Both the lotdars and chakdars were absentee landlords. Only a few chakdars lived permanently in the area. They employed their agents, known as *naibs*, managers and other persons to look after the estate and these people became the actual rulers.

For reclamation, the lotdars made some initial expenses and did only the preliminary works namely, *ak katai* (the first step of deforestation) and boundary *bandh* (construction of embankment around the lot to stop water inlets). And only after the initial stage of deforestation, they hired landless cultivators from Midnapur with the assurance of giving them tenancy right over the land they would bring under cultivation. Allured by this assurance, peasants of the lowest category came and started reclaiming their allotted lands in right earnest, but ultimately they were denied of the promised right.[7] In this connexion one writer on this subject has rightly remarked, 'Before deforestation the bhagchasis (sharecroppers) were assured of tenancy rights but even after the expiry of five years following it they were not given the ownership rights'[8].

This deprivation was, as we shall see later, the immediate cause of tension leading to peasant organization and movement in one village. In view of our investigation in the area it is well-nigh impossible on our part to accept the opinion of Dr Radha Kumud Mookerjee when he writes, 'In general, it may be stated that zamindars brought the waste and jungle under cultivation ... at their expense'.[9]

Most of the peasants who came in the hope of land had no other means save their hands and hence could not purchase land by cash.[10] Consequently, the system of production that developed in the area since the beginning was 'bhag chas' (share-cropping) at the rate of half share of the produce for each party. The total yield should be stacked at the landowner's *Khamar* (yard) instead of cultivator's. All the landlords wanted to get it introduced since they would be the party to derive the maximum from the system with the least labour and risk.

On the other hand, the cultivators, compelled by their helplessness, had submitted themselves to the yoke of share-cropping system. From our investigation in the area we have found that two main factors, namely, landlords' economic interests and cultivators' helplessness were responsible for the development of share-cropping system. It is interesting to point out that in interpreting the development of share-cropping system Dr Radhakamal Mukherjee did not see the economic factor behind it.[11] Our investigation confirms the opinion of Dr K. Mukherji who observes, 'The moneylender will not cultivate the land himself and prefers produce-rent to cash-rent since the former gives him more than the latter at the present level of prices.'[12]

The extra-ordinary development of share-cropping system in the area might be illustrated by our survey in two villages namely Budhakhali and Haripur. Out of 70 and 31 investigated families in two villages respectively it was found that 89% of the former and 64.5% of the latter were share-cropping families. It was also found that 46.4% and 54.5% families in the villages respectively were absolutely dependent on rented land. It was the picture of land-relation in two villages in which the tebhaga movement was remarkably intensive.[13] The landowners not only took away the best quality of the grains in their share, but also they looted the share-croppers as well as tenants as much as they could by extorting and exacting various subscriptions, interests on advance, *selami*, *abawbs* etc.

From individual statements of more than 40 local peasants and also some landlords' agents and police officers, we see below the types of exactions and their approximate rate prevailing in Kakdwip area before the tebhaga movement.[14]

Nos.	Name	Meaning	Approximate rate per bigha
1.	Dera-bari	(enforced borrowing by the share-croppers at the rate of 50% interest in kind subject to increase at compound rate)	1½ maund ″ ″
2.	Kayali	(wage of the weightman of share-cropping crops)	3 to 5 seers ″ ″
3.	Khamar Chwilani	(charge for preparation of landlord's yard)	2 to 4 ″ ″ ″
4.	Prachir ghera	(charge for making walls around the yard)	2 to 5 ″ ″ ″
5.	Naibiana Hisabana	(charge for account-keeping by landlord's agent)	3 to 6 ″ ″ ″
6.	Dwaroani	(charge for the service of landlord's darwan or guard)	1 to 3 ″ ″ ″
7.	Nazrana	(occasional presentation to the landlord)	1 to 4 ″ ″ ″
8.	Parbani	(charge for village festivals)	1 to 3 ″ ″ ″
9.	Selami	(annual charge for rented land)	1 to 1¼ maunds or Rs 4 to 7 ″ ″
10.	Education cess.		3 to 4 seers ″ ″

11.	Golakamti	(Paddy charged for its loss of weight that resulted from its being dried up in the landlord's barn preserved for advance to the share-croppers)	2 to 3 seers " "

It was highly illegal to exact anything from the tenants but the agents did not discriminate between the share-croppers and the tenants in so far as exaction was concerned.[15]

The number and the respective rate of exactions varied from one village to another just because of differences in the attitude of the agent concerned. The most remarkable exaction prevalent in every village was 'dera-bari'. It was compulsory for every share-cropper to take advance at the rate of 50 per cent. Interest in kind and refusal to accept advance led to eviction of share-croppers in many cases since they had no tenancy right and there was no law to protect them.[16] Another factor that brought distress to all sections of peasantry was the loss of crops by inundation of saline water due to failure or negligence of lotdars and chakdars to keep embankments in an efficient state for which they were legally responsible.[17] The pitiable plight of the cultivators of this region was reflected in the settlement Report of Sundarbans and some relevant portions of it have been stated below: 'The paddy harvested is stacked in the landlord's own barn and what he receives after deduction of landlord's half share and his previous debt to him will hardly keep his body and soul together for three or four months.... It is difficult to extricate himself from the clutches of the landlord and mahajans if he once incurs any debt from them.

In this manner the landlord can easily manipulate a large amount of cheap labour who are more submissive than assertive'.[18]

The peasants of Kakdwip, mainly the great bulk of share-cropping cultivators, were enchained to the lands of their master and the actual position of them may be compared to that of 'serf' with 'half-free status.'[19]

The social system of Kakdwip itself had certain peculiarities unfavourable for the growth of organization of the peasants at least in the initial stage. These were first, lack of unity resulting from rigid caste structure; village factional quarrels, and communal feelings; secondly, in spite of all oppressions, the allegiance and dependence of the peasants to the landlord's agents; thirdly, the attitude of the peasants to the existing socio-economic system as immutable which accounted for their passivity and conservative outlook and finally, their fear of landlord's power of money, police and *lathials* (goondas).[20] But we see that these unfavourable factors could not impede the peasant organization and movement at a time that saw the emergence of a local leader with a few followers in a village backed by some members of the Communist Party.

III

When the Kakdwip peasants had gone below the subsistence level, a heavy cyclone accompanied with devastating flood broke out on the 17th October, 1942 which affected a population more than one lakh, razed all their modest dwellings, destroyed cattles and the standing aman crops of 1942-3; this along with the great Bengal famine brought additional sufferings to the Kakdwip peasantry already in a state of ruin.[21] It was in this background that along with others Satyanarayan Chatterjee and Jyotish Roy as members of People's Relief Committee, a voluntary organization sponsored by the Communist Party, came to Kakdwip for relief work and recruited Jatin Maity of Budhakhali who had political background as a terrorist worker, sought his help in forming peasant organization in the area under the banner of Kisan Samiti of the Communist Party.[22] With the help of Kangsari Halder, Manik Hazra, Abdur Rajjak Khan, Nityananda Chowdhury who came as relief workers of the said Committee, Jatin Maity had begun to organize the peasants of Budhakhali. In 1951 B.S. Satis Shau, a share-cropper of Budhakhali, allied himself with Jatin Maity, the first local leader of Kakdwip. Next year they were joined by five other peasants of the village and the cumulative effect of all these was the formation of a secret organization in the area.[23] That the peasant organization at Budhakhali, though not operating openly, created some impact was proved by a joint petition filed secretly by some peasants of the village before the SDO against the manager Bijoy Banerjee's rack-renting. The SDO acted upon it which went in favour of the peasants, the Officer warned the manager and thereby the peasants foiled the manager's attempt to evict his share-croppers involved in the matter.[24]

This success, however minor, at the initial stage created the most favourable situation for organization in the village.

The resentment caused by rack-renting was further accentuated by Bata Krishna Shau's (a chakdar as well as usurer of Budhakhali) calculated violation of the customary principle of 'dera-bari' (50 per cent interest of advance). How vicious was his attempt appears from his insistence that the peasants were required to pay in advance in cash rate of 50 per cent interest to be charged on the market price of paddy borrowed. Besides, those who begged for advance, received ill-treatment. The condition arising out of it facilitated a better prospect for organization.[25]

The District Committee of Kisan Samity of the Communist Party then decided to hold a peasants' conference in 1944 at Budhakhali and vigorous propaganda was carried on to ensure its success. Addressed by Nityananda Chowdhury, Kangsari Halder, Manik Bazra, Jyotish Roy to name some of the leaders, led to the formation of Kisan Samity at Budhakhali, in the same year.[26]

The formation of peasant organisation at Haripur can be attributed to the complete identity of Gajen Mali's personal cause with those of his community. Deprived of his land of one hundred fifty bighas and its crops, because of Dwarik Samanta's (landlord) conspiracy, Gajen, who had urban background, in a bid to have legal redress set for Diamond Harbour Court. When in the midst of way, he was persuaded by Jatin Maity of Budhakhali to give up this idea and urged him to set himself to the task of organising the village peasants for redress.[27] Consequent to that, a meeting was held to protest against the various atrocities including dishonouring of their women at 'Tankpukur Ground' of Haripur. This led to the formation of Kisan Samity organization in this village of which Gajen became the president, Balaram the Secretary and eleven others including Kshirode Bera, Atul Santra, Ananta Kuiti, Girish Mandal ordinary members.[28] Sharply reacting against the growing unrest and protest of the peasants, so long submissive, Dwarik Samanta took the help of the police to nip the peasant organization in the bud. To serve the interest of the landlord the police arrested three share-croppers involved in the protest movement on charge of dacoity which, however, could not be established in the court and the result was acquittal and release of the arrested peasants. This situation immediately paved the ground for peasant organization.[29]

Our study of peasant organization and movement in two selected villages show that organization of the peasants in the initial stage is dependent on some factors: (i) quality of local leadership, (ii) political party's support, (iii) initial success of movement against the landlords or their agents (as happened at Budhakhali in foiling the manager's attempt of eviction) (iv) the reaction of peasants against the violation of customary practice (as happened at Budhakhali in the case of Chakdar) (v) sudden attack of grievous nature (as the case of Dwarik Samanta of Haripur).

Another factor which had influenced the Kakdwip peasant movement was the impact of the Midnapore Salt movement and heroic mass movement of August 1942. Since most of the peasants of Kakdwip (86% of Budhakhali and 60% of Haripur) came from Midnapore, many of them had experience and background of movements.[30] The local leaders of Kakdwip movement, namely, Jatin Maity, Ananta Kuiti, Sujoy Barik had political background due to their involvement in movements which broke out at Midnapore.[31]

When the peasant organization in some form had already been developed in a few villages, Bengal Provincial Kisan Sabha gave its 'Tebhaga Call' in September, 1946. In this connexion it may be pointed out that what Sunil Sen says about the origin of the Tebhaga[32] runs counter to Bhowani Sen's opinion which is as follows: 'Since 1938 Bengal Provincial Kisan Sabha had been persistently porpagating for the abolition of Zamindari and also for conceding the demand for Tebhaga. I am adding by way of supporting the former's conclusion in regard to the origin of the Tebhaga demand that it owed more to recommendations of the Land Revenue Commission of 1938 than to the igenuity of the Sabha.'[33]

Since Tebhaga was for the interest of share-cropping cultivators, the peasants of Budhakhali of whom about 89% were share-croppers first responded to the call. Along the tebhaga, other slogans were '*Zamindari Khatam Karo*' (abolish Zamindari), '*Nij Khamare dhan tolo*' (stock crop to own yard), '*Samasta Zulum Bandh Karo*' (stop all oppression), *Bhag jamir rasid chaii* (give record of rights on rented land), etc. The tebhaga slogan became so popular that the movement spread in all parts of the area. In Kakdwip, where it became remarkably intensified were Munsif's lot, Fatikpur, Bamanagar, Bisalakshmipur, Dwariknagar, Berar lot, Sibrampur, Radhanagar, Durganagar, Chandanpiri, Layalganj, Haripur, Rajnagar, Debnibas and from Lakshmipur to Fragarganj. Everywhere the share-cropping cultivators were being organized almost spontaneously under the leadership of Kisan Samity. Inspired by Kakdwip, peasants of Mathurapur and Sagar Island started tebhaga movement spontaneously without Samiti's leadership. This is to indicate the popularity of the call.[34]

Everywhere in Kakdwip Kishan Samitis were formed on Union basis; at the bottom was the local committee. Each Union Kisan Samiti had a working Committee consisting of 6/7 members. During tebhaga, tebhaga Committees were formed with the consent of common peasants in the village meetings. As most of the peasants were illiterate public meetings, gharoa meetings (indoor meetings) processions, tebhaga songs and geets, tarja (a type of rural song) on tebhaga were the main vehicles of propaganda.[35] They used to sing tebhaga songs early in the morning through the village paths and meetings were held regularly for awakening the sharecroppers.

As regards economic resources, the Kakdwip peasant movement at the outset had to depend on financial assistance of the Communist Party. But later on the organisation became financially self-sufficient. The local peasant found interest in collecting 1 to 2 sheers of paddy per bigha and one anna as annual subscription of the Kisan Samiti. It is reported that peasants did not always pay their subscription generously.[36]

Decision-making is an important factor in every movement. In the Kakdwip peasant movement, the Communist Party leaders took decisions which were expressed through the Kisan Samiti. But it was not always true that what the C.P.I. leaders decided was always followed by the peasants of Kakdwip. As regards decision-making, the Communist Party's decision regarding the movement had to undergo a change when the peasants of Kakdwip took a different attitude from that which the Party in its policy sought to adopt. This might be illustrated by the fact that due to severe repression in 1947 the Communist Party had to decide that the share-croppers of Tebhaga movement should stock paddy at the Jotedar's yard. But the Kakdwip share-croppers' movement reached such a height that the peasants of this area were reluctant to follow the party's decision. Consequently, the Party had to modify its policy and asked the peasants of different areas to act as the situation warranted.[37]

The Kakdwip peasantry, though most of whom were share-croppers, did not constitute a homogeneous group. They regarded themselves as 'poor', 'middle' and 'rich' in terms of their existing poverty and prosperity. The term 'poor' stood for those families which could not support themselves for several months of the year. Most of the poor peasants had no land of their own and were absolutely dependent on rented land. They themselves worked and did not employ agricultural labour. The landless wage-labourers belonged to this category. The 'middle' category was almost self-sufficient in food-stuff; some had a few maunds' surplus, while others had a little deficit. Generally, the families of the category had some bighas (20-70 bighas) of their own, some bighas of rented land and a few of them employed wage-labourers.

The rich family was one which possessed considerable amount of land (70-125 bighas) and did not rely on rented land. On the contrary, some of them supplied land to share-croppers for rent and they employed agricultural labourers and used to advance 'bari' for incurring interest.

Now let us see the attitude of each section of the peasantry to the Tebhaga movement. Investigations in two villages, namely Budhakhali and Haripur show that about 65% of the former and 41.7% of the latter were 'poor' families. And of the 'poor' category about 89% at Budhakhali and 100% at Haripur actively participated in the movement. It is clear that amongst the poor, there was the maximum support and involvement. Of the poor families we also see that 64.29% at Budhakhali and 100% at Haripur were *bhag chasis* (share-croppers). The reason for the maximum involvement of poor section was that since tebhaga movement was intended to bring to the share-croppers an additional gain of one-fourths of the total produce, it was the prospect of gain that led them (89% at Budhakhali and 100% at Haripur) to be champions of the movement.

Of the poor sections of Budhakhali peasants which remained

or sought to remain passive was 6.6%. Their passivity was attributed to the fact of their being wage-labourers, and seeing no prospect of economic gain in the Tebhaga movement, they did not join the movement. Among the poor who opposed the movement was 4.45% and their attitude of opposition was due to the fact of their being supporters of the Congress which was the rival to the Communist Party that led the movement.

The percentage of middle category families at Budhakhali and Haripur was 27.1% and 54.8% respectively. Of this category, 66% at Budhakhali and 32.29% at Haripur actively supported the movement.

The nature of attitude of this section was largely determined by the prospect of gain from the lands they cultivated as share-croppers.

Among the peasants of middle section, 31.6% and 23.5% families in the two aforesaid villages respectively remained passive and were not involved in the movement. At Budhakhali some of the 'middle' families remained passive due to the fact of their having modest dwellings very near to the *Kutchery* of the Manager. At Haripur it was reported that since some families of this category could support themselves through the customary rate, they did not join the movement in order to avoid conflict with the landlords' agent.

Among the middle category, peasants who opposed the movement were 5% at Budhakhali and 29% at Haripur. The main cause of their opposition was that they belonged to Congress.

The rich families formed 8.6% and 3.2% of the total families investigated at Budhakhali and Haripur respectively. Of such families of the first village only 33.3% took part in the movement. This was because of the past grievances they had against the Manager, Bejoy Banerjee led them to identify themselves with the anti-lotdar movement. Half of the rest were passive as they did not like the Communist movement and the other half were vocally opponent because of their uncomfortable position they found themselves in, because of the share-croppers' demand for the two-third of the produce in their rented land.

At Haripur, only 3.2% rich families were against the Communist Party and opposed the movement.[38]

Now from analysis of relevant data we may make certain conclusions and generalizations regarding the attitude of different sections of the peasantry to the tebhaga movement.

1 Apart from other considerations, a peasant movement that incorporates in its programme one main demand which can assure maximum benefit to the largest number of a peasant society can ensure the largest participation (the case of involvement of the poor who formed the great bulk of Kakdwip population).

2 The rich peasants' past grievances against the landlords can be a factor to have an extra bit to their support for the movement.

3 Another contributory factor determining an attitude of support was the sense of fellow-feeling or community-sentiment generated by the *boisterous* course of the agitation.

4 Apart from economic motivation, political belief of one brand or another is a factor that determines the attitude of a small section (not large in number) to the movement.

The factors that account for an attitude of passivity and non-involvement are: (1) the remote possibility of any perceptible gain; the non-involvement of a section of the poor (the case of poor wage-labourers) is a case in point; (2) a state of self-sufficiency in the *statusquo* (the case of some middle peasants); (3) the desire to avoid conflict can lead a section of the peasantry to remain passive and non-involved (the case of some peasants belonging to the middle category); (4) fear from the landlord class may keep a section inactive and passive.

In general, the fear of economic loss is the main cause of reaction in the case of lotdars and chakdars.

With regard to the nature of leadership of this movement, we could clearly distinguish them into two groups—the leaders who came as members of the Communist Party to uphold the peasants' cause without personal interest; and those local leaders who personally suffered because of the extant socio-economic system. At the initial stage of organization, the leaders of the first group was less effective and had little direct contribution.[39] It was the local leadership that was most effective in the formative stage. The leaders of the first group assumed bigger role when the organization and movement developed to a certain extent.

Another fact regarding leadership was that it was the poor section of the peasantry which constituted the leading cadre of the movement. At Budhakhali, among the five initial leaders, it was found that four belonged to the poor and one to the middle section.⁴⁰ The case was similar at Haripur. Here out of the thirteen leaders who were associated with the movement from the very start, the three including Gajen belonged to the category of middle peasantry and the rest with the exception of one (whose actual economic position could not be ascertained) belonged to the poor category.⁴¹

The relationship between the leaders and the participants was very cordial. The peasants followed what the leaders said them to do. They were very simple. Unlike its middle class counterpart, they followed their leaders without reservation. The simplicity of the peasants might be illustrated by the fact that when the peasants were told that the police did not possess the key to their rifles to open fire, they took it to be true.⁴²

The share-croppers in hundreds assembled in the harvesting field of those land-owners who were unwilling to concede their demand. The peasants armed themselves with traditional weapons, namely, *lathi*, *vali*, arrows etc. while women depended on jhanta, (brooms), boti (sharp cutters), sand and chillipowder. In the harvesting session of 1946-7 the peasants could seize paddy and stacked them to their own *khamar* or *panchayat khamar*. The unity, militancy and organizational strength forced the land-lords to concede the demand. One of the factors that helped the success was the attitude of the then Suhrawardy Government which did not take severe steps to suppress it nakedly. Instead, the Government had conceded the tebhaga demand and the Bengal Bargadars Temporary Bill was notified in *Calcutta Gazette* on 22.1.1947 and the Bill was also introduced in the Assembly.

In February-March 1947 came the police party in the villages of Kakdwip and they were housed at landlords *kutcheries*. The landlords agents and Chakdars also bore the expenses for the police since they got immense help from them.⁴⁴ Apart from police help, they gathered *lathials* (goondas). In the harvesting session of 1947-8, the landlords' agents immediately took the help of Police who promulgated Section 144 Cr. P.C. in many harvesting fields thus preventing the share-croppers from harvesting. More cases—both Civil and Criminal—were instituted against the militant cadres and leaders. In the latter part of the year 1947, the Congress came to power, and many leaders and cadres including

Jatin Maity were arrested on grounds of security. But the peasants could not be subdued. Defying the prohibitory order they assembled in the field with their traditional weapons for harvesting. Some were deputed to watch on the police and they used conch to alarm the peasants when police was found approaching. But as a result of combined attack by landlords' lathials and armed police, the peasants could not protect their crops. The Government of West Bengal on 1st January, 1948 declared the whole area under the jurisdiction of Kakdwip and Sagar Police Station as disturbed area.[45] And police repression became so severe that the peasants failed to harvest and crops of many share-croppers were destroyed in the field. Ultimately the Kakdwip Tebhaga movement failed to withstand the combined attack of police and landrolds' lathials and thus the Tebhaga movement ended.

In Kakdwip movement women had played a remarkable role. Their courage and sacrifice are worth mentioning. It was found that out of 70 families of Budhakhali, women of 25 families took active part in the movement and developed leadership.[46]

The Tebhaga movement, the most significant event in the Kakdwip area, had brought about immediate as well as far-reaching changes.

i) In the harvesting session of 1946-47, the movement was successful and in the next session, it was partly successful.
ii) It was the movement by which all illegal exactions were done away with for ever.
iii) 'Dera-bari' and eviction ceased.
iv) All sorts of ill-treatments, ranging from physical torture to the dishonouring of women came to be a story of the past.
v) The movement brought Kakdwip to the attention of the Government. To take the edge out of the Communist movement, the B.C. Roy Ministry provided in its budget for the financial year of 1952-3 a portion of Rs. 1,50,000 earmarked for 'the Communist affected area', which seemed definitely to be the Kakdwip area.[47]
vi) The tebhaga movement of Kakdwip had undeniably contributed towards the agrarian land-reform laws of the subsequent years.
vii) Over and above all, what is more significant was that within a few years the peasantry of Kakdwip underwent a revolu-

tionary change in their thinking and outlook in that they were not only able to shake off their servile and submissive mentality, but also elevated themselves from the 'half-free' status of a serf to the status of a Citizen.

References

1. Written statements by Smt Laksmipriya Sautia and Purna Chandra Samanta of Budhakhali, 11.10.71.
2. Written statement by Krishna Binode Ray, president of Bengal Provincial Kisan Sabha (1946), 30.6.72.
3. *Tebhaga Sangram Rajat Jayanti Smarak Grantha* (in Bengali), p. 64; also see *Diamond Harbour Hitaishee* (a local fortnightly in Bengali), 15.4.58.
4. Speech by Patiram Roy, *Bengal Legislative Assembly Proceedings*, Vol. LXIX, No. 2, 12.3.45.
5. F.E. Pargiter, *Revenue History of the Sundarbans* p. 93, Superintendent, Government Printing, Bengal Govt. Press, Alipore, Bengal, 1934.
6. Written statement by Sachindra Chandra Ghose, Chakdar of Layalganj, 24.10.73.
7. Written statement by Gunadhar Mali, brother of Gajen Mali of Layalganj, 30.1.74.
   Written statement by Srinath Ranjit of Layalganj, 1.12.73; also see Kalantar (Special issue), p. 46.
8. Suprakash Ray, *Kakdwip Sonarpore Bhangorer Krishak Sangram* (in Bengali), p. 5 Radical Book Club, Calcutta, 1967.
9. *Report of the Land Revenue Commission*, Bengal, Vol. 2, p. 234, 1940.
10. Interview with Charu Bhandari, an Ex-Minister of Congress Government, 22.6.72.
    Written statement by Sachindra Chandra Ghose, 24.10.73.
11. Radhakamal Mukerjee, *Land Problems of India*, p. 361-62, 1933.
12. Karuna Mukherjee, *Land Reforms*, p. 189. Calcutta, H. Chatterjee & Co., 1952.
13. The Survey was made by the present writer.
14. Individual statements were given by Jatin Maity (local leader), Jagannath Maity (local leader), Kumud Shau (local leader), Dhananjoy Das (a militant cadre), Gunadhar Maity (local leader), Prahlad Samanta (an ordinary cadre), Gagen Barik, Kanai Bera, Bhusan Jana (ordinary cadre), Satish Shau (local leader), Banamali Mandal (ordinary cadre), Sahadeb Karan (ordinary cadre) Smt Kaishalya Mandal, Nitya Jana, Kanan Das (women leaders) of Budhakhali; Katrick Chandra Mali (elder brother of the late Gajen Mali), Gunadhar Mali, Jagatmohan Kauti, Bijoy Mandal (local leader), Kshirode Bera (local leader) of Haripur, Jhatu Charan Rahul (cadre), Lakshmikanta Chatterjee (a *mohurar* of lotdar), Bhupati Mohan Biswas *(Naib)*, Bhabaranjan Bhattacharjee (President of Budhakhali Union Board, 1942 to 1951) to name a few of them.
15. Act X of 1859, (B.T. Act) Section 10, *West Bengal Code* (as modified upto 13th June, 1951).

16 Statement of Laksmi Sautia (a peasant woman) of Budhakhali, 11.10.71. She stated that her father was evicted on account of refusal to take 'bari'. Also statements of many local peasants of Budhakhali, Haripur and other villages.
17 Bengal Legislative Assembly Proceedings, Vol. LXVII, No. 3, 29.3.44. T.N. Mukherjea, Minister of Revenue Department admitted that due to negligence of lotdars and jotedars, the embankments had occasionally remained in damaged condition as a result of which the peasants suffer from loss of crops.
18 *Settlement Report*, 24 Parganas para 30.
Also see Bengal Legislative Assembly Proceedings, Session 1, Vol. 71, p. 28.
19 Mr Charu Bhandary has assessed their position as serfs.
20 Written statement by Manik Hazra, a leader of Kakdwip Movement. For casteism, communalism etc. a personal letter (21.5.52) of the late Ananta Kuiti of Haripur; also statements of Jatin Maity and Jagannath Maity of Budhakhali.
21 Bengal Legislative Assembly Proceedings, 1944 Vol. LXVIII No. 1.
In the area there was loss of 1390 human lives, cattle—23,743 and damage of houses 25, 201. For an account of collection of funds of the people's Relief Committee which worked in the field, see *Amrita Bazar Patrika* 18.11.1942.
22 Interview with Jatin Maity of Budhakhali.
23 Written statement by Satish Shau, 13.10.73.
24 Interview with Jatin Maity.
25 Written statements by Gunadhar Maity of Budhakhali, (also by some other peasants) 13.10.71.
26 Written statement by Manik Hazra (one of the leaders) 26.12.74.
27 Written statements by Gunadhar Mali (younger brother of the late Gajen Mali) and Kshirode Bera. Also interview with Jatin Maity.
28 Written statement by Kshirode Bera (a local leader), 2.2.74.
29 Written statement by Kshirode Bera, 2.2.74.
30 The investigation was made by the present writer.
31 Interview with Jatin Maity.
32 Sunil Sen holds; "It was from this recommendation (the recommendation of the Land Revenue Commission, 1940) that tebhaga, the battle cry of bargadars in 1946-7, originated"—*Agrarian Struggle in Bengal*, People's Publishing House, New Delhi, 1972, p. 15.
33 *Tebhaga Sangram Rajat Jayanti Smarak Grantha* (in Bengali), p. 10, Calcutta, 1973.
Also see Abdullah Rasul's *Krishak Sabhar Itihas* (in Bengali) p. 103, National Book Agency, Calcutta.
For the relevant portions of Land Revenue Commission's Recommendation, see *Report of the Land Revenue Commission, Bengal* Vol. 1, p. 69. The relevant portion of the recommendations is the following:
'Our recommendation is that provision of Sir John Kerr's Bill should be resorted by which it was proposed to treat as tenants bargadars who supply the plough, cattle and agricultural implements. ... We shall recommend that the share of the crop legally recoverable from them should be one third instead of half ...'
34 Statement by Manik Hazra, 26.12.74.
35 Written statement by Bhowani Sen (member of the Politbureau of the C.P.I. in 1948-9, Secretary of Bengal Provincial Committee of the C.P.I. in 1943-8), 25.9.41.
Also written statements by Kangsari Halder, Manik Hazra and others. Dhananjoy Das of Budhakhali has given manuscripts of some tebhaga *geet, tarja,* etc.
36 Written statements by Jatin Maity, and also by some local peasants.

37 Written statements by Bhowani Sen, Abdur Rajjak Khan, Jatin Maity and Kangsari Halder.
38 The survey was conducted by the present writer.
39 Statement by Jatin Maity, 19.10.71
40 Investigation was made by the present writer.
41 Interview with Kshirode Bera of Haripur. He was one of those who formed the Kisan Organization, 2.2.74.
42 Written statements by Smt. Kanan Bala Das, a woman leader of Budhakhali and also by Dhananjoy Das of Budhakhali, 14.10.71.
43 Written statements by Bhowani Sen, Abdur Rajjak Khan, Kangsari Halder and Jatin Maity; also *West Bengal Assembly* Proceedings, Official Report, No. 2 Vol. 72, 10.3.47.
44 Interviews with Sachindra Chandra Ghose, a chakdar of Layalganj and Bhupati Mohan Biswas, a naib of Budhakhali.
45 From the High Court Judgment *Kangsari Halder-vs-the State*.
46 Investigation was made by the present writer.
47 Government of West Bengal, *West Bengal Budget* 1952-3, p. 26.

25 Social Origins of the Peasant Insurrection in Telangana (1946-51)

D.N. Dhanagare

THE REVOLT in Telangana and the adjoining districts of the Andhra delta was one of the two post-war insurrectionary struggles of peasants in India.[1] It was launched by the Communist Party of India (CPI) as a sequel to the shift in its earlier policy of collaboration with the Congress giving way to a strategy of encouraging or initiating insurrectionary partisan struggles. The revolt began in the middle of 1946 and lasted over five years till it was called off in October 1951. It resulted in land reform legislation produced some perceptible changes in the agrarian social structure of the region.

The Telangana peasant revolt is often considered as paradigmatic and has attracted widespread attention.[2] In this paper we shall examine both its general and specific features. The focus will be mainly on the structural setting and the class character of the revolt and on the specific historical conditions that shaped its character.

To very briefly outline the framework of the study, we define as 'peasant' anyone who earns his livelihood from cultivation of land; the class of absentee landlords and rentiers are, however, excluded. Peasantry is not itself an internally homogeneous social category. The contradictions existing within a peasant or agrarian society and its internal differentiation and conflicting interests have been viewed here from the Marxian angle of 'class' and 'class conflict'. The model of agrarian classes consisting of the 'rich', 'middle', and 'poor' peasants in addition to the landless labourers is usually drawn from the works of Lenin and Mao Tse-tung. However, its application to the Indian and specially to the Telangana

Reproduced from *Contributions to Indian Sociology (NS)* Delhi, Number 8, 1974.

situation calls for caution. First, like all other social classifications, this model is also regionally specific. Here the extent of property owned in land becomes a crucial variable. We have considered peasants owning 25 acres of land (or 10 acres of irrigated land), or more, as rich, those having an average (in that region) holding or below as poor and the rest as middle peasants. Secondly, we also realize that in India a host of social cleavages other than class, such as caste, kinship or ethnic ties ('community type bonds') cut across the economic class situations. Our use of the term 'agrarian class' does not imply that these primordial loyalties are either non-existent or play no part in class formation. In other words, it implies Marx's notion of 'class in itself' i.e., unity of economic interests only and not his notion of 'class for itself'. We do not suggest that those who occupy the same class position are necessarily aware or politically conscious of their collective interests.

I

Land Control and Social Structure in Telangana under the Nizams

Hyderabad was one of the largest princely states in India before independence. A political structure from medieval Muslim rule had been preserved intact till the state merged into the Indian Federation in 1948 (GOI (i), Smith 1950: 27-8). After the advent of the British in India, the Nizams in Hyderabad simply retained in form a semblance of sovereignty which they exercised with the tacit consent of the representatives of the British Crown. Right from the troubled days of the Mutiny (1857) through the two world wars, the Nizams liberally contributed to and ardently supported the British Empire.

The Hyderabad state covered a substantial part of the southern plateau in the Indian peninsula. Its total area was some 82,000 square miles; its predominantly Hindu population totalled 18.6 million in 1951. There were three linguistic regions in the state: (*i*) Telangana—nine districts of Telugu-speaking people; (*ii*) Marathwada—five districts of Marathi-speaking people; and (*iii*) three Kannada-speaking districts. The first formed a majority of 47 per cent in the total population while the other two regions shared the rest except the 12 per cent accounted for by Urdu-speaking Muslim (Qureshi 1947: 30-1).

The agrarian social structure in Hyderabad was like a page out of feudal history. There were two main types of land tenure:

(*i*) *Khalsa* or *diwani* tenures implied what in some parts of India is called *raiyatwari*, that is the peasant proprietary system. About 60 per cent of the total land was held under these tenures in 1941. The landholders were not called owners *per se* but were treated as *pattadars* (registered occupants). The actual occupants within each *patta* were called *shikmidars*, who had full rights of occupancy but were not registered. As the pressure on land grew, the shikmidars, previously the cultivators, began to lease out lands to subtenants (*asami-shikmis*) for actual cultivation. The latter were tenants-at-will having neither legal rights in land nor any protection against eviction (Narayan 1960: 58-9). As we shall see later, the process of subinfeudation had steadily penetrated deep into the system of raiyatwari tenures, particularly from 1920 to 1950.

(*ii*) There were some special tenures called jagirs. *Sarf-e-khas* was obviously the most important of them being assigned to the Nizam himself as Crown lands. Scattered in several parts of the state, these covered a total area of 8,109 square miles (1,961 villages), and fetched revenues totalling about 20 million rupees, which met the Nizam's household, retinue and other expenses and also partly met the cost of his army (Khusro 1958: 4-5; Roth 1947: 1-2).

There were various other types of jagirs, besides Sarf-e-khas but their details are not relevant for our purpose. The jagirdari system of land administration was the most important feature of the political organization of Hyderabad. The Nizam created his own noblemen and bestowed on them a distinguished rank and order—each with a large grant of land. In return the trusted noblemen undertook to maintain an army for the Nizam to rely on in time of need. These jagirs were thus typically feudal tenures scattered in different parts of the State, including 6,500 villages and covering some 25,000 square miles, about a third of the state's total area (Qureshi 1947: 112-18). Over the years the number of jagirdars steadily multiplied. In 1922 there were 1,167 jagirdars in the Nizam's dominion; in 1949 their number had gone up to 1,500 (Khusro 1958: 4).

The conditions were, however, far more oppressive on the jagir lands than on the Sarf-e-khas. The civil courts had no jurisdiction over the former and therefore the jagirdars and their agents were free to extort from the actual cultivators a variety of illegal taxes and thus to fleece them. The conditions remained practically unchanged until the jagirdari system was abolished in 1949 (Khusro 1958: 5).

The khalsa land produced no better alternative. On such lands, *deshmukhs* and *deshpandes* were the hereditary collectors of revenue for groups of villages. As the system of direct collections was introduced in the last quarter of the nineteenth century, these intermediaries were granted *vatans* (annuities) based on a percentage of the past collections. This only propped up their position in the agrarian hierarchy. Very often the deshmukh landlord—a figure roughly half-way between the bureaucratic official and the feudal seigneur—himself became the newly appointed village revenue official or had at least an access to land records. His influence thus permitted him to grab lands by fraud which, in countless instances, reduced the actual cultivator to the status of a tenant-at-will or a landless labourer.

Nowhere in Hyderabad was the feudal exploitation of the peasantry more intense than it was in the Telangana districts.[3] Here some of the biggest landlords, whether jagirdars or deshmukhs, owned thousands of acres of land each. Such concentration of land ownership was more pronounced in Nalgonda, Mahbubnagar, and Warangal districts than elsewhere (Sundarayya 1972a: 9-18). Significantly, it was this region which was the locus of the peasant insurrection in 1946-51.

In the local idiom these powerful jagirdars and deshmukhs were called *durra* (also spelled as *dora*), meaning 'sir', 'master' or 'lord of the village'. A durra, often a combination of landlord, moneylender, and village official, traditionally enjoyed several privileges including the services of occupational castes in return for some payments either in cash or in kind. But he tended to exact these services free owing to his power and position (Gray 1970: 119-20). Such exactions had become somewhat legitimized by what was known as the *vetti* system under which a landlord could force a family from among his customary retainers to cultivate his land and to do one job or the other—whether domestic, agricultural or official—as an obligation to the master. The vetti exactions were thus a symbol of the dominance of landlords in

Telangana. Most of the agricultural labourers, on whom the vetti obligations fell, were from the lower and untouchable castes of Malas and Madigas (Sundarayya 1972a: 12-4).

Like the vetti, the system of *bhagela* serfdom was prevalent in Warangal and Nalgonda districts. Similar to the Pannaiyals of Tanjore or the Dublas of Gujarat, the bhagelas, drawn mostly from aboriginal tribes, were customary retainers tied to their masters by debt. Working as domestic or menial labourers, they could never repay the debts and hence had to work for their masters generation after generation on a pittance. Legislation passed in 1936 to limit and curb bhagela serfdom had remained largely ineffective (Qureshi 1947: 72-3). It seems that the vetti and bhagela arrangements were perversions of the traditional Hindu *jajmani* system which was based on the principle of reciprocal exchanges. Its Telangana variant was highly exploitative, being based on the economic power wielded by those jajmans, like durras, who owned land.

Among the substantial landowners and pattadars in Telangana districts, Brahmins were once predominant. With the rise of the Reddis and Kammas—the two notable castes of peasant proprietors—the influence of Brahmins as a landowning caste declined, although in the field of politics they continued to be powerful. Komtis, a caste of traders and moneylenders, had considerable influence on the economic life in the countryside. From the turn of the century, however, Marwadi *sahukars* gradually penetrated rural Telangana and established their ascendancy as moneylenders although the Komtis still remained on the scene as traders, shopkeepers, and merchants. The bulk of the rural masses—poor peasants, unprotected tenants, share-croppers, and agricultural labourers—came either from lower untouchable castes, such as the Malas and Madigas,[4] or from tribal groups like the Hill Reddis, Chenchus, Koyas, Lambadis, and Banjaras.[5] These tribal communities had longstanding grievances against the government on account of its taxes and levies, against moneylenders and revenue officials who usurped their lands, and also against private contractors who exploited the tribal labourers in the forestworks, on construction sites, or in mines and collieries (Furer-Haimendorf 1945: 5-7, 39-46, 66-75).

Two important aspects of the agrarian economy of an otherwise backward region like Telangana must be noted here. First, the development of irrigation facilities and cultivation of commercial crop was taking place since the late nineteenth century. The main commercial crops of Telangana—ground-nuts, tobacco, and castor-seeds—were grown in Nalgonda, Mahbubnagar, Karimnagar, and Warangal districts. Both the total acreage and the produce of commercial crops increased steadily and after 1925 commercial farming assumed an increasingly greater importance in the regional economy (Narayan 1960: 27-41). Secondly, the development of commercial farming was not, however, matched by any corresponding growth of towns, of industrial enterprise, and markets, nor even of transport and communication facilities. Consequently, the cultivators had to depend almost entirely on urban moneylenders, traders, merchants, and businessmen who controlled the few and highly centralized markets in Telangana for the sale of their produce. Local retailers, agents, and village sahukars helped the urban commercial interests in securing the produce from the cultivators and thus managed to have a share in the profits of the marketing enterprise.

Land alienation increased considerably between 1910 and 1940, particularly during the economic depression, when much land, previously owned by tribal peasants, passed into the hands of non-cultivating urban interests, mostly Brahmins, Marwadis, Komtis, and Muslims (Furer-Haimendorf, 1945: 41-3). Economic investigations carried out in 1928-30 showed that in Warangal district alone nine per cent of the total land and 25 per cent of the irrigated land had changed hands. Most of the land thus transferred went either to big landlords and deshmukhs or to sahukars (from the Marwadi and Maratha castes), traders and non-cultivating pattadars who dominated the economic life of the district (Iyengar 1930: I, 34).

As a result of the growing land alienation many actual occupants or cultivators were being reduced to the status of tenants-at-will, sharecroppers or landless labourers. This trend dominated till 1930 or so. Thereafter, the proportion of non-cultivating occupants and of cultivators of land, wholly or mainly unowned, began to decline. Owner-cultivators and agricultural labourers, on the contrary, steadily increased in number in Hyderabad state as a whole. Their proportions in 1951 were 61 and 25 per cent respectively (for details see Narayan 1960: 10). These shifts in the agrarian class structure point to the gradual development of the rich peasant sector of the agrarian economy.

Significantly, the decline of the number of non-cultivating occupants and the increase in the number of cultivating owners and landless labourers were more marked in the Telangana districts, particularly in Mahbubnagar, Nalgonda, Nizamabad, and Warangal (Iyengar 1951: 37).

The rise of the 'rich-peasant' sector, however, did not supplant the 'landlord-tenant' sector of the rural economy completely.[6] The absentee landlords were very much there though their number was declining after 1930. Nor did it signify any fundamental change in the modes and relations of production. In fact, where rich pattadars held holdings too large to manage, they tended to keep a certain amount of irrigated land to be cultivated with the help of hired labourer and turned over most of their dry lands either to bhagela serfs or to tenant cultivators on very high produce rents. (Bedford 1967: 126-7, 150-52).

What was happening on the agrarian scene in Telangana from the last quarter of the nineteenth century till 1930 or so could be summed up thus: the system of subsistence agriculture had undergone a gradual transformation giving way to the new market or cash economy, without any corresponding change in the social arrangements on land. The modes of production and exchange remained pre-capitalist or semi-feudal and emerged as the major source of discontent among the poor peasantry. During the economic depression (1929-34) even the well-to-do cultivators, substantial pattadars or rich peasants, were badly affected owing to the fall in whosesale prices. Although the prices recovered slightly between 1936 and 1940, they were not even half as high as the price level of 1922. Throughout the 1930s, therefore, the cash incomes of all those cultivators who produced for the market fell considerably. The price-trends strengthened the position of moneylenders and traders who tightened their grip on indebted small pattadars and tenants. A committee appointed in 1939 for investigating the status and conditions of tenants in the State recommended a minimum tenurial security but without any results till 1945. Fearing accrual of tenants' occupancy rights on their lands, the landlords had resorted to large-scale evictions of tenants. A Tenancy

Act, passed in 1945, remained practically a defunct piece of legislation (R.V. Rao, 1950: 618) which only further aggravated the agrarian discontent.

The number of landless labourers in Hyderabad increased phenomenally in the first half of this century. The first Agricultural Labour Enquiry (1951-2) estimated that over 42 per cent of the rural population of Hyderabad was engaged in agricultural labour (19.5 per cent with and 22.6 per cent of them without land) (GOI, (vi): 56 and (vii), I-A: d-e). The proportion of agricultural labourers was much lower in 1929-30 when the first rural economic enquiries were conducted in some of the districts of Hyderabad state (Bedford 1967:123). The landless labourers did not constitute a homogeneous class. Not only was their caste and ethnic composition complex, but also several occupational categories such as rural artisans, craftsmen, and tenants-at-will were swelling their ranks. Widespread seasonal unemployment and acute competition for work kept the agricultural wages low in Telangana. Towards the end of the Second World War food prices, which increased faster than the wage rates, affected the conditions of landless labourers adversely and augmented their distress further (Iyengar 1951: 216-17).

II

Political Development in Hyderabad and Mobilization of the Peasantry in Telangana from 1936 to 1946

The despotic rule of the Nizam permitted neither political freedom nor any representative institutions. Harassment of suspected political activists, detention of leaders and potential agitators were so common forms of repression that a straightforward political movement was almost ruled out in the state till 1930 or so. However, after 1920 several members of the intelligentsia and liberal professional class in Hyderabad, inspired by the Indian national movement, formed three different cultural-literary forums, one each for the three linguistic regions of the State. The Andhra Conference, which operated in the Telangana districts, was set up in 1928 and began to mobilize public opinion on issues like administrative and constitutional reforms, schools, civil liberties, recruitment to services, etc., reflecting partly the regional economic and political aspirations and partly the urban middle class and elitist charactar of the new political commotion (Sundarayya 1972a: 18-19).

Congressmen and their sympathizers operated chiefly through the three 'mask organizations'. Political developments in India in the thirties prepared the background for a nascent movement for constitutional reforms in Hyderabad also where the political conditions were being slightly liberalized. The Hyderabad unit of the Congress started a satyagraha in 1938 for political reforms. But the agitation came to be dominated by the Arya Samaj and the Hindu Mahasabha and the Congress, acting on Gandhi's advice, abandoned it to lessen political confusion (GOI, (iii) -a and -b: 1-4; Tirth 1967: 93-107). The rise of the Hindu nationalist opinion was clearly a reaction to the growing dominance of the Majlis Ittehad-ul-Musalmin—a communal organization of Hyderabad Muslims committed to the idea of Muslim supremacy—in the State's politics (Wright, Jr. 1963: 234-43).

During the Second World War, the Andhra Conference expanded its network, in the Telangana villages by taking an active interest in agrarian problems such as vetti labour. Just across the border, in the Andhra delta districts of the Madras Presidency, a political movement for unification of all Telugu-speaking regions into a separate Vishalandhra was launched by the Andhra Mahasabha. In the Telangana region the branches of Andhra Conference and Andhra Mahasabha functioned in close collaboration (Bedford 1967: 196-97). Following the satyagraha the Congress was banned in 1938, and so was the CPI, with the result that the Andhra Conference and the Andhra Mahasabha had the entire field of politics wide open for their activities.

The communists arrived on the Telangana scene only during the latter half of the war period. They had been active in the delta districts since 1934 when the Andhra CP was established. The party drew its strength from the famous caste of Kammas—well-to-do peasant proprietors—for whom other political alternatives did not exist as their archrivals—Brahmins and Reddys—dominated the Congress. (Harrison 1956: 378-404). Between 1928 and 1933, Professor N.G. Ranga had laid down a framework of regional level peasant organizations which, later in 1936, were affiliated to the All India Kisan Sabha, CPI's front organization. This, for the CPI, was the period of the 'United Front' strategy which made strange political alliances possible and helped it to infiltrate the Congress and the Congress Socialist Party and to capture a host of peasant organizations all over India, including those in the Andhra delta. Consequently the Indian Peasant Institute, started by Ranga at Nidubrolu, imperceptibly turned into a training centre for CPI cadres (Ranga 1949: 76). By 1940 the communists were firmly entrenched in the Andhra delta politics. During the ban (1940-2) they operated through 'front' organizations like the Kisan Sabha, Andhra Mahasabha, and so on. But the rich Kamma *Kulaks* formed the class base of the Andhra CP and provided the party with funds and workers (Harrison 1962: 204-10).

The growing influence of the communists in the delta naturally had its spill-over in the adjoining Telangana region; this was visible in the changing complexion of the leadership and of the workers of the Andhra Conference. Some of the newly emerging leaders had earlier participated in the civil disobedience movement (1930-2) and later in the Hyderabad satyagraha (1938). But they could no longer look to the Gandhian Congress for ideological orientation and guidance as the Congress itself eschewed mass movements and refrained from committing itself to a definite economic and political programme. The young radical elements within the Andhra Conference therefore turned to communism and converted the cultural forum into a mass militant organization—a united front of the youth, peasants, middle classes, and workers—against the Nizam's government (Sundarayya 1972a: 19-20).

Economic conditions of the different strata of Telangana peasantry had deteriorated, first due to the depression and later due to the war. The peasant groaned under the tyranny of landlords, deshmukhs, and sahukars, an unsympathetic police force and an unfair revenue, judicial, administrative machinery that added misery to his poverty. Any organization espousing his cause could have won his gratitude and support. Through the Andhra Conference young communists voiced the peasant's grievances, paid more and more attention to the agrarian problems in Telangana, and mobilized opinion in favour of abolition of landlordism and the oppressive vetti system.[7] But before 1940 the Andhra Conference had done practically no work to build a peasant organization as such. Students, leaving college, were being recruited to the party cadres but the organizational network of the Conference and the Mahasabha until 1942 was dominated by some liberal and moderate politicians. The agrarian radicalism that the communists vocalized on the Conference platform made little impact on the rural masses before them. But after the Government of India lifted the ban on the CPI in 1942, the communists were able to oust the right-wing elements and establish their hold on the Andhra Conference and the Mahasabha. The process was complete when, at the Bhongir session of the Andhra Mahasabha, two young communists, Ravi Narayan Reddy and Badam Yella Reddy, were elected as the President and Secretary respectively (Sundarayya 1972a: 20-21).

The agrarian slogans and demands of the communists included abolition of vetti, prevention of rack-renting and of eviction of tenants, reduction in taxes, revenues and rents, confirmation of occupancy (patta) rights of cultivating tenants, and so on, which naturally attracted the poor peasants, tenants, and labourers to the Andhra Conference. All the same, till 1945 even the communists did not come out openly against the Nizam's autocratic rule, nor did their demands include a radical programme of distribution of land to the landless labourers (Sundarayya 1972a: 27). But the pro-government campaigns like 'Grow More Food', and translation of the Marxist classics into Telugu and their distribution in the Telangana countryside continued to be their preoccupations (Sheshadri, 1967: 389-90). Between 1944 and 1946, the Andhra communists organized annual conferences of the All India Kisan Sabha (Vijaywada, 1944), All India Students' Federation (Guntur, 1946) and Railwaymen's Federation (Secunderabad, 1946) making Andhra the citadel of the CPI. However, all these enthusiastic activities could not go very far in building up a mass following in the countryside and in mobilizing the peasantry into a revolutionary organization.

Between 1944 and 1946 the communist activities did spread far and wide in Nalgonda district, enmeshing numerous villages in the Bhongir, Suryapet, Jangaon, Nalgonda, and Huzurnagar *talukas*. Soon after capturing the Andhra Mahasabha and the Andhra Conference, the communists lowered their membership fees so as to draw large numbers of agricultural labourers, poor tenants and small landholders closer to their ideology and programme. The effort paid some dividends. Apart from Nalgonda, the Andhra Conference gained considerable ground in Warangal and Karimnagar districts. All over Andhra and Telangana membership enrolment figures for all the CPI-led organizations showed remarkable improvement (Harrison 1960: 222).

As in Andhra, the leading communists in Telangana were, by and large, wealthy landholders, pattadars of substantial holdings, and men of some hereditary standing in their villages and talukas. Both Ravi Narayan Reddy and B. Yella Reddy, referred to earlier, were prominent landlords. D. Venkateshwar Rao, leader of the Suryapet taluka, could be cited as yet another example. Of course, not all the Telangana communists were landholders. Some, like Dr Raj Bahadur Gaur and Mukaddam Mohiuddin, came from the urban intelligentsia (Bedford 1967: 201-2). They had shown some generosity toward poorer sections of the peasantry whom, in fact, they hired either as tenants on temporary leases or as agricultural labourers. Hence both in Andhra and in Telangana the class interests of the leading communists lay in promoting a class alliance between the rich and small holders, tenant cultivators and the landless labourers against those isolated landlords and rich landholders who were either inconsiderate to their tenant-cultivators or paid poor wages to their labourers. Such a class alliance remained the central theme and concern of the Telangana communists as was evident in their radical agrarian demands made subsequently.

Another issue concerning food scarcity had arisen in 1946. The shortage of food was partly the result of the growing cultivation of commercial or cash crops. Until the war ended no measure whatsoever was taken to curb the extent of commercial crop production (Qureshi 1947: 284-94). This resulted in high consumer prices and in an acute food shortage. The government's bid to resolve the food crisis by rationing and by procuring foodgrains through a compulsory levy only aggravated the general agrarian discontent (Sundarayya 1972a : 304-5). Procurement, which affected mainly the rich and middle peasants, was, in effect, an invitation to the police and officials to resort to fraud, corruption, and favouritism. In collusion with them, many landlords evaded the compulsory levy, hoarded foodgrains, and profited from the rising prices (Bedford 1967: 210-11). The worst affected were the poor peasants and landless labourers. Those rich and middle peasants who were being subjected to harassment under the procurement levy regulation had every reason to make common cause with the poor whose wages did not increase at the same rate as prices. A stage was thus set for a class alliance and spontaneous peasant upsurge in early 1946 in Telangana. The agrarian social structure was certainly conducive to an insurrectionary movement, but the post-war political developments and economic crisis provided an impetus to a sustained peasant revolt that lasted nearly five years.

III

The Beginning and Growth of the Telangana Insurrection: July 1946 to September 1948

The communist effort to build strong party bases yielded good results in Nalgonda and Warangal districts which were their strongholds. Between 1942 and 1946 their influence among poor peasants, tenant-cultivators, and landless labourers grew steadily. In certain parts of these districts the Nizam's writ had virtually ceased to run at the beginning of 1946. The officials as well as the landlords who did not pay 'protection money' were afraid of visiting those areas of their jurisdictions or estates where the communists had established strongholds (Zinkin 1962: 62). The presence of a number of landlords owning large estates extending over thousands of acres of land had facilitated the expansion of communism in this area (Sundarayya 1972a: 15).

In the post-war crisis, the local branches of the Andhra Conference, called *sanghams*, launched village level struggles for better wages for labourers and against the vetti labour, illegal exactions, evictions and also against the newly imposed grain levy. These struggles were located mostly in the Nalgonda district on the estates of some of the most notorious landlords and deshmukhs. Militant action in this early insurgence included a few isolated instances of forcible seizure of the lands of those landlords who had evicted some Lambadi (tribal) tenant-cultivators and also involved non-compliance of the demands of vetti labour, illegal taxes, and the procurement levy. The extent of the peasants' spontaneous action did not always carry the approval of sangham leaders. The landlords either fled to safety, resorted to litigation, or summoned their own goondas and the police to deal with the rebellious peasants. Many pitched battles occurred between the two sides (Sundarayya 1972a: 28-35).

One such major incident occurred in July 1946 when over a thousand peasants, armed with lathis and slings, took out a procession in a village that formed part of Vishnur Deshmukh's estate. The hired goondas of the landlord fired at the procession and killed Doddi Komarayya, the village sangham leader and injured a few others. The procession, now turned into an angry crowd, went to the landlord's house which was about to be set on fire when the police arrived and dispersed it. Komarayya's martyrdom sparked off the conflagration and thus marked the beginning of the Telangana insurrection (Sundarayya 1972b: 11-12).

It is significant that by the end of July 1946 peasant resistance and militant action against landlords, deshmukhs, and village officials spread to some 300 to 400 villages (in Nalgonda, Warangal, and Khammam districts) which, the communists claimed, were under their control (Sundarayya 1972a: 39). The CPI press launched a massive propaganda campaign, voiced the demands of the Telangana peasantry, and exposed the oppression and brutalities.[8] The propaganda was further intensified after October 1946 when the Andhra Conference was banned by the Nizam's government. Several hundred CPI workers were arrested and more police reinforcements sent to the troubled areas. But so determined was the resistance that the landlords and deshmukhs found it difficult to get the villagers to perform vetti; small holders did not hand over a part of their paddy crop as required under the procurement levy regulation and foiled all the coercive attempts of village officials; and landless labourers and evicted tenants sat tight on the lands they seized (Bedford 1967: 213-22). In all, some 156 cases of assault were registered by the police against peasants, and some 10 rebels in four separate incidents of police-peasant battles were killed by the end of 1946 (Sundarayya 1972a: 38).

The salient features of the insurrection in its initial phase could be summed up thus: large masses of peasants spontaneously participated in the struggles directed against the government, landlords and deshmukhs and their agents. The insurgents had neither firearms nor the training required to use them. A few volunteer groups had come into existence. They were not well-organized guerrilla squads as such, but were rather extempore formations in response to the situation. Initially, therefore, the revolt was spasmodic. The communist or Andhra Conference sanghams and *dalams* (batches) acted as morale boosters for the peasant action but beyond that, there is little evidence to suggest that they had succeeded in channelling the spontaneous upsurge into systematically planned offensives. The emphasis in the slogans being on a variety of agrarian matters, already referred to, all the strata, whether rich and small pattadars, cultivating tenants or landless labourers, were united. The peasant militancy till the end of 1946 had not turned into a cataclysm but whatever violence occurred in the process of resistance it was the doing of poor peasants, including the tribal Lambadi elements. (Sundarayya 1972a: *passim*). Although a few isolated areas of Warangal, Karimnagar, and Khammam districts were under the rebels' influence, in general the stage on which the first scenes in the insurrectionary drama were acted was undoubtedly Nalgonda district, mainly the Suryapet and Jangaon talukas.

Mere agrarian slogans of purely local relevance were not enough for the Telangana communists. Major events and constitutional developments in 1946-7 were shaping the political future of India, whereas the destiny and future status of Hyderabad, like all other princely states of the subcontinent, hung in suspense. As mentioned earlier, until 1946 or so the communists did not come out openly against the Nizam's autocracy and feudal political structure, but any further silence on such vital issues would have only alienated them from the masses. Inside Hyderabad the people were being swept by the new tides of nationalism and political freedom that gathered momentum with the announcement in February 1947 regarding the transfer of power in India. But the British gave the princely states an option between remaining autonomous and joining either India or Pakistan. On the eve of independence all the princely states, except Hyderabad, Jungadh, and Kashmir, had exercised the option (Menon 1956).

In Hyderabad the Nizam, the Muslim nobility, and also the Majlis-i-Ittehad, which rallied the bulk of the ruling minority, wanted to preserve the state's autonomy. The Hindu majority, however, wanted its merger with India so that they could enjoy political freedom and participate in the processes of self-government. The parleys that took place between the Nizam's government and the Indian government both before and after the transfer of power reflected the conflicting aspirations of the powerless majority and the ruling minority of the state. Communal propaganda and the fanaticism of the Ittehad, and to a certain extent of the Arya Samaj and the Hindu Mahasabha, led to a sudden deterioration of the communal situation which was at its lowest ebb when a 'Standstill' Agreement was signed in August 1947 by the Hyderabad and Indian governments (Menon 1956: 319-29).

As the above political developments were taking place, the communists aligned with the anti-Nizam and pro-merger forces including the Congress, the only known, if not well-organized, body of the nationalist opinion in the state. The Congress embarked on a satyagraha to seek the merger of Hyderabad. The communists, despite their inherent dislike for Gandhian agitational methods, had to go along, but, perhaps, they never anticipated that the state's accession to India would ever become a reality.[9] Their involvement in the peaceful and non-violent satyagrah caused them considerable embarrassment in view of the fact that they had already launched the peasant insurrection on the Telangana front. The setback to the communists due to the alliance with the Congress was perhaps more than psychological. In course of the satyagraha, the Congress and communist workers began to cut down toddy trees partly as a symbolic defiance of the Nizam's government, for whom the trees were an important source of excise revenue, and partly as propaganda against toddy drinking which the Gandhian ethic prohibited.[10] The communists, however, later realized that by cutting down *toddy* trees they were depriving a great many active members of their own dalams and sanghams of their livelihood. Fearing a withdrawal of their support to the insurrection the communists soon dissociated from the satyagraha and the alliance with the Congress (Sundarayya 1972a: 57). A radical wing of the Congress led by Swami Tirth was, in fact, drawing closer to the communists and their insurrectionary tactics, but the political cross-pressures within the Congress prevented him from cultivating the relationship any further. Consequently, the alliance practically ceased to operate in January 1948 (Tirth 1967: 168, 196-7).

The growing militancy and power of the Majlis Ittehad were evident in the activities of the Razakars, a para-military voluntary force organized by Kasim Razvi, the leader of the Ittehad. In January 1948 more than 30,000 Razakars were enrolled and by August 1948 their number was about 100,000 (GOI, (iii), c: 1 and d: 31). As the peasant insurrection was spreading in rural Telangana, the Nizam's government sent batches of Razakars, sometimes with, but many a time without, any police or army, in order to deal with the recalcitrants and to protect the frontier as well as the distressed landlords and officials. But the Nizam's authority was too nominal to check the Razakar squads in action. They raided and plundered the troubled villages, arrested or killed suspected and potential agitators, terrorized the innocent, and also abducted women as part of the campaign of punitive measures aginst the turbulent villages all over Hyderabad, but particularly in Telangana where the rural mass of peasantry was coming under the communist influence. (GOI, (iii), d: 60-77). Having neither will nor ability to restrain the terroristst trio—Ittehad, Razakars, and the police—that had come to govern the day-to-day affairs in the state, the Nizam and his government had no course open but to endorse their operations and to support them morally and materially (Menon 1956: 319-29, 341-56). This epitomizes the conditions of political instability and near-anarchy in Hyderbad throughout the first eight months of 1948.

The authority crisis helped the communists in Telangana to spread the insurrection and to set up village republics ('soviets') which functioned as parallel governments in the areas under their control. Groups of volunteers were organized to ensure the internal security of a village, or group of villages, and to act as fighting squads when the Razakars and/or the police raided. Tired of the atrocities the villagers joined these groups (dalams) enthusiastically in the communist stronghold districts of Nalgonda, Warangal, and Khammam. By April 1948 the communists were able to organize six 'area-squads' (each with 20 fighters), and 50 to 60 'village squads' (Sundarayya 1972a: 90). Consequently the insurrection expanded territorially. Till the Government of India resorted to the 'Police Action' in Hyderabad, the armed resistance of peasants was carried to almost all the parts of Nalgonda, Warangal, and Khammam districts. In about 4,000 villages a parallel administration was established by the communists (C.R. Rao 1972: 14-5). Parts of Adilabad, Karimnagar, and Medak districts, where the Tirth group of the Congress had set up some bases during the alliance, were captured by the Andhra Conference/communist dalams (Bedford 1967: 263). In the same period when the Razakar terrorism was at its peak the Telangana armed insurrection also turned both grimmer and more effective.

Besides the growing anarchy and political crisis, other factors also contributed to the strength and spread of the insurrection. First, in the months of February-March 1948 the Second Congress of the CPI ratified a new 'left' policy while supplanting the 'United Front' strategy that the party had followed for well over a decade. The shift only conformed to the 'Zhdanov line', newly prescribed by the International Communist movement, which decreed unequivocal guerrilla offensives throughout Asia. Under the dispensations of the new radical left revolutionary policy, the CPI's attack was no longer concentrated on imperialism alone, but was diffused to cover all the manifestations of the power of the bourgeoisie and landed aristocracy. The new leader—B.T. Ranadive, who replaced P.C. Joshi, the chief architect of the 'United Front' policy—now came out strongly in support of every revolutionary upsurge and popular struggle (Kautsky 1956: 46-85). With the swing from the 'right' to the 'left' strategy also came an ideological justification for and a legitimization of the Telangana insurrection which had commenced a year and a half earlier. Secondly, the deteriorating law and order situation was conducive to undetected crossing of the borders. The Telangana and Andhra communists seized the opportunity, set up revolutionary headquarters in Mungala estate, an enclave of the Hyderabad State surrounded by the territory of the Krishna district (Madras Presidency), and smuggled in and out arms, funds, propaganda literature, and, above all, workers. Without this activity the massive expansion of the insurrection might not have been possible. Thus, the Andhra 'delta' had become the supply base of the peasant struggle in Telangana (Harrison 1956: 390-91; C.R. Rao 1972: 12). Thirdly, *gram-rajyams* ('village soviets') set up by the rebels, functioned very efficiently; the lands, seized forcibly, were distributed among the land-hungry agricultural labourers and also among evicted tenants. Although the land distribution work was not free from arbitrariness and practical problems, it certainly helped to build the morale of the rebels and the popular image of the revolt itself. The guerrilla squads protected the villages under their control whereas the village *samitis* settled disputes and coordinated activities at the local level. The sanghams also discouraged, and later even prohibited, the primitive forms of torture and retribution. By the end of August 1948 about 10,000 peasants, students, and party workers actively participated in the village squads and some 2,000 in the special mobile guerrilla squads (Sundarayya 1972a: 60, 65, 91-3).[11]

Yet another factor in the growth of the insurrection till August 1948 was that in May the Hyderabad government lifted the ban on the CP. The gesture aroused suspicion in the minds of many that the CPI had secretly come to terms with the Nizam, revoking its earlier policy to work for the liquidation of his autocratic rule and for merger of the state with the Indian Union (GOI, (v): 2-3). Perhaps a section of the Telangana CP, particularly the City Committee of Hyderabad headed by Gaur, Mahendra and others, did come to some understanding with the Nizam's government when it issued a press statement denouncing the Indian government as 'pro-landlord and pro-bourgeoisie' and proclaimed its resolve to fight against all those forces which were then working for Hyderabad's integration with India. But this reconciliation with the Nizam by some communists had neither the concurrence of the Telangana insurgents, nor of the Andhra CP under whom the Telangana leaders were technically operating (Sundrayya 1972a: 179). It is also significant in this context that the ban was not reimposed (Bedford 1967: 277), a fact which has gone unnoticed in all the accounts of the insurrection prepared recently by those communist leaders who were directly or indirectly involved in conducting the insurrection. Nevertheless, it seems reasonably clear that the removal of the ban facilitated the work of securing arms and ammunition, from whatever sources possible which the squads and dalams needed badly if they were to hold on to their positions in the face of a serious offensive by a well-trained superior army.

IV
The Decline of the Insurrection

On 13 September 1948 the Indian army marched into Hyderabad and within less than a week the Nizam's representatives surrendered. The Nizam outlawed and banned the Razakars and lifted the ban on the State Congress. On India's part the 'Police Action' was taken to put an end to the conditions of anarchy within the state and to ensure the internal security of the neighbouring Indian territory. The 'Police Action' was, therefore, unsavoury but essential (Menon 1956: 341-82). However, it became apparent later that the Indian government's concern over the undemocratic feudal regime of the Nizam and over the Razakars' terrorism was really secondary to their fears of the Telangana peasants' insurrection and of the possibility of a communist capture of power right in the heart of the Indian territory. The apprehension was not expressed openly until February 1949 (GOI, (iv), 1-71), but it is more than likely that it contributed to the Indian government's intervention far more than any other consideration.[12]

As the Indian army was advancing and rounding up the Razakars, the communist dalams on the Telangana front acquired a large amount of arms and ammunition abandoned by the latter (Menon 1956: 384). This naturally strengthened the rebels' position but only for a while. Once the Razakars were overpowered, and a military administration set up, the offensive was immediately directed at the peasant rebels in the troubled districts of Telangana. Describing the extent of the repression Sundarayya (1972a: 199) writes: 'In more than 2,000 villages of Nalgonda, Warangal, Karimnagar, Khammam and Hyderabad districts ... 300,000 people were tortured, about 50,000 were arrested and kept in [detention] camps for a few days to a few months. More than 5,000 were imprisoned for years'.

Fighting with the Indian army over 2,000 peasants, and party workers, were killed. By July 1950 the number of communists and active participants detained had reached 10,000 (Pritt 1950: 319-20). This should suffice as an index of the degree of intensity of the insurrection.[13]

The army action had successfully liberated Hyderabad and, at least apparently, fulfilled the political aspirations of the people by ending the feudal and anachronistic reign of the Nizam and by paving the way for the state's integration in the Indian Union. The people welcomed the troops enthusiastically and their attitude to the Telangana insurrection changed drastically. The Telangana revolt was no longer a liberation struggle but became mainly the peasants' partisan struggle (Sundarayya 1972a: 425). Similarly, in less than a year after the Indian military took over the administration of Hyderabad, it issued the Jagir Abolition Regulation (August, 1949) and appointed an Agrarian Enquiry Committee to recommend a comprehensive land-reform legislation. These seemingly progressive measures were taken promptly but primarily with the intention of neutralizing the communist influence among the rural masses (Menon 1956: 385, Khusro 1958: 12-13).

September 1948 to October 1951 (when the insurrection was called off) was essentially the phase of decline but somewhat paradoxically it was also the most significant phase since it revealed the strength and the weakness of the Telangana revolt.

Who were the principal participants in the Telangana insurrection? What were the social origins of the squad leaders, party workers, and the men who fought? Why did they resist at all? Was it the question of their immediate grievances and privations that stirred the peasantry into the violent resistance or was it the broader and ultimate issue (of radically transforming the system) that motivated the rebels? Finally, why is it that, after a sustained fight for nearly five years, the withdrawal of the struggle became indispensable? These are some of the questions which we shall try to answer, although some of the answers that follow must be treated as tentative in the absence of ampler and still more authentic source material than has been available to us.

It seems reasonably certain that the Telangana revolt was not staged by peasants of a single agrarian stratum. Its adherents had a mixed class character (Harrison 1956: 390). As mentioned earlier, the leading communists of the Andhra delta and Telangana were well-to-do peasants and came from either the Kamma or the Reddy caste of peasant proprietors.[14] It was, therefore, basic to the interests of rich peasants, who dominated the party, that all other subordinate agrarian classes, such as the small holders (middle peasants) and the tenants and sharecroppers (poor peasants), quite as much as the landless labourers, formed an alliance and launched a combined offensive against the handful of big absentee landlords whose power and dominance could not be threatened otherwise. The multiple grievances of all the sections of the peasantry during the post-war economic crisis had opened up the possibility of such an alliance.

From the beginning of 1946 the communists began a three-pronged attack on the enemies of the peasants: first, they wanted to put an end to the vetti and demanded wage increases. Second, they condemned the large-scale eviction of tenants and demanded both abolition of landlordism and a moratorium on all debts. Third, the communists adopted a dual policy on the question of 'the procurement of grain through compulsory levy'. On the one hand, they deplored the landlords' and deshmukhs' evasion of the levy regulation and their hoarding and profiteering. On the other hand, rich peasants, well-to-do and small holders, who supported the party, were encouraged to withhold the grain-levy (Sundarayya 1972a: 54-59). Such a three-fold appeal alone could hold the diverse agrarian class interests together. The alliance was certainly not free from conflicting interests or cross-pressures. For example, the demand for increased wages was bound to affect the well-to-do peasants whose primary interests lay in keeping the wage level down and avoiding the grain levy. But those rich peasants who were with the party and had sympathetically met the demands of their sharecroppers or labourers were treated as 'neutralized' and their lands and paddy stocks went unscathed (Harrison 1956: 391).

As the insurrection developed, the poor peasants (particularly the tenants and sharecroppers) and the landless labourers began to seize lands from the landlords and deshmukhs and to occupy waste-lands which later they distributed among themselves. In deciding which surplus land to seize, the sangham leaders made liberal concessions to the rich peasants who sided with the rebels. Ceilings on landholdings were also generously fixed. Initially the ceiling was fixed at 500 acres; it was reduced later to 200 acres and then to 100 dry acres and 10 wet acres. These revisions, which were already effected by mid-1948, when the final phase had not yet started, made two things abundantly clear. First, the spontaneous seizure and distribution of land changed the course of the insurrection and enlarged its scope considerably. A revolutionary change, which the alliance did not contemplate while launching the revolt, now seemed plausible. Secondly, it also brought to the surface the conflicting interests within the alliance. That such a class alliance was inherently weak seems reasonably clear. Initially the communist leaders promptly promised adequate compensations to the owners for the surplus lands seized although this could not be pursued further. This shows that the land ceiling question and the way it was settled finally in favour of the rich peasants 'reflected a reformist understanding of the agrarian problems of Telangana' on the part of the communist leaders (Sundarayya 1972a: 58-9, 116-8).

It thus seems that the alliance of different agrarian strata was made possible by their immediate grievances and demands, and not by any grand ideas of total transformation of the system. The alliance worked so long as more fundamental issues such as land seizures, ceilings, and distribution did not threaten its solidarity. Significantly enough, even these fundamental issues cropped up only as a result of certain historical circumstances in which the poor peasants' spontaneous seizure of land, which was not part of the original design, became possible. It can therefore be surmised that cracks in the alliance began to show with such seizures of land. It was only to the chagrin of the rich peasants, and not without reluctance, that the central party bosses legitimized the seizure and distribution of lands as an ingredient of the revolutionary programme' (Sundarayya 1972a: 118).

After the military action the rich peasants increasingly deserted the alliance in which the agricultural labourers and tenants (poor peasants) together with some smallholders (middle peasants) were left to carry on the insurrection. The split occurred also among the Telangana communist leaders. Revi Narayan Reddy, the most popular of them, later dissociated himself from the revolutionary struggle and joined the critics of the Telangana insurrection. Being a defender of rich peasant interests within the party, Reddy criticized the seizure of land as ill-conceived and advocated withdrawal of the struggle which, to him, became redundant after the Indian Army took over Hyderabad (Basavapunniah 1972 (I): 6-7).

The principal participants in the sustained revolt were thus unquestionably the poor peasants and the landless labourers. Most of the recruits in the dalams came from the untouchable castes (Malas and Madigas) and from among the tribals. The caste Hindus treated them as socially inferior. The deprived and peripheral groups had also lost all their rights in land owing to the fact that for the past several decades the power and instruments of justice were in the hands of the landlords and deshmukhs.

Lack of alternative avenues of work had rendered them weak in bargaining for their rights. They were doubly exploited, culturally as well as economically. By joining the communist dalams and revolting against the oppressive system they had nothing to lose and everything to gain.[15]

The role of the rich peasants was anything but revolutionary. In the first two years of the insurrection, they gained a great deal from the alliance. Thus, they were able to ward off the grain-levy. But despite the gains, many of them were reluctant to increase the wages of their own labourers in pursuance of the party directives. After the army take-over, the grain-levy issue was no longer focal anyway. Moreover, as the grip of the military administration tightened, and the troops began to suppress the dalams ruthlessly, some rich peasants, while continuing to be apparently loyal to the party, providing food and shelter to the squad-leaders and guerrillas, also acted as informers to the army and the police. (Sundarayya 1972a: 125, 259).

The role of the middle peasants could not be researched into adequately and therefore we shall be able to say little. Our sources, however, do not suggest that the middle peasants played any spectacular part. On the whole, they did not constitute a very significant social category in Telangana either numerically or politically. Thus, the poor peasants and the labourers were the backbone of the resistance right from the beginning and till the very end.

Some data on the local (village) level leaders (see Sundarayya 1972a: 354-90) active either in actual squads or in *samitis* enable us to examine the social character of the leadership. Sundarayya has sketched life-histories of some 80 squad and party leaders who were killed while fighting the army. Unfortunately, the details of their social origin have not been recorded by him uniformly. Occupation has been mentioned in 47 cases: of these 12 were 'rich' peasants, four 'middle' peasants, seven 'poor' or 'small' landholders (including tenant cultivators), 20 agricultural labourers and allied groups, and four others, including a village patel.[16]

Most of these leaders were recent followers of the party. Only five of them had come in contact with the CP or the Andhra Conference/Mahasabha prior to 1946: nine joined the party in 1947 while a great majority joined the dalams and sanghams in course of the insurrection itself between 1948 and 1951. This confirms, at least partially, the point made earlier that the Telangana revolutionary movement was not a product of a sustained political organization of peasants, and that the participation of peasants as well as of their leaders was spontaneous.

This brings us to the most important question as to why the withdrawal of the insurrection became necessary. Disunity in the class alliance and the military repression constitute only a part of the story. The intra-party differences over the ideological issues and over the broad objectives of the revolutionary struggle in Telangana should provide us some clues. After the 'Police Action' in Hyderabad, a section of the CPI leadership, the Ranadive group, which had earlier hailed the Telangana insurrection as 'a big landmark in the Communist movement', openly disowned it. Their objection was that the predominantly peasant upsurge did not conform to the classical notion of the 'leadership of the proletariat'. Moreover, their naive hope that the working class in the cities all over the country might rise simultaneously with the Telangana peasants did not materialize (Kautsky 1956: 49, 57). At the ideological level, the question whether the Telangana revolt was 'antilandlord', 'anti-Nizam (and therefore pro-liberation)', 'antibourgeoisie, anti-imperialist and therefore anti-Indian Army', 'the agitation for Vishalandhra' or whether it was uneasy mixture of two or more of these, was never settled.

The Andhra Committee of the CP, which was responsible for directing the upsurge in Telangana, defended strongly its reliance on the peasantry in the revolutionary movement. This, is argued, was in keeping with the Maoist theory of 'new democracy' which propounded a multi-class alliance as the correct strategy for advancing the socialist revolution in colonies and semicolonies.[17] No matter what the ideological polemics, the practical dilemma of the Andhra and Telangana communists was whether or not to continue the insurrection. The final split came on precisely this issue; Ravi N. Reddy, B. Yella Reddy, and C. Rajeshwar Rao favoured abandonment as they saw in the struggle symptoms of degeneration into 'left adventurism', and 'infantile disorder' or 'individual terrorism' (C.R. Rao 1972: 24-25). On the other side were P. Sundarayya and M. Basavapunniah who criticized the former for their 'right reformism' and advocated continuation of the struggle as a peasant partisan struggle. The latter thought that without continuing the fight, the party might lose the ground gained and the goodwill earned through the seizure and distrubution of lands and through the 'village soviets'. The Indian army's presence enabled the landlords and deshmukhs to recapture some of their lands. An abandonment of the struggle would be tantamount to political surrender and betrayal of those peasants who stood resolutely behind the party fighting till the end (Sundarayya 1972a: 177-82, 391-400; Basavapunniah, 1972 (I): 6-7 and (II) 4,10). These intra-party conflicts became endemic after 1950 and weakened the insurrection considerably from within.

In the first two years of the insurrection rising expectations provided the major inpulse to the revolutionary peasant masses in Telangana, but from the time of the 'Police Action' till the end it was essentially a revolt of desperation. The general political instability and the rapidly developing crisis of authority and legitimacy were the most immediate circumstances that facilitated a revolutionary mobilization of peasant masses in Telangana but organization, which plays a vital part in sustaining revolutionary *elan*, such as land seizure and establishment of gram rajyams, and in making the mass politically effective, did not exist.[18] To cite an example, the village committees, which ran the parallel governments, were isolated from each other and lacked proper coordination. Although they distributed land to the landless labourers and to the evicted tenants for cultivation they had no access to the market, not to speak of control over it. For trade and essential supplies the rebels had to depend on the urban merchants and traders whose agents at the village level had to be bribed by the samitis for marketing the produce of the rebel villages (Sundarayya 1972a: 128-9).

When desperation faces a revolutionary mass, petty reprisals become rife. The revolutionaries, who persist in the tactics of desperation, intensification of violence being one of them, do not realize how they damage their own cause. 'An expression of diffuse rage against peripheral targets often provides the forces of order a widespread public support' (Moore Jr. 1972: 176), and this seems to have happened in Telangana. The communists were never able to muster support from the urban middle class and the working class whereas the rural masses who had so enthusiastically responded initially began to withdraw their support. Consequently, only isolated squads of peasant guerrillas and party workers remained but they could not sustain the revolt long.

Early in 1951 the Congress government made several conciliatory gestures towards the CPI as it knew well that any further repression would not only add to the popularity of the communists in Telangana, but would also cast doubts on its own credibility as a democratic government. Except in the troubled areas of Telangana the democratic processes and institutions then functioned normally. Even the CPI Polit bureau had acknowledged this (see 'Strategy and tactics', *Communist* (Bombay), 4, 1949 quoted in Chaudhuri 1950: 41).

In April 1951 Acharya Vinoba Bhave, the leader of the bhoodan movement which began in Telangana villages about the same time, met some CP leaders who were under detention (Ram 1962: 45-55). Although very little is known as to what passed between him and them, it is not without significance that soon a number of detainees were released by the government. Within months (i.e. in October), the CPI formally declared the struggle withdrawn. The preparations for the first Indian elections, under the Constitution recently adopted, were under way. The prospects of the ban being lifted were in view, and the CPI hoped to participate in the elections, test its political strength and try the constitutional alternative for consolidating the gains of the five-year long insurrection.

Although the CPI in Andhra and Telangana won impressive electoral victories (Gray 1968: 409-10: M. Rao 1973: 4-6), they could do little in introducing any radical changes or modifications in the land reform legislation which was then afoot in the Hyderabad assembly. Jagirdari was abolished, but in anticipation of comprehensive land reform legislation, many substantial landowners had resorted to subdivision and transfer of lands to avoid any losses on account of the ceiling provisions. Very few of the tenants actually registered themselves as tenants and claimed occupancy rights; a majority of them were either evicted from lands before the actual enforcement of the new statutes, or had surrendered their lands voluntarily. They and the landless labourers now found it increasingly difficult to secure land from landlords and rich pattiadars on tenurial lease for cultivation (Nair 1961: 58-68).[19]

The judgment about the success or failure of a revolutionary movement is not easy to pass as it depends largely on the meaning we give to the words. If seizure of power and sustaining it for a considerable period of time is taken as the touchstone of success then, perhaps, no other peasant revolt or movement in India was more successful than the one in Telangana. If, however, a lasting dent in the agrarian structure and change in the conditions of its principal participants are viewed as the criterion then perhaps the Telangana insurrection was not more successful than other peasant resistance movements in India (Dhanagare, 1973: 406-26). Like all other movements, though, the Telangana struggle too has become the source of legends and inspiration for the radical left in India. Recently there has been a renewed interest, academic as well as political, in the study of the struggle. Its silver jubilee, celebrated by all the shades of Communist parties in India, however, became an occasion for mutual mud-slinging, but that must be left out of this paper.

Notes

1 The other was the Tebhaga movement in Bengal, 1946-7 which has been discussed by me elsewhere (Dhanagare 1973: 316-59).
2 Thus, Moore, Jr (1965: 380-5) discusses only the Telangana rebellion and ignores all other instances of peasant struggle in contemporary India (1920-1950).
3 The nine districts of Telangana are: Adilabad, Hyderabad, Karimnagar, Khammam, Mahbubnagar, Medak, Nalgonda, Nizamabad, and Warangal.
4 For the economic activities of the various caste groups in Telangana villages, see Dube 1965: 57-73.
5 The 1951 tribal population in Hyderabad state as a whole accounts for 1.90 per cent of the population, a higher proportion than in the past. The increase was more striking in Nalgonda, Warangal, Adilabad, Khammam, and Mahbubnagar districts than elsewhere and was notable in case of the Koyas and Hill Reddis. See GOI (ii):249, and also (vii), IX, Part II-A:158-9.
6 Alavi (1965: 245-55) has distinguished three different sectors of agrarian economy, namely: (*i*) landlord-tenant, (*ii*) rich peasant-labourers, and (*iii*) subsistence sector.
7 For details of the initial attempts of the Andhra Conference for mobilizing the peasantry, see 'The Communists in Hyderabad', Part III (in series), *The statesman* (Calcutta), 11 May 1950, 8.
8 Numerous reports and despatches that appeared in *The people's age* (Bombay) from 1 May to 31 December 1946 bear this out.
9 See 'The Communists of Hyderabad', Part III, *The Statesman*, 11 May 1950. For details of the Congress satyagraha see Tirth 1967: 179-83; and also Laik Ali 1962: 30-37.
10 Some 19,000 toddy trees were cut down during the satyagraha. See *The Statesman*, 9 September 1947, 7.
11 The claims regarding the land distribution, etc. are now admitted even by an extreme left-wing opinion in India. See M. Rao 1973: 6.

12 Evidently, 'The immediate intention of India's forces in Hyderabad was (a) *to round up the communists in the south-eastern districts; (b) to go round, taluk by taluk*, tracing out the Razakars and *disarming the population so that the Nizam could be retained as the head of State*' [GOI, (iii), e. No. 937: 2, emphasis added].

13 Sundarayya has produced a complete list of 2,517 'martyrs of the struggle'. However, not all of them were killed by the Indian Army; some were killed by the Razakars. See Sundarayya, 1972a: 447-506. M. Rao (1973: 6) claims that some 4,000 communists and peasant fighters were killed either in the encounters or in prison-camps.

14 For example, G. Rajeshwar Rao, M. Basavapunniah, N. Prasad Rao, M. Hanumant Rao, C. Vasudeo Rao were all Kammas, and P. Sundarayya, Ravi Narayan Reddy, and B. Yella Reddy, who were directly involved in conducting the insurrection, were all Reddies. They were either rich landowners themselves or came from such families. See Harrison 1956: 381-2; Sheshadri 1967: 388.

15 Sundarayya's account, almost in entirety, supports the contention that the Telangana revolt was predominantly the poor peasant and landless labourer's affair. See Sundarayya 1972a: 90-91; Bedford 1967: 232.

16 Here we have relied on the occupational descriptions given by Sundarayya and have grouped them into five categories, on the assumption that his subjective judgment about the 'rich', 'middle', and 'poor' peasants etc. at least broadly corresponds with the objective meaning given to these concepts in this paper. The 'allied groups' in the fourth category include shepherds, toddy-tappers, hunters, ferry-driver, and handloom weaver which normally form part of the rural proletariat.

17 For details of the differences between the Central Committee of the CPI and the Andhra Committee see Kautsky 1956: 60-80. For the 'Theory of new democracy' see, Mao Tse-tung 1967, II: 339-80, and IV: 411-23.

18 Moore (1972: 176-8) had discussed in greater detail the role of the organization in revolutionary movements in his recent work.

19 Khusro (1958: 24, 40-42), however, claims that the Telangana upsurge not only speeded up the land reform but also helped create an awareness of their rights among the tenants. Under the provisions of the land reforms the tenants of Telangana, more than their counterparts in Marathwada region, asserted their rights.

References

The following abbreviations have been used in this paper (GOI stands for Government of India):

GOI (i). 1909. *The Gazette of India—Hyderabad state*.

GOI (ii). *Census of India*—1931, *XXIII, Part I (Hyderabad state)*.

GOI (iii). Information Department—File No. 25/8 (1931-48), Hyderabad. The file is available at the India Office Library and Records, London No. L/I/1/176. Its contents cited in this paper are: (a) *The Arya Samaj in Hyderabad* (a pamphlet); (b) *Indian social reformer*, 8 July 1939 (an old periodical); (c) *India Today* (monthly magazine of the India League of America), July 1948; (d) *White paper on Hyderabad*—1948; (e) 'Inward telegrams to Commonwealth Relations Office'.

GOI (iv). 1949. *Communist violence in Hyderabad*. New Delhi: Ministry of Home Affairs.

GOI (v). 1950. *Communist crimes in Hyderabad*. Hyderabad.

GOI (vi). 1952. *Agricultural labour enquiry report, 1950-1*, Delhi.

GOI (vii). *Census of India*—1951 *(Hyderabad)*.

ALAVI, H. 1965. *Peasants and revolution*, in Miliband, R. and Saville, J., eds. *The Socialist register 1965*: pp. 245-75. London, Merlin Press.

ALI, M. LIAK. 1962. *Tragedy of Hyderabad*, Karachi, Pakistan Cooperative Book Society.

BASAVAPUNNIAH, M. 1972, 'Are these lessons of Telangana struggle, or bankrupt conclusions?' *People's Democracy* 8(44): pp. 6-7 (Part 1); 8(45) : 4, 10 (Part II).

BEDFORD, I. 1967, *The Telangana insurrection: a study in the causes and development of a communist insurrection in rural India, 1946-51*. Unpublished Ph.D. dissertation (history). Australian National University, Canberra.

CHAUDHURI, T. 1950. *A swing back—a critical survey of the devious zig-zags of C.P.I. political line (1947-50)*, Calcutta: Revolutionary Socialist Party Publication.

DHANAGARE, D.N. 1973. *Peasant movements in India, c. 1920-50*. Unpublished D. Phil. dissertation (sociology). University of Sussex. Brighton.

DUBE, S. C. 1965. *Indian village*. London: Routledge and Kegan Paul.

FURER-HAIMENDORF, C. Von. 1945. *Tribal Hyderabad*. Hyderabad: Government of H.E.M. Nizam.

GRAY, H. 1968. Andhra Pradesh. In Weiner, M., ed. *State Politics in India*. Princeton: Princeton University Press. pp. 398-431.

———. 1970. The landed gentry of the Telangana, Andhra Pradesh. In Leach, E. and MUKHERJEE, S. N. eds. *Elites in South Asia*. Cambridge: Cambridge University Press. pp. 119-37.

HARRISON, S. S. 1956. Caste and the Andhra communists. *The American political science review* 50(2): 378-404.

———. 1960. *India: the most dangerous decade*. Princeton: Princeton University Press.

IYENGAR, S. K. 1930. *Economic investigations in the Hyderabad state, 1929-30*. Vols. I-III Hyderabad: Government of the H.E.M. Nizam.

———. 1951. *Rural economic enquiries in the Hyderabad state, 1949-54*. Hyderabad: Government Printing Press.

KAUTSKY, J.H. 1956. *Moscow and the communist party of India—a study in the post-war evolution of international communist strategy*. New York: M.I.T. Press and John Wiley.

KHUSRO, A. M. 1958. *Economic and social effects of jagirdari abolition and land reforms in Hyderabad*. Delhi: Atmaram and Sons.

MENON. V. P. 1956. *The story of the integration of the Indian states*. London: Longmans Green and Co.

MOORE, JR., B. 1969, *Social origins of dictatorship and democracy—Lord and peasant in the making of the modern world*. London: Penguin.

———. 1972. *Reflections on the causes of human misery*. London: Allen Lane. The Penguin Press.

NAIR, K. 1961. *Blossoms in the dust—the human element in Indian development*. London: Gerald Duckworth.

NARAYAN, B. K. 1960. *Agricultural development in Hyderabad state 1900-1956, a study in economic history*. Secunderabad: Keshava Prakashan.

PRITT, D. N. 1950. Oppression in India. *The labour monthly* 32 (7): 319-20.

QURESHI, A. I. 1949. *The economic development of Hyderabad*. Vol. 1 (rural economy). Bombay: Orient.

RAM, S. 1962. *Vinoba and his mission*. Kashi: Akhil Bharat Sarva Sewa Sangh. Revised edition.

RANGA, N. G. 1949. *Revolutionary peasants*. New Delhi: Amrit Book Co.

RAO, A. R. 1969. *The Telangana movement: an investigative focus*. Hyderabad: Teachers' Association Research Forum.

Rao, C. R. 1972 *The historic Telangana struggle: some useful lessons from its rich experience.* Delhi: C.P.I. Publication.
Rao, M. 1973. Telangana and the revisionists *Frontier* 5(52): 4-7.
Rao, R. V. 1950. A new deal for the farmer in Hyderabad. *The Economic and Political Weekly* 24 June: 617-9.
Roth. A. 1947. Peasant revolt in Hyderabad. *Modern Review* 82(3): 1-2.
Sheshadri, K. 1967. The communist party in Andhra Pradesh. *In* Narain. I., ed. *State politics in India.* Meerut: Meenakshi Prakashan. pp. 388-96.
Smith, W. C. 1950. Hyderabad: Muslim tragedy. *The Middle East Journal* 4(1): 27-51.
Sundarayya, P. 1972. *Telangana people's struggle and its lessons.* Calcutta: C.P.I. (M) Publication.
———. 1972b. Telangana people's struggle and the right communists. *People's democracy* 8(43): 11-2.
Tirth, Swami R. 1967. *Memoirs of Hyderabad freedom struggle.* Bombay: Popular Prakashan.
Mao Tse-Tung, 1967. *Selected Works.* Vols. I-IV. Peking: Foreign Languages Press.
Wright, J., T.P. 1963. Revival of the Majlis-Ittehad-ul-Musalmin of Hyderabad. *The Muslim world* 3(3): 234-43.
Zinkin, T. 1962. *Reporting India.* London: Chatto and Windus.

26 The Postwar Situation and Beginning of Armed Struggle

C. Rajeshwar Rao

I

THE CPI UNIT in Telangana, along with the party unit in Marathwada, organised vigorously the workers under the leadership of Comrades Makhdoom Mohiuddin and Raj Bahadur Gour. Later on, it succeeded in organising the All-Hyderabad Trade Union Congress under whose flag the workers were organised in the Karnataka region of the state also.

Along with this the students were also organised under the flag of the All-Hyderabad Students' Union. Women were organised into their organisation in a few towns, apart from Hyderabad.

The communist movement thus became an important factor in the political life of Hyderabad, specially in the Telangana area by the end of the second world war and beginning of the postwar political upsurge in India.

The end of the second world war brought about basic changes in the international scene and the correlation of forces. The fascists had been routed. The other sections of the imperialist powers who were in the antifascist coalition were weakened. For the first time, a socialist camp, as opposed to the camp of imperialism, came into being, exercising profound influence on the international scene. Anti-imperialist national-liberation movements and national-liberation wars began raging in the enslaved countries of Asia, Africa and Latin America.

In our country also, a powerful anti-imperialist wave swept from one end to the other. Militant mass demonstrations on the issue of the trial of the INA prisoners were the first shot. Then followed the historic RIN mutiny and outburst of simmering

Reproduced from 'The Historic Telengana Struggle—Some Useful Lessons from Its Rich Experience,' by C. Rajeswara Rao, Freedom Jubilee Series No. 3. Communist Party Publication, No. 29, October, 1972 pp. 5-17, pp. 25-9, pp. 30-32.

discontent in the Indian army and air force. The British imperialists realised that they could no longer rely on the armed forces whom they had so long carefully fostered to prop up their rule. The strike of the post and telegraph workers and the proposed all-India strike of the railway workers were the last straw.

The British imperialists were clever enough to see the writing, on the wall and divided the country on a communal basis and handed over power to the Congress and Muslim League in the two parts. They declared the native states independent and helped their stooges, the princes, to balkanise our country. Through these vile manoeuvres, they sought to impose their neocolonialist domination over our country. But they did not succeed, which is another matter.

The mighty anti-British upsurge in the Indian subcontinent had its own reflection on the people of Hyderabad state. The long simmering discontent was bursting up in 1946. Different sections of the people were coming into mass actions on their demands. Workers came out on strikes in a number of places on their pressing demands. Peasants and agricultural workers also resisted the depredations of the landlords and government officials. The notorious incidents of Machireddypalli and Akhnur took place, where the Nizam's armed police resorted to inhuman terror against the people and the raping of women, because they dared resist the looting of their paddy in the name of 'levygalla'. These incidents shook the people in the whole state. Not only the Andhra Mahasabha and the Communist Party but other mass organisations and progressive-minded people also protested against these atrocities and rallied to the support of the people of these villages.

Similarly, the peasants of Mundrai in Jangaon taluk also took back their lands which had been occupied by the notorious landlord Vishnur Ramchandra Reddy who had let loose his goondas. These were only the portents of the coming storm.

The Nizam of Hyderabad understood this and started arresting political workers and resorted to repression against the people. He let loose gangs of his stooge organisation, the Ittehad-ul-Mussalmeen, in order to nip in the bud the rising upsurge of the people. In the context of the British quitting India, as explained earlier, he was conspiring with the British imperialists to make his state independent, which many other princes were also trying to do.

He refused to accede to the Indian union even when almost all the princes were forced to do so. He declared his independence and on 12 June, 1947 he issued a firman that after the lapse of British paramountcy, he would become a sovereign monarch over his state.

With that, the political scene inside Hyderabad state heated up. It acted as the danger signal for all democratic and progressive forces and people. They saw what was in store for them if they did not act quickly to foil the conspiracy being hatched by the Nizam and the British imperialists.

The Telangana and Andhra state units of the CPI did not take any chances. They reviewed the situation, clearly understanding the game of the Nizam, and came to the conclusion that the mass upsurge, which had already started bursting against the Nizam's autocracy and the feudal lords, should be given a proper shape. They decided to organise mass resistance and local volunteer squads equipped with the traditional weapons of the peasants— the lathi, spear, slings and a few muzzle-loaders—to beat back the goonda gangs of the landlords.

In a number of places like Kadivendi, Devaruppula, Patasuryapet in Jangaon and Suryapet taluks and a number of other places in other districts the goonda gangs were beaten back. A number of comrades laid down their lives in these resistance actions. The first martyr in this struggle was Comrade Komarayya of Kadivendi in the successful resistance against the goonda gangs of the notorious Vishnur deshmukh. As the goonda gangs of the feudal landlords failed to suppress the peasant upsurge, the Nizam's armed police entered the scene and launched severe repression.

A mass upsurge burst out in the princely states. In some of them armed actions also took place to force their rulers to accede to the Indian union. Using this mass upsurge and armed actions of the people and the state power they had acquired in their hands, the Congress forced all the princely states—except Hyderabad— to join the Indian union sooner or later. The Nizam was bent upon remaining independent, which would have remained as a dangerous ulcer in the body politic of India if he had succeeded.

Even before 15 August 1947, accession of Hyderabad state to the Indian union had become the main issue before the people of the state. The State Congress, instead of uniting with all other democratic forces and canalising the mass upsurge for an all-out struggle against Nizam's autocracy and his henchmen, sought to plough a lonely furrow. Further, it wanted to turn the mass upsurge into a mere protest satyagraha, preventing it from developing into militant mass actions. The liberal section inside the State Congress was against even this type of mass action and they were putting all sorts of obstacles in its way. The State Congress urged upon the Nizam to join the Indian union and it issued a call for hoisting the national flag everywhere as a form of struggle, which the Nizam banned.

The CPI, the Andhra Mahasabha, the All-Hyderabad Trade Union Congress, the All-Hyderabad Students' Union, which had been urging upon the State Congress to have united struggle all these days, joined in this movement of hoisting the national flag. It caught like wildfire because the people were restive and wanted to go into action on any issue against the Nizam's autocracy. In many towns and villages, national flags were hoisted. In the villages the movement took the form of cutting down toddy palm trees in the fields over which the peasants had no legal right according to the law of those days and preventing forcible collection of grain levy by the government. Workers, peasants, students and the general mass of people, men and women, participated in this struggle. A number of Muslims also joined, braving all the fury of Muslim fanaticism fanned by the Majlis.

The Nizam government retaliated with its might. Shooting, killing, raping of women, trampling down of the national flag, largescale arrests, looting and burning of houses became the order of the day. Hundreds of patriots laid down their lives, including women. There was no safety of life, property and honour in those days. The leadership of the Majlis not only fully supported this carnage but its armed gangs actively participated in these actions along with the armed police force of the Nizam.

While the people of Hyderabad were fighting their life and death battle, the Congress central leadership, which wielded power in Delhi, was negotiating with the Nizam for a settlement on the basis of his joining the Indian union, conceding subjects like defence, foreign affairs and communications to the Indian government and retaining the rest of the powers in his hands. This virtually meant that the Nizam was to be left free to suppress the people's movement in blood.

The Nizam did not agree even to this.

Finally in November 1947 the Indian government signed a standstill agreement for one year with the Nizam. This was a stab in the back of the people of Hyderabad. According to this agreement, the government of India would not interfere in the internal affairs of Hyderabad state. That meant, he could do whatever he liked with the lives of the people. The government of India, on the other hand, would 'wholeheartedly cooperate' with the Nizam 'to promote communal harmony and to maintain peace and security' in the state. In return for this, the Nizam would condescend not to set up embassies in foreign countries. But he could set up offices of agent-general, which in effect would mean the same thing. After one year, a permanent settlement was to be negotiated.

This standstill agreement gave a one-year breathing space to the Nizam in which he could carry on his conspiracy for practically achieving his evil design of an independent Hyderabad. He utilised the opportunity to the fullest extent. While, on the one hand, he was ruthlessly suppressing the freedom movement in the state, on the other he was feverishly enlarging and modernising his armed forces by importing arms from Pakistan, Britain and other countries. He also helped Kasim Rizvi, the leader of the Majlis, to organise and arm his Razakar forces as an auxiliary of the state's armed forces in suppressing the people's movement.

Even after the betrayal by the Congress central leadership, the State Congress leadership dared not come out boldly rejecting the standstill agreement and build a united movement along with other democratic parties and mass organizations to fight the Nizam's evil rule.

It was precisely in this critical situation that units of the Communist Party played a historic role in properly assessing the fighting mood of the people and coming out boldly for armed resistance against the depredations of the Nizam's armed forces and Razakar gangs of the Majlis in defence of the life, property and honour of women and ending the satanic rule of the Nizam once for all.

Comrades Makhdoom Mohiuddin, Ravi Narayan Reddy, Baddam Yella Reddy, Devulapalli Venkateswara Rao, Chandragupta Chowdhury and V.D. Deshpande (the last two communist leaders of Marathwada) gave a call for armed resistance on behalf of the Communist Party, the Andhra Mahasabha, the Marathwada Kisan Sabha and the All-Hyderabad Trade Union Congress.

On behalf of the All-Hyderabad Students' Union, which was led by communists, Comrade Onkar Prasad, general secretary, and Rafi Ahmad, joint secretary, a call was given to the students to take up the challenge thrown by the Nizam and organise and carry on armed resistance. This inspiring call fell on fertile soil and it galvanised the entire situation in the state.

Side by side with this call, a concrete programme of action was chalked out for various sections of the people, which gave flesh and blood to the movement. The programme consisted of abolition of forced labour, reoccupation of lands of the peasants illegally grabbed by the deshmukhs, jagirdars and other landlords, distribution of government lands among the agricultural workers and poor peasants, fair rent for tenants, fair wages for agricultural workers, abolition of exorbitant interest on grain and cash loans given by the landlords to the peasants and agricultural workers. The minimum demands of the workers were also included in this programme. It also included smashing up of the customs outposts which were acting as instruments for harassment of people and obstruction in the way of free trade between the people on both sides of the border and acting as an artificial barrier, dividing the people of the same nationality—the Andhras, the Maharashtrians and the Kannadigas. A call was also given against the looting of grains from the peasants in the name of levy.

In order to assist in the implementation of this programme, the immediate organisation of people's committees and armed guerilla squads was started. In the Telangana region since the Andhra Mahasabha (called by the people 'Sangham') had already become a mass political organisation, committees of the Mahasabha were organised as people's committees to lead the armed guerilla movement.

People of Hyderabad state responded enthusiastically to the ringing call of the CPI and other mass organisations led by it. They rose like lions in Telangana and the armed guerilla movement spread like wildfire, because the people had already gone through the first stage of mass resistance against the armed police and goonda gangs of the feudal lords by taking up traditional weapons which people use in their defence. The CPI and the Andhra Mahasabha commanded the confidence of vast sections of the people in Telangana, especially the rural masses.

The Andhra Mahasabha spread to new areas and new sections of people. Its committees were organised in most of the villages. Some modern weapons were procured and permanent guerilla squads were organised and trained along with local squads. Armed resistance began. In several places the armed guerilla squads retaliated effectively against the armed forces of the Nizam and Razakar gangs of the Majlis when they were on their way to villages for pillage. Sometimes their arms were also snatched away and they were put on the run.

In a number of places the customs outposts were smashed. The looting of grain from peasants in the name of levy collection was also foiled to a large extent.

In thousands people helped the guerilla squads whenever it was necessary. Guerilla squads were moving in the villages quite openly. People gave them food, shelter, information about the movements of the enemy, etc. The guerilla squads moved like fish in water.

Thousands took part in sabotage work by digging up roads in order to hamper the movement of the Nizam's armed forces and Razakars. They also accompanied the squads whenever the fortresses to the feudal lords had to be attacked and razed to the ground. In this way the people played a very active part in the armed struggle against the Nizam.

In the course of the armed struggle, a number of most oppressive landlords and their agents who were actively aiding the Nizam's forces to perpetrate inhuman atrocities on the people were also punished and in some cases put to death. Some of them were tried in people's courts also. Consequently, many landlords ran away to towns, leaving the areas where guerilla struggle was going on, just to save their lives. They left behind their officials to run their establishments and farms, and operated from the towns.

Thus the field was left free for the people in these areas. There was government only when the armed forces were present. Otherwise, the Andhra Mahasabha committees were the rulers. People used to say that there were two governments—one by day and the other at night. Usually the Nizam's armed forces used to move only in day time and before nightfall they would take shelter in the camps. In far-off places where there were no communications, they came but rarely. Hence the strategic roads were dug up by the people in order to prevent the armed forces of the Nizam from moving.

This gave an opportunity to the people to throw away the oppressive yoke of the jagirdars, deshmukhs and other feudal lords. The agrarian programme was fully implemented in the areas where armed resistance was successfully going on. Forced labour was abolished. Illegally occupied land of the peasants was taken back from the feudals. Government lands were distributed to the agricultural workers and poor peasants. Rackrenting and usurious grain loans were abolished. People were thus relieved of feudal oppression in the areas of armed resistance.

The armed resistance was carried on in most parts of the famous Nalgonda district, vast tracts of Warangal district (which at that time included the present Khammam district), the present Hyderabad district (which at that time was the personal jagir of the Nizam) and some areas of Karimnagar, Medhak and Adilabad districts. The armed struggle was going on within even a few miles of Hyderabad city, the capital of the state. These areas comprised about 4,000 villages which were considered as liberated areas. In this area, about ten lakh acres of land were distributed among the people.

Armed resistance was fast spreading to the other areas of Telengana. Of course, in Hyderabad and other towns the Nizam was holding his sway and the people were at the mercy of the Razakar gangs. Even there people organised selfdefence squads to defend their life and honour.

In the same way, armed actions took place in Marathwada and even in the Karnatak part of the state. The Nizam was getting more and more isolated and his power was dwindling.

This was the situation before the 'police action' of the Indian army which entered the state in September, 1948.

Armed actions became possible mainly because the Nizam was defending an autocratic feudal social order, hated by the general mass of people. He and the other feudal lords were completely isolated from the people. He had a very narrow social base with only sections of Muslims poisoned by communal fanaticism supporting him. Even sections of Hindu feudal landlords were against him and they were in sympathy with the anti-Nizam movement in general because of the communal policy the Nizam had been pursuing to get the support of the Muslim minority and the atrocities committed by the Razakar hordes on the people.

A second factor to be taken into consideration was that administrative set-up based on the outdated feudal autocratic social order was inefficient. It could not stand the onslaught of the mass upsurge and armed guerilla resistance. The armed forces of the Nizam were mostly old-fashioned, not modernised. This could be seen from the very fact that even a large number of tahsil offices and even some district centres did not have even telegraphic facilities, not to speak of telephone and wireless.

Alarmed at the growth of the armed resistance movement in Telangana under the leadership of the CPI, they took anti-communist positions and were pressing the State Congress leadership to dissociate themselves from the resistance movement. Simultaneously, they attacked the Andhra state unit of the CPI at the end of January 1948, utilising the clashes between our party and the RSS at Vijayawada following Gandhiji's murder. They made widespread searches of party offices and a number of leading cadres of the Andhra state unit of the CPI were arrested. As a result, delegates from Andhra to the Second Party Congress which was held in Calcutta had to go there secretly. This repression was launched in order to see that the Andhra area did not act as the base for the Telangana armed struggle. It was not only the communists and people under their influence who were supporting the armed struggle in Telangana. The general mass of people also supported this struggle and liberally contributed funds. This unnerved the Congress central leadership. Even communist guerilla squads taking shelter on the border were arrested.

The Hyderabad State Congress leadership was a house divided. The liberal section was dead-set against any sort of resistance, they were for any compromise with the Nizam. They fell for the overtures of the Nizam floated by his prime minister Laik Ali and other Hindu stooges in the so-called interim government he had set up. Confabulations were going on under the active guidance of K.M. Munshi. They responded to the call for fighting the 'communist danger' issued by the Nizam and propagated that if no compromise was arrived at soon, Telangana would go Red.

Despite the fact that the Congress central government in Delhi offered full autonomy to the Nizam in internal matters, provided he was prepared to concede subjects like defence, foreign affairs and communications to the Indian union and agree to join it, he was adamant. Cleverly utilising the weak-kneed policies of the Congress central leadership and the standstill agreement which, in fact, was a surrender to the Nizam, he was frantically trying to assert his independence. He utilised the inactivity and timid behaviour of the central and State Congress leaders to suppress people's upsurge and the armed resistance movement spreading under the leadership of the Communist Party.

II

Armed Struggle Retreats to Forests

Taking up the thread of the narration of the Telangana struggle again, it has to be stated that with the above understanding of the path of the Indian revolution, the leadership of the Andhra unit of the Communist Party decided to continue the armed struggle. As stated earlier, the government of India made all preparations to suppress the Telangana struggle. The armed forces attacked the communist strongholds and the guerilla squads with all their might at the end of 1948. A number of comrades and guerilla fighters were killed in encounters with the Indian armed forces. Naturally, the Telangana movement could not withstand such a political and military offensive any longer. We were faced with the problem of either withdrawing the armed struggle or finding a way out.

As the communist movement in both the regions of Telangana and Andhra had reached a dead-end and it became impossible for comrades and guerilla squads in the plains where they had been operating till then to continue armed struggle, a call was given for all the able-bodied comrades to go to the forests. Others were asked to remain underground if they could in their place of work or move from their own village to other areas where they were not known and take up some job to survive. Many regional party committees of the plains even moved to the border province. This was done for sheer survival in the middle of 1949.

The comrades of Warangal, including the present Khammam district, some taluks of Nalgonda district adjacent to Warangal district and Krishna, West Godavari and East Godavari districts of Andhra region were sent to the dense forests on the Godavari river. Comrades from Medhak and Karimnagar went to the forests in Karimnagar. The comrades of the major part of Nalgonda district and Guntur, Nellore, Kurnool districts of Andhra region went to the dense Nalgonda forests on both sides of river Krishna.

In these forests, the main mass of the people were tribals. In the petty urban centres in the forests, the landlords, contractors and merchants, who exploit and loot the tribal people utilising their ignorance and backwardness, were living. Though the area was vast, the population was very thin. The landlords grabbed the best lands of the tribals mainly by giving loans at exorbitant rates of interest. The merchants looted the people through the exchange of the forest produce like tamarind, honey, etc. for salt, cloth, etc. fully making use of the ignorance of the tribal people of prices and calculation. The forest contractors exploited them by paying low wages for plucking bidi leaves or cutting bamboos and wood.

The government apparatus in these areas was also very weak. It consisted of police outposts here and there and the forest rangers and tahsil offices in the headquarters of these forest tahsils. Though their effective control over the tribal people was not much, they were also collecting illegal gratifications in the form of forest produce and making them do forced labour.

When our guerilla squads went to the forest, at first the tribal people would not repose their confidence in them. When they found that the merchants, landlords, contractors and government officials stopped coming to the tribal villages for fear of the guerilla squads, they became our friends and began helping our squads with food and shelter. But as their economy is primitive, they could not support all our guerilla squads and political workers. Therefore, our squads attacked the landlords' houses in the villages on the border of forests to get grain and other foodstuff. They hunted forest animals also for food.

Our squads lived in this state of affairs till the end of 1949. Then the Congress administration became wise and set up military and armed police camps in the key centres of the forest regions. Then they adopted the socalled Briggs plan, which the British imperialists had used to suppress guerilla movement in Malaysia, in some of the dense forest regions, especially in the forests on the Godavari river. They burnt down about 2,000 tribal hamlets and herded the tribal people into concentration camps. They were allowed to go outside the camps only during day time. But they had to return to the camps long before sunset. Otherwise other members of their family who were held as hostages would be taken to task. Many of these tribal people died in these camps because of semistarvation and undernourishment.

The Congress administration adopted this tactic to physically isolate our squads from the tribal people and eliminate our squads. Our squads harassed the armed forces and kept them on tenterhooks whenever they dared to come out of the camp even in day time. In a number of such engagements, our squads fought bravely and skilfully. The armed forces rarely dared enter the dense forests. But the squads could not remain in the dense forests all the time. They had to get food and water. In the engagements with the armed forces, many a comrade lost his life. They enrolled some tribal youth and girls into the squads and gave them training.

Some of the squads moved to newer forests. Thus our squads went even to the vast and dense forests of Adilabad district. Some crossed the Godavari river and went to the forests of Bastar. But they had to return after suffering some losses because they did not know the language of the tribes in the region.

Thus, by the middle of 1951, the situation again became critical for the guerilla squads and political workers in the forests. Procurement of food, water and other absolute necessities of life for mere physical survival became the sole daily job of the squads.

When comrades went to the forest, the idea was to keep contact with the plain areas of Telangana armed struggle from these bases. In the beginning this was tried. But it became impossible. In Telangana area, the government organised local defence squads to help the police to capture communists and suppress the communist movement. The landlords dared not come back to the villages even after that. They only kept close contact and tried to demoralise people, saying that the communist movement had been suppressed and it would never rise again. Home Minister Sardar Patel made a speech at Hyderabad in 1950, a few days before his death, saying that he would not allow a single communist to be alive in Telangana. This was utilised to the fullest extent.

Though the masses were still sympathetic to the communists, they lost faith that the communists could ever return and help them. So they came to a compromise with the landlords and bought the lands which they had occupied at very cheap rates. This became possible because of the strength of the Telangana resistance movement which had shaken the very foundation of the feudal set-up and the landlords did not think that they could ever get back the lands so easily. Therefore, they sold them at cheap prices to the occupiers.

Had we understood the situation properly, we would have changed our tactic and withdrawn the armed struggle and utilised the mass upsurge to force the Congress government to implement the two important land legislations they had themselves issued—for the abolition of the jagirs and protection to the tenants—under pressure of the Telangana armed struggle and the general democratic movement in the state. That would have not only helped the strengthening of the communist movement, but also the unification of all the progressive forces for democratic advance. The other course of continuing the armed struggle helped the Congress government and the reactionary forces to suppress and weaken it.

In Andhra area, there were no favourable conditions for any sort of armed guerilla struggle. There were only some sporadic actions, here and there, against the atrocities of the landlords, and some famous raids on police stations on the borders of the forests where arms were captured. In Andhra area, the government armed the landlords in the villages and organised all able-bodied males into local defence squads for suppressing the communist movement. Many communists and sympathisers were captured with the help of the landlords and their gangs. They were tortured in the armed police camps and some were killed in cold blood. Thus the communist movement in Andhra area was suppressed. But the guerilla squads maintained themselves and continued to survive somehow in the forests.

Thousands of communists were arrested in Telangana and Andhra area and they were put in jail. Jails were a hell, especially in Telangana. They had to undergo inhuman sufferings. A number of comrades were killed in firings inside jail.

III

Historic Significance of Telangana

In conclusion the following important aspects of the Telangana struggle can be highlighted.

Firstly, the significance of the historic struggle was that it was a struggle for ending the autocratic rule of the Nizam and for the establishment of democracy and for foiling the conspiracy of the Nizam to make Hyderabad an independent state. The struggle played a very significant role in ending the Nizam's rule and for unifying the country.

Secondly, it was a revolutionary agrarian armed struggle for ending inhuman and outdated feudal order, presided over by the Nizam, and for giving land to the agricultural workers, peasants and adivasis. Though it was not able to fully realise this aim, it greatly helped in eliminating forced labour, illegal taxes and oppression of various types by feudal lords. It greatly helped in eliminating the jagiri system at one stroke and giving full ownership rights to the jagiri peasants and occupancy rights to the tenants-at-will of the deshmukhs.

Thirdly, it was a struggle for division of the state into linguistic zones and formation of unified linguistic states of Andhra, Maharashtra and Karnataka with the people of adjoining areas speaking the same language so as to facilitate all-round political, economic and cultural development of these people.

This struggle greatly helped the subsequent struggle for the formation of linguistic states in India. With the success of the struggle not only the Hyderabad state but other provinces of India were divided into unified linguistic states, along with Vishalaandhra, Samyukta Maharashtra and Samyukta Karnataka states.

Fourthly, it was an armed struggle fought under the leadership of the Communist Party over a vast area in which about 20 districts, both of Telangana and Andhra area, were involved. In this struggle 4,000 Communist Party cadres and sympathisers laid down their lives and millions of people participated and underwent terrible sufferings. The armed struggle not only enhanced the prestige of the Telangana and Andhra units of our party, but of the entire party. The struggle made our party in Telangana and Andhra areas a revolutionary party. The armed struggle set revolutionary traditions among the Telugu people—a great capital for our party.

Fifthly, the struggle had two phases—anti-Nizam and anti-Congress-government. So far as the anti-Nizam struggle was concerned, it was a struggle in which millions of people took part and it was started on the crest of a mass upsurge.

The extension of this struggle to the second phase was done with a wrong understanding of the situation obtaining in the state, our country and the world at that time. Though our party extended to the forest regions in this phase of struggle, yet because of this wrong understanding, we were cut off from our main base both in Telangana and Andhra area where we had been building our movement for decades.

Extension of the armed struggle in desperation to Andhra districts was also wrong. In the Andhra area, there was no mass wave at all as in Telangana.

If we had changed our political line after the police action in Telangana and utilised the opportunities which came at that time, our party's position and movement would have been far stronger than what it became by continuing the armed struggle.

Lastly, there was never any difference in the Telangana and Andhra units of our party over the anti-Nizam phase of the struggle. But when some leading comrades saw the bad effects on the second phase, they differed and wanted the withdrawal of the struggle. But the major section of the leadership thought otherwise and the struggle continued up to the end of 1951.

The glorious traditions and achievements of this heroic struggle are the common heritage of the entire united communist movement. Those who led and took part in this struggle are today inside the Communist Party of India, Communist Party (Marxist) and in the extremist movements.

27 Telangana

P. Sundarayya

Introduction

IT IS NOW 20 years since the Telangana peasants' armed struggle was withdrawn on October 21, 1951. There is no authentic narration, even in outline, of how this struggle developed in that Nizam-governed feudal Hyderabad state into a peasants' and people's armed revolt, the intervention by the Indian Army on September 13, 1948, and the heroic armed resistance put up by the peasant masses for three years to defend the lands they gained earlier from being seized by the landlords backed by the Nehru Government's armed forces. Avowed enemies and hostile critics of this great movement have produced tons of literature denouncing the struggle as Communist 'violence, banditry and anarchy'.

The Right Communists are vociferous in depicting it, particularly the stage of the partisan resistance during the years 1949-51, as sectarian, dogmatic and individual terrorism in the main. The Naxalite leaders are busy carrying on the smear campaign that the leadership of the Telangana struggle betrayed it in calling it off in October, 1951.

To present, in brief, an overall balance-sheet of this heroic peasant uprising: it exacted tremendous sacrifices from the fighting peasantry of Telangana and the Visalandhra state unit of the Communist Party which was destined to lead this popular peasant uprising. As many as 4,000 Communists and peasant militants were killed; more than 10,000 Communist cadres and people's fighters were thrown into detention camps and jails for a period of 3-4 years; no less than a minimum of 50,000 people were dragged into police and military camps from time to time to be beaten, tortured and terrorised for weeks and months together; several

Reproduced from *Telangana People's Struggle and its Lessons* by P. Sundarayya, Published by Desraj Chadha, on behalf of the Communist Party of India (Marxist), Calcutta, December, 1972, pp. 1-5.

lakhs of people in thousands of villages were subjected to police and military raids and suffered cruel lathi-charges; the people in the course of these military and police raids lost properties worth millions of rupees which were either looted or destroyed; thousands of women were molested and had to undergo all sorts of humiliations and indignities; in a word, the entire region was subjected to a brutal police and military terror rule for full five years, initially by the Nizam and his Razakar armed hordes, and subsequently by the combined armed forces of the Union Government and the State Government of Hyderabad. After the police action, a huge 50,000 strong force of armed personnel of different categories was deployed to violently suppress the movement and restore the shattered landlord rule. According to some unofficial estimates, the Government of India had spent as much money and resources in Hyderabad then as it had spent in its war with Pakistan over the issue of Kashmir during the years 1947-8.

Of course, the picture is not complete without its second side, the picture of an impressive record of achievements and gains to the credit of the peasant uprising. During the course of the struggle, the peasantry in about 3,000 villages, covering roughly a population of 3 million in an area of about 16,000 square miles, mostly in the three districts of Nalgonda, Warangal and Khammam, had succeeded in setting up gram raj, on the basis of fighting village panchayats. In these villages, the hated landlords—the pillars of Nizam's autocracy in the rural areas—were driven away from their fortress-like houses—gadis—and their lands were seized by the peasantry. One million acres of land was redistributed among the peasantry under the guidance of the people's committees. All evictions were stopped and the forced labour service was abolished. The plunderous and exorbitant rates of usury were either drastically cut down or altogether forbidden. The daily wages of agricultural labourers were increased and a minimum wage was enforced. The oppressive forest officialdom was forced to abandon the entire forest belt and the tribals and the people living in the adjoining areas of these forests were able to enjoy the fruits of their labour. For a period of 12 to 18 months the entire administration in these areas was conducted by the village peasant committees. During the course of this struggle against the Nizam's autocracy, the people could organise and build a powerful militia comprising

10,000 village squad members and about 2,000 regular guerilla squads, in defence of the peasantry against the armed attacks of the Razakars and the Nizam's police. Lakhs of peasants, for the first time in their life, could have their regular two meals a day. In a word, this historic peasant rebellion shook the medieval autocratic regime of the Asafjahi dynasty to its roots, delivering death-blows against it.

To this heroic peasant resistance movement goes the credit of pushing the question of the agrarian revolution into the forefront, compelling the unwilling hands of the Congress leaders to embark upon various agrarian reforms, however halting, half-hearted and pitiful they were. It was during the course of this struggle that the bhoodan utopia was conceived by Sri Vinobha Bhave, the sarvodaya leader, who was sent there by the Congress leaders for the so-called pacification campaign and anti-Communist propaganda among the peasantry. It was in the course of this bitter and prolonged struggle that people came into grasp the truth that the land problems can never be really resolved by the honeyed phrases and pompous promises of the bourgeois-landlord rulers but a powerful organised militant mass struggle alone can do it.

Let us also remember again that not a small share of credit goes to the Telangana struggle for forcing the pace of states' reorganisation on a linguistic basis, enabling the several disunited and dismembered nationalities to realise their long-cherished democratic demand for separate statehood. The powerful blows that this struggle delivered to the biggest princely regime of Hyderabad, inspired the struggle which won the Andhra state, after the martyrdom of Potti Sreeramulu in 1952 and this, in turn, paved the way for the formation of linguistic states throughout India in 1956, forcing the ruling Congress leadership to demolish the unprincipled and arbitrary division of the country made by the former British rulers. The heroic Telangana peasant struggle thus made its unique contribution to redrawing the political map of India on a national, democratic, and sound linguistic basis.

In this connection, it is very necessary to realise that the Communist Party which had the proud role of leading this historic Telangana revolt and had to bear the brunt of the repression with tremendous sacrifices, the Communist Party which was at the head of the Vayalar-Punnappra struggle in Kerala, which was at the head of the postwar peasant struggles and the working class struggles in Bengal, emerged as a result, on the national political scene as a widely recognised and effective political force to be seriously reckoned with. From a small force of militant working class trends that it used to be till then in shaping the destinies of India's multi-millions, the Communist Party earned the prestige and honour of emerging as the single biggest opposition group in the first Parliament, following the 1952 general elections.

Finally, the single biggest contribution made by the Telangana peasant revolt to the Communist movement in India is of tremendous importance—that this struggle brought to the forefront of the Indian Communist movement almost all the basic theoretical and ideological questions concerning the strategy and tactics of the Indian people's democratic revolution for correct and scientific answers and realistic and practical solutions. A series of issues such as the role of the peasantry in the people's democratic revolution, the place and significance of partisan resistance and rural revolutionary basis, the question of concretely analysing the classification among the peasantry, and what role is played in the revolution by the different strata of the peasantry, the perspective for the Indian revolution, the specific place and role of the working class and urban centres in our revolution, the precise meaning and import of the concept of working class hegemony and the part played by the Communist Party in realising it in an underdeveloped and backward country like ours, where the modern working class does not exceed one per cent of the population, etc., were thrown up for serious inner-party debate and decision. Life and experience, after a prolonged inner-party struggle, enabled the Party to arrive at a fairly correct political line, with satisfactory answers to most of the problems posed.

It is relevant to mention here that during the course of the struggle, particularly during the phase of its last two years, the Communist Party from top to bottom was sharply divided into two hostile camps, one defending the struggle and its achievements and the other denouncing and decrying it as terrorism, etc. Those who opposed this struggle had even openly come out the press, providing grist to the mill of the enemies in maligning the struggle and the Communist Party that was leading it. This sharp political-ideological split though enveloping the entire Party in the country, was particularly sharp and acute in the Party's Visalandhra unit which was directly and immediately involved in this valiant peasant uprising. Subsequently, history demonstrated that the inner-party unity achieved, following the withdrawal of the Telangana armed resistance in October, 1951, was only formal, superficial and temporary and the division, actually, got crystallised into two distinct hostile political trends. It was not just accidental, and may be of interest to note, that in the Party split that came about in the year 1962-3, the division in the state Party unit of Visalandhra remained, more or less, of the same character and with the same composition as was witnessed during the 1950-51 inner-party strife. With the exception of a handful of individual Communist leaders and cadres, who might have changed their loyalties and political convictions, the bulk that stood opposed to the Telangana struggle, on one count or the other, opted out to the side of the right reformist and revisionist Right Communist Party; while the overwhelming majority, that defended the struggle to the last, rallied firmly behind the Communist Party of India (Marxist). No serious student of the Indian Communist movement can succeed in getting to the root cause and reason that inevitably paved the way for the split in 1962-3 if he were to bypass the struggle of Telangana and the various inner-party controversies that broke around the issue of conducting this valiant peasant resistance movement.

28 Hyderabad State—its Socio-political Background

P. Sundarayya

Multi-lingual State

THE HYDERABAD state consisted of three linguistic areas, the eight Telugu-speaking districts with Hyderabad city, the capital of the state, constituting the Telangana area; five Marathi-speaking districts, in the north-west of the state, constituting the Marathwada region; and three Kannada-speaking districts in the south-western part.

The Telangana region occupied 50 per cent of the area, as against 28 per cent of the Marathwada region, and the remaining 22 per cent of the Kannada region. The Telugu-speaking population in 1951 was 9,000,000 (50 per cent), Marathi-speaking about 4,500,000 (25 per cent) and Kannada-speaking 2,000,000 (11 per cent) while the Urdu-speaking population was 2,100,000 (12 per cent).

Conflict Between the Muslim Ruler and the Hindu Subjects

The Nizam of Hyderabad state, though a vassal of the British imperialists, being a Muslim and the vast majority of the people of Hyderabad belonging to the Hindu religion and its various sects, got reflected in the administrative set-up. Though the Muslim population was about 12 per cent, in the whole administrative set-up, especially in the higher echelons, the overwhelming majority, more than 90 per cent, were Muslim bureaucratic officials. The Nizam and mullas tried to instil a feeling that the Muslims were the ruling class and they had a right to lord it over the rest of the people of the state. Against this, the growing middle class intellectuals, and the growing Hindu business and industrial interests took up the cudgels, and the Arya Samajists became the champions of the 'Hindu masses' against the 'Muslim oppressors'.

Reproduced from *Telangana People's Struggle and its Lessons* by P. Sundarayya. *op. cit.* pp. 7-13 and 16, 17, 21, 22, 23.

There were large numbers of conflicts and clashes between these sections.

In the early days, till the 1940s, the Indian National Congress refused to take up the struggle of the people against the 'princes and nawabs' of the native states. This also left the field free for the Arya Samajists to come forward as the champions of the struggle against autocracy and enabled them to divert the democratic awakening of the people, to a considerable extent, on to communal lines.

One of the aspects of this Muslim feudal rule was reflected in the language policy of the state, making Urdu dominate, at the cost of major languages, which were the mother-tongues of the overwhelming majority of the people of the state.

Later, during the Telangana struggle of 1946-7, the Nizam and his feudal administrators, his armed Razakars, tried to rally the Muslim masses to support them as against the 'Hindus'. But thanks to the leadership of the Communist Party, large numbers of the Muslim peasantry and rural artisans and the rural poor were rallied behind the fighting Telangana peasantry, though it has to be admitted that a vast section of Muslims in the towns and cities supported the Nizam and the Razakars. It was again thanks to the Party's leadership, that the reprisals against Muslims, after the 'Police action' were prevented in the Telangana area, whereas in the Marathwada region, in many areas, where the democratic movement was not so strong as in Telangana, they occurred on quite a large scale.

The utter isolation of, the 'Muslim ruler' from the vast mass of his 'Hindu subjects' was an important factor that enabled the rallying of various sections against the hated ruler.

The Feudal Oppression

The basic feature that dominated the socio-economic life of the people of Hyderabad and especially in Telangana was the unbridled feudal exploitation that persisted well-nigh till the beginning of the Telangana armed peasant struggle.

Out of the 53,000,000 acres in the whole of Hyderabad State, about 30,000,000 acres, i.e., about 60 per cent, were under governmental land revenue system, (called 'diwani' or 'khalsa area'); about 15,000,000 acres, i.e., about 30 per cent, under the 'jagirdari' system, and about 10 per cent as the Nizam's own direct estate, i.e., sarf khas system. It was only after the police action that the sarf khas and jagirdari systems were abolished, and these lands were merged in diwani (brought under governmental land revenue system).

The income or loot from the peasantry, from the sarf khas area, amounting to Rs. 20,000,000 annually was entirely used to meet the expenditure of the Nizam's family and its retinue. The whole area was treated as his private estate. He was not bound to spend any amount for economic and social benefit or development of people's livelihood in that area. If anything was spent, it used to be from other general revenues of the state. In addition, the Nizam Nawab used to be given Rs. 7,000,000 per annum from the state treasury.

After the police action when the 'sarf khas' area was merged in the 'diwani' area, the Nizam and his family offspring were to be paid Rs. 5,000,000 per annum as compensation, apart from another Rs. 5,000,000 as privy purse. The peasants in these areas were nothing but bond-slaves, or total serfs under the Nizam. Even whatever little rights existed in the 'diwani' area were denied to them.

The 'jagir' areas constituted 30 per cent of the total state. In these areas, paigas, samsthanam, jagirdars, ijardars, banjardars, maktedars, inamdars, or agraharams, were the various kinds of feudal oppressors. Some of these used to have their own revenue officers to collect the taxes they used to impose. Some of them used to pay a small portion to the state while some others were not required to pay anything. In these areas, various kinds of illegal exactions and forced labour were the normal feature. Some of these jagirs, paigas and samsthanams, especially the biggest ones, had their own separate police, revenue, civil and criminal systems; they were sub-feudatory states, under the Nizam's state of Hyderabad which was itself a stooge native state under the British autocracy in India. In jagir areas the land taxes on irrigated lands used to be 10 times more than those collected in diwani (government) areas, amounting to Rs. 150 per acre of 20-30 maunds of paddy per acre.

The paigas were estates granted to Muslim feudals, especially the Nizam's relatives, for recruiting and maintaining armed personnel to help the Nizam in his wars. The jagirs and samasthanams were those given to reward officers, who distinguished themselves, in serving the Nizam. Maktas, banjars, agraharamas and inams were given for various services, and these owners were entitled to fleece the peasantry and take as much as they could extract. There used to be 'deshmukhs' and 'deshpandes' who were earlier the tax collectors for the Government, but later on, under the Nizam Government's Salar Jung diwanship (Chief Ministership), when direct tax collection by the state apparatus was introduced, these 'deshmukhs' and 'deshpandes' were granted vatans or mash (annuities), based on percentage of the past collections, in perpetuity. These deshmukhs and deshpandes as collectors of taxes, grabbed thousands of acres of the best fertile cultivated land, and made it their own property. The peasants cultivating these lands were reduced to the position of tenants-at-will.

How did they come to own these lands? These feudal landlords had acquired them by all foul means from the ordinary people. The major portion of the lands cultivated by the peasants came to be occupied by the landlords, during the first survey settlement. These people who had power in their hands got lands registered in their names without the knowledge of the peasants who were cultivating them and the peasants came to know of it only afterwards when it was too late to do anything. Thus, these feudal lords got possession of unlimited vast lands and made them their legal possession.

Even lands which were left out in possession of the peasants in the survey settlement, were occupied by the landlords in the years of the economic crisis of 1920-22 and 1930-33, when the peasants either due to bad harvests or unfair prices for the crops were unable to pay the taxes; these feudal landlords used to torture the peasants who were unable to pay the taxes and get hold of their lands. Many a time this acquisition used to take place even without the knowledge of the peasants. They used to lend agricultural products like grain, chillies, etc., to the peasants at fantastic usurious rates and later under the pretext of non-repayment of these loans, used to confiscate the lands. This system was prevalent at the time of the Telangana struggle.

These landlords are not only deshmukhs but also village chiefs, patel, patwari, mali patel—with hereditary rights. Each one used to get five to ten villages under him as vatan.

These vatan villages were controlled through clerks or agents (seridars) appointed by the deshmukh. They enjoyed the rights of an officer. These seridars used to collect the products from the peasants by force, and do all other jobs including supplying all information about the village. If there was any quarrel or friction amongst the villagers, it could not be settled without the knowledge of the landlord. Depending upon the nature of the quarrel, the deshmukhs used to decide whether it should be settled in his house (gadi) or outside in the village centre or elsewhere. If it was a small matter, the deshmukh's agent would be entrusted with it, but if it was a big affair, then it was settled in the presence of the deshmukh in his house. To this category of rich landlords belonged people like the Babasahebpeta landlord, Visnoor Ramachandra Reddy, etc.

Pingali Venkatrama Reddy (Waddepalli deshmukh) got excise contracts for the whole of Telangana all for himself. In those days, excise (abkari) contract meant full control over the villages.

Vetti System

The vetti system (forced labour and exactions) is generally taken to be confined to tribal areas or some of the most backward social communities in other areas. But in Telangana vetti system was an all-pervasive social phenomenon affecting all classes of people, in varying degrees. Each harijan family had to send one man from the family to do vetti. In a small hamlet (palle) each house will send one man. Their daily job consisted of household work in the house of the patel, patwari mali-patel or deshmukh, to carry reports to police stations, taluk office (tehsil); keep watch on the village chavadi and the poundage. Besides these, there used to be more work for them whenever an officer came to the village chavadi. In village Chilukur, daily 16 harijans used to do vetti. They used to collect wood for fuel from the forests and carry post also. For carrying post or supplies they were supposed to get an anna for two and a half miles, which was of course not even honoured in practice. This system was known as 'kosukuvisam' in Telugu (i.e., 1/16th of a rupee for a distance of $2\frac{1}{2}$ miles).

Further the harijans, who carried on the work of cobblers, tanning of leather and stitching shoes, or preparing leather accessories for agricultural operations, for drawing water from wells or yoke belts for plough cattle, or for draught bullocks, were forced to supply these to the landlords free of cost while the rest of the peasantry used to pay them fixed annuities in grain and other agricultural produce.

Wretched Conditions of workers and Middle Class Employees

In 1941, in the Telangana area, there were about 500 factories employing about 28,000 workers. Many of the big factories like textiles, mines, paper mills, engineering factories were heavily subsidised and large amounts of loans granted by the Government to these owners—Salarjung, Babu Khan, Lahoti, Alauddin, Dorabji, Chenoy, Tayabji, Laik Ali, Pannalal Pitti, etc. They made huge profits during the war, selling their goods in the black market.

But the workers were miserably paid, the textile workers' wage being Rs. 10 to 15 per month. Eighty per cent of the wage earners got Rs. 15 per month. In the Azamjahi Mills of Warangal, 4,000 workers' wage bill was Rs. 13.63 lakhs in 1943, while the managing agent's commission amounted to Rs. 7.44 lakhs; in the Ramgopal Mills of Hyderabad 1,500 workers' wage bill was Rs. 4 lakhs while the managing agents' commission was Rs. 1.35 lakhs.

The higher government officials, numbering 1,500, were paid Rs. 50 million per year, while the wages for many lower categories varied between 12, 16, 30 and 60 rupees per month.

Second World War and People's Struggles in Hyderabad State

The second world war had broken out in 1939. It spread all over the world, with Hitler attacking the Soviet Union in June 1941, and the Japanese imperialists, in collaboration with the Hitlerites, attacking the American naval base in Pearl Harbour, thus starting its Pacific war against American, British and French positions.

The British rulers of India automatically declared India to be at war, without even consulting the national leadership and elected legislatures. The Indian National Congress decided not to cooperate with the British war effort, till their demand for National Government at the Centre and the British Viceroy to act in accordance with the national Ministry thus formed, was met, and the pledge that after the war was over full transfer of power would take place. It asked the Congress Ministries in the provinces to resign and started individual satyagraha to bring pressure on the British Government.

The British did not bother much about the ineffective individual satyagraha movement. It went on with its war effort, intensified its exploitation of Indian resources and manpower, and the Indian army was sent abroad to fight for the British in many key sectors in Europe, Africa, West Asia, and later on in Burma, Malaya, etc. The militant section of the Indian National Congress led by Subhas Chandra Bose was opposed to these mild steps of the Congress leadership. They advocated a militant mass movement, Subhas Bose left India in disguise and later organised the Indian National Army with the aid of the Japanese and marched into Manipur and Assam in 1942-4.

The Communist Party of India also advocated militant struggle for complete overthrow of the British imperialist Government in its Proletarian Path. It had to go underground and work. It could only carry on propaganda in most of the states as it was a small force; in Andhra it brought out secretly a magazine, Swatantra Bharat, and circulated widely 2,000 copies in about the same number of villages throughout the State. But the prestige of the Party had tremendously grown because of this militant line and the underground organisation and campaigns it carried on against the British imperialist war effort.

But with the Hitlerite attack on the Soviet Union, and its rapid and deep penetration into the Soviet Union, it became the duty of every democratic force and especially the Communist movement to chalk out a programme of how, while effectively fighting the British imperialist domination in our country and other colonies, to help the Soviet Union and its allies to defeat the Hitler-Mussolini-Tojo fascist tri-combination, its onslaught on the bastion of Socialism and the world democratic camp.

Sri Jawaharlal Nehru and those who followed him in the Congress were for support to the war effort and help to the Soviet side to win, but to effectively do it, to rouse the Indian people, they felt that effective power should be transferred to the Indian leadership, with the definite proviso for full transfer of power after the war. Certain other leaders of the Indian National Congress felt that it was the opportune time, when the British were in a tight corner, to bring maximum pressure, to get maximum concessions from the British. Since the British imperialists were not prepared to grant even the minimum which the Indian National Congress leadership demanded, the 1942 Quit India movement was launched.

The British imperialists launched full-scale repression to suppress this movement violently.

It was in December 1941 that the Communist Party came out with its assessment of the new situation, six months after Hitler's attack on the Soviet Union. It was not easy for the Communist Party to come to a quick decision. It was clear to the Party that the war was no more between two groups of imperialist powers (one of the groups being fascist) as it had been from 1939 to 1941. The attack on the Soviet Union, the only socialist power then in the world, by the Hitler-Mussolini fascist combine, was the calculated, though desperate act of these fascist powers to clear their way for world domination by destroying the Soviet Union, which was blocking it, determinedly.

29 The Communist Movement in Andhra: Terror Regime 1948-51

P. Sundarayya

Historical Background

ANDHRA is a contiguous area to Telangana. Now in 1971, it has a three-crore population and 12 districts. The 12 districts in the Andhra area can be divided again as follows: Circar or coastal districts (8); Rayalaseema districts (4); with the nine Telangana districts, now they constitute Andhra Pradesh. The boundaries now are: east-sea coast: south-Tamil Nadu, West-Karnataka; North-Maharashtra; North-east-Bastar area of Madhya Pradesh and Orissa State.

Andhra had a predominantly peasant economy. While the Circar districts were comparatively more developed economically, socially and politically with a number of projects and other irrigation facilities, the Rayalaseema districts are backward in all respects, with a backward agriculture, no big projects and more domination of feudal relations and oppression. There were hardly any big industries except in Vizagapatnam district, where the shipbuilding yard owned by the Scindias and two jute mills owned by Europeans, were situated, and railways in the whole of Andhra. The rest of the working class was mostly dependent for its livelihood on petty industries such as tobacco, mica mines, foundries, rice and oil mills, etc. Ninety per cent of the whole population lived on agriculture in villages.

The Communist Party

The Communist Party in Andhra was officially organised in September 1934. The development of the Communist movement

Reproduced from *Telangana People's Struggle and its Lessons* by P. Sundarayya, op. cit. pp. 154-5, 158-64, 168-71.

in India was a terror for the imperialists and they banned it in 1934, even before its branches could be organised in Andhra.

The Communists, while working in the Congress organisation, conducted agitation on the demands of agricultural labour and poor peasants in the villages and the working class in towns and could build up their independent base among them, to a considerable extent.

Forced by the anti-fascist war situation, the imperialists lifted the ban on the Communist Party in 1942. Communists came out legally and directly plunged into the battle against fascism. While ceaselessly campaigning for the release of Congress leaders and formation of a National Government they took up the day-to-day issues of the people: conducted agitations, led deputations, organised demonstrations, and held meetings on such issues as supply of agricultural implements, repairs of tanks, roads and canals, against blackmarket and for strict price controls, against hoarding and corruption. They led a number of agricultural labour struggles and the 'grow more food' campaign. In the towns, wide support was mobilised behind the working class demands and the Party led some of their strike struggles successfully. Volunteers of the Communist Party were able, in many towns, to successfully unearth the hoards of blackmarketeers, and force the Government to distribute them to the people.

Communists fought on the political, economic and social issues of every section of the toiling people; on such peasant demands fair price for his produce, for supply of agricultural implements and fertilisers; on working class demands for supply of all necessities of life at controlled rates and increase in wages; on student demands for supply of white paper, kerosene at controlled rates, against detentions, for amenities such as tiffin sheds, rest rooms, in the educational institutions; on such women's demands as provision of separate sanitary facilities in villages, for maternity and welfare centres, for strict implementation of the anti-child-marriages Act, for educational facilities and for equal rights; on middle class issues against high house rentals, housing scarcity, etc. In one word, wherever and whenever people were in difficulties there you could see a Communist with a red flag on his shoulder. That was a common phenomenon in those days.

All through these campaigns, the main political task of the people—the struggle against fascism—was specially stressed and achievements of the Soviet Union were widely popularised. For carrying on a ceaseless campaign for the release of Congress leaders, a large number of our leading cadre were kept in prison all through the period.

It was this constant and ceaseless work on people's issues, close ties with the people through thick and thin, that enabled the Communists to rally 100,000 people at the All-India Kisan Sabha Conference, held in Bezwada in 1944 and the next year, 50,000 to the Provincial Kisan Sabha Conference in Tenali.

These ever-growing activities and increasing influence of the Communists was a bitter pill to the Congress leaders, mainly coming from liberal landlord sections, who had just come out of jails. They realised that if the Communists were allowed to grow at this rate, their social order of class exploitation would be at an end. So, 'under the open instigation of Dr Pattabhi Sitaramayya and N.G. Ranga, all-India Congress leaders, raids were organised on party offices, attacks were made on individual Party members and important leaders, and Party rallies were disturbed. The Communist Party scented the danger underlying these goonda attacks, organised the PVB (People's Volunteer Brigade) and gave the slogan: 'defend the people', 'beat back the goondas', and 'expose the reactionary Congress'. Under the leadership of the anti-Communist fire-eater Ranga Party the mass rallies in Krishna and Guntur districts were attacked. There was not a single meeting, demonstration or cultural performance that was not attempted to be disrupted by them. But, thanks to the timely sensing of this menace and immediate mobilisation and defensive actions, they were everywhere put on the run, the Party was saved and the revolutionary movement was defended and extended.

Elections and After

World War II was terminated with the smashing of Nazi Germany and fascist Japan. The working class in India began to rise. There was a gigantic mass upsurge and a huge strike wave, highlighted by INA demonstrations, the RIN Revolt, the all-India Postal workers' strike, etc. The British imperialists saw this as a challenge to its colonial rule and in order to divert the attention of the people from the revolutionary path, announced elections to provincial legislatures.

In Andhra, the Communist Party put up 35 candidates (in half of the total constituencies) and fought the elections with the two main slogans of 'land to the tiller' and 'Vishalandhra in a people's India'. Goondas were freely employed against the Communist election campaign and the Congress-Justice Party-zamindar alliance littered money all over to buy votes. Unashamedly, they sought police and goonda help to frighten the voters. But the PVB volunteers were rallied and the Congress volunteers and goondas were kept at bay.

The results of the elections showed that the Communist Party was the biggest and the most influential party after the Congress in Andhra. The party polled 2.5 lakh votes in all, and 22 per cent of the total votes polled in the constituencies contested by Communists. In the strongholds of Krishna and Guntur districts, the percentage was 35 and 25 respectively of the total votes polled. And, at the time, franchise in India was limited to only 13 per cent, the vast mass of toilers, who form the bulk of the supporters of the Communists, were deprived of their voting right.

A wave of strikes swept Andhra, both in the villages and the towns. Agricultural labour and farm servants in hundreds of villages struck work demanding increase in their yearly and daily wages, wages in kind to be given with correct measures, for holidays and regular hours of work. The peasants in Munagala and Challapalli occupied zamindari lands and began to fight the repression that ensued.

The strike of ten thousand tobacco workers (which broke out the very next day after the Congress Ministries took office); one thousand textile workers of Pandalapaka, the cart-pullers in Rajahmundry, the cigar workers and a host of other workers belonging to other trades came out on the streets on strike for their minimum demands; of particular importance was the province-wide strike of 20,000 municipal workers, who were paid a pittance of Rs. 4.72 per month.

As a result of its all-sided mass work, the Party was able to draw over to its side the wide strata of urban poor and the rural toilers, especially the agricultural labours and poor peasants, for whose rights the Party was fighting ever since its inception in 1934. It could stand face to face with the Congress in the elections and poll 2.5 lakh votes.

The Party came out as the stalwart defender of toilers' rights by leading their day-to-day struggles on urgent economic issues. The Communist Party stood against all injustices, inequality, and suppression of fundamental rights. Such was the influence of the Party in the villages that not only on economic demands, but for every trifling matter such as kerosene or rice ration cards, or excess municipal taxes or some social injustice, etc., they used to rush to the office of the Party and seek redress of their grievances.

In the social sector, it had fought the devil of untouchability. Members of the Party shared food with untouchables, lived with them and shared their sorrows and joys. Moreover, the very nature of the class struggle was such that it had unified under one banner the touchables and untouchables as well. Marriage ceremonies were simplified, doing away with priests and mantrams; widow-remarriage and inter-caste-marriages were widely popularised and members of the Party were always in the forefront. Equality between men and women was advocated.

A new culture was introduced. The youth of the towns and villages were drawn into the new life of activity. They were mobilised under the flag of the Andhra Youth Federation, the only organisation of its kind. They participated in games, yearly sports on the occasion of national festivals, joined volunteer squads, trained themselves in the use of lathi, took part in drama and burra katha squads, and were also imbued with the fighting consciousness against imperialism. The Communist Party's name had become so synonymous with all good youth in the villages that even some of the old folk in the houses used to prevail upon their sons or grandsons to go and join the Youth Leagues so that they might be schooled and disciplined as good citizens.

The Communist Party had revived languishing cultural forms like burra katha, veedhi bhagavatham, etc., and through them approached the masses. Hundreds of squads and drama groups functioned all over Andhra. Through these cultural forms, stories peasants' lives, biographies of national heroes, militant struggles of the Andhra people, heroic exploits of Soviet guerrillas, were all popularised. The number of people that attended the cultural performances ranged from 3,000 to 10,000. There were many instances when the middle class people and intelligentsia preferred to attend a burra katha performance to a cinema. This had changed the tastes of the people so much that the professional dramatists had to adapt themselves to this change, partly giving up their religious and 'ethical' performances.

Through innumerable mass meetings, through Prajasakti, organ of the Communist Party, the peasants had been politicalised; they came to know much about the Soviet Union, the fortress of socialism, and about the heroic struggle of the Chinese people. Prajasakti Publishing House published a record number of nearly 300 books on various topics: politics, theory of Marxism, histories of various countries, on literature, on science, on economics, short stories, dramas, burra kathas, etc., which no other organisation could do up till then. On every burning problem of the people and the country, on every significant event in the international field, PSPH came out with a pamphlet and constantly kept the people abreast of events, and brought the general masses to a higher political level.

The following figures of membership give an idea of the development of the Communist Party and various mass organisations during 1945-6.

Communist Party	20,000	(in 2,000 villages)
Andhra Prov. Kisan Sabha	175,000	
Andhra Prov. Agri. Labour Union	60,000	
" " Students' Federation	12,000	
" " Youth Federation	50,000	
" " Mahila Sabha	20,000	
" " Trade Union Congress	30,000	

Thus, in spite of certain reformist mistakes and politics, the Communist Party in Andhra became a broad mass party, came forth as the champion of the toiling masses, as the unquestioned leader of the workers, as builder of the revolutionary peasant movement, as a staunch fighter for social justice and as the beacon light of a new culture in Andhra.

Black Act Promulgated Repression Begins

The Prakasam Ministry, which was then in office in Madras province, promulgated the 'Public Safety (Prajarakshana) Ordinance', popularly known as the 'Public Disaster (Prajabhakshana) Ordinance' on January 22, 1947, on the eve of Independence Day on January 26. Hundreds were arrested and detained without cause, without trial. Offices of the Communist Party, trade unions and Kisan Sabha were raided and records were confiscated.

Here it is necessary to note that the Communist Party was neither preparing for the overthrow of the Government by force, nor was it indulging in violence of any sort, as was slandered by the Congress Government. The Party was just championing the day-today interests of the workers, of agricultural labour and poor peasants; it was leading their struggles for their just demands, the elementary right of the people even in a bourgeois parliamentary democracy. And for this 'crime' the Congress Ministry replied with this Black Act. Thus it was the Congress Government that started the unwarranted offensive against the Communists and the people and not the other way round, as the Government shamelessly propagated in its lies later.

The democratic toiling masses could not tolerate this foul offensive on the fundamental rights of the people and parties. Ten thousand workers in Rajahmundry came out on a one-day strike demanding unconditional release of their leaders. The railway workers of Bitragunta and other centres also stopped work. Workers in Bezwada, Guntur, Pandalapaka, Vizag, Chittavalasa, the Kisan Sabha, the Agricultural Labour Association sent strong protest notes against this arbitrary action of the Government and demanded its withdrawal.

Nor had they been cowed down with the detention of their leadership. The economic crisis, the pro-capitalist and pro-landlord policies of the Congress Government and the intensifying repression on the peaceful population, forced them into further bitter struggles.

In Gajullanka of Divi taluka, Krishna district, the peasants began to assert their right on the lanka lands (riverbed lands). What did the Congress Government, which waxed eloquent promises during the elections, do? It did not come to the rescue of the poor peasants against the high-handedness of the Challapalli zamindar, who after the elections had overnight turned into a Congressman, but went to the assistance of the zamindar, with its police force and opened fire on the unarmed peasants, killing four, including a woman leader, Viyamma, and wounding scores of others. And note again, it was not the Communist guerrillas that started the shooting, it was the Congress Government that fired the first shot on the unarmed people. It was not the Communists but the Congress Government that started the armed offensive.

In Buchampet of West Godavari district, the tribal peasants started a fight against the zamindar. The police came and shot four of them dead.

In Kanur and Pandyala and other centres of West Godavari district, the peasants stood against the oppression of the landlords and zamindars. The peasants' demands were so just that the Taluka Congress Committee and some members of the District Congress Committee came to their support and formed joint action committees. The Congress Government promulgated orders under Section 144 and lathi-charged the peasants. The landlords and the Government let loose goondas throughout the district. As a result of this free reign of the landlord-goondas, in 'Pedapadu' village in another part of the district, Raja Ram Mohan Roy, a militant peasant youth and a member of the Party, was killed.

In 'Munagala', an enclave of Andhra in Hyderabad state, a traditional militant agrarian base, the peasants, under the influence of the sweeping land struggle of the Telangana peasants, seized 4,000 acres of zamindari lands. The police came and opened fire, killing two and injuring several others.

In Divi taluka of Krishna district, the peasantry in Challapalli estate occupied thousands of acres and the Congress police rushed to the aid of the zamindar and let loose terror on the fighting peasantry. In Munagala and Challapalli estates, over 50 were kept as detenus besides the arrest of several hundreds of people.

Independence and After

It was constantly dinned into the people's ears that India had now achieved independence and the condition of the people would be bettered. But the toiling masses found the real class character of this independence. The Communist Party's influence went on increasing. Municipal elections were held all over Andhra only three months after the Mountbatten Award. The Communist Party contested these elections. In such important towns as Bezwada and Rajahmundry, Communists won 1/3 of the total seats. Altogether the Communists won 36 seats all over Andhra, in half a dozen municipalities.

These victories of the Communists, that, too, within 3 months of independence, made the bourgeois-landlord Government panicky. As it was, the sweep of the struggles of the agricultural labourers, farm-servants, the working class and the peasantry during the one year of the Congress regime in the provinces was enough of an indication of the anti-people character of the regime of the Congress.

Heroic Telangana—A Constant Terror to the Congress Government
Already in the '40s, Communists in Krishna district of Madras Andhra had come into contact with the disillusioned left-oriented youth in the state (Hyderabad) and ever since then, had been tirelessly working for the cause of the peasants, who were most feudally exploited and oppressed under the Nizam-Deshmukh rule. They took up such immediate issues of the people as vetti, illegal exactions, bribery, etc., and fought against the local deshmukhs. When the deshmukhs left loose goondas, people resisted and drove them back. Then the Nizam's police and military came on the scene. They began to loot the property of the people, commit arson, murder and rape on a mass scale. In order to save their hearths and homes and their own lives from the murderous attacks, people formed into guerrilla bands and began putting up militant resistance under the political, organisational and ideological leadership of the Communist Party. The rule of the exploiters was coming to an end. Thousands of acres of land were being confiscated and distributed and people's committees were being established. The Razakar armies were let loose on the people. People under the leadership of the Andhra Mahasabha and Communist Party began heroically resisting the Nizam regime.

The Communist Party in Andhra, especially in the four coastal districts which were on the borders of Nalgonda and Warangal districts, served as a rear base for the Telangana fight. The Party in Andhra gave a call for all-out assistance to the struggle of the Telangana people against the Nizam, to help them overthrow the feudal regime and establish Vishalandhra. Thus, it sought to implement the election slogans of 1945-6, unlike the Congress whose promises evaporated into thin air. The call was responded to on a mass scale.

The Communist Party, the Andhra Provincial TUC and the Kisan Sabha welcomed and organised relief for the people from Telangana who sought protection from torture, rape and loot. The guerrilla fighters and leaders got the guidance and help they wanted. The whole movement was under the ideological, political and organisational leadership of the Communist Party. In the whole of Andhra, a national fervour to fight and liquidate Nizam's rule and unify Andhra had been roused. With what eagerness and readiness people came forward to help their fighting brethren across the border can be understood from the single fact, that in just three days, in Bezwada town alone, Rs. 20,000 were collected for purchase of arms to the guerrillas. The Communist movement and the Party had become the backbone of the Telangana people's armed struggle.

The play, 'Ma Bhoomi' (Our Land), depicting the life of Telangana peasants, the exploitations of deshmukhs and Nizam, police atrocities and the people's resistance and fight for land, which was written to popularise the agrarian revolt in Telangana, played a particularly significant role in rallying the people to the assistance of Telangana. Two hundred squads staged this play all over Andhra, in villages as well as towns. Lakhs of people saw it: lawyers, doctors, intellectuals, scientists, Congressmen, cinema stars, writers, one and all acclaimed the play as most effective. The funds collected through the staging of this play ran into a lakh of rupees. The Ministers, prevailed upon by the Congress MLAs, invited this drama squad and got the play staged in the Rajaji Hall (Government House in Madras). They saw with their own eyes what a powerful message it was giving to the people and banned it afterwards, though praising it to the skies on the spot.

In the course of a conversation in Bezwada town, Congress leaders were being criticized by a person who desired strongly the creation of the Andhra province. The Congress leaders ridiculed him saying that he was talking like a Communist and joked, 'wait, the Communists will get you Vishalandhra.' To this, he retorted, 'It is the Communists that propagated the demand for Vishalandhra in 1946, and they have taken up arms and have been fighting for it during the last four years, while the Congress has been promising the Andhra province for the last 40 years and refuses even that much today'.

While on the one hand, the Nehru-Patel Government stabbed in the back the fighting people of Telangana by entering into a stand-still agreement with the Nizam and agreeing to supply arms to this butcher of the people, the Communists were leading the people fighting in the battle-fields and shedding their blood for the cause of the people, for the cause of Vishalandhra. This placed the Communist Party in Andhra not only as the workers' and peasants' leader but also as the champion and unifier of the Andhra people.

Two Years of Terror-Rule in Andhra

It was on January 31, 1948, that the Madras Congress Government launched its long-prepared offensive against the militant people's movement in Andhra and its leader, the Communist Party. The assassination of Gandhiji, and the consequent clashes between the people and the RSS gang, were only an excuse to carry out its fascist offensive. That night, the police swooped down on the office of the Prajasakti, Communist daily in Bezwada, the Party's City Committee office and the offices of the Krishna District Committee and the Andhra Provincial Committee of the Party and on the houses of many prominent Communists and their sympathisers and effected large-scale arrests. It hoped to bag the whole of the Communist leadership of Andhra—an extended meeting of the Provincial Committee was in session then just after the Provincial Conference. But it failed in its objective in spite of its sudden swoop.

The reason behind this swoop, the first of its kind in the whole of India, was that the Communist Party in Andhra and the militant mass movement that was led by it and especially, the powerful people's movement in Krishna district was the strong base of support for the Telangana people's struggle for liberation against the Nizam and his Razakar gangs. So, when the Government of India entered into the stand-still agreement with the Nizam, and when the Telangana Communists and the Telangana Andhra Mahasabha repudiated the stand-still agreement and continued to wage the struggle with even arms in hand, the Congress got frightened.

It was determined to crush and extinguish the Telangana people's struggle, so that it might not become the beacon-light to the oppressed masses of the rest of India. So, while on the one hand, it was helping the Nizam by supplying arms, on the other hand, it prepared to clean up the rear base of the Telangana people's struggle in Andhra, especially in the Krishna, Guntur and Godavari districts.

After the first raid on the Communist and trade union offices in Bezwada, the Madras Government arrested 79 persons on the false charge of murdering one of the RSS men in the January 31 clashes. How false this charge was and how it was just no more than a pretext to round up the militant leadership was proved when in the above case, after two years of delaying the trial during which time many of the accused were refused bail and kept in jail or under detention, ultimately only 17 were convicted for forming an unlawful assembly and sentenced to two to three months' imprisonment in January 1950.

The Madras Government continued its preparations to liquidate the people's struggle in Krishna. It concentrated its armed police, the Malabar Special Police, in Krishna District while the Government of India was massing Gurkha and Sikh battalions to intervene against the Telangana people's struggle under the proclaimed cover of protecting the Hyderabad people against the Nizam and his Razakar gangs.

In Krishna district, the people's movement in support of Telangana became intensified. The mass of agricultural labour, in more than 400 villages, were preparing for strike struggles to win their demands. Their demands were 30 bags of paddy, 8-hour day and 30 paid holidays. The peasants in the zamindari tracts refused to pay rent to zamindars and demanded that their rent be scaled down and the zamindari system be abolished. The Madras Government resorted to mass raids, mass beatings, arrests, destruction of properties and utensils, burning and razing down of houses, raping and murders. The Congress Seva Dal 'volunteers' were pressed into service along with the Special Armed Police.

The usual technique in the raids was for a force of 200-300 policemen to surround a village during the night, not to allow anybody to go out from the house even to answer the calls of nature, gather men and women of the village in a cattle-shed and beat them, while some other batches of police entered the houses and began looting, breaking the furniture and utensils, tearing up sarees, shirts and dhoties to pieces and mixing dal, rice and pickles with kerosene and urine. They burnt and razed to the ground many houses, prevented cultivation of the lands of Communist workers and their relatives. Agricultural labour hamlets were the special targets in these raids. These raids continued for full three months from May to July. Though the main concentration was in Krishna district, raids took place in Guntur, Godavari and even Kurnool districts as they all bordered on Telangana.

And the people, in spite of the terror, began to fight for their demands. Agricultural workers in Krishna district in about 90 villages went on strike or prepared themselves for strike and won wage increases of 3 to 5 bags of paddy. In Guntur district, in about 70 villages, and in Nellore in about 20 villages, they went on strikes and won their demands. In East Godavari district, in Razole and Ramchandrapuram talukas, agricultural workers struck work and won wage-increases. In Pithapuram taluka of East Godavari, during the replanting season, agricultural labourers in a few villages won from Rs. 2 to Rs. 3 per day. The movement for higher wages and holidays spread to the Rayalaseema districts, Cuddapah and Anantapur. In West Godavari, Nellore, Cuddapah and Anantapur districts, banzar lands (waste lands) to the extent of hundreds of acres were occupied by agricultural labourers and poor peasants.

The Congress bourgeois-landlord Government panicked and banned the Communist Party in Madras province, the Provincial Kisan Sabha, the Andhra Provincial Agricultural Labour Association, the Andhra Provincial Youth Federation and all strong TUs in the province. The Government sent orders to all the heads of high schools and colleges in the province to drive out all Communist minded students and their sympathisers from the educational institutions.

Anything in the nature of civil liberty was totally absent in the areas where the militant people's movements existed. In a word, these areas were declared disturbed areas with orders to the police to shoot at sight anybody whom they suspected as Communists. The couriers, pilots, contacts, shelter keepers, etc., who accidentally fell into the hands of the police were subjected to sadistic torture like thrusting pins under fingernails, hanging them upside down, and all sorts of devilish brutalities. . . .

Thus, the years 1949 and 1950 saw a new pitch of intensified terror of mass raids, beatings, lootings, rapings and shootings of important people's leaders and Communist leaders after their arrest, and these murders were announced to the press as 'shot dead in encounter with the police'.

People Fight Back
The Party during the whole of 1948 was calling upon the Party ranks and the people to bravely face the police attacks, not to leave the villages but assert their right to demonstrate and right to hoist red flags and fight back the police brutalities with whatever weapon they could lay their hands on. But the police came in hundreds and this call of frontal resistance reduced itself to militant satyagraha with backs and bones of our comrades broken and a number of important cadres arrested.

The people and the party ranks were fed up with this form of resistance. In Jupudi village in Guntur district, they organised themselves into squads, retreated into neighbouring villages when the police came in large numbers, but the moment they went away, came back and attacked the landlords and their agents. This dingdong battle continued for more than a year.

In Davajigudem, Krishna district, the local cadre adopted similar tactics.

It was in November 1948, in Pedamuktavi village in Divi taluka, Krishna district, which was the worst target of Congress police brutalities, that the comrades mobilised themselves and entered the village, dragged out of their beds the landlords and their agents who were terrorising the whole neighbourhood, and gave them a good thrashing.

People's reaction was 'how long could the Communists keep mum in the face of the torture they were being subjected to: they have decided to fight back'. This was the thought in everybody's mind . . . . That meant that they could shoot any Communist they could lay hands on. The Congress Seva Dal and the landlords in villages were being armed and there was open talk in Congress offices that the Communists would be taught a lesson.

It was under these conditions that in July 1949, the Party gave the call 'a tooth for a tooth' and 'an eye for an eye', to fight back the landlord-police terror that had been going on for so long.

The Andhra State Committee of the Party was opposed during the whole of 1948 to resort to arms in the Andhra area, as the people there had not yet developed to the stage of waging a struggle for land and defending it by arms as in Telangana. It also argued that the political-economic situation in the Andhra area under Congress regime was entirely 'different' from that prevailing in Telangana under the Nizam. But it yielded to this demand from the lower ranks and from the Telangana comrades to take up arms, and develop guerrilla movement to help the Telangana movement as well. But it was soon found that there was no mass participation and fighting as in Telangana, only squad actions, which were easily suppressed by brutal violence by the Congress regime. The Party later came to the conclusion that these tactics were wrong and caused the Party great loss and damage; though by its brave fight against terror and immense sacrifices, it gained the respect of the toiling people and middle classes.

The Party at the time was still thinking that it was possible for the exposed leadership and ranks to function from neighbouring areas by taking up some profession as cover and eking out a living. It was a costly mistake to have entertained such ideas when the people there were not participating and not ready to fight back the armed forces of the Government actively and protect the cadres. We should have withdrawn to our Telangana bases in the forests and mountainous territory of a strong safe area, most of the exposed cadres and squads and continued the work in the old areas with entirely unexposed cadres. This bitter lesson the Party learned only after a few months of severe losses of cadre and Party leaders during March-June 1950.

The Government was ready with its plans to deal a heavy blow to the Party and the mass movement in the coastal districts. It was ready with increased police camps and with orders to shoot and kill any Communist leader and guerrilla and squad member who fell into their hands. During the year 1950, the coastal districts of Andhra were the scene of heroic, struggles of the people, with people's resistance actions against the landlords and their agents on the one hand, and the mass butchery of the Congress Government to drown in blood the people's fight on the other.

People's Actions in Andhra

In Krishna district, in Divi taluka, in the village Velivolu, goonda leader Basavayya destroyed property worth Rs. 50,000, collected a fine of Rs. 25,000 and stole hens and ducks. He enforced the wage rate of 8 annas (50 paise) when the normal rate was Rs. 1.50. His goonda camp was raided by the people and he was beaten and crippled for ever and two of his lieutenants were killed.

In Katur village of Gannavaram taluka, Ramalingayya was a Home Guard, a goonda, a landlord agent and an informer. His name was associated with all the loot, arson, attempts at raping, and other atrocities committed on the people during 1948-9. Tens of villages were raided under his leadership. A special police camp was opened in Katur village. Men and women who passed that way were caught and belaboured. This scoundrel used to jump over the compound walls into the homeyards when women were taking their baths. He was presented with a revolver by the Government. But he was killed right in the village, with the armed police camp in the vicinity. In buses, coffee houses, trains the talk went round but not a word of sympathy for him was heard. People who saw the corpse at Vuyyur bus stand on the way to Masula Hospital for post-mortem were heard saying 'he did such atrocious things and has got the just punishment for it'.

In Gannavaram taluka, right on the main Bezwada-Masula road, in the village Chinna Vogirala, two hated landlords were killed, right in front of the police camp, and their guns were seized. The police in Kankipadu station—just 10 miles away—locked themselves up and did not dare move out, in spite of frantic knocking of the door by the local landlords to come out and give them protection. Their reply was that they had to guard their station and after all, 'we too have our families and children and our lives are dear to us'.

In Tiruvur taluka, Krishna district, in December 1949, and again, in March 1950, people raided 20 villages and confiscated gold and guns from the landlords and killed a few of them, with the help of Telangana guerrillas.

In East Godavari district, in Razole taluka, Lingamurthy Raju, a big landlord, who usurped 1200 acres of temple land, fertile deltaic soil, along with a few other big landlords organised some guards and instituted a reign of terror. These goonda landlords tried to seize the crops on lanka lands. The Government forcibly took over these lands that were being cultivated by agricultural labourers for 20 to 30 years and auctioned them to these landlords. Women and men led by the Party fought many a glorious struggle and saved their crops on the fields. Again and again, agricultural labourers went on strike struggles for higher wages. Women were in the forefront. They too got training in self-defence. When the husbands of some wanted to prevent them, the reply these brave women gave was: 'You cannot save our honour or life. Yet you try to obstruct us from taking training to defend ourselves'. Women acted as couriers, kept watch on police movements and conveyed information to Party leaders and protected them from the police.

After months of undergoing regular torture, agricultural labourers and poor peasants began to retaliate. Twenty of Lingamurthy's goondas were beaten to pulp. Some of them were maimed for life. One goonda who used to participate in raids all day, used to come at night and boast before his wife, 'I have kicked men all day and my legs are aching. Come and wash my legs with hot water'. The people broke his legs for good.

Telangana guerrilla squads helped the people to raid the Atchampet police station. They shot dead two constables, took possession of 70 guns. This was the first major action against a police station by guerrillas in the coastal districts.

This action was followed by other actions in about 15 villages where the hated landlords were killed by the guerrillas. Most of these actions took place in the border talukas of Guntur-Palnad-Sattenapalli; the Telangana guerrillas made the forests nearby their base of operations.

Telangana guerrilla squads aided their colleagues from Andhra area to operate throughout the whole forest region of Nallamala covering Kurnool and Guntur districts on the banks of the Krishna River.

In the whole of Andhra, in about 100 villages, people attacked landlords or their agents, killed some of them, destroyed property of some others and seized guns from them.

It had been the common practice in every raid to burn all the debt and mortgage bonds of the hated landlords. This fact was announced to the villagers by leaflets and they were asked not to re-write the bonds or pay their debts. The landlords concerned were threatened with direr consequences if they tried to collect the debts with the help of the police.

In many villages, the agricultural labour and the poor raided landlords' granaries and distributed the grain. In a number of other villages, the paddy crop was cut and taken away.

The people hated the landlords and police agents. They helped to destroy the enemy properties. The villagers, especially agricultural labourers and poor peasants, gave shelter to party leaders and cadres at great risk to their life and property. They guarded and sheltered them as their own sons. In Antarvedipalem, East Godavari district, when a group of 20 villages was surrounded by 3,000 armed police and Congress Home Guards, not one single party comrade was caught. The people saved them all, though for one full week, the police went on arresting and beating every male in that whole area. It was the agricultural labour women that came forward to act as couriers. In spite of this white terror, hundreds of party members and tens of organisers continued to live in the villages. This was possible only because of the tremendous cooperation of the people and especially the agricultural labour and poor peasants.

All the poorer classes considered that the Communist Party was their party. They believed that only under a people's Government headed by the Communist Party would their sufferings come to an end. In the talukas bordering Telangana, they were eagerly awaiting the Communist guerrillas to come and distribute the land. Even in far-off Cuddapah, where in a few villages the agricultural labourers and poor peasants occupied waste lands under Communist Party leadership, the talk went round that Nalgonda Communists had come and were distributing the land. In Palnad taluka, Guntur district, when squads were going through new areas where no movement had ever existed, poor peasants approached the squads and asked them to drive away the landlords and agraharamdars and rid them of this feudal pest. The moment the guerrillas began to raid the hated landlords' houses and the police station and seize arms, the enemy became terror-stricken. The hated landlords, the moneylenders began to leave the villages and flee to the towns. This was a very common feature in many villages of Krishna and Guntur and the two Godavari districts. The remaining goondas in the village slept together at a place, guns by their side and with sentries posted all night, changing their places frequently.

With the raid on the police station of Atchampeta, the confusion and terror of the enemy increased by leaps and bounds. 'The Communists captured 70 guns, how can we live now?' This was what Sri N.G. Ranga exclaimed! This same Congress leader who had demanded that the Communists must be hunted down and wiped out by declaring Martial Law, did not dare move out without a police lorry to protect him on his tours in Guntur district. Vallabhbhai Patel, the Congress leader of fascist terror in India, had to admit in Parliament in Delhi 'that the people of Andhra are not co-operating with them in suppressing the Communists'.

Some statements on repression in Andhra

Sri Vemula Kurmayya, former Congress Minister for Harijan Uplift, member, Madras Legislative Assembly, issued a statement on the shameless police atrocities in the village of Yelamarru, an extract from which is given hereunder:

'Before day-break on 14th July, 1949, 200 MSP raided the village of Yelamarru. They surrounded the village and did not allow anybody to leave. After daybreak, they gathered the villagers in three batches in the local high school compound. They stripped them naked and each was given ten stripes. Then, they forced the villagers to parade throughout the village, in their nakedness. When some tried to hide their shame with their hands, they were beaten again. Some of them were made to lie prostrate before a Gandhi statue and were given more blows. Even after this, the clothes were not returned but they were asked to go home and appear before their womenfolk naked and to come back attired in new clothes. Both untouchables and touchables were among the people who were subjected to this atrocious humiliation and beating.

'All the women in the harijan colony were made to stand in the maidan and were beaten. The menfolk in their nakedness were asked to go to them and each to bring his wife. One was ordered to strip naked his wife who was 16 years old. He refused. They threatened the woman and asked her to strip herself naked. She refused and replied, 'You may kill me but I will never debase myself'. Thereupon a policeman was about to strip her naked, when the village munsiff prevented him, warning that it would lead to trouble. After this, the women were beaten again, and were allowed to go home.

'In all the villages of the district, the people are asking about these village atrocities, which they say, are worse than Punjab atrocities perpetrated by the British imperialists in 1919.

'I want the Premier and the Telugu Ministers to tour these villages in the district which are subjected to police raids and vouchsafe peace and protection for the people. Otherwise, the people may revolt in sheer exasperation'. (*Andhra Prabha*, July 23, 1946)....

Andhra Prabha, a leading Telugu daily of Andhra, in its editorial dated July 26, 1949, wrote:

'Uncivilized, atrocious, unspeakable—these may be very strong words; but even these words are not sufficient to describe the barbarous raids by police in Krishna district.

'The same gruesome and sordid story from every village—gather all people, indiscriminately beat them, strip some of them of their clothes, parade those people in the streets in nakedness.

'... By doing such things, it does not result in suppressing the Communists; but only creates hatred against the Congress. Loyalty towards the Congress does not increase but only makes the people think that British raj is better.

'In their efforts to suppress the Communists in Krishna district, civil liberties are not only infringed but a situation is created when people have to feel shame for being born as people of India.

'... Besides stopping such atrocities, the officials responsible should be punished.

'We came to know that Sri Madhava Menon (Minister of Law) has brushed off these incidents as Communist propaganda. It is not correct. Those who have written letters to our office are all Congressmen and they wrote only after personally visiting the villages and after enquiry'.

30 Entry of Indian Army and Immediately After

P. Sundarayya

On the eve of the Indian Army Intervention

BY THE MIDDLE of 1948, all the developments pointed to the possibility of the Indian Government intervening in Hyderabad to force the Nizam to accede to the Indian Union and to suppress the spreading Telangana peasant movement. The question arose as to what we should do with regard to this problem.

We were sure that after the Indian army intervention, Hyderabad state would be forced to accede to India, and the Razakar terror would end, but at the same time a terrific attack on our Party and Sangham and on the Telangana movement would be made, to liquidate it. We had a foretaste of it in the way the Congress Government had been attacking and suppressing our Party in the Andhra area. So, should we continue the armed struggle against Nehru's armies and its attack on the Telangana peasants to snatch away all the gains? Or should we withdraw armed struggle and try to adopt normal legal forms of agitation and struggles, to win partial demands and retain partially the achievements of the Telangana peasants, such as no evictions, no forced labour or exactions; patta rights for waste lands that were being cultivated, and confine ourselves to agitation and mass mobilisation for agrarian legislation, for ceilings, rent-reduction, and for civil liberties, elected local bodies, elected ministry for the state, etc?

But if we withdrew the struggle unconditionally, and immediately after intervention, would the Indian Government declare amnesty and not persecute thousands of guerrilla squads and cadre and members of the Party and Sangham, who had carried on confiscation of land and properties of the big landlords, their agents, Nizam's police and Razakars? Would it leave in the possession of the peasants the lands they had seized and cultivated? We were sure that it would not and if that was so, would not the peasants resist such

Reproduced from '*Telangana People's Struggle and Its Lessons*' by P. Sundarayya, *op. cit.* pp. 177-182.

attempts at seizure and if we did not stand by them and defend them even with arms as we did in the past, would they not consider us as betraying them?

But if we decided in favour of carrying on the armed struggle, our squads would be no match to and could not stand at all in the field before the well-trained, disciplined Indian army with its high morale. Further, the rich peasants, small capitalists and liberal landlords and quite a section of others who were with our struggle against the Nizam would definitely go over to the side of the Indian Government at that stage, as these sections had great hopes that the Government of Independent India under Nehru would fulfil their aspirations for economic betterment. With no working class actions in the state, no possibility of a general strike or armed uprising, would it not be disastrous to continue the armed struggle?

If the armed struggle was to be continued, how could it be for anything less than liberation? (Then the concept of partial partisan struggle for partial economic demands, as distinct from and not to be confused with the armed struggle for liberation, was not there at all in our understanding. Armed struggle meant liberation struggle or revolutionary armed uprising.)

Could the Telangana struggle, then, be the beginning of the liberation struggle? Was it the Yenan of India? Is our path of revolution to proceed along the Chinese path or the Russian path? What are the classes that will be in our revolution and against which classes? That is, what is the class character of the state that was ushered in in 1947 and the stage and strategy of the revolution?

Let me add here that though Sri Ravi Narayan Reddy and Ella Reddy were for withdrawal of armed struggle, once the Party decided to carry it on, they tried to obey it and carry it into practice. Sri Ella Reddy was arrested within a few months of the police action. Sri Ravi Narayan Reddy was underground till 1950 October and then later left his den (centre) without informing the State leadership and reached the Party Headquarters in Bombay and started a campaign against the Telangana armed struggle being continued through the Central Committee of the Party on December 13, 1950, had adopted the following resolution on the Telangana struggle:

'The Telangana people are carrying on a revolutionary struggle, arms in hand, against the oppressors, who have been exploiting them for generations, for their land and freedom, under the leadership of the Communist Party. The C.C. deplores all those statements by some persons demanding the withdrawal of the struggle. The C.C. warns all Party members that when the enemy is trying to drown the Telangana struggle, which heralds the beginning of the People's Democratic Revolution, to make statements demanding its withdrawal will only go to help to disrupt this revolutionary struggle.

'The C.C. appeals to Party members and to all people that they must do everything in their power to help and strengthen and sustain the Telangana struggle. The Great Telangana stands as the beacon call to all of us, blazes the way for us, to build the powerful unity of the people under the leadership of the Communist Party and to advance forward. It will continue to be so in future as well'.
(Retranslated from Telugu).

Let it be also noted that both Sri Ravi Narayan Reddy and Ella Reddy, when their brothers were killed, in the course of the partisan struggle, justified and defended the action of the guerrillas publicly.

Decision to continue the armed struggle

The Andhra Provincial Committee of the Party decided to continue the armed struggle even against Nehru's armies. Apart from other aspects, it had felt the immediate practical necessity of defending the gains of the Telangana peasantry against the attempts of deshmukhs and landlords who would be returning with the support of the Indian army, to seize the lands from the peasantry. Not to continue the armed struggle would have been betrayal of the fighting peasantry and damaging the cause of the Telangana people's movement irreparably.

So, on the eve of the 'police action', the Party instructed all the areas and guerrillas squads not to come into clash with the Indian army as long as they were attacking the Razakars and Nizam's armed forces, but to launch independent attacks against Razakar and Nizam's police camps, destroy them, seize weapons, re-equip he squads with modern weapons and retain them; wait for a few weeks, by which time the attacks on the Telangana peasantry by the Indian armed forces and their landlord-deshmukh gangs would shatter the illusions and hopes roused among the masses.

They would be ready and demand the squads to go to their protection and fight with arms as well.

Actually, within a week after the entry of the Indian army, the attacks began. There was a general and determined attack to destroy all the guerrilla squads and the Party and Sangham organization. Unfortunately, many of the squads and political organisers of the Party and Sangham were not in a position to meet the offensive, having developed illusions about the character of the intervention by the Indian Union.

Some of the area committees and their leaderships like Huzurnagar (led by Dodda Narasayya), Bhuvanagiri (led by Arutle Ramachandra Reddy and Katkur Ramachandra Reddy), Palvancha area (led by Nallamala Giriprasad and Pullanna), State leaders like Ravi Narayan Reddy and Baddam Ella Reddy advocated withdrawal of armed struggle and taking to legal and other forms of agitation. Only the Suryapet-Khammam-Manukota area stood firm for continuing the armed struggle and defending the gains of the Telangana struggle. But all these comrades as well as most of the others who held similar views, carried on the armed struggle when the decision to continue was finally taken. Some were arrested and imprisoned. Almost all of them are now with the Right Communist Party.

31 The Liberation Movement Among Varlis

S.V. Parulekar

THE BASIC CAUSE of the mass upsurge of the Varlis lay in their abominable condition of wretchedness and their suppression by the tyrant landlords. They had rotted in these conditions for a century unnoticed and uncared for. They were nursing in the innermost corner of their hearts inextinguishable fire of hatred for these conditions. But they dared not express it. Fear and helplessness had suppressed the smoldering fire. They saw nowhere on the horizon any ray of hope of their liberation. They lived in a mood of bitter despair. They were anxious to end their slavery. But they did not know how to do it. They needed somebody who would extend to them his helping hand, show them the road to their freedom, guide them, take their side against their oppressors and stand by them and lead in their fight to be free men.

This need was fulfilled by the Kisan Sabha. When it went to work among them, they rose to resist their oppressor. Their movement of liberation started in May, 1945, when they raised their Red banner of revolt against serfdom.

An Abortive Attempt.
Crushed under the burden of the last world war, the economic conditions of these serfs, who were living on the lowest conceivable level of human existence, deteriorated. The prices of the meanest necessaries of life had shot up by 400 p.c., while the daily rate of their wages even in 1944 remained at the pre-war level of one anna per day. Their conditions of life became so intolerable that they were driven to resort to the weapon of strike for securing an increase in their daily wages. About 3,000 Varlis in Umbergaon taluka struck work in 1944 when the harvesting season began and demand-

---

Reproduced from *Revolt of the Varlis*, by S.V. Parulekar, People's Publishing House, Bombay., 1947, Chapter IV.

ed a daily rate of wages of annas 12 for agricultural operation, cutting grass and felling trees.

For the first time in the course of a century the Varlis had dared raise their voice of protest against in-human exploitation and wretched condition of life by refusing to slave for the landlords and the timber merchants for daily wages which would not fetch them even half a cup of tea. The strike was a spontaneous outburst. But the source of inspiration for the strike was the propaganda of Mr Save, the government-appointed Assistant Backward Class Officer for Varlis. Quite fresh from the University, he was new in government service. He was not then contaminated with the spirit and practices of bureaucracy. He took the job of the welfare of the Varlis for which he was appointed, seriously and literally. He advised the Varlis not to do any forced labour and to demand annas 12 as a daily rate of wages. He further promised to help them in leading their struggle for securing the demand.

Encouraged by this promise, the Varlis raised their banner of struggle. They struck work and the strike continued for nearly two months. But the help promised by Mr Save was not forthcoming. When he went amongst them again, he did not go to lead their struggle but to betray it. Because, Mr Save had changed in the meanwhile. He was chastised by the bureaucracy for giving a wrong lead to the Varlis and was asked to settle the strike by persuading them to accept a daily rate of annas 6. He was also transferred from the area for having misunderstood his job as the Welfare Officer of the Varlis. In obedience to instructions from above, Mr Save advised the Varlis to call off the strike and accept the daily rate of annas 6. The Varlis were rudely shocked by the betrayal. It demoralised and disheartened them. But they were in no mood to listen to the advice of Mr Save. They spurned it and continued the strike. But in the end it fizzled out as they received help from no other quarter in conducting it.

Though the strike failed, it helped them to have a glimpse of the strength their unity possessed. Their sense of utter helplessness decreased. They became conscious that if they were united their unity did possess the strength to fight their oppressors successfully. This consciousness was, however, vague. It expressed itself in their courage to speak about their oppression to one who approached them. For the first time the dumb had found a voice to speak, frankly and without fear, of his agony and misery, his exploitation and oppression.

Kisan Sabha Contacts the Varlis

The Maharashtra Kisan Sabha decided to hold its first provincial conference at Titavala in Thana district on 12th January, 1945. In persuance of this decision the Kisan Sabha workers in Thana district had planned to mobilise at the conference the representatives of the peasants from all the talukas in the district. While campaigning for the conference, the Kisan Sabha for the first time came in contact with the aboriginal hill tribes of Umbergaon taluka in December, 1944. Late Dr Sane visited some villages in Umbergaon taluka and I addressed a meeting of about 300 Varlis at Zari some time in the third week of December.

Their response to my invitation to attend the conference in the beginning was so cold that it chilled my enthusiasm. Their strike had just then fizzled out. They had been betrayed and they spoke bitterly about it. They told us with their characteristic frankness that they did not trust us. They distrusted all. They had become sceptical and cynical in their attitude towards all outsiders....

After they had heard me for an hour, there was a distinct but slight change in their attitude towards us. My speech had loosened the barrier that stood between us. They started their narration and narrated at great length and in great detail how wretched were their conditions and how they were inhumanely tortured and tyrannised by the sowkars.

In the end they told us that they would give us a chance. Of their own accord they proceeded to tell us what had changed their attitude. They told me that in my speech I had roused their feelings. I had spoken what they felt deeply but could not express. What had appealed to them most was the reason which I had given for their poverty.

They promised to send a few representatives to attend the conference at Titavala. But they laid down a condition and demanded from us its acceptance. The condition was that one of the Kisan Sabha workers must stay in their midst to help them after the conference. They were afraid and justifiably so that sowkars would inflict most brutal punishments if they were to know that they had

Titavala Conference

Fifteen Varlis, representatives from Umbergaon taluka attended the Titavala conference. The mobilisation of 7,000 peasants at the conference, which included representatives of peasants of all the districts in Maharashtra, had a magical effect on the Varlis. It inspired and transformed them. One of them, Com. Maya Dhangada of Zari, who had never spoken more than a few words in all his life, volunteered to speak on the resolution of abolition of forced labour. He trembled while he spoke but he spoke with determination. His pent up feelings had found an outlet and they burst out in torrents. He held the conference spell bound by his pathetic narration. In conclusion he solemnly declared that Varlis would end serfdom and resist their oppressors.

The Varlis who returned home from the conference were not the same as those who attended it. The conference had changed them beyond recognition. They no longer trembled in the presence of their oppressors but started defying them. They had returned convinced that abolition of forced labour was an easy job and started efforts in right earnest for achieving that end without waiting for the Kisan Sabha workers to arrive in Umbergaon to help them. They had carried with them a few Red Flags which had decorated the pandal of the conference. They felt that they would serve as their guide, friend and philosopher. They discarded their routine mode of life and went as missionaries from village to village, holding group meetings of Varli peasants and preaching the message of the conference. The message stirred the whole mass of Varli peasants and the whole jungle tract of Umbergaon vibrated with the echo.

The Umbergaon Conference

The Varli Conference which met at Zari on 23rd May, 1945 under the auspices of the Kisan Sabha was a significant landmark in the history of the liberation movement of the Varli serfs. Com. Dalvi and Godavari Parulekar campaigned intensively in the jungle tract for a month before the conference. Their identification with the Varlis was so complete that the Varlis regarded them as one of them. The campaign roused the entire mass of Varlis; but it also awakened their oppressors. They started opposing bitterly the Kisan Sabha and resorted to social persecution of the Kisan

Sabha workers. Their attitude of hostility which increased in intensity with increasing volume of enthusiasm of the Varlis confirmed the belief of the Varlis, as nothing else did, that at last they had their real friends who would take up their side and help them to break their chains of bondage. The landlords, then in their own way, helped the Red Flag to win the loyalty of the Varlis.

While campaigning for the conference the Kisan Sabha workers helped the Varlis to resist the demand of the sowkars for Veth (forced labour) and to stop it. It helped them to realise vividly how feeble were their oppressors who had appeared to them omnipotent, in the face of their united strength. The stray victories which were easily won in the first round of struggle roused their spirit of resistance in all the stratas of the Varli population and installed confidence in them that they could easily defeat their enemy. A new awakening and consciousness was being born. The Varlis were enthused and their enthusiasm knew no bounds.

The conference took momentous decisions. It adopted the immediate programme of abolishing serf-tenure and forced labour. It urged the Varlis to resist their oppressors with their united strength and formulated the following four main and simple slogans.

'DO NOT CULTIVATE THE PRIVATE LAND OF THE LANDLORD UNLESS HE PAYS IN CASH THE DAILY WAGE OF ANNAS 12. DO NOT RENDER ANY FREE SERVICE TO THE LANDLORD! RESISTS HIM IF HE ASSAULTS YOU. YOU MUST ALL UNITE.'

The resistance of the Varlis to the demand of the landlords for forced labour commenced on a mass scale the moment the conference had concluded. They returned home shouting along the way that forced labour (Veth) was buried in the conference. The slogan and the message of the conference reached all the nooks and corners of the jungle tract within 24 hours of its conclusion. The Varlis forged 100 per cent unity. The timid were persuaded. The few recalcitrants were threatened with social boycott. Their resistance swept the jungle tract so swiftly and it gathered strength so rapidly that within three weeks of it forced labour became an event of the dead past. The system had become so rotten to the core and the unity which the Varlis had forged was of such irresistible strength that it collapsed. The Varlis did not have to exert for ending it.

Assaults and torture of Varlis which had been quite routine and common occurrences in their life stopped automatically. Their strength instilled such a dread in the hearts of the sowkars that they dared not raise their finger against the Varlis. The sowkars were convinced that the erstwhile tame and timid Varli would not hesitate to defend himself and resist them if they persisted in their inhuman practices.

Abolition of Serf Tenure

It was the month of June and the rainy season had set in. The aboriginal serf had abolished forced labour. He proceeded to abolish serf-tenure. The victory which he had easily won in the first encounter against forced labour had made him fearless and audacious. He launched a full blast offensive against the oldest and strongest citadel of the enemy which crumbled as easily as forced labour had collapsed. He bluntly refused to cultivate the land of the sowkars free and demanded the rates of wages fixed by the Kisan Sabha. His offensive gathered the strength of a whirlwind in the whole of the jungle of Umbergaon taluka and the sowkar was swept away. The sowkar found himself utterly at the mercy of his serf and he retreated without even attempting to offer resistance. Serf-tenure was abolished. It was hardly two months since the Varli serf had risen to break his chains of bondage. Abolition of serf-tenure was a glorious victory. It regained him his freedom which he had lost a century ago.

The Liberation Movement Spreads to Dahanu

The Kisan Sabha had planned to extend its sphere of activities to Dahanu taluka in 1946 after it had consolidated and organised its work in Umbergaon. But the Varlis of Dahanu upset its plan. They did not allow the Kisan Sabha to take the initiative in launching their liberation movement. They launched it themselves on their own initiative in September, 1945.

The Umbergaon conference was their source of inspiration. A few Varlis of Dahanu taluka from the adjoining villages of Umbergaon taluka had attended the conference out of curiosity. It inspired them. But the inspiration lacked the intensity which could impel them to march simultaneously along with the Varlis of Umbergaon in the common battle against their bondage. They did not share the confidence of the Umbergaon Varlis which was born in the course of the campaign and in the close contact with the Kisan Sabha workers that they could easily win the struggle on the strength of their unity. The conference enthused them but could not imbibe them with confidence. They had doubts in their minds as to the certainty of success. They had decided, therefore, to wait and watch the progress and the result of the battle waged by the Umbergaon Varlis.

When the news of the victorious march of the Umbergaon Varlis crossed their borders, their hesitation ceased and they became impatient. Without waiting for the Kisan Sabha, they moved on the march. They launched their offensive against their oppressors unaided. The Red Flag which they had carried from the Umbergaon conference was their only guide and they felt that they could achieve their liberation under its inspiration.

They launched their movement by the middle of September by holding mass meetings daily. The reports from Umbergaon which had percolated throughout the area had so roused the Varlis that the meetings attracted large crowds. The audience varied between 2 to 3 thousand. In the initial stages they did not feel the need for inviting any one for addressing the meetings. They addressed their own meetings. Those who had attended the Umbergaon conference used to be the speakers. Their speeches were short. They simply repeated the slogans formulated by the Umbergaon conference and the audience was satisfied. But as the movement gathered momentum the attendance swelled. It varied between 8 to 15 thousand. Mere slogans no longer satisfied the audience. But the organisers did not know what else to speak. It was then that they realised that they needed the Kisan Sabha workers for addressing meetings. They sent their frantic invitations which used to be in the form of commands. "A meeting is to be held on such date. The meeting orders you to come and address it". But no Kisan Sabha worker was able to attend their meetings as the invitations never reached the destination in time. The movement, however, did not pause nor falter. It marched ahead and took historical strides. When the Kisan Sabha workers went there for the first time in the first week of October they found to their surprise that the whole area was in the grip of a gigantic mass upheaval.

Liberation of Debt-Slaves in Dahanu

Before the Kisan Sabha workers had arrived on the scene, the Varlis of Dahanu had marched ahead of the Varlis of Umbergaon. They had not only abolished forced labour but had liberated the debt-slaves.

The problem of debt-slavery was very acute in Dahanu. The decision to liberate debt-slaves was prompted by none. The Kisan Sabha was not aware either of its existence or of its acute nature. The Varlis had understood the movement of the Red Flag as the movement of their liberation and liberation of debt-slaves was its integral part.

In the mass meetings which were held at Akharmal and Narpud and which were attended by 6,000 Varlis, they took the decision to liberate the debt-slaves. They also decided not to return home without implementing the decision. The plan which they chalked out was simple, effective and characteristic of their boundless enthusiasm.

Those who could not be away from their homes for urgent reasons returned with the permission of the meeting. The rest divided themselves into four batches. The batches marched in a procession in different parts of Dahanu taluka with the Red Flag. As they marched, they stopped at the door of the landlord's buildings and called out the debt-slaves. The slaves came out and the landlord dared not stop them. The procession declared in the name of the Red Flag that they were free men from that moment and asked them to join the procession. The slaves walked out of their prisons with their bag and baggage which consisted of a couple of tattered clothes and accompanied by their wives. The procession proceeded further. Thus they marched for three days and returned home after liberating about a thousand debt-slaves.

The movement of liberation of debt-slaves had another important aspect. It restored to the slave his freedom. But more important than that it rescued his wife from the lust of the landlord.

The Strike

The liberation movement entered its second phase when the Varlis went on strike in the first week of October, 1945. The season for cutting grass had approached. The Kisan Sabha had demanded the minimum rate of Rs. 2-8 for cutting 500 lbs. of grass. The sowkars refused to concede the demands. The Varlis refused to cut the grass. The strike in both the talukas of Umbergaon and Dahanu was so complete that grass cutting would not commence. The sowkars would not get a single Varli to cut their grass.

Landlords' Efforts to Crush the Strike and Movement

In the initial stages of the movement, the sowkars had used all the weapons in their armoury for disrupting the solidarity of the Varlis. They had tried in vain to check the surging torrent of the revolutionary upsurge and to regain the ground which had swept off under their feet. They tried to frighten the Varlis by launching false, frivolous and vexatious complaints in the criminal courts against them. They starved them during the rainy season by refusing to advance Khavati. But to their utter disappointment they found that their measures had not the desired effect of compelling the Varlis to retreat. On the contrary these measures made the Varlis more bitter and march forward more doggedly and with redoubled determination and energy.

The strike stunned the landlords. In their helplessness they pleaded with bureaucracy to render them assistance in suppressing the movement. They vilified and misrepresented the activities of the Kisan Sabha. They harped on the prejudices against Communists. They falsely accused that the Kisan Sabha workers were inciting Varlis to violence. They requested the District Magistrate several times to ban the meetings but the District Magistrate refused to believe the allegation, to ban meetings and to intervene on the ground that the movement was peaceful.

The sowkars decided to utilise the situation created by the strike. But the strike was exemplarily peaceful. They had to design a plan which would provoke bureaucracy to intervene inspite of the peaceful situation. Secondly the plan must be such as to provoke maximum bureaucratic repression. Because the sowkars imagined that the movement could not be suppressed unless bureaucracy resorted to ruthless repression, to firing and to killing a few Varlis, they felt that the movement needed to be drowned with blood of the Varlis.

The sowkars did succeed in hatching a most wicked, treacherous and heinous plot. And the plot did succeed. There was firing. There were murders. There were mass arrests. There was torture. There was inhuman repression.

The Landlords' Plot

The landlords had correctly judged the intensity of the loyalty of the Varlis to the Red Flag. They based their plot on this basic fact. They knew that the Varlis could be easily misled in the name of the Red Flag. And they decided to mislead them by treacherous trick. On 10th October, 1945, at about 8 p.m. the sowkars through their hirelings organised to raise a false cry simultaneously at several places within an area of 1,500 sq. miles that 'Com. Godavari was coming to Talawada, a village near Bhilad in Umbergaon taluka. She was to address a meeting at midnight. The sowkars have brought goondas for breaking the meeting. The Red Flag wants every Varli to attend the meeting and he should come armed with lathis and sickles'.

The cry about the meeting was totally false and baseless. The Kisan Sabha had not even thought of holding any meeting. Com. Godavari was then lying ill at Kalyan. Com. Dalvi was at Kosbad in Dahanu taluka. Com. Ranadive had arrived at Khattalwad on the night of the 10th itself.

The naive and innocent Varlis believed the cry in the name of the Red Flag to be true and was lured. They ran to Talawada for reaching there in time for the meeting. At midnight more than ten thousand Varlis had arrived. Many of them had walked a distance of about 30 miles. They continued to pour in till 3 a.m. According to the report of the District Superintendent of Police the attendance had mounted up to 30 thousand.

Luring the Varlis for the meeting at Talawada was one part of the plot of the sowkars. Its counterpart was to inform the police that a violent and armed mob of Varlis had collected at Talawada for killing the landlords and the lives of the landlords were in danger.

Firing

Armed police arrived at the place of the meeting at about midnight on 10th October and opened fire on the peaceful gathering of the Varlis from the roof of a moving motor van. The gathering did not disperse though one of them was killed and a few were wounded in the firing. The police continued to open fire at intervals indiscriminately and in all directions from a moving van till 3 p.m. on

11th October. They opened fire thrice during the interval of fifteen hours on the same gathering at the same spot. Five Varlis were killed in the firings. The number of the wounded was large. Among the wounded there was a boy of twelve years of age. And still the gathering refused to disperse.

This episode was a thrilling exhibition of the reckless defiance of death by the Varli, his loyalty to the Red Flag and the birth of rare courage in him. For fifteen hours he had defied bullets which were showered on him from time to time. Firing failed to influence him to move from the place and it was difficult to guess how long he would have continued to remain there if the Kisan Sabha worker had not arrived there at 3 p.m. on 11th October and dispersed the gathering.

For fifteen hours they had protected the Red Flag which they had hoisted by shielding it with their bodies. As the police van used to pass by the spot and the police opened fire, they crowded round the Red Flag. They thought that the police were aiming to shoot the Red Flag, and they felt it to be their sacred duty to protect it at the cost of their lives.

Firing did not and could not have succeeded in dispersing the meeting. A word from the Red Flag for dispersal was necessary for the purpose. The gathering believed that the meeting was called by the Red Flag. They felt that their loyalty to the Red Flag required of them not to disperse till they were asked to disperse by the Red Flag. They would rather pay any amount of price in life rather than disperse without the permission of the Red Flag.

They waited for the Kisan Sabha worker to arrive for addressing the meeting till morning broke out. But as none arrived they sent a messenger to the office at Khatalwada which was at a distance of about 12 miles from Talawada. Com. Kamalakar Ranadive happened to be in the office. He hurried to Talawada where he reached at 3 p.m. while he was addressing the gathering and advising them to disperse peacefully, the police van passed by. The police opened fire; one Varli was killed and several were wounded.

The gathering dispersed. The realisation that they had been deceived by the treachery of the landlords dawned on them. Then they returned home full of bitterness against the landlords and the government who together had killed five innocent Varlis and wounded several.

The Reign of Bureaucratic Repression and Terror

The attitude of imperialist bureaucracy which was one of non-intervention in the initial stages suddenly changed as soon as the significance of the liberation movement dawned on them. From non-intervention it turned to ruthless repression. Firing signalled the turning point. Under the mask of restoring law and order a reign of police terror was let loose against the Varlis.

Meetings, processions and assemblies of five or more persons in the area were banned on 13th October, 1945 for a period of two months under the Defence of India Rules.

On the 14th October, the landlords requested the District Magistrate to extern all the communists from the area. In obedience to the sowkar's request, the District Superintendent of police externed on 15th October, Godavari Parulekar, Kamalakar Ranadive, Jashwant Thakkar of the Indian People's Theatre Association, Sunil Janah, the photographer of the People's War, V.M. Bhave of the Lok Yudha and myself on the ground "that our presence in Dahanu and Umbergaon talukas were prejudicial to public safety, industry, machinery and buildings in the above areas".

Com. Dalvi was arrested for treason. But when it was realised how absurd and ludicrous was the attempt to charge him with treason, it was changed into dacoity. Comrades Phadke, Patki and Pradhan were arrested in the Kisan Sabha office on 12th October where they had arrived just a few hours before from Thana for the first time for enlisting voters to the Legislative Assembly, on a charge of alleged dacoity which had taken place in Umbergaon on 9th October. A Varli who had gone to the office for complaining that his son was missing was also arrested along with them.

The police repression in Dahanu taluka knew no bounds. Some of the methods employed by them were as crude, brutal and matchless as those employed by the Nazis. Several Varlis were mercilessly hammered. The Varli women were threatened to be raped. Kerosene was poured on the buttocks of one of the Varlis and they were set fire to.

The main object of the repression was to terrorise the rising movement of the liberated Varlis and to drown it in blood.

The Movement Forges Ahead

Undaunted the Varlis marched ahead. Firing and repression had failed in its object of crushing their movement. They had emerged stronger, more united and with a better understanding as to who were their real friends and who their enemies. The report of the Adivasi Seva Mandal for 1945-6 describes the morale and mood of the Varlis after the firing and the repression. It says, 'they are not in a mood to tolerate any further oppression by the landlords and the sowkars. They have realised that organisation is their only strength. After a long dark and dreary night, the jungle seems to have awakened and has given a call'.

The strike succeeded in spite of the firing and repression. The Varlis secured the rate of Rs. 2-8 for cutting 500 lbs. of grass which they had demanded. Some of the landlords had to pay over Rs. 3.

The landlords were jubilant over the success of their plot. But their joy was very shortlived. Because, they soon realised to their utter disappointment that the Varlis held their ground firmly. Their disillusionment demoralised them.

A conference of the Varlis of Dahanu and Umbergaon talukas was held at Mahalakshmi on 21st January, 1946. 15,000 Varlis attended the conference. Many had walked a distance of 30 miles. Consciousness of their strength born out of the victorious resistance to the repression of the government and the landlords was widely in evidence. The conference considered the problem of current year's rent and decided that they should pay only one year's rent and refuse to pay any arrears of rent which had accumulated. The conference also took the decision that they should pay as rent only the quantity of paddy which they had contracted to pay and refuse all the other legal and illegal exactions.

The decisions of the conference marked a new step of advance in the development of the movement. And the Varlis advanced with a firm step in obedience to the decisions. All arrears of rent were wiped out. All exactions other than the rent of paddy stopped. The roaring success of the conference made the landlord feel so helpless that he meekly submitted.

The Mahalakshmi conference furnished with yet another evidence of the loyalty of the Varlis to the Red Flag. The Kisan Sabha workers had appealed that they should contribute a rupee per family towards the funds of the Communist Party for building up their movement. The call could not reach all. Those to whom it had reached had brought with them a rupee. The esteem in which they held the Red Flag, their appreciation of what it had helped them to achieve, their conviction that it would stand by them in their struggle to the end, were to be seen in the enthusiasm, eagerness and devotion with which they paid their contributions. They stood in long queues for hours. Collection had to be discontinued when it was time for the conference to meet in session. The disappointment of those whose contribution could not be received was great. They needed to be comforted with the assurance that the Kisan Sabha worker would later go to their villages for collecting it. The total collection on the day exceeded Rs 3,000.

32 The Struggle of 1946

S.V. Parulekar

THE STRUGGLE of the Varlis which brought them on the political horizon of the province, secured recognition to the problem of the aboriginal hill tribes which had been ignored, as one of the important items in national reconstruction and became an epoch making event in the history of the struggle for their emancipation started at the end of September, 1946.

The Transformation of the Varlis
The experience of the bitter struggle through which the Varli had to wade had rapidly transformed him. His transformation had been so radical that he became a new being. He had been quite an innocent infant in understanding and consciousness. Straight from infancy he stepped into maturity. He has advanced with a breathless speed to overtake the peasants who had been far ahead of him by omitting many an intermediary step.

He had developed a thirst for knowledge. He had become very keen to know all about Soviet Russia. It was the landlords' campaign of slander against the Kisan Sabha workers which kindled in him this desire. They had been circulating the news that Com. Godavari Parulekar received huge sums of money from Soviet Russia and that she was misappropriating it instead of distributing it among them. They had never heard of Soviet Russia and they were, therefore, very eager to know who was this philanthropic 'person'.

The struggle had not only made him conscious of his rights in the economic domain, but that it had also made him understand and value civic and political rights. On the occasion of the election to the Bombay Legislative Assembly in March, 1946, he showed such enthusiasm and interest in them as none else in the district did. The Red Flag had set up a candidate. Very few of the Varlis had votes. But hundreds of them marched to the polling station in procession, defying the ban imposed by government, and camped there the night before the day of the election. When the polling

Reproduced from *Revolt of the Varlis*, by S.V. Parulekar, *op. cit.* Chapter V.

started, they could not understand why all of them had no votes while all the rest had. They were indignant to see that all of them were not voters while all their exploiters were.

One of the Varli youth could not control his indignation. He went to vote for his ailing father who had not come. The Polling Officer explained to him that he could not vote for his father. But the explanation could not satisfy him. He insisted on voting and voted. He was prosecuted and sentenced to one month's regorous imprisonment. But even the conviction could not convince him that it was wrong to vote for his ailing father. When he was released after the expiry of his sentence he remarked in disgust:

'The laws are made by the landlords. They are intended to keep their grip over us. The laws, the courts, everything belong to the landlords'.

The Red Flag candidate was defeated and the landlords tried to humiliate the Varlis, saying that the Congress Flag had defeated the Red Flag. The Varlis, however, retorted: 'All the members of your family have votes, your women, children, old men, all have votes, while even our grown-up men have no votes. Give us all votes and let us see who defeats whom'.

Both the change in the political situation and the awakening of the new consciousness among the Varlis constitute necessary clues to understand the course of development of the historic struggle of the Varlis.

The Nature of the Struggle

The dispute was purely a simple economic dispute in its origin.

But the popular ministry, in their Press communique, characterised it as a political dispute instigated by those 'who advocated violence to bring about a political change, namely the ushering in of a Communist state'.

This charge was most frivolous and fantastic. So long the bogey of communist menace had been most unscrupulously utilised by imperialism for crushing the legitimate and just struggle of the oppressed. It was now adopted by the popular ministry without the slightest compunction for suppressing the merits of the dispute and for crushing the just cause of the most downtrodden section of the population in the province.

The popular ministry was led to make the baseless charge for various reasons. It placed blind faith in the false, distorted and mischievous report of the bureaucracy. It allowed itself to be led astray by its prejudices against the Kisan Sabha, its activities and its workers. And lastly it was tempted to make the accusation as it served as a very convenient devise for invoking to its rescue the anti-Communist prejudices. Because, the communique quite inadvertently admits that it was an economic dispute. It says that a dispute arose ' in October, 1946 in connection with the terms offered by the communists for grass or paddy cutting, timber cutting and other varieties of labour '.

The Issue of the Dispute

The dispute which arose when the season for grass cutting and felling trees in forest approached, was confined only to two issues. One of these was between the Varlis and the landlords regarding the rate for cutting grass. The other was between the timber merchants and the Varlis regarding the rate for felling trees in the forest.

The Kisan Sabha had demanded a minimum rate of Rs 2/8 for cutting 500 lbs. of grass and a daily rate of Rs 1/4 for forest work.

A number of landlords, even this year, readily conceded the demand and grass cutting had started. Some of them had engaged Varlis on a higher rate of Rs 3 per 500 lbs. The dispute was however confined only to a small section of landlords who were most reactionary and were not willing to pay the minimum rate of Rs 2/8. They too would not have resisted if they had not been encouraged by the attitude of bureaucracy of stiffen their own attitude.

As regards the daily rate of Rs 1/4 for forest work it was the minimum which the Kisan Sabha could demand. Because, what it had demanded was quite inadequate to cover the cost of living of a Varli family on the lowest economic level. Secondly, it was below the level of wages which prevailed for similar kinds of very hard and strenuous work. Lastly, the timber trade which had yielded fabulous profits to the merchants could easily afford it. The timber merchants would not agree to pay more than a rupee as daily wage for forest work. All work in the forest had therefore stopped.

Who was Responsible for the Dispute?

Bureaucracy was more responsible for the origin, development and the prolongation of the dispute than either the landlord or the timber merchants. They played only a secondary and supporting role in the game. The dispute would never have assumed the serious proportion it did if bureaucracy had remained impartial, neutral or even had assumed the same bureaucratic indifference which it had in 1945 during the initial stages of the dispute. But it had changed its policy. It was anxious to intervene. It was quite unconcerned with the merits of the dispute but not with the fate of the dispute. The intervention had a definite purpose behind it. To crush the influence of the Kisan Sabha and its strength was what prompted it to intervene. It did not intervene to settle the dispute but to create a situation which would necessarily make settlement impossible and to prolong it so that it may be utilised for the achievement of its ulterior object.

The Landlords' Role

The most reactionary and the notorious landlords still clung to the dream of smashing the solidarity of the Varlis and of reimposing on them conditions of serfdom and bondage. They indulged in the same devilish designs as those of the last year for achieving their object. They employed the old methods which failed to yield any result, because the Varlis had grown wiser. Their strength was irresistible and their solidarity was unassailable.

With the approach of the grass cutting season the landlords started intimidating and provoking the Varlis. They lodged false and frivolous complaints in Criminal Courts against several active Varlis, workers of the Kisan Sabha. The goonda agents of the landlords who had been the mainstay of serfdom became active once again and started assaulting the Varlis. There was a plan behind these moves of the landlords. It was to provoke the Varlis and create a situation in which government would be led to resort to firing and to adopt repressive measures for crushing the solidarity of the Varlis and their organisation. In short, the landlords desired the repetition of the history of October, 1945. But the Varlis refused to be provoked. They foiled the game of the landlords by remaining peaceful and by not losing their composure of mind. As a countermove they started demonstrating their strength and solidarity by assembling in large numbers and marching in processions in the area, and thus had a temporary but salutory effect on the landlords.

The landlords took their next move in the first week of October. It occurred to their fertile imagination to take advantage of 11th

October, which was the 'martyrs day'. They gave currency to a false and baseless rumour that the Kisan Sabha had organised to commemorate the memory of the Varli martyrs who had fallen victims to the firing on 11th October, 1945 by holding a meeting at the place of firing and by wholesale acts of violence against the landlords on the area. The Kisan Sabha had convened no meeting on or about the 11th of October. But the prejudices of the bureaucracy against the Kisan Sabha led it to believe the rumour. The District Magistrate and the District Superintendent of Police rushed to the area with 150 armed constables. The Kisan Sabha took precautions to see that the Varlis would not be duped by false cry about the meeting and assemble in large numbers in any place on 10th and 11th of October. Nothing untoward happened. The game of the landlords was foiled. Bureaucracy was disappointed.

Once again as a last resort the landlords resorted to acts of intimidation, provocation and violence. Between 15th October and 8th November a number of Varlis were assaulted by the hired hooligans of the landlords. One of them was so brutally hammered near Vanagaon that he died in the hospital on the fourth day. The Varlis, however, behaved with admirable restraint. They would not walk into the snare. In spite of provocation, they remained peaceful.

Peaceful Struggle of the Varlis

The unique character of the dispute was that it was conducted most peacefully. The strike in the forest work began by the middle of October. There were 120 coups in the forest. They were spread over an area of 1000 square miles. The number of Varlis involved in the strike were 15 thousand. The villages which were affected by the strike were over 200 and the population over a lakh. The message of the Kisan Sabha that the Varlis should not start forest work unless the timber merchants conceded its demand was conveyed by the Varlis to their villages. They used a stick to which toddy leaves and the chit conveying the message were tied at the top. The stick went from village to village and the Varlis stopped going to work wherever it reached. Only in four out of 120 coups a few Varlis, to whom the message of the Kisan Sabha had not reached and who were weak to resist the pressure of the hooligan agents of the timber merchants, had started work. To enable them to drive away the fear from their minds, the Varlis took out processions to the coups. No sooner the procession reached the coup than they stopped work and joined the procession in joy. Thus within 48 hours after the message was given by the Kisan Sabha, there was complete stoppage of all forest work in the whole area. It is alleged by the timber merchants that the Varlis in the procession assaulted three of their agents. Since the subject matter of this allegation is sub-judice, its merits cannot be discussed. But assuming the allegation to be true, an impartial observer will come to the only conclusion that but for the remarkable sense of discipline among the Varlis, their loyalty to their organisation and their willingness to participate in the strike, it could not have been so complete and successful in so short a period and in such a vast area.

The strike regarding cutting grass was equally complete and peaceful. The landlords who refused to pay the minimum rate of Rs 2/8 per 500 lbs. of grass and who had lodged false and frivolous complaints against the Varlis, could not secure the services of a single Varli in the whole area to work for them. They relied on the efforts of the bureaucracy for securing the services of the Varlis. But its efforts met with dismal failure. The District Magistrate had instructed his subordinates to campaign among the Varlis by holding meetings for acceptance of the rate fixed by him. But no Varli attended the meeting. No Varli went to work. The grass as well as the paddy of these landlords rotted in the fields.

The Varlis not only refused to work in the forest for the timber merchants and cut grass for the landlords who refused to pay the rate fixed by the Kisan Sabha, but that they also refused to ply carts. The timber merchants and the landlords employ about 5000 carts during the season. The stoppage was so complete that not a single cart moved on the road. When some of them argued with the Varlis that they should not stop plying carts as cartage was not an issue of the dispute, the Varlis replied, ' Bring the permit from the Kisan Sabha allowing plying of carts '. The landlords in Dahanu taluka rushed to the Kisan Sabha for securing permits. The ' permits ' soon assumed such a general character that the landlord had to secure the ' permits ' from the Kisan Sabha for every little thing which they wanted to get done by the Varlis. Nothing moved without permits. Everything stopped in its absence.

The spectacle of the solidarity and strength of the Varlis frightened the landlords who had a guilty conscience. All of them who had their place of abode in the Varli area came to live in the towns.

Kisan Sabha's Efforts.

About the 1st of November one of the landlords filed a complaint of robbery against two Varlis. The Sub-Inspector of Police went to the village with a police party for investigation. He proceeded to make a panchanama which the resident Varlis of the village who had assembled there believed to be false. They objected. They were innocent and honest and were not yet used to all the dishonest and false ways of the civilised world. They could not understand how a false panchanama could be made of an offence, which was never committed, when a popular ministry was in power. The Sub-Inspector returned without completing his investigation. On the third day of the alleged incident the Superintendent of Police went to the village in the early hours of the morning with large police force. He arrested the Varlis met on the road while proceeding to the village. In the village he arrested some and thereafter arrested a number of Varlis from the villages situated round about. In all 55 Varlis were arrested and they were brought to Dahanu. The news of the arrest of innocent Varlis spread throughout the area. And the Varlis decided to go to Dahanu for demanding their release. Five thousand of them proceeded to Dahanu. The Kisan Sabha workers met the Varlis on the outskirts of Dahanu. They explained to them how bureaucracy was waiting only for an opportunity to open fire on them and persuaded them to disperse peacefully. The Varlis were agitated and excited. Still they responded to the appeal.

Demoralisation Among the Landlords

The landlords were completely demoralised. They saw the futility of continuing the dispute. Some of them approached the Kisan Sabha for the settlement of the dispute, realising that it was no longer possible to fight the solidarity of the Varlis and that continuation of the dispute would ruin them economically. They suggested that they would withdraw the cases they had lodged against the Varlis. The Varlis were, however, in no mood to settle the dispute on such terms. They agreed to permit the landlords to withdraw the cases and settle the disputes on fulfilment of two conditions. One of them was that the landlords must pay Rs. 3 for cutting 500 lbs. of grass. And the second one was that they must pay compensation to the village and each of the Varlis against whom complaint was lodged. They agreed to these terms and the dispute was settled. Only those landlords who were still conspiring with the bureaucracy to find out adequate repressive measures for suppressing the struggle continued to resist the demand of the Kisan Sabha. But the number of such landlords was reduced considerably.

The Offensive of the Bureaucracy

The bureaucracy was taking the side of the landlords and the vested interests from the beginning of the dispute. In its initial stages it used measures of indirect pressure for disrupting the solidarity of the Varlis, for assailing the influence of the Kisan Sabha and for settling the disputes on the terms of the landlords and the timber merchants. The Special Officer appointed for the welfare of the Varlis who would not enthusiastically support its policy was got transferred to another province. The whole state machinery in the district was set in motion for campaigning against the Red Flag. But it failed dismally and had to be abandoned.

When indirect pressure failed to yield the desired results, bureaucracy launched measures of direct intervention and repression. The district Magistrate started interfering in dispensation of justice and procedure of courts and using his discretionary powers for suppressing the legitimate struggle of the Varlis. He issued directives to the Criminal Courts which are subservient to the executive, to hear the cases in which the Varlis were alleged to have committed offences of violence and intimidation from day to day. The discretion was intended in effect to put the Varli at a great disadvantage in defending himself and send him to jail undefended. It is the general practice of bureaucracy to use such directives for causing to its subordinate courts to convict the accused irrespective of the merits of the case. The District Magistrate issued another directive to the courts which was more repressive in character. It was to the effect that the courts should demand heavy bail from the Varlis. In effect the directive meant that the release of the Varlis on bail was to be denied. It was intended to make the Varli rot in jail before his guilt was formally proved against him. There was a third directive. The courts were asked not to release the Varlis on bail unless they agreed not to attend any meeting and to participate in any communist activities. This directive was intended to penalise the Varlis for participating in legitimate activities and movements without declaring them illegal and constituted a grave encroachment on the civic rights of the citizen and a menace to legitimate democratic movements. There were other directives of minor character. The object of all of them was to terrorise and frighten the Varlis.

But the repression failed to make any impression on the Varlis. The jail no longer held any terror for them. They continued the struggle with unabated enthusiasm, vigour and courage. Bureaucracy was utilising the prolongation of the disputes for fabricating a case against the activities of the Kisan Sabha and presenting to the popular ministry a false, distorted, mischievous and misleading picture of the situation.

The End of the Dispute

The strike which had lasted for about a month and showed no signs of weakening spread among the timber merchants. They were anxious for a settlement of the dispute, since its continuation would involve them in irreparable financial loss. The Special Officer for the welfare of the Varlis who had not yet handed over his charge to his successor intervened to bring about the settlement. The strike was settled on 10th Novemeber 1946 on terms which secured to the Varlis earnings much higher than what the Kisan Sabha had demanded and concessions which it had not demanded. The agreement was first signed by the representatives of the Kisan Sabha. The Special Officer took it to the representatives of the timber merchants who also signed it. It was also signed by Mr. V.B. Karnik, B.A., the principal of the high school, Dahanu as an independent witness. The Welfare Officer immediately left Dahanu in a hurry with the agreement bearing the signatures of all the parties for acquainting the District Magistrate and the popular ministry that the dispute had been settled. He had promised to furnish the Kisan Sabha with the copy of the agreement, later. He could not, however, fulfil his promise for reasons which up to this day have remained mysterious.

The Timber Merchants' Association ratified the agreement in its general meeting held on 14th November, 1946. The Kisan Sabha called off the strike on 11th November and advised the Varlis to resume work. The Kisan Sabha workers were busy till the 20th November in informing the Varlis of the settlement of the dispute and explaining to them the terms of agreement. Varlis started resuming work. Normal conditions of work were being restored.

Thus the dispute ended on 10th November, 1946. It was a great victory for the Varlis. They had successfully fought and met the offensive of the landlords, the timber merchants and the repression of the bureaucracy and had conducted their struggle most peacefully to a successful end.

PART VI

An Overview

Some Centres of Peasant Revolts

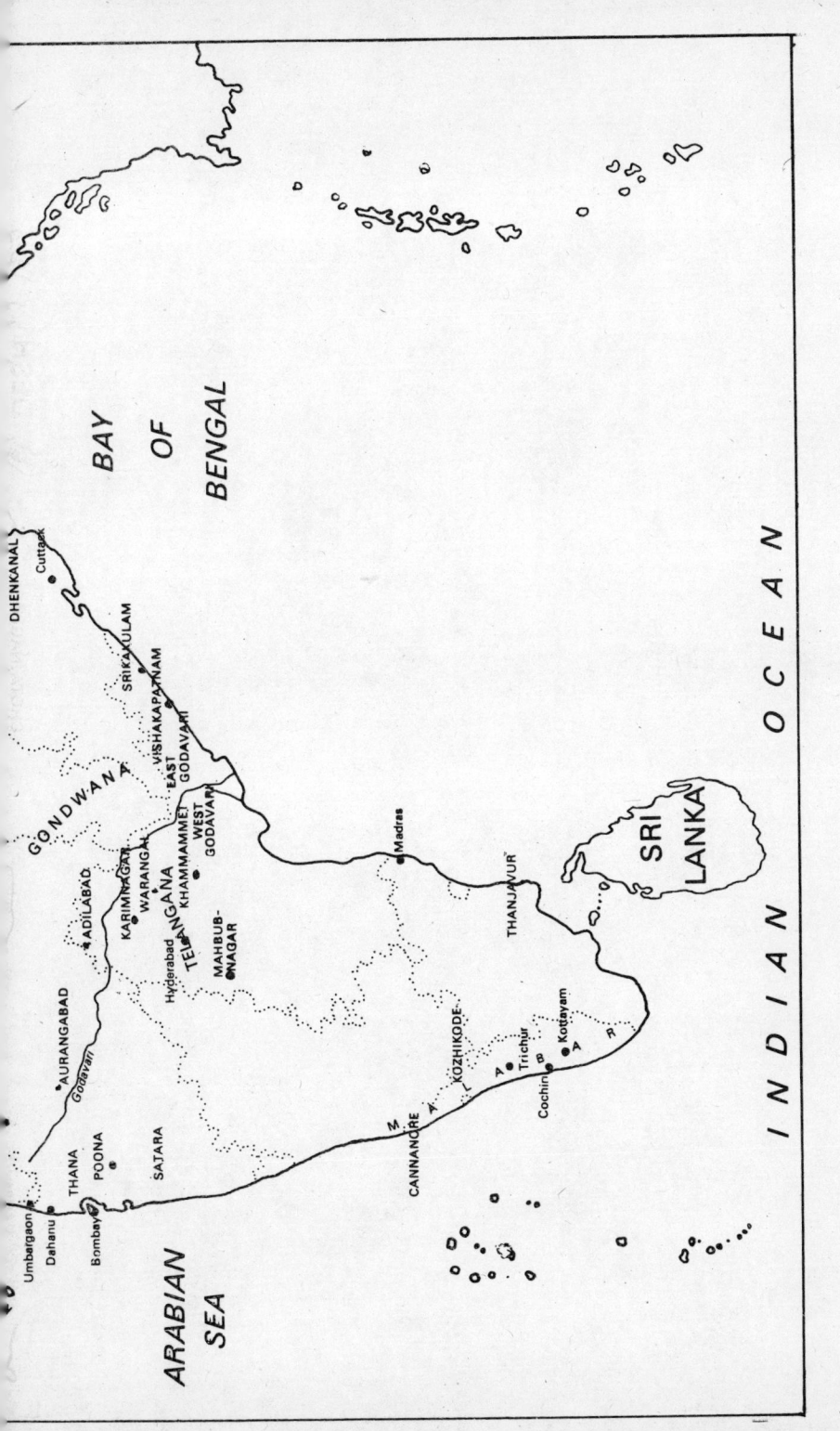

Introduction

(1)

OUR SELECTIONS have dealt with peasant struggles in different parts of the country during different periods. The first two selections reproduced here provide a picture of successive peasant struggles in the same district or province throughout the entire British period. They thus highlight the need to construct a history of districts, regions and provinces. Such detailed studies of various areas will generate an appropriate basis and material for a comprehensive social history of India.

(2)

Essays by Hamza Alavi, Kathleen Gough and Uday Mehta, highlight some of the crucial theoretical debates emerging among the scholars and activists of peasant struggles. These discussions deal with the role of the peasantry in the anti-colonial nationalist movements and also in the class battles of the exploited strata.

The end of the first world war, the historic proletarian-socialist revolution in Russia, the large number of national liberation movements in colonial and semi-colonial countries, the intense struggles of these colonial and semi-colonial countries during the Second World War, including struggles against the changing imperialist masters, and the post-war emergence of anti-imperialist struggles in Asia, Africa, Latin America, have posed the problem of the role of the rural classes in bourgeois nationalist and proletarian socialist revolutions that are erupting in many parts of the world. In fact an animated controversy is underway with regard to the role of the national bourgeoisie, the proletariat and the various categories of rural classes in shaping the Third World countries which have emerged after the Second World War. In these countries the newly emerged states are pursuing a policy of development based on a 'mixed economy'. The questions of the nature and the stages of revolution in these countries, the position of various classes and the class character of the state in these, the problem of the relation between the newly emerged states with the imperialist 'First World,' non-capitalist 'Second World' and the 'Third World' countries, have acquired crucial importance. Similarly the problems of the role of proletariat, landlords, kulaks and rich farmers, middle peasants, the vast bulk of poor peasants, comprized of sub-marginal cultivators, tenants, sharecroppers and agricultural labourers and ruined pettie bourgeoisie in the form of artisans and workers connected with informal sections in rural and urban areas have also become a subject of controversy.

These controversies shape the programmes, policies, strategies and tactics of various forces engaged in the struggle to transform societies. It is indisputable that in the third world, the agrarian population plays a crucial part in shaping the future of these countries. However there is a powerful debate going on with regard to the exact role of the various strata in rural areas in different periods, different phases and different stages of Revolution.

The three articles reproduced here examine this problem in the context of the Indian development by analysing the role of peasant struggles in the context of the British and post-independence period. It is unfortunate that neither Alavi nor Gough clearly state what they mean by revolution in the context of which they are evaluating the role of the peasantry. Do they evaluate the role of peasantry in the context of a national democratic, people's democratic, new democratic or socialist revolution? Further, they do not distinguish between revolution, created by people of the colonial countries, particularly India, in the context of their struggles against the British and other foreign rule, and the Revolution created by the same people in the context of their struggles against the newly emerged state after the withdrawal of foreign rule.

Further there is no clear analysis of even the two paths of anti-imperialist struggles viz. the path of bargain and pressure adopted by the political party representing the indigenous bourgeoisie in India, and the path of militant anti-imperialist, national freedom movements based on class struggles under the influence of Marxist parties. The post-war developments, the policies pursued by the Indian National Congress in securing a transfer of power, the vascillations of the Communist Party of India during the entire period following 1928 to 1951, and their impact upon the nature of participation by different classes in rural areas are not analysed with the care and precision that is necessary to define the nature of the anti-British and the post-independence phase of revolution.

However, Hamza Alavi and Kathleen Gough have posed the question which has profound theoretical and tactical importance. They have also stressed the problem of viewing the role of various categories of rural classes, particularly the relative role of the middle peasantry, the poor peasantry and the agricultural labour. The differences in the assessment of the role of the middle peasant between Hamza Alavi and Kathleen Gough also deserves careful understanding. Uday Mehta's work, though not directly focussed on theoretical issues of the role of specific classes in the context of revolution, indirectly contributes to the same discussion through a survey of the phases of the peasant struggles in India.

A proper understanding of the role of the proletariat, the class which is to lead the revolution, the role of various rural classes and their function in either providing leadership or following two different phases of revolution, is immensely important for a clear understanding of the nature of revolution viz. national democratic, people's democratic, new democratic or socialist Revolutions.

(3)

The last two selections are presented to round up the theoretical problems involved in appraising the role of peasantry in the context of the nature of social transformation and the conception of the stages of revolution as discussed by different groups of Marxists. The article 'The Two-Stages Theory of Revolution in the Third World' reflects the views held by the editor with regard to the discussion going on about stages of revolution today.

The selection 'Unconventional Anthropology of the "Traditional" (?) Peasantry' is a review of the findings of six peasant wars in 20th century by E.R. Wolf. It is a critique of the established social-anthropological study of the peasantry on the basis of an ahistorical structural-functional approach. It also points out how a systematic study of peasant struggles has become necessary to appraise the nature of leadership under which the poor peasants and the agrarian labourers can really abolish a historically dwarfed capitalist order which utilizes feudal and semi-feudal institutions and culture and usher in a healthy socialist order which alone can lead to their emancipation. Findings of Wolf, based on the case studies of six major peasant wars, provides an illuminating perspective on this crucial issue.

33 Peasant Revolts in Malabar in the Nineteenth and Twentieth Centuries

K.N. Panikkar

THE NATURE and extent of peasant revolts in India during the British colonial rule have not yet received adequate attention in historical writings on India. The early colonial historians and their modern disciples have drawn the picture of a docile and contented peasantry living under the shelter and comfort of *Pax Britanica*. Apart from the security to life and property provided by British rule, it was argued that the peasants were the beneficiaries of a more benevolent revenue system compared to the surplus extracted by the 'Indian despotic rulers' like the Sultan of Mysore, the Nawab of Oudh and the Nizam of Hyderabad. Even the nationalist historians, who have recognized the severity of the colonial and feudal exploitation of the primary producers, have generally ignored the struggle of the peasantry against this exploitation. The peasantry bore the burden either with stoic indifference or with fatalistic resignation. In spite of occasional outbursts against moneylenders and landlords, it is argued that religious influences and caste loyalties had ensured social harmony in rural India.

This, however, is a misleading picture. Kathleen Gough has recently identified 77 peasant revolts in various parts of India, 'the smallest of which probably engaged several thousand peasants in active support or combat'.[1] Gough's estimate is perhaps very modest. A more detailed survey would show a substantially larger number. The details of many of these revolts lay shrouded in the official records of the British government, entered under rather misleading titles like religious disturbances, communal riots, fanatical outbreaks etc. Some of these revolts, though basically agrarian in character, assumed communal dimensions due to land

This article was especially written for this volume.

being controlled by a dominant religious group. In such a situation, in the absence of class consciousness and proper leadership, ideological influences of religion provided the necessary moral force and justification for struggle against exploitation and oppression. The revolt of the Mappila peasantry of Malabar during the 19th and 20th centuries is a good example of such a phenomenon.[2]

I

Malabar was ceded to the East India Company in 1792 by Tipu Sultan after his defeat in the third Anglo-Mysore war. After a brief spell of administration under the Bombay Government it formed a district of the Madras Presidency. Covering an area of 5795 square miles and stretching over a distance of 150 miles along the Arabian Sea. It was bound in the north by the South Canara District of the Madras Presidency, in the south by the former Cochin State and in the east by the Western Ghats.[3] According to the Census of 1921 the total population of the District was 3,098,891 with a density of 535 per square mile—2,039,333 Hindus and 1,004,327 Mappilas. The religion-wise distribution of the population in the ten *taluks* of the district was as follows:—

Taluk	Hindus	Mappilas
Calicut	1,96,435	88,393
Chirakkal	25,498	87,337
Cochin	7,318	4,999
Eranad	1,63,328	2,37,402
Kottayam	1,75,048	55,146
Kurumbranad	2,59,799	96,463
Palghat	3,15,432	47,946
Ponnani	2,81,155	2,29,016
Walluvanad	2,59,979	1,33,919
Wynad	67,845	14,252

The above table shows that roughly 60% (600,337) of the Mappila population was concentrated in Eranad, Walluvanad and Ponnani *taluks* where the rebellion was most intense in 1921 and the remaining 40 per cent was distributed over the remaining seven *taluks*.

The number of the literate in Malabar in 1921 was 393,020 amounting to about 13% of the total population. Out of this Mappilas were 62,344 or about 16% of the total literate population. In other words, while the Mappila Hindu population ratio was 1 : 2, the ratio of literacy was 1 : 6. Generally speaking, education was comparatively backward in the internal *taluks* like Eranad and Walluvanad. The data relating to religion-wise distribution of literacy is not available and therefore it is not possible to find out the number of literate Mappilas in these two *taluks*. But the literacy level of the population as a whole was as follows:[5]

Literate in Malayalam

Taluk	Male	Female	Literate in English	Total	Percentage
Eranad	25,072	5,099	960	31,131	7.5
Walluvanad	35,019	9,825	2,249	47,093	12

The literacy level of these two *taluks* was below the district average. Literacy, however, should not be confused with English education leading to job opportunities both inside the district as well as the metropolitan cities outside. The literate in English as evident from the above table were negligible in number and it is reasonable to assume that they came mostly from the Hindu land owning class. The Christian missionary educational activities were not extended to the predominently Mappila *taluks* like Eranad and Walluvanad and the Mappilas generally attended *madrasas* attached to the mosques, where education was primarily religious in nature.

A study of the occupational structure reveals that the Mappilas were mainly engaged in cultivation in the inland regions and fishing in the coastal belt. The following table shows the occupations of the Mappilas in 1921.[6]

	Male	Female
Agriculture	1,41,617	58,843
Special Products and Market Gardening	5,677	1,521
Forestry	2,375	30
Raising of Farm stock	1,542	19
Fishing and Hunting	9,617	297
Mines & Quarries	57	—
Textile	1,442	3,714
Hides, skins etc.	20	—
Wood Industries	1,702	2,174
Metal Industries	269	8
Post and Telegraph etc.	40	—
Banks	55	33
Army	20	—
Police	292	—
Public Administration	600	—
Trade	63,929	8,252

In the internal *taluks* where the Rebellion became intense the Mappilas depended solely on land for their subsistence, whereas in the coastal *taluks*, where they had other occupational possibilities like fishing, the rebellion was either weak or non-existent.

Tenurial System and Agrarian Relations

The traditional structure of agricultural society in Malabar was based on fragmented feudalism' hierarchically ordained reaching down to the lowest stratum. The *jenmi* (landlord), *Kanakkaran* (protector)[7] and the peasant shared the produce equally, working out a social equation, on the basis of mutual dependence and reciprocal interests, within the confines of a feudal system of exploitation. The introduction of British administrative institutions led to the dissolution of this system by the substitution of a strong central power for the divided authority of feudal chieftains. The British land revenue policy and land settlement further helped this process by recognizing the *jenmies* as freehold proprietors, a position which they had never enjoyed before. The *Kanakkaran* was considered a mortgagee or a lessee and was treated as such. On the basis of this erroneous assumption the principles which guided the early revenue settlements recognized the interests of the *jenmi* and the cultivator, but the traditional share of the *Kanakkaran* in the produce was overlooked.[8] Though this did not have any immediate repercussions, in the long run it created considerable pressure on land and also deprived the cultivator-cum-*Kanakkaran* of a part of his income.

The land revenue system introduced in Malabar was basically different from the pattern in other parts of the Madras Presidency. In the ideal system envisaged by Munro, the classes of labourer, farmers and landlords were combined in the *ryot* with whom the settlement was made. In Malabar they were distinct and separate. Because the absolute ownership of land, including waste, was vested in the *jenmi*, he was left free to exact as much as he could from the tenants and under-tenants. The most common features of exploitation were through the enhancement of rent, eviction and imposition of renewal fees. Those who held land directly from the *jenmi* under a variety of tenures like *Kanam*, *Kuzhikanam* and *otti* and sub-tenants and tenants-at-will like *pattakkar* and *verumpattakkar* were all subjected to the rapacity of the landlord.

The *Kanam* tenure, for instance, which was considered by the British as a mortgage or lease against a pecuniary payment, came in for particularly harsh treatment. In the traditional tenurial system the *Kanakkaran's* relation with his superior was liable to be reconsidered or readjusted only on succession. On the basis of the erroneous assumption regarding the *jenmam* title which informed the British land revenue policy, the judicial courts decreed the renewal of *Kanam* tenure at the end of every twelve years. The automatic terminability of the contract implied in this decision was not in conformity with past practice. It therefore introduced fundamental changes in the structure of land relationship. The traditional notions of reciprocity and interdependence received the final jolt.

The second quarter of the century recorded a steep rise of prices amounting to about 27% during a period of two years.[9] There was a further increase in the fifties. The following table gives an idea of the spurt in prices.

Years	Paddy per grace Rs.	Gingly per grace Rs.	Coconut per 1000 Rs.	Pepper per Candy (560 lb) Rs.	Coffee per Candy Rs.	Green Ginger per Candy Rs.
1851-2	78	266	12	51	75	11
1856-7	108	311	16	85	98	21
1857-8	149	392	21	100	130	23
1858-9	166	407	22	95	121	25

Over a period of nine years the price of almost every produce increased by more than hundred per cent.[10] Naturally the value of land and its demand suddenly increased. It was then that the land owning class realized the significance of their newly acquired status and power. The British revenue policy had bestowed upon the *jenmi* the absolute ownership of land and the British courts had recognized his right to expel the tenant at the end of every twelve years. Armed with these powers the landlords not only demanded exhorbitant rents and renewal fees but also introduced several provisions which facilitated eviction earlier than the stipulated period. There were also several other easements like presents during the time of marriages, births and festivals which the landlords exacted from the tenants. The failure to give rent or even to provide a present to the satisfaction of the landlord were considered sufficient reasons for eviction. The rent receipts were not generally given and to demand them was taken as a hostile action. The tenants were clearly at the mercy of the landlords. The proceedings of the British courts and the elaborate rules and regulations which guided their decisions only added discomfiture to the disadvantages of the peasantry. The land owning class freely resorted to the means of litigation for the exercise of their rights. The country, as William Logan, the Collector of Malabar, remarked, 'teemed with false deeds and the courts were crowded with litigants.' During a period of four years, 1862-6, there were as many as 10,196 suits regarding land registered in the various courts in the district. This, however, does not bring out the full extent of the evictions or other related harassments. Ejections without resorting to the judicial procedure were even more numerous. Due to financial incapacity and the lack of judicial evidence the tenants found it impossible to defend their rights in the courts. Moreover, the tenants, especially the Mappilas, had no faith in the justice of the courts, since most of the *munsiffs* were Nairs, who were in some way or the other related to or under the influence of the landlords. A Mappila tenant told Logan that he did not expect the Hindu *munsiff* to give a verdict against his landlord, Azhuvancherry Nambudiripad, 'who was worshipped by Hindus as a God'.[11] A large number of cases were, therefore, decided ex-parte.

In these circumstances the tenants had no other alternative but to submit to the exactions of the landlords or to be deprived of their land, their only means of subsistence. The choice was between total deprivation and a possible survival. Even when the exactions were directed against the *kanakkar* who in most cases were intermediaries the financial burden was in the end borne by the peasantry. The *kanakkar* passed on their exactions to their under-tenants and rack-rented them for satisfying the demands of their superiors. The under-tenants could meet these demands only by taking recourse to the money-lender. This resulted in large scale agrarian indebtedness in Malabar. Out of 7994 cultivators interviewed by Logan in 1881, 4401 were in debt. The total amount of debt was about 10 lakhs at an interest ranging from 12 to 36% per annum. The reasons for indebtedness were:[11]

	Number	percent
Agriculture, House and Land improvement	736	12
Loss and Purchase of stock	396	6.9
Excessive Rent	221	3.9
Excessive fines etc. on renewal of leases	644	11.3
Bad season	1,222	21.4
Accidents	7	0.1
Family trade, wedding and other ceremonies	671	11.8
Sickness	114	2.0
Family maintenance	1,498	26.2
Trade losses	108	1.9
Misc.	92	1.6

In view of the oppressions and exactions of landlords it was indeed strange that only 15.1% of the tenants should have attributed their indebtedness to excessive rents and excessive renewal fees. Logan felt that the number of cultivators whose indebtedness was due to the exactions of the landlords was much higher than actually recorded. But since they gave their evidence in the presence of the agents of the landlords, most of them preferred to blame the weather or the expenses of maintaining their families rather than their landlords.[13] In a sense, the reason for indebtedness was immaterial. What was relevant was that the large bulk of the peasantry was not getting enough even for bare subsistence.

Agrarian Uprisings in The 19th Century

The tenants and under-tenants thus oppressed and harassed rose up in revolt against their landlords. There were as many as 45 uprisings during the course of the 19th century. Most of them were in the Eranad and Walluvanad *taluks* of South Malabar. The peasantry in these two inland *taluks* were mostly Mappilas holding land either directly from a Hindu *jenmi* or from an intermediary. The land was almost exclusively held by the Hindus. The following table gives the number of principal *jenmies* holding more than 100 pieces of land in 1881.[14]

Taluks	Rajas	Brahmins	Nayars	Mappilas	Total
Eranad	6	62	43	2	113
Walluvanad	14	111	54	—	179
Ponnani	9	142	54	10	219
Palghat	11	30	52	—	96

The number of *jenmies* in Chirakkal, Kottayam, Kurumbranad, Wynad and Calicut *taluks* were only 42, 32, 66, 26 and 56 respectively. In Eranad, Walluvanad and Ponnani *taluks* the number of principal *jenmies*, most of them Hindus, was very high. In Eranad there were only two Mappila *jenmies* and none in Walluvanad. This indicates that in these taluks land was concentrated in fewer hands compared to the other parts of the district.

The Mappilas were at the bottom of the tenurial structure and all the higher steps of the ladder were occupied by the Hindus either as intermediaries or as *jenmies*. Hence the conflicts between the Mappila peasantry and the Hindu land owning class superficially appeared to be the result of communal tensions. The Madras Government described them as 'Mappila Outrages'.

In 1851 a Special Commissioner, T.L. Strange, was appointed 'to trace out the causes which have produced or influenced the unhappy state of feeling between the Moplahs and the Hindu population' and to suggest remedial measures to prevent similar outbreaks in future.[15] The Commission was specifically asked 'to consider whether with reference to the position of Hindus and Moplahs in their relation of landlord and tenant, mortgager and mortgagee, any measure seemed to be necessary for defining the landed terms of the country and placing them on a better footing.'[16] During his enquiry the Commissioner was told by the Mappilas that 'destitution, oppression and exactions of the Hindu landlords have been the causes of these outbreaks.'[17] Yet the conclusion arrived at by Mr Strange was that 'the general character of the dealings of the Hindu landlords towards their tenantry, whether Moplah or Hindu, is mild, equitable and forbearing.'[18] He, therefore, attributed the 'Outrages' to Mappila fanaticism fanned by Muslim priests who glorified the murder of Kafirs for the sake of religion. He also saw the hand of some land-hungry rich Mappilas who exploited the religious sentiments of their illiterate and poor brethren for their selfish ends.

The mass of evidence collected and incorporated by Mr Strange in his report, however, does not warrant these conclusions. Let us, for instance, have a look at the Kolathur uprising of 1851. On the 22nd of August 1851 six Mappilas murdered Kottuparampath Komu Menon, the *karyasthan* of Walluvanad Raja and himself a landlord of substantial wealth. The Mappilas then went to Ittunni Ramu Menon's house, about two miles away, and murdered him and Kadakkatil Nambudiri, a Brahmin landlord, who happened to be present in Ramu Menon's house. The insurgents, whose number had by now swelled to 19, marched to Kolathur, a distance of about 13 miles. There Kolathur Warrier, the most important landlord of that locality, was attacked and murdered. There are two features discernible in the proceedings of the rebels whom the

Special Commissioner described as 'fanatics'. First, they killed only the head of the family; no other member was murdered or even injured. In fact, at Kolathur Warrier's house women and children were asked to leave the premises. Secondly and—more importantly—the account books were invariably burnt.[20] It is also significant that these nineteen 'fanatics' allegedly looking for salvation by killing Hindus travelled about fifteen miles through a region well populated by Hindus and in the process murdered only four wealthy landlords. Evidently, religious fanaticism was not the motive force.

A closer look at the character and economic status of the victims and their relationship with the insurgents is extremely instructive. Komu Menon, Ramu Menon, Kodakkatil Nambudiri and Kolathur Warrier were the biggest landlords of that region. Komu Menon was addicted to intoxication, and 'in both his drunken and sober hours, his behaviour to those about him was generally overbearing and abusive' especially towards the Mappila tenants.[21] With all his wealth and power as the *karyasthan* of Walluvanad Raja and the former *adhikari* (village official) of Mangada *amsom* he did not lose any opportunity of increasing his property by eviction, over-mortgaging or acquisition of land against loans advanced to his tenants. This was true of Ramu Menon also. He was an 'extremely avaricious man and lent money and grain to a large extent and often on most usurious interest.'[22] Kolathur Warrier was the richest of all. He received nearly 20,000 rupees per annum as rental and considering the value of grain at that time it was a very substantial amount.[23] He had started from scratch in the beginning of the century. He was one of those who had left for Travancore during the Mysorean invasion and had returned after Tipu Sultan's defeat to regain their land from the Mappilas who had occupied it during their absence. He had even acquired lands which were granted to mosques by Tipu Sultan. He also became the *parvathikar* (Government Accountant) during the early period of British rule, a position which he later passed on to his nephew. With the aid of the influence he had thus acquired with the Government officers he ejected Mappila tenants rather indiscriminately by means which were not always honourable.[24] Moreover, a good number of suits instituted by these four for eviction and acquisition of property were pending in the courts at the time of the uprisings.

Most of the insurgents were the discontented Mappila tenants and debtors of these four *jenmies*. Some of them had lost their lands during their life time. Some others had become landless by the ejection of their parents. The rest were burdened with outstanding debts at extremely high usurious rates and hence the transfer of their land into other hands was only a matter of time. Faced with this bleak prospect and finding no alternative employment they rose up against their oppressors. These poor, persecuted and frustrated peasants were further exploited by their materially better placed co-religionists. The comparatively rich Mappilas, who saw the advancement of their personal and class interest in the annihilation of the wealthy Hindu landlords, instigated them to take to violent action. The instances of Melu Mamil Emalukutty in Kolathur case and Kallatil family in Mattannur case are instances in point.[25] These interested parties very cleverly used religion to provide justification for their action against the landlords. The Assistant Magistrate in his report on the Kolathur uprising observed:

> The late enquiries have shown that there is a notion prevalent among the lower orders that according to Mussalman religion, the fact of a *Jenmi* or landlord having in course of law ejected from his lands a mortgagee or other substantial tenants, is a sufficient pretext to murder him, become *Shahid* (Saint) and so ensure the pleasures of Muhammadan paradise. This opinion has been openly stated before me by Moplahs, some indeed making a distinction as to whether the ejection was accompanied by fraud or otherwise, but others believing that the fact of the tenant being thus reduced to poverty, was sufficient.[26]

The religious belief thus aided the peasantry and gave them the necessary moral strength to act against their immediate exploiters. It is pertinent that religion in this case only helped to accentuate the existing economic antagonism rather than that economic antagonism deepened the communal cleavage. In the absence of proper leadership, class organization and class consciousness, it is not surprising that religious sentiments of the peasantry were exploited and that religion also became a factor, though contributory and secondary, in a struggle which was essentially agrarian.

The remedial measures, recommended by the special Commissioner on the basis of his conclusion that fanaticism was the main driving force behind these uprisings, were repressive in nature.[27] Accordingly 'Moplah Outrages Act' and 'Moplah War Knives Act' were passed in 1854. These enactments sanctioned repressive steps such as mass scale fines and confiscation of property of the activists. The possession of *vettukathy*, a longish knife used in Malabar for domestic purposes, was banned. The most vital problem, namely, the tenurial relationship was left untouched and unsolved. Needless to say, these measures only accentuated the economic deprivation of the Mappila peasantry and thus sharpened their economic antagonism, with the Hindu landlords.

II

Relief Acts and Their Results

The legislation, naturally, did not achieve the desired objective. The outrages not only continued to occur, but their extent and intensity slowly but steadily increased. The Madras Government, therefore, instituted another enquiry and William Logan, a former Collector of Malabar and the famous author of *Malabar Manual*, was entrusted the task of conducting it. Logan undertook a meticulous enquiry and in his report running into three volumes exploded the myth of Mappila fanaticism and pointed out that agrarian discontent was the basic cause of these uprisings. He observed:

> The Moplah outrages was an organization designed, in my opinion, to counteract the overwhelming influence, when backed by the British courts, of the *Jenmies* in the exercise of the novel powers of ouster and of rent raising conferred upon them. A *Jenmi* who through the courts, evicted, whether fraudulently or otherwise, a substantial tenant was deemed to have merited death, and it was considered a religious virtue, not a fault, to have killed such a man, and to have afterwards died in arms fighting against the infidel Government which sanctioned such injustice.[28]

Logan, therefore, suggested a number of measures for improving the condition of the cultivators, including permanency of tenure, a free hand to exploit the soil for agricultural purposes and a right to sell or transfer his interest in the soil. These were considered by many in the Government as being too harsh on the landlord. An acrimonious debate ranging over a period of five years followed. Ultimately, though the recommendations of Logan were the

'Malabar Compensation for Tenants' Improvement Act' was passed in 1887. The Madras Government followed the maxim that 'the best solution of the agrarian question was that which involved least interference'. The Act, therefore, simply provided that 'every tenant who is ejected from his holding shall notwithstanding any custom to the contrary, be entitled to be compensated for improvements to be made by him or his predecessors.' The amount of compensation was left to be determined by the court ordering the eviction.[29]

Working of The Act of 1887

The assumption behind the Act was that by ensuring the tenants the full market value of their improvements the growing practice of eviction would be effectively checked. But the working of the Act belied this hope. It neither ensured the tenants the full market value of the improvements nor succeeded in minimising evictions. The interpretation by the civil courts of the provisions regarding the value of compensation considerably differed from the original intentions of the Government. Some of them determined the compensation on the basis of the capital and labour actually expended in effecting the improvement. Others totally dismissed the idea of the market value, but held that the improvement to be paid for was the 'work' of planting, protecting and maintaining the tree and not the tree which was the result of that 'work'.[30] It was also contended that the *jenmi* too as entitled to a share of the increased produce as a result of the improvement since there could not be any improvement without the land of which the *jenmi* was the sole proprietor.[31] Apart from this, the *jenmies* invented two very subtle devices to circumvent the provisions of the Act. First, at the time of the renewal of a lease, a considerably enhanced rent was fixed and then a clause was inserted remitting a portion of the rent for improvements to be effected in future. Secondly, the tenants were allowed to retain the land for a few years beyond the period of contract. A new lease was then executed in which all or nearly all the trees were entered as landlord's improvements.[32]

The procedure adopted by the courts to ascertain the value of improvement was extremely defective. The clerks and *amins* of the courts, appointed Commissioners for valuation, were notoriously corrupt. They changed their evaluation according to the gratification received. For instance, in one particular case the first Commissioner valued the improvements at Rs. 2900/-, the second at Rs. 800 and the third at Rs. 700. The discrepancy was not only in the fixation of value, but also in the number of trees each one of them noticed in the garden. The tenants complained that 'owing to the corruption of the Commissioners on whose reports the courts rely, the decree goes in favour of the longest purse, is therefore ruinously expensive, and very often leads to the transfer of the *kanakkar's* improvement to the *jenmi*.'[33] The Commissioners only added another brick to the tenants' oppressive burden.

A reference to the incidence of eviction will help to highlight the inadequacy of the Act both to provide compensation as well as to prevent evictions. The total number of evictions in the district during 1890, 91 and 92 were 4227, 4132 and 4620 respectively out of which 3268 (77%), 3112 (75%) and 3524 (76.4%) were without compensation. The following table gives the details for the munsiff courts of Shernad, Eranad, Bettutanad and Kuttanad which roughly comprise the Eranad and Walluvanad *taluks*.[34]

Name of the Court	Year	Total evictions	Eviction without compensation	Percentage
Shernad	1890	343	263	76
Eranad	"	246	205	83.3
Bettutanand	"	401	348	86.7
Kuttanad	"	278	237	85
Shernad	1891	319	264	82
Eranad	"	218	183	83.9
Bettutanad	"	331	249	75.2
Kuttanad	"	328	279	85
Shernad	1892	387	346	89
Eranad	"	296	253	85.4
Bettutanad	"	355	289	81.4
Kuttanad	"	310	273	88

The evictions, as evident from the above table, were mostly without any compensation. Even in those cases in which compensation was awarded the amount granted was very negligible. The average amount granted in 1887 there were 2819 evictions whereas in 1892 the number rose to 4620.[35]

The amendment to the Compensation Act passed in 1900 failed to mitigate these evils. In view of the mounting tension among the agrarian classes, the Government of India had desired immediate steps to be taken 'to secure permanency from arbitrary ejectment to all.'[36] But the Madras Government did not undertake a comprehensive legislation for safeguarding the interests of the peasantry. The amendment only sought to rectify the ambiguous and confusing language of the Act of 1887 and to lay down principles for the award of compensation. The champions of the landowning interests indulged in so much quibbling about the nature of the tenurial rights and relations, the clarification really went against the interests of the tenants.[35a] The Act did not recognize the payment of compensation to the extent of full market value of improvements. Instead, it was held that a fruit tree grown by the tenant could have no value apart from the soil on which it grew and that the tenant had no claim to be compensated for the value contributed by the soil. It was therefore decided to give the landlord 25% of the surplus over the cost of improvements.[37] Thus, in effect, the Government, in the name of precision, transferred a further share of the cultivators' labour to the landlord.

The Relief Acts, therefore, did not register any improvement in the condition of the tenants. All the malpractices and oppressions of the landlords noticed in the mid-nineteenth century continued unabated. Charles Innes, the Collector of Malabar, during his enquiry in 1915, noticed the deplorable condition of the peasants due to rack-renting, inadequate compensation, insecurity of tenure, exhorbitant renewal fees and above all the social tyranny of the *jenmies*. In fact, capricious and arbitrary evictions considerably increased during the post-1900 period. The number of eviction suits instituted in the various courts in the district in 1919, 1920 and 1921 were 5074, 5142 and 4490 respectively.[37a] There were several factors which contributed to this spurt. The most important of them were the emergence of a tenant movement, demands and discussion regarding the permanency of tenure, scarcity of grain and the increase of prices during the First World War. In other parts of the country, occupancy rights of some sort had already been conferred upon the tenants. In Bengal, Punjab and the North-Western Province Tenancy Acts were passed in 1885, 1889 and 1901 respectively. The Travancore State had conferred occupancy rights on *kanam* tenure as early as 1867 and Cochin State in 1914. The *zamindari* tenants of the Madras Presidency also got occupancy rights in 1908. The landlords in Malabar naturally knew the way the wind was blowing.

The Mappila peasantry of the inland *taluks* of South Malabar were the worst hit by these trends. To them even the marginal benefits of the Compensation Acts were not available. About 70% of the grain crop cultivation of the district was in these taluks and in grain crop lands no improvement could be effected. Hence the ejected tenants in this region could claim no compensation. The incidence of eviction without compensation was naturally higher in these *taluks* compared to other parts of the district.[38]

Thus, by the end of the second decade of the century the condition of the cultivators in South Malabar had become extremely miserable. Therefore, there were signs of mounting tension among the agricultural classes. The local British officers apprised the Government of the grave agrarian situation. The newspapers repeatedly wrote about the necessity of immediate and decisive remedial measures. *Kerala Sanchari* and *Mitavadi* warned that if the Government continued to be 'hesitating, halting and debating' on the tenant question and 'pursued a policy of neglect, indifference and drift', a storm might break out any day.[38]

It did. At Pukottur on the 1st of August 1921.

III

Beginning of The Rebellion

Pukottur, a thickly populated village, about five miles north west of Manjeri in the Eranad *taluk* of South Malabar, was inhabited predominantly by the Mappilas. There were 2170 Mappilas and 993 Hindus.[39] The major part of the land in the village was held by Nilambur Raja, one of the richest landlords in South Malabar. He maintained a *Kovilakam* (Palace) at Pukottur and a member of his family, Thirumulpad, the Sixth, lived there to collect rent. Most of the Mappilas in Pukottur were tenants, under-tenants or wage labourers of Nilambur Raja. In the last week of July 1921 Kalathingal Mammad, a tenant and erstwhile rent collector of Nilambur Raja, accompanied by a good number of Mappila peasants, approached Thirumulpad for the realisation of a sum of Rs. 350/- due to him. Thirumulpad who at that moment had no money with him escaped their fury by borrowing money from a rich Mapilla neighbour. But immediately after, Thirumulpad, in collusion with the village official, registered a case of house-breaking and theft of a rifle against Mammad, whose house was consequently searched. Mammad and about two hundred Mappilas remonstrated with the Police Inspector who had gone to Pukottur on the 1st of August to investigate the case and had called him to the *kovilakam* for interrogation. Mammad, being the local leader of the Khilafat movement, considered it an act of reprisal on the part of the landlord—Government combine and therefore decided to resist his arrest. The Police Inspector sensing the mood of the Mappilas quietly withdrew from the scene giving an assurance that no action will be taken against them.[40]

The Inspector of Police, in his report to the District Magistrate, drew an alarming picture of the communal situation in south Malabar. The Mappilas, according to him, were busy organizing volunteer corps and were manufacturing and collecting arms and weapons. He indicated the possibility of a 'Mapilla Uprising' in Eranad *taluk*, if quick and decisive action was not taken. The District Magistrate, E.F. Thomas, concurred with the assessment of the Police. To him the situation appeared so serious that he requested the Madras Governor for military assistance for the maintenance of peace in the district. His assumption was that a large number of potential Mappila insurgents will have to be disarmed and arrested by combing village after village in South Malabar.[41] Though in response to this request the First Lienster Regiment was despatched to Kozhikode, the Governor forbade the District Magistrate from taking general action against the Mappilas. He only authorised him to arrest the leaders in order to obviate any further trouble. The anxiety and impatience of the District Magistrate was evidently not shared by the Government. A.R. Nap, a member of the Governor's Executive Council, who visited Kozhikode to make an on the spot enquiry, did not consider the Eranad situation to be really alarming. But Thomas was one of those British officers who could not be accused of pacific inclinations in their public dealings. What distressed him most was perhaps not the communal tension in Eranad but the progress of Khilafat and Non-Cooperation movements and the slight and disregard with which the public and the leaders treated him.[42] He soon unleashed a reign of terror and, as K.V. Pillai wrote in the *Muslim*, 'out-Dyered Dyer' in his oppressive measures against the Khilafat and Non-Cooperation workers.[43]

Tirurangadi Incident

On the 19th of August 1921 Thomas proceeded to Tirurangadi with a contingent of Army and Police to arrest the Mappila leaders, including Ali Musaliar, a highly respected and popular priest of Mambrath mosque. He also carried with him warrants to search mosques and houses and confiscate war knives. On the 20th morning Thomas and his party reached Tirurangadi and searched the Kizhakkepalli mosque and arrested three comparatively unknown Khilafat volunteers. Ali Musaliar was not in the mosque at that time and hence could not be arrested. Meanwhile the news about the arrest of the Khilafat volunteers and the entry of the police into the mosque spread with amazing rapidity into the adjoining regions and was embroidered all the way. What the Mappilas of Tanur, Parappanangadi, and Kottakkal heard was that Mambrath mosque, one of the oldest and perhaps the most important religious centre in Malabar, had been fired at and destroyed by the British army. It was the day of weekly fair at Kottakkal and the Mappilas who had assembled there marched towards Tirurangadi in utter amazement to discover the truth. Similarly, people from Tanur, Parappanagadi and, in fact, from all the adjoining regions, who came to know about the incident, proceeded to Tirurangadi. The illiterate Mappilas who had already heard that the British were desecrating the Muslim religious shrines in Turkish territory readily believed the rumour about the destruction of the Mambrath mosque.[44] Their action was spontaneous and voluntary. There was no leadership, no organization.

A large crowd of Mappilas thus assembled at Tirurangadi. They were all unarmed except for sticks in their hands.[45] Their representatives met the British officers for the release of the arrested volunteers. The mob also followed them. They were peaceful and committed no violence. They even agreed to squat on the ground when so ordered by the Police. But the moment they sat down the army opened fire and a good number of unarmed Mappilas were killed.[46] An already excited crowd now broke into violence and attacked the army and the Police. The Government offices were destroyed, treasury looted and records burnt. The District Magistrate and his party withdrew to Kozhikode in panic. Thus began the Malabar Rebellion at Tirurangadi which soon spread to the Eranad, Walluvanad and Ponnani *taluks*. The District Magistrate in his communique characterized the Rebellion as 'an outburst of religious fanaticism directed first against European officials and non-officials and laterly against Hindu *jenmies* and others. Public offices have been looted everywhere, *manas*[47] and *kovilakams* pillaged, Hindus murdered and forcibly converted'.[48]

The fury of the Rebellion during its early phase was indeed directed against the Hindu landlords and the symbols of British authority, namely, treasuries, *katcheries* and police stations. Let us return to Pukottur for elucidation. On the 21st of August the Mappilas of Pukottur marched to Nilambur, about twenty three miles away, where the Raja of Nilambur, the landlord of the Pukottur Mappilas, resided. No outrage was committed against any Hindu either at Pukottur or on their way to Nilambur. In fact, at Pukottur, they gave a patient hearing to K. Madhavan Nair, a Congress leader, who advised them against violence. On their way to Nilambur they attacked a police station. When they approached the *kovilakam*, one of the guards fired at them. A skirmish followed in which seventeen were killed. After overcoming this initial resistance they entered the *kovilakam* and went straight to the record room and burnt all the records.[49] No harm was done to any member of the Nilambur family, even though they had met the heir-apparent in the house. On their return journey to Pukottur also they did not murder any one nor plunder any Hindu house.[50] It is indeed significant that the 'fanatic' Mappilas of Pukottur chose to go to Nilambur about twenty three miles away and burn their landlords records and not to march to Tirurangadi, only a distance of twelve miles, for the help of their religious brethren.

This was the pattern of rebel activity during the initial stages throughout South Malabar. At Tirur, Perinthalmanna, Manjeri, Malappuram, Mannarkad and all other places, the rebels attacked, demolished and plundered the British treasuries and offices.[51] The *jenmies* who were notorious for usurious and oppressive measures were not spared. Generally no injury was done to the poor Hindus and lenient landlords.[52] The rubber estates owned by the British planters also became the targets of attack. The labourers of Kalikav and Chembrasseri attacked the Pullengad and Kerala Rubber estates. While beating Mr Eatten, the proprietor, the rebels recounted the atrocities committed by him on the workers.[53] At Mannarked, there were a good number of Hindus among the rebel ranks who were active in attacking the police stations and demolishing road bridges.[54]

Rebel Leaders and Their Attitude

The most important leaders of the Rebellion were Variam Kunnath Kunhammad Haji, Kalathingal Mammad and Ali Musaliar in Eranad and Sithi Koya Thangal and Embichi Koya Thangal in Walluvanad. In Eranad region 'Republics' were established and Kunhammad Haji and Mammad proclaimed themselves as 'Presidents'. They recruited armies, organized police and instituted courts for trying criminals. Kunhammad Haji proclaimed the liberation of the country from the British. A moratorium on all taxes for one year was granted. Passports were issued for those wanting to travel outside his 'republic'. A fee was charged for the passport which was determined by the financial ability of the applicant. The peasants were ordered to harvest the paddy crops of the landlords.[55]

Sithi Koya Thangal installed himself as the Governor of the Khilafat Province in Walluvanad. He issued *fathwas* proclaiming that the country now belonged to the people and that nobody should indulge in any criminal activities. So did Imbichi Koya Thangal who held courts in various places in Walluvanad for trying criminals.[56] In short, Eranad and Walluvanad *taluks* by and large came under the control of these leaders. The Chief Secretary to the Government of Madras observed:

> the whole interior of South Malabar except Palghat *taluk* is in the hands of the rebels..... situation from the point of view of civil administration is that local machinery of Government has broken down. Throughout the affected area the Government offices have been recked and looted and records destroyed.

Communications have been obstructed.... All Government offices and courts have ceased to function and ordinary business is at stand still.[57]

Kunhammed Haji proclaimed himself as the Raja of the Hindus, the Amir of the Muslims and the Colonel of the Khilafat army.[58] He treated all his 'subjects' alike and no discrimination was allowed to be practised. Those who took advantage of the unsettled conditions for indulging in plunder and harassment of the innocent population were publicly flogged and plundered articles were returned to their owners.[59] The punishment for molestation of women was chopping of hands.[60] When Madhavan Nair complained that Mappilas were plundering and killing innocent Hindus, Haji told him that he would cut off the hands of all such criminals.[61] In fact, he went around Eranad *taluk* to prevent atrocities and assured the Hindus that nothing will be done against them.[62] The statements recorded by a good number of Hindus of Eranad *taluk* show conclusively that Kunhammad Haji was free from any communal hatred. To cite one of them, C. Gopala Panikkar of Chathankot village, observed in his statement:

> Variam Kunnath Kunhammad Haji ordered the Mappilas who had indulged in plunder to be produced before him. Except one, named Kunjali, all others returned the plundered articles to their owners. Kunjali refused to do that. He was flogged 125 times and it was only then that he confessed his crimes... Plundered articles were recovered. They were shown to Marath Nambudiri and Kavungal Nambudiri and enquired whether they belonged to them. Kunhammad Haji did not do any harm to the Hindus.[63]

The activities of other rebel leaders also fell into the same pattern. In Pukottur, Mammad punished all those who exhorted money from Hindus or removed their cattle and he arranged the money so taken to be returned.[64] So was the case of Ali Musaliar, Sithi Koya Thangal and Imbichi Koya Thangal.

This, however, is not to suggest that there were no murders or conversions of Hindus or plundering of their property during the Rebellion as a whole. The very fact that the leaders had to punish the Mappilas point to their incidence. According to Pandit Hrishi Ram, an Arya Samaj worker, who went to Malabar for *Sudhi* and relief work, there were about 2500 forced conversions. No official figures are available for the death of civilians but it is estimated to be about 600.⁶⁶ It is indeed significant, as E.M.S. Namboodiripad has pointed out, that in a region inhabited by about four lakh Hindus only 600 were killed and 2500 converted.⁶⁷ Considering the fact that the rebels had complete control over the region for a period of six months, it will not be wrong to say that the number of killed and converted was remarkably small, if the Rebellion were to be considered a communal conflict. Even in case of these murders and conversions the timing of their occurrence is extremely significant.

During the early phase of the Rebellion the fury of the rebels, as is evident from the Nilambur incident described above, was primarily directed against the *jenmies*, and the British Government. All contemporary observers, including British officials, agree that among the Indians 'the victims chiefly were the Hindu propertied class'.⁶⁸ Except for the wanton crimes committed by certain undersirable elements, whom the leaders promptly punished, the general Hindu population was not affected at all. But a change did take place during the latter part of the Rebellion. The proclamation of the Martial law and the arrival of the British army thrust a wedge in the communal relationship. Some Hindus were coerced to help the army and give information about the rebels whereas a few did so voluntarily. Understandably, the Mappilas now grew suspicious of even the innocent Hindus, and some of the rebels began to take revenge on them. For instance, Imbichi Koya Thangal tried forty Hindus who were accused of helping the army by giving them milk and tender cocoanuts. Thirty eight of them were awarded capital punishment. The Hindus thus suspected and harassed wreaked vengence on the Mappilas with the assistance of the British army and the police. The rebels in turn retaliated in greater fury. Madhavan Nair in his reminiscences remarked: 'For the attack of the Mappilas the revenge of the Hindus and the Police; for that revenge a counter revenge by the Mappilas; followed by a stronger retaliation by the Police and the Army—this in short was the history of the Malabar Rebellion'.⁶⁹ A similar observation was made by Mahmood Schamnad Sahib Bahadur during his speech in the Legislative Council: 'The rebellion was started as a joint concern of some Moplahs, Nayars and others of the non-cooperation party, and in the beginning all were arrested and punished indiscriminately.... Laterly, however a change came on. These Nayars and others were somehow or other made to feel the safer course for them would be to desert the Moplahs and show themselves as their foes...they went along with the police and military and joined them in looting Moplah houses and outraging their women. When the Moplahs saw their co-workers turning against them, they considered it a treachery. Therefore, when the military retired in the evenings, they took revenge by killing them or confiscating their properties.'[70]

It was thus that a rebellion which was initially directed against landlordism and imperialism assumed a communal colour. In a feudal-Colonial multi-religious society such a transformation was not in the least surprising.

It is not true, however, that only the Hindus were punished for pro-British leanings. Kunhammed Haji started his rebel career with the murder of Khan Bahadur Chekutty, a retired Police Inspector. He ordered the execution of Iythru Haji, a popular physician of Eranad, who was reported to have helped the police. He also punished a good number of other pro-British Mappilas.[71]

That a total communal cleavage ever existed during the Rebellion cannot be accepted. In many villages the Mappilas protected the Hindus from the rebels coming from outside. Individual cases of the Hindus being saved by unknown Mappilas were numerous.[72] In Ponnani the Hindus and the Mappilas jointly persuaded the rebels from Tanur to depart. Even in Eranad, during the thick of the rebellion, Hindus and Muslims lived together in peace. Madhavan Nair could even reprimand the rebels for indulging in violence and they departed without even a note of protest.

IV

The foregoing analysis suggests that the Rebellion of 1921 cannot really be interpreted in communal terms. On the contrary, in the background of the economic condition of the peasantry, the pattern of rebel activity and the classes to which the participants belonged, it is reasonable to suggest that the Rebellion was a continuation of the agrarian conflicts of the 19th century. Rao Bahadur C.S. Subramanyam speaking in the Legislative Council observed:

There is one peculiarity of this rebellion: the better classes of

> men, men who own property, are not in it..... I wish to draw particular attention to the fact that the men who are now in jail, the men who have died, the men who have been arrested, the men in exile, are men with little property.[73]

Even Lord Reading, the Viceroy, recognized the influence of the agrarian conditions on the Rebellion. In a letter to Lord Wellingdon he wrote:

> It is possible to argue that agrarian grievances were at least a predisposing factor, and a perusal of certain reports prepared some years ago on the subject suggests that even if there is no substratum of truth in the argument, some revision of the existing land tenure system may be desirable in the interests of future peace of Malabar.... We have in regard to Malabar to aim not merely at the restoration of order but also at the conversion of the Moplahs into peaceful and loyal citizens, and it may be that agrarian reform would be a powerful influence in this direction.[74]

The step taken by the Government to obviate the recurrence of rebellion was indeed not the enactment of another 'Moplah Outrages Act' but of a comprehensive tenancy legislation in 1930.

There was, however, a remarkable difference between the agrarian conflicts of the 19th century and the Rebellion of 1921. While the earlier uprisings were localized in extent and limited in scope the Rebellion of 1921 was more intense and widespread. It embraced almost the whole of the Mappila peasant population of Eranad and Walluvanad *taluks*. The official estimate of Mappila casualties was 2337 killed and 1652 wounded.[75] The unofficial sources, however, put this number above 10,000.[76] The number of Mappila rebels captured and surrendered was 45404.[77] Needless to say, the actual participants must not have been fewer than double this number.

Khilafat Agitation and Tenant Movement

An explanation for this transformation lay in the interaction between the political and economic forces in Malabar in the second decade of the 20th century. The nationalist agitation gathered momentum during this period and the Congress activities slowly penetrated into the rural regions.[78] Mahatma Gandhi and Shaukat Ali visited Malabar in August 1920 and addressed a public meeting at Kozhikode. Though their call for non-cooperation did not arouse much enthusiasm among the middle and upper urban strata the Khilafat movement received immediate response from the Mappilas, especially in South Malabar. The Malabar District Congress Conference held in Manjeri in April 1920 was attended by a large number of Mappilas. Though Mrs Annie Besant wanted a resolution on the Reforms Act to be discussed first, the majority of the delegates pressed for a resolution on Khilafat which was hence taken up for consideration. Mrs Beasant, Manjeri Rama Iyer and a host of others denounced the British attitude towards Turkey and dilated upon the great injustice done to the Muslim community as a whole. The Manjeri conference marked the beginning of extensive Khilafat agitation and movement in Malabar. Soon after, Khilafat committees were established and meetings were convened at Kozhikode, Kondotti, Tanur, Vengara, Pulikkal, Tirur, Tirurangadi, Kottakkal, Kodur, Ponnani, Malapuram, Manjeri, and Mampad which were attended by thousands of people. The Hindu participation in these meetings was either meagre or non-existent.[79] In all these meetings—the Khilafat resolutions demanding the integrity of holy places and proclaiming that 'the Indian Muslims will not rest and will not allow the enemies of Islam to rest' were read out.[80] At Cannanore E. Moidu, one of the prominent leaders of the Khilafat, reminded the audience that 'the Indian Muslims ought to have fought a war in revenge for the wrongs done to Islam' and he 'deplored the want of arms' to undertake such a venture.[81]

Though the Mappilas were thus aroused to action against British imperialism, the general character of the movement controlled by the urban based middle class continued to be non-violent non-cooperation. But the District authorities disturbed by the increasing popularity of the movement and the consequent solidarity among the Mappilas imposed prohibitory orders on all Khilafat meetings. The prohibitory notice issued by the District Magistrate on the 5th of February 1921 stated that the Khilafat meetings would not only arouse the ire of the Mappilas against the British Government but also against the Hindu *jenmies* of Eranad *taluk*.[82] On the 16th of February all important Congress and Khilafat leaders including Yakub Hassan, U. Gopala Menon, P. Moideen Koya and K. Madhavan Nair were arrested. The arrest of the prominent leaders and the prohibition of meetings transferred the leadership into the hands of the local Mappila leaders as well as alienated them from the general milieu of the Congress non-violent non-cooperation influence and politics. When the leaders returned from jail after three months they found to their dismay that the militant Mappilas had slipped out of their influence. Though the British officials in Malabar described the revolt as 'the fruit of the seed Annie sowed and Gandhi watered',[83] by July 1921 the Mappilas had become sceptical about the effectiveness of non-violent non-cooperation. To the Mappilas the Swaraj which Gandhi had promised within a year seemed a possibility though not through 'Gandhism' but through an armed struggle.

The choice of this alternative was influenced by several factors. The illiterate Mappilas readily lent their ear to the rumours current in the countryside. It was common talk that the British Army was crippled by the First World War and was no more in a position to take serious military action. The transfer of the British regiment from Malappuram gave credence to this belief. While moving out, the property of the Regiment was auctioned which created an impression that the British were in dire financial crisis. The retrenched Mappila soldiers also contributed to the anti-British feeling in the countryside as well as to the general economic discontent and frustration.

The tenant movement in South Malabar was closely connected with the Khilafat agitation. The tenant question was first raised in the District Congress Conference in 1916. But the landed interests in the Congress did not allow its discussion till 1920.[84] It was only in the Manjeri conference attended by a large number of Mappilas that a resolution demanding legislation for regulating the tenant-landlord relations was passed.[85] Immediately after that a tenants' association was formed at Kozhikode. Similar associations soon started functioning in other parts of Malabar. The most important activity of these associations was the organisation of public meetings in which the grievances of the tenants were graphically described. A meeting convened at Kottakkal in September 1920 was attended by about five thousand tenants.[86] Similar meetings were held throughout Eranad and Walluvanad *taluks*, including a mammoth public meeting at Pukkottur in January 1921. In these *taluks* the bulk of the peasants being Mappilas, those meetings assumed the character of tenant-cum-Khilafat agitation. Most of the Khilafat leaders, namely, Kalathingal Mammad, Kunhikadar, Kattlasseri Muhammad Musaliar, Chembrasseri Thangal and so on were active workers of the tenant movement also. The political developments in 1921, as discussed earlier, led to the merger of Khilafat and tenant interests representing anti-imperialism and anti-landlordism.

This coalition created a sense of cohesion and solidarity among the peasantry. It also provided them an effective organization. The peasantry having thus acquired solidarity and organisation, the conflict arising out of economic antagonism developed into a wide spread rebellion against the landlords and the British imperial power.

References

1. Kathleen Gough, 'Indian Peasant Uprisings,' *Economic and Political Weekly*, Special Number, August 1974. (Reproduced in this volume)
2. An earlier version of this paper was presented in a seminar organised by Nehru Memorial Museum and Library in March 1972.
3. The Cannanore, Kozhikode, Palghat and Malappuram districts of the present state of Kerala roughly comprise the former Malabar District.
4. *Madras Census Report*, 1921, Part II, p. 350.
5. *Ibid.*
6. *Ibid.*, p. 254.
7. *Jenmam* means birth. *Jenmi* is one who possesses a birthright. *Kanakkaran* is derived from the word *Kanuka* (see). For an excellent study of the evolution of *Jenmi* system, see Elemkulam P.N. Kunjan Pillai, *JENMI Sampradayam Keralathil* (Malayalam), (Kottayam, 1959). For a description of the development of different types of tenures see Baden Powell, *Land System of British India*, iii, pp. 162-77
8. For a brief survey of the land revenue policy, settlement and assessment see William Logan, *Malabar Manual*, pp. 625-89. Also see T.A. Varghese, *Agrarian Change and Economic Consequences*, pp. 20-32 (Bombay, 1970), pp. 20-32 and Thomas W. Shea (Jr), *The Land Tenure Structure of Malabar and its Influence upon Capital Formation in Agriculture*, pp. 94-166, Unpublished Ph. D. Dissertation of the University of Pennsylvanya.
9. Report of the Malabar Special Commission, pp. 1881-2, i, para 257.
10. *Ibid.*, ii, Appx. ii, p. 194.
11. *Ibid.*, para 263.
12. *Ibid.*, pp. XXII-XXVI.
13. *Ibid.*, para 92.

14 *Ibid.*, page lvi. Logan does not give the measurement of holdings. He has used numbers for purposes of comparison. Though inadequate it is mentioned here to indicate the nature of land holdings.
15 Madras Government Minutes of Consultation, 17th February 1852; *Correspondence on Moplah Outrages in Malabar for the Year 1849-53*, (Madras 1863), pp. 268-73.
16 *Ibid.*, p. 509
17 *Ibid.*, p. 408.
18 *Ibid.*, p. 441.
19 The principal servant of a landlord who looked after his landed interests and collected rent from the tenants. He was not only the instrument of landlords' oppression but an oppressor himself. Well versed in judicial matters he was dreaded by the tenants for his dubious ways.
20 Report by C. Collet, Assistant Magistrate to H.V. Connally, Magistrate, 20 September 1851, *Correspondence on Moplah Outrages*, i, pp. 177-80
21 *Ibid.*, p. 187.
22 *Ibid.*, p. 188.
23 See the table of prices given above.
24 *Correspondence on Moplah Outrages*, i., p. 191.
25 Robinson to Connally, 13 February 1852, *Ibid.*, p. 285.
26 Collet to Connally, 20 September 1851, *Ibid.*, p. 195.
27 Report of T.L. Strange, para 42-72, *Correspondence on Moplah Outrages*, pp. 454-74.
28 *Malabar Special Commission Report*, 1881-2, i, para 280.
29 Clause No. 4 & 5 of the Act of 1889.
30 *Legislative Department Proceedings*, Jan. 1900, Nos. 1-4 *National Archives of India*, New Delhi.
31 Opinion of Justice Parker of the Madras High Court, *Ibid.*
32 Madras Govt. Revenue Dept. G.O. No. 4114 (Conf) dated 25.10.1894.
33 Legislative Dept. Proceedings, n. 30.
34 *Ibid.*
35 Rev. Dept. n. 32.
36 Denzil Ibbetson to Secretary, Madras Government, 29th Aug. 1895; *Legislative Department*, Part B, Sept. 1895, No. 25.
36a See the debate on the Bill in the Madras Legislative Council on 24 Jan. 1899, especially the speeches of S. Sankara Subbayar, Ratna Sabhapati Pillai and Vijya Raghavachariar.
37 *Legislative Dept.*, Jan. 1900, Nos. 1-4.
37a *Report of the Malabar Tenancy Committee*, 1928, i, Chapter II
38 Rev. Dept. n. 32.
38a *Native News Paper Reports*, Madras 1921, pp. 394, 584 and
39 *Madras Census Report 1921 Village Statistics for Malabar District*.
40 K. Madhavan Nair, *Malabar Kalapam* (Malayalam) (Kozhikode 1971) pp. 94-7.
41 *The Madras Mail*, 8 August 1921.
42 On the 17th August 1921 three important leaders of Non-Cooperation and Khilafat movements—Gopala Menon, K. Madhavan Nair and Moideen Koya were released from Jail after a six months' term. They were accorded a grand reception at Kozhikode. The processionists clapped in derision when they saw the Collector while passing through the Collectorate. K. Madhavan Nair, n. 40. p. 101.
43 *Muslim*, 8 Sept. 1921, Madras Native News Paper Reports, 1921, p. 1111.

44 Kunhi Kadar, the local leader of the Khilafat at Tanur, told Brahmadattan Nambudiripad that he and his followers went to Tirurangadi on hearing about the destruction of the Mambrath mosque. Mozhikunnatha Brahmadattan Nambudiripad, *Khilafat Smaranakal* (Malayalam) (Kozhikode, 1965), pp. 43-4. Kanjirappali Ali Musaliar, a participant in the Rebellion of 1921, whom the authors interviewed on 30.6.43 mentioned the same.
45 The Madras Govt. in its communique issued on 24 August said: 'Police charged, with fixed bayonets and were met with sticks in self defence'. *Home Poll.*, 1921 F. No. 241, Part I, A., p. 123. Also see K. Madhavan Nair, no. 40, pp. 110-26.
46 *Ibid.*,
47 House of a Nambudiri Brahmin.
48 *Home Poll*, 1921, F. No. 241, Pt. I-A. Appx. III.
49 *Home Poll*, 1922, F. No. 23.
50 K. Madhavan Nair, No. 40.
51 *Ibid.*, p. 129-52.
52 *Ibid.*
53 *Ibid.*
54 K. Madhavan Nair, n. 40, p. 164.
55 C. Gopalan Nair, *Moplah Rebellion*, pp. 76-80.
56 *Ibid.*
57 Chief Secy., Madras Govt. to Secy, Govt. of India, 30th August 1921, *Home Poll.* 1921, File No. 241, Part 1-A, p. 146.
58 *Ibid.*
59 Statement of Puliyali Krishnan Nair recorded at the Malabar Congress Office quoted by K. Madhavan Nair, n.40, p. 260.
60 *Kerala Patrika*, 24 Oct. 1921. Quoted by K. Madhavan Nair, n.40, p. 260.
61 K. Madhavan Nair, n. 40, p. 171. Also see Mozhikunnatha Brahmadattan Nambudiripad, n. 44, p. 54-5.
62 E. Moidu Maulavi is an important Congress leader and had visited Eranad and Walluvanad *taluks* in the beginning of the Rebellion. In an interview with the author on 26.6.73 further detailed the efforts made by the rebel leaders for maintaining communal harmony.
63 K. Madhavan Nair, n. 40, p. 261.
64 Message of a correspondent, a Hindu Resident, of Kozhikode, *Leader*, 14 Sept. 1921 see *Home Poll.* 1922, f. No. 232.
65 Quoted by E.M.S. Nambudiripad: *Keralathile Deshiya Prasuam* (Malayalam) pp. 232-3 (Ernakulam 1951)
66 C. Gopalan Nair, n. 55, p. 58.
67 Quoted by E.M.S. Nambudiripad n. 65 p. 232.
68 Account given by a Judicial officer belonging to an aristocratic family for publication in *Hindu*, *Home Poll*, 1922, F. No. 23. For the opinion of British officers see *Home Poll*, 1921, F. No. 241, Part I-A.
69 K. Madhavan Nair, n. 40, p. 216. Kanjirapalli Ali Musaliar told Madhavan Nair that in his region, i.e. Manjeri, also the Hindus who were attacked by the rebles were mainly those who had helped the British army.
70 Mahmood Schammad Sahib Bahadur's speech in the Legislative Council, 8 February 1922.
71 K. Madhavan Nair, n. 40, p. 169.
72 *Reading Papers*, Microfilm, R. No. 1, Nehru Memorial Museum, New Delhi, p. 236.
73 *Legislative Council Debates*, 8 February 1922.

74 Lord Reading to Lord Wellington, 26 May 1922, *Home Poll*, 1922 F. No. 23.
75 Home Poll, 1923, F. No. 129, IV.
76 *The Statesman*, 2 September 1922. In contrast to this, the number of Hindus killed during the Rebellion was estimated to be around six hundred only.
77 *Home Poll*, 1923, F. No. 1929-IV.
78 For a brief survey of the history of the National Movement in Kerala. See Perunna K.N. Nair, Keralathile Congress Prasthanam (Malayalam) (Tri 1967).
79 K. Madhavan Nair, n. 40, p. 65.
80 *Home Poll*, 1921, F. No. 241, Part I-A.
81 *Ibid.*
82 Quoted by K. Madhavan Nair, n. 40, p. 68.
83 H.B. Jackson to C.A. Innes, 4 September 1921, *Home Poll*, 1921, F. No. 241, Part I.A.
84 V.R. Menon: *Mathrubhumiyude Charitram*, Vol. i, (Malayalam) p. 34. (Kozhikode, 1973)
85 K. Madhavan Nair, n. 40, p. 88.
86 K. Madhavan Nair, n. 40, p. 83.

34 Peasants of the Parganas

Ashim Mukhopadhyay

I

THE PRESENT STRUGGLES of the peasantry in the Parganas can be understood well if the past is known. Like other parts of undivided Bengal this region also saw, from time to time, severe conflicts between the peasantry on the one side and the zamindars, mahajans (moneylenders) and their paid agents on the other. Knowledge of this background is essential for a correct assessment of the present happenings.

Before the advent of the British, the Mughals were the real masters of this land, and before them the Hindus and the Turko-Afghans. Even at that time the peasantry revolted against oppression. Sincere and serious students of history will never forget the 'Kaibarta revolt' during the reign of King Rampal. They will not label Dibbak and Bhim, the leaders of that revolution, as mere rebels. On the contrary they will adore these two leaders as champions of the cause of the poor peasantry.[1]

In lower Bengal which comprized the Parganas, Howrah, Midnapore, Khulna, Dacca, Bakhargunge, several leaders arose from the lowest rung of the social ladder at different times to oppose the tyrants. The peasants and artisans formed the rank and file of their army, fought for them and helped them to seize power. In almost all cases a new monarchical set-up came into existence and the gains were short-lived, but in that extreme feudal structure of society nothing better could have been obtained. In the Parganas and Howrah there were many such local leaders of humble origin. They are now mere legendary figures.[2]

Even the folk gods were once such leaders. If the religious side of the history of their origin is rejected, the things to consider are economic and political factors. Dakshin Roy, Panchanan, Panchu Banbibi, all these folk gods were once connected with the economic

Reproduced from *Frontier* Vol. 2 No. 37 to 42, (Calcutta), Dec. 1969-Jan. 1970.

and political struggles of the common people. But as days went on, people began to worship them as gods. The upper classes, who used to exploit them, constantly encouraged this process, because they knew that by putting a religious coating on the real facts they would be able to hoodwink the next generations of their victims. Thus what was an economic struggle was turned into a religious feat. However, these folk gods and 'Kaibarta' or 'Bagdi' leaders were the first peasant agitators in Bengal. This is an untold story of our social history.

In the Turko-Afghan period there were many possiblities of peasant movements on a large scale in the Parganas and also in other parts of the province, but things happened otherwise. Stories of conversion of the Hindus have been always misunderstood by our pundits. Behind this countrywide conversion were the age-old economic grievances of the common people. Most of them were peasants. They were ready for revolt. But they were disorganized. The newcomers understood the situation very well. They planned not to organize those peasants against the existing feudal system which they themselves had decided to run. But they thought of setting them upon the Hindu feudal lords. To serve both these purposes they urged the ignorant and oppressed peasants to embrace Islam, by doing which they would be placed in 'behest' (heaven). But in reality this call for conversion was a sound strategy of the Muslims. In this way they isolated the militant Hindu peasants and artisans from their community; feeling helpless, isolated they submitted to their new masters and with every passing day began to lose their militancy. In Harao-Balanda (northern part of 24-Parganas) and in Baruipur, Khari etc. (the southern part) peasant revolts could have been staged in the early period of the Turko-Afghan rule. Pir Gorachand of Haroa, Mubarak Ghazi of Ghutiar-i-Sharif, Bara Khan Gazi of Khari were nothing but local Muslim leaders who cleverly canalized the grievances of the local peasantry into campaigns against the ruling Hindu lords. But they never tried to organize the people for a struggle through which they could have improved their own lot. However, these pirs and ghazis are now worshipped as folk gods.[3]

Nothing to choose
During the Mughal rule, the peasantry in the Province (including

its lower portions) occasionally rose in rebellion against the local fauzdars and talukdars. Those rebellions were ruthlessly suppressed. Men of the upper stratum of society always deceived those brave but simple peasants and exploited them to serve their own interests. The 'Bara-Bhuians' of Bengal had many peasants soldiers in their army to fight Akbar and Jehangir. They ignited a spirit of nationalism in the minds of the ignorant peasants, made them communal and then set them upon the Mughals but they themselves were no less tyrants. Pratapaditya, one of the 'Bara-Bhuian' who ruled over the present Jessore, Khulna and a large part of the Parganas, was a tireless oppressor of his subjects. After the battle of Plassey, Robert Clive wrote to the authorities of the East India Company that when the small Company-infantry was moving to the Nawab's palace at Murshidabad, several thousand natives gathered on the highway. They could have easily crushed Clive and his followers if they had so wished, but they remained silent spectators.[4] Clive could not understand the reason for their remaining silent. Actually to the toiling masses of Bengal replacement of the 'Nawab' by the 'Sahib' was nothing but replacement of one oppressor by another. Neither did the Nawab approach them, nor did they extend their help to him. From their past lessons they realized that they were the exploited. It was only when they organized themselves to struggle against their oppressors and exploiters that they succeeded in securing some concessions.

On December 20, 1757, Mir Jafar, the new Nawab of Bengal, surrendered to the Company the zamindari or landholder's rights over the Parganas.[5] Clive, who was then master of Bengal, had his eyes on this fertile tract. He had already written to the Court of Directors that 'the annual income in this area I will venture to estimate at ten lacs per annum.'[6] He got his chance when in June 1765 Mir Jafar conferred on him the 'Jagir' or zamindari of the Parganas.[7] From that time began the real story of the Parganas, an ugly story of unlimited exploitation of its people by the English and their native agents.

The southern section of the district was wild and uncultivated. It was an ideal habitat of ferocious animals, reptiles and pirates. The first attempt to reclaim it by granting leases to individuals was made between 1770 and 1773. The next attempt at reclamation was carried on by Mr. Tilman Henckle, the judge and magistrate of

Jessore. Between 1811 and 1823, this region of the Parganas, together with the lower part of Jessore and Bakhargunge or the Sunderbans in short, was surveyed by several English officers. Their object was the same, i.e., reclamation and cultivation of the Sunderbans.[8] But that was hampered by flaws in the system of land distribution and the ill-defined character of the lands distributed on lease. These again encouraged the opportunist zamindars to start boundary disputes. The Company felt the need of a correct survey, and in 1830 for the first time the Sunderbans came to exist as a clearly defined area. Since then many rules have been passed at regular intervals up to the end of the 19th century (1853, 1863, 1879, 1897) to reclaim and cultivate this wild but fertile tract.[9] But the mission proved a grand failure. The entire region turned into hell.

The system of land distribution and collection of revenue in the northern part of the Parganas was completely different. To that part were extended the rules of the Permanent Settlement (1793). From that time onwards, the northern portion of the Parganas along with other districts was repeatedly subjected to revisions of the land and land revenue system, for instance the Act of 1799, the Act of 1812, the Act of 1845, the Act of 1859, the Act of 1885 etc. However none of these Acts could solve the basic problem. 'Who is the real owner of the soil'?—remained an unsettled question. The zamindars and mahajans prospered at the expense of the ryots, the latter gradually became paupers.

'The Baboos'

Introduction of the Permanent Settlement permanently unsettled the future of the poor peasantry. It smashed the village community system, created a class of landlords and middlemen and established the concept of private property on a solid footing. In introducing this Settlement the Company had two definite objectives. One was economic and the other political. The Company, which was a typical colonial power, sought to create some staunch supporters of its activities. Lord Cornwallis, the inventor of this Settlement, wrote in his letter to the Court of Directors that for its own interests the Company should make the native zamindars its allies. Lord William Bentinck, for whom the pundits have great respect, said that the

Permanent Settlement had created a large number of rich zamindars who would preserve the rule of the Company in India and if necessary would exert their influence over the countrymen[10]. All these expectations were fulfilled. Whenever there was a rising in any part of the country, the 'Bengalee Zamindar baboos' served their masters like faithful dogs.[11]

The increasing demands of the shareholders of the Company and the huge expenses of wars against the militant peasantry of Bihar and Bengal were a constant headache of the Court of Directors. The propertyless revenue farmers could not quench the Company's thirst for money. Hence the Directors planned to replace these persons by a new class of collectors. Thus the Permanent Settlement came into existence. 'The total collections from 1794 to 1798 amounted to sicca Rs 2,65,00,000'.[12]

The subsequent regulations were of the same vicious nature. 'Section XV of Regulation VII of 1799 or the 'Haptam' gave the zamindars the power of arrest before decree, which they had used to serve the worst purposes. 'It greatly helped the ruthless landlords to squeeze the last penny out of rackrented peasants in order to meet the revenue demands of the British as well as to make their own money'.[13]

Regulation V of 1812 gave unlimited power to the zamindar to enhance rent provided he gave a formal written notice to the cultivator or tenant at the beginning of the Bengali year of the rent he was to pay for that year.

Act No. 1 of 1845 or the 'Sunset Law' gave ample authority to the purchaser of an estate to enhance at discretion the rents of all under-tenures in the said estate and to eject all tenants thereof.

The provisions of Act X of 1859 raised great expectations, but could give no practical relief. Even the Europeans themselves admitted these failures.[14]

The Bengal Tenancy Act of 1885 was also a failure. The zamindars continued to wallow in wealth and the peasants, in poverty.[15]

The systems in the Sunderbans were no less injurious, creating several dozens of big landowners. Those zamindars were more interested in profiteering than in reclamation or cultivation. Their peasants and labourers had to lead a miserable life in the jungles.[16] Not only that, the defects of the land distribution systems led to the growth of an undesirable class of speculators and middlemen and to the grinding down of the actual cultivators by excessive rent.[17]

Thus with the advent of the Company, an era of heinous oppression ensued. The 'Diarchy' or the dual rule of Clive descended on the poor Bengal peasant as a curse. In the famine of 1770-1 when about one third of the population perished, the Company collected sicca Rs 1,40,06,030. During 1771-2 the collection was sicca Rs 1,57,26,576. From Warren Hastings' letter to the Directors we know that the loss of revenue due to the death of one third of the population was made up by severe exactions from the remaining two-thirds.[18]

As has been stated earlier, in the pre-British period land in Bengal was jointly possessed by the entire village community. At that time 'the revenue farmers were not actually proprietors of land'. So there was very little scope for the development of landholder-cum-sharecropper and supervisory farmer-cum-agricultural labourer relationships. There were two economic classes connected with land and cultivation, one was the revenue farmers or Class I and the other, the self-sufficient, self-cultivating peasantry working within the periphery of the village community or Class II.

But due to the defects of the Permanent Settlement and the subsequent Settlement regulations following it a great change came over the prevalent land system and its connective class structure. The revenue farmers gave way before the zamindars and middle-men and thus Class I lost its previous character. The disorderly situation also effected a speedy dissolution of Class II and emergence of Class III or a propertyless class of cultivators. By severe exaction and gradual enhancement of rent the zamindars evicted the peasants from their land and reduced them to the position of mere sharecroppers. This distressing condition of Class II also brought the moneylenders or mahajans to the forefront. Although they were not unknown in Hindu or Muslim India, their social role underwent a great change in the Company-regime.

As the systems of land transfer and mortgage were prevalent, the rackrented peasants frequently approached them for loans, the mahajans thus got a good opportunity to enrich themselves. Firstly, as suppliers of loans at excessively high interest they accumulated huge wealth. Secondly, they forced the peasants to sell their crops at a very cheap rate and then started a monopoly business. Thirdly, they deprived many peasants of their 'Vastoobhita' and in course of time became owners of huge landed property.

Thus one great achievement of the Company Raj was the destitution of the once self-supporting peasantry and mushroom growth of loyal landholders 'brought up in the women's apartment and sunk in sloth and debauchery'. In the words of Marx it was an 'unsuccessful and really absurd (and in practice infamous) experiment in economics'.[18a]

The zamindars, talukdars, gautidars, jotedars and other middlemen seemed to have the least respect for law and order. Besides the rent, they used to collect forcibly a number of illegal cesses. For instance: (a) Road cess—usually realised by the big landlords (Roy Chowdhurys of Baruipur, Das Mandals of Bawali—south 24 Parganas); (b) Tahari or collector's fee; (c) Agaman or Nazar (collected whenever a new naib or superior officer visited the cutchery); (d) Malik basha kharcha (fee for the zamindar's chair); (e) Hishab kharcha (fee for the accountant); (f) Mela kharcha (free for the fair); (g) Maricha (fee for marriage in the zamindar's family); (h) Parbi or bhet (fee for puja expenses collected everywhere in the Parganas); (i) Mamooly (fee for puja and other festivals); (j) Batta or exchange for sikka coin. (k) Dak kharcha (fee for the expenses of the Zamindar's mail); (l) Proja kharcha or tol kharcha (fee realised from the peasants for permitting them to sit in the cutchery); (m) Dakhila kharcha (fee for rent receipt).[19]

No excuse of natural calamities or poverty or ill health could soften the heart of the zamindar or his agent. Oppression and forcible exaction continued. The lives and properties of the peasants were left at their mercy. In their private life these zamindars, talukdars, jotedars and other middle men were addicted to all sorts of crimes. The contemporary literature gives a very good exposure of their private life.[20] Among the various means of torturing the subject population was violating the honour of their womenfolk. Once a notorious zamindar of the Sunderbans said that he had made the entire village his 'harem' and every newly married girl before she entered her husband's house had to lie with him repeatedly until she conceived.[21]

Thus day by day the Bengal village stumbled from one crisis to another. But it will be wrong to think that the peasantry silently submitted before these misdeeds. On the contrary, they never intended to remain under the black veil which was drawn over them by their oppressors and exploiters. From the very beginning of the Company's rule they revolted against its oppressive nature.

II

Within thirty years of the Battle of Plassey (1757) millions of peasants in the Sunderbans region rose to challenge the misrule of the East India Company.

Together with the agony of the famine of 1770, which was an artificial creation of notorious 'Writers', the repression by the Company of the weavers, saltmakers, silk growers and other classes of artisans made life unbearable for the peasants. Towards the end of the 18th century the peasants of the Parganas, Khulna and Jessore defied the authority of the English.[1] They attacked the "Khuthis" (warehouses) and plundered carts and boats carrying the merchandise of the Company and distributed the booty among the poor people. Although this movement was sporadic and disorganized, those who led it were very sincere and serious in their actions. Realising their limitations they followed the tactics of guerilla warfare. Whenever the enemy overpowered them, they hurriedly retreated to the dense jungles of the Sunderbans. A section of them reclaimed the jungles and settled there permanently.

After the Permanent Settlement (1793) the struggle between the Company and the peasantry intensified. The newly created zamindars and middlemen came forward to help the Company, their masters. On the other hand, the disgruntled revenue collectors whom the Company replaced by the zamindars sided with the fighting peasants. At a time it seemed as if the English would have to pack up and quit lower Bengal. This state of affairs continued till the end of the 18th century. However the movement failed and its failure was almost certain for one obvious reason: the combination of propertyless cultivators and wealthy revenue farmers was a great obstacle in the way of success. A parallel instance can be given from the revolt of 1857. On several occasions the sepoys and peasants who challenged the Company's authority were betrayed and deserted by their feudal leaders. The revenue farmers and petty landlords who joined the peasants of the Parganas and Jessore stopped fighting as soon as they lost patience. The ignorant and helpless peasants either submitted or fled to the jungles.

The next movement in the Parganas was that of the salt makers. As has been stated earlier, the Company had been running a monopoly business in tobacco, paddy, textiles, silk and salt and making huge profits out of it.[2] According to William Bolts, during the reign of Alivardi, the price of salt per 100 maunds was between 40 and 60 sicca rupees. But in 1773 it went up to 170 sicca rupees and in 1798 to 380. To the poor peasants salt became something as precious and scarce as gold and they used to consider themselves lucky enough if they could ever collect a handful of it to feed their cattle. Paradoxically enough, it was the Bengal peasants who used to manufacture this salt but could not taste even a grain of it.[3] During 1781-6, the price of salt was twelve times higher than that of rice. The chief salt-manufacturing centres in Bengal were Midnapore, the Parganas (south-east parts), Khulna, Bakhargunge and the sea-coast of Cittagong. Everywhere at these places the Company practised various cruel methods to collect workers for its factories.

The plan followed in salt manufacture in the Parganas and Khulna was that the government Salt Agent contracted with the Malangis or middlemen (in Midnapore the middle were called Huddadar') for the engagement of people as salt boilers or Mahindars. In most cases the Mahindars were forced to take advances and the Malangis were vested with certain powers to enable them to drive the Mahindars cruelly to work. These powers the Malangis cruelly abused and gross oppression was perpetrated by the officials. They insisted on receiving back Rs 20 for every Rs 4 which they had advanced.[4] The most notorious among those salt officers was Mr Euart, head of the Raimangal division salt agency. The Mahindars in the Sunderbans were actually landless peasants. It was only for their survival that they used to take advance from the contractors. Otherwise they had no attraction for the profession (salt manufacturing). The entire Raimangal belt was full of tigers and venomous snakes and above all there was the jungle fever. So it was quite natural that the Mahindars were reluctant to stay there. But it was Mr Euart who forced them to stay and kept a constant watch on their movements.[5] At last the Mahindars revolted, stopped work and within a few months the situation became so critical that the Malangis and Sahibs hurriedly retreated to the town areas for safety. Mr Tilmen Henckell, the then judge-magistrate of Jessore, intervened and a compromise was arrived at. The main points were: (a) Salt manufacturing areas must be fixed and definitely located. (b) No one should be forced to accept advance against his will. (c) If it was seen that the people were reluctant to manufacture salt, then the business should be stopped, etc.[6]

Meanwhile the salt manufacturers of Midnapore had started similar movements. At Derduman, Birkul, Balasay, Mirgodha and many other areas salt factories had to be closed. Strikes, processions and hand-to-hand fight between the workers and the sepoys annoyed the Company. Ultimately it set its entire coercive machinery upon the Malangis. It is really interesting to note that during those fateful years the peasants of the Parganas extended their helping hand to the salt manufacturers of Midnapore. In 1793 several hundred Malangis of Derduman came to Murgachha (south 24 Parganas). The peasants of Murgachha gave them shelter, fed them for a long time and also gave assurance of such friendly treatment in future. Next year (1794) another batch of the Malangis of Ajura crossed the River Hooghly and entered Tentulberia. This time also they were treated kindly by the local peasants.[7]

Thus the movements of the salt makers show the sowing of the seed of class consciousness, an essential pre-requisite for class struggle. The salt makers of Midnapore were actually landless peasants and the people of the Parganas from whom they received help were also the same. As this class consciousness hardened day by day, the peasants wars in Bengal also intensified. The indigo movements of the 19th century reflected this noticeable feature.

Blue Mutiny

The indigo planter of Bengal extracted blood from the body of the helpless peasant and transformed its glowing red into the deep blue of indigo through a process unbelievably hellish and unthinkable even in the animal world.

The indigo industry was transported to India from the West Indies in the last quarter of the 18th century. In 1778, one Carel Blume (English) built a factory somewhere in Bengal and submitted a memorandum to the Governor General pleading for the extension of indigo cultivation.[8] At that time, England was passing through the phase of the Industrial Revolution and her textile industries needed indigo. The Company, which was exploiting India, both as a supplier of raw materials needed for British Industries and as an ideal market for the finished produce, availed itself of this opportunity and started financing individual planters to extend cultivation. Thus like other articles of trade, indigo also became a monopoly of the Company.[9]

In 1819, the Company, as it had done in the past, once again misused its 'prerogative'. By regulation VIII it gave the zamindars the right to lease their lands and thus encouraged further subinfeudation of cultivable areas. The zamindars, who had been growing like mushrooms since the Permanent Settlement and living like parasites on the body of the peasantry, welcomed the Regulation. They leased their lands to the indigo planters and with plenty of money settled in the cities to enjoy an easy-going life.[10]

From the very beginning, the planters started a very repressive regime. In a journal printed and published from Mazilpur (south 24-Parganas) they were described as 'Kings and killers of the natives.'[11]

Very soon the zamindars themselves felt the weight of repression. The planters began to press them for further transfers of land and even demanded their 'khas possessions', This led the zamindars to submit a memorandum to the British Parliament pleading for the Crown's help. But it went unheeded, because 'some most faithful servants'[12] of the English had by this time started a movement demanding settlement of the 'Sahibs' in India. Among them were Rammohun Roy and Dwarkanath Thakur. Their activities greatly encouraged their bosses, i.e., Charles Metcalfe and William Bentinck, who wrote to England that a section of educated and wealthy natives would be helpful for the settlement of the English in India, and therefore the Government should consider the matter seriously.[13] Ultimately, it was due to the earnest efforts of the Roys and Thakurs that in 1833 the Crown allowed the planters of the West Indies to settle in India. An international entente was thus formed between two groups of feudal exploiters against the toiling masses of a chained country.

As days rolled on the crisis deepened. The seasoned planters of the West Indies, backed by the Company, continued their land-grabbing practice and extended indigo cultivation over a vast area of the province. The Bengal Indigo Company, the largest—in the country, became the owner of a huge landed property, (594 villages)[14] which it used to control by its various 'concerns'. Of these, the Mollahati Concern (now in Bongaon PS, 24-Parganas) had factories and several thousand bighas of land. R.T. Larmour, the notorious manager of the Company, had his residence here.[15]

In his evidence before the Indigo Commission in 1860, Mr Ashley Eden, the Magistrate of Barasat (24 Parganas), admitted that 'till then 20,40,000 bighas of fertile land had been used for indigo cultivation and thus to a country, regularly visited by famine, a great wrong had been done.'[16]

Regarding cultivation, the planters generally followed two systems: Nij Avadi and Ryoti Avadi or Dadani Avadi (also known as the Khatai jami system). In the former, the planter had to cultivate his Khas possessions and bear all expenses including labour charge and therefore the profit never came up to his expectations. But in the 'Avadi' or 'Khatai' system it was the ryot who had to supply all means of production including labour, 'the Shahib had no other responsibility except that two rupees of advance.'[17] According to the Indigo Commission in the 'Nij Avadi system' a planter had to spend Rs 2,50,000 for every 10,000 bighas, whereas in the Ryoti Avadi or Khatai jami system has expenditure never exceeded Rs 20,000.[18] Quite naturally, the planters preferred the 'Ryoti'. The guiding principle of their business was 'maximum gain at minimum pain'.[19] It was one of the important factors which formed the back-drop of the indigo tragedy.

The planters who had been running a serfdom in the West Indies started the same sort of business in Bengal with renewed vigour. The government and the zamindars threw the peasantry at their mercy. To a peasant 'the Khatai jami system was as harmful as poison and he who submitted to it, drank poison with his own hands'.[20] In this system a ryot had to spend near-about Rs 11 for every 2 bighas. But the outturn could not be more than Rs 4. However, this sordid tale did not end here. After the deduction of the 'Dadan' (advance) and 'Dasturi (bribe) this little amount of Rs 4 was reduced to a few annas and the helpless ryot had to crawl back to his broken hut only to beat a starving and accusing wife. There was none to protect him. The agony of the Bengali peasants was aptly echoed by a native (Harish Chandra Mukherjee?) who wrote, 'How shall I describe the atrocities committed especially by certain zamindars—native and European—who stand high in the esteem of the English community and who contain only rottenness and bones beneath the external polish of specious philanthropy and pretended enlightenment.'[21] But much more interesting was the confession of Mr Forde, Magistrate of Faridpur, who said, 'The expression: 'not a chest of indigo reached England without being stained with human blood' is mine and I adopt it in the fullest and broadest sense of its meaning, as the result of my experience as a Magistrate in Faridpur.'[22]

The nilkars (planters) became a living curse in the everyday life of the peasants. Those who refused to obey their orders were subjected to inhuman tortures and even their wives and daughters had to lose honour. The situation was depicted in Nildarpan.

Peasants hit back

The peasants could not allow this tyranny to go on. From the very beginning of the 19th century they offered the indigo planters stiff resistance. In 1810, they compelled the government to send back four notorious planters to England and the then Governor General himself admitted that the atrocities committed by the planters had undoubtedly lowered the prestige of the Crown. A British observer of those earlier events wrote in 1848 that even in the first decade of the 19th century hundreds of clashes took place between the planters and the peasants. On several occasions the latter gave the former a good beating and destroyed the factories.

In 1810, Biswanath Sardar, a peasant leader of Nadia, organized a large number of oppressed ryots against the local planters and punished many of them. It is a shame indeed that the bourgeois historians describe Biswanath as a 'mere dacoit'. In 1838 the Faraji leader of Faridpur—Dudu Mian revolted against the local zamindars and planters and continued struggles till his death in 1860. In 1843, the ryots of Kagmari (Mymensingh, now in East Pakistan) attacked the local factories and kidnapped King who had earned notoriety as a planter. In 1840, the ryots of Hogla (Khulna, East Pakistan) had a serious clash with Renny, a local planter. The situation worsened so quickly that the government intervened and effected some administrative divisions of the district.[23] In the Parganas, the most interesting of the earlier movements was that of the Wahabis.[24] Here one thing must be admitted—that the movement was waged not only against the planters but also against the local zamindars and mahajans and the question of religion was never raised. It was definitely a commendable feature of the movement, because the Wahibs, themselves being ardent Muslims, championed the cause of the fellow Hindu peasants. This unique development of class consciousness among the backward sections prepared the ground for future class struggles.

To the Wahabis, a zamindar or a mahajan, (he might be a Hindu or Muslim) was an oppressor of the peasants and therefore a class-enemy. Although they were men of humble origin, they were united and well disciplined and became a terror to the rich. It was Titu Mian or Titu Mir (his original name was Mir Nishan Ali) who organised this movement in the Parganas. From his boyhood he had a definite idea about the mission of his life. He wanted to be the oppressor of the oppressors and began to build up a good physique. William Hunter who had not done enough justice to Titu said that he (Titu) 'earned an ignominious livelihood as a boxer in Calcutta' and also joined a band of dacoits. But what better could be expected from a member of the ruling class when his own countrymen misunderstood him?[25]

From 1830 Titu and his followers were engaged in serious clashes with the local zamindars and planters. In November 300 armed Wahabis attacked the residence of Krishnadev Ray, a notorious zamindar of Purra (Baduria Ps., 24 Parganas). This incident terrified other zamindars. They now approached the planters. Babu Kaliprasanna Mukherjee of Gobardanga (Bongaon subdivision) joined hands with Davice, the manager of the Mollahati factory (Bongaon Ps.). However, the combined force of Davice and Kali suffered a humiliating defeat at the hands of the peasant warriors. Several planters, deserted their factories, cultivation of indigo came to a halt, peasants recovered their lands and refused to pay rent. Titu declared the entire area a free zone and assumed the title of 'Badshah' (Emperor). At Narikelbaria he built a fort with bamboo and mud and mobilised more than 1,000 peasants for its defence. Here on November 14, 1831 a battle took place between Titu and the English. He suffered defeat and died on the spot. His lieutenants were hanged and others jailed.[26] Thus ended the Wahabi movement, a brilliant attempt by the Pargana peasants to retaliate against their oppressors. In spite of its religious origin, it was one of the earliest challenges to English rule in India and at the same time a class struggle of the peasents against the feudal lords.

By the middle of the 19th century the indigo movement reached its climax. Although everywhere the peasants were up in arms, their struggles intensified mainly in three districts, i.e., the Parganas, Nadia and Jessore. In the Parganas, the peasants attacked and destroyed the factories at Mollahati, Barasat, Baruipur and Boral. The managers of Mollahati and Boral were severely beaten. The important leaders during this period were Vishnu Charan Biswas, Digambar Biswas, Mir Ali etc. A contemporary missionary who witnessed the clashes gave an idea of the indigo fighters in action: 'They had divided themselves into about six different companies. One company consisted merely of bowmen, another of slingsmen, another of brickwallas, another of balewallas (their business was to send unripe bale fruit to the heads of the lathials). Another division consisted of thalwallas (who fling their brass rice plates in a horizontal way at the enemy) and another of rolawallas who received the enemies with whole or broken well burned earthern pots.'[27]

The movements raised a great controversy among the rulers regarding further continuation of indigo cultivation, and although the majority of the educated natives remained indifferent onlookers, a few daring Bengalis started an agitation in support of the suffering peasants. *The Patriot* of Harish Chandra Mukherjee became the mouthpiece of the ryots and Nil Darpan, Dinabandhu Mitra's work, became a magic mirror reflecting at a time two faces, the face of the tyrant and the face of his victim. Ultimately the government yielded to public opinion, and on March 31, 1860 set up the historic Indigo Commission. From May 18 to August 14 (1860) 136 persons gave evidence before the Commission. Among them were 15 government servants, 21 planters, 8 missionaries, 13 zamindars and 77 ryots. Hearing the statements the Commission came to this conclusion: 'The whole system is vicious in theory, injurious in practice and radically unsound.' The then Lieutenant Governor of Bengal declared that the peasant of Bengal was not a mere serf but a real owner of land. In spite of these vocal sentiments no new regulation was issued for the restriction of indigo cultivation; the government simply shelved the problem and new troubles broke out in north Jessore. However, the planters whose powers had been considerably curtailed by the peasant wars could not regain their former position and by 1895 their activities came to be restricted within the small periphery of 17 factories. Finally, after the preparation of synthetic blue by the Germans, cultivation of indigo gradually came to an end.²⁸

Link with Mutiny

It is very often asked whether the Bengal peasantry had ever participated in the Great Revolt of 1857. The so-called pundits, both here and abroad, have tried hard to prove that during 1857 peasants in Bengal were as mute as corpses and what happened at that time was merely a sepoy mutiny. Surely, a better analysis of a mass movement cannot be expected from people whose fathers and forefathers belong either to the ruling class or to its most faithful servants. The peasants were definitely fighting against the English during 1857. This they were doing in the villages through their anti-indigo movements. Striking the planters they wanted to weaken the economic base of the ruling power. Therefore, in their struggles there was a unique combination of diplomacy and strategy. Not only that, during the Great Revolt, the situation was really very tense all over Bengal and in the districts adjacent to Calcutta, including the Parganas, thousands of peasants assembled to join the sepoys. In 1858, a large number of peasants assembled at Baruipur (the Parganas), submitted a memorandum to the Magistrate demanding immediate release of all the prisoners. Even the rulers themselves admitted this countrywide unrest and said: 'the districts immediately in the neighbourhood of Calcutta and even the Presidency itself, have been subject to periodical panics during the whole progress of rebellion.'

'Hardly a single district under the government of Bengal has escaped either actual danger or the serious apprehension of danger.'²⁹

The rapidly increasing strength of the peasants and the intensification of their struggles against vested interests became a constant headache to the government. In order to counteract 'this great evil', the then Governor General and his advisers discovered a unique formula, which came to be known as the 'Indian National Congress'. From the statement of Allan Octovian Hume, the so-called father of the Congress, we know the real motive of the government. He said that thousands of reports warning the government about a serious mass upsurge poured into the capital from every corner of the country. Therefore he thought that something must be done without any delay and the starving people should not be given any chance to organize themselves.[30] Thus the reactionary rulers and their reactionary Indian supporters joined hands to set up the Congress. But the millions of starving peasants and artisans could not forgive this entente. A spirit of revenge continued to burn in their hearts.

Throughout the 19th century, the educated and westernised Bengali 'baboos' played a role which was both loathsome and ignoble. They supported and encouraged all the misdoings of the English. It was they and not the English who really betrayed their countrymen, and hampered the progress of the peasant movements. Yet our pundits appreciate their activities and describe them as messengers of the 'Indian renaissance'. The term renaissance means reawakening or rebirth—reawakening of the sense of humanity, fellow feeling, patriotism and sacrifice. Paradoxically, these qualities were not present in those so-called great men. Although they were well acquainted with the revolutionary ideas of the West, they carefully avoided their inner meaning and what they sincerely imported from Europe was Western feudalism. Previously they had been 'babu' feudals, now they wanted to become sahib feudals. The net result of this so-called renaissance was the replacement of the Indian feudal way of life by its European counterpart. Rammohun, Dwarkanath, Bankim Chandra, Vivekananda, all those 'heroes' of the 19th century served the British. It is a tragedy that Rammohun and Dwarkanath supported the indigo planters, encouraged their settlement in India, it is an ugly truth that 'Rishi' Bankim Chandra opposed the peasant wars and Vivekanda identified socialism with Hindu advaitabad. Although there were a few exceptions—(Harish Chandra Mukherjee, Dwarkanath Ganguly etc.), it was the real picture of the day.[31]

III

As the nineteenth century lapsed into the twentieth the number of landless people increased at an unusual pace. It happened mainly because of the destitution of the share-croppers or bargadars and their demotion to the position of paid-labourers or khet majurs.[1] In 1902, in 'A Memorandum on the Land Revenue Policy of the Indian Government', the existing tenancy Acts were severely condemned for placing the tenants unreservedly at the mercy of the landlords. In 1905, a member of the Bengal Provincial Civil Service, referring to the vindictive nature of the land settlement, said, 'To leave the rights of property of the vast majority of the people at the pleasure and will of a miscroscopic minority is only a retrograde step and tends to check the development and prosperity of the country. Therefore, I appeal to the government which is ever ready to protect the weak, to look up for the amelioration of the condition of the peasantry'.[2] Although there was enough truth in the speech of that civil servant, he intentionally described the government as the saviour of the peasants. Being a member of the judicial branch, he was well acquainted with the abounding hypocrisy of the alien rulers who, as a typical colonial power allowed their native agents to prey upon the poor people and thus secured their help to strengthen their own position in the country. Actually, the government was unwilling to redress the grievances of the peasants. Apart from routine recitals of its failures, as in the Report of the Land Revenue Commission of 1940, it cleverly sidetracked the problems originating from its land settlements.[3]

As days passed the landless labourers gradually went down to the lowest rung of the social ladder. By the twenties of this century their number went up to 30 per cent of the entire agricultural population. They became, quite literally, slaves of their masters. Still they could not save themselves. Their humble earnings could not keep pace with the rocketing cost of living. Up to 1922 their wages increased four to sixfold but the price of their staple diet increased eightfold.[4]

As a logical corollary to the destitution of the peasantry, their indebtedness also shot up. Land transfers by mortage or sale became very common. The number of transfers effected by registered deeds rose from 43,000 in 1844 to $2\frac{1}{2}$ million in 1913 and the number of unregistered transfers was even greater. According to the Report of the Bengal Banking Enquiry Committee, by 1929 the total rural debt of Bengal amounted to Rs 100 crores; per capita it amounted to Rs 160. According to this report, in Jessore and north 24-Parganas, 80 per cent of the population were in debt, the average debt ranging between Rs 150 to Rs 175. The report further said that the per capita income of the then Bengal cultivator was only Rs 84 and therefore less than enough to meet his daily expenses, which meant that he always lived a hand-to-mouth existence.[5]

In order to shelve these grave problems or to hoodwink the millions of ignorant peasants, the government decided to amend certain clauses of the Bengal Tenancy Act of 1885. But in doing so, it did not forget the interests of the landed aristocracy whom it considered one of the pillars of its strength. Thus the Amending Act of 1928 outwardly strengthened the rights of under-ryots but in reality gave the zamindars enough power to evict them from land. In the report of the land Revenue Commission of 1940, government officials themselves admitted the defects of the Act of 1928.[6] Janab Abdul Kashem Fazlul Haq, the then Chief Minister of Bengal, who was mainly responsible for the passing of that Act, himself served the interests of the zamindars. However, he was not entirely responsible for the failure of the Act. Most of the native members of the Legislative Council were landlords or had direct interests in land and it was due to their pressure that the under-ryots received no definite right over land.[7] Those reactionary persons openly declared that they would never allow the government to give occupancy rights to the propertyless peasants. One of them unhesitatingly said, 'if occupancy rights are given to bargadars, it would be giving them something for which they have not paid, and it would encourage dishonesty and indolence. They might not make any effort to cultivate the land, thereby making their landlords suffer. They might also try to deprive the landlords of the proper share of the crops.'[8] The zamindar baboos advised the British Government to beware of agrarian socialism, and described the Permanent Settlement as a lasting barrier between the state and Bolshevism.[9] The government in its turn never frustrated those zamindars, because to it also the unending series of agrarian revolts, if not Bolshevism itself, posed a great threat. Quite naturally, it kept enough loopholes in its land legislation. In 1936 it set up a board of arbitration on rural indebtness. The board gave the peasants some privileges but no right to prevent the auction of their lands and thus the government neglected one of their vital problems. In November 1938, Janab Fazlul Huq appointed a commission under Francis Floud, a Civil Servant, to examine the existing land problems. The commission submitted certain proposals regarding the improvement of the condition of landless peasants, in practice, it looked for an effective solution to the evils of the Permanent Settlement which had by that time dragged the landowners to the brink of extinction thanks to absentee landlordism, excessive sub-infeudation and accumultion of arrear rents.[10] This pro-zamindar policy was also revealed in the Act of 1938 which amended certain sections of the Act of 1928. The Act of 1938 contained nothing in favour of millions of bargadars, *khet majurs* and 'Uthbandi prajas' (Jessore).[11] This indifferent attitude of the government towards the subject population and its patronage of a class of bloody leeches, were the main factors which formed the backdrop to the peasant revolts of the twentieth century.

Peasant Revolts

In the early thirties nothing significant took place. From the second phase of the indigo movement (1889) till 1938, there was more or less a lull in the rural areas of Bengal. It is not true, however, that in this period the peasants silently yielded to the relentless oppression. Even at that time in the remote villages of the Sunderbans the bargadars and *khet-majurs* were engaged in armed clashes with the lotdars, jotedars and their agents.[12] Unfortunately, very little is known about this phase of the peasant movement, but whatever cumulative evidence can be gathered, reveals an interesting story of the bravery of the Pargana peasantry. The late Mr Kalidas Dutta who conducted several archaeological expeditions in the dense forests of the Sunderbans and frequently visited lower Bengal, recorded some such clashes between the peasants and the jotedars.[13] According to him trouble often broke out at Satkhira, Raimangal, Pathar, Basanti and Kakdwip. Significantly enough, it was Kakdwip which in 1946 came to the forefront of the famous Tebhaga movement. However the peasant movements of this period had many limitations and were isolated, taking place in certain corners of the country. But those which began in the late thirties were of a completely different nature. Unlike the earlier movements, these were spontaneous, widespread and in spite of the presence of many geographical barriers separating one place of agitation from another, they bore a semblance of unity. This difference in character between the two phases of the peasant movements was mainly due to the efforts of the Bangiya Pradeshik Kishan Sabha, formed in August 1939. Although in different periods of the last century there was a close understanding among the peasants of distant districts and the men they fought were often their common enemies, still the spirit of discipline so vitally needed in such cases, was absent in them. Also, the peasant warriors of the last century had no proper political training and therefore their class consciousness could not get sharper in time. During the indigo agitations, they allowed many petty zamindars, their class enemies, to join them simply because they turned for the time being anti-planter or anti-British. To be frank, it was the synthetic blue invented by the Germans and not the opportunist zamindars, which actually helped the peasants to win the long-drawn battle.

The birth of the Bangiya Kishan Sabha and its activities inspite of their many setbacks marked a new chapter in the history of the peasant movement.

As has been stated earlier, the National Congress was a feudal-bourgeois organization. Its leaders, both the moderates and extremists, played the role of impotent constitutional agitators and howled at the top of their voices for the grace of their masters. 'At dawn they drew up a plan for a mass rally, at noon their oratory pushed the mercury of the thermo-meter to a point of no return, at dusk they set out for the Governor's House to join his cocktail party and finally at bed prayed for His Majesty's grace.'[14]

Naturally, the peasants did not benefit from the emergence of such an organization. On the contrary they began to doubt its mission. They had enough grounds to do so. From 1917 onwards Mohandas Karamchand Gandhi tried to canalise the militancy of the peasants into satyagraha or non-violent movements. The pact Gandhiji signed with Lord Irwin in 1931 did not include even a single demand of the country's worker and peasant population! This moral bankruptcy of the 'National' Congress led the Congress socialists, communists and other leftist leaders to think about the formation of an effective organization to champion the cause of the peasantry. In January 1936 they formed an All India Peasant Committee at Meerut and called an open conference at Lucknow in April. The Bengali delegates, Chhunnu Mian, Kamal Sarkar, Ananta Mukherjee, Niharendu Dutta Majumder, who joined the conference, decided on their way back to set up in Bengal a provincial peasant committee. In August peasant representatives from 20 districts gathered at the Albert Hall at Calcutta and in their presence the Bangiya Pradeshik Kishan Sabha, the parent body of the present Krishak Sabha (CPI-M) and the Krishak Samity

(CPI) came into existence. Soon after its birth the BPKS tried to extend its activities to every remote corner of Bengal. Sister committees at district level were formed at the Parganas, Howrah, Murshidabad, Faridpur, Chattagram and Khulna. The local peasant organizations of Tripura and Noakhali also joined them. In March, 1937, the BPKS held its first annual conference at Patrasayar (Bankura) and demanded abolition of the zamindari system without any compensation, speedy end of colonial exploitation, establishment of a democratic State in which real power would rest in the hands of the people, improvement of the condition of the rural population and unconditional transfer of land to the landless peasants. The conference also declared itself against imperialism and identified the British Government as the enemy of the nation.[15]

Prior to Tebhaga (1946) the important movement led by the BPKS were those for khas land in the Parganas, against a canal in Burdwan, the agitation of the adhiars in North Bengal and those against 'hat tola' or 'Mela tola' which began simultaneously in Rangpur, Dinajpur, Jessore, the Parganas, Malda and Mymensingh.

It has already been stated that at the outset of the present century, the peasants of the Parganas occasionally fought pitched battles with the lotdars and jotedars. The issues were forcible eviction of bargadars and quick transformation of their lands into khas possessions of the zamindars, illegal exactions and violation of the honour of peasant women. Even before the birth of the BPKS, they set up local krishak samitis (peasant committees) in their areas and used them against the oppressive landlords and moneylenders. On February 14, 1932, the peasants of Hasnabad (Basirhat Subdivision) assembled at the local bazaar and observed a Peasants Day. Their activities terrified the local jotedars and they summoned the police. Dozens of armed constables rushed to the bazaar and fired upon unarmed peasants and killed five on the spot.[16] Many such incidents took place in other villages.

After 1936 the movements against eviction and khas lands received further impetus from the emergence of the BPKS. In that year the peasants of Daudpur (Sandeshkhali Police Station) attacked the cutchery of the local zamindar, killed the Naib (Manager) and burned all documents. The government quickly interfered and Umasankar Maity, the local peasant leader, died in an encounter with the police.[17] But neither the BPKS nor the peasants lost hope.

The Port Canning Zamindary Company evicted thousands of poor peasants from their lands and home-steads and became owner of vast fisheries and cultivable fields. At Minakha, Uchila-Haroa and some other places it carried on inhuman repression on the peasantry. Quite naturally the Company, for its misdeeds, became a target of attack. The men of the BPKS who led the movement against the Company were Bankim Mukherjee, Mansur Habibullah, Naliniprabha Devi and Siris Ghosal. In April 1938 a large number of peasants who had been evicted by the Company came to Calcutta and demonstrated before the Legislative Council for immediate redress of their grievances. Their movement continued until 1942-3 but could not gain anything significant.

Leadership

The leadership of the BPKS was responsible for the failure. While the movement was in full swing, the local BPKS leaders allowed certain rich peasants to join their camps. One of them, is still alive and, strangely enough, possesses 5,000 bighas of benami land.[18] It was mainly because of their personal interest that they joined the BPKS. Otherwise they themselves were no less oppressors of the poor peasantry. The Port Canning Company effectively used them as their agents. It returned their land and even offered them substantial amounts of money and they in their turn served it well by sabotaging the peasant movement. The entire episode proved the unsoundness of the tactics of the BPKS and its lack of effective political training.

The next important movements in which the Pargana peasants took part were those against hat tola or mela tola. In several districts of Bengal, the local zamindars, talukdars, ijaradars and their paid servants amassed vast wealth by illegal exactions from the local periodical markets or 'haats'. The poor peasants who used to sell their paddy, vegetables and cattle in those markets had to pay various kinds of fees both in cash and kind. Not only the landlords, their servants also indulged in illegal exactions. Although this practice had started much earlier, the peasants could not check it and their sporadic clashes with the paiks and peadas (paid servants) of the zamindars led to further oppression. But from 1936, after the birth of BPKS, their movement against such illegal exactions received a fresh tempo. In the Parganas the movement intensified at Falta, Bongaon, Gopalnagore, Khatura, Diamond Harbour, Burul and Bishnupur and those who led the local peasants were Naliniprabha Ghose, Jyotish Roy, Pravash Roy, Ajit Ganguly and Hemanta Ghosal.[19] In North Bengal, Malda, Murshidabad and Jessore, wherever the people were affected by the system, a movement flared up with equal vigour. In 1939 at a fair in Dinajpur, the BPKS men encircled the paiks of a local zamindar and gave them a severe beating, as a result of which some of the paiks died on the spot.[20] At Diamond Harbour the situation became so tense that government officials interfered and settled the dispute in favour of the local peasants. Ultimately the zamindars submitted to the organized movement of the people and today though the system still continues it has lost it's previous repressive nature.

With the beginning of the Tebhaga movement (for a three-fourth share of the crop) in 1946, the militancy of the Pargana peasants reached further heights. The main factors responsible for the new outburst were the continuous oppression of the peasant population by the landlords, and ineffective and injurious land system, outbreak of the Second World War, the famine of 1943 and the rapid deterioration of the condition of the common people.

At Kakdwip, during this period, Dwarik Samanta, Aditya Samanta, Pulin Das, Paresh Das, Srinath Das, Haren Raychoudhury, Naren Dalal, Sanat Choudhury and many other lotdars were carrying on jungle rule. The lotdars evicted many peasants from their land and reduced them to the position of humble labourers, raped every pretty woman of the locality and if necessary tortured both the children and the old in cold blood.[21] Devi Raychoudhury of Gurguria (Jainagar Police Station) invented a unique method of repression. He used to offer his victims a drink called 'Sakhi Rakshitar Prasad' (Sakhi was the mistress of Devi Raychoudhury). The main ingredients of the 'prasad' were the urine of the woman and cowdung. The reluctant victims were forced to swallow it. Another equally notorious zamindar was Ayub Peanda of Kulpi (Diamond Harbour Subdivision). A tireless raper of women, he became a nightmare in the everyday life of the local peasantry.[22] The same was the character of the landlords in other districts.

After the outbreak of the Second World War, hoarding and blackmarketing of foodgrains received special patronage of the British Government. Many unscrupulous Indians availed themselves of the opportunity and started a very lucrative business of supply of foodgrains to the British army. Thus they threw millions of men and women into starvation and became owners of palatial buildings and cars. In its memorandum to the Land Revenue Commission, the BPKS made a very witty remark. It said: 'It is a joke in Bengal that the Government has by executive order abolished "famine" and substituted for it when occasion arises "shortage".'[23] It was this 'shortage' which finally brought about the famine of 1943.

The Famine

In course of a single year $3\frac{1}{2}$ million hungry people perished; $1\frac{1}{2}$ million men, women and children turned into beggars. The following data collected by BPKS relief workers reveal a dangerous increase in the number of beggars.

Percentage of beggars among the total number of the families

1939	1943	1944
1.72	3.69	6.78
4.00	7.33	8.33
2.1	2.1	2.9[24]

One contemporary observer of the famine has given a very touching account of the destitution of the poor peasants: 'It is the good earth which is the very life of the kisans—nothing is more sacred, nothing more attractive than it ... in 15 areas alone 5 lakhs of kisans have sold off Rs 10 crores worth of land in the course of a single year'.[25] The following table gives an idea of land sales in the Parganas during 1943.

Holding valued at not more than Rs 250

Area	Tenancy land			Tenancy land with occupancy right		
	Number of sellers	Price of sale	Number of holding	Number of sellers	Price of sale	Number of holdings
24 Parganas	19,438	46,68,132	14,848	48,558	9,05,595	39,091[26]

The observer again says: 'The scarcity of cattle is so acute and the desire to live on the part of the kisan is so strong that at places the spectacle of the kisan yoking his own son or brother to the plough has been witnessed'.[27]

Yet during those dark days the Congress, the Muslim League and the Hindu Mahasabha were engaged in fratricidal bickerings, most of the 'patriots' thinking that they had no part to play in the relief work. And so the famine spread like pestilence all over Bengal. At least 6 million people were directly affected by its evils. Of them 2.7 million were agricultural labourers, 1.5 million poor peasants, 1.5 million village artisans and 25,000 school teachers.

At Chandanpiri, Loilgunge, Budakhali, Burul, Hasnabad, Sandeshkhali and other parts of the Parganas the jotedars and lotdars prepared false sale deeds and handnotes and deprived the peasants of their last belongings. Finding no other way out, they sacrificed the honour of their women-folk to the carnal pleasure of their oppressors.[28]

At last their accumulated grievances burst into open conflicts with their oppressors, leading to the Tebhaga movement.

IV

In the Parganas, the storm centre of the Tebhaga movement (movement for three-fourths share of the crops) was its southern part. The oppressed peasants of Kakdwip, Haroa, Sandeshkhali, Canning, Bhangor, Sonarpur and other Sunderban areas displayed during that movement a militancy, a vigour, a grim determination the like of which the people of Bengal had never seen before. Not only that, their call for "Tebhaga" greatly inspired the peasants of North Bengal who were equally oppressed and exploited by the local landlords and moneylenders and had an equally brilliant tradition of struggle against all sorts of oppression and injustice. Ultimately, the North Bengal peasants, following the foot steps of their comrades of the Parganas, started agitation for 'Tebhaga', and other demands. From 1946 to 1950, these two distant regions remained hotbeds of a violent mass upsurge.

In the Parganas, it was the Kakdwip peasantry who suffered most and sacrificed most during the movement. There, many villagers of Loilgunge, Chandanpiri and Budakhali died, bathing the good earth with their blood.

From the very beginning of the harvesting season of 1946, the British Government mobilised a strong police force at Kakdwip. To the people of Kakdwip, who were still suffering from the devastating floods of 1942 and amongst whom the BPKS volunteers had done enough 'brain-washing', it was the last straw on the camel's over-burdened back.[1] Within a short time bloody encounters started between the peasants on one side and the lotdars and jotedars backed by the hired goondas of the 'Congress Seva Dal' and the police on the other. At Loilgunge, the police fired on unarmed peasants and killed 16 on the spot. At Chandanpiri 36 Gurkhas attacked 15 peasant women. The entire Gurkha community, well known for their bravery, will be ashamed to learn that at Chandanpiri their men, armed with rifles and grenades, killed some unarmed and helpless village girls and did not spare even the pregnant!

Soon the movement spread to other districts. In North Bengal, including East Dinajpur, Rangpur and Mymensingh (which are now in East Pakistan) thousands of peasants who had been suffering from the vicious Tanka, Nankar and Bhawal systems, raised the slogan of 'Tebhaga' and revolted against the landlords. Pitched battles started between them and the police. Several hundred peasants died in encounters and nearly 10,000 were injured.[2]

Finding the situation going out of control the Muslim League Ministry issued a Press note and acknowledged the legality of the Tebhaga demand. After a few days a Bill was published in the Government gazette regarding abolition of the zamindari system and evictions. The Bill also gave assurances about distribution of land among the landless. But it did not get the sanction of law and therefore the movement continued.[3]

On August 15, 1947, the Indians achieved 'independence,' but in reality power shifted from the hands of the British to their native agents, the Congress. Nothing therefore changed. On the contrary, the Indian leaders, following the proverb, 'servants always try to supersede their masters', set in a more oppressive regime. As soon as the harvesting season of 1947 began, the notorious lotdars and jotedars of Kakdwip sought police help from the West Bengal Government and in doing so were earnestly backed by the local Congress leaders—Charu Bhandari, Paresh Das and Bhusanpati. Charu Bhandari, who was well known for his double-dealing, advised the peasants to make peace with the jotedars.

He used to say, 'Zamindars and mahajans are your guardians, don't quarrel with them.' But at the very bottom of his heart, he was a tout of the local landlords and moneylenders.

In the month of December, with the connivance of Bhusanpati, a local leader of the Congress Seva Dal and a seasoned raper of women, a large number of armed police spread over the Budakhali Mauja to help the jotedars to carry away the paddy from the fields. On the night of December 15, 50 armed police and 4 inspectors launched a sudden attack on the peasants, mercilessly beat their leaders—Sibu Mandal, Harish Mandal, Gabua Nandapati and others—raped dozens of girls, burned several huts and threatened further torture in the near future. But the peasants of Budakhali did not lose heart. On the midnight of December 30 they assembled in the field and began to harvest the paddy. The police and the goondas of the 'Seva Dal' rushed to the spot and a bloody encounter followed. Many peasants died, many received injuries, but the enemies were not allowed to snatch away the golden crop.[4]

At Loilgunge, Chandanpiri and other parts of the province, the situation was equally tense and everywhere the peasants were fighting with equal vigour and seriousness. The Prafulla Ghose Ministry sharply reacted. Most of the members of the Bidhan Sabha (Legislative Assembly) were pro-Congress and had interest in land and it was mainly due to their hue and cry that the Ghose Ministry passed the Security Bill and planned to use it against the Tebhaga agitators. Immediately the peasants hit back. On December 10 they came to Calcutta and demonstrated before the Assembly. The police opened fire and killed Sisir Mandal. But the incident could not frighten them. Within a few days, they again came to the city and this time in far greater numbers (6,000). On their way to the Assembly they were beaten and tear-gassed by the police. They dispersed but the bitter experience they gathered made them more aggressive and violent. The repercussions of that incident were soon felt in fresh fighting at Kakdwip and other regions.[5]

Early in November, 1948, Dwarik Samanta, Srish Nandy, Kunja Ganta, Kangal Haldar, Gopi Giri and some other notorious jotedars of Loilgunge imported hundreds of lathials from different places and set them upon the peasants. Meanwhile 500 armed police and many hired goondas of the 'Seva Dal' had encircled the entire area. Yet, nothing could stop the peasants. They drove the enemy back, cut away the paddy from almost all fields and finally on August, 15, 1949 declared Loilgunge a 'free land'. At an open meeting, called on that day, several important resolutions were adopted: the lands recovered from the jotedars would be distributed among the local peasants; everybody would have his own home-stead where he would live without any interference from outside, he would also till his own plot of land and its entire produce would be his own; no action would be taken against the petty jotedars and middle peasants if they agreed to assist the fighting peasants, but if they conspired with the enemies, 'they would be sent to hell' the people of Loilgunge would always be ready to help the aggrieved peasants of other places; they would henceforth boycott the Congress Government and start their own rule. Life almost along the lines of a commune began at Loilgunge and continued till the end of the Tebhaga movement.

At Chandanpiri, in spite of the presence of the District Magistrate, the Police Commissioner and 500 Gurkha soldiers, the peasants continued their struggle and killed two local Congress leaders—Basanta and Paresh Das.

At Sandeshkhali hundreds of *khet majurs* attacked the cutcheries of Ramanath, a jotedar, destroyed all documents and seized 500 maunds of paddy. Their next victim was Dwarik Sharma of Sukodoani. Within a few days of the first incident, peasants from Durga mandap, Gabberia, Daudpur, Sukodoani and other villages attacked the residence of Dwarik. His men were beaten black and blue and his granaries were looted. In that 24-hour operation the peasants distributed amongst themselves 1,000 maunds of paddy, 800 pairs of 'dhotis' and a huge quantity of kerosene, sugar and salt. After two or three days a strong police force went to Sandeshkhali and started a counter-attack. Even now the humble peasants of Sandeshkhali spit with utter indignation when they recall the ghastly incidents of police operations in those days.

Story of Burul

The story of Burul is more, interesting, because, here, what started as a mere students' affair, soon flared up as a peasant movement. Most of the local students were from the bargadar or khet majur communities and had no good relationship with Chandi Ghose, the founder-president of the school and a Congressite jotedar. As time passed Chandi's position in the village became very weak and he rushed to Writers' Building to seek the help of Dr Bidhan Roy, the then Chief Minister of West Bengal. He got a favourable response, because Burul was one of the oldest strongholds of the Congress in the Parganas and most probably its birth place. For about 70 days the people of Burul passed through a nightmare. On August 13, 1948 Bijoy Singh Nahar, the 'Veteran' Congress leader, entered the village to organize the celebration of Independence Day. In reality, he had been sent by Dr Roy to restore the influence of the Congress there. This fact was well proved by the sight of military convoys plying along the village roads of Burul. However, the peasants, who had by that time sided with the students, came out to oppose. Mr Nahar and the latter who was then addressing his local followers had to jump down from the dais with the ease and vigour of a champion sportsman and fled through the backdoor. On August 15, the police showered bullets on the villagers, killed and wounded many on the spot yet the demonstration did not stop. At last the killers retreated, Chandi Ghose and his follower Murari Saran left Burul. 'In the evening, under the red-sky and in the presence of a red sun the people of Burul hoisted their dear Red Flag at the local bazaar.'

At Sonarpur and Bhangar the landless peasants organized themselves against Bhupati Naskar, Hemchandra Naskar, Sricharan Napte and other jotedars. Fierce pitched battles continued for several weeks.

At Tiuri, Nayabad, Kheada, Shaheber Abad peasants occupied fisheries, attacked cutheries, seized and distributed paddy among themselves. Everywhere peasant volunteers, armed with spears, bows and arrows fought with the police who were well equipped with rifles, grenades and other weapons and in spite of heavy casualties, in almost all cases came out victorious.

Ultimately the State Government felt the gravity of the problem. In 1949 it passed an ordinance extending some concessions to the bargadars. The ordinance later became known as the Bargadar Act. This Act, however, did not provide the peasants with the tebhaga or three-fourths of the crop for which they had borne so much hardship. It only arranged a 60-40 division which soon proved vague and the Board of Arbitration for sharecropping, which was born out of this Act, did not do away with the possibilities of eviction of the peasants from their lands. Their many other grievances remained unredressed.[6]

Along with the granting of these small concessions the Bidhan Roy Ministry also resorted to repressive measures. Every day it arrested a large number of peasants in different parts of the state and threw them into jail. Dozens of police camps were set up in strategic areas and murder, arson, loot and rape continued in the name of restoration of peace. Only a few leaders succeeded in remaining outside the prison. Day by day the peasants lost their militancy and morale and finally yielded in utter frustration.[7]

The failure of the Tebhaga movement was due to several factors. The landlords and moneylenders against whom the movement was directed had enough resources at their disposal which they utilised against the poor peasants who had neither money nor any modern arms and fought with simple spears, arrows and lathis. The Congress government itself patronized the landlords during the movement and its participation changed the character of the agitation; previously it was anti-landlord, but later it became purely anti-government. The resolution of the Loilgunge peasants to boycott the Congress Government was a proof of this. Not only that, the role of the Government in the movement caused so much indignation amongst the people that ever since they have been suspicious about its every action. However, it was the support of the ruling party which strengthened the hands of the landlords against the peasants.

The movement itself suffered from some internal weaknesses. In its earlier period many middle peasants joined the bargadars and khet majurs. The BPKS leaders who were well aware of the opportunism of such people thought otherwise. They decided to use the middle peasants and their resources against the jotedars and for the time being succeeded in doing so, because up to that time their only target of attack were the big landlords. But as the movement intensified and the bargadars raised many fresh demands including the requisition of 'Khas lands', the middle peasants sought to change their side. In the Parganas Chandra Patra, Gadadhar Singh, Nagendranath Jagulia and many other middle peasants joined the Congress and became good friends of the big landlords. The same thing happened in other areas. The strategy of the BPKS thus failed.

The peasants who participated in the movement were no doubt brave and good fighters but instead of resorting to guerilla tactics they followed the usual practice of face-to-face fighting and that was a big blunder. Their bravery and fighting skill proved fruitless before rifles and machine-guns.

Although in many cases the students co-operated with the peasants and shared their sufferings, no serious attempt was made to influence the working classes in the cities. In the Parganas, Khulna and some other districts were not very far away from the busy towns, an alliance between the two classes could have been easily formed. But the BPKS leaders did not avail themselves of that chance, and therefore instances of such co-operation are very rare. Had there been a good understanding between the workers and peasants the result of the movement would have been quite different.

In spite of these defects the Tebhaga movement opened a new horizon in the history of the peasant movement in Bengal. It revealed the real nature of the Congress Government and threw a challenge to all vested interests. Moreover during 1946-1947, when the entire Bengal was passing through a devastating communal riot, the humble Tebhaga agitators, both Hindus and Muslims, fought together and died for the same cause and thus proved that though they were at the lowest rung of the social ladder, they were much better than the 'educated beasts of the high society'.

V

The lessons of the countrywide Tebhaga movement proved fruitful. The tension and unrest among the peasant population heightened every day. They became more aggressive and assertive. So far as the Congress Government was concerned, the movement also influenced its policies. Even the over-zealous Congressites, who had so long believed in bullets and batons as good remedies for all problems, realized the futility of further repression. They deicded to hoodwink the people in a way which would not involve them in further trouble. Other Congressites, who were rather peace-loving but equally unscrupulous, expressed the same views. So in April 1953, the people of West Bengal came to learn that Dr B.C. Roy's Ministry had adopted a 'revolutionary resolution'. It would pass the Estate Acquisition Act and thereby abolish permanently the age-old zamindari system. The emotional Bengalis were quick to hail the Congress as a true lover of the peasantry, and the prestige of the Roy Ministry rose. The pro-Congress newspapers worked very hard during this period and it was mainly due to their propaganda that the people did not doubt the sincerity of the Government. They failed to see the inner truth of the resolution, that it was nothing but a farce, pre-arranged by the Government in collaboration with the landlords.

In reality it turned out to be so. The Congress, as has already been said, emerged as a party of the rich, controlled by the rich for the rich and therefore, apart from occasional loud-sounding resolutions, it could not go far. Dr Roy and his cabinet had no intention of losing the patronage of the big landowners and the latter also knew it well that the puppet Roy Ministry would never injure their interests. So when the Bill for Estate Acquisition was still under preparation, its contents did not remain secret to the zamindars or perhaps the Ministry itself informed them of what was going to happen. Within a short time illegal transfers of land properties shot up in every district. The zamindars and their revenue officers invented numerous techniques of illegal transfer False documents were prepared and lands were shown even in the names of distant relatives, servants and pets. In North Bengal, a zamindar kept several acres of land in the name of his favourite animal.[1] In the Parganas a khet majur made a very biting comment on such transfers. He said: 'Although my master has raped my wife and kept us in starvation, in his document I am now an owner of ten acres of land, good heavens!'[2]

Throughout these years, the Government intentionally remained silent and when the zamindars gave the all-clear signal, it started a mock fight against the wind. Thus by 1955, when the Estate Acquisition Act was actually put into operation, most of the landowners had succeeded in dispersing their land through fake transfers.

Although the Act fixed the ceiling of cultivable land and homesteads no limitation was placed on orchards, tanks and fisheries and this encourageed the landowners to evict unwanted bargadars. In every district evictions went on unabated. Knowing that the government would never react, the zamindars or jotedars forced their rack-rented bargadars or neighbouring small peasants to sign labour contracts or 'majur kabuliat'. Those who refused to yield to such pressures were either killed or driven out. In the Parganas, the Naskars, the Baghs, the Rays and other notorius jotedar families evicted many small peasants and bargadars and flooded thousands of acres of land with the saline water of the Vidyadhari and thus became owners of vast fisheries.[3] The peasants of the scheduled castes and tribes suffered most. According to the Tenancy Act of 1885 none could purchase their land without the consent of the district magistrate or subdivisional officer. But in both parts of the Parganas, the jotedars and rich peasants deprived them of their land in a very inhuman way.

In almost all cases those people, commonly known as the Adibasis, were offered liquor, drinking which they temporarily lost their mental balance and signed sale deeds of their land. In such documents they were always shown with the titles of higher castes. This ugly exploitation still continues in the Bongaon subdivision and there the peasant organizations of the CPI (M) and the CPI are trying to fight it out.[4]

Apart from evictions, the miseries of the landless peasants increased manifold. In October 1952, the Government imposed a levy on the peasants for collection of foodgrains. Outwardly there was nothing sinister in the proposal but when the actual operation began, almost all big jotedars and rich peasants hoarded their paddy and escaped the levy. Only the small peasants and poor bargadars were victimised by the collectors. Everywhere they were tortured by the police. The words, 'levy' and 'seize' created a stir in rural Bengal and the Congress became more unpopular. Thus eviction and levy or the landowners and their puppet Congress Government became the peasants' targets of attack. On July 17, 1952, the entire West Bengal observed a 24-hour hartal. Movements against eviction and hoarding continued. In the Parganas, skirmishes went on between the peasants and jotedars at Haroa, Sandeshkhali, Gosaba, Canning, Bhangar, Sonarpur, Mathurapur and other Sunderban areas. In some cases the jotedars were forced to surrender. For instance, Debi Roychoudhury of Gurguria,[5] who had so long oppressed his peasants, this time tried to appease them by throwing some concessions. The latter forced him to leave his estate. He then came to Calcutta and in utter frustration committed suicide.[6] As the situation was taking an awkward turn, the Government hurriedly passed an ordinance against evictions in June 1954. Next year it passed another Bill on land reform. In both cases the peasants were granted certain privileges but they were not given any guarantee against eviction and the declaration regarding sixty-forty division of the food-crops also proved to be a bluff, because the Government gave no assurance that during the harvesting season it would help the bargadars to get their legitimate share (60 per cent of the paddy). So the situation tended to deteriorate. In the Parganas the jotedars carried on evictions in a subtle way. They did not drive out the bargadars but forced them to enter into labour contracts whereby the latter would have no claim over crops and henceforth would work as ordinary day-labourers.[7]

One typical characteristic of the Congress Government was that its sense of duty was reawakened only on the eve of the general elections. The same thing happened in 1957. As the general elections neared, the number of 'promises' also increased. At a meeting Dr Roy, the Chief Minister, said: 'We the Congressites believe in socialism. But we do not want to hit the rich. We however expect that they will give up a major portion of their wealth in the interests of the poor. This is the eternal preaching of India'.[8] At Delhi, the then Congress President, Mr U.N. Dhebar, said: 'The Congress is serving the Indians with the devotion and sincerity of a devoted wife.'[9]

However, the devotion of the devoted wife disappeared after the elections, and she again turned into a prostitute.

In 1959, the Communist Party of West Bengal sent a memorandum to the President of India and warned him about the ill-fate of the Congress in the State. The memorandum also contained charges against some Ministers. It said: 'Among those who have resorted to benami transfers are Sri Hemchandra Naskar, Sri Ardhendu Naskar, Sri Hrishikesh Tripati, a near relation of the Cabinet Minister, Sri Ajoy Mukherjee, a near relation of Sri Jadabendra Panja, the President of the West Bengal PCC, Sri Khagen Das, Congress MLA and Srimati Ila Palchoudhury, Congress MP.'... 'They have effected fake transfers of thousands of acres of land in the names of their friends and relations.'[10]

From August onwards fresh trouble broke out all over the province. Upto September 2, at least 7,776 persons were imprisoned in different districts. On September 3, the city of Howrah was placed in the hands of the army and there 17 people died of bullet injuries. The people of Calcutta also experienced some ghastly incidents.[11]

As a result of Dr Roy's misrule the number of dependents on test relief increased from $1\frac{1}{2}$ lakhs to 5 lakhs and the deficit of food grains showed a sharp rise.[12] Nothing concrete was done for the common people. On the contrary they were left to suffer and starve. During the following years jotedars, hoarders, black-marketeers and other anti-social elements turned the State into a paradise of their own choice. Mr Prafulla Sen, who had meanwhile succeeded Dr B.C. Roy, pursued the same old policy of 'see and sleep'. As a result, fresh movements broke out in February, 1966. On February 16 about 2,000 students and peasants demonstrated at the Bashirhat court and demanded supply of food rations and kerosene. They also condemned police raids on hats and bazaars. The police chased the demonstrators and injured six by firing and causing the death of Nurul Islam. Within two days trouble spread over the entire Parganas. At Bongaon, Gobardanga, Chandpara, Naihati, Baduria and Garia, violent crowds consisting mostly of students and peasants clashed with the police, attacked the thanas and set fire to the 'black vans'. From March 5, the people of Nadia also started a similar movement. On that day a serious clash took place at Krishnagar and the local DM sent an SOS to Calcutta. As a result, the city was placed under the army. The Government arrested 30 opposition leaders, including Jyoti Basu, Somnath Lahiri and Jatin Chakravarty. On March 9 the people observed hartal in every district. On that day tension reached its climax. Fierce fighting between the police and people caused many deaths. In industrial areas, hundreds of factory workers joined the demonstrators and a large number of them sacrificed their lives.[13] The movement continued up to the middle of March. The Prime Minister, Mrs Indira Gandhi, instructed Mr Sen to appoint a high power commission to enquire into the causes of the 'disturbances'.[14]

The fourth general election was approaching. In order to influence the ignorant voters of rual areas, the Sen Ministry withdrew levy, cordoning and other restrictions on foodgrains. But the villagers did not benefit from the measures. The jotedars, rice mill owners, hoarders and blackmarketeers had lucrative business in paddy.

Naturally the food problem became more acute and the deficit in the government's collection increased.

The following table will make the point clear

Year	Month	Amount of collection (in tons)
1966	January	87,000
,,	February	1,76,000
1967	January	17,300
,,	February	25,100
,,	March	12,500[15]

In spite of their best efforts the Congress leaders failed to win the election and gave way to the United Front, a composition of different opposition parties, including the CPI (M), CPI, RSP, SUC, Bangla Congress, Forward Bloc etc.

References

I

1 *Dacca History of Bengal*, Vol. 1.
2 *Census Handbook*—Howrah (1961) (see the history portion).
3 *Bangla laukik Devata* by Gopendra Krishna Basu.
  Bengal District Gazetteers (24-Parganas, Khulna, Jessore) by L.S.S. O'Malley; *Pashim Banger Sanskrit* by Benoy Ghosh (In these books the religious side of the history of the Ghazis is described).
4 Clive's Letters to the Court of Directors.
5 Bengal District Gazetteer (24 Parganas), by L.S.S. O'Malley (See history portion)
6 Clive's Letters, *op. cit*
7 Papers of the 'Select Committee of the House of Commons on the affairs of the East India Company, Vol. 1, pp. cxi-cxii.
8 *The Calcutta Review*, 1858, vol. xxxi, pp. 384-411.
9 District Census Handbook (24 Parganas) 1951, appendix II p cxi, appendix IV, pp. cxlii-clix. *The Calcutta Review*, 1858, Vol. xxxi.
10 *Bharater Krishak Vidroha O Ganatantrik Sangram*, by Suprakash Roy, pp. 134-5.
11 *Ibid*, pp. 135.
12 *The Dynamics of a Rural Society* by Ramkrishna Mukherjee, p. 33.
13 *Ibid*.
14 Report of the Field Commission, 1879, Quoted in *Florence Nightingale's Indian Letters*, edited by Priya Ranjan Sen, p. xv.
15 'What does the Bengal Peasant want?' by a member of the Bengal Provincial Civil Service—Judicial Branch (1905), p. 46.
16 See note 8.
17 See notes 8 and 9.
18 *Ramtanu Lahiri O Tatkalin Banga Samaj*, by Shivnath Sastri, pp. 92-3.

18a Karl Marx, *(Capital)* — quoted in the Report of the Land Revenue Commission, Vol.—vi, p. 8.
19 *Some Social and Economic Aspects of the Land System of Bengal* by Nalini Ranjan Pal, p. 134.
20 *Nava Babu Bilas and Nava Bibi Bilas* by Bhabani Charan Banerjee.
Hutom Penchar Naksa by Kapliprasanna Sinha.
Nil Darpan etc. (Almost all books and journals of the day revealed the real story of the private life of the then wealthy section of society).
21 Interview: Late Kalidas Dutta, a pioneer in the study of local history of Bengal.

II

1 Bharater Krishak—Vidroha O Ganatantrik Sangram by Suprakash Roy—pp. 112-5
2 See note 1, pp. 91-4.
3 *Joshar, Khulnar Itihas* by Satish Chandra Mitra, Vol. 2, pp. 697-9.
4 Bengal District Gazetteers by L.S.S. O'Malley (Khulna), pp. 43-4.
5 See note 3, pp. 697-9.
6 *Ibid.*
7 See note 1, pp. 98-9.
8 *Ibid*, p. 86.
9 *Ibid.* p. 87.
10 See note 3, p. 761.
11 *Mazilpur Patrika*, March 1865.
12 See note 1, pp. 24-5.
13 *Nil Vidroha* by Promod Sengupta.
14 See note 3, pp. 769-71.
15 *Ibid*, p. 771.
16 See note 1, p. 250.
17 See note 13, p. 45.
18 *Ibid.*
19 *Ibid.*
20 See note 1, p. 255.
21 'A speech delivered at Midnapore by a Native'—printed from the *Patriot Press*, Bhowanipore, 1856—p. 9.
22 Mr Forde's statement quoted in Nil Darpan by Dinabandhu Mitra p. vi.
23 See note 1, pp. 256-60
24 *Ibid*, p. 260.
25 *The Indian Musalmans* by W.W. Hunter, p. 37.
26 See note 1, pp. 280-81.
27 Letter of Rev. C. Bornwetsch, *Indian Field*, January 1860.
28 Reports of the Indigo Commission (1860), p. 5. in *Ichhamati* by Bighutibusan Banerjee.
29 Bengal under the Lieutenant Governors by C.E. Buckland, Vol. 1, pp. 67-8.
30 See note 1, pp. 378-9.
31 *Ibid*, pp. 204-15.

III

1 They have different names in different districts.
2 'What does the Bengal Peasant want?' by a member of the Bengal Provincial Civil Service, Judicial Branch 1905, p. 46.
3 Report of the Land Revenue Commission, Bengal, Vol. 1, pp. 30-43.

PEASANTS OF THE PARGANAS 669

4 *Ibid*, Vol. VI, p. 49, Banglar Chashi by Santipriya Basu, p. 30.
5 Report of the Bengal Banking Enquiry Commitee (1929) quoted from *The Problem of Agricultural Indebtedness* by N.R. Sarkar, pp. 8-9; and also Report of the Land Revenue Commission, Vol. VI, p. 52.
6 See note 3.
7 *Ibid*, p. 30.
8 Oral evidence of the 24-Parganas Bar Association, Report of the Land Revenue Commission, Vol. VI, p. 311.
9 *The Statesman*, 26-1-1929.
10 See note 3, pp. 33-9.
   Krishak Sabhar Itihas by Md Abdullah Rasul, pp. 71, 99 and also *Statistical Account of Bengal* by W.W. Hunter, Vol. 1, pp. 162-3, Vol. 3, p. 368, Vol. 2, p. 278, Vol. 8, p. 81, Vol. 6, p. 319.
11 *Krishak Sabhar Itihas*, op. cit. p. 84.
12 Interview: Kshudiram Bhattacharya (CPI-M).
13 Interview: the late Mr Kalidas Dutta of Jainagar-Mazilpur.
14 'The So-called Renaissance', quoted from *Now*, Vol. 4, Nos. 3-5, 6-10-1967, p. 57.
15 See note 12, pp. 52-62.
16 *Ibid*, p. 153.
17 See note 13.
18 *Ibid*.
19 *Ibid*.
20 Interview: Muzaffar Ahmed (CPI-M).
21 *Ibid*, and also *Kakdwip, Sonarpur Bhangarer Sangramer Itihas* by Suprakash Roy, pp. 1-6.
22 Interview: Yaqub Pailan (SUC).
23 'Memorandum of the BPKS', *Report of the Land Revenue Commission*, Vol. VI, p. 39.
24 *Rural Bengal Ruins* by Bhawani Sen, p. 18.
25 *Ibid*.
26 *Ibid*.
27 *Ibid*.
28 See note 21.

IV

1 *Krishak Sabhar Itihas* by Abdullah Rasul, p. 112.
2 *Ibid*., pp. 156-8.
   Gram Banglar Pathe Pathe by Satyen Sen—1965, Muktadhara Publications, Dacca, pp. 3-14.
   Mukti Yuddhe Adibasi by Pramatha Gupta, pp. 35-6.
3 See note (1), pp. 155-6.
4 *Kakdwip, Sonarpur Bhangarer Krishaker Sangram* by Suprakash Roy, pp. 27-32.
5 See note (1), p. 177.
6 See note 4, pp. 18-41.
7 Interviews: Kshudiram Bhattacharya (CPM) and some villagers of Sandeshkhali.

V

1 Interview: Muzaffar Ahmed (CPI-M).
2 Interview: Villagers of Dattapukur (24-Parganas).

3 Interviews: Kshudiram Battacharya (CPI-M), Hemanta Ghosal (CPI-M), Sibdas Bhattacharya (CPI-M), Yaqub Pailan (SUC), Deshhitaishi, July 11, 1969.
4 Interview: Ajit Ganguly and Gobinda Dev (CPI).
5 See Part 3 of this series, Frontier, January 3.
6 Interview: Yaqub Pailan (SUC).
7 Krishak Sabhar Itihas by Md. Abdulla Rasul, p. 192.
8 Jugantar, February 11, 1957.
9 *Ibid.*, February 18, 1957.
10 Memorandum of the Communist Party of India, 1959, p. 78.
11 *Jugantar*, September 2-4, 1959.
12 *Ibid*, August 25, 1959.
13 *Dainik Basumati*, February 16 to March 15, 1966.
14 *The Statesman*, March 9, 11, 12, 1966.
15 *Paschimbanger Gramin Arthaniti* by Ranen Nag, p. 13.

35 Peasants and Revolution

Hamza Alavi

In colonial countries the peasants alone are revolutionary, for they have nothing to lose and everything to gain. The starving peasant, outside the class system, is the first among the exploited to discover that only violence pays. For him there is no compromise, no possible coming to terms.

—Frantz Fanon[1]

THE ABOVE VIEW of the revolutionary potentiality of the peasantry was expressed by Frantz Fanon, ideologue of the Algerian revolution. From time to time, throughout the centuries, the peasant has indeed risen in rebellion against his oppressors. But history is also replete with examples of peasants who have borne silently, and for long periods, extremes of exploitation and oppression. At the same time occasional outbreaks of peasant revolt do raise the question of the conditions in which the peasant becomes revolutionary.

We cannot speak of the peasantry in this context as a homogeneous and undifferentiated mass. Its different sections have different aims and social perspectives, for each of them is confronted with a different set of problems. The constellation of peasant forces that participate in a revolutionary movement depends upon the character of the revolution, or, as Marxists would see it, the 'historical stage' which it represents. Thus, when a revolutionary movement progresses from 'bourgeois-democratic revolution' to 'socialist revolution,' the roles of the different sections of the peasantry no longer remain the same.

As a generalization about the revolutionary potential of the peasantry, Fanon's statement thus begs many questions. Equally question-begging are those generalizations which dismiss the peasantry as a backward, servile, and reactionary class, incapable of joining hands with forces of social revolution. The peasants

Reproduced from *Imperialism and Revolution in South Asia*, *(ed)* Kathleen Gough and Hari P. Sharma, Monthly Review Press, New York, pp. 291-337.
An earlier version of this article appeared in *The Socialist Register 1965*, Monthly Review Press.

have in fact played a role, sometimes a crucial and decisive role, in revolutions. The Chinese Revolution is a case in point.

The question that needs to be asked, therefore, is not whether the peasants are or are not revolutionary but, rather, under what circumstances they become revolutionary or what roles different sections of the peasantry play in revolutionary situations. These are questions which greatly interest socialist movements in countries with predominantly peasant populations. The main tradition of Marxist theory, until the turn of the century, took its stand firmly on the dominant, or even exclusive, revolutionary role of the industrial proletariat. But Marx and Engels were painfully aware of the fact that if the industrial proletariat was to fulfill its historic tasks by leading the forces of revolution, it would have to mobilize peasant support, especially in countries with predominantly peasant populations. For socialists, moreover, the question is not merely that of mobilizing peasant support as a *means* to achieve success in their struggle. The question is not just that of *utilizing* the forces of the peasantry. The free and active participation of the peasantry in transforming their mode of existence and giving shape to the new society must be an essential part of the socialist goal itself.

We propose in this essay to consider the roles played by different sections of the peasantry in the cases of Russia, China, and India. We shall examine the preconditions that seem necessary to bring about a revolutionary mobilization of the peasantry in the struggle for socialism, whether it be peaceful and constitutional or insurrectionary. We shall put forward hypotheses which, in our view, throw fresh light on certain aspects of the problem. These hypotheses require further consideration, especially in the light of the experiences of other countries.[2] We would like to emphasize at the outset that these propositions are being advanced tentatively and in order to open up a discussion on certain aspects of the problem that have so far been obscured.

Our hypotheses concern the respective roles of the so-called *middle peasants* and *poor peasants* and the preconditions that we find are necessary for a revolutionary mobilization of *poor peasants*. These terms have been defined in Marxist literature to refer to various classes of the peasantry. But they are fraught with ambiguity and, as we shall see later, they have sometimes been reinterpreted to alter their denotation to suit ideological exigencies of political tactics or the personal predilections of particular writers.[3] For a meaningful and scientific discussion of the subject, it is essential that the terminology used should be unambiguous. I have continued to use the above-mentioned terminology only because it is in common use. But, before we proceed further, the precise meaning of these terms should be clarified. This terminology appears to focus attention on relative differences in the wealth (or poverty) of various strata of the peasantry without any indication of the criteria by which the strata may be distinguished from each other as classes. Stratification on the basis of simple difference in wealth, on a single linear scale, is often the basis of differentiation of 'classes' in academic sociology. But that is not the basis on which Marxists distinguish classes. The Marxist concept of class is a structural concept; classes are defined by relations of production. Where several modes of production coexist, classes cannot be arranged in a single linear hierarchical order because they must be structurally differentiated. The division of the peasantry into *rich peasants*, *middle peasants*, and *poor peasants* suggests an array of the peasantry with the different strata arranged one over the other, in a single order. This is misleading: middle peasants (i.e., independent peasant proprietors), for instance, do not stand *between* rich peasants and their employees, the poor peasants; they belong to a different sector of the rural economy.

In the transitional historical situations we shall deal with, a broad distinction may be made between three 'sectors' of the rural economy, or three modes of production. In the first place, we have the sector whose essential distinguishing feature is that the land is owned by landlords who do not undertake cultivation on their own account. Their land is cultivated by landless tenants, mostly sharecroppers who are classed as *poor peasants*. The second sector is that of independent smalholders who own no more land than they cultivate themselves and enough of it to make them self-sufficient. They do not exploit the labor of others; nor is their labor exploited by others. They are the *middle peasants*. A special case of middle peasants was that of the allotment-holding peasants in Russia who were obliged to work for landlords because of various disabilities imposed upon them, as discussed below. A third sector is that of capitalist farmers, also described as rich farmers, who own substantial amounts of land and whose farming is primarily based on the exploitation of wage labor, although they may participate in farm work themselves. Unlike landlords, they undertake the business of farming and employ capital in it.

Farm laborers who are paid wages are referred to as the agricultural proletariat, but they are usually included with that other exploited section of the peasantry—the sharecroppers—in the term *poor peasant*. The use of the terminology makes it quite clear that the essential distinctions are those of relations of production and not simply those of relative differences in wealth or property. This is exemplified by the inclusion in the term *middle peasant* of an independent smallholder whose income may be very small but who does not work for others; whereas a sharecropper with a large holding, who may earn more than he does, is classified as a *poor peasant*. The terminology is clearly unsatisfactory. It would avoid a great deal of unnecessary confusion if we were instead to adopt structurally descriptive terms, such as *capitalist farmers*, *independent smallholders*, *sharecroppers*, and *farm laborers*. But in the statements and writings that we must discuss in this essay, the terms *rich peasants*, *middle peasants*, and *poor peasants* are widely used and for that reason we cannot avoid using them ourselves.

While using that terminology, we would like to emphasize the critical distinction between the class situation of the independent peasant smallholders, the *middle peasants*, on the one hand, and the exploiting and exploited sections of the rural population, namely, the *landlords* and capitalist farmers or *rich peasants*, and their sharecroppers and laborers, the *poor peasants*, on the other. The sector of *middle peasants* is characterized by their *economic independence* (from landlords and rich peasants), whereas in the other two sectors —sharecropping and capitalist farming—the mode of production is characterized by the exploitation of the poor peasants and their *economic dependence* on their masters. This distinction between the economic dependence and subordination of the *poor peasants* and the economic independence of the *middle peasants* is critical for our analysis.

We should qualify this threefold classification of the different sectors of the agrarian economy (or the different modes of production) by pointing out that there is a great deal of overlapping between these categories and the actual demarcation between them is by no means sharp and clear. In practice it is often the case that a person may enter into more than one relation of production. Ownership of his own patch of land does not by itself suffice to classify a peasant as a *middle peasant* if he also works as a sharecropper or a laborer to supplement his livelihood. The difficulty in classification is met (by Mao, for example) by attempting to determine the *principal* relation of production from which a person draws his livelihood. Thus a peasant who owns a tiny patch of land, but depends for his livelihood mainly on sharecropping for a landlord or on working as a laborer, is classed as a *poor peasant*, he is not classed as a *middle peasant* even though he owns some land. Again, a *middle peasant* who employs casual labor occasionally to cope with peak operations is classified as a middle peasant, for his livelihood does not depend principally on the exploitation of the labor of others. A similar problem arises in the case of a landlord who employs sharecroppers on part of his land and undertakes cultivation on his own account on another part of his land, say, by mechanized farming and wage labor. He engages in two modes of production at once. Lenin described such situations as 'transitional.' In Pakistan and India one finds that the two modes of production are not separate and simply coexistent; the two are structurally integrated because landlords who engage in mechanized farming retain sharecroppers on diminished holdings, insufficient for their livelihood, in order to have a tied source of the seasonal labor they require in the mechanized farm sector. The two modes of production are thus structurally integrated.[4] But we do not propose to pursue the question of transition from the one mode of production to the other. The relation that is essential to the analysis which follows is that of the economic exploitation and dependence of the poor peasantry, and this exists in either case. The crucial distinction we wish to reiterate is that of the economic independence of the middle peasant and the economic dependence of the poor peasant. We propose to examine their respective roles in the Russian and Chinese revolutions and in the peasant movements in India.

I

The peasants were given a definite place in the Bolshevik revolutionary strategy under Lenin's slogan of 'Alliance of the Working Class and the Peasantry.' However, the role of the peasantry in the

Russian Revolution is sometimes exaggerated out of all proportion. Thus, Lichtheim writes: 'The uniqueness of Lenin—and the Bolshevik organization which he founded and held together—lay in the decision to make the agrarian upheaval do the work of the proletarian revolution.'[5] Neither the facts of the Russian Revolution nor Lenin's theoretical formulations support such a judgement. It was in the towns and the cities that the Bolsheviks first seized power, for the class struggle in the countryside had not yet developed.[6] That was the conclusion Lenin reached after the October Revolution. His attitude toward the peasantry evolved continuously, in response to the developments taking place in the Russian countryside. From the point of view of the role assigned to the peasantry in Bolshevik revolutionary strategy, one can broadly distinguish three periods, in each of which we find a distinct theoretical stand. The first period was that up to the 1905 Revolution, although we can see the change in Lenin's views already beginning to take place after the peasant upsurge of 1902. The second period was between 1905 and 1917. The third period, one of reassessment, was after the October Revolution.

The central feature determining the perspective of the first period was Lenin's view of the dynamic growth of agrarian capitalism in Russia and the decay of the feudal economy. As early as 1893, young Lenin had begun to see the new economic developments in peasant life, which became the subject of the earliest of his writings to be preserved. In 1899 he published his first major work, *The Development of Capitalism in Russia*, two-thirds of which is devoted to a brilliant and thoroughly documented analysis of the capitalist revolution in the Russian countryside, the decay of the feudal economy, and the complex variety of transitional forms that had emerged. Without going into details of the rural economy of Russia at the turn of the century, we must, for our purposes, point out some of its salient features.[7]

A crucial factor that inflamed the Russian countryside, in 1905-7 and again in 1917, was the peculiar problem, a legacy of the emancipation of 1861, of the allotment landholder, the Russian middle peasant. By the edict of emancipation the serf had received as 'allotment' the land he had cultivated before, but with a portion of it withheld by the landlord; such withheld portions were called 'cutoff lands.' For Russia as a whole the proportion of 'cutoff' land is estimated to have been about a fifth of the peasants' original holdings. The crucial fact, however, about the 'cutoff lands' was not their relative size but the type of land that was taken away from the peasant and its role in the peasant economy. The peasant was deprived of meadows and pastures, water courses, and access to woods—all essential to the peasant economy. Moreover, the peasant was required to pay for the allotment land. He could do so by giving labor to the landlord or he could opt to make money payments, which considerably exceeded the rental value of the allotment lands. He could terminate his 'temporary obligation' by making a 'redemption payment,' which again was in excess of the market value of the land; moreover, he had to borrow to make such a payment. The need to work off these obligations to the landlord, together with such surviving feudal laws and institutions as the commune, tied the peasant to the village and his land, and forced him to work for his landlord on unfavorable terms. This relationship between the middle peasant and landlord, a source of deep and direct conflict, was a feature peculiar to Russia.

Much of the landlords' land was, however, cultivated by sharecroppers—poor peasants—who had little or no land but who possessed some farm implements and horses. A distinction between the situation of such poor peasants and that of the middle peasants, as described above, is important. The middle peasant had a substantial allotment as well as access to communal grazing and woodland. His livelihood did not depend totally on the landlord, but his obligations to the landlord were an insufferable burden. In the case of the poor peasant, the sharecropper, his livelihood depended on his being able to get the land from the landlord for cultivation. Although he was exploited, he was too dependent on the landlord to be able to oppose him as the middle peasant could.

Some landlords' lands were cultivated by hired farm laborers—already a transition to capitalist farming. But it was the industrious kulaks, the rural bourgeoisie, who conducted farming as a business and employed the rural proletariat as wage labor. In the growth of agrarian capitalism in Russia, Lenin saw a powerful force for the bourgeois-democratic revolution which would open the door for the socialist revolution.[8] Plekhanov, and even more so some of the extreme Mensheviks, had looked exclusively to the growth of industrial capitalism for the maturation of the forces of revolution. This offered socialists the rather dismal prospect of an interminably long interlude of capitalist development before Russia could be ripe for the socialist revolution. The Mensheviks looked upon the peasantry as a conservative and reactionary force. Seen against the background of such ideas, the Narodnik view—that the peasant commune provided Russia with a unique opportunity for a direct transition to a socialist order—was not altogether without its attractions; even Marx and Engels were not altogether without sympathy for it.[9] Lenin rejected this idea as utopian. He saw the commune as a survival of the old feudal order which was to be swept away. The middle peasant, the mainstay of the commune, was disintegrating as a class. With the inexorable advance of capitalism, the middle peasant was being pauperized and the peasantry as a whole was being polarized into two classes, capitalist farmers and the rural proletariat. The immediate task, in Lenin's view, was to assist and speed up this process by fighting for the removal of those survivals of feudalism which tended to slow down the advance of agrarian capitalism.

Lenin thus looked to the classes in the capitalist sector of the agrarian economy, rather than to the disintegrating class of middle peasants, to provide the forces for the struggle against feudal survival and the completion of the bourgeois-democratic revolution. However, in 1901 he tended to discount even the rural laborer as an effective revolutionary force. In his *Iskra* article of April 1901, which set out the agrarian program of the Iskra-ists, he wrote: 'Our rural laborers are still too closely connected with the peasantry, they are still too heavily burdened with the misfortunes of the peasantry generally, to enable the movement of rural workers to assume national significance either now or in the immediate future.'[10] Thus, he argued, 'The whole essence of our agrarian program is that the rural proletariat must fight together with the rich peasantry for the abolition of the remnants of serfdom, for the cutoff lands.'[11] It was for the industrial proletariat to provide revolutionary leadership, while in the agrarian field it was the rural bourgeoisie who would provide the main force for the bourgeois-democratic revolution.

The central issue of the agrarian program was the demand for the restitution of the cutoff lands and the abolition of the remnants of serfdom. But Lenin overestimated the role of the rural bourgeoisie in this struggle and curiously ignored the role of the middle peasant, who was most directly concerned with it. The challenge of the kulak to the feudal system was economic—it lay in his greater efficiency, his ability to pay higher wages to the farm laborers, and his competitive strength in bidding for land available for buying or leasing. But he was outside the feudal sector and was not directly involved in conflict with the landowners. Although he resented being accorded an inferior social status by the nobility, this was not cause enough for him to engage in battle.

When the great peasant upheaval began in 1905, it was the middle peasant who provided its main force in the fight for cutoff lands. In February, soon after Bloody Sunday, January 9, 1905, the peasants rose in revolt. Peasant *jacqueries* flared up all over Russia and continued to inflame the countryside in 1905 and for two succeeding years, long after the revolution in the towns had been extinguished. The respective roles of the different sections of the peasantry in this revolutionary upsurge are described by G.T. Robinson:

'Such revolutionary leanings as existed in rural Russia had chiefly come out of the relations of small, land-short, farmers with large land-holders rather than the relations of proletarians and "half-proletarian" laborers with capitalist cultivators.... Sometimes the better-off peasants joined with the rest in depredations upon the estates, and particularly in the cutting and carting-off of timber and in the illicit pasturing of cattle. However, there were at least a few cases in which the attacks of the peasants were directed against the richer members of their own class rather than against the landlords; and no doubt because of a fear of loss to themselves, the richer peasants...were often indifferent or openly hostile to the agrarian movement.... On the other hand the agricultural wage workers who had no land...were not usually the leaders of the agrarian movement in general or even of the labor strikes on the estates.... Indeed there developed in certain instances a definite hostility between the agricultural proletariat and those peasants who divided their time between the landlords' fields and their own.'[12]

The kulak's role in the peasant uprising was ambivalent. He did not lead the attack on the landlords for the restitution of cutoff lands, for that was a matter which concerned the middle peasants. Indeed, as Robinson has pointed out, he was himself sometimes the target of attack and was often indifferent or openly hostile to the peasant uprising. On the other hand, he often found the tide too strong not to go along with it, and he participated in the attacks on landlords' manors and the looting that followed.

Until 1905 the Bolsheviks had looked upon the rural bourgeoisie, the kulaks, to provide the forces for the bourgeois-democratic revolution in the countryside. They had not paid much attention to organizing the broad mass of the peasantry themselves. In the *Iskra* article he had written in 1901, Lenin had virtually written off the rural proletariat as a force which was 'still wholly in the future.' He added that 'we must include peasant demands in our program, not in order to transfer convinced Social-democrats from the towns to the countryside, not in order to chain them to the village, but to guide the activity of those forces which *cannot* find an outlet anywhere except in the rural localities....'[13] After the peasant upsurge of 1902, however, Lenin's outlook changed. He wrote: 'The purely practical requirements of the movement have of late lent special urgency to the task of propaganda and agitation in the countryside.' The basic strategy of the bourgeois-democratic revolution still was that 'the rural proletariat must fight *together with* the rich peasantry for the abolition of the remnants of serfdom.' Only the completion of the bourgeois-democratic revolution would lead to the 'final separation of the rural proletariat from the landholding peasantry.'[14]

By 1905 the bourgeois-democratic revolution was still far from being completed. But with the peasant uprisings of that year, the Bolshevik attitude changed fundamentally. Writing in March 1905, Lenin issued a call to organize the rural proletariat in the same manner as the urban proletariat had been organized. He added: 'We must explain to it that its interests are antagonistic to those of the bourgeois peasantry; we must call upon it to fight for the socialist revolution.'[15] Lenin subsequently repeatedly exhorted the Bolsheviks to organize the poor peasantry, but they had little success in doing so.

The basic unit of peasant organization was the traditional village assembly. Ordinarily, rich peasants—the kulaks—controlled collective decisions made by the assemblies. In revolutionary situations, in times of violent action, however, it was the middle peasants whose militant views prevailed in the assemblies; the poor peasant remained in the background. The peasants' organization at the national level was the All-Russian Peasants' Union, which was also largely under kulak influence. At its first congress in the summer of 1905, 'the delegates themselves indicated that in most places the work of organizing the peasants had hardly begun as yet.'[16] The political leadership of the peasantry was in the hands of the Social Revolutionaries, who primarily represented the rich peasants. The Bolsheviks never quite managed to get a firm foothold among the peasantry.

By 1917 we find Lenin more cautious and less certain about the possibility of organizing the poor peasantry independently. In his historic 'April Thesis' he stated:

> Without necessarily splitting the Soviets of Peasants' Deputies at once, the party of the proletariat must make clear the necessity of organizing separate Soviets of Poor (semi-proletarian) Peasants, or, at least, of holding constant separate conferences of peasant deputies *of this class status* in the shape of separate fractions or parties within the general Soviets of Peasants' Deputies.

He was, however, by no means confident that this task would be accomplished; in the 'April Thesis' he continues:

> At the present moment we cannot say for certain whether a powerful agrarian revolution will develop in the Russian countryside in the near future. We cannot say exactly how profound is the class cleavage within the peasantry.... Such questions will be, and can be, decided only by actual experience.[17]

The pattern of peasant upheaval which did develop in 1917 is rather complex. There were two sets of struggles—between peasants and landlords and among the peasants themselves—where the alignments cut across each other. The main peasant struggle in 1917, as in 1905-7, was that of middle peasants against landowners for the cutoff lands and for the abolition of the surviving feudal restrictions. The intervening years had been relatively quiet. Now, once more, peasant struggle was precipitated by the decay of agriculture, the depletion of stocks and food shortages, and the high prices of goods. This time the struggle was more intense and violent than in the earlier period; in some respects, but only occasionally, it was more advanced in character.

A factor which possibly contributed to the greater militancy of the middle peasant in the second period was the fact that Stolypin's agrarian policy, in the intervening years, had loosened many of the feudal bonds which had tied down the middle peasant, thus giving him the taste of more freedom. Also, Bolshevik ideas had had a big impact on the soldier, the peasant in uniform, who participated with the industrial worker in making the socialist revolution. Deserters returning to the countryside from the front carried with them the ferment of new ideas and an attitude of militancy.

Now, as before, the struggle was concentrated on the meadows and forests; the most frequent forms of action consisted of seizures of hay and wood, More manors were looted and burned than before. An advance on the previous situation, however, was that in some cases village land committees (set up by the provisional government to mediate disputes between peasants and landlords) became vehicles for the seizure and distrubution of land. Maynard suggests that 'there was, paradoxically, a certain system, even a certain order, in the proceedings. Peasants did not seize the land which had not been cultivated by them or their forebears.'[18] It is more likely that in actual practice the proceedings were not quite so orderly as Maynard imagines; there was little to stop the peasants from taking an optimistic view of their claims, except the competing claims of their fellows. However, the fact that the peasant, even in revolution, invoked only his claim to what was rightfully his, refleets his conservative respect for private property and the fact that, in the main, the seizures of land were confined to the cutoff lands. Once again the middle peasant was in the forefront of the struggle. The attitude of the kulak remained, as before, a contradictory one: fear and even hostility combined with not-too-reluctant participation in sharing the loot. The rural proletarians similarly joined with the others in the looting, but did not emerge as an independent force and did not rise against their masters, the kulaks.

There was another, quite distinct, struggle in the rural districts, in which the middle peasant found himself mostly in conflict with the other two sections of the peasantry. This was the struggle of those who wished to preserve the communes against the 'separators.'

During the inter-revolutionary years legislation had been promulgated providing for the dissolution of repartitional tenure in communes and for the establishment of hereditary holdings, which would make possible the establishment of individual farms free from communal restrictions. The pressure to break up the communes came from the enterprising 'communal kulaks' (the other kulaks held their land outside the communes) who wished to be free from communal restrictions. It also came from the poor peasants whose tiny holdings served only to tie them to the village but gave them no livelihood. The middle peasant, however, had little to gain and much to lose by a breakdown of the commune. He staunchly opposed the 'separators,' and passions ran high. The middle peasants often resisted successfully the attempts to 'separate,' and in many cases peasants who had left were forced to return and pool their land again. Thus in these cases the middle peasants were once again the effective force in the village.

These divisions and conflicts among the peasantry evidently did not allow the formation of 'revolutionary peasant committees,' as Lenin had urged. The peasant Soviets, where they existed at all, existed at the county and provincial level and were mostly dominated by right-wing Social Revolutionaries, the spokesmen of the kulaks. The role of the peasantry in the revolution was an indirect one, though by no means an unimportant one. The Bolshevik formula was that they seized power in alliance with the peasantry as a whole. If the role of the peasantry must be called an 'alliance,' it was, from the side of the peasantry, undeclared, unorganized, and without a clear direction. Moreover, it could hardly be called an alliance with 'the peasantry as a whole,' for the peasantry was deeply divided. In a later controversy Stalin argued that the proletarian revolution was carried out by the proletariat 'together with the poor peasantry.' He supports this by quoting Lenin's repeated post-1905 calls for mobilizing the poor peasantry. As we have seen, this does not mean that the Bolsheviks actually succeeded in achieving that objective. Lenin's own postrevolutionary assessments make it quite clear that this was not so.

In October 1918, looking back on the experience of the Revolution, Lenin explained the Bolshevik failure to mobilize the poor peasants:

Owing to the immaturity, the backwardness, the ignorance,

precisely of the poor peasants, the leadership [in the Soviets] passed into the hands of the kulaks.... A year after the proletarian revolution in the capitals, and under its influence and with its assistance, the proletarian revolution began in the remote rural districts.[19]

But why did the Bolsheviks fail to break down the backwardness and ignorance of the peasantry, despite at least a decade of commitment to just that task? Lenin perceived that the true explanation lay beyond the subjective factor. He became aware of the existence of what we have referred to as the necessary preconditions for the mobilization of the poor peasantry—although he expressed it in a form which refers only to the Russian experience. Thus, in 1920, he referred to such preconditions as:

a truth which has been fully proved by Marxist theory and fully corroborated by the experience of the proletarian revolution in Russia, viz. although all the three above enumerated categories of the rural population (i.e. the rural proletariat, semi-proletarians and small peasants)... are economically, socially and culturally interested in the victory of socialism, they are capable of giving resolute support to the revolutionary proletariat only *after* the latter has won political power, only *after* it has resolutely dealt with the big landowners and capitalists, only *after* these downtrodden people see in practice that they have an organized leader and champion, strong and firm enough to assist and lead them and show them the right path.[20]

Lenin was generalizing here from the Russian experience; he was not elaborating a Marxist text. The Chinese experience, as well as examples from India, show us, however, that the prior seizure of state power by the proletariat is only one of several alternative forms in which the necessary preconditions for the mobilization of the poor peasantry may be realized.

II

The Chinese Communist Party set out on its revolutionary course in the Leninist tradition. But in the first few years of its life its work was concentrated largely on the urban proletariat and on students and intellectuals; very little was done among the peasantry. Jane Degras quotes a report of the Executive Committee of the Comintern according to which, in 1926, the working class membership of the

CCP was 66 percent of the total and peasant membership no more than 5 percent.[21]

It was also among the industrial proletariat that Mao Tse-tung began his work, to use his own words, as a 'practical Marxist.' As secretary of the Hunan party he organized miners, railway workers, municipal workers, etc. He did very little work among the peasantry at the time, and it was not until 1925 that he became aware of their revolutionary potential. 'Formerly,' he told Edgar Snow, 'I had not fully realized the degree of class struggle among the peasantry. But after the May 30 (1925) incident, and during the great wave of political activity which followed it, the Hunanese peasantry became very militant. I... began a rural organization campaign,'[22] A new chapter had opened in the history of Chinese communism.

Peasant riots and uprisings were endemic in China at the time. Several factors had precipitated such a situation. Perhaps the most important was the constant civil war among warlords and the excessive taxes and levies extracted by them as well as by government tax collectors. Another factor of some importance was that in those 'troubled times' many of the old 'gentry' had moved to urban centers and were no longer present in the village to exercise their direct personal authority, which they had enjoyed by virtue of their wealth as well as traditional social status. The removal of the men who had exercised on-the-spot power loosened social control in the villages, enabled the peasants to gain more confidence, and allowed peasant militancy to develop. However, perhaps the most decisive factor lay in the operations of the Revolutionary Army, which had been established in 1923 by the Kuomintang government of Dr Sun Yat-sen, with the support of the Chinese Communists and with help from the Soviet Union. In February 1925 the Revolutionary Army launched its First Eastern Expedition, the first of several against the warlords. This was followed by the Southern Expedition and, in the summer of 1926, by the famous Northern Expedition. It is significant that on the eve of the Northern Expedition nearly two-thirds of the nearly one million members of the peasant associations were in Kwangtung province,[23] one of the principal areas of operation of the Revolutionary Army during the Eastern and Southern expeditions.

The peasant movement was not created by the Communist Party or by the genius of one man. Mao was drawn into the peasant movement only after it had already begun. But Mao's organizing genius enabled it to reach new heights. In 1925 he began to train cadres for the peasant movement at the Institute of the Peasant Movement. At the end of the year he took his students to Hunan, established contacts with active elements among the peasantry, and set up peasant associations in the townships. A solid foundation was laid to provide leadership and organization for the peasant movement so that when it arose again in the following year, it arose with full force.

Mao summed up his experience of the peasant movement in two essays that are regarded as classics of Maoism. The first was an article entitled 'An Analysis of the Various Classes of the Chinese Peasantry and Their Attitudes Toward Revolution,'[24] published in January 1926. The other was the celebrated 'Report of an Investigation into the Peasant Movement in Hunan,' written a year later. Stuart Schram has pointed out what at first sight appears to be a rather curious 'deviation' from the Marxist-Leninist orthodoxy in the original versions of these two texts. In the original versions the leading revolutionary role of the industrial proletariat is not specifically mentioned; appropriate references to that effect were not added until 1951. Does this mean that at this stage Mao had abandoned the basic principle of Marxism-Leninism, the principle of proletarian revolutionary leadership? In his analysis of Maoism, Isaac Deutscher has referred to the fact that 'Mao...recognized more and more explicitly the peasantry as the sole *active* force of the revolution, until to all intents and purposes he turned his back on the urban working class.'[25] But this, as Deutscher has shown, came later. It came after the defeat of the revolution when, following the autumn-harvest uprising of 1927, Mao and his comrades, with the core of what later became the Red Army, marched to the Chingkang Mountains and established a revolutionary base there. At first, as Deutscher has argued, the 'withdrawal into the countryside' was thought to be only a temporary strategy, a marking of time until conditions for an urban insurrection revived. It was only 'gradually [that Mao] became aware of the implications of his move.' In 1926, thus, the point of departure of Maoism had not yet arrived. And it came two years later, not as a premeditated change of strategy but as one that was imposed by the logic of the situation.

To return to Schram's point, what explanation can we find of Mao's omission, in 1926 and 1927, of references to the leadership of the proletariat? Schram's explanation is that 'Mao's position at this time constitutes neither orthodox Leninism nor a heresy *beyond* Leninism, but rather the gropings of a young man who has not yet thoroughly understood Lenin.' He continues: The Hunan Report is neither "orthodox" nor "heretical" Leninism; it is essentially a-marxist.'[26] Such a contention is quite untenable. It was his understanding of Marxism that led Mao, son of a peasant, to spend his early years of revolutionary work among the urban proletariat. Moreover, the issue of proletarian leadership in the revolution was a central issue in the CCP at the time. One cannot presume that the question was simply not in Mao's mind. However, two facts may suggest an explanation. First, if Mao had brought up the issue of the leadership of the revolution, he could hardly have avoided a frontal attack on the view then being put forward by the Comintern; evidently, young Mao did not wish to take that course. Second, the two documents were written in the heat of a controversy in which Mao wanted to establish 'the agrarian revolution as constituting the main content of the Chinese bourgeois-democratic revolution and the peasants as its basic force.'[27] He did no more in these documents than portray the revolutionary potentialities of the different sections of the peasantry. He did not engage in a theoretical analysis of overall revolutionary strategy. Moreover, it should be added that there is nothing in these documents to compare with the careful and detailed analysis Lenin made of the processes which were transforming Russian rural society. Mao learned his lessons in the field; the essence of his thought must be sought in his revolutionary practice rather than in writings which do not always reflect accurately his own practice in so far as he had to pay lip service to Comintern orthodoxy in order to gain the freedom to follow the demands of the Chinese situation. Mao the 'theoretical Marxist' had a role which did not always coincide with that of Mao the 'practical Marxist.'

The paradox of Mao is exemplified particularly by his attempt to make the facts of the Hunan Movement fit Comintern orthodoxy by the simple device of redefining categories, as we shall see below. In his Report Mao was at pains to demonstrate that both leadership and the main force of the peasant movement came from the poor peasantry, which, in theory at least, made the facts of the Hunan Movement fit Stalin's conception of what was to be expected. But to appreciate the true character of the Hunan Movement, we must briefly consider the pattern of China's rural society and the main problems of the peasantry.

Capitalist farming had not yet developed in China, as it had in Russia. According to figures given by Mao, the size of the agricultural proletariat in China was less than 2 percent of the total number of peasants.[78] There were thus two main sectors of the rural economy. One was dominated by landlords, who controlled a large proportion of the land (Mao says 60-70 percent) that was cultivated by the poor peasants, i.e., sharecroppers, who had no land or very little land. Big landlords, those who owned more than 500 *mou* (i.e., 83 acres), were less than 0.1 percent of the rural population. Small landlords made up 0.6 percent of the rural population. The 'semi-proletariat,' who worked for them, consisted, according to Mao's classification of (1) semi-landholders (16 percent), who owned too little land for their subsistence; (2) sharecroppers (19 percent), who owned no land but owned the implements, etc., with which they worked the landlords' lands; and (3) the poor peasants (19 percent), who owned neither land nor implements. The other sector was that of the independent peasant landholders, i.e., the middle peasants (38 percent), whom Mao further classifies into three subclasses: (1) those with an annual surplus (3.7 percent of the total peasantry); (2) those who were just self-sufficient (19 percent); and (3) those who had an annual deficit (15 percent).

Three problems dominated the Chinese countryside. The first was that of putting an end to the exploitation of the landlords, or at least of easing its burden by reducing the share of the crop taken by them. Then there was the problem of rectifying the very uneven distribution of land among cultivators, providing secondary employment in order to relieve pressure of population on land, and improving the level of technique so that all cultivators could enjoy a reasonable livelihood. The solution to that problem would have to await the socialist revolution. Finally there was an immediate problem, one that in fact gave rise to the peasant movement and determined its character: the problem of the excessive demands made by warlords and tax officials on the peasantry. The aftermath of Yuan Shih-kai's unsuccessful attempt to restore the monarchy in 1916, the revolt of the generals which had thwarted it, and the constant imperialist intervention and intrigue resulted in a collapse of governmental authority. The warlords became a power in the countryside and began to dominate it. Before that time, prudence had restrained the landlords and the government from raising their demands on the peasantry beyond the limits of endurance, but there were no limits on the warlords. Everyone in the village was affected by their excessive demands, except for those big landlords who were in league with them.

Despite the continued extortions of the warlords, no major peasant movement arose to resist them until the various expeditions smashed the power of the warlords and their allies in the villages and the peasant uprisings began. The aims of the peasant movement that arose in 1926 went little beyond putting an end to the extortions by the warlords and their local allies. 'The peasants attack as their main targets the local bullies, bad gentry and lawless landlords, hitting in passing against patriarchal ideologies and institutions, corrupt officials in the cities and evil customs in the rural areas.'[29] In those words Mao gave the gist of the achievements of the Hunan Movement of 1926-7, which he describes in some detail in his Report.

Of all the actions of the peasantry described by Mao in his Report, the weakest are dealt with under the heading of 'Dealing Economic Blows Against Landlords.' The central issue here, as we pointed out, was that of reducing, or indeed abolishing, the landlords' rent. Mao claims that the peasants' associations succeeded in preventing *an increase* in rent! Surely, in a revolutionary situation, there should have been no question of the landlords even thinking of increasing the rents further. Mao then adds that *after November* the peasants went a step further and began to agitate for a reduction in rent. But this was after the autumn harvest and the year's rent had already been collected. At that late stage, even if a demand for rent reduction was voiced by a few peasant organizers, it had no immediate practical value. The fact that the peasants' associations had not yet begun to challenge the fundamental class positions of the landlords is also indicated by Mao's reference to the fact that many landlords were trying to join the peasants' associations! Again, there is a suggestion made by Mao in his original essay,

'Analysis of the Various Classes of the Chinese Peasantry,' that some of the small landowners could be 'led toward the path of revolution.'[30] What kind of 'revolution' could that be? It is clear that the movement aimed at little more than smashing the power of the warlords and their local allies, whose victims included, of course, the smaller landlords.

Landlords preserved not only their economic positions but also their armed forces. One of the achievements Mao claimed for the peasant movement in his Report is the 'overthrowing of the landlords' armed forces.' But what we actually find under this head is a tacit admission that, by and large, the landlords' militias continued to exist. What is said here is only that their armed forces had largely 'capitulated' to the peasant associations and were 'now upholding the interests of the peasants'! It is only with respect to 'a small number of reactionary landlords' that the Report says that such forces would be taken over from them and 'reorganized into the house-to-house regular militia and placed under the new organs of local self-government under the political power of the peasantry.' It is evident that the continued existence of the armed power of the landlords, as well as their hold over the sections of the peasantry directly dependent on them economically—the sharecroppers, etc.—prevented the peasant movement from becoming a peasant revolution and brought about its subsequent collapse.

In the Hunan Report, Mao emphasizes repeatedly that both the leadership and the main force of the movement came from the poor peasantry. If the poor peasants had in fact provided both the leadership and the main force of the movement, it is inconceivable that such demands as the reduction and the abolition of rent would not have come to the forefront of the struggle. After all, that would not have antagonized the middle peasantry; indeed, it would have found support among them. And the landlords were only 0.7 percent of the rural population: in fact, it was their economic power and their hold over the poor peasantry which gave them power in the countryside. The demands put forward in the peasants' movement were those which affected the middle peasants far more than the poor peasants. The landlords, while exploiting the tenants to the limit, adopted a paternal attitude toward them and even afforded them some protection against extortions by such third parties as warlords and tax men. On the other hand, the independent smallholders, the middle peasants, stood exposed and weak, and were the principal victims of the warlords and tax men. More than the poor peasants, the middle peasants could squeeze out a surplus of income, and this marked them as the more likely victims of extortion.

In fact, when Mao uses the term 'poor peasant' in the Hunan Report, he redefines it in such a way as to include some middle peasants. The original eleven categories of the rural population, as described in his January 1926 article, were, in the Hunan Report compressed into three categories. In doing so, he included under the term "poor peasants" not only the peasantry directly exploited by the landlords, but also a section of the independent smallholders, the middle peasants. He says in the Hunan Report that the poor peasants were about 70 percent of the peasantry. This figure could be arrived at only by totalling the following categories, as described by Mao earlier: (a) farm laborers, 2 percent; (b) poor peasants, 19 percent; (c) sharecroppers, 19 percent; (d) semi-landholders, 16 percent; and (e) the poorer section of the independent peasant small-holders, 15 percent. But only the first three categories can be properly called poor peasants. The category of semi-landholders is an intermediate category, for their landholdings were too small for an independent livelihood and they had to depend on other sources to supplement their income. Peasants in the last category are middle peasants and not poor peasants.

Mao's redefinition of the term 'poor peasants' is only implicit in his altered statistics; he does not describe his new categories in any detail. But by including a section of the middle peasants under the label of poor peasants, he gave at least a formal validity to his statement that the leadership and the main force of the movement came from the poor peasants. This only confused the issue. It is a spurious confirmation of his earlier prediction that peasants were the most revolutionary, and is understandable only if we consider the fact that such a characterization of the movement made inacceptable in terms of Comintern (Stalinist) orthodoxy, which called for an alliance of the proletariat and the poor peasantry. The Report was written in the heat of party controversy, and evidently Mao was more preoccupied with the task of swinging party opinion on the subject than with formal niceties. Unfortunately, the supposed militancy and the leadership said to have been shown by the poor peasantry in the Hunan Movement have been made into a myth which glosses over the actual practice of the Chinese Communists and, indeed, Mao's own many statements in later years which contradict it. If anything is to be learned from the Chinese Revolution, we must turn away from this myth.

The poor peasantry were mobilized only after a new phase of the Chinese Revolution opened with the establishment of a new base in the Chingkang mountains, after the successful counter revolution led by Chiang Kai-shek in 1927 forced the Communists to take refuge there. Under the umbrella of Red power, albeit in a very small area, the peasant revolution went a step forward. In the light of his new experience Mao came to the conclusion that 'positive action is taken in the village against the intermediate class (i.e., small landowners) only at a time of real revolutionary upsurge, when, for instance, political power has been seized in one or several countries, *the reactionary army has been defeated a number of times, and the prowess of the Red Army has been repeatedly demonstrated.*'[31] Echoes of Lenin, 1920!

The creation of the Red Army was a decisive factor in the new situation. The Red Army did not, however, arise spontaneously out of the peasant movement, although its intimate relationship with the peasantry gave it its special character. The nucleus of the Red Army came from sections of the Kuomintang Revolutionary Army that had come over to the Communist side after the counter-revolution. Thus relatively well-trained, experienced, politically educated fighting units provided an essential core. One might contrast their situation with that of the armed forces of the Telangana Communists in India who were suppressed, after some brave fighting no doubt, by the Indian forces (who took three years to do it though). The Chinese Red Army was able to fight back against the far greater forces deployed against them.

Another factor which made possible the creation and the building up of the Red Army in China was that armed conflict had been endemic in China for at least a decade. In most villages there were armed units, although they were controlled by the landlords. Their importance and character are indicated by Martin C. Yang, a social anthropologist, in his description of a prerevolutionary village in Shantung province: 'The first village-wide organisation [was] the village defence programme ... Wealthy families [were] expected to equip themselves with rifles ... etc .... The very poor [were] asked for nothing except that they behave themselves and obey the defence regulations.'[32] Although the village self-defense units were controlled by landlords, they had accustomed the peasants to the idea of arming themselves. Many of the village militias could also be taken out of the power of the landlords and absorbed in the Red Army. Moreover, the Red Army fitted easily into the rural setup. The people were accustomed to bear the burden of maintaining armies, and the burden of the Red Army fell lightly on their shoulders. It created conditions for the emancipation of the peasantry from extreme exploitation, and it drew its tribute from the exploiters rather than the exploited.

Finally, a factor of no mean importance was the collapse of central authority, which could not act immediately and swiftly to destroy the nucleus of the Red Army. When the blows finally came, backed with all the might and the resources of imperialism, the Red Army not only survived but was eventually victorious largely because of the existence of mass movements and the active support of the people. The actions of the proletariat in areas under Chiang Kai-shek, actions that impeded and sometimes disorganized his machinery of repression, were also no doubt of great value.

From the nucleus of the red base in the Chingkang Mountains the revolution developed. With all its vicissitudes, it extended and deepened until it had transformed the whole of China. The progress of the revolution and the precise content of the agrarian changes at its different stages is a long and complex story that we can hardly attempt to survey in these pages.[33] But one crucial aspect needs to be noted: land reform was implemented by peasant committees and not by a Communist bureaucracy. Thus the implementation of the land reform varied at different times and at different places; it reflected the unevenness in the growth of revolutionary consciousness and in the organization of the peasantry in different areas of the country, as well as changes in the overall strategy of the Communist Party that were determined by a number of factors, one of which was the rate at which the revolutionary movement was going forward. But more than the changing scope of the land reform at different stages, what interests us particularly is the actual process by which it was carried out.

The success of Mao and the Chinese Communists in bringing about a revolutionary mobilization of the peasantry lay in their subtle dialectical understanding of the respective roles of the middle peasants and the poor peasants. The task confronting them was to raise the level of revolutionary consciousness of the poor peasantry, a task that called for skill as well as much devoted effort. This was necessary precisely because the poor peasants were initially the more backward section but were, at the same time, potentially the more revolutionary section of the peasantry. On the other hand, Mao and his comrades had to take full account of the fact that it was the middle peasant who was initially the more militant and his energies had to be mobilized fully in carrying forward the intial thrust of the agrarian revolution. Precisely because the middle peasants were not a revolutionary class, the revolutionary initiative had to be maintained independently of them by the revolutionary leadership, while fully utilizing their energies, and without antagonizing them. This initiative was then to be carried forward to a second stage of the agrarian revolution by the newly aroused poor peasants. Mao and his comrades showed, in practice, a masterly understanding of this dialectic. Yet in some of Mao's formal texts it seems to be missing altogether. The poor peasant is depicted as spontaneously and unconditionally playing a revolutionary role, a picture that obscures the crucial role of the Communist Party as a party with a proletarian revolutionary perspective, and of the Red Army which broke the existing structure of power in the village and prevented the Chinese revolution from degenerating into an ineffective peasant uprising.

It was during the period 1950-3, with the consolidation of Communist rule, that a major wave of land reform set in motion a new dynamic in the rural society of China and transformed the face of the countryside. Embodying the lessons learned in the struggle, on the eve of this final phase the Agrarian Reform Law and related regulations were promulgated; these were explained in a report made by Liu Shao-chi.[34] While correctly emphasizing the need to mobilize the poor peasants, we see here a concern that the party cadres should appreciate the role of the middle peasants, especially at an early stage of the proceedings. The importance that was attached to the middle peasant was made even more clear in the speech of Teng Tse-hui, Director of Rural Work of the CCP, at the Eighth Congress of the CCP in 1956. He said:

> If we had confined our attention to relying on the poor peasants and neglected to unite with the middle peasants, if we had not

firmly protected the interests of the middle peasants during the land reform ... or, if we had not made efforts to draw the representative figures among the middle peasants into the leadership of the peasants' associations and cooperatives, *then our Party as well as the poor peasants would have been isolated* ...[35]

A mere recognition of the role of the middle peasants, drawing them initially into the leadership of the peasants' associations and fulfilling some of their immediate demands, might not in itself have enabled the agrarian movement to develop further and enter the next stage, the stage of proletarian revolution. The success of Chinese agrarian policy lay precisely in following a dialectical strategy, ensuring at each stage that conditions were created for a further advance to the next stage.

The actual process by which this was achieved is described very vividly in two studies by social anthropologists, whose findings corroborate each other and are in turn corroborated by the general conclusions drawn by Teng Tse-hui in his above-quoted speech. One of the two studies is by David and Isabel Crook, pro-Communist Anglo-Saxons who work in China. The other is by an anti-Communist Chinese, C.K. Yang, who works in the United States.[36] Yang gives a picture of a village newly liberated by the Red Army. 'Their first task was to "set the masses in motion" in order to develop a situation of "class struggle," the basic step being to select 'active elements' amongst the peasants to serve as a core for the organization of the peasants' association and the new "people's militia".' Yang shows that middle peasants were initially selected to head the peasants' association and the militia 'primarily because they had been active in village affairs.' He argues, however, that 'the selection of these [middle peasants] to lead the vital new peasants' association primarily on the basis of their active part in village affairs appeared to deviate from the official Communist policy of using only elements from the poor peasants and agricultural laborers as the core of the new village leadership.'[37] This is precisely where Yang betrays his lack of understanding of Communist policy. It would have been all too easy for local party officials to nominate individual poor peasants to these posts and to issue directives in their name. But that would not have brought into being a vigorous peasant movement in which the poor peasants *as a class* could play an active role. Precisely for this reason, the regional and local authorities in China were under orders not to carry out land distribution by force or by mere orders, but only in accordance with the decisions of the peasants in each village and in conformity with local conditions. After peasant associations were established, initially under middle peasant leadership, Communist Party cadres encouraged poor peasants to press their demands, both through their representatives on the peasant associations as well as collectively through demonstrations, such as one described by Yang, when 'noisy angry peasants appeared at the door' of the middle peasant head of the association with their demands. It was by means of this process that the level of consciousness of the poor peasants was raised to a point where they could take the initiative in local government. Otherwise the peasants' associations might have degenerated into merely an extension of the bureaucratic apparatus.

This sequence reveals a crucial underlying condition. The energies of the poor peasants were released only after the landlords and the rich peasants were isolated (which happened as a result of the coming of the Red Army and the Communist leadership) and finally eliminated as a class as a result of land reform. Only then was a new stage in the local struggle opened up; only then did the poor peasant leadership acquire a new perspective and a new confidence and begin to come forward to displace the middle peasants. This process is the vital process which transformed the agrarian upheaval in China into a proletarian revolution. It would not have grown as it did from its agrarian base but for the crucial role played by the Red Army and the Chinese Communist Party in releasing the revolutionary energies of the peasantry. Unfortunately, the mythology about the revolutionary leadership the poor peasant is supposed to have shown right from the beginning obscures this most important feature of the Chinese Revolution, one made possible by its special conditions.

In India, to which we turn next, we find that even those peasant uprisings in which, for a variety of reasons, the poor peasant had played an important part could not develop into a proletarian revolution.

III

The situation in India at the turn of the century was different from that of China. In India, inter-imperialist rivalry had long ended with the supremacy of the British. No warlords or private armies roamed the Indian countryside. The rising nationalist movement, with its modest constitutional aims, did not seek to arm itself as Sun Yatsen's Kuomintang had done. Until the 1920s the nationalist movement stood isolated from the potent forces of the peasantry, although there had been much peasant unrest and occasional uprisings. Nor was there that crucial contact between the Indian nationalists and the Soviet Union which played such an important role in China, although the Russian Revolution had had a big intellectual impact on the minds of many young nationalists such as Nehru.

The radicalization of the nationalist movement in India just before and especially after World War I increasingly began to draw the masses into the movement. Gandhi, above all, who emulated the simple life of the peasants, spoke their language, and engaged in symbolic activities which captivated their imagination, played a vital role in mobilizing peasant support for the Indian National Congress. But if he made the peasant speak for the Congress, he did little to make the Congress speak for the peasant. When in 1921, during the first Civil Disobedience Movement, the peasant began to extend the struggle against British imperialism to a struggle against the landlord and the moneylender, Gandhi invoked the principle of nonviolence to call an abrupt halt to the movement. He was not prepared to do more than to back, at certain times, a call to the peasantry to refuse to pay taxes, a slogan which evaded the issue of class exploitation in the village but was strong enough to rouse the peasantry. But his most powerful appeal to the peasantry was through the millennial concept of 'Ram Rajya' (God's Kingdom), which would be established in India after the expulsion of the British.

Gandhi's accent on the peasantry in his political language did, however, lead many middle class intellectuals to 'go to the people,' very much in the spirit of Russian populism. The effect of this is described by Nehru:

> He sent us to the villages and the countryside hummed with the activity of innumerable messengers of a new gospel of action. The peasant was shaken up and he began to emerge from his quiescent shell. The effect on us was different, but equally far reaching, for we saw for the first time, as it were, the villager ... We learnt.[38]

The growth of an urban working class movement, the new involvement with the peasantry, the ferment of new ideas—especially the impact of the Russian Revolution—and the disillusionment with the Congress after Gandhi's decision to halt the Civil Disobedience Movements of 1921 and of 1930, each time precisely when the movement was gathering momentum, caused many middle class intellectuals to shift leftward in their outlook. In 1934 the Congress Socialist Party was constituted within the parent organization. Several streams of ideas had influenced the young Socialists, but in its early stages the influence of Marxist thinking was strong. Although the Socialists had begun to take an interest in the problems of the peasantry, they concentrated on fighting within the Congress for recognition of peasant demands rather than on mobilizing the peasants themselves to fight for their demands. Isolated peasant struggles did, however, develop from their local roots, and some assumed major importance. But little progress had yet been made to build up a class organization of the peasantry.

The Communist Party of India (a unified Communist Party bagan to take shape only in the thirties) had, in the twenties, concentrated mainly on organizing the industrial working class. The peasant upheavals of the 1920s did not produce a fresh orientation, as in China. During the Civil Disobedience Movement of the thirties, when it could have developed peasant struggles, the Communist Party found itself crippled and isolated both because its main leadership was in prison, following the Meerut conspiracy case, and because the Comintern line at the time did not permit its participation in a movement led by the Indian bourgeoisie. Thus the Communist Party did very little work among the peasantry precisely at a time of ferment because of the economic crisis of the thirties and the impact of the Civil Disobedience Movement throughout the country.

In 1936 the Congress Socialist Party decided to admit Communists to membership. The coming together of the Left forces was the background to the setting up in 1936 of the All-India Kisan Congress, later renamed the All-Indian Kisan Sabha (Peasant Congress). Two other groups of peasant leadership also joined (and later contended along with the Socialists and the Communists in the AIKS). These two groups, along with the Socialists, spoke for the rich peasant and the middle peasant and eschewed struggle for the special demands of the poor peasants. Thus Professor Ranga, one of their leaders, spoke of a 'common front to be put up by both the landed and landless *kisans*' and of the 'common suffering of all classes of the rural public.'[39] The Socialist Acharya Narendra Deva made this even more explicit in his presidential address to the AIKS Conference in 1938:

> Our task today is to carry the whole peasantry with us .... If romantic conceptions were to shape our resolves and prompt our actions, we would aspire to organise first the agricultural laborer and the semi-proletariat of the villages, the most oppressed and exploited rural class ... but if we do so ... the peasant in the mass would, in that case, remain aloof from the anti-imperialist struggle.[40]

If, for the Socialists in the 1930s, the postponement of the struggle for the poor peasants was a matter of political expediency because of the primacy, as they understood it, of the anti-imperialist struggle, after independence the ideologues of Indian socialism abandoned the struggle for the poor peasant altogether. Thus Ashoka Mehta, who was Chairman of the Praja Socialist Party (heir to the Congress Socialist Party) and its most influential ideologue, wrote:

> Should the Socialists, as the Communists are wont to do wherever they are in power, foment class conflict in villages even after landlordism is removed and use the wide array of tactics developed from Lenin to Mao Tse-tung to use one section against the other? ... If that is the line chosen, democratic rights and socialist values cannot survive. Then must come the whole complex of communist paraphernalia: people's courts, liquidation of kulaks, forced levies and the attendant violence. The other alternative is to help the village to recover its community solidarity and foster autonomy of the village community .... The organic needs of village community cannot be met by sharpening class conflicts or party rivalries.[41]

Such an outlook acquiesces in and perpetuates the exploitation of the poor peasant by the rich peasant.

The Communists, on the other hand, did speak of setting up a a separate organization of agricultural laborers, and in the Kisan Sabha they put a special emphasis on the organization of the poor peasantry. But in practice several factors stood in their way. First, after the mid-1930s they were guided by the 'popular front' line of the Comintern and were not inclined to force the issue with their colleagues in the AIKS. Secondly, Indian Communists took an essentially 'Menshevik' view of the revolutionary perspective in India. In the 'Joint Statement' of eighteen Communist leaders issued at the time of the Meerut trial, an important statement of Communist policy, it was argued that because of an insufficiently developed industrial base, an indefinite period would elapse between a 'bourgeois-democratic revolution,' which was the immediate objective, and an eventual 'socialist revolution' in India. In effect this meant that the task of organizing the rural proletariat and the poor peasants did not have any special urgency. Finally, the Communists, like the others, had to face the fact that the poor peasants, desperately exploited and literally starving, were nevertheless too strongly dominated by their masters to be able to emerge, in the political context of the time, as an independent force.

Thus the main direction of Communist practice was similar to that of the Socialists and their other colleagues in the Kisan Sabha. They concentrated on agitation for broad peasant demands, especially for security of tenure, debt relief, and cheaper credit facilities, etc., and sought to influence government policy rather than to bring about direct peasant action. This tradition largely continues to this day. But the Communists did lead many local struggles, some of which assumed proportions of major uprisings. We shall examine very briefly two major peasant uprisings, particularly with a view to throwing light on the respective roles of middle peasants and poor peasants.

The two major peasant uprisings occurred toward the end of World War II and the early postwar years, with the Communist Party providing the leadership in both. Apparently, they were both movements of poor peasants and therefore could be cited as examples that contradict the thesis advanced in this essay about the role of middle peasants. However, a closer examination of the two movements shows the crucial role played by middle peasants in each case, both in providing their initial thrust and in their eventual collapse. We must point out, however, that the published material available on these movements at the moment of writing is rather limited and insufficient for an adequate historical account. But their salient features are clear enough to provide a basis for an interpretative essay such as this.

The first of these two movements was the Tebhaga movement, which arose in North Bengal, including the districts of Dinajpur and Rangpur in East Bengal and Jalpaiguri and Maldah in India; it was concentrated mainly in the region which became East Pakistan. The slogan of the movement was the demand for reduction of the proprietors' share of the crop from one-half to one-third. The 'proprietors' of the land, the *jotedars*, were 'occupancy tenants' who possessed transferable and heritable rights to the land, and paid a fixed money-rent to the *zamindars*, the great landlords. Over the years, the fixed money-rent had become a relatively small part of the value of the crop so that, in course of time, the *jotedars* appropriated the largest share of the crop which they extracted from the cultivators of the land, the sharecroppers. The latter were called *adhiars* or *bargadars*; the number of landless in Bengal has been variously estimated at between a fifth and a quarter of the rural population. But the Tebhaga movement enveloped the bulk of the peasantry in the areas in which it arose. The vast majority of the Bengali peasantry consists of small peasant proprietors with tiny holdings, many of whom supplement their incomes by share-cropping. The bulk of them are under a heavy burden of debt, the lenders generally being the rich *jotedars*; and any analysis of class conflict in the Bengal countryside must especially take into account the effects of usury on the situation of the middle peasants. The situation of most of them is precarious, for they live from hand to mouth and a crop failure or the death of a farm animal may easily overwhelm them. *Jotedars* are only too eager to seize their lands when they are unable to meet their liabilities. As Bhowani Sen, a Communist theoretician and leader of the Tebhaga movement, expressed it: 'The middle peasant of today is the share-cropper of tomorrow.' And the peasant is painfully aware of this prospect. The situation of the middle peasant in Bengal is far more precarious than in many other regions. He was, therefore, only too willing to throw in his lot with the sharecroppers in the struggle against *jotedars*.

In fact, the movement did not begin as a movement of share-croppers: initially it was a movement of middle peasants in their own behalf, and later drew in the sharecroppers. According to Bhowani Sen, the origins of the peasant unrest which eventually led to the Tebhaga movement can be traced back to 1939. The first movement began in Dinajpur district and it was not about sharing the crop. It arose on the issue of the illegal imposts levied by the *jotedars* and their manipulation of produce markets to the detriment of the small peasants. According to Bhowani Sen:

> In this movement the *jotedar's* share of fifty-fifty was not challenged. Only illegal exactions were challenged; and by their successful struggle they put an end to them. A big victory. That happened in 1939, against the background of the War and a spontaneous rumor that the Government was going to collapse, which gave confidence to the peasants. Prices had also begun to rise. The movement was very big but did not develop further; it subsided after winning some concessions. Things were then quiet until 1943.[42]

In 1943, 3.5 million peasants perished in the great Bengal famine. Bhowani Sen points out that because the rich *jotedars* were also the principal hoarders of food grains, hatred against them was intense and universal. He writes how he was struck by the contrast between the acquiescence and resignation of the starving peasantry during the famine, when millions died without a struggle, and the later militancy of the same peasantry during the Tebhaga movement. But he does not attempt to analyze the reasons for that difference, merely ending with the comment that "the intolerable condition of the *adhiars* (sharecroppers) awakened them to a new sense of solidarity."[43] Their condition could not have been more intolerable than in 1943 during the famine, but the Tebhaga movement started later. According to the CP it did not start (officially) until 1946, although in fact the movement had been gathering momentum since 1945.[44] Local Communist and Kisan Sabha cadres participated in these early actions; but the Communist Party did not put its full weight into the movement until the end of the war with Japan. When they did so in 1946, the movement went forward with overwhelming force.

Although the great famine found the peasantry unprepared and unable to rise up against profiteers and food hoarders, and much food had already vanished into the cities or military stocks, many of the unique features of subsequent years which helped the rise of the Tebhaga movement arose as a consequence of the famine. First, the weak peasant organizations were disrupted and disorganized by the overwhelming calamity of the famine. The Bengal peasant, used to semi-starvation, was helpless in the face of the disaster and evidently proved too weak to fight back. When the Kisan Sabha units recovered from the initial blow, they were quickly drawn into famine relief work. It was only in the following years that a new determination gave impetus to their organization. Secondly, large numbers of students and people from the educated middle classes were drawn into the voluntary relief work during the famine and into large-scale medical relief in the following year. This brought about a new contact between the peasantry and educated youth, provided social education for both, and was a very important factor in creating new cadres for the Communist Party and the Kisan Sabha. Third, a factor of vital importance, was that, following the famine, the Kisan Sabha renewed its drive against hoarders and black marketeers of food with fresh vigor. Now its hands were stronger inasmuch as the authorities also began to view the activities of the hoarders with a fresh concern because of the magnitude of the famine as well as the fact that in the spring and summer of 1944 the Japanese had invaded Assam and parts of East Bengal. The *jotedar*, who had the food to hoard and sell on the black market, could no longer count on the connivance of the authorities. The power of the *jotedar* was thus seen by the peasant to crumble in the face of the Kisan Sabha leadership, which gave the peasant a new confidence in that leadership and in the possibility of fighting back against the *jotedars*. An additional factor was that some tribal people, such as the Hajangs of North Mymensingh, who have a long tradition of militant struggle, participated in the movement. A further significant factor was that there developed a change in the bargaining power of sharecroppers. During the famine more sharecroppers had died than peasants of any other class, because they had the least reserves with which to get through the famine. Apart from the millions who died, large numbers had drifted to towns and cities in search of work and food and did not come back. The reduction in their numbers created a relative shortage of labor. The invasion of Assam and parts of East Bengal by the Japanese and the consequent large-scale military operations in the region also opened up alternative avenues of employment for sharecroppers. Their bargaining position vis-a-vis the *jotedars* was strengthened.

In the end, however, it was the role of middle peasants that was crucial, according to the account given by Bhowani Sen. The movement had begun in Thakurgaon subdivision of Dinajpur district as a middle peasant movement against the oppression of *jotedars*. During the 1939-40 movement, these middle peasants had been politicized and the CP had recruited many of them. The intervening years had forged them into an effective political cadre. The sons of middle peasants had little difficulty in persuading their people that their fight against the *jotedars* could succeed only if they rallied the entire rural poor. They espoused the cause of sharecroppers, which was also their own cause, for many of them supplemented their incomes by sharecropping. According to Bhowani Sen, most leading members of Tebhaga committees were middle peasants and not poor peasants, but all participated in the movement. It was difficult, he said, to hold meetings of cadres because 'everyone turned up. Meetings were held in somebody's house and everyone in the village came to know, with the result that every meeting tended to become a mass meeting.'

The crucial battles of the Tebhaga movement were fought at harvest time, when the crop was shared out. But the fight did not always end then because the sharecroppers had to resist attempts by *jotedars*, with the support of the police, to deprive them of their gains. This continuing struggle was led by peasant committees, which became a power in the villages. They legitimized their authority in the name of a 'new Raj.' As Bhowani Sen put it;

> Peasants are not happy about doing anything illegal. When they were told that *a new authority* existed, namely that of the *Kisan Sabha*, they came to the *Kisan Sabha* and applied for a Red Flag to be given to them so that they too could proclaim the authority of the *Kisan Sabha* in their village and enforce the demands of the Tebhaga movement. They even 'arrested' police parties in the name of the Kisan Sabha. They understood that there was now a new Raj and no longer the old one.[45]

The peasant committees began to administer the affairs of the village and to administer justice. The Muslim League government of Bengal, with the connivance and support of the Congress, tried to repress the movement and eventually succeeded. On the other hand, the League was also compelled to make the gesture of introducing a bill in the Provincial Legislature in January 1947 to legalize the two-thirds share for the sharecroppers. The bill did not become law; the *jotedars*, through both the Congress and the Muslim League, fought back.

By the summer of 1947 the movement collapsed. Bhowani Sen called to the peasants not to launch direct action that year, pleading that after independence the new governments of India and Pakistan were to be given an opportunity to fulfil their pledges to the people. It was clear to all that those promises would not be fulfiled. Bhowani Sen's call merely formalized the fact that the Tebhaga movement, which he described as 'one of the biggest mass movements of our time,' had come to an end.

In his article, Bhowani Sen, with much candor and political courage, lists the 'Main Failings of the Leadership' in the movement. In his self-criticism he argues that the failure of the movement was due to its inability to win the support of the 'middle class' and the working class. Working class 'support' could have been little more than a gesture of solidarity, for its practical contribution under the circumstances of the time could not have amounted to much. His remarks about antagonizing the 'middle class' are significant, for both in the beginnings of the movement, as well as in its ultimate collapse, the role of the middle peasants proved to be crucial.

Concerning the role of middle peasants, Bhowani Sen wrote:
> Many of them are poor and petty *jotedars* who, while they recognise that the system is bad, feel that they would be done for if the system is liquidated without at the same time opening other avenues for their employment ... We should have advised the *adhiars* (sharecroppers) to exempt petty *jotedars* from the operation of Tebhaga and concentrated against the richest and the biggest.[46]

As it stands, this argument is somewhat unrealistic. What Sen says about the plight-of the small *jotedar* is only too true. But if the movement had been strong enough to force the biggest *jotedars* to accept a one-third share of the crop, it would have been very difficult indeed to dissuade the sharecroppers who tilled the lands of small *jotedars* from demanding the same. However, Bhowani Sen's argument does point to the narrow base of the movement; it failed to generate slogans that could have sustained the active participation of middle peasants who had not been unsympathetic to the movement insofar as it had challenged the power of the landlords and rich peasants.

Two major changes in the situation also made it no longer possible for the Tebhaga movement to continue. First, with the end of the war with Japan, the authorities were no longer interested in supporting the anti-hoarding drives which had weakened and demoralized the *jotedars*. The full force of the government's machinery of repression was turned on the peasantry; and the movement, with its limited class base in the village, was not able to fight back effectively. Second, a deciding factor in the situation was that whereas the peasantry in the area in which the Tebhaga movement arose, both *jotedars* as well as sharecroppers, were mostly Muslim, the cadres of the Communist Party and of the Tebhaga movement were mostly Hindu. With the approach of independence, the full force of Muslim nationalism was sweeping through Bengal, as through other areas with a Muslim majority in India. This tended to isolate the Hindu cadres. With the establishment of Pakistan, most of the Hindu cadres went over to India and the movement was virtually decapitated.

The other great peasant uprising in India since the war was the Telangana movement. In character and political objectives, it was the most revolutionary peasant movement that has yet arisen in India. The movement began rather modestly in 1946 in the Nalgonda district of Hyderabad state, which was ruled by the Nizam under British suzerainty. The movement then spread to the Warrangal and Bidar districts of the state. The Hyderabad state was dominated by a backward, oppressive, and ruthless aristocracy. The initial modest aims of the Telangana movement reflected the broad demands of the whole of the peasantry against illegal and excessive exactions of the feudal lords, the Deshmukhs and the Nawabs. One of the most powerful slogans of the movement was the demand that all peasant debts be written off.

The repression let loose by the feudal lords and their government was met by armed resistance by the peasantry. The movement then entered a new revolutionary stage. Local Communists had participated in it vigorously, although it did not receive the official sanction of the Communist leadership until later. By the time of the Second Congress of the CPI in March 1948, the Telangana movement had already entered its revolutionary phase and was one of the factors that influenced the leftward swing in the Communist Party line at the Congress.

By 1947, the Telangana movement had a guerrilla army of about 5,000. The peasants killed or drove out the landlords and the local bureaucrats, and seized and redistributed the land. They established a government of peasant 'Soviets' which were regionally integrated into a central organization. Peasant rule was established in an area of 15,000 square miles with a population of four million. The movement of the armed peasantry continued until 1950; it was not finally crushed until the following year. Today the area remains one of the political strongholds of the Communist Party.

There are several special factors in the Telangana situation which at the time favored the rise of a militant peasant movement and its subsequent transformation into a revolutionary movement. The political situation in Telangana in 1946 provided the right political climate for such a movement. With the independence of India in sight, the future of the Hyderabad state and its place in the Indian Union became a dominant political issue in the state. The nationalist movements in the subcontinent of India had looked to the eventual absorption of the 'princely states' in free India or Pakistan, as the case may be. Hyderabad was the largest and the richest of them all. The majority of the population, which was Hindu, as well as its geography, favored Hyderabad's union with India. The feudal aristocracy, both Hindu as well as Muslim, favored the idea of an independent Hyderabad. So did the small Muslim middle class, which had enjoyed a favored position and had fears about its future in the Indian Union. They organized armed bands, called Razakars, to fight for an independent Hyderabad under the Nizam. Kasim Rizvi, leader of the Razakars, was looked down upon by the feudal lords, who considered him to be an upstart, but they used the Razakars against the peasants when the movement arose. The leadership of the Telangana movement, in its first stages, had supported the idea of Hyderabad's union with India; the Nizam's rule and the idea of an independent Hyderabad were identified with the feudal aristocracy of the state. The peasant movement at that stage thus drew great strength from the Indian nationalist upsurge in the state. But later, when union with India seemed to be inevitable and it became clear that the government of India would deploy far larger and more effective forces against them, the Telangana leadership, in panic, switched their political allegiance to the support of the Nizam and the demand for an independent Hyderabad. The Communist Party in Hyderabad was legalized for the first time, and Communists and Razakars fought together against

Indian troops. Now the movement was aligned with the forces which it had fought in the past, and it was running counter to the nationalist sentiment. This created a great deal of political confusion and split the Communist leadership of the movement. Nationalist sentiment, a powerful factor in the rise of the Telangana movement, thus became an important factor leading to its eventual downfall.

Another factor which contributed to the initial success of the movement was that the feudal aristocracy was demoralized by the fact that union with India seemed inevitable, despite its desperate bid for autonomy. The state apparatus was corrupt and inefficient. On the other hand, there was general political unrest. The peasant movement, directed against the ruling aristocracy, drew much popular support and was able to withstand repression. But later, confronted with a more powerful army of India, it also lost popular support.

The movement developed its initial momentum from the fact that its demands were broad-based and it drew in the middle peasant as well as the poor peasant. Later, when the peasant 'Soviets' were established and land was redistributed, conflicts of interest between different sections of the peasantry came to the surface. Some Communists argue that this was a hasty and ill-thought-out policy which the Telangana leadership sought to impose from above, instead of preparing the ground carefully and helping the peasantry to advance the movement from below. The disruption of their peasant base proved disastrous when they were under heavy military attack.

Among the special factors which favored the rise of the Telangana movement are those which favored the guerrilla struggle. Telangana is a very poor area, much of it covered by thorny scrub and jungle, interspersed with relatively more prosperous settlements in a few favored basins with tank irrigation. It also has a substantial tribal population, among whom there is a greater sense of solidarity and fighting spirit than there is among the stratified peasant societies in frontier areas. Thus when an attempt was made in 1948 to extend the movement to the neighboring rich delta region of Andhra, it failed. However it should be added that this failure was due also to the fact that by that time the movement had moved away from its broad slogans, had become sectarian, and thus lost the support of the middle peasant. By that time the movement was also running counter to the nationalist sentiment on the Hyderabad issue.

The Tebhaga and the Telangana movements had both risen from local roots rather than from any initiatives by the Communist Party, although the Communists provided the leadership and played vital role in both. After the Communist Party Congress of 1948, the party was committed to launching insurrectionary forms of struggle but was not able to organize any movement on the scale of the Tebhaga or Telangana movements. Between 1948 and 1952 the Communist Party was banned in many states. On the peasant front, as on other fronts, party workers were subjected to severe repression. Most AIKS workers were either in jail or underground during this period, and the organization virtually ceased to function. Despite that, local peasant unrest continued to manifest itself throughout India; but it remained localized and limited in scope. It was clear that peasant insurrections could not be launched merely by party decisions, but required certain preconditions before they could develop.

In the period that followed 1952, the Kisan Sabha and the Communist Party moved away from the idea of direct peasant action except for demonstrations and agitation. Instead, they put the emphasis on exerting pressure on the Congress government for implementing effective land reforms and on parliamentary political struggle for the Communist Party, which, if brought to power, would itself reform. At the Congress of the Communist Party in 1958 at Amritsar, the party adopted a program of 'peaceful road to socialism'; at the Congress in 1961 at Vijaywada it proposed the concept of *national democracy* as the most suitable form to solve the problems of national regeneration and social progress along the *noncapitalist path* of development.' Thus the CPI cow seeks to replace the present government of '*bourgeois democracy* in which the leadership of the national bourgeoisie is decisive' by a government of national democracy. The latter is to be distinguished also from '*people's democracy* in which the leadership of the working class is decisive, that leadership having won the support of the overwhelming majority of the people.' National democracy is distinguished from these two other concepts by the fact that in it 'the proletariat *shares* power with the national bourgeoisie.'[47] This conception does not appear to be very different from that of the

Praja Socialist Party, which is also prepared to share power with the Congress in the hope of consolidating the Congress's 'left wing.' The fundamental differences between the Praja Socialist Party and the Communists now seem to lie almost entirely in the field of international relations rather than in domestic policy. The effect of this realignment of political forces has been to limit the peasant movement to agitation about government policies instead of undertaking any direct action.

Both the Communists and the Socialists are largely in agreement with the principles of land reform adopted by the Congress. Their main criticism is directed at the manner of its implementation, which defeats its objectives. The Report of the Congress Land Reform Committee, published in 1949, is a radiFal document. It took as its guiding principles the elimination of exploitation and giving the land back to the tiller. It sought to establish independent peasant landholdings and, on that basis, to develop a cooperative system of agriculture. That document, however, reflected the views of the Congress's 'left wing' rather than those of the main body, much less the views of the various state governments which were to undertake the land reforms. The character of the land reforms, as implemented rather unevenly in the various states over the last decade, is very different indeed from the recommendations of the Agrarian Reforms Committee. The actual result of the land reform is the subject of some controversy. The Chinese view[48] is that it has 'abolished only the *political privileges* of some of the local feudal princes and *zamindari (tax farming) privileges* of some landlords,' but that 'the Indian feudal land system as a whole was preserved.' Such a view underestimates the profound changes which have in fact taken place in the Indian agrarian economy over the last decade. Land reform in the different states of India has, in varying degrees, eliminated or limited exploitation by noncultivating landlords and has encouraged the growth of capitalist farming. The changes in the different states are too numerous and complex to permit an attempt to present them here even in outline. Moreover, although numerous studies have examined the changes in detail, an overall statistical picture of the present situation is still not available. Sulekh Gupta points to the fact that, in 1953-4, 75 percent of the peasant households operated holdings of less than 5 acres. On the other hand, 65 percent of the land was farmed by 13 percent of the households; of the latter, at the top, 3.6 percent of the households possessed 36 percent of the land.[49] Gupta points to the increasing disparity between the growing prosperity of capitalist agriculture and the stagnation and bankruptcy of the small peasant economy, in which the vast mass of the peasantry live in increasing poverty. Gupta perhaps overestimates the extent of the capitalist sector. This picture is qualified by Bhowani Sen, who, while recognizing the trend toward the growth of the capitalist sector, also points out that 'the *upper limit* of employment in India's capitalist cultivation is 16 percent of the rural labor force (40 percent of the agricultural workers—the rural proletariat).'[50] The many survivals of the old system are pointed out by Sen, as well as by Kotovsky and Daniel Thorner, whose works provide a very useful survey of the land reforms.[51] The existence of survivals of the old system is also indicated by the continued emphasis in official documents, such as the Mid-Term Appraisal Report on the Third Five-Year Plan, on such questions as the problems of tenancy reform, security of tenure, regulation of rents, etc.[52]

Two aspects of land reform have a direct bearing on the question of political mobilization of the peasantry. First, an upper stratum of tenants was able to acquire ownership of land and have become employers of labor. Kotovsky argues: 'Before the reforms, this stratum of tenants energetically advocated abolition of the *zamindari* system; it played an important role in the peasant movement.... After the reforms were put through it withdrew from active peasant movement.'[53] Second, one of the principal results of the land reform has been the mass eviction of tenants, on an unprecedented scale, by landowners taking over land for 'self-cultivation.' These peasants, deprived of their land and livelihood, might have been expected to have become an explosive force in the countryside. The issue did greatly agitate some local Kisan Sabhas and provoke some local demonstrations, but it did not develop into a militant movement. The peasants did not launch direct action to resist eviction. Indeed, from 1955 to 1958, when the land reforms were in progress, 'there was a temporary decline of the organized peasant movement.'[54] In criticizing the Congress land reform, the Communist Party has criticized its bureaucratic method of implementation, which resulted in widespread evasion. The party advocated instead the implementation of the land reform through peasant committees. But their appeal was evidently directed only toward the Congress government, for they took no steps to organize direct action by the peasants for this purpose.

The prospect that is being held out to the Indian peasantry today by the Communist Party of India is one of 'revolution from above' rather than 'revolution from below.' Although the CPI distinguishes between the 'peaceful realization of the socialist revolution' and 'the parliamentary way of the reformist conception,' it is clear that its commitment to a constitutional struggle leaves it with few alternatives of struggle beyond agitation against the existing Congress government to mobilize electoral support. On the question of the ruling classes relinquishing power, the CPI takes this view:

> 'Everything will depend on whether the force of peaceful mass struggle, isolating the ruling classes, compels them to surrender or whether they hit back with their armed might.... The class aspect (of the struggle) consists in *exposure* of capitalism...*showing how* the class aspirations of the national bourgeoisie conflict with the national aspirations.'[55]

As far as the peasant masses are concerned, however, the policy of agitation and 'exposure' of the Congress government has met with little success and has failed to mobilize a majority of peasant votes for the Left in the several elections that have been held in the decade and a half since independence. Nor has the agitational struggle generated a force which may isolate the ruling classes and compel them to surrender. This has been the situation, notwithstanding the fact that the Communist Party has, from time to time, launched massive demonstrations in towns and in the countryside on such issues as rising prices and tax relief. Thus, one of the most successful mass demonstrations launched by the Kisan Sabhas in recent years was the 1959 struggle in the Punjab against the 'Betterment Levy,' a tax that was levied on the enchanced value of land which has benefited from new irrigation. But if the Kisan Sabhas have had some success in launching such *'mass* struggles,' they have had little success in launching any *class* struggles of the exploited peasantry. Moreover, success in such struggle, involving the entire peasantry, has not brought in its wake any substantial increase in electoral support. The reasons for this lie in the power relationships which operate in the rural society and in the structural conditions governing the political behavior of the peasantry; these cannot be changed merely by an 'exposure' of the ruling Congress Party.

The pattern of political behavior of the peasantry is based on factions that are vertically integrated segments of the rural society, dominated by landlords and rich peasants at the top, and with poor peasants and landless laborers, who are economically dependent on them, at the bottom. Among the exploited sections of the peasantry there is little or no class solidarity. They stand divided among themselves by their allegiance to their factions, led by their masters. Political initiative thus rests with faction leaders, who are owners of land and have power and prestige in the village society. They are often engaged in political competition (even conflict) among themselves in pursuit of power and prestige in the society. The dominating factions, who by virtue of their wealth have the largest following, back the party in power and in turn receive many reciprocal benefits. The opposition generally finds allies in factions of middle peasants who are relatively independent of the landlords but often find themselves in conflict with them. Many factors enter into the factional picture: kinship, neighborhood ties (or conflicts), and caste alignments affect the allegiance of particular peasants to one faction or another.[56] But broadly speaking, it does appear that in one group of factions the predominant characteristic is that of the relationship between masters and their dependents, while other factions are those of independent smallholders. The number of votes that the Left can hope to mobilize depends primarily not on the amount of agitation it conducts (although this must affect the situation partly), but on the relative balance of the factions. Above all, the decisive question here is that of winning over the votes of the large number of poor peasants and landless laborers who are still dominated by their masters. This cannot be done unless the factional structure is broken, for the allegiance of the poor peasants and the farm laborers to their masters is not merely due to subjective factors such as their 'backward mentality,' etc. It is based on the objective fact of their dependence on their masters for their continued livelihood. Thus it seems hardly likely, in the absence of any direct action by the peasantry or any action by a government which might break the economic power of the landlords and rich peasants, that effective electoral support can be won by the Left. This is a paradox of the parliamentary way, and a dilemma for a party which renounces direct action.

We have raised a number of questions in the above analysis. There is, however, one theme which runs through our discussion: the respective roles of the middle peasants, the independent peasant smallholders, on the one hand, and the various categories of poor peasants on the other.

We have found that the poor peasants are *initially* the least militant class of the peasantry. Their initial backwardness is sometimes explained in purely subjective terms, such as servile habits ingrained in the peasant mind over centuries or the backward mentality of the peasant, etc. But in fact we find that when certain conditions appear, the peasants are very quickly liberated from such a servile mentality. Clearly, the subjective backwardness of the peasantry is rooted in objective factors. There is a fundamental difference between the situation of the poor peasant and that of the industrial worker. The latter enjoys a relative anonymity in his employment and a job mobility which gives him much strength in conducting the class struggle. (Where the industrial worker's relative independence is reduced by such devices as tied housing, etc., his militancy is also undermined.) In the case of the poor peasant, the situation is much more difficult. He finds himself and his family totally dependent upon his master for their livelihood. When the pressure of population is great, as in India and China, no machinery of coercion is needed by the landlords to keep him down. Economic competition suffices. The poor peasant is thankful to his master, a benefactor who gives him land to cultivate as a tenant or gives him a job as laborer. He looks to his master for help in times of crisis. The master responds paternalistically; he must keep alive the animal on whose labor he thrives. When, in extreme and exceptional cases, the exploitation and oppression are carried beyond the point of human endurance, the peasant may be goaded into killing his master for this departure from the paternalistic norm, but he is unable to rise, by himself, against the system. His dependence on his master thus undergoes a paternalistic mystification and he identifies with his master. This backwardness of the poor peasant, rooted as it is in objective dependence, is only a relative and not an absolute condition. In a revolutionary situation, *when anti-landlord and anti-rich peasant sentiment is built up by, say, the militancy of middle peasants, his morale is raised and he is more ready* to respond to calls to action. His revolutionary energy is set in motion. When the objective preconditions are realized, the poor peasant is a potentially revolutionary force. But the inherent weakness in his situation renders him more open to intimidation, and setbacks can easily demoralize him. He finally and irrevocably takes the road to revolution only when he is shown *in practice* that the power of his master can be irrevocably broken; then the possibility of an alternative mode of existence becomes real to him.

The middle peasants, on the other hand, are initially the most militant element of the peasantry, and they can be a powerful ally of the proletarian movement in the countryside, especially in generating the initial impetus of the peasant revolution. But this social perspective is limited by their class position. When the movement in the countryside advances to a revolutionary stage, they may move away from the revolutionary movement unless their fears are allayed and they are drawn into a process of cooperative endeavor.

Our hypothesis thus reverses the sequence suggested in Maoist texts—although it is in accord with Maoist practice! It is not the poor peasant who is initially the leading and main force of the peasant revolution, with the middle peasant coming in only later when the success of the movement is guaranteed, but precisely the nature of the conditions required to mobilize the poor peasants must be vital to the formulation of a correct strategy vis-a-vis the peasantry.

Finally, we would like to conclude by emphasizing again that our conclusions are purely tentative and are intended to open up a discussion of the problems by raising several questions rather than suggesting cut-and-dried answers. The answers will no doubt be forthcoming from a fresh spirit of inquiry and, above all, from actual experience; and they will be proved by the success of those who lead the peasant struggle.

References

1. Frantz Fanon, *The Wretched of the Earth* (New York, 1963), p. 48.
2. Since the initial publication of this article, these hypotheses have been corroborated by the findings of various writers. They have been reaffirmed, in particular, by Eric Wolf in his article, 'On Peasant Rebellions,' in UNESCO's *International Social Science Journal*, Vol. XXI, No. 2, 1969, and reprinted in T. Shanin (ed.). *Peasants and Peasant Societies* (London, 1971). Wolf has corroborated the theses in the light of the experiences of a number of other countries in his *Peasant Wars of the Twentieth Century*, 1969.
3. In the present version of this article, I have slightly elaborated, in this and the two following paragraphs, on my original statement so as to clarify this important issue which has been misunderstood by some—for example by Saghir Ahmad, whose article appears elsewhere in this volume. It is essential to emphasize that, in defining social classes, Marxists do not participate in the apparent consensus among 'social scientists' which Saghir Ahmad assumes; for the Marxist concept, unlike that of academic sociology, is a 'structural' concept. Secondly, Saghir Ahmad's redefinition of the terms 'rich peasants' and 'poor peasants,' which departs, for example, from the usage adopted by Lenin or Mao, illustrates the looseness of the terminology, which lends itself to such arbitrary and idiosyncratic redefinitions. If everyone were to choose his own definition, meaningful debate would become impossible and we would have semantic chaos.
4. See Hamza Alavi, 'Elite Farmer Strategy and Regional Disparities in West Pakistan,' in R.D. Stevens, H.A. Alavi, and P. Bertocci (eds.), *Rural Development in Pakistan* (to be published).
5. George Lichtheim, *Marxism, a Historical and Critical Study* (London, 1961), p. 333.
6. V.I. Lenin, *Selected Works*, Vol. II (Moscow, 1947), pp. 456-7.
7. For a fuller picture readers should consult the following works: Lenin, *The Development of Capitalism in Russia* (Moscow, 1956); G.T. Robinson, *Rural Russia Under the Old Regime* (New York, 1949); and Sir John Maynard, *The Russian Peasant* (New York, 1962).
8. See J. Stalin, *Problems of Leninism* (Moscow, 1953), pp. 213-36.
9. Marx and Engels, Preface to the Russian edition of *The Communist Manifesto*, in *Selected Works* (London, 1950), Vol. I, p. 24.
10. Lenin, *Collected Works* (Moscow, 1961), Vol. IV, p. 424.
11. Ibid., Vol. VI, p. 444.
12. Robinson, op. cit., pp. 206-7.
13. Lenin, *Collected Works*, Vol. IV, p. 427.
14. See 'The Agrarian Program of Russian Social Democracy' and 'Reply to Criticism of Our Draft Program,' ibid., Vol. VI, pp. 109-50, 438-53.
15. Ibid., Vol. VIII, p. 231.
16. Robinson, op. cit., p. 161.
17. Lenin, *Selected Works*, Vol. II, p. 37.
18. Sir John Maynard, *Russia in Flux* (New York, 1962), p. 332.
19. Lenin, *Selected Works*, Vol. II, pp. 414-7.
20. Ibid., p. 647.
21. Jan Degras, *The Communist International—Documents* (London, 1960), Vol. II, p. 336.

22 Edgar Snow, *Red Star Over China* (London, 1963), p. 157.
23 Ho Kan-chih, *A History of the Modern Chinese Revolution* (Peking, 1959), p.100.
24 The article included in the *Selected Works of Mao Tse-tung* (London, 1955), as 'Analysis of Classes in Chinese Society,' and dated March 1926, is a revised and consolidated version of two articles which appeared in *Chung-Kuo Nung-min* in January and February 1926. Much of value in the original article has been lost in the revised version. Our references are to the translation of the original article, as given by Stuart Schram in *The Political Thought of Mao Tse-tung* (New York, 1963), pp. 172-7.
25 Ralph Miliband and John Saville (eds.), *The Socialist Register 1964* (Monthly Review Press, New York, 1964), p. 19.
26 Schram, op. cit., pp. 28 and 33.
27 Ho Kan-chih, op. cit., p. 139.
28 The percentage figures of the various classes of the Chinese peasantry are derived from the data given by Mao Tse-tung in the original article referred to in note 25.
29 Mao Tse-tung, *Selected Works* (London, 1955), p. 23.
30 Schram, op. cit., p. 173.
31 Ibid., p. 88. (Emphasis added).
32 Martin C. Yang, *A Chinese Village* (London, 1947), p. 143.
33 See Chao Kuo-chun, *Agrarian Policy of the Chinese Communist Party* (London, 1960).
34 *The Agrarian Reform Law of the People's Republic of China* (Peking, 1950).
35 *Eighth National Congress of the CCP*, Vol. III (Peking, 1956), pp. 182-3. (Emphasis added).
36 David and Isabel Crook, *Revolution in a Chinese Village* (London, 1959); C. K. Yang, *A Chinese Village in Early Communist Transition* (Cambridge, Mass., 1959).
37 C.K. Yang, op. cit., pp. 143-5.
38 Jawaharlal Nehru, *The Discovery of India* (London, 1956), p. 365.
39 N.G. Ranga, *Revolutionary Peasants* (New Delhi, 1949), p. 89.
40 Acharya Narendra Deva, *Socialism and the National Revolution* (Bombay, 1946). pp. 46-7.
41 Asoka Mehta, *Studies in Asian Socialism* (Bombay, 1959), pp. 213-5.
42 Bhowani Sen, "The Tebhaga Movement in Bengal," *Communist*, September 1947, p. 130.
43 Ibid.
44 Ibid., pp. 124 ff.; also All India Kisan Sabha, *Draft Report for 1944-5* (Bombay, 1945), pp. 9-13.
45 Bhowani Sen, op. cit., p. 130.
46 Ibid.
47 G. Adhikari, 'The Problem of the Non-Capitalist Path of Development of India and the State of National Democracy,' *World Marxist Review*, November 1964.
48 'More on the Philosophy of Pandit Nehru,' *People's Daily*, October 27, 1962.
49 Sulekh Gupta, 'New Trends of Growth in Indian Agriculture,' *Seminar* (New Delhi), No. 38, October 1962.
50 Bhowani Sen, *Evolution of Agrarian Relations in India* (New Delhi, 1962).
51 G. Kotovsky, *Agrarian Reforms in India* (New Delhi, 1964); Daniel Thorner, *The Agrarian Prospect in India* (Delhi, 1956) and *Land and Labour in India* (London, 1962).

52 Government of India, Planning Commission, *The Third Plan, Mid-term Appraisal* (Delhi, 1963).
53 Kotovsky, op. cit., p. 80.
54 Ibid., p. 82.
55 Adhikari, op. cit., p. 39. (Emphasis added).
56 For reasons of space we are unable to enlarge on this question, which deserves more attention than it has received so far from the Left. The following works provide a useful introduction to this subject: Ralph Nicholas, 'Village Factions and Political Parties in Rural West Bengal,' *Journal of Commonwealth Political Studies*, November 1963; Oscar Lewis, *Village Life in Northern India* (Urbana, III, 1958), Chapter IV; T.O. Beidelman, *A Comparative Analysis of the Hindu Jajmani System* (New York, 1959); and Frederick Barth, *Political Leadership Among Swat Pathans* (London, 1959). Since the original publication of this article, we have analyzed this question further. See Hamza Alavi, 'Politics of Dependence: A Village in West Punjab,' *South Asian Review*, January 1971, in which we commented on Nicholas' 'pluralist' thesis.

36 Peasant Resistance and Revolt in South India

Kathleen Gough

WITH A THIRD of the world socialist, and guerrilla movements active in more than a dozen countries, some social scientists in the West have turned their attention to the role of peasants in revolution.[1] This article stems from work by Hamza Alavi, Eric Wolf, and A.G. Frank.[2] It tries to supplement Alavi's analysis of peasant revolts in two areas of India—Telengana and Bengal—with an account of some peasant actions in the northern part of the state of Kerala, with references for purposes of comparison to Tanjore, a district in southeast Madras.

The questions of principal concern are, first: is rural class struggle endemic in these South Indian regions, or is it engendered by self-interested political parties, especially the communists? Second: in modern peasant insurrections, what have been the respective roles of landlords, rich peasants, middle and poor peasants, and landless labourers? Third: what is the potential for future peasant revolt?

Kerala has a large number of types of land tenure, which vary, moreover, as between Malabar, Cochin, and Travancore. The most common traditional tenure has been 'kanam', in which the tenant surrenders a fixed rent, often about a third of the crop, to the landlord, in addition to a cash renewal fee every twelve years. In pre-British times this 'superior' tenure was confined to Nayars and other high caste Hindus of similar rank and to relatively high ranking Muslims and Christians. The most common 'inferior' tenure is 'verumpattam', in which the tenant pays a fixed rent, usually amounting to about two-thirds of the net produce, to the landlord or the 'kanam' tenant, whichever is immediately above

Reproduced from '*Pacific Affairs*', Vol. XLI, No. 1, 1968-9, (University of British Columbia), pp. 526-44.

him. 'Verumpattam' and similar tenures have traditionally been accorded mainly to members of the large, relatively low ranking cultivating caste of Tiyyars or Iravas; very seldom to the lowest, 'Untouchable' castes such as Pulayas and Parayas, almost all of whom are landless labourers.

In Tanjore the most common types of tenure have been 'kuthakai', in which the tenant traditionally paid a fixed rent usually amounting to about three to four-fifths of his net produce, and 'varam', an older, share-cropping tenure in which the tenant retained one-fifth of his net produce each year, regardless of the size of his crop.[3]

This analysis cuts somewhat cavalierly through the details of land tenure to apply Mao Tse-tung's categories, which are useful for the sake of comparison with other areas. Thus, in 1933 Mao analyzed the classes in rural Chinese society as follows:

A landlord is a person who possesses land, who does not engage in labour himself or merely takes part in labour as a supplementary source of income, and who lives by exploiting the peasants. The landlord's exploitation chiefly assumes the form of collecting land rent; besides that, he may also lend money, hire labour, or engage in industrial or commercial enterprise. (2) The rich peasant as a rule possesses land. But there are some who possess part of the land they farm and rent the remainder.... The rich peasant as a rule possesses comparatively abundant means of production and liquid capital, engages in labour himself, but regularly relies on exploitation for a part or the major part of his income. The exploitation the rich peasant practises is chiefly that of hired labour. In addition, he may also let a part of his land for rent, lend money, or engage in industrial or commercial enterprise. (3) In many cases the middle peasant possesses land. In some cases he possesses no land at all and rents all the land he farms.... The middle peasant relies wholly or mainly on his own labour as the source of his income. As a rule he does not exploit other people; in many cases he is even exploited by other people and has to pay a small amount of land rent and interest on loans.... The middle peasant as a rule does not sell his labour power. (4) In some cases the poor peasant possesses a part of the land he farms...in other cases he possesses no land at all, but only an incomplete set of instruments. As a rule the poor peasant has to rent land for cultivation... While the middle peasant need not sell his labour power, the poor peasant has to sell a small part of his—this is the principal criterion for distinguishing the middle peasant from the poor peasant. (5) The worker (including the farm labourer) as a rule does not possess any land or implements.... A worker makes his living wholly or mainly by selling his labour power.[4]

Alavi distinguishes three sectors of the rural economy in India. In the first sector, land is owned by landlords who do not themselves undertake cultivation. They rent land to poor peasants, mainly sharecroppers. In the second sector are independent small-holders or middle peasants, who own the land they cultivate and do not exploit the labour of others. In the third sector, land is owned by capitalist farmers or rich peasants, who manage the land themselves and employ hired labour. Alavi's argument is that it was the independent middle peasant who, in Russia and China, played the most active role in the early stages of revolution; the poor peasants, both more backward and potentially more militant, were drawn in along with the middle peasants in later stages. In India, he sees the poor peasants as having been most active in the Bengal and Telengana movements of 1946-8; he attributes their failure in part to a failure to draw the middle peasant into the struggle.

This analysis differs from Alavi's on two counts, First, the situation in Kerala and Tanjore do not allow a clear distinction between the 'landlord' and the 'capitalist' sectors, nor can either of them be separated from the sector of the middle peasant. In both regions there has been, over the past hundred years, a gradual increase in the proportions of landlords and rich peasants who employ hired labour, and in the proportions of hired labourers to poor and middle peasants. This tendency has not declined, and may even have been stepped up, with the land reforms of the past decade. At least since the late nineteenth century, however, it has been common for both landlords and rich peasants to lease out portions of their lands to poor peasants and to have other portions cultivated by labourers. It is, moreover, common in these regions for both rich and middle peasants to lease at least part of their land from landlords, a fact which makes it virtually impossible to separate Alavi's three 'sectors'. The attempt to do so probably stems from a 'dual economy' (in this case 'triple economy') thesis which sees the capitalist and precapitalist (sometimes called 'feudal') sectors of the economy as existing side by side, with the former gradually overtaking the latter. But while some 'features' of pre-capitalist relations (payments in kind, debt-labour, special levies, etc.), may undoubtedly continue to exist here and there in rural India the system as a whole has been a colonial capitalist system, incorporated into, and affected by, the fluctuations of world markets, since at least the last third of the nineteenth century.

The distinction between landlords and rich peasants rests, therefore, not on whether tenants or hired labourers are engaged, although it is true that rich peasants tend to have most of their land cultivated by labourers, and that big landlords rent out substantial amounts of land. Instead, the distinction is made in terms of whether or not the owner or holder actively engages in management of his lands and contributes some of his own manual labour to their cultivation.

In Kerala and Tanjore, a landlord is thus a land owner ('janmi' in Kerala, 'mirasdar' in Tanjore) who himself does no cultivation, who almost always rents out part of his land, but who in addition often employs hired labourers; the latter are usually managed by overseers. A landlord may own anything from about eight to several thousand acres; if he own less than eight acres, he is likely to have clerical, professional, or mercantile work in addition, and will thus not be primarily a landlord. A rich peasant is likely to own or to lease from about eight to thirty acres of land. He manages most of it himself, usually does some manual labour, and regularly hires a number of labourers; he may also rent out small plots to tenants. Rich peasants in Kerala are likely to be either 'kanam' tenants or to own some acres and to lease more on 'kanam'. In Tanjore they are usually small 'mirasdars' who may in addition lease land on 'kuthakai'. Middle peasants in Kerala and Tanjore may own a little land of their own, but almost all lease some from landlords, on 'kanam' or 'verumpattam' in Kerala and on 'kuthakai' in Tanjore. 'Pure' middle peasants who hire no landless labourers are actually almost non-existent in these regions. Most have one or two regular workers and engage more at peak seasons. They are thus somewhat hard to separate from the rich peasants and are involved in both of Alavi's first and third sectors—as tenants and as hirers of labour. Poor peasants in Kerala lease all their lands, usually on 'verumpattam' or one of the less favourable variants of 'kanam'; in Tanjore they may be 'kuthakai' or 'varam' tenants. They are too poor to survive on these lands and work either half-time or seasonally for landlords, or for rich or even middle peasants. Most poor peasants come from relatively low or 'backward' castes (in Kerala, Iravas or low-ranking Muslims or Christians; in Tanjore, Konar, Nadar or relatively low-ranking subcastes of Kallar or Vanniyar) whose ancestors have traditionally served as tied labourers or semiserfs of landlords. Substantial numbers of high caste people such as Vellalas and Naidus in Tanjore, or Nayars and Syrian Christians in Kerala, have, however, become middle or poor peasants in recent decades. Landless labourers, finally, include almost all members of the Harijan or 'Untouchable' castes of former agricultural slaves: Pallas and Parayas in Tanjore; Pulayas, Cherumas, and Parayas in Kerala. Many Muslims and Christians in Kerala, and many 'clean' caste Hindus in both Kerala and Tanjore, have, however, become landless labourers during this century. Landless labourers possess no land, and lease at best only a minute plot as a house-site. They work full time for wages, either in cash or kind, and either for long periods or casually by the day.

A second difference from Alavi's analysis derives from the different course taken by the revolts in Bengal and Andhra as described by Alavi, and those in Kerala and Tanjore. In the latter, while poor peasants and also landless labourers were drawn into the struggle, there was still a tendency on the part of the communists to rely on the middle peasants for local leadership. It is true that it has always been difficult to combine middle and poor peasants and landless labourers in a united struggle. Nevertheless, in these regions, the failure of the revolts of the late 1940s was due more to vacillations of policy on the part of the communist leadership, and to the fact that only isolated sectors of India were at that time ripe for agrarian revolt, than to a 'sectarian' preference for poor peasants and landless labourers on the part of the communists. If anything, it would seem that the communists have so far failed fully to utilize the militancy of poor peasants and landless labourers in Southern India. Today, the increasing proportions and restlessness of these agrarian classes are causing some communist groups and leaders to reconsider their policies in this regard.

Collective acts of violence or non-violent resistance by Indian peasants against landlords and higher authorities were common during British rule. They included spontaneous killings of landlords or officials by small groups of peasants; organized non-violent strikes; and prolonged armed attempts to seize the land and establish peasant self-government. The largest revolts were the Mappilla (Moplah) or Muslim rebellions of Malabar District in North Kerala of 1836-98. Muslim tenants revolted twenty-five times, killing many Hindu landlords, British officials, and soldiers. Before 1920, such actions emerged from the peasants themselves, with some of them focusing around local charismatic leaders. After 1920 peasant revolts tendered to come under the guidance of regional, national, or urban-based political movements.

Peasant revolts during British rule appear to have stemmed from the increasing exactions of the colonial economy. During the first two-thirds of the nineteenth century the British instituted capitalist agrarian relations throughout most of India. These relations involved private ownership of land by its former managers, the right of the landlord to sell his land in the market, the right to evict unwanted tenants and freely to undertake contractual leases, the freeing of serfs and slaves, and their conversion into landless wage labourers.[5] The sale of cash crops, whether for foreign or local markets, developed in both Tanjore and Kerala in response to the government's extraction of a heavy revenue from the landlords. In Tanjore's deltaic rice area, landlords began to sell grain to other regions, retaining enough to feed their families and labourers. In Kerala the second half of the nineteenth century saw a great increase in the agricultural population and a vast expansion of export crops such as coconuts, spices, lumber, and later tea, rubber and cashewnuts. Much of this expansion took place in former forest lands but long-settled villages were also affected. Pulled by the rising prices of export crops and pushed by the need to pay high revenues, landlords extracted more and more produce from their too-numerous tenants and labourers and evicted them when they were unable to pay their rents. Many of those evicted starved. Others eventually found work in the towns, in the new lumber industry in the forests, or on the export crop plantations developed in the last third of the century by British firms. Tenancy Acts passed after 1887 gave increasing security to those holding superior tenures—often themselves non-cultivating middlemen—but did little to stay the insecurity of the poorest tenants and landless labourers.[6]

The first modern politically-sponsored revolt took shape under the Congress-Khilafat movement of 1920-1. Guided by the Indian National Congress and the Muslim League, Kerala's new middle class of students, rich peasants, middle ranking merchants, and professionals encouraged cultivators and hand-mill workers to engage in non-violent strikes and boycott of British goods. The goals were Home Rule for India and for Turkey, at that time struggling against European hegemony. The British responded with violent repression. At this, poor Muslim tenants, heirs of the nineteenth century rebels, organized in village assemblies round their religious leaders and with knives, spears, clubs, and homemade firearms drove out or killed both Hindu and Muslim landlords, government servants, and police. Muslim leaders of middle peasant rank took over the government of 220 villages for several months. They killed five to six hundred landlords, police, and others who had aided the British military. Once violent revolt occurred, Congress leaders under Gandhi withdrew their support. The British defeated the movement and deported or executed many rebels. About 10,000 died in this rebellion.[7]

In the 1920s and 1930s, a gulf widened between rightwing Congressmen who wanted Home Rule with a minimum of internal changes, and left-wingers, often of Marxist persuasion. The latters' bases lay in the modern labour unions they had formed among handmill, industrial, and transport workers in the coast towns, among peasants in villages of the midlands, and among wage-earning plantation workers on the large British-owned tea and rubber estates in the highlands. In 1934 leftwing Congressmen formed the Congress Socialist Party within the Congress Party. The socialists dominated the Kerala Provincial Congress Committee until 1940, when they were expelled by the national leadership and openly declared their affiliation to the Communist Party.

This period of the late 1930s, together with the postwar period of 1947-50, saw the most intense politically sponsored activity among middle and poor peasants that has occurred in South India. Most of it was organized by communists, although socialist, Congress and independent peasant unions sponsored some peasant boycotts and strikes. Communist peasant actions were inspired not only by immediate economic goals but also by a belief in revolutionary class struggle. Peasants came to hope and expect that it would eventually culminate in seizure of the land by its cultivators and of the country by the Communists.

Communist influence strongly affected the Kerala branch of the Socialist Party by 1940. In that year the communists tried to precipitate Indian independence by paralyzing the British wartime administration. The national bourgeoisie within the Congress was now seen not as allies but as 'cowards' to be 'isolated',[8] and the urban proletariat was expected to lead the struggle. There were urban strikes and sabotage throughout India, and supporting actions by peasants. On September 15, 1940, during widespread demonstrations, a number of police, socialist leaders, and peasants died in armed clashes in several towns and villages of Malabar. Responding to these events, the national Congress leadership expelled the Kerala socialists from the party. All of them thereupon joined the Communist Party. Those communists who escaped imprisonment went underground, and the 'proletarian struggle' petered out in early 1941.

Shortly after the Soviet Union entered the war in mid-1941, Indian communists opted to support the war effort and entered into limited collaboration with the British. Until the end of the war, they refrained from militant struggles. At the same time, with the Congress leadership in jail for non-cooperation, the communists expanded their leadership in labor and peasant unions in Kerala, and at war's end they emerged in control of most of these bodies.

In 1946-7, revolts broke out in the Indian Navy, among the urban classes in many cities, and among the peasants in large regions of Bengal, Telengana, Tanjore, and Kerala.[9] The CPI national office did not support these revolts, for its leadership was divided and its official policy was now one of cooperation with the Congress in the transition to independence. Rural communist leaders were, however, active in the revolts. In Telengana in the princely state of Hyderabad (now part of Andhra State) guerrilla warfare led to the seizure of some 3000 villages in two whole districts, and to their administration for six months by peasant soviets. These revolutionary institutions were crushed by the Indian Army, which under orders from the new Congress government, invaded Hyderabad and annexed it to the Indian union in 1948.

The Communist leaders in Telengana were influenced by the Chinese theory and practice of peasant guerrilla warfare. This differed both from the path of proletarian uprising and from that of United Front constitutional opposition which the Indian communists had hitherto alternately pursued. Chinese influence also affected the leadership of Tanjore and Kerala. In these regions the struggle never attained the proportions seen in Bengal and Telengana. Nevertheless, communist-organized groups of middle and poor peasants did drive out the landlords and take over a block of villages in eastern Tanjore for several weeks early in 1948.[10] In many other villages, unions of tenants and labourers struck during the harvest season until they had compelled the landlords to halve rents and double wages. The Tanjore revolt was put down by armed police in the course of 1949. In Kerala, too, there were strikes of tenants and labourers for lower rents and higher wages, large demonstrations, and organized seizures of blackmarket grain-stocks from rich landlords and merchants. Both in Tanjore and Kerala, landless labourers as well as poor peasants were now drawn into the struggles and played a militant role. Many of them came from the lowest castes of Harijans, hitherto ostracized and exploited by the somewhat higher Hindu castes of middle and poor tenants. In Tanjore, Harijans (called Adi Dravidas) form about one-third of the population and live in segregated streets on the outskirts of villages. The communists organized these streets into unions on the basis of their existing caste-assemblies. The Adi Dravidas acted separately, although in alliance, with the unions of higher ranking middle and poor peasants, thus raising the struggle to new heights of militancy. In Kerala, thousands of Harijan and Backward Caste landless labourers struck for the first time on the cash crop farming estates of big village landlords in 1947. Both men and women came out. Their discipline and militancy were remarkable. In one North Malabar village sprawling over four square miles of mountains and valleys only one labourer went to work on the first day of the strike. He had heard of it but did not really think the people would be united. His caste members approached him before the second day and he stayed away thereafter.

The peasant revolts of 1947 took place without support from

the central leadership of the Communist Party. In 1948, however, as in 1940, the CPI line changed to one of revolutionary upsurge led by the urban proletariat. In theory, the peasants were still neglected. B.T. Ranadive, the Party's general secretary, in fact described Mao's theories as 'horrifying', 'reactionary', and 'counter-revolutionary'.[11] In practice, however, communist revolutionary action in this period was more successful in the countryside than in the cities, and South Indian rural leaders clung to the Chinese line. Finally, in mid-1950, a reconstituted central committee briefly adopted the Maoist approach of armed revolution based primarily on guerrilla warfare. By this time, however, the main revolts had been crushed. The Congress government was firmly in control and most villagers appear to have been made hopeful by the prospect of universal franchise under the new constitution. In 1951 the communists changed their approach to one of parliamentary opposition. They renewed their attempts to unite the workers, all classes of peasants, and the "patriotic" bourgeoisie to bring about a mixed economy under government regulation, with a democratic parliamentary structure. Beginning with the Indian elections of 1952, the communists have followed the parliamentary road up to the present time, in spite of the party-split of 1964 and a variety of fundamental disagreements on international and national problems.

During the period of parliamentary democracy, many communist peasant unions have been allowed to lapse. In 1964 I found that local communist leaders in Kerala absorbed in electioneering, legal work, and ideological meetings and conflicts, often had little time for day-to-day organization in their villages. Union meetings were infrequent and in many villages peasants had ceased to pay their dues. Some militant struggles had been waged by the communists, however, and also by a new Christian Peasants and Workers' Party which has since joined a United Front with the communists. These struggles were especially prominent among some 30,000 peasants in hill areas, who had occupied government and private forest lands and whom the Congress government of 1960-64 had tried to evict.

It is important to notice that even in the absence of their communist leaders, peasants often revert to their traditional forms of joint action and resistance in crises. Two examples illustrate this point. In eastern Tanjore in late 1948, after the peasant revolt had been crushed, police arrived one day in a village to see that everything was under control. The Village Headman, a high caste landlord, summoned the elected headman of the Untouchable landless laborers' community. He intended to impress on the low caste headman the fact that the revolt was over and that the laborers should peacefully resume their tasks. On hearing the summons all the landless laborers of the village downed tools and marched to the landlords' street with the communist flag, fearing that their leader might be intimidated or beaten. When they saw the police trucks they angrily climbed into them, shouting that their lives were wretched and that they wished all to be taken to prison. In the ensuing melee the police drove off with thirty of them. They were sent to jail in Trichinopoly, some hundred miles away, and held without trial for four months. A deputation of local landlords eventually went to plead for their release so that the harvest work could go on. Laborers in this region continued with periodic strikes, stackburning, and even attacks on the homes of landlords until 1952, when their communist leaders were released from jail and the peasant unions were formally reconstituted. Under communist leadership the unions then pressed, through strikes and legal channels, for implementation of a newly enacted land regulation.[12]

In Kerala my Irava cook, who hailed from a British tea plantation, told of an incident in 1962. A woman in a nearby house in the plantation coolies' barracks began to give birth to a child and was taken to the plantation hospital. The surgeon refused to leave a movie he was attending and the nurses gave the woman injections to try to delay the birth and to ease her pain. She became unconscious and seemed at the point of death. The cook summoned one hundred of his street fellows and they marched to the cinema, dragged out the doctor, and forced him to return to the hospital, where he safely delivered the child. 'If you act thus again we shall kill you next time', they told him. This pattern of 'encirclement' or 'gherao' by groups of laborers of an official or landlord until he submits to their demands has recently spread throughout India and is currently a potent form of direct action.

In Kerala, as is well known, the Communist Party came to power in the state government in 1957 with 41 percent of the vote.

It was ousted by the Central government in 1959 on grounds of inability to maintain law and order. Through its policies of land ceilings, minimum wages, rural debt cancellations, and welfare provisions, the Party increased its support among the poor tenants and the propertyless classes. Even while pursuing the parliamentary road, the communists deepened the class struggle, by encouraging the poor to put forward their claims. In the sixteen years of parliamentary struggle the communists have continued to help tenants and landless labourers by filing suits on their behalf, leading strikes and boycotts within the constitutional framework, and counselling them on their rights under the various land reform laws.

In 1964, Left and Right communists split on the fundamental question of approaches to the Congress Party. These were in turn, of course, linked with Rightist support of the Soviet Union, which gives aid to the Congress government and hopes for a peaceful transition to socialism. The Left communists (CPI-M) oppose Soviet revisionism and any compromise with the Congress Party, and give critical support to China. They foresee the possibility of armed revolution if the Indian government succumbs to American penetration and closes all avenues to constitutional and parliamentary struggle. At the same time, the CPI-M continues to participate in elections. In Kerala, the Right communists have rather weak support from the urban lower middle classes and the industrial unions; the Left communists have much stronger support from middle and poor peasants and from landless laborers in villages and export crop plantations. While bitterly opposing each others' ideology, the two parties have forced electoral or post-electoral alliances in a number of states.

Communist-led United Front governments came to power in Kerala and Bengal in the Indian elections of early 1967. The Bengal government was ousted by the Center in the autumn of 1967 after defection from the Front of some individual non-communist legislators. In Kerala the Front remains in power but in deepening trouble because of food shortages. With over 40 percent of its land under export crops, Kerala must import half its food. In the general food crisis in India the Central Government has failed to maintain supplies. Adults in Kerala consider twelve to seventeen ounces of rice per day an adequate diet. Under the present informal rationing scheme they receive only three ounces in ration shops and must obtain the remainder at prices which exceed the wages of landless laborers.

Meanwhile, further serious divisions of policy have appeared among Left communists. In May 1967 a revolt broke out among sharecroppers and landless laborers in the mountainous district of Naxalbari in West Bengal. It arose because landlords refused to cede land taken from them by the government under the land-ceiling laws, and sent police and armed bands against the cultivators when they tried to occupy the lands. Many of the cultivators were Santal tribespeople who countered the landlords' attacks with bows and arrows. Plantation workers on nearby foreign tea plantations struck in sympathy. The revolt was led, or at least supported, by local Left communists. It appears to have followed traditional patterns: expropriation of the land, driving out of the landlords, attempts to set up peasant soviets and to immobilize local government officials. One policeman and ten peasants were killed. The West Bengal Minister of Land and Land Revenue, a Left communist, tried to bring about a compromise but it was foiled by police who continued to attack and by local Left communists and peasants who continued to defend themselves. The revolt at one point affected some 42,000 people in 70 villages over an area of 80 square miles. It appears to have been temporarily put down by the police, although rebel Left communists claim that a revolutionary framework has been maintained. The United Front government condemned the revolt as adventurist, and the Left Communist Party expelled the rebels.[13] The United Front Government was, however, ousted by the Central Government in November, 1967.

The rebel policy has since triumphed in the Left Communist Party-plenum in Delhi, and spread to a number of Left communist district and village committees in Bengal, Orissa, Bihar, Punjab, Uttar Pradesh, Maharashtra, Andhra, Mysore, Madras, and Kerala.[14]

The rebel approach includes the following: the organization of peasant-based guerrilla warfare as the main path to revolution in India, with the assistance of the urban working class; rejection of parliamentary participation as revisionist; and an analysis of Indian society which sees the Congress Central Government as the captive of American imperalism, and India as already a neo-colonial state. This last contrasts with the orthodox Left communist view of India as under the class-rule of the landlords and the bourgeoisie, led by the big bourgeoisie which, so far, is only 'increasingly collaborating' with imperialism.[15]

The rebels accept the Left communist distinction between a 'fedual' sector of the economy dominated by the landlords, an 'imperial' sector dominated by foreign monopoly capital with the assistance of an Indian comprador bourgeoisie, and a 'national capitalist' sector led by an independent national bourgeoisie, at least part of which is seen as a potential revolutionary ally. I would question such distinctions, arguing instead that the various sectors of the economy are fully integrated with one another in a colonial-style capitalism which is itself part of world capitalism and whose main features of underdevelopment derive from its satellite relationships with the metropolitan powers.[16] Correspondingly, it is questionable whether there is, or is any longer, a sizable independent national bourgeoisie in India, for the increasing penetration of the economy by American and European capital since the second world war has co-opted to the imperialists' side virtually the whole Indian bourgeoisie, whether mercantile, farming, or industrial. This means that while private industry and trade would, as in China, probably need to be retained for some time after a revolution, no substantial section of the Indian bourgeoisie can realistically be relied upon as potential revolutionary allies at the present time.

The rebel analysis does, however, give greater weight to foreign penetration of the Indian economy than does the orthodox Left communist analysis. Thus the rebels, like the Chinese Communist Party, argue that substantial elements of the Indian industrial bourgeoisie are part of the comprador bourgeoisie as a result of American, British, and other foreign penetration of Indian industry.[17]

It seems probable that much of the rebel Left communist analysis will appeal to poor peasants and landless laborers in Kerala. In 1964 I found on the one hand that support for the communists, especially the Left communists, had become virtually universal among landless laborers and had increased among poor and middle peasants. This resulted from the deterioration of food supplies and real wages in these classes in the 1960s and from the communists' record of 1957-9. On the other hand, there was a growing impatience and a wish to return to the militant actions of the late 1930s and 1947. My fieldnotes abound in statements by poor peasants and laborers that nothing will solve Kerala's problems except armed revolt against the landlords and sharing of land among those who cultivate it. Similarly, workers on the foreign export crop estates insisted that programmes for improved wages and benefits were at best temporary. Eventually, they held, a communist government must expropriate the planters and either divide the land among the plantation workers or run it cooperatively for their benefit. These and similar sentiments were shared by many of the village level communists whom I interviewed. A number of them complained about what one communist called 'this confusing, treacherous period of bourgeoisdemocracy'. Many admitted uneasiness over opportunistic electoral alliances and though that eventually the Left communists would be forced by repression to abandon the constitutional road and to arm and organize the peasantry. With this background, I was not surprised to read that a majority in four out of nine district committees in Kerala tend to favour the 'rebel' path.[18] The party-plenums in Kerala in January 1968 re-endorsed E.M.S. Namboodiripad's communist-led United Front government, but this unity is apparently precarious. The All-India Peasant Union President, A.K. Gopalan of North Kerala, has since called for intensive organization among peasants, especially landless labourers, recruitment of peasant and worker volunteer forces, and psychological preparation of the peasantry for a prolonged struggle against the landlords and the imperialists.

What conclusions can be drawn from this analysis? In Kerala and Tanjore, peasant revolts occurred frequently during British rule. These revolts appear to have been responses to increased exactions from poor and middle peasant brought about by colonial capitalist relations. When they achieved scope and intensity the revolts aimed at throwing off the authority of the state and of landlords, and at setting up a local government drawn from the peasantry.

When modern reform or radical parties have coordinated the peasants without constricting them, peasants have tended to follow the same pattern of overthrow of landlords, seizure of the land, and removal or neutralization of officials of the existing state.

The difference has been that radical parties, especially the communists, have been able sometimes to link these revolts over wider areas and to infuse them with a revolutionary ideology and a new conception of the state.

In relatively traditional villages, peasants have readymade bases of organization in their caste assemblies, composed of the heads of households of one caste within each village or group of villages. These assemblies were traditionally organized for the settlement of internal disputes; in addition, the assembly of the dominant high ranking caste usually governed the village as a whole. During British rule, the assemblies of middle or low castes of tenants or laborers often provided a framework for revolt or resistance. The communists have appreciated the value of caste assemblies and, especially in Tanjore, have managed to unite the assemblies of several middle and low ranking castes in groups of villages to form labor unions capable of either organized revolt or constitutional agitation. Caste assemblies have their greatest strength and unity on large village estates where a majority of poor tenants or landless labourers fill the same role and are exposed to the same forms of oppression. Such assemblies are especially strong, egalitarian, internally democratic, and militant among Untouchable landless labourers. On foreign export crop plantations, in spite of caste, linguistic, religious, and kinship diversity, workers of the same street or barracks tend to form assemblies to settle their internal disputes along lines similar to their old caste assemblies. Such multi-caste, local assemblies also provide a ready basis for union organizing by leftwing parties.

Communist Party cadres operating in villages have come mainly from families of less successful landlords and rich peasants, from the children of priests and literati whose authority had been challenged by new bureaucratic and market-oriented institutions, and from such local and low-paid intellectual workers as school teachers and village clerks.

The communists were first able to recruit tenant cultivators of middle peasant rank into their peasant unions, and have hitherto tended to rely on the village leadership of this class. In Kerala and Tanjore, middle peasants come mainly from the middle to high castes of Hindus, Christians, and Muslims. Their early responsiveness to socialist ideas can probably be attributed to various factors mentioned by Eric R. Wolf.[19] These include their comparative literacy and knowledge of the wider society, their enjoyment of relatively greater security and autonomy than the poorest sharecropping tenants or landless laborers, yet their experience of uncertainty and of new kinds of exploitation in the market economy. In the agitations of the 1930s, as apparently during Malabar's 19th century peasant revolts, Kerala's middle peasants were able to organize large numbers of poor peasants to throw off some of the more traditional exactions of landlords. From about 1947, landless laborers were also, apparently for the first time, drawn into political struggles and organized into unions on a large scale. Difficulties exist because middle peasants themselves often exploit landless laborers. In many contexts, the interests of the two classes are opposed, and landlords have used every opportunity to keep them at enmity. In South India the extremely deep social and ritual barriers between middle or poor peasants of middle to low Hindu caste on the one hand, and those landless laborers who are of the lowest, Untouchable castes on the other, made the rapprochement between tenant and landless laborer peculiarly difficult. By the late 1950s, however, both in Kerala and Tanjore, the two were beginning to amalgamate within the same peasant unions and thus to reinforce each others' demands.

It is noteworthy, moreover, that the communists (and since 1964, the Left communists) have drawn their greatest support from states and districts where landless laborers are numerically most prominent, for example Bengal, Kerala, Andhra, and Tanjore. In Tanjore and Kerala, further, it is to my knowledge the landless laborers who, once they are aroused, most completely and consistently vote for the communists. In Tanjore, landless laborers, chiefly Untouchables, formed about one third of the total population in 1952; their proportion has certainly increased since then. In Kerala, landless labourers and their families increased from 12.5 percent of the total population in 1931 to 21.6 percent in 1951.[20] This figure is much higher today, even excluding the hundreds of thousands of workers on foreign export-crop plantations. In Malabar (North Kerala), the proportion of landless laborers to the total agriculturally dependent population increased from 38 percent in 1931 to 44 percent in 1951 and 47 percent in 1961. In contrast to Alavi, I would argue that the Indian communists have never accorded sufficient weight to the poor peasants and landless laborers in their organizational and revolutionary efforts. A change may, however, be underway among both rebel and orthodox Left communists. In a recent speech to the All-India Left Communist Kisan Sabha (Peasant Association), A.K. Gopalan stated that agricultural laborers now form 25-40 per cent of the population in most of the states of India. Gopalan's conclusion seems warranted, namely, 'We have to make them (the landless laborers) the hub of our activity. Reluctance to take up their specific demands, fearing that this will drive the rich and middle peasant away from us, will have to be given up.'[21]

Over the past sixteen years, the communists' pursuit of the parliamentary path has allowed them to increase the numbers of their supporters in several states. At the same time, it has placed serious difficulties in the way of organizing peasants and workers 'from below'. Concern with canvassing for national, state, and village elections takes village communist workers away from day-to-day organizational work among the propertyless. It causes even village communists, let alone national leaders, to focus on budgetary problems, short-term reforms; and the arithmetic of seats and votes. As a result, they tend to neglect socialist education and the deeper political and ethical problems of class struggle. In one North Kerala village, for example, a Left Communist Party member and panchayat president admitted to me that his task had become difficult because of electioneering. Between elections he tried to persuade Muslim poor peasants that the Communist Party had more to offer them than the non-socialist Muslim League. In the 1963 panchayat elections, however, the communists supported a number of League candidates, as the Left communists did later in the state elections of 1965 and 1967. In such ways the policy of "unity from above" through electoral alliances and adjustments with nonrevolutionary social democratic or non-socialist ethnic parties seriously damages the potential for class unity, with clear ideological direction, from below. It makes many peasants cynical about the sincerity of communist analyses of class struggle and suspicious that the communists, after all, are interested less in revolution than in power. When communists have actually attained power at the state level, as in Kerala in 1957-9 and, in 1967, their efforts to protect and to redistribute benefits to the poorest classes have brought them the gratitude of poor and middle peasants, landless laborers, and urban workers. These efforts are, however, too meagre to make a substantial difference. Confined within the provisions of the Indian constitution, it is impossible for the communists to transform property relations, allocate resources, and plan production. This means that they can compensate the propertyless only at the expense of the petty bourgeoisie, the rich peasants, and even some of the middle peasants, without increasing production. Further, their welfare-state efforts foster dependency and helplessness rather than active self-organization among the common people.

Meanwhile, during the last sixteen years, India's socio-economy has changed so that its problems are not the same as those of 1952. Although they have not given land to the tiller, the Congress Party's land reforms have changed relations in the countryside. As A.G. Frank suggests for Brazil, there seems to be some likelihood that social democratic land reforms can actually help to polarize property relations with regard to land. The upgrading of superior tenures and the guarantee of security of tenure mean that a small proportion of middle and rich peasants imporve their position. With inflation such as has occurred in Kerala in recent years, however, many more peasants have to sell out to usurers, landlords, merchants, or bureaucrats to keep their families alive. Again, landlords manage to evict large numbers of poor peasants and turn them into wage labourers before land reform laws come into effect, in order not to lose control of their land to their tenants. Similarly, measures to get rid of non-cultivating middle-tenants and rent-collecting landlords both produce a higher proportion of landlords and rich peasants farming with hired labor. The fact that most export crops are exempt from land-ceiling means, finally, that in an export-crop producing region like Kerala, an increasing proportion of the land is turned over to cashewnuts, rubber etc. The swelling numbers of poor tenants and landless laborers are thus left stranded, are crowded on to ever smaller plots, or are forced into squatting on forest lands, where they must fight an uneven battle against landlords, plantation managers, and government. Finally, the failure to industrialize with sufficient rapidity means that an increasing proportion of the population becomes dependent on agriculture and that landless laborers become the largest section of these.[22]

These conclusions are amply borne out in the North Malabar village that I surveyed in 1948 and 1964.[23] In spite of all the land-reform acts that have been passed in Kerala, the biggest landowning Nayar matrilineage has increased its share of the ownership of the total village lands from 31.5 percent in 1948 to 44.6 percent in 1964. Its holdings in this village now form part of a total estate of about 30 square miles. In the same village, 21.9 percent of the land has remained in the ownership of a Hindu temple located some ten miles away and managed by a small number of wealthy high caste Hindu families. The remaining 33.5 percent of the village land was, by 1964, divided between 206 other owners of middle and poor peasant rank. The total acreage of the village was 1,351 acres, and the population had increased from 1,176 in 1949 to 1,478 in 1964.

Among the villagers, the percentage of landlords and rich peasants had dropped from 4.3 percent in 1948 to 2.6 percent in 1964. The proportion of middle peasants, together with persons of middle peasant rank who retained a little land and ran some other occupation, had fallen from 23.6 percent to 9.2 percent of the total. This meant that in 1964 only 11.8 percent of the villagers owned or leased enough land to maintain themselves and their families, while 27.9 percent could maintain themselves from their lands in 1948.

Coming to the poor peasants and landless laborers, we find in this village that poor peasants, that is, persons who lease or own one substantial garden for their own use but hire themselves out as laborers for at least half of each day when they can, formed 36.7 percent of the villagers in 1964, as against 41.7 percent in 1948. This does not mean that some poor peasants have risen in wealth since 1948. It means, rather, that while the poor peasants category has received some new people from the former middle peasant rank, a larger number of poor peasants have completely lost their land since 1948 and have become landless laborers. Such people lease no land and own only a small shack together with the use-right of one-tenth of an acre of garden on their landlord's property. Even this latter privilege they owe to the communist government of 1957-9 and they are not always accorded it in practice. In all, 29.3 percent of villagers were landless laborers in 1948; 51 percent were landless laborers in 1964.

A further significant fact is that in 1964, a high proportion of the landless laborers were no longer even farm workers, for there was no room for them on the land. Instead, they had dropped into the poorest category of casual laborers who pick up jobs when they can, usually cutting timber in the forests, or cutting out and transporting blocks of laterite for urban building programmes. In 1948, 5.5 percent of the villagers were in such casual manner work, but in 1964, 25 percent were either in such work or were unemployed. This North Kerala village thus demonstrates conclusively an increasing polarization in land-relations, and thus in incomes, between 1948 and 1964.

Increasing polarization between agricultural classes knocks out the middle peasants as a significant social category. It breaks down the barriers between poor peasants and landless laborers, and, among these classes, between "clean" castes, 'backward' castes, and Harijans. There are definite signs that increasing polarization of agrarian relations also breaks down religious barriers between Hindus, Muslims, and Christians among the propertyless in villages. The prolonged food shortage and the ever growing inflation in Kerala of the last five years have brought these rural classes, and their urban counterparts, to a pitch of anger and militancy in which they take action independently along traditional lines or along lines laid down by their Marxist leaders of the 1930s and 1940s. Strikes, 'encirclements' of cabinet ministers and government officials, attacks on transport and food stores, and threats or assaults against landlords and plantation managers have become common, and a fairly large revolt occurred on the Munnar tea plantation in Travancore in January and February, 1968. Incipient revolt among the peasants in turn produces counterattacks by the landlords, usurers, and big merchants, poses problems of "law and order" for the United Front Government, and brings on the threat of intervention from the Central Government.

The precise details of ideological and policy crises within the Left Communist Party and between the Party and its expelled rebels cannot be fully assessed by observers from the outside. In the past few months, however, communist leaders in Kerala, while officially endorsing the United Front Government, have formed volunteer corps among the peasants and urban workers to carry out public works projects and to fend off violent attacks. With Indonesia, 1966, as an object lesson, it is possible that these measures are being taken none too soon.

References

1 This paper was first read at a meeting of the South Asia Colloquium of the Pacific North-west held at the University of Washington on April 23, 1968. The research is based on field-work in Kerala and Madras in the late 1940s and early 1950s, and in Kerala in 1964. Fieldwork in Kerala was made possible by grants of William Wyse and Anthony Wilkin Studentships from the University of Cambridge in 1947-9, and by an Auxiliary Research Award from the Social Science Research Council and a gift from my mother-in-law, Mrs. David W. Aberle, in 1964. The Tanjore research was financed by a British Treasury Studentship. My thanks go to all of these bodies and persons.
2 Hamza Alavi, 'Peasants and Revolution' reproduced above, Eric R. Wolf, 'Peasants and Revolution', a paper read at the Socialist Scholars' conference, New York, September, 1967; and Andre Gunder Frank, *Capitalism and Underdevelopment in Latin America; Historical Studies of Chile and Brazil*, New York, Monthly Review Press, 1967.
3 For Studies of agrarian relations in the two areas, see Adrian C. Mayer, *Land and Society in Malabar*, Oxford, Oxford University Press, 1952; Thomas W. Shea, 'The Land Tenure Structure in Malabar and its Influence on Capital Formation in Agriculture', unpublished Ph.D. thesis, University of California Press, 1965; Dagfinn Sivertsen, *When Caste Barriers Fall*, London, Allen and Unwin, 1963; Kathleen Gough, 'Caste in a Tanjore Village', in Edmund R. Leach (ed.), *Aspects of Caste in South India, Ceylon and Pakistan*, Cambridge, the University Press, 1962. E.M.S. Namboodiripad, *Kerala Yesterday, Today and Tomorrow*, Calcutta, National Book Agency, 1967, and A.K. Gopalan, *Kerala, Past and Present*, London, Lawrence & Wishart, 1959, provide especially valuable 'inside' views.
4 Mao Tse-tung, 'How to Analyse the Classes in the Rural Areas', *Selected Works*, New York, International Publishers, 1954, I, pp. 138-40.
5 See Daniel and Alice Thorner, *Land and Labour in India*, New York, Asia Publishing House, 1962, pp. 51-70. The free sale of land and labor came about at different dates in different regions. Kerala had had some wage labor and considerable sale of land before the British conquest of 1972, but they had been restricted by law to particular castes. Land sales appear to have been rare in Tanjore before British rule began in 1799. Under British law, land seems to have been freely marketable in Kerala by about 1830; in Tanjore by 1865. (W. Logan, Malabar, Madras, the Government Press, 1951, Vol. I, p. 582; F.R. Hemingway, Madras District Gazetteers, Tanjore, Madras, the Government Press, 1906, p. 184.) The various kinds of slaves and agricultural serfs were gradually freed between 1812 and 1854.

6   Unfortunately we lack comparative data since we do not know much about revolts or famines among peasants in Tanjore and Kerala before British rule, nor do we know the precise amounts of their real incomes before the nineteenth century. We do know, however, that the population of Malabar District increased from an estimated 465,594 in 1802 to 2,261,000 in 1891 and 4,758,300 in 1951, and that there were severe famines almost every year between 1836 and 1896, especially in the years of the worst revolts. Since I have not found accounts of large-scale evictions and unemployment, of prolonged famines, or of revolts of peasants against their landlords (rather than on their behalf, against other authorities) for pre-British Kerala, I conclude that the upheavals and disasters of the nineteenth century did spring primarily from the introduction of colonial capitalism. It is true, of course, that productivity must have increased in order to support such a rapidly expanding population, but that fact does not bear on the rate of exploitation of the peasantry. It is also equally true that the eighteenth century saw other kinds of disasters, particularly massive reductions of the population through wars. These wars were themselves, however, largely a result of competition between the European mercantile powers and between them and the indigenous rulers.
7   A.S. Memon, *Kerala District Gazeteers*, Trivandrum, Government Press, 1962, p. 180.
8   P.C. Joshi, 'Unmasked Parties and Politics', March, 1940, quoted by Gene D. Overstreet and Marshall Windmiller, *Communism in India*, Berkeley and Los Angels, University of California Press, 1959, p. 181.
9   For accounts of these revolts, see Overstreet and Windmiller, *op. cit*., pp. 276-312 and Alavi, *op. cit*.,
10 John F. Muehl was an eye-witness of this revolt, which he describes in Interview With India, New York, John Day, 1950.
11 B.T. Ranadive, 'Struggle for People's Democracy and Socialism—Some Questions of Strategy and Tactics', *Communist, II*, June-July, 1949, p. 71, quoted in Overstreet and Windmiller, *op. cit*., p. 287.
12 The Tanjore Tenants and Pannayals Protection Ordinance, 1952, which raised the wages of tied laborers and raised the tenant's share of the crop from one-fifth to two-fifths. The Ordinance did not, however, affect the wages of the increasingly large number of day-laborers, nor did it strengthen the claims of tenants who had no written leases.
13 For articles relevant to the Naxalbari revolt and the official Left communist attitude towards it, see *People's Democracy*, Calcutta, Vol. 3, Nos. 23, 24, 25, 26, 27, 28, 29, and 30.
14 See 'Notes', *Liberation*, Calcutta, No. 3, January 1968, pp. 95-6; 'Revolutionary Comrades on the March', *Liberation*, No. 4, February 1968, pp. 77-82; 'Rebellion is Right!' *Liberation*. No. 5, March, 1968, pp. 92-6; and '*Rebellion is Right!*' *Liberation*, No. 6, April 1968, pp. 96-109.
15 Programme of the Communist Party of India, Calcutta, 1964, p. 23.
16 This view is partly influenced by A.G. Frank's analysis of the Brazilian economy (op. cit.) and by his argument that the character of the capitalist metropolitan countries' monopoly of the world capitalist economy is changing from a monopoly ownership of most branches of industry itself to a monopoly of the technology of industry. This gives the metropolitan powers, especially the United States, increasing control over the new industries recently established in underdeveloped regions. My view is also based partly on the observation that in 1964 I found a marked sense of economic, military, and psychological dependence on the United

States among almost all members of the Indian bourgeoisie whom I met, in contrast to the views I heard expressed in 1947-53.
17 See Bowani Pathak, 'Character of the Indian Bourgeoisie', *Liberation*, No. 2, December 1967, pp. 76-82. An official Left communist argument against this position is made in 'Is the Indian Big Bourgeoisie Comprador?' *People's Democracy*, Vol. IV, No. 17, April 28, 1968, pp. 6-8.
18 *Link*, New Delhi, January 14, 1968, p. 13.
19 *Op. cit.*, see note 2.
20 *Techno-Economic Survey of Kerala*, Trivandrum, the Government Press, 1962, p. 211.
21 *People's Democracy*, Vol. IV, No. 6, February 11, 1968, p. 5.
22 Between the Census of 1931 and the Census of 1951 the percentage of Kerala's population dependent on agriculture is reported to have increased from 34.2 percent to 53.84 per cent. *Techno-Economic Survey of Kerala*, p. 211.
23 The village, which I have called Parambur, lies sixteen miles inland from the coast in Cannanore District in the foothills of the Western Ghats. For further references to the village see my articles, 'Village Politics in Kerala', *Economic and Political Weekly*, February 20, 1965, pp. 363-72, and February 27, 1965, pp. 413-9.

37 Peasant Movement in India

Uday Mehta

A PROPER APPRAISAL of the peasant movement in India becomes difficult on account of the paucity of comprehensive data on the subject. With this basic limitation, an attempt is made here to analyse it in terms of its historical evolution in India. This article is written in the hope that it will provoke further discussions on the subject by more competent persons.

Evolution

Historically the peasant movements in India can broadly be grouped in the following three distinct phases:

1. *The Initial Phase (1857-1921)*: This phase was characterized by the sporadic growth of peasant movements in the absence of proper leadership.

2. *The Second Phase (1923-1946)*: This phase was marked by the emergence of the class conscious peasant organisations. Its distinct feature was that during this period peasant movements were led by people who gave priority to kisan problems in the struggle for national liberation.

3. *Post-Independence Phase*: This era witnessed the uninterrupted continuity of the agrarian movements due to the failure of the ruling party to resolve any of the basic problems of the toiling masses in rural India. The peasant struggles in this period were led predominantly by left political parties like the CPI, the PSP and the SP through their kisan organizations.

The Initial Phase

The tyranny of zamindars along with the exhorbitant rates of British land revenue led to a series of spontaneous peasant uprisings in different parts of the country during this period. The periodic recurrence of famines coupled with the economic depression during the last decades of the 19th century further aggravated the situation in the rural areas and consequently led to numerous peasant revolts.

Reproduced from *The Call*, Delhi, May, 1965, Vol. XVI 12, pp. 14-6.

The following were the notable agrarian movements of this phase: 1. The Santal Rebellion of 1855 against the oppression by the British Government; 2. The Deccan riots of 1875 against the moneylenders; 3. The Bengal tenants struggles against zamindari tyranny during 1870-85; 4. The Oudh Insurrection; and 5. The Punjab kisan struggles against the moneylenders in the last decade of the nineteenth century.

In 1917-18, under the leadership of Mahatma Gandhi, the Indian National Congress led two significant peasant struggles. It organized the struggle of the peasants of Champaran in Bihar against the indigo planters, most of whom were Europeans. Thereafter, it launched the satyagraha movement of peasants in Kaira against the collection of land revenue which they were unable to pay due to failure of crops.

The Role of the Indian National Congress in Peasant Movements

Despite the fact that the Indian National Congress came into existence in the late 19th century, it took cognizance of the peasant problems only in the second decade of the 20th century. In the initial years, the Congress laid exclusive stress on the needs of the Indian industrialist class, ignoring the urgency of agrarian problems. Its manifesto just reiterated some of the superflous demands such as permanent settlement of land revenue and the abolition of salt tax etc. But the Congress leaders remained scrupulously silent about the problems of the vast bulk of tenants in zamindari areas during the earlier phase of the movement. With the appearance of Mahatma Gandhi on the Indian political scene, the Indian National Congress experienced a metamorphosis. Its sphere of influence was extended and it assumed a mass character. The Congress formed peasant committees in rural areas and took note of peasants' grievances. However, the peasant movements initiated by the Congress were invariably restricted to seeking relief against the excessive rates of land revenue, and were in no case directed against the zamindars.

The Second Phase: Emergence of Class Conscious Organizations

The Congress policy of safeguarding the interests of zamindars and landlords led to the emergence of independent class organizations of kisans in rural India. Radical sections in the peasant movements increasingly realised that the Congress was solicitous of the interest of the capitalists and land magnates. They felt that to protect the interests of the kisans, their own class organizations and leadership must be evolved. Consequently, the kisan organizations came into existence in different parts of the country.

The first Kisan Congress held at Lucknow in 1935 led to the formation of the All India Kisan Sabha. The programme of the Sabha reflected the aspirations and needs of the entire peasantry in agrarian India. The All India Kisan Sabha was composed of radical petty bourgeois individuals, within and outside the Indian National Congress. It was also supported and strengthened by the Congress Socialist Party and later on by the Communist Party of India. We shall now refer to some of the significant struggles launched by the Kisan Sabha in different parts of the country during the initial period of their inception.

In Andhra Pradesh it launched an anti-settlement agitation against zamindari 'zulum' in 1927. Swami Sahajanand, one of the eminent leaders and pioneers of the All India Kisan Sabha led a heroic movement for the abolition of zamindari in Bihar. A powerful struggle was initiated against the oppressive forest laws in South India in 1927. Similarly, in UP and other parts of India agitations were launched against the tyranny of zamindars.

The growth of peasant movements exercised considerable pressure on the Indian National Congress. Despite this, the Karachi Congress charter did not touch even the fringe of the peasant problem. But the political pressure of the Kisan Sabha succeeded in the Faizpur Congress and paved the way for the formulation of the Congress agrarian programme. However, the Congress could not, under the pressure of the native bourgeoisie grant any radical consessions to the peasant demands, at the cost of jeoparadizing the interests of zamindars. This was amply demonstrated by the performance of the Congress ministries during the short period that they were in office before independence.

The Provincial Ministries and Peasant Struggles

In Bihar, the Congress-zamindar agreement prevented the Ministry from adopting any radical measures in the interest of the peasants. Similarly, in Central Provinces and Bombay, the Congress Ministries refused to entertain any such proposals. The enactment of the ambiguous land legislations by the Bengal Ministry resulted in widespread eviction of the tenants. Thus the miserable performance of the Congress Ministries worsened the plight of the peasants and the resultant growing unrest led to a series of uprisings in different parts of the country. The massive agitation launched by Bihar kisans against the betrayal by the Congress Ministry, anti-settlement campaign in UP, debt relief struggle in Bengal, the Koya revolt, the Bhil disturbances in Mayurbhanj are instances of heroic peasant struggles. This in turn led to a chain of Kisan revolts in Indian States against feudal brutalities during 1937-46. The Mysore and Travancore struggles for responsible government, the Orissa agitation against princes, the Jaipur, Udaipur, and Gwalior revolts against local Thakurs are some of the glorious events in the history of the Indian peasant movement. However, it should be noted that during this phase too the All India Kisan Sabha with its roots in the upper section of the peasantry could not develop any effective struggle for the problems of the submarginal farmers and agricultural labourers. Secondly, in the absence of a clear Marxist perspective the Kisan Sabha movements at times took even communal turns.

In 1942, Indian kisans responded to the Congress call of Civil Disobedience movement most heroically. In Uttar Pradesh, Bihar, Bengal, Maharashtra and Tamilnad, they formed parallel governments. Nevertheless, the outstanding achievement was in Midnapore in Bengal where for years the British rulers were unable to regain their control. It may not be an exaggeration to say that if the peasant movements had received proper guidance from a mature Marxist leadership, Indian history would perhaps have taken a different course.

Post-Independence Era

The failure of governmental measures in resolving agrarian problems has been widely recognized and admitted today. The land reforms and community programmes meant for promoting capitalist farming in India have only succeeded in intensifying the agrarian crisis. The Congress Government has not only failed in providing relief to the vast bulk of deficit farmers and agricultural proletariat, but its agrarian policy has aggravated their miseries. This fact has been sufficiently demonstrated by the various Government

Evaluation Reports and non-official enquiries on the impact of welfare measures on rural society. Consequently, Indian agrarian society is seething with discontent even after independence. This has led to a series of peasant struggles in different parts of the country. We shall briefly refer to the principal movements organized by major left parties through their kisan organizations in recent years.

Agrarian Movement of Kisan Sabha

The All India Kisan Sabha under the influence of the CPI led numerous struggles. The following are some of the more significant amongst them.

On the eve of independence, the All India Kisan Sabha led a very heroic battle of the peasants in the Telangana district of the erstwhile Hyderabad State. Over 2,000 villages set up their own people's committees, took over the land and maintained their own administration and armed defence over an area of 15,000 sq. miles and resisted the onslaughts of the notorious bands of Nizam for a considerable period. It is hardly necessary to point out that in the absence of preparation on All India basis and poor response of the toiling masses, this isolated and adventurous action resulted in massive massacre of innocent tillers who responded to the call of the Kisan Sabha. Tebhaga movement of crop-shares for reduction of landlord's share in Bengal, Warli revolt against forest contractors and moneylenders in Maharashtra anti-betterment levy against excessive rates of irrigation in Punjab, agitation against food-hoarders and rise in food-grain prices in Bihar, struggles for proper implementation of land ceilings in Bengal, and agitation for fixing higher prices of sugarcane are some of the instances of significant movements initiated by the Kisan Sabha since independence. Besides this, the Sabha led an agitation for higher wages for agricultural labourers in Tamilnad and Maharashtra. In Kerala, it led numerous struggles for land reforms. In Andhra, it launched a movement for rehabilitation of landless labourers on waste lands in recent years.

Peasant Struggles under the PSP and the SP

Now we shall briefly enumerate the principal struggles under the leadership of the Praja Socialist Party in rural India.

In 1958, the PSP launched a satyagraha for relief measures in the famine-stricken areas of UP and further organized protest movements against irrigation cess levies from UP peasants. A struggle for proper implementation of land ceilings in Bihar, an agitation against heavy water tax in Rajasthan, a movement against food scarcity and for rehabilitation of landless labourers in Madhya Pradesh, and the Bhil agitation against oppressive forest lands in Rajasthan are some of the significant peasant movements organized by the PSP in recent years. Besides this, the PSP organised a massive satyagraha for the settlement of the landless labourers on grassland in the Paradi taluka of Gujarat State.

In contrast to the CPI and the PSP the Socialist Party prepared a comprehensive plan for launching civil disobedience movements simultaneously in different parts of the country. 'Ghera Dalo' movement, started in Uttar Pradesh during 1956 was a part of this broad programme. These struggles were mainly directed against high prices of food grains and for relief measures in the famine-stricken areas in Uttar Pradesh. The demands of the SP included (a) free kitchen and cheap foodgrain (b) fixation of reasonable prices by the Government and legal action against the hoarders and profiteers (c) remission of taxes, levies, rents etc., in famine-stricken areas (d) fixation of ceiling and completion of land redistribution programme within the prescribed time, and scaling down of irrigation rates and (e) abolition of taxes on profitless agriculture, etc.

According to the Socialist Party, the movements led by the CPI and the PSP are mere symbolic protests against the government's agrarian policy while the 'Ghera Dalo' and other struggles launched by the SP involved direct action by hungry peasants themselves.

The Supra-class Approach of the CPI and the PSP

It can be seen from the peasant movements led by the CPI and PSP that there is no basic difference between them. Not only are the forms and demands of the struggles the same but even the approaches of both remain essentially identical. Both the parties suffer from illusions of 'progressive aspects' of the Congress Govt. Both have betrayed their faith in the consolidation or strengthening of the national economy as a result of the state policy of the public sector. This illusion restricts the scope of the movements initiated by them. It also explains their arbitrary suspension and sudden withdrawal of the movements for appeasing the so-called progressive bourgeoisie in the Congress government. It can be also observed that most of the struggles initiated by these parties were limited to the effective and speedy implementation of agricultural legislations. The supra-class approach of the CPI at the national level also prevents it from organizing any genuine tillers' movement which would jeopardise the interests of the rich peasantry. Its sole object seems to be the preservation of a mythological village unity even if it involves the persistence of the sufferings of the vast bulk of deficit farmers and agricultural labourers. In consonance with its policy to woo the rich peasantry none of the Communist-led agrarian movements was launched for the specific problems of the large bulk of the submarginal farmers, like abolition of taxes in uneconomic farms. Even the CPI enthusiasm for land ceilings seems to be notivated from its desire to assist or accelerate the development of small-scale capitalist farming in rural India. From the point of view of the CPI, the only obstacle to development of productive forces in Indian agriculture is survival of feudal mode of cultivation, as if the elimination of feudal remnants from Indian agriculture would usher in a new era of progressive peasant proprietorship as in European countries in the 17th and 18th centuries during the hey-day of capitalism. Nothing seems to be more unhistorical and arbitrary than this borrowed belief in the possibility of a healthy growth of small-scale capitalist farming within the matrix of underdeveloped Indian economy. It is no wonder that with its reformist approach the peasant movements led by the CPI today remain ill-organized and sporadic in nature without even assuming a national level.

In this connection it is interesting to note that even a non-Marxist American scholar, Myron Weiner has distinctly pointed out the supra-class approach of the Communist kisan organisations in his recent work, *Politics of Scarcity*. He observes: 'The Fifteenth Provincial Conference, meeting in 1957, announced that the Kisan Sabha favoured compensation for those small intermediaries whose holdings were confiscated by the Government. It further declared that the organization would launch agitation for agricultural loans, improved irrigation facilities, manure, education, health and drinking water, and would continue agitation against excessive irrigation taxes and other taxes, including a proposed development tax. The Sabha also announced that it would work within the existing legislative framework, would take the initiative in forming panchayats (local govt. councils) under the new Panchayat Act, and would support credit co-operatives, marketing societies, handicraft co-operatives, and even the government's community development programme and National Extension Service. In short, the Kisan Sabha proposed to minimise agitations and maximise the benefits, peasant (and the Kisan Sabha) might receive by working within existing legislation, while at the same time putting pressure on the State government for greater rural expenditures. Rural harmony rather than class conflicts was the new theme of the West Bengal Kisan Sabha". (P. 159). Further, 'a similar position now guides the national All India Kisan Sabha. The groups in Kerala, Bihar, Assam and Tripura all want a moderate Kisan position.'

It must be said to the credit of the Socialist Party that its approach towards peasant movement appears to be more dynamic than that of the CPI and the PSP. Nevertheless, the absence of a clear perspective and resultant inconsistent and contradictory policy prevents its leadership from developing any effective agrarian movement on a national plane.

The paradox of the Indian situation is that non-Marxist organizations like the Republican Party today champion the cause of the agrarian proletariat and even lead their struggle at an all India level, while the so-called vanguards of the toiling strata in the rural society vie with each other in subserving the interest of richer peasantry.

Under the circumstance it becomes all the more imperative for the Revolutionary Socialist Party to build up class organizations of the rural poor and agricultural labourers and champion their cause.

38 The 'Two-Stages' Theory of Revolution in the Third World: Need for its Evaluation

A.R. Desai

Lenin on Stages of Revolution

LENIN MADE a profound statement in his famous work, *Proletarian Revolution and Renegade Kautsky*:

'.... beginning *April 1917*, long before the October Revolution, that is, long before we assumed power, we publicly declared and explained to the people: the revolution cannot now stop at this stage, for the country has marched forward, capitalism has advanced, ruin has reached unprecedented dimensions, which (whether one likes it or not) will *demand* steps forward, *to Socialism*. For there is no other way of advancing, of saving the country which is exhausted by war, and of *alleviating* the sufferings of the toilers and exploited.

'Things have turned out just as we said they would. The course taken by the revolution has confirmed the correctness of our reasoning. *First*, with the 'whole' of the peasantry against the monarchy, against the landlords, against the mediaeval regime (and to that extent, the revolution remains bourgeois, bourgeois-democratic). *Then*, with the poorest peasants, with the semi-proletarians, with all the exploited, *against capitalism*, including the rural rich, the kulaks, the profiteers, and to that extent the revolution becomes a *Socialist* one. *To attempt to raise an artificial Chinese Wall between the first and second stage (Ed), to separate them by anything else than the degree of preparedness of the proletariat and the degree of its unity with the poor peasants, means monstrously to distort Marxism, to vulgarise it to substitute liberalism in its place. It means smuggling in a reactionary defence of the bourgeoisie as compared with the Socialist proletariat by

---

Reproduced from '*A Positive Programme of Indian Revolution*', C. G. Shah Memorial Trust Publication, No. 2.

means of quasi-scientific references to the progressive character of the bourgeoisie as compared with mediaevalism.' (Italics in the original).

Since Lenin made this epoch-making generalization, about the character of revolution, stages of revolution and the driving force of revolution, in Russia in 1917, history has vindicated without exception the validity of this crucial Marxist theoretical observation, with regard to the bourgeoisie, not merely of advanced capitalist countries but also with regard to the bourgeoisie of all underdeveloped countries.

Whenever the proletarian vanguard in the form of a Marxist party has followed this path—either consciously or pragmatically by empirically correcting the errors in the process of struggle—ruin of unprecedented dimension caused by capitalism has been stopped and a path of advancement taken. The history of all the countries, where the capitalist system has been abolished and a transitional economy based on a non-capitalist socialist path has been launched, has borne out the truth of Lenin's generalization. The section of the world comprised of the USSR, the People's Republic of China, Yugoslavia, East European countries, North Korea, North Viet Nam and Cuba etc. *has convincingly established that the path of economic advance beneficial to the people, and unstrangled by the imperialist-capitalist shackles, can start only after making a Socialist Revolution.* The experience of these countries had proved that even the elementary bourgeois-democratic tasks, like the agrarian problem, education and others which were resolved by the bourgeoisie in advanced capitalist countries through the democratic revolution can be resolved in colonial and semi-colonial countries only through Socialist Revolution and only when the society has taken to non-capitalist socialist path after the overthrow of capitalism.

Further, the experiences of the countries of Latin America, Africa and Asia which are characterized as Third World and which have taken to a 'path of mixed economy' capitalist development led by the bourgeoisie have also proved *by their failure either to charter a path of independent economic development or to relieve the burdens on the people*, the validity of Lenin's path-breaking generalization about the entire epoch. The experiences of the last twenty-five years after World War II, wherein the overwhelming majority of ex-colonial and semi-colonial countries have secured formal political freedom, wherein an effort to reshape the economy and society on the mixed economy capitalist path have been adopted, have increasingly established that even the elementary bourgeois democratic tasks cannot be fulfilled by the bourgeoisie, whatever be the category of the bourgeoisie that wields power. Even in countries where the economy exhibits some growth in terms of production compared to that when they were under direct or indirect rule of the imperialist masters, the rate of growth is very slow, and that also on the basis of a massive and extensive exploitation and oppression of the local producers. Even this development is either coming to a dead end or is losing its initial limited momentum, even though propped up by outside assistance. In these countries, the economy is being transformed into a neo-colony of the aiding powers.

This truth has to be restated firmly and with clarity today for a number of reasons.

(1) Communist parties claiming to follow a Stalinist line before his death, but claiming after Krushchev's exposures to follow the 'Marxist-Leninist' line are not acknowledging (in a large number of countries) the profound truth formulated by Lenin, and are really elaborating a massive sophistry by means of what Lenin characterized as 'quasi-scientific references to the progressive character of the bourgeoisie' as compared with mediaevalism and are thus 'smuggling in a reactionary defence of the bourgeoisie against the socialist proletariat.'

These parties are elaborating a complex group of arguments, are also weaving out a labyrinth of data and subtle defences to build up a Chinese Wall between two stages of revolution. They have even gone to the extent of proclaiming that a peaceful transition to socialism via pressurizing the progressive, national, anti-feudal, anti-imperialist, anti-comprador bourgeoisie to complete the National Democratic Revolution or People's Democratic Revolution is not only possible, but is the immediate task of the Communist parties. According to these parties, the stage of development in the Third World is that of a National Democratic, or People's Democratic Revolution and not of Socialist Revolution. According to them the advance now is not to be towards the goal of socialism or the overthrow of capitalism. In their view the stage of revolution does not depend only upon the preparation of the proletariat and the degree of its unity with poor peasants. These parties though sometimes refusing verbally, do in effect, therefore, erect a Chinese Wall between the first and the second stage of revolution i.e. between the Democratic and the Socialist stages. They, therefore, come to the conclusion that the proletarian parties have to concentrate today on completing the first phase of the revolution by pressurizing the progressive bourgeoisie or by allying with them under the hegemony of the proletariat and on completing the National Democratic or People's Democratic by strenghtening the progressive national bourgeoisie, and thereby assist the process of generating an independent economic development on bourgeois lines, free from the trammels of imperialist and feudal forces.

(2) There is a second reason for restating this truth formulated by Lenin. Communist parties in various countries of the Third World have elaborated their strategy and tactic of struggles on the assumption of their theory of two stages of revolution and have shaped their parliamentary and non-parliamentary movements on the basis of this fundamental postulate. These parties are elaborating their programmes of action, organizational manoeuvres, types of united fronts, and slogans for agitation on the assumption that the immediate tasks for the next stage of the revolution is to push the bourgeoisie—the progressive national bourgeoisie—towards completing the independent capitalist development, by elaborating the public sector, by coming in closer association with socialist countries, and by freeing economy, polity and social structure from the imperialist and feudal domination. The disastrous consequences of such a line for the exploited and toiling masses, based on 'dualeconomy' postulates and its significance in strengthening the bourgeoisie and thereby intensifying the capitalist exploitation and oppression of the toiling masses, are becoming more and more glaring. The strategy based on the thesis of two-stages revolution in weakening and disorganizing the fighting will of the exploited masses and channelizing the struggles of the masses into disastrous economism or unplanned anarchic outbursts have not been properly appraised.

(3) There is a third reason for restating the truth propounded by Lenin.

The experiences in all the countries of the Third World of Latin America, Africa and Asia where the bourgeoisie have secured formal political freedom from imperialism, and have organized the state machinery for developing their economy and social structure on the mixed-economy capitalist path, that is the path of economic development on the basis of 'relying on the rich' i.e., on strengthening the propertied classes, is worth noting. The bourgeoisie—whatever the hue—have invariably intensified the economic exploitation of the masses, and have astutely evolved the strategy of depending on foreign capital. If the resistance of the masses against their growing burden becomes more powerful, the ruling bourgeois class whether 'progressive-national or reactionary-comprador' or their henchmen, have let loose a reign of terror. The ruling classes of the Third World have not hesitated to seek assistance from imperialist powers or even secure military-political aid from the 'socialist' countries to suppress the militant class and mass movements in their own countries. The bourgeois ruling groups of a few of these countries have even openly embraced the imperialist powers, have invited them to protect them and have practically surrendered their political sovereignty to imperialist powers. They, have, in fact, left the governance of the country to the military-diplomatic arm of the imperialist bourgeoisie.

(4) There is a fourth reason for explicitly remembering the vital truth of Lenin's generalization.

During the last 25 years after the second World War, all efforts to reconstruct the economy and culture by the bourgeois national states in the Third World have proved that in the epoch of the declining phase of world capitalism, the weak, colonial bourgeoisie, even with the active help of their own national state, or even with assistance from 'socialist' or imperialist countries, cannot carry out even the elementary bourgeois-democratic tasks. They cannot industrialize their countries at a rate which would relieve the burden on the agrarian sector; they cannot develop at a tempo which would create conditions for a 'take-off'. They have neither the internal market, nor the external market to expand the economy at a buoyant rate even by the yard-stick of capitalism. Under the present circumstances, they cannot simultaneously exploit their own labouring masses and generate purchasing power among them. They cannot undertake major industrialization projects even by resorting to large doses of foreign aid in a manner that would not increase the growing burdens on the people. They cannot resolve elementary problems like freeing the masses from semi-feudal forms of exploitation or solve the agrarian problem. The bourgeoisie of the Third World, product of belated, distorted colonial development have developed so 'slothfully' and 'cravenly' that while they felt the cramping effect of foreign capital and its direct and indirect political domination, 'they were menacingly' faced by the proletariat and agrarian poor of their own countries on whose plunder they thrived. The colonial bourgeoisie were not capable of becoming heroic and truly revolutionary leaders like the bourgeoisie of France or Britain in the 17th and 18th centuries, who really formed the vanguard leaders of the anti-feudal democratic revolution. They always played a vacillating role, they wanted change, but basically by bargain and compromise. The colonial bourgeoisies, when they led the national independence movement against foreign imperialist rule, headed the mass and class movement only in order to divert this movement from the path of a thoroughgoing revolutionary struggle to the path of reformist oppositional pressure for bargaining with the foreign rulers. The bourgeoisie in the colonial countries, in the epoch of world capitalist decline, do not symbolise the victory of a new social order, but represent a system which has become old and superannuated. It trembles before and is haunted by the spectre of the Socialist Revolution and communism. As Paul Baran has rightly pointed out and David Horovitz, Gunder Frank and others have ably expounded, propertied calsses of all types, including the most progressive national bourgeoisie in underdeveloped countries are instilled with 'a mortal fear of expropriation and extinction.' This fear has been driving all more or less privileged, more or less well-to-do elements in the newly independent Third World society in one 'counter-revolutionary coalition'. 'In brief whatever differences and antagonism exists between various sections of domestic and foreign interests, they are generally subordinated and submerged on all crucial occasions by the overwhelmingly common interests of staving off socialism and of preventing and curbing socialist revolution. All of them, including the national bourgeoisie in underdeveloped areas unite against the growing menace of communism and, therefore, generate a hybrid conservatism, which degenerates liberalism into anti-communism'. The bourgeoisie of these countries are, therefore, denied the power of 'solving the economic and political deadlock prevailing in the underdeveloped countries on the lines of a progressive capitalism'.

Ernest Mandel, Hansen, Novack, Paul Baran, Paul Sweezy, David Horovitz, Gunder Frank and a large number of eminent Marxists have pointed out that the countries comprising the Third World cannot be regarded as underdeveloped in the orthodox sense, that is in the sense of being at an earlier stage of the development passed through advanced capitalism. On the contrary, their typical characteristic are not the characteristics of the immature stages of the newly developed capitalist societies, but of the combination of advanced and backward stages produced by partial penetration of capitalism in a backward semi-feudal colonial society. 'These economies are not dual (part capitalist, part feudal), as it sometimes suggested but 'hybrid' or 'mutant'. Their problems stem not from failure to develop, but from a distorted development, one that leads not along a path to eventual self-sustained growth but to an economic cul-de-sac. Real growth, in these mutant economies cannot be achieved by organic, evolutionary processes within the basic existing structures (least of all by an influx of foreign capital), but only through a revolutionary transformation of the structures themselves and cutting of dependent and dependency-generating ties.'

The findings of the UNO, the 4th International led by followers of Trotsky, and Baran, Sweezy, Gunder Frank and a host of Marxists, and even some of the critical bourgeois and petty bourgeois thinkers like Myrdal and others, have revealed the failure of the bourgeoisie of the ex-colonial countries to develop during the last 25 years to solve the economic and social-cultural problems. These studies have also proved that they cannot generate a self-sustained economic advance. They have further established that the national bourgeoisies of the Third World countries, because of the peculiarities as a result of their belated arrival on the historic scene, are not in a position to undertake the revolutionary tasks necessary to solve the urgent problems of national development within the confines of a capitalist social framework.

Imperialist subjugation of these colonial countries has skewed the internal socio-economic formations of these weakened, industrially backward countries. It has altered the class structures in such a manner, that even after securing politcal freedom from imperialism formally and securing the political reins of their countries, the national bourgeoisie (or any section of it) cannot lead the countries to the self-sustaining development and growth.

Self-sustained growth, economic and social advance, unfettered development of productive forces, and the rise in the standard of living of the masses would now become possible only when capitalism has been destroyed and a Marxist party of the proletariat backed by poor peasants, seizes power and launches the economy on the non-capitalist socialist path.

(5) There is a fifth reason for clearly grasping the profound implication of Lenin's formulation. The Communist parties which propagate the theory of two-state revolution are themselves unclear about the nature of the two stages of revolution. As rightly pointed out by Kathleen Gough in her article, 'Imperialism and Revolutionary Potential in South Asia', all the communist groups including the CPI, the CPM and the various Maoist groups in India, who postulate a 'two-stage' revolution differ over the precise character of the stages, over which classes will bring the two stages to completion, and above all, about how the stages are to be realized. As she emphatically asserts, the analyses formulated by these groups 'seem imperfect, partly because there is no dual economy and partly because the separation into two revolutionary stages is unnecessary and mechanical'. She rightly points out 'the time for an independent capitalist or even a 'non-capitalist' (but non-socialist), stage is past—that bus has been missed'.

Conclusion

The lesson of twenty-five years of bourgeois rule in the Third World has also vindicated the truth of Lenin's statement, which was formulated even earlier by Trotsky in his famous thesis of *Permanent Revolution*. Neither National Democratic Revolution, nor People's Democratic Revolution, but Socialist Revolution is the task on the agenda of history, and that strategy and tactic derived on the basis of pseudoscientific evaluation of colonial bourgeoisie as comprised of a section of progressive bourgeoisie and mortally in combat with feudal and imperialist forces are nothing but a monstrous distortion of Marxism and are leading to disastrous consequences for the exploited and toiling masses.

A methodical discussion on the theory of two-stages of revolution has, therefore, become urgent. I wish this discussion is started in India as it has profound implications for evolving a correct startegy and tactic for developing class and mass struggles in a country which envelops nearly one-fifth of world humanity.

39 Unconventional Anthropology of 'Traditional' Peasantry

A.R. Desai

(1)

ERIC WOLF in his *Peasant Wars of the Twentieth Century* (Faber) focusses attention on the role of peasantry from a new angle. As an anthropologist, Wolf attempts in his book to 'review the evidence of six cases of rebellion and revolution in our time in which peasants have been the principal actors'. He seeks a more sophisticated understanding of the political involvement of peasant groups, a subject hitherto ignored or viewed as incidental to the major focus of anthropology.

(2)

In the preface, Wolf reasons as to why anthropologists have to change their focus of studies, their objects of study and also ruthlessly break through biases that have imprisoned anthropologists in the West. As Wolf points out, anthropology, 'once conceived as the study of the primitive, of that radically "other" beyond the pale of civilization, this comparative science of savages and barbarians is now experiencing a major change in its subject matter: the far and distant populations "out there" have become participants in a drama set upon our stage. They are no longer exotic and hence capable of being admired or despised at a safe distance. They wear our own robes, address us in our own idiom, affect in tangible and immediate ways the outcome of a play we so willingly began with a sense of our own enduring superiority.'

Wolf also distinguishes himself from the entire group of social and cultural anthropologists who adopt an ahistorical approach to the study of peasants in the Third World, and who have adopted an 'ideal typical index' approach, or psychological approach to study the peasantry as 'little communities' which are treated as passive, unchanging, superstitious and traditional and further considered as major obstacles to the modernization of the Third World. Scholars adopt an attitude of superiority, and examine the peasantry as objects to be changed from outside by larger forces of capitalist modernization. Wolf urges anthropologists to return to history: 'we need a new kind of history, as an account of our growing existential involvement with one another. There is need for a history which will draw upon several specialized disciplines and yet transcend them, a history capable of telling us how the modern world was made in the systematic interaction of bush and town, of city dweller and peasant, of metropolis and satellite, of colonizer and colonized'.

Wolf then enumerates how anthropology can contribute to the reconstruction of such a unified account of contemporary mankind. According to him, anthropology offers (a) 'a history of populations long thought to be people without a past, but whose past is now very much a part of our present'; (b) 'a holistic perspective... without falling prey to the tendency to apportion human reality among several sets of rival specialists', (c) 'a lively sense of the importance of life as lived in small groups and ordered in narrow social networks and a recognition that life in such social microcosms persists in a powerful dialectic with the engulfing social macrocosm. In this recognition it not only draws attention to the many layered character of a complex society, but also emphasizes its sense that these layers and segments affect each other in a continuous process of the 'interpenetration of the opposites'.

(3)

The detailed account of Wolf's postulates as an anthropologist are given here with a view to highlight one significant development in the USA.

A section of the anthropologists have been shocked into a new sensitivity after the heroic struggles of the peasantry of Vietnam. This heroic peasantry which was described by the US Military as 'ragged little bastards in black pyjamas', confronted and defied in an unparallel manner the mightiest military machine in history. This peasantry, which was assumed to be the bearer of tradition and obstacle to modernization, was becoming a force which was shattering not merely the socio-cultural and politico-economic structure of Vietnam itself, but triggered some of the most profound movements in the very heart of the bastion of imperialism.

Wolf, belongs to a section of concerned anthropologists, who though still not avowedly Marxist, have been increasingly accepting, consciously or unconsciously some of the major elements of a Marxist approach to contemporary social reality. Wolf undertakes this study no longer in the tradition of 'pure scholarship' but adopts an approach and a methodology which comes closest to a Marxist approach, though Wolf himself is still not aware of it. He attempts to understand the role and activities of the peasantry under the impact of the world-wide spread of capitalism with its emphasis on production for profit and market, and producing its shattering impact in an uneven manner for various segments of feudal and pre-feudal social structures both in metropolitan countries and colonial and semi-colonial hinterlands. He focusses on the impact of capitalism on the peasantry in various parts of the world, and the reactions including participation in rebellions and revolutions that have taken place during this phase of human history. Wolf considers this as a global phenomenon. However he attempts to examine the problem through a few case studies of mighty upheavals in the twentieth century in which the peasantry took a very active part.

The six case studies examined by Wolf are (1) Mexico; (2) Russia; (3) China; (4) Vietnam; (5) Algeria; (6) Cuba.

After undertaking the review of the six case studies, Wolf in a very thought provoking chapter entitled 'Conclusion' highlights certain common and unique features of these six great upheavals. He also draws certain tentative generalizations which are fruitful for those who want to extend the studies to other countries or go deeper into the studies of the same cases taken by Wolf.

Wolf realizes the value of secondary sources, and need for properly utilizing such sources for understanding such events in which one cannot always proceed as participant or non-participant observer. His account of the case studies are based on secondary sources.

The case studies are carefully documented. They provide an exciting account of rebellions and revolutions in six countries. The accounts are lively, provide insightful details, endeavour to highlight the relative importance of various objective and subjective forces operating in each country. Each case reads like a poignant, heroic, and still authentic saga of a great event.

The Chapter on 'Conclusion' is most thought provoking and has raised issues which have very significant implications.

(a) The revolutions and rebellions described in the six case studies, though belonging to the twentieth century, were the product of tensions which had their roots in the past.

(b) This concrete historical experience 'bears the stigma of trauma and strife, of interference, rupture with a great past as well as the boon of continuity of successful adaptation and adjustment of events not easily erased and often only latent in the cultural memory until some greater event serves to draw them forth again.'

(c) 'In all our six cases this historical experience constitutes in turn, the precipitate in the present of a great overriding cultural phenomenon, the worldwide spread and diffusion of a particular cultural system—that of North Atlantic Capitalism'.

(d) The impact of capitalism as a world-wide system based on production for the market and operation on the principle of profit, meant that everywhere 'land, labour and wealth' have to be slowly transformed into commodities.

(e) This implied that land 'which was not regarded as a commodity in most of the other kinds of societies, but where rights to land are aspects of specific groups and its utilization, the ingredient of specific social relationship, 'if it had to become a commodity in the capitalist market... it has first to be stripped of these social obligations'. This was achieved either by force, through colonization of new lands or indirectly accomplished by furthering the rise of 'the strong and sober entrepreneurs within the peasant communities, who could abandon their ties to neighbours and kin, and use their surpluses in culturally novel ways to further their own stand in the market'. 'The spread of capitalism necessarily produces a revolution of its own'.

(f) 'This revolution from the beginning takes the form of an unequal encounter between the societies which first incubated it and societies which were engulfed by it, in the course of its spread. The contact between the capitalist centre, the metropolis, and the pre-capitalist or non-capitalist periphery is a large-scale cultural encounter, not merely an economic one'.

(g) Historically unique factors which gave rise to metropolitan advanced capitalist societies, were not to be repeated in other parts of the world. The contact between North Atlantic Capitalist Countries and the colonial and semi-colonial countries subjected to the forces generated by the former, created a situation in the latter countries wherein the old social structure and cultural systems were shattered, without being replaced by the more advanced capitalist system. The West disintegrated the old fabric but initiated distorted new subordinated ones shaped by its own requirements. This was a new experience uprooting the entire past and necessitating the creation of a new social order, which will eliminate the combined ravages of distintegrated old societies and destroy new forms of exploitation and oppression.

Wolf sums up this change in a very apt manner when he says: 'Where previously market behaviour had been subsidiary to the existential problems of subsistence, now existence and its problems became subsidiary to market behaviour'.

The impact of colonization created stratification, produced economic, political and socio-cultural situations, wherein the toiling strata, particularly middle peasants, poor peasant, agricultural labourers, tenants, city proletariat and lower middle classes could not attain security or improve their conditions by going back to the past, nor could they better their positions in the emerging new belated capitalist formations, which in the context of the historically declining phase of the capitalist system as a whole, had lost the ability to even fulfil the bourgeois-democratic tasks. Wolf emphasizes this point vividly in his own technical language and draws significant conclusions.

(a) Peasantry by itself would be rebellious, would launch gigantic upheavals, even wars, but if it is lead by parties or groups wedded to the capitalist path of development, would be a part of a capitalist order wherein its problems would only be aggravated as the Mexican and the Algerian cases reveal. If the peasants are guided by a party or a group firmly committed to destroying capitalism and take the social order to a non-capitalist path, the powerful rebellions launched by the peasantry, culminating in peasant wars can usher in conditions for the liberation of the peasantry and make it a part of the larger social order where the exploited strata would usher in a new epoch of non-capitalist socialist development, whatever the super-structural deformities arising out of faulty policies of the leaderships.

Wolf draws this conclusion from two cases of Mexico and Algeria where the leadership of the mighty peasant wars did not transcend the capitalist framework in their conception of a new order and from four cases where the leadership, was consciously Marxists, was disciplined, and inspite of numerous errors, pragmatically, pushing the movement from bourgeois-democratic limitations to a socialist revolutionary stage.

Wolf comes to this conclusions without recognizing that these conclusions were drawn theoretically by Trotsky in 1905 and explicitly stated as a guiding principle by Lenin in his *April Thesis* in 1917. Wolf also pragmatically states a profound truth which history after October Revolution has proved a number of times. This truth is stamped on our life vividly viz. wherever the colonial or semi-colonial countries have carried the anti-imperialist or anti-colonial battles to their successful socialist stage, and ushered in a non-capitalist path of development, the cycle of underdevelopment and distorted capitalist development have ceased and the societies have been launched to a historically higher stage. The leap from colonial backwardness to non-capitalist socialist development is ushered in, skipping over the period of the bourgeois stage. Wherever the peasant wars have been led by the forces wedded to the capitalist path of development and so channelled even by communists, these wars have ushered in an era of capitalist development which intensifies the exploitation of the peasantry, and leaves the tasks of the toiling strata unresolved. The story of Mexico and Algeria are evidence of this fact. One can multiply evidence from countries of the Third World, where the leadership has taken to a capitalist path of development.

INDEX

Abdul Gafar Khan 305
Acharya Narendra Deva, on peasantry 699
A.K. Gopalan 120, 733
All India Kisan Sabha (AIKS) 4, 7, 63, 238, 286, 289, 349–50, 428–41, 444; and Congress 428; and Congress Socialist party 428; and Communist 429–33, 436–8 and Kshatriya Sabha 433–4; and land reforms after Independence 709–13; and local leaders 433; and Muslim league 433–4; and Peasant's Struggles in Bengal 354–62; in Bihar 363–7; in Tebhaga 443–52, 461–8, 701–06; and revolutionaries 354–5; and Second World War 438–9; collective affiliation with I.N.C. 436–39; demands of 238, 430; Gaya Session 436–37; Hamza Alavi on 698–713; Memorandum to Flood Commission 434–36
Alluri Sitaram Raju 59, 60, 62, 74, 77, 277–8, 291–302
Andhra Mahasabha, demands Visal Andhra 494
Andhra Pradesh Revolutionary Committee 113–15, 126
Anti-Partition Movement (Bengal) 212
Anti-Rawlatt Act agitation 213, 217–18
Arya Samaj 421, 494
Bangiya Pradeshik Kisan Sabha 650–51; and Tebhaga in Pargana 656–662
Bannerjee, Tarun Kumar, Desai A.R. on 288–90; on Damodar Canal Tax movement (with others) 375–412
Basu, Jyoti 453
Beasant, Annie 64, 214, 222
Bhave, Vinoba 423, 438, 512
Bhoodan 423, 438, 512
Bose, Subhash Chandra 543
Brij Kishore Prasad 225–6
Buddhadeb Bhattacharya 287 Desai A.R. on 288–90; on Damodar Cannal Tax movement (with others) 375–412
Charu Mazumdar and A.J.K.S. 438; and Tebhaga 446; death of 116
Chatterjee Bankim Chandra 53
Chaudhary Sukhbir 221, 237 Desai A.R. on 211–22; on alliance of peasantry and nationalist intelligentsia 234; on Champaran struggle 223–34; on Chaurichaura episode 262–8; on Gandhiji 237, 263–8; on peasant struggles in 1905–18, 221–36; 1919–21, 237–374; Bengal 260–1; Gantur (Karnataka) 261–2; Moplah revolt 259–60; the United Provinces 238–59
Chaudhury, Binay Bhusan 282–7; on agrarian movement in Bengal and Bihar (1919–39) 337–74; on agrarian programmes of Congress 339–41; on aims of Peasant Movement 352–3; on depression and peasantry 346–8, 357; on hetrogeneity of peasantry 361–2; on impact of money rent 347; on importance of Peasant and Worker's Party 343–45; on land relations after amendment of Bengal Tenancy Act—1855, 343–5; on limitation of earlier struggles 339; on limitation of peasant struggles 367–70; on new features of peasant movement in 1919–39, 338–39; on Swami Sahajanand Saraswathi 348–50
Civil Disobedience Movement 1930s 8, 64, 213, 217, 218, 219, 263–8, 279, 285, 286, 292, 303–36, 353, 363, 417, 697, 698, 746; (1940–41) 439, 441
Communist Party of India (unified) 8, 11, 113, 116, 125, 133, 285, 289, 429, 441, 453, 582, 598–9, 651–2, 665, 667; and Commintern 285, 417, 418, 421, 422, 429, 503, 724; and Electoral Game 712–13; and Kisan Sabhas 418, 428–39, 443–52; and Naval Revolt (1946) 442; and

Quit India Movement 422; and Peasant struggles in Kerala 723–30; in Tebhaga 418–20; 443–52, 463–6, 701–06; in Tebhaga (Kakwdip) 469–70, 474–8, 480–4; in Telangana 421–4, 486, 494–513, 517–31, 706–09; Impact of split in International Communist Movement 730; Inner party struggle 510–11, 728–30; Kathleen Gough on 723–30; Randive line 510, 728; United Front Govt. in Kerala 728–30;
Communist Party of India (Marxist) 11, 85, 113–16, 125, 126, 426, 531, 552, 536, 651, 664, 667; and Krishak Sabha 651; and left adventurists in Bengal 731; and struggles of Kerala peasants 730–9
Communist Party of India (Marxist-Leninist) 113–116, 118, 124, 125, 126, 175, 426, 532
Congress Socialist Party 428, 495, 725, 745
Dange S.A. 266, 273; on Gandhism 266
Das C.R. 62
Das Dipak Kumar 275, 288–90; on Damodar Canal Tax Movement 375–412
Deutscher Issac on Mao's relation with peasantry 686
Dhanagare D.N. 486 Desai A.R. on 422; on definition of peasantry 486–7; on Marxism 486–7; on results of Telangana movement 512–13; on role of peasants in the Telangana movement 506–10; on Telangana struggle 586
Dutt R.C. 52–5, 120
Dutt R.P. 429–30, 440, 452
Forced recruitment in Army and Collection of funds (World War I) 212, 214–15, 221–3
Forward Block Party 667
Frank A.G. 719, 737; on changing pattern of World Economy 741–2
Frantz Fanon 671 on revolutionary potentiality and peasantry 671 Hamza Alavi on 671–2
Gandhi M.K. 4, 5, 6, 7, 59, 61, 84, 111, 152, 157–58, 235–37, 281–82, 335–36, 371, 415, 494, 501; and Civil Disobedience movement 279, 305–12, 438; and Dandi March 285; and Kheda-Satyagraha 55–56, 72–73, 230–34; and Khilafat Movement 110–12, 259, 624; and Indigo-cultivator's struggle (Champaran) 20, 54–55, 72, 223–30, 237, 340; and non-cooperation movement 56, 237, 263–68, 342, 349; and peasant struggle in U.P. 246, 247, 250; betrayed peasant 214, 219–20, 262–68; Chaudhuri Sukhbir on 237, 263–68; death of 525; Hamza Alavi on 697–98; Marxist estimates of 280–1; method of Satyagraha 54, 72–3, 213–14, 218; Mukhopadhyay Ashim on 651; on Adivasis 16–17; stratagist of ruling class 213–16, 219–20, 279–82, 439
Gokhale 54
Gough Kathleen 85, 119, 120, 122, 125, 627, 719; Desai A.R. on 9–11, 597–9; on agricultural labourers 91, 121, 737–39; on caste and peasant struggles 113–14, on Kerala 723–39; on Kerala (unified) 723–30; in Kerala (CPIM) 730–39; on compulsion to cultivate for export 90, 120; on 'de-industrialization' 90; 119–120; on ill-treatment of revolutionaries 126; on impact of British-Rule 88–94; on Kerala land-relation 719–23; on messianic movements 123; on messianic movements and cultural minorities 100–01; on limitation of peasant revolt 87–8; in pre-1920 period 112; in post 1920 period 112–13; on Naxalbari movement 731–3; on peasant revolution and socialism 118–19; on peasant struggles, 96; in 1765–1857 period 122; in pre-British period 88; in Kerala 719–42; lessons of 116–18; types of 94–6; Statistics of 86, 94, 96, 100, 103, 108–9; on pattern of world economy 741–2; on similarity between religious peasant struggles and social banditry

105–07; on social background of Kerala Communists 734–5; Panikkar K.N. on 601–02
Gunnar Myrdal 374 impact of caste system 368
Gupta Sulekh on capitalist farming 710–11
Hamza Alavi 122, 125, 126, 671, 719; on role of middle and poor peasants 672–75; Kathleen Gough on 721–25; on agrarian relations in China 688–91; in Russia 676–78; on Bhowani Sen's evaluation of middle peasants 701, 705; on condition of success of Chinese Communists 692–3; on definition of peasantry in Marxist literature 673–5, 716; on difference between Chinese and Indian situation 696–7; on Frantz Fanon's view of revolutionary potentiality of peasantry 671–2; on impact of Gandhi on Indian Nationalist movement 697; on land reforms 711; on Marx-Engels views on peasantry 672; on Mao 685–9; on pattern of political behaviour of peasantry 713–16; on peasant and revolution 671–718; on peasant upheaval in China 685; in Russia 679–83; on place of peasantry in Leninist revolutionary strategy 675–84; on process of agrarian revolution and role of Communist bureaucracy 693–6; on Red Army (China) 692–6; on role of Mao and Maoists in agrarian revolution in China 693–6; on Tebhaga and role of Communists 701–06; on Telangana and role of Communists 706–09
Hindu Mahasabha 494
Hobsbawn 99, 103, 106, 122–4
Home Rule agitation 212, 214–15, 221–3
Home Rule League 215, 221
Hume A.O. 171–2
Hutton J.H. on reasons of Tribal struggles 17
Indian National Congress 5, 53–54, 61, 71–4, 84, 158, 167, 171–2, 212, 238, 254–55, 260, 263, 265, 272, 283–5, 289, 292, 335, 342, 415, 441, 518, 598–9; agrarian programme of 339–41; and Kisan Leaders 362–3; and civil disobedience movement 279, 303–14, 329; and non-cooperation movement 56, 237, 263–8, 342, 349; and peasant struggle in Champaran 20, 54–5, 72, 223–30, 237, 340; Damodar Canal Tax Movement 381, 386, 392, 397, 400–09, 412; in Kheda 55–56, 72–73, 230–34; in Pargana 657–67; in Tebhaga 419, 449, 421, 494, 501, 505, 519–21; in U.P. 246, 247, 250; in Warli 425; betrayed the masses 62–8, 214, 219–20, 284, 342, 356, 415–18, 542–6; Chaudhury Binoy Bhushan on 339–41; Desai A.R. on 213–20, 279–82, 415–18, 426; disillusionment with 220, 262–68, 268–69; Hamza Alavi on 697–98; initiated land-reform 710–12; Ministry of 73–5, 356, 362, 363–, 415, 434, 453; Mukhopadhyay, Ashim on 647–48, 651; national government of 542, 546; on affiliation with AIKS 436–39; Ranga on 6–7, 54, 61–2; rural strategy of 215, 284, 327–8, 428
Indian Wars of Independence (1857) 5, 8, 12, 20, 22, 61, 86, 87, 98, 100, 123, 153; and peasantry 66–9
Jallianwallah Bag massacre 213, 217; Jayakar M.R. 265, 273 Jayaprakash Narayan 428 Joshi N.M. 231, 329, 336 Joshi P.C. 436, 441, 503 on United Front with I.N.C. 437;
Justice Party 58, 59, 548;
Kanpur and Meerut Conspiracy Cases 285;
Khusro 488, 489, 506, 514–15;
Krishak Proja Party 351–2;
Krishak Smiti (Communists 385, 403–10, 433
Lenin 675, 683, 684, 699; on Agrarian Programme of Iskra-ist 678–80; on Bolshevik failure to mobilize Poor Peasantry 683–84; on Method of organising Peasantry 681; on Perspective of Development of

Capitalism in Rural Russia 676; on Pre-condition of Mobilizing Poor Peasantry 684; on Slogan of 'Alliance of the Working Class and the Peasantry' 675; on Stage of Revolution 751–2;

Liakat Hussain 214, 222

Malavia, Madan Mohan 234, 265, 273

Mao, Tse Tung 510, 514, 516, 675, 685, 689, 699; activity in Peasantry of 685–86; and Hunan Movement (Report) 687–88, 690–92; and Lenin's view on peasantry 684–5, 692; former view on peasantry of 685; ideological development of 685–6; on class differentiation in rural China 688, 691, 720–1

Mass Emigration 47, 80; to avoid forcible recruitment in Army 214

Mass insurrections 108

Mehta Ashok on strategy of communists 699;

Mehta Ferozshah 54

Mehta Uday 743; Desai A.R. on 597–99; on characterization of phases of Indian peasant movements 743–4 on C.P.I. and P.S.P. 747–50;

Menon M.S.N. 22, 58, 60, 124

Menon Sreedhara 111

Moore Barrington 86, 118, 374, 511, 513 compares Chinese and Indian Revolts 86; on the effects of caste system on peasant movement 118, 367–8 Mukherjee Ramkrishna 119, 120, 471, 483 Mukhopadhyay Ashim on I.N.C. 647–8, 651 Munshi K.M. 525 Muslim League 350–1, 372, 415, 418, 426, 468, 518, 657 Ministry of 453, 464 Muzharul Haq 225

Nair M. Krishnan 58, 59

Namboodripad E.M.S. 119, 125, 230, 235, 266–7, 272–3, 629, 733

Natrajan L 19, 123; an overview of peasant struggles in India 170–3; on Deccan Riots 159–69; Indigo Cultivators' Strike (1860) 148–58; Santhal Insurrection 136–47

Nehru Jawaharlal 268, 270–3, 283, 305, 341, 371, 415, 543, 555, 567; and peasant movements 240, 245, 254–6, 262–3, 341; on I.N.C. with A.I.K.S. 436; on nature of his politics 341; on pauperization of peasantry 239

Nehru Motilal 62, 64, 255

Non-Cooperation Movement 56–7, 61, 75, 157–8, 167, 213, 217, 218, 219, 237, 277, 292, 341–2, 349, 417, 618; and No-Tax agitation in Guntur 261–62; and peasant struggle in U.P. 246–61; Chaudhury Binoy Bhushan on 341–2; Swami Sahajanan Sarswathi and N.G. Ranga on 6

Panikkar K.N. 601 on Peasant Revolts in Malabar 601–30

Parulekar Godavri 592, 578, 583

Parulekar S.V. 569, 583; Desai A.R. on 424–5; on Warli Revolt 569–82, 583–92;

Patel Vallabhbhai 65, 73, 81, 231, 305, 309, 366, 415, 422, 555

Patel Vithalbhai 231

Pattabhi Sitaramayya 157, 158, 169, 547

Peasants and Workers Party (1926–28) 284–6, 343–5 Programme of 285, 344

Peasant Struggles; before Indian War of Independence (1857) 122–3; in Bengal (19th Century) 189–207, 744; in Bengal (20th Century) 75, 217, 260–61; in Bengal (Pabna-1873) 19, 20, 117, 179–88, 189, 337, 453; in Bengal (Parganas) 631–62; in Bengal (Tax-Movement of Damodar-Canal) 75, 375–412; in Bengal (Tebhaga 1930's) 114, 115; in Bengal (Tebhaga 1946) 113, 114, 117, 125, 418–20, 434, 438, 439, 442–68; in Bengal (Tebhaga-Kakdwip) 419–20, 469–85; in Bihar (Champaran 1916–18) 20, 54, 72, 152, 157, 215, 223–30, 237, 238, 283; in Bihar (Indigo Cultivator's Strike—1860) 19–20, 110, 132–3, 147, 148–58, 170, 171, 172, 453; in Bihar (land satyagraha 1939) 75;

INDEX

in Gujarat (Kheda 1919–21) 55–6, 60, 65, 70, 77, 73, 75, 152, 223, 230–4, 238, 283; in Karnataka (against forest law) 75; (No Tax campaign and civil disobedience) 57, 58, 71, 75, 217, 261–2; 719–43; 21–22, 97, 100–01, 123, 170, 608–16, 724; in Kerala (Mopla 20th Century) 58–59, 62, 72, 102, 110–18, 217, 259–60, 284, 616–27, 719–43; in Kerala (Mopla-Khilafat) 110–12, 125, 217, 238, 259–60, 618, 623–7; in Maharashtra (Deccan Riots 1875) 19, 20, 21, 51, 57, 70–71, 109–10, 125, 147, 159–69, 170, 171, 172, 744; in Pre-British India 88; in Princely States (1937–46) 78–81, 87, 519; in Telangana (1946–51) 113, 114, 115, 117, 125, 420–25, 486–516; in United Provinces 57, 237, 238–59, 744; sponsored by Communists 113–16

Police action 142–6, 165–7, 178, 233, 241–6, 249–50, 295–9, 303–04, 314–34, 461–2, 563–4, 578–80, 590–1

Praja Socialist Party (P.S.P) 699, 710

Prasad Rajendra 54, 55, 225, 228–9, 230–5

Quit India Movement 8, 82–3, 415–17, 422

Qureshi 487, 488, 490, 515

Raghavaiah V.R. 3, 4, 12, 174; Chronology of Tribal revolts 23–7; Tribal revolts, background of 12–22; in Andhra Pradesh 174–8; in Andhra Pradesh (Alluri Sree Ram Raju) 291–302

Rajagopalachari 54

Ranade 54

Randive B.T. 503, 510, 728

Ranga N.G. 47, 66, 428, 439, 440, 494–5, 515, 547, 563; and A.I.K.S. 428; and kulaks 8; on co-operatives 8; on Gandhi (with S.S. Swami) 4; on I.N.C. (with S.S. Swami) 54, 61–2; on method of organizing peasantry 699; on type, nature, strategy and 66, 68, 83; limitations of peasant movements

Rao C. Rajeshwar 502, 503, 510, 514, 516; Desai A.R. on 422–23; on Telangana 517–31

Report of India League Delegation (1932) 278, 303–36

Ryots Association 62–4, 260, 380–6, 391–2, 402–07

Russel Bertrand 278, 303 Presided India League Delegation (1932) 278, 303–36

Sanyal Kanu 125

Sarkar Krishnakant 469; Desai A.R. on 419–20; on condition of Kakdwip 470–4; on structural aspects of Peasant Movement 476–80; on Tebhaga in Kakdwip 469–85

Schram 687, on Mao and Leninism 687

Sen Bhawani 122, 270; Hamza Alavi on 701, 705; on class nature of peasantry 701, 704, 705; on growing capitalist farming in India 711

Sen Sunil 428; Desai A.R. on 418–19; on condition of duars area 457–60; on Kisan Sabha 428–51; demands 433; nature 430; political orientation 436; on relation of peasantry and revolutionaries 428; on the Bargadars Bill 453–60;

Sengupta Kalyankumar 179, 189; Desai A.R. on 135; on agrarian disturbance in 19th century Bengal 189–207; on Pabna struggle 179–188;

Simon Commission 305

Social Banditry 10, 103–08, 115 117, 119–24

Stalin 683 on alliance with peasantry 683

Stephen Fuchs 4, 28, 100, 105, 119, 122–5; on nature of Messianic movements 28–43;

Sun Yat-Sen 685

Sundarayya P. 490, 495–6, 498–9, 502, 504–5, 507–11, 514; Desai A.R. on 423–4; on Telangana 532–68;

Swami Sahjanand Saraswathi 47, 286, 439; and peasant movement 348–50, 370–1, 745; on Gandhi (with Ranga) 4–5; on Government of India Act

(1936) 363; on I.N.C. (with Ranga) 54
Swaraj Party 62-3
Thakkar Bapa 329
The All-India Adibasis and Excluded Areas Association 75-6
Thomas Munro 48
Tilak 214, 221
Tribal population statistics 12-13, 174-5
Tribal struggles Andaman revolt 27; Assamese revolts 23-4; Bihar revolts 23; Bhil (Gujarat) revolts 23, 25, 27, 43, 45, 75, 301-02; Khandesh 1808-09 revolt 122; Malva 1846 revolt 122;
Chaudhri (Bihar) movement 23
Chota Nagpur revolt 23;
Chronology of 23-27;
Chuar (Midnapore 1799) 97, 122
Daflas (NEFA) Revolt 24, 26;
Dhalbhum (1769-74) revolt 122;
Gonds (Bastar) revolt 25, 27, 132, 301-02;
Gonds (Adilabad, A.P.) revolt 27;
Hos (Singbhum 1831-32) revolt 13, 17, 123;
Jaintia Hills (Assam 1860-62) revolt 13, 24, 26, 123;
Jharkhand movement 11, 113;
Juang revolt 26;
Kallar (Madura 1710-84) revolt 122;
Khampti (Assam) revolt 24;
Khasi (Assam 1829-58) revolt 13, 24, 123;
Khewar (Bihar) revolt 24;
Khondh (Orissa) revolt 13, 25, 122, 123;
Kolam (Adilabad, A.P.) revolt 27;
Koli (Maharashtra) revolt 23-4;
Kols revolt 17, 123;

Koraput (Orissa) revolt 27, 78;
Koya (Andhra Pradesh) revolts 175-6; Rampa (1802-03) 23, 87, 97, 175-6; led by Tammandora (1879-80) 26, 176-8; led by Sree Ram Raju (1922-24) 27, 61, 75, 291-302;
Lushai (Assam) revolts 13, 24-6;
Mal Paharia revolt 13, 23;
Manipur revolt 27, 77;
Mayurabhang revolt 75;
Mishmis (Assam) revolt 24-5;
Mizo revolt 27, 132;
Munda (Bihar) revolt 24, 27, 101, 102, 123, 301-02;
Mymenisingh revolts 75, 103, 117, 189, 447;
Naga revolts 19, 26, 27, 132
Naikdas (Gujarat) revolts 24, 25, 26, 101, 102, 132;
Naxalbari revolt 27, 85, 113-16;
Oraons (Jarkhand movement) 113, 458-60;
Panchet revolt 23;
Phulaguri revolt 26;
reasons of 13, 14-19;
Santhal revolts 12, 13, 14, 26, 51, 75, 76, 85, 113, 117, 119, 744; of 1811, 1820, 1831, 138; insurrection (1855-56) 20, 21, 25, 69-70, 97, 98, 112, 131-2, 136-47, 150, 162, 170-2; Jarkhand movement 458-60
Sentinal island revolt 26-7;
Singphos (Assam) revolts 24, 25;
Tamar Rebellions 17, 23;
Varli revolt 27, 45, 132, 424-5, 569-82, 583-92;
Verrier Elwin 14, 17; on reasons of tribal struggle 17;
Wolf E.R. 599, 719, 735 on peasantry 599-600
Yagnik Indulal 55, 231, 430